JUNIOR
PEARS
ENCYCLOPAEDIA

ILLUSTRATED BY

E. BROOKS
DAVID CHARLES
FRANK CLIFFORD
HILARY EVANS
CHARLES GORHAM
DONALD GREEN
DAVID HUGHES
STAN MARTIN
DAVE NASH
FREDA NICHOLS
HAZEL POPE
CHRISTOPHER REYNOLDS
BRUCE ROBINSON

JUNIOR

PEARS

ENCYCLOPAEDIA

EIGHTEENTH EDITION

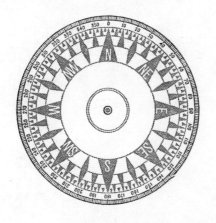

EDITED BY EDWARD BLISHEN

First published 1978

© Pelham Books Ltd. 1978

All enquiries to be addressed to
Pelham Books Ltd.,
52 Bedford Square, London, WC1B 3EF

ISBN 0 7207 1076 6

*Printed and bound in Great Britain
by Richard Clay (The Chaucer Press), Ltd., Bungay, Suffolk*

About This Book

'Oh,' said a stranger at a party. 'You're JUNIOR PEARS, aren't you?' I felt very flattered. It was like—not much like, but a bit like—someone coming up to Shakespeare and saying, 'You're HAMLET, aren't you?' 'I edit it—yes, that's true,' I said, modestly. 'I've still got,' he said, 'the edition I had when I was a boy. The second, I think.' My smile slipped. *When he was a boy?* He had this moustache, and a wife on the other side of the room, and at least one child of his own. It was talk of his child (*he'*d been doing the talking) that had led to his identifying me as JUNIOR PEARS incarnate. He'd said it was nice, when you were a father, to introduce your children to the books you'd read yourself when young. Now he said: 'I think our lad's nearly ready for your encyclopaedia.'

I felt terrible. Not, I hasten to say, because I think there's anything awful about anyone's lad (or lass) having a copy of JUNIOR PEARS. Far from it. I incline to think that *everyone*'s lad (or lass) should have one. No: I felt terrible because JUNIOR PEARS has been going on for so long that one of our earliest readers (and there must be others) is going about with a moustache and a wife and a lad: and that means I'm old, old, old. I haven't just got readers: I've got grand-readers. It also means that JUNIOR PEARS is old: but then it's easy for a book. Especially for a book that's fitted out with a new body annually. . . . I must say, standing there at that party, pleased and displeased at once, I found myself wishing furiously that I, too, could be completely revised, overhauled and brought up-to-date every year.

That's what happens to JUNIOR PEARS. Which brings me (leaning heavily on my stick and stroking my long white beard) to the purpose for which the book exists. It's an encyclopaedia, of course: which literally means a volume, or set of volumes, that tells you everything about everything. But the days when anyone could do that, if ever they existed, are long since over. Today, despite their name, most encyclopaedias have to be much more modest.

This, in fact, is a specialised encyclopaedia, for a particular audience. It's for young people, and is intended to provide information on the main topics in which, as we judge, young people are likely to be interested. Partly we hope it will be found a helpful handbook by students: thus the sections on history, geography, and so on. But no young reader is simply a schoolboy, or a schoolgirl, or a student: and though we hope your schooling is so wide-based that sections on sport and ships, and railways and music, may often have some bearing on what you're studying, still these and other similar sections are there mainly to supply information about out-of-school or out-of-college activities.

But if our basic purpose is to provide information, we've never wanted the book to be merely a bulging collection of facts. We've tried to make it pleasant to read as well as easy to consult: here, for example, are all the main facts about motor cars, but imbedded in a history of the motor-car, and an account of the workings and makings of the motor-car, that form, we hope, more than a dry assemblage of information.[1]

Nevertheless, we've tried to bear in mind that you ought to be able to track down as quickly as possible any single piece of information for which you have some desperate need: therefore each section is arranged so that it yields any particular fact as easily as possible. The list of contents on the title-pages of some sections will be found useful; and other sections, which lend themselves to such treatment, are in dictionary form.

But, of course, a single-volume encyclopaedia is not and could not be a substitute for deeper reading. You can learn from JUNIOR PEARS that five hundred years ago, in 1478, the Inquisition began in Spain; but to discover exactly what the Inquisition was, and why it began at precisely that moment, and why it began in Spain, you must look beyond this volume. This is one kind of book—aiming to give the gleaming bare bones of information. For the flesh you must look to the other sorts of book to which we provide pointers here and there in our lists of 'Further Reading'.

Now and then, alas, a reader fails to find the bone he is after, or finds something amiss with the bone itself. If this happens to you, write to me about it. Complaints or comments of any kind—addressed to 52 Bedford Square, London, WC1B 3EF—will be taken into account in next year's revision. Behind certain changes in this 18th edition lie the very helpful suggestions made by many readers. On the whole, I'd be glad if you wouldn't ask me to carry out extensive research on some subject or other: I'd have to be twenty men to provide such a service. And now and then I've had the mean suspicion that I was being asked to do someone's homework. ('Please tell me everything about the French Revolution and let me have it, with maps, diagrams and time-charts, by next Monday at the latest.') But simpler inquiries, and certainly any criticism you wish to make, will be most welcome. A book like this ought to be shaped not only by a body of contributors but also by a body of readers, and all of us who are responsible for JUNIOR PEARS will welcome your collaboration.

---

[1] It may be worth giving our usual warning that this section has been found so useful by some fathers that the true owners of the book have been deprived of it. Keep it in a safe place.

Contents

The World

1: ITS HISTORY

A Diary of World Events

THE story of man, who first appeared on the Earth a little less than a million years ago, can be traced back only about 6,000 years. For earlier times there are no written records (nor have archaeologists made discoveries) to help the historian to form an accurate or detailed picture of human activity.

This diary is planned not only to be referred to if you are hurriedly searching for a particular event (or revising a particular period) but also to be read as a story. And a hair-raising story it is, with its empires rising and falling, its barbarian Franks and Goths and Vandals becoming the French and Germans and Italians of today, and the uneasy groupings of nations against one another becoming the enormous anxious grouping of our own time. Read the diary through, and consider what a tiny pinch of time these 6,000 years are when measured against the total life of our planet. And remember, as you read, that the diary doesn't cease to be written simply because we have had to break off at 1978 to put it in this book. This diary is now your diary; History is your history.

The first reference to any historical figure in this account is printed in black type. So that if you are interested in, say, Napoleon, and come across his name in ordinary type, you will know that you are somewhere in the middle of his story, and must look back to **Napoleon** in order to find its beginning. The names of battles are printed in small capitals, like this: WATERLOO. If you wish to refer to a particular battle there is an index of battles at the end giving the dates under which you should look for them.

Some of the most important events of all, the passing of great Acts of Parliament and achievements of exploration and discovery, are omitted because they are dealt with separately elsewhere in this section.

B.C.

4000–3000 First settlements in the river valleys of the Nile in Egypt, the Tigris and Euphrates in Mesopotamia, the Indus in India and the Yellow River in China.

By 2000 Chinese civilisation, oldest in the world, covers practically the whole of China.

In the Indus valley the Dravidians have established an orderly system of government; they are often invaded, but out of the give and take of ideas between conquerors and conquered, Hinduism begins to emerge. In Mesopotamia the Sumerians have invented a form of writing (cuneiform),

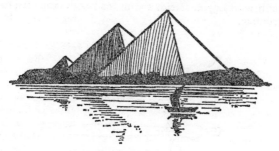

The Great Pyramids

divided the circle into 360°, a degree into 60 minutes and a minute into 60 seconds, and discovered how to extract copper and make bronze. Their knowledge lives on despite their absorption into the Babylonian Empire, whose best-known king, **Hammurabi**, extends the authority of Babylon as far as Syria and codifies his country's laws.

In the Nile valley the Egyptians have already built the Great Pyramids at Gizeh and the Sphinx (2600) and divided time into solar years.

The spread of knowledge from Egypt has helped to create the Minoan civilisation in Crete (named after the legendary king **Minos** (see DICTIONARY OF MYTHOLOGY), whose magnificent palace at Knossos was discovered in 1900).

In Britain the great stone circles at Stonehenge and Avebury are still used for religious worship.

1800–1700 First use in Egypt of papyrus, an early form of paper. Nile valley overrun by Hyksos ('princes of the desert').

The Babylonian empire is overrun by the Hittites; but there is conflict, lasting several centuries, between these and other invading tribes based on Babylon, Nineveh and other cities.

1580 Hyksos driven out of Egypt. Founding of the 'New Kingdom', under which Egypt is to be at her greatest.

1400 Moses leads the Israelites out of Egypt. Knossos destroyed by earthquake or enemies, and Cretan civilisation at an end.

1300–1200 Hittites, now controlling all Mesopotamia, discover how to smelt iron, equip their troops with iron weapons, and clash with Egypt. Neither wins, and both empires begin to crumble.

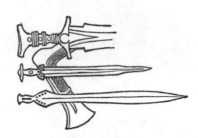

1180 Siege of Troy: one of the wars by which the ancestors of the ancient Greeks settled themselves round the Aegean, and the only one of which an account survives (in Homer's *Iliad*).

c. 1060–c. 970 David king of Israel.

c. 970–c. 940 Solomon king of Israel. He uses his enormous wealth, gained through trade, to build the Temple at Jerusalem.

800 The Phoenicians, whose cities of Tyre and Sidon are nearly 1,000 years old, found Carthage.

776 First Olympiad.

753 Rome founded.

750–550 Greek city states emerge on Greek mainland and around the coasts of Mediterranean and Black Sea.

691 Assyrians (already lords of Mesopotamia, Syria, Palestine, Arabia) conquer Egypt.

660 First Mikado in Japan.

612 Chaldeans conquer Assyrians and establish second Babylonian Empire.

597 Nebuchadnezzar, mightiest Chaldean emperor, captures Jerusalem and carries off the Jews into captivity.

594 Solon lays the foundations of Athenian democracy.

560 Buddha born.

551 Confucius born.

539–525 Cyrus, king of Persia, makes himself master of Asia Minor, captures Babylon, founds the Persian empire and allows the Jews to return to Jerusalem.

525 Cambyses, Cyrus's successor, conquers Egypt.

510 Rome becomes a republic.

490 Athens has helped Greek cities on the coast of Asia Minor to revolt—unsuccessfully—against their Persian overlords. **Darius I** of Persia lands a force in Greece to punish Athens; is beaten at MARATHON.

480 Xerxes makes a second attempt to crush Greece; exterminates a Spartan army under **Leonidas** at THERMOPYLAE and occupies Athens; but the Persian fleet is destroyed at SALAMIS.

479 Persians defeated at PLAETAEA.

461 Pericles becomes the most important person in Athenian politics. Under his leadership Greek civilisation, free of the Persian menace, has its 'golden age'; it is now that the Parthenon is built (447–438). But removal of the Persian danger leads to quarrelling among the Greek city states.

431–404 Peloponnesian War between Athens and Sparta, ending with capture of Athens.

The Parthenon

390 Gauls capture Rome except for the Capitol, but Romans regain the city by paying huge ransom.

359 **Philip** becomes king of Macedonia; sets out to make himself overlord of quarrelsome Greek cities.

338 Philip defeats combined armies of Athens and Thebes, becomes master of Greece.

336 Philip assassinated; succeeded by his son, **Alexander the Great.**

333 Alexander defeats **Darius III** of Persia and conquers Egypt, where he founds Alexandria.

327 Alexander extends his empire as far as the Indus.

323 Alexander dies; his empire is divided among his generals.

280 **Pyrrhus**, king of Epirus, aids Greek cities in S. Italy against Rome; defeats the Romans twice but himself suffers heavy losses (hence the term 'Pyrrhic victories', meaning victories won at great cost).

275 Defeating Pyrrhus, Rome becomes mistress of S. Italy, and thus comes into conflict with Carthage.

264 First Punic War between Rome and Carthage for control of Sicily.

260 Roman sea victory at MYLAE.

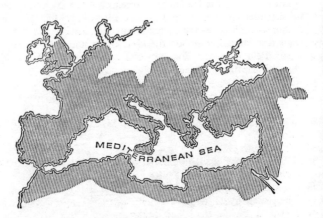

The Roman Empire at its furthest extent

256 Roman landing near Carthage repulsed.

246 Great Wall of China built.

241 Remainder of Carthaginian fleet defeated; Carthage sues for peace and loses control of Sicily.

238 Carthage sets out to create new empire in Spain.

225 Gauls invade Roman territory and are defeated. To prevent this happening again, Rome extends her frontiers northwards by conquering Cisalpine Gaul (modern Lombardy); is now mistress of all Italy.

219 Second Punic War. A 26-year old Carthaginian general, **Hannibal**, crosses the Alps into Italy, where he is unbeaten for 15 years.

217 Hannibal destroys a Roman army at LAKE TRASIMENE.

216 Hannibal destroys a second Roman army at CANNAE, but is unable to capture Rome itself.

210–206 Roman army wipes out Carthaginian forces in Spain and conquers the country.

204 Romans cross from Spain to Africa.

202 Hannibal returns to Africa to save Carthage, but is defeated at ZAMA.

201 Carthage surrenders her fleet and hands Spain over to Rome.

166 Tartar invasion of China.

149 Third Punic War. Uneasy at the steady recovery of Carthage, Rome resolves to destroy her rival.

146 Carthage destroyed.

102 **Marius** drives back invading German tribes.

91 Revolt of Italian cities belonging to Rome but with no say in government.

89 All Italians become Roman citizens.

88 Civil war in Rome between plebeians (people's party), led by Marius, and patricians (nobles), under **Sulla**. Sulla wins and Marius escapes to Africa.

87 While Sulla is fighting in Greece, Marius seizes power in Rome.

86 Marius dies.

82 Sulla returns, massacres his enemies, strengthens the power of the Senate, becomes dictator.

78 Sulla dies.

73 **Spartacus** leads revolt of 60,000 slaves.

71 **Crassus** crushes Spartacus revolt.

70 Crassus and **Pompey** reduce power of the Senate.

66–62 Pompey captures Jerusalem, conquers Syria and advances to the Euphrates.

60 Pompey, Crassus and **Caesar** divide the government of Rome's dominions, becoming the First Triumvirate (rule of three men). Caesar begins conquest of Gaul.

55 Caesar's first visit to Britain.

53 Crassus defeated and killed by Parthians.

51 Caesar completes conquest of Gaul.

49 Caesar crosses the Rubicon, boundary of his own command, to overthrow Pompey, now his only rival.

48 Caesar defeats Pompey at PHARSALUS. Pompey escapes to Egypt and is murdered.

44 Caesar is murdered.

43 **Octavian**, Caesar's nephew, **Antony** and **Lepidus** form Second Triumvirate.

42 Octavian and Antony defeat **Brutus** and **Cassius**, chief plotters against Caesar. The government of Rome's dominions is divided, Octavian taking the West, Antony the East (which he rules from Egypt with **Cleopatra**) and Lepidus, Carthaginian Africa.

31 Octavian defeats Antony and Cleopatra at ACTIUM.

30 Deaths of Antony and Cleopatra.

27 Octavian, now known as Augustus, becomes first Roman emperor.

4 True date of birth of **Jesus**.

A.D.

14 Augustus dies.

30 Jesus crucified.

43 Emperor **Claudius** sends force to conquer Britain. The South is soon subdued, despite resistance from **Caractacus**, who is captured and sent to Rome. The Romans work their way northwards.

61 **Boadicea**, queen of the Iceni, revolts against Romans, burns their settlement at London; but her army is annihilated and she takes poison.

68 **Nero**, last emperor of the house of Augustus, commits suicide.

70 Emperor **Titus** captures and destroys Jerusalem, drives the Jews from the Holy Land.

79 Pompeii and Herculaneum destroyed in eruption of Vesuvius.

82 **Agricola**, governor of Britain, attempts conquest of Scotland.

93 **Trajan** adds Dacia (modern Rumania) and Mesopotamia to Roman empire, now at its largest.

117 **Hadrian** tries to keep barbarians out of Roman territories by building permanent fortifications, including 70-mile-long wall (Hadrian's Wall) from Tyne to Solway.

164–80 Plagues ravage Roman and Chinese empires.

180 Century of war and disorder begins for Rome, during which a succession of generals, many not even Roman by birth, are made emperors by troops in their pay. Perpetual invasions by Franks, Goths, Parthians, Vandals and Huns.

226 **Artaxerxes** founds new dynasty in Persia.

284 **Diocletian**, last Roman emperor to persecute Christians, re-organises the empire with two joint emperors and two subordinate emperors.

312 **Constantine** defeats his joint emperor, **Maxentius**, and becomes sole emperor in West.

313 Constantine legalises Christianity; later makes it State religion.

324 Constantine defeats emperor in the East, becomes sole ruler of Roman world.

328 To celebrate victory, Constantine founds 'new Rome' by enlarging ancient Greek city of Byzantium, calls it Constantinople.

330 Constantine moves capital to Constantinople.

337 Constantine dies, and empire is again ruled by succession of joint (and rival) emperors.

379 **Theodosius the Great**, emperor in the East, drives Goths from Greece and Italy.

382 Theodosius makes peace with Goths.

394 Theodosius becomes last sole emperor of Roman world.

395 Theodosius dies; division of empire into West and East becomes final.

407 As barbarians pour into Western empire, Roman legions are withdrawn from Britain in last attempt to defend Rome. Britain is left easy prey to Angles and Saxons.

410 Visigoths under **Alaric** plunder Rome. Waves of barbarians sweep into Spain, Portugal, Italy, Gaul and North Africa.

434 **Attila** becomes king of the Huns, Mongolians whose invasion of Europe is death-blow for Western empire.

449 **Hengist** and **Horsa**, Jutish chiefs, invade England, set up kingdom in Kent.

451 Invading Gaul, Attila is defeated by army of Goths and Romans at CHALONS.

452 Attila invades Italy; is persuaded by **Pope Leo I** to spare Rome.

453 Attila dies.

455 Vandals sack Rome. In next twenty years ten different emperors rule.

476 Last Roman emperor deposed; Western empire comes to an end.

482 **Clovis**, king of Salian Franks, makes himself first king of Frankland (France), with Paris as his capital.

496 Clovis baptised; Franks become Christians.

527 **Justinian**, whose codification of Roman law is basis for much later Western law, becomes emperor in Constantinople. Attempting re-conquest of Western Empire, he recovers North Africa, S.E. Spain and Italy.

536 **Belisarius**, Justinian's famous general, captures Rome.

565 Justinian dies.

568 Lombards invade Italy, settle in the north.

570 Birth of **Mohammed**.

590 **Gregory the Great** becomes Pope; declares Rome supreme centre of the Church.

597 **St Augustine** lands in England, baptises **Ethelbert**, king of Kent.

601 St Augustine becomes first archbishop of Canterbury.

c. 616 Mohammed proclaims himself the apostle of Allah.

618 Great T'ang dynasty founded in China.

628 Mohammed writes to all rulers of the earth, demanding that they acknowledge the One True God, Allah, and serve Him.

632 Mohammed dies; his friend **Abu Bakr**, first Caliph ('successor'), leads Arabs out of the desert to achieve Mohammed's aim of making the world submit to Islam.

637 Arabs defeat Persians at KARDESSIA. Soon after, Mesopotamia, Syria, Palestine and Egypt fall to them.

638 Jerusalem surrenders to Arabs.

641 Arabs capture Alexandria. Its famous library is destroyed.

643 The Arabs defeat armies of the Eastern empire at YARMAK.

669 Arabs unsuccessfully attack Constantinople from sea.

711 Having conquered East and North Africa, Arabs cross into Spain.

720 Spain subdued, the Arabs (with the Moors) invade France.

732 **Charles Martel** drives Arabs out of France.

751 **Pepin**, son of Charles Martel, crowned King of the Franks, founding Carolingian dynasty.

762 Baghdad founded; becomes capital of Arab empire.

768 Pepin dies; his kingdom divided between his sons Charles (later known as **Charlemagne**) and **Carloman**.

771 Carloman dies and Charlemagne takes possession of his lands. From then onwards Charlemagne enlarges his dominions until his power reaches from the Pyrenees to the river Elbe in Germany, and from the Atlantic to the Danube and Tiber.

786 **Haroun-al-Raschid** becomes Caliph at Baghdad; under him Arab empire is at its greatest.

800 Charlemagne crowned in Rome emperor of the Holy Roman Empire.

802 **Egbert** king of Wessex, one of seven Anglo-Saxon kingdoms fighting for supremacy in England. Others are Northumbria, Mercia, Kent, Sussex, Essex and E. Anglia.

809 Haroun-al-Raschid dies; beginning of 200 years of chaos and civil war in Arab empire.

Viking Ship

814 Charlemagne dies.

829 Egbert unites England for first time under one king.

840 Frankish empire is divided between Charlemagne's sons and grandsons, whose quarrels lead to its breaking up.

871 Alfred the Great king of Wessex, practically the only part of England not in Danish hands.

878 Alfred defeats Danes, compels them by Treaty of Wedmore to stay in their settlements in N.E. England and become Christians.

900 Alfred dies.

919 Henry I king of Germany; completes the separation of the Frankish empire into Germany and France.

987 Louis V, last Carolingian king of France, dies, and is succeeded by **Hugh Capet**, first modern French king.

1013 Sweyn of Denmark conquers England, is accepted as king.

1015 Canute, Sweyn's son, defeats **Edmund Ironside**, son of last Anglo-Saxon king, and divides realm with him.

1016 Edmund dies; Canute becomes sole king.

1042 Edward the Confessor returns to England as king from Normandy, where he has been living at the court of the Norman duke. Leaves government to **Earl Godwin**, devotes himself to religion.

1054 Eastern Orthodox Church breaks with Church of Rome.

1065 Westminster Abbey, rebuilt by Edward the Confessor, consecrated.

1066 Edward the Confessor dies; **Harold**, son of Earl Godwin, elected king. **William** of Normandy invades England and kills Harold at HASTINGS.

1071 Seljuk Turks, having seized Baghdad, sweep across Asia Minor and take fortress of Niceaea opposite Constantinople.

1075 Turks take Jerusalem and Holy Places.

1086 Domesday Book, a survey of England, completed.

1095 Pope Urban II summons Christian nations to First Crusade.

1098 Crusaders take Antioch.

1099 Crusaders take Jerusalem.

1135 England plunged in civil war when **Stephen**, grandson of William the Conqueror, allows himself to be elected king although he had previously recognised **Mathilda**, Henry I's daughter, as heir to throne.

1149 Second Crusade ends in failure.

1153 Stephen acknowledges Mathilda's son as his heir.

1164 **Henry II** tries to bring English clergy into the power of the royal courts and clashes with **Thomas à Becket**, his chancellor and Archbishop of Canterbury, who flees to France.

1170 Becket returns, but the quarrel breaks out afresh, and he is murdered in Canterbury Cathedral.

1174 **Saladin** proclaimed caliph; launches a holy war of all Muslims against Christians.

1187 Saladin recaptures Jerusalem.

1189 Third Crusade, under **Philip Augustus** of France and **Richard I**, fails to retake Jerusalem. Siege of Acre.

1191 Crusaders capture ACRE.

1192 Richard concludes armistice with Saladin.

1202 Fourth Crusade; Constantinople captured.

1206 Mogul empire founded in India.

1215 **King John** is forced at Runnymede to accept Magna Carta, which lays it down that no freeman may be imprisoned or punished except by the law of the land.

1218-21 Fifth Crusade captures Damietta, in Egypt, but loses it again.

1228-29 Sixth Crusade recovers Jerusalem by negotiation.

1264 **Henry III**, whose misrule has caused barons to revolt, is taken prisoner at LEWES by **Simon de Montfort**.

1265 De Montfort summons first Parliament in which towns are represented; is defeated and killed at EVESHAM.

1273 **Rudolf of Hapsburg**, founder of dynasty that is to reign in Austria until 1918, elected Holy Roman Emperor.

1280 **Kublai Khan** emperor of China; encourages trade and teaches religious tolerance. Visited by **Marco Polo**.

1282 **Edward I** completes conquest of Wales.

1291 Acre, last Christian stronghold in Syria, is lost.

1295 Edward I summons Model Parliament, so called because for the first time King, Lords and Commons meet.

1296 Edward I attempts to annex Scotland.

1297 **Sir William Wallace** defeats Edward at STIRLING.

1298 Edward defeats Wallace at FALKIRK.

1301 Edward makes his son Prince of Wales.

1304 Wallace captured and executed, but **Robert Bruce** raises another revolt against Edward.

1306 Robert Bruce crowned king of Scotland.

1309 Papacy falls into French control; residence of the Popes moved to Avignon.

1314 Edward II defeated at BANNOCKBURN by Robert Bruce.

1328 Robert Bruce recognised by England as king of Scotland.

1337 Outbreak of 'Hundred Years' War' between England and France. Causes: a conflict of commercial interests and Edward III's claim to French throne.

1340 English defeat French by sea at SLUYS.

1346 Edward III defeats French at CRECY.

1347 Edward captures Calais.

1348–49 Black Death, the bubonic plague, reaches England, killing nearly one half of the population, and causing acute shortage of labour and social unrest.

1356 Edward, the Black Prince, defeats French at POITIERS.

1369 French renew the war; reconquer province after province.

1372 English fleet destroyed. Impoverished by war, weakened by quarrels between Black Prince and his brother, **John of Gaunt,** England loses all her French possessions except Bordeaux and Calais.

1378 Rival Popes elected in Rome and Avignon.

1381 Heavily taxed, tied to the land as serfs, the peasants revolt under **Wat Tyler.** Tyler is murdered and the rising crushed, but from this time serfdom gradually declines.

1384 Death of **John Wycliffe,** who has attacked abuses in the Church of Rome and ordered a translation of the Bible into English.

1385 Scots invade England; **Richard II** takes Edinburgh.

1388 Scots again invade; are victorious at OTTERBURN.

1397 Richard II executes or banishes leaders of the barons. Among those banished is **Henry, Duke of Hereford, John of Gaunt's** son and heir.

1399 John of Gaunt dies; Richard II confiscates his estates. Henry, Duke of Hereford, returns to England to lead revolt of the nobles. Parliament deposes Richard and accepts Henry as king—the first to speak English (grown out of Norman French and Anglo-Saxon) as his mother-tongue.

1400 Welsh revolt under **Owen Glendower.**

1403 Scots defeated at HOMILDON HILL. Henry IV crushes revolt at SHREWSBURY.

1415 Henry V renews war against France, captures HARFLEUR and is victorious at AGINCOURT.

1420 Henry V recognised by French king as his heir; marries French princess.

1422 Henry dies. French refuse to recognise his one-year-old son, **Henry VI**, as king of France; Henry V's brother continues war.

1429 English overcome all French resistance except in ORLEANS; they besiege the town, but are driven off by an army led by **Joan of Arc**.

1431 Joan of Arc, captured by the English, is burned at the stake; but French advance continues.

1445 **Johann Gutenberg**, first European printer, sets up business in Mainz.

1453 The Eastern empire is at an end when Constantinople falls to the Ottoman Turks, who sweep into Greece and across to the Danube.

1455 Disastrous end of Hundred Years' War has made the English government unpopular, and the **Duke of York** (white rose) claims the throne from Henry VI, a Lancastrian (red rose). So begin Wars of the Roses. Yorkists win at ST ALBANS, but are then defeated; York flees to Ireland.

1460 York returns, is victorious at NORTHAMPTON, but is defeated and killed at WAKEFIELD.

1461 Edward, York's son, proclaimed king in London as **Edward IV**. Defeats the Lancastrians at TOWTON; Henry VI is captured and imprisoned.

1464 Lancastrians defeated at HEXHAM.

1470 Yorkist **Earl of Warwick**, the 'Kingmaker', quarrels with Edward IV, frees Henry VI. Edward flees to Flanders.

1471 Edward returns, defeats and kills Warwick at BARNET and routs Lancastrians at TEWKESBURY.

1476 **Caxton** sets up as printer.

1478 Inquisition begins in Spain.

1483 Edward IV succeeded by 12-year-old son, **Edward V**. Richard, Duke of Gloucester, Protector of the Realm, has himself proclaimed king as **Richard III**. Edward V and his brother are murdered in the Tower.

1485 Henry Tudor, Earl of Richmond, lands in England and defeats Richard III at BOSWORTH. As **Henry VII**, he founds the line of Tudors, breaks the power of the nobles and establishes strong central government.

1492 **Ferdinand** of Aragon and **Isabella** of Castile, whose marriage unites Spain for the first time, finally free the country

The *Santa Maria* 1492

from the Moors by capturing GRANADA.

1513 James IV of Scotland invades England, is defeated at FLODDEN.

1517 Martin Luther, founder of Protestantism, nails to church door at Wittenberg his condemnation of many practices of the Church of Rome.

1519 Cortes conquers Mexico.

1520 Luther publicly burns the Papal Bull excommunicating him, and refuses to go back on his teachings. Protestantism spreads; is adopted in Sweden in 1527, in Denmark in 1536. In Switzerland it is established by **Calvin**, whose followers in France, the Huguenots, wage bitter wars with the Catholics between 1562 and 1598. In Scotland the Reformation, as this great movement is called, triumphs by 1560, largely owing to teaching of Calvin's disciple, **John Knox**.

1526 Baber, Moslem warrior king, captures Delhi.

1528 Conquest of Peru.

1529 The Ottoman Sultan, **Suleiman** the Magnificent, having taken Belgrade, the island of Rhodes and Budapest, attempts

The Tower of London

to storm Vienna but is beaten back.

Cardinal Wolsey, Henry VIII's chief minister, fails to persuade the Pope to grant Henry a divorce from **Catherine of Aragon,** and Henry dismisses him.

1533 Archbishop Cranmer dissolves Henry's marriage and crowns **Anne Boleyn** as queen.

1534 Henry VIII, though no Protestant, repudiates authority of the Pope, proclaims himself head of the Church and dissolves the monasteries, confiscating their wealth.

1536 Death of Catherine of Aragon; execution of Anne Boleyn. Henry marries **Jane Seymour.**

1538 Henry VIII excommunicated.

1540 Henry marries **Anne of Cleves;** later in the year marries **Catherine Howard.**

1542 Catherine Howard executed; Henry marries **Catherine Parr.**

1547 Ten-year-old **Edward VI** succeeds Henry VIII.

1549 & 1553 First Prayer Books in English are issued by Cranmer.

1553 Mary, Henry VIII's daughter and a Catholic, becomes Queen. **Lady Jane Grey,** to whom Edward VI had bequeathed the crown to avoid return to Catholicism, is also proclaimed Queen, but is arrested and executed. Cranmer is burnt at the stake and succeeded by a Catholic Archbishop of Canterbury. Supremacy of Pope again acknowledged. Persecution of Protestants marking Mary's reign wins her the nickname of 'Bloody Mary'.

1558 Calais, last French possession still in English hands, falls.

Elizabeth succeeds Mary and repudiates authority of the Pope. To spare England the bitter religious wars with which

Europe is being ravaged, she begins working out a religious compromise, in which the Protestant doctrines of the Church of England are mixed with many Catholic elements in its ritual.

1568 Mary Queen of Scots, Catholic and heir to Elizabeth, forced to flee to England; imprisoned by Elizabeth.

1571 Fleet of the Christian League, led by Spain, defeats Turkish fleet at LEPANTO and destroys Moslem sea power in Mediterranean.

1585 Elizabeth lands English army in Netherlands to support Dutch in their revolt against Spanish rule, and this brings into the open the undeclared war England has been fighting with **Philip of Spain** as a result of trade rivalry and religious differences.

1586 Battle of ZUTPHEN; **Sir Philip Sidney** slain.

1587 Mary Queen of Scots executed.
Drake attacks Cadiz.

1588 Philip of Spain sends Great Armada against England; it is destroyed by the English fleet under **Howard of Effingham**, Drake, **Hawkins** and **Frobisher**.

1603 Elizabeth dies; James VI of Scotland becomes king as **James I.** His High Church views displease the Puritans, and the powerful new merchant class is offended by his insistence on the Divine Right of Kings.

1605 Gunpowder Plot, a Catholic conspiracy to blow up James and his Parliament, is discovered.

1609 Holland frees herself from Spain; is soon to be a great power, leading the world in trade, art and science and founding an empire in East and West Indies.

1618 Outbreak of the Thirty Years' War, last attempt of the Catholics to stamp out the Reformation in Europe. The Catholics are at first successful, but the tide turns against them when in 1629 **Gustavus Adolphus** of Sweden comes in on the Protestant side.

1620 Pilgrim Fathers sail from Plymouth in the *Mayflower* to found the first colony in New England.

1628 Parliament refuse to vote **Charles I** any money until he has accepted their Petition of Right, which declares taxation without consent of Parliament and imprisonment without trial illegal.

1629 Charles dissolves Parliament, imprisoning its leaders. He

The *Mayflower* 1620

reigns without parliament for the next eleven years, raising money by means regarded as illegal, and suppressing all opposition by special royal courts.

1632 Gustavus Adolphus wins the battle of LUTZEN but is slain.

1640 England invaded by Scots; Charles I obliged to recall Parliament to raise money for the war. The 'Short' Parliament insists on airing its grievances before voting money, and is dismissed. Charles has to summon new Parliament and this (the 'Long' Parliament lasting until 1660) sets out to make personal government by a monarch impossible.

1641 Irish rebel against English.

1642 Charles I goes to House of Commons to arrest his enemies, finds them gone. Slips out of London and the Civil War begins. First battle, at EDGEHILL, is indecisive.

1644 Royalists defeated at MARSTON MOOR by **Cromwell.**

1645 Cromwell wins decisive victory at NASEBY.

1646 Charles surrenders to Scots.

1647 The Scots, having made alliance with Parliamentarians, hand Charles over.

1648 Scots, uneasy about their alliance and encouraged by Charles, invade England, are defeated by Cromwell at PRESTON.

1648 Thirty Years War ends without victor.

1649 Charles I executed. England, calling itself a Commonwealth, becomes a republic. Cromwell ruthlessly restores
English rule in Ireland.

1650 Charles I's son, later **Charles II**, lands in Scotland, is
crowned King of Scotland.

1651 Prince Charles invades England, is defeated by Cromwell
at WORCESTER, and escapes to the continent.

1652–54 Trade rivalry between English and Dutch leads to war.
Cromwell's navy, commanded by admirals like **Robert Blake**,
holds its own against the mighty Dutch fleet.

1653 Cromwell becomes Lord Protector.

1655 Cromwell seizes Jamaica from Spain.

1658 Cromwell dies; is succeeded by his son, **Richard Cromwell**.

1659 Richard Cromwell resigns.

1660 **General Monk**, Commonwealth commander in Scotland,
occupies London and invites Prince Charles to return as
Charles II.

1664 War between Britain and Holland; British capture New
Amsterdam and rename it New York.

1665 Great Plague of London.

1666 Great Fire of London.

1667 Dutch fleet sails up the Medway and destroys British squadron. Britain makes peace but keeps New York.

1670 Charles II makes secret Treaty of Dover with **Louis XIV** of France, promising to declare himself a Catholic, restore Catholicism in England and support Louis against the Dutch; in return Louis agrees to help Charles with money and, if necessary, troops.

1672 Charles suspends all laws against Catholics, and joins with France in attacking Holland. The Dutch, under **William of Orange,** hold up the French by piercing the dykes; the Dutch admiral **De Ruyter** puts the Anglo-French fleet out of action in SOUTHWOLD BAY.

1673 Charles II forced to summon Parliament to ask for money; is compelled to accept Test Act excluding all Catholics from office and to end war with Holland.

1678 **Titus Oates** announces 'Popish plot' to restore Catholicism in England. Attempt is made to exclude from the succession Charles's brother, **James,** a Catholic convert.

1681 **William Penn** establishes colony of Pennsylvania as refuge for persecuted Quakers.

1683 Turks make final effort to carry Islam into the heart of Europe; are defeated at VIENNA.

1685 Charles II dies; James, though a Catholic, becomes king as James II. **Monmouth,** illegitimate son of Charles II and a Protestant, tries to seize the throne, but is defeated at SEDGE-MOOR and executed.

1688 **William of Orange,** married to **Mary,** James's Protestant daughter, is invited to come over with an army to save the English constitution and Church. William lands at Torbay, and James II flees to France.

1689 The Crown is accepted by William and Mary after they have agreed to the Bill of Rights, limiting royal power. James II lands in Ireland to lead an Irish rising.

1690 William defeats James and the Irish at the battle of the BOYNE.

1701 Parliament passes the Act of Settlement confining the succession to Protestants.

Louis XIV uses a dispute over the succession to the Spanish throne to resume his plan to make France strongest European power. William forms Britain, Holland and Austria into 'Grand Alliance' to stop him.

1702 William dies; succeeded by **Anne**.

1704 **Marlborough's** victory at BLENHEIM saves Vienna from the French.

1704 **Admiral Rooke** captures Gibraltar.

1706 Marlborough defeats French at RAMILLIES.

1707 Act of Union between England and Scotland.

1708 Marlborough defeats French at OUDENARDE.

1709 Marlborough victorious at MALPLAQUET.

1710 Replacement of Whigs by Tories, who want to end the war, leads to Marlborough's downfall.

1713 War ends. Britain receives Newfoundland and Hudson Bay territory from France; Gibraltar and Minorca from Spain.

1714 Anne dies and Elector of Hanover becomes king as **George I**. He cannot speak English and has no interest in English affairs; his reign helps to make Parliament even more powerful, leads to the modern pattern of government by a cabinet of ministers.

1715 The 'Old Pretender', son of James II, lands in Scotland to find his supporters have already been defeated.

1720 A financial crisis, the 'South Sea Bubble', produced by wild speculation, ruins thousands.

  Sir Robert Walpole becomes first Prime Minister.

1739 Walpole, though anxious to preserve peace, is forced into war with Spain (the 'War of Jenkins' Ear').

1740 Hapsburg emperor, **Charles VI**, dies. The European powers have agreed to accept his daughter, **Maria Theresa**, as his heir; but France, Spain and Prussia ignore the arrangement. Prussia attacks Austria; France invades Germany. Britain and Holland enter this War of the Austrian Succession on Maria Theresa's side.

1743 **George II** defeats French at DETTINGEN—the last time a British king is personally in command in a battle.

1745 French defeat Austro-English army at FONTENOY. **Prince Charles Edward**, the 'Young Pretender', lands in Scotland and wins victory at PRESTONPANS. He invades England, but finds little support; his army returns to Scotland.

1746 The Jacobites (Charles Edward's followers) defeated at CULLODEN; the 'Young Pretender' escapes to the continent.

1748 War of the Austrian Succession ends. Prussia under **Frederick the Great** has emerged as the strongest power in

N. Germany; Britain has proved herself superior at sea over the French, with whom she continues a struggle for supremacy in India and America.

1756 Seven Years' War breaks out. Maria Theresa, helped by France and Russia, seeks to win back Silesia from Frederick of Prussia, who is supported by Britain under the elder **Pitt. The Nawab of Bengal** captures Calcutta; locks 140 British men and women into small military guardroom—the 'Black Hole of Calcutta'—where most suffocate. In America French capture Fort Oswego, main British trading centre on Great Lakes.

1757 Clive defeats Nawab of Bengal at PLASSEY.

1758 Fort Oswego recaptured; British take Fort Duquesne, renaming it Pittsburgh in honour of Pitt.

1759 French defeated at MINDEN; in America **General Wolfe** is slain capturing QUEBEC. There are British naval victories at LAGOS and QUIBERON BAY.

1760 French defeated in India, leaving British supreme. George II succeeded by his grandson, **George III**, first Hanoverian king to speak English and to regard himself as king of England rather than Elector of Hanover.

1761 George brings about downfall of Pitt.

1763 Seven Years' War ends, leaving Britain with her conquests in India and America.

1773 'Boston Tea Party' brings to a head the long quarrel between George III and American colonists. Colonists maintain they should not be taxed without their consent. When Britain imposes tax on tea, a group of colonists, disguised as Indians, board ships in Boston and throw their cargoes into the harbour.

1775 First shots exchanged between colonists and British troops at Lexington. **George Washington** made American Commander-in-Chief.

1776 The 13 American colonies issue Declaration of Independence (July 4).

1777 General Burgoyne, marching from Canada to New York, forced to surrender at SARATOGA. France and Spain declare war on Britain.

1781 British army under **General Cornwallis** forced to surrender at YORKTOWN, Virginia.

1783 Britain recognises American independence.

1788 Founding Fathers draw up American constitution.

1789 George Washington first U.S. President. French Revolution breaks out. Faced with bankruptcy, **Louis XVI** is compelled to summon the States-General (French Parliament) for first time since 1614. States-General turns itself into National Assembly, determined to abolish absolute power of king, and proclaims principles of Liberty, Equality, Fraternity. Louis calls in soldiers; people of Paris retaliate by storming Bastille prison (July 14).

1791 Louis XVI flees, but is caught and brought back to Paris.

1792 Austria and Prussia, wishing to restore Louis, make war on France; Louis is deposed and imprisoned, France becoming republic. Extreme revolutionaries (the Jacobins) gain control.

1793 French occupy Austrian Netherlands (now Belgium); Britain joins in war against France with Holland, Spain, Austria and Prussia. Louis XVI is executed; Reign of Terror begins. In Britain the government, afraid that revolutionary ideas will spread, suppresses all societies in favour of reform.

1794 Execution of **Robespierre** ends Reign of Terror.

1795 Prussia has withdrawn from war, Holland been conquered and Spain defeated; only Austria and Britain are left. **Napoleon Bonaparte** becomes French C.-in-C. in Italy, where he rapidly masters the Austrians. Britain takes Cape of Good Hope, formerly Dutch.

1797 Napoleon threatens Vienna; Austria makes peace. **Jarvis** and **Nelson** defeat Spanish fleet at CAPE ST VINCENT; **Duncan** the Dutch fleet at CAMPERDOWN.

1798 Bonaparte eludes a British fleet under Nelson, lands in Egypt and defeats Mameluke Turks in BATTLE OF THE PYRAMIDS. Nelson destroys French fleet anchored in Aboukir Bay, in BATTLE OF THE NILE. Bonaparte advances into Syria, is stopped by **Sir Sidney Smith** at ACRE.

1799 Britain, Turkey, Austria and Russia combine against France. Bonaparte abandons army in Egypt and returns to France, where he makes himself First Consul.

1800 Bonaparte defeats Austrians at MARENGO. Ireland made part of United Kingdom.

1801 Austria sues for peace. Russia has withdrawn from war and, with Denmark, Sweden and Prussia, has taken measures against Britain for searching neutral ships to ensure that they

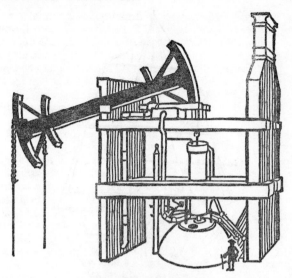

Early Watt's Pumping Engine

do not carry cargoes useful to France. Nelson smashes Danish fleet at COPENHAGEN.

1802 Peace returns for a time. Britain restores Cape of Good Hope to Dutch, but keeps Ceylon (formerly Dutch) and Trinidad (formerly Spanish). Bonaparte made First Consul for life.

1803 War between Britain and France renewed, with Spain on France's side. Bonaparte sells Louisiana to the U.S.A.

1804 Bonaparte becomes Emperor Napoleon.

1805 Younger **Pitt** builds alliance against Napoleon with Austria and Russia. Napoleon gathers army at Boulogne to invade England. Nelson defeats French and Spanish fleets at TRAFALGAR. Napoleon defeats Austrians and Russians at AUSTERLITZ. Pitt dies.

1806 Austria again sues for peace; **Francis II** drops title of Holy Roman Emperor, becomes Emperor of Austria. Napoleon crushes Prussia at JENA; is master of Germany.

The *Victory*, Nelson's flagship

1807 Napoleon defeats Russians at EYLAU and FRIEDLAND; forms an alliance with Russia at Tilsit. Britain now his only enemy; he seeks to ruin her by excluding British goods from Europe. Britain replies by blockading all countries under Napoleon's control; forces surrender of the Danish fleet by bombardment of Copenhagen. Napoleon occupies Portugal, which has thriving trade with Britain.

1808 Napoleon makes brother Joseph king of Spain. Spain and Portugal revolt; Peninsular War begins.

1809 Sir Arthur Wellesley (later Duke of Wellington) defeats French at TALAVERA. Austria re-enters war; is defeated at WAGRAM and again sues for peace.

1812 Napoleon invades Russia; occupies Moscow after battle of BORODINO, but the Russians burn the city and he is forced to retreat in winter, his 'Grande Armée' being destroyed. Wellington defeats French at SALAMANCA; occupies Madrid.

Dispute arising out of Britain's insistence on searching neutral ships leads to war between Britain and U.S. Britain occupies and burns Washington.

1813 Prussia and Austria drive Napoleon from Germany. Wellington defeats French at VITTORIA; drives them out of Spain.

1814 Britain and America make peace.

Austria, Russia and Prussia invade France, occupy Paris; Wellington marches into S. France. Napoleon abdicates, is banished to Elba. Bourbon dynasty restored.

1815 Napoleon escapes, resumes power, but is defeated at WATERLOO. Banished to St Helena. **Louis XVIII** returns to Paris.

1819 At 'Peterloo Massacre' in Manchester cavalry charge an open-air meeting of supporters of parliamentary reform.

1821 Greeks revolt against Turkish rule. Death of Napoleon.

1822 The poet **Lord Byron** is among many volunteers who go to Greece to help her in her war of independence.

1823 Spain tries to regain her American colonies; Britain recognises their independence, threatens to use British navy to prevent interference from Spain. **President Monroe** of the U.S.A. issues what is known as the 'Monroe Doctrine', saying that any interference by European powers on the American continent would be regarded as unfriendly to the U.S.A.

1827 British, French and Russian fleets destroy the Turkish fleet at NAVARINO, making it impossible for the Turks to put down the Greeks.

1829 Greece becomes independent kingdom.

1830 **Charles X** of France, who has tried to re-establish absolute monarchy, is driven from the throne and replaced by **Louis-Philippe**. Belgians revolt against Dutch rule and become independent. Unrest in Italy and Germany; in Britain the struggle for parliamentary reform becomes intense.

1832 Great Reform Bill is passed (see HISTORIC ACTS OF PARLIAMENT).

1833 Slavery abolished throughout British Empire.

1835–36 Boers undertake their 'Great Trek' to escape from British rule in the Cape; set up republic in Transvaal.

1837 Queen Victoria ascends the throne.

1846 Faced with famine in Ireland, **Sir Robert Peel** repeals Corn Laws (SEE HISTORIC ACTS OF PARLIAMENT).

1848 A year of unrest: revolt against Austrian rule by Hungarians, Czechs and Italians; Rome declared a republic; Sicily and Naples rise against their King. All these revolts suppressed. The crown of a unified Germany offered to **Frederick William IV** of Prussia, but as a believer in Divine Right of Kings he refuses because crown is offered by representatives of the people. He is forced to give his own subjects a constitution. Louis-Philippe of France deposed; republic proclaimed. In Britain the Chartists demand the vote for all.

1851 Great Exhibition in London.

Paxton's Crystal Palace, home of the Great Exhibition

1852 Louis-Napoleon makes himself French emperor as Napoleon III.

1853 Britain, seeing her position in India threatened by Russian ambitions, and France, under Napoleon III, who wants to strengthen his power by military triumphs, declare war on Russia. Anglo-French and Turkish force landed in the Crimea to capture Sevastopol. In the battles of BALACLAVA and INKERMANN, the Russians fail to drive out allied force. The harsh winter exposes the inefficiency of the British army, especially of its medical services, which **Florence Nightingale** does her best to remedy.

1855 Sardinia, wanting French and British support in the struggle to unite all Italy, joins war against Russia. Russians abandon SEVASTOPOL.

1856 Crimean War ends.

1857 Indian Mutiny breaks out. Delhi seized by rebels, besieged and captured by the British; Lucknow defended by British garrison. Last Mogul emperor is deposed and British Crown takes over administration of India from East India Company.

1859 Sardinia, under **Victor Emmanuel II**, and France declare war on Austria; defeat her at MAGENTA and SOLFERINO. Sardinia receives Lombardy, gives Nice and Savoy to France.

1860 **Garibaldi** overthrows Kingdom of the Two Sicilies (Naples and Sicily), which, with four remaining Italian duchies, are annexed by Sardinia.

    Abraham Lincoln elected U.S. President. Eleven southern states, wishing to maintain State rights against the central government, particularly on the issue of Negro slavery, claim the right to break away from the Union. Lincoln denies this right; American Civil War breaks out.

1861 Victor Emmanuel proclaimed first king of a United Italy.

1862 **Bismarck**, foreign minister of Prussia, sets out to unify Germany.

1863 **General Robert E. Lee**, commander of Southern forces in the American Civil War, defeated at GETTYSBURG. Lincoln proclaims abolition of slavery.

1864 **Maximilian of Hapsburg** made emperor of Mexico by Napoleon III. Mexican republicans, under **Juarez**, bitterly oppose him.

1865 General Lee surrenders to **General Grant** and American Civil War is over. Abraham Lincoln assassinated.

1866 U.S.A. insists that French troops be withdrawn from Mexico. Maximilian shot.

    In brief campaign against Austria, ending in overwhelming victory at SADOWA, Prussia smashes Austria's influence over Germany and insists that Venetia be handed over to Italy.

1867 Canada becomes Dominion.

1869 Suez canal opened.

1870 Napoleon III declares war on Prussia. French army surrounded at METZ and another, with Napoleon in command, surrenders at SEDAN. Napoleon's Empire collapses; is followed by Third Republic.

1871 United Germany proclaimed with king of Prussia as Emperor. France forced to give Alsace-Lorraine to Germany.

1872 Voting becomes secret in Britain.

1875 Disraeli wins control of Suez Canal for Britain by buying shares of the Khedive of Egypt. The Khedive's misrule has made Egypt bankrupt, and Britain and France have to pour money into the country to save it from collapse.

1877 Queen Victoria becomes Empress of India. Russia comes to aid of Serbs, Montenegrans, Rumanians and Bulgarians, risen against Turkish rule. Turks defeated; only under threat from Britain and Austria does Russia stop the war.

1878 Bulgaria established as a separate principality under Turkey; Serbia and Montenegro become independent kingdoms; and Bosnia and Herzogovina, both with largely Serbian populations, pass into Austrian hands, thus causing bad blood between Serbia and Austria. Britain receives Cyprus.

1881 At MAJUBA HILL Boers defeat British force trying to occupy Transvaal. Transvaal is recognised as independent republic under British authority.

France occupies Tunis as part of her policy of creating an empire for herself in Africa and Indo-China. Following discovery of the interior of Africa by **Livingstone** and others, 'scramble for Africa' becomes intense.

1882 Britain occupies Egypt and is drawn into the affairs of the Sudan, where **Mohammed Ahmed** has proclaimed himself Mahdi (Messiah) and declared a holy war against Egypt and all non-Moslems.

1884 Germany joins in 'scramble for Africa', acquiring S.W. Africa, Cameroons, Togoland and Tanganyika.

1885 General Gordon, sent to evacuate British and Egyptian garrisons in the Sudan, killed in Khartoum by Mahdi's forces.

1886 Royal Niger Company formed to open up interior of Nigeria.

1888 British East Africa Company secures what is now Kenya and takes over Uganda.

William II becomes German emperor.

1890 Cecil Rhodes, founder of Rhodesia, who hopes to see

British territory extend from the Cape to Cairo, becomes Prime Minister of Cape Colony.

In Germany William II drops Bismarck as Chancellor; the German drive to 'win a place in the sun' becomes fiercer.

1896 **Jameson**'s raid into the Transvaal in support of the British there, whose lives the Boers are making difficult, is a failure. Rhodes, suspected of backing Jameson, has to resign as Prime Minister of Cape Colony.

Italy, having established herself in Eritrea as part of the 'scramble for Africa', tries to conquer Ethiopia; is defeated at ADOWA.

1898 British General **Kitchener**, having defeated the Mahdi's forces at OMDURMAN and recaptured Khartoum, encounters a French force at Fashoda. The 'Fashoda incident' brings Britain and France close to war; but France, fearing the growing strength of Germany, gives in.

Grievances of British settlers in the Boer republic lead to the Boer War, beginning with a series of British defeats.

1900 **Lord Roberts** wipes out main Boer forces, but Boer guerilla units continue war.

Failure of the Boxer rising in China (a revolt against European and Japanese interference in Chinese affairs) speeds the collapse of Chinese imperial rule.

1901 Queen Victoria dies.

Australia becomes self-governing dominion.

1902 Boer War ends; Boer republics annexed by British Crown.

1904 'Entente Cordiale' ('warm understanding') established between Britain and France.

Russia which, after completion of the Trans-Siberian Railway, has extended her influence into Manchuria and Korea, clashes with Japan, which is trying to secure for herself as much of the decaying Chinese empire as she can. Japan declares war on Russia, and in a series of brilliant land and sea victories crushes Russia's Far Eastern forces.

1905 Russia forced to make peace and evacuate Manchuria.

1906 In Britain Liberals win great electoral victory and embark on sweeping programme of social reform.

1907 New Zealand becomes dominion.

Alliance between Britain and France extended to include Russia. There are now two great power blocs in Europe—Germany and Austria on one hand, Britain, France and Russia

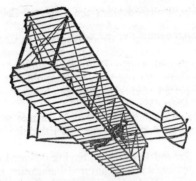

Wright Brothers' biplane 1907–8

on the other. Tension increases, and the powers begin an armaments race.

1908 Austria annexes Bosnia and Herzegovina, offending Serbia and Russia, since both provinces have largely Serb (or Slav) populations.

1910 Union of S. Africa formed of Cape of Good Hope, Natal, Orange Free State and Transvaal; becomes a dominion.

1911 In Britain the powers of the House of Lords are sharply cut.

Italy, seeking colonies, makes war on Turkey in order to seize Tripoli.

Germany tries to prevent French penetration of Morocco by sending a warship to Agadir. Backed by Britain, France refuses to give way.

1912–13 Two Balkan wars result in the expulsion of Turkey from Europe.

British government introduces an Irish Home Rule Bill which nearly leads to civil war in Ireland.

Tripoli is yielded to Italy.

1914 Assassination of the heir to the Austrian throne at Sarajevo triggers off First World War.

The Germans sweep through neutral Belgium; are halted only a few miles from Paris. The Allies force the Germans back in the battle of the MARNE; by October the struggle has settled down into trench warfare. Russians invade East Prussia, are stopped by **Hindenburg**'s victory at TANNENBERG.

1915 Both sides make costly attempts to break through, without success.

On the eastern front the Germans push the Russians further back.

Turkey, fighting on Germany's side, tries to cut the Suez Canal, but fails. The British fail to open communications with Russia through the Black Sea by forcing the Dardanelles and landing troops on the Gallipoli peninsula.

Italy enters the war on the Allied side. Germans announce that their U-boats will sink all merchant ships in British waters.

1916 Trench warfare continues; huge losses on both sides. British and German fleets meet off JUTLAND; the Germans are so battered that they remain in port for the rest of the war.

Following the sinking of the *Lusitania* with many Americans on board, the Germans are forced to abandon their unrestricted submarine campaign. The Arabs, aided by **T. E. Lawrence**, revolt against Turkish rule. In Britain **Lloyd George** becomes Prime Minister.

1917 Anti-war feeling in Russia leads to overthrow of the Czar; but the provisional government's attempt to continue the war enables **Lenin** and the Bolsheviks to seize power.

The Germans renew unrestricted submarine warfare, and in April the U.S.A. declares war.

British and French troops are sent to Italy after the Germans and Austrians have broken through the Italian front at CAPORETTO.

General Allenby captures Jerusalem.

1918 Germans launch their final offensive, but fail to break through. Allies counter-attack under **Marshal Foch** and force Germans to sue for armistice in November. William II, the Kaiser, abdicates; Germany becomes republic. Hapsburg monarchy in Austria comes to an end.

1919 Under peace treaties France regains Alsace-Lorraine; Germany loses the 'Polish Corridor' to the new Polish republic; Austria and Hungary are separated; Serbia is enlarged and becomes Yugoslavia; Czechoslovakia is created; the Ottoman empire is broken up, leaving only Turkey itself, which becomes a republic; a League of Nations is created, but its founder, **President Wilson**, fails to persuade his own country, the U.S.A., to become a member; Germany's colonies become League of Nation's mandates; and Germany has limits set on the size of her armed forces.

1921 Ireland, with the exception of Northern Ireland, which remains linked to the U.K., is made a dominion after nearly three years of disturbances.

1922 **Kemal Ataturk** seizes power in Turkey, sets out to modernise his country.

  Mussolini becomes head of the Italian government, establishes Fascism.

1924 Lenin, having established Communist rule in Russia despite famine and foreign intervention, dies; **Stalin** emerges as his successor and sets out to make Russia a great industrial power.

  In Britain **Ramsay MacDonald** forms the short-lived first Labour government.

1926 General Strike in Britain collapses after six weeks.

1929 World-wide economic crisis causes millions to be thrown out of work in the U.S.A. and Europe. In Germany **Hitler**'s National Socialist ('Nazi') party makes large gains.

1931 In Britain the second Labour government is replaced by a largely conservative National Government.

  In Spain the monarchy collapses and a republic is established.

  Japan invades China, sets up a puppet regime in Manchuria. China appeals unsuccessfully to the League of Nations, from which Japan resigns.

1933 **Franklin D. Roosevelt** becomes U.S. President and launches his 'New Deal' of social and economic reform to help America out of the Great Depression. Hitler is appointed Chancellor and makes himself dictator of Germany.

1935 Hitler denounces the terms of the Versailles Treaty limiting the size of the German armed forces.

  Mussolini invades and conquers Ethiopia, which appeals in vain to the League of Nations. Mussolini leaves the League.

1936 Military rising against the left-wing government in Spain leads to the outbreak of the Spanish Civil War. Germans and Italians fight openly on Franco's side, and the government receives aid from Russia.

1938 Hitler occupies Austria and claims the Sudetenland in Czechoslovakia. Under the Munich Agreement, signed by Britain, France, Germany and Italy, the Sudetenland is given to Germany; the new frontiers of Czechoslovakia are guaranteed.

1939 The Spanish Civil War ends with the surrender of Madrid; Fascist dictatorship established under **General Franco**. Hitler seizes the rest of Czechoslovakia. Mussolini seizes Albania.

Hitler makes a pact with Stalin and invades and crushes Poland, which is divided between Germany and Russia. Britain and France declare war; the Second World War has begun.

Russia makes war on Finland (in order to bring the approaches to Leningrad under her control), but her armies are beaten in the winter campaign.

1940 Russians break through; Finland sues for peace. Hitler occupies Norway and Denmark. In Britain **Chamberlain** is brought down, and **Winston Churchill** forms a coalition government. Sweeping through Holland, Belgium and Luxembourg, Hitler crushes France, which sues for armistice. Free French under **General de Gaulle** continue to fight from Britain. Britain, having extricated her army from France at Dunkirk, fights on alone. Hitler's plan to invade Britain collapses when his air force (the Luftwaffe) fails to win control of the air in the Battle of Britain; but the Luftwaffe continues its effort to smash Britain by 'blitz' bombing.

Italy enters war on German side, attacks Greece. British troops begin the capture of Italian colonies in E. Africa; reconquer Ethiopia.

1941 Hitler conquers Yugoslavia and Greece; in June, attacks Russia. Germans sweep to gates of Moscow and Leningrad, are caught by the winter. German force under **Rommel** arrives to strengthen Italians in N. Africa and becomes a dangerous threat to Egypt, the Suez Canal and Britain's position in the Middle East.

In December Japan attacks the U.S. Pacific Fleet at Pearl Harbor, bringing the U.S.A. into the war, and invades Malaya, Siam, the Philippines, Burma and Indonesia. Hong Kong falls.

1942 In Russia the Germans conquer the Ukraine and penetrate deep into the Caucasus, but winter sets in again, and a German army of over 300,000 is trapped and wiped out at STALINGRAD.

In Africa Rommel defeats the British and gets within 60

American Eagle

miles of Alexandria, but in the battle of ALAMEIN **Mont-gomery** defeats him decisively. An Anglo-American force under **Eisenhower** takes French N. Africa. Singapore falls, and by May the Japanese are masters of S.E. Asia, but their advance in the Central and S.W. Pacific is halted by American naval and air victories in the CORAL SEA and off MIDWAY.

The Americans begin to roll back the Japanese across the Pacific, capturing Guadalcanal in 1943, the Gilbert, Marshall and Mariana Islands in 1943 and 1944, the Philippines in 1944 and Iwo-Jima and Okinawa in 1945.

1943 German forces sent against Eisenhower in Africa, together with what remains of Rommel's force—altogether over a quarter of a million men—are forced to surrender.

The Allies invade Italy, but the Germans put up stiff resistance, and the Allied advance becomes a long, bitter push up the mountainous Italian peninsula, lasting until the end of the war. Mussolini is deposed and imprisoned; Italy joins the Allies. With Hitler's help, Mussolini escapes.

1944 Russians push Germans out of Russia and advance into Europe.

The Western allies, under Eisenhower, land in Normandy and sweep across France almost to the Rhine. A group of German officers attempt to assassinate Hitler, without success.

The British foil a Japanese attempt to invade India from Burma and launch a drive for the reconquest of Burma, Malaya and Singapore: completed successfully in 1945.

1945 The Allies cross the Rhine; the Russians invade Germany from the East. Hitler commits suicide as the Russians take Berlin. Germany surrenders. Japan surrenders after atom bombs have been dropped on Hiroshima and Nagasaki.

In Britain the Labour party wins an overwhelming victory

and sets out on a programme of social reforms designed to produce the 'welfare state' and to give self-government to non-white colonial peoples.

The United Nations organisation is formed.

1947 India, Pakistan, Burma and Ceylon become independent. **General Marshall**, U.S. Secretary of State, pledges American aid for Europe's recovery provided the European nations unite in a co-operative effort. With help given under this Marshall Plan living standards in nearly the whole of Western Europe rise within three years well above those of before the war. Russia and countries under her control boycott the Plan.

1948 Communists take over government in Czechoslovakia. There is now an 'iron curtain' between east and west. The Russians try to squeeze the Western Allies out of Berlin by cutting road and rail communications. The Allies supply Berlin by airlift until the blockade is lifted.

The state of Israel is proclaimed.

1949 The U.S.A., Canada, Britain, France and eight other W. European countries join together for mutual defence in the North Atlantic Treaty Organisation (NATO). Chinese Nationalists, under **Chiang-Kai-Shek**, are driven from Chinese mainland and take refuge in Formosa; Communist Chinese People's Republic is set up in China.

1950 N. Korea, under communist control, invades S. Korea. United Nations Security Council (from which the Russian delegate happens to be absent) calls upon its members to stop the aggressor; and American, British and other U.N. forces land just in time to save Korea from being overrun. The communists are driven back into N. Korea, but as they near the Chinese frontiers the Chinese intervene to drive the UN forces back into S. Korea.

1951 In Britain the Conservatives under Churchill defeat Labour.

1952 In Egypt **King Farouk** is forced to abdicate by **General Neguib**.

Elizabeth II succeeds her father, **George VI**.

1953 General Eisenhower becomes first Republican president for twenty years.

Stalin dies; there is a struggle for power inside Russia.

In Egypt Neguib is replaced by **Nasser**.

United Nations Build-
ing, New York

Korean War ends.

1954 After seven years of war between French and communists
in French Indo-China, an armistice is arranged. At the
Geneva Conference, French rule in Indo-China is ended, and
Laos, Cambodia and Vietnam become independent; but N.
Vietnam is left under communist control.

1955 Heads of government of the U.S.A., Russia, Britain and
France hold a 'summit' meeting at Geneva, and tension is
temporarily eased.

1956 Kruschev denounces Stalin's methods in a speech at the
20th Congress of the Soviet Communist party. His speech
causes the downfall of the Stalinist government in Poland; and
in Hungary it leads to a popular uprising, put down by Russian
tanks.

In Egypt Nasser seizes the Suez Canal. Goaded by the
aggressive attitude of the Arabs, who refuse to recognise her,
Israel invades Egypt and advances on the Suez Canal. Britain
and France demand an immediate cease-fire and, when their
demand is disregarded, land at Port Said. Their action is condemned by the United Nations, who order the Anglo-French
forces to withdraw. This they do.

1957 Ghana and Malaya become independent.

Russia launches into space the first man-made satellite, Sputnik I.

1958 In France, on the brink of civil war as a result of the disobedience of the Algerian settlers and sections of the army, de Gaulle is returned to power, remodels the constitution, and gives independence within the French community to France's colonies.

1959 Macmillan visits Kruschev in Moscow, and Kruschev becomes the first Soviet head of government to visit the U.S.A.

In Cuba **Fidel Castro** ends the **Batista** regime.

Fidel Castro

1960 Belgian Congo given independence; sinks almost immediately into chaos. U.N. intervenes, but disagreement between the great powers and the African nations hampers its work.

Nigeria becomes independent.

1961 John F. Kennedy, the youngest candidate ever to be elected to the White House, is installed as President of the U.S.A.

Man's first flight into space is made by **Major Yuri Gagarin**, Soviet airman, who circles the earth at 25,000 miles an hour before landing safely in Russia.

South Africa leaves the Commonwealth because of the opposition of the African and Asian Commonwealth countries to her racial policies. Sierra Leone and Tanganyika become independent. Cyprus joins the Commonwealth.

In Algeria extremists among the European settlers and French Army make two attempts to seize power, but President de Gaulle reasserts his authority on both occasions and continues his efforts to reach a settlement with the Algerian Arabs. The extremists form a Secret Army (the O.A.S.) and launch a terrorist campaign in Algeria and France.

World tension mounts when the Communist East German authorities build a wall across Berlin to stop the flow of East German refugees to West Berlin.

Dag Hammarskjoeld, the U.N. Secretary-General, is killed in an air crash in Africa, and is succeeded by a Burmese, **U Thant.**

Britain applies to join the European Common Market.

1962 **Colonel John Glenn,** American astronaut, successfully circles the earth three times in his Mercury space capsule.

Two Russian astronauts, **Major Nicolaev** and **Colonel Popovich,** are launched into space, the former orbiting the earth for 94½ hours and the second for 71 hours.

France and the Algerian Arabs sign a cease-fire, and Algeria becomes an independent country.

Jamaica and Trinidad become independent. Tanganyika declares itself a republic but stays within the Commonwealth.

The world's first communications satellite, Telstar, is launched.

Three thousand Cardinals and Bishops of the Roman Catholic Church meet in Rome to discuss Church problems and Christian unity under **Pope John XXIII.**

The Soviet Union establishes atomic missile bases in Fidel Castro's Cuba, President Kennedy orders Cuba to be blockaded, and the world seems to be on the brink of nuclear war. War is avoided, and tension eases, when Kruschev orders the dismantling of the Soviet missile bases.

1963 President de Gaulle objects to Britain's proposed entry into the Common Market, and the negotiations between Britain and the Common Market 'Six' are broken off.

U.N. military forces seize the main towns in Katanga, **President Tshombe's** secessionist province in the Congo, thus breaking the power of the biggest of the many separatist governments which have been defying the authority of the Central Congolese Government since independence in 1960.

Valentina Tereshkova, of Russia, becomes first woman in space.

Signing of Test Ban Treaty in Moscow between U.S.A.,
Russia and Britain marks easing of East-West tension.

Pope John XXIII dies. His successor is **Pope Paul VI.**

New state of Malaysia, comprising Malaya, Singapore,
Sarawak and parts of Borneo, is set up despite strong opposi-
tion of **President Soekarno** of Indonesia. Kenya and
Zanzibar become independent members of Commonwealth.

Harold Macmillan resigns for health reasons and is succeeded by Lord Home who relinquishes his peerage to become **Sir Alec Douglas-Home.**

President Kennedy is assassinated. His Vice-President,
Lyndon B. Johnson, takes over.

1964 In Zanzibar the Sultan is expelled and Zanzibar unites
with Tanganyika to form the new state of Tanzania.

Kruschev falls from power. As Secretary General of the
Russian Communist Party he is succeeded by **Brezhnev** and
as Chairman of the Soviet Council of Ministers by **Kosygin.**

Labour Party narrowly defeats Conservatives in General
Election. **Harold Wilson** becomes Prime Minister.

Lyndon B. Johnson, the Democratic candidate, wins a land-
slide victory in U.S. presidential election over **Senator Barry
Goldwater,** the Republican candidate.

1965 Sir Winston Churchill dies and is given a State funeral.

Russian **Colonel Leonov** becomes first man to 'walk' in
space, American **Major White** the second.

Fighting breaks out between India and Pakistan over
Kashmir. A cease-fire is arranged after three weeks.

The Government of **Mr. Smith** in Rhodesia, a British
colony, declares independence without Britain's consent, and
is condemned as 'illegal'.

Singapore leaves Malaysia to become independent state
within Commonwealth.

1966 Mrs. Gandhi, Nehru's daughter, becomes India's first
woman Prime Minister after **Mr. Shastri's** death.

Nigeria's unity is shaken by a series of military coups in
which many of the country's leaders are killed. A colonel in
his thirties, **Yakubu Gowon,** emerges as Head of State.

President Nkrumah of Ghana is deposed by a military
coup while on a visit to China.

The fighting in Vietnam, already some years old, between
the Communist Vietcong supported by the North Vietnamese,

and the South Vietnamese supported by the Americans, becomes fiercer and casualties mount on both sides.

Mr. Wilson and Labour Party win substantial victory in General Election.

England wins World Cup in football.

Dr. Erhard's Christian Democrat Government in West Germany collapses. Christian Democrats under a new leader, **Herr Kiesinger,** form a coalition government with the main opposition party, the Social Democrats.

1967 Britain applies for membership of the Common Market for the second time but again General de Gaulle says no.

A military junta seizes power in Greece.

Israel routs the armed forces of Egypt, Jordan and Syria in six days but, despite a hurriedly arranged cease-fire, there is no relaxation of tension in the Middle East.

Civil war rages in Nigeria between the Federal Nigerian Government and the breakaway state of Biafra.

1968 In Czechoslovakia **President Novotny,** a 'Stalinist hardliner', is ousted by **Alexander Dubcek** and other Communist 'liberals' who introduce political, social and economic reforms. The Russians invade and occupy Czechoslovakia and arrest Dubcek and many of his followers, but when they fail to find any Czechoslovak Communist willing to run the country for them they are forced to reinstate Dubcek. But Dubcek's powers of government are drastically reduced.

Britain announces her intention to withdraw from all her bases East of Suez by 1971 (with the exception of Hong Kong).

France is brought virtually to a standstill by violent student riots and strikes by more than 8 million workers, and it is several weeks before General de Gaulle restores his authority.

Peace talks to end the Vietnam War begin in Paris.

Dr. Martin Luther King, the American Negro leader, and **Senator Robert Kennedy,** the late President Kennedy's brother, are assassinated.

Three American astronauts, **Frank Borman, Bill Anders** and **Jim Lovell,** become the first men to circle round the moon.

1969 Richard M. Nixon, a Republican and President Eisenhower's Vice-President, is installed as US President. He begins withdrawal of American troops from Vietnam.

Alexander Dubcek is ousted as First Secretary of Czechoslovak Communist Party and replaced by **Dr. Husak.** 'Hard-line' Communists tighten their control in Czechoslovakia.

American astronauts **Neil Armstrong** and **Edwin Aldrin** become the first men to walk on the moon.

General de Gaulle, defeated in a referendum on local regional reform, retires from public life. **Georges Pompidou,** a Gaullist, is elected President.

After general elections in West Germany, the Social Democrats become the dominant partners in a coalition government for the first time since the foundation of the West German Federal Republic, with **Willy Brandt** as Chancellor.

Greece withdraws from Council of Europe to avoid being expelled because of the undemocratic and repressive nature of its military regime.

1970 The Nigerian civil war ends with the capitulation of Biafra.

Treaty, limiting spread of nuclear armaments, comes into force after ratification by 43 states, including Britain, the U.S.A. and the Soviet Union, but excluding France and Communist China.

In Britain the Conservatives, led by **Edward Heath,** defeat Labour.

Britain, for the third time, begins negotiations to join the Common Market.

President Nasser of Egypt dies and is succeeded by **Anwar Sadat.**

Serious riots in the Polish ports on the Baltic, sparked off by large increases in food prices, cause downfall of **Gomulka** and his replacement by **Gierek**.

1971 Commonwealth Prime Ministers' Conference meets in Singapore, the first ever to be held in Asia.

In East Pakistan, the Awami League, victorious in the previous year's elections, demands first autonomy for the eastern province and then independence as the Republic of Bangladesh. **President Yahya Khan** treats this demand as sedition. The Awami League's leader, **Sheik Mujibur Rahman**, is arrested and flown to West Pakistan. West Pakistani troops are flown to East Pakistan to suppress all support for independence. Millions of refugees flood across the border into India. India intervenes with its armed forces. The war between India and Pakistan is short. In East Pakistan the West Pakistani forces surrender, and Bangladesh is proclaimed. In the West of the Indian sub-continent, a cease-fire is arranged between India and Pakistan. Yahya Khan resigns and hands over the presidency to **Zulfikar Ali Bhutto.**

Britain reaches agreement on the main points in her negotiations for joining the Common Market, and Parliament votes in favour of the principle of Britain becoming a member.

Communist China replaces Chiang-Kai-Shek's government as the official representative of China in the U.N.

Kurt Waldheim, an Austrian diplomat, is elected fourth Secretary-General of the U.N. in succession to U Thant.

1972 President Bhutto releases Sheik Mujibur Rahman who becomes Prime Minister of Bangladesh.

Pakistan leaves the Commonwealth when some Commonwealth countries recognise Bangladesh as an independent state.

Britain signs a Treaty of Accession to the Common Market. Eire, Denmark and Norway sign similar treaties.

President Nixon visits Peking at the invitation of the Chinese Communist Government, and later Moscow at the invitation of the Soviet Government.

Edward Heath's Conservative Government takes over direct rule of Northern Ireland, suspending the powers of the Northern Irish Government and Parliament.

West German Parliament ratifies treaties of reconciliation between West Germany on the one hand and on the other the Soviet Union, Poland and East Germany.

Elizabeth II becomes the first British monarch to visit a Communist country when she pays a State Visit to Yugoslavia.

Willy Brandt calls for a general election in West Germany and wins a majority for his Social Democrats and his coalition partners, the Free Democrats (Liberals).

The British Parliament ratifies the Treaty of Accession to the European Economic Community. Eire and Denmark vote in favour of joining but Norway votes against.

President Amin of Uganda expels tens of thousands of Asians from his country in pursuit of his policy of 'Africanisation'. Britain receives nearly 30,000 Ugandan Asians.

1973 Britain, Eire and Denmark become full members of the enlarged European Economic Community.

President Nixon is sworn in for a second term of office after his sweeping victory over **Senator George McGovern.**

Cease-fire agreement in Vietnamese war is signed between U.S., North Vietnam, South Vietnam and Vietcong.

President Nixon is suspected of being involved in the attempt, during the 1972 Presidential campaign, to break into the headquarters of his political opponents in a building called Watergate, and several of his top assistants resign.

Vice-President **Spiro Agnew,** after pleading guilty to tax evasion, resigns his office.

Dr Henry Kissinger is appointed U.S. Secretary of State, the first non-U.S.-born citizen to be appointed to this office.

Leonid Brezhnev, General Secretary of the Soviet Communist Party, visits the United States and stresses the importance of detente between the super-powers.

The Conference on European Security and Co-operation opens in Geneva; and talks begin in Vienna between East and West on the reduction of forces in Central Europe.

Elections for a new local assembly are held in Northern Ireland; a 12-man executive is created, and the setting-up of a Council of Ireland is agreed.

In Argentina, **Juan Peron** returns to power.

In Chile, **President Allende's** Marxist government is overthrown by a military junta. Allende is killed.

In Greece, **President Papadopoulos,** having deposed **King Constantine** and the monarchy and declared his country a republic, is overthrown by a rival military junta.

Egypt and Syria attack Israel on Yom Kippur, the Jewish Day of Atonement, and, after initial successes, are fought to a standstill. The United States and the U.S.S.R. agree to bring the fighting to an end to prevent a worldwide conflagration. The Soviet–U.S. agreement is approved by the U.N. Security Council; but before the fighting is stopped, a second cease-fire agreement has to be negotiated. On Dr Kissinger's initiative, a Middle East peace conference convenes in Geneva.

The oil-producing states of Kuwait, Saudi Arabia, Algeria, Abu Dhabi and Libya cut back oil deliveries to countries declared to be pro-Israel. The use of the 'oil weapon' causes an acute energy crisis—particularly in Britain, where it is made worse by the overtime ban imposed by miners and railway drivers.

1974 The British Government announces that the working week for most of British industry has to be cut to three days. The miners vote in favour of a national coal strike.

The U.S. government convenes a conference of oil-consuming countries to discuss the world energy crisis.

Edward Heath calls an election on the issue 'Who governs Britain?' Labour wins 301 seats, the Conservatives 296, and others (including 14 Liberals) 38, and Harold Wilson takes power at the head of a minority Labour Government. The miners accept a settlement of over £100,000,000.

Harold Wilson calls a second election in the autumn and wins a narrow majority over all other parties. The British government presses ahead with re-negotiating the terms of British membership of the European Economic Community.

High oil prices cause the economies of many industrial countries, including Britain, to slow down.

President Nixon is forced to resign because of his involvement in the Watergate break-in and the manoeuvres to cover it up—the first President in U.S. history to resign his office. He is succeeded by **Gerald Ford.**

Mrs Golda Meir resigns as Prime Minister of Israel and is succeeded by **Yitzhel Rabin.**

President Makarios is forced to leave Cyprus after a coup organised by Greek Cypriots who support union with Greece (*Enosis*), encouraged in their action by the military junta in Athens. The Turks invade Cyprus and occupy the northern part of the island. The Turkish invasion leads to the collapse of military junta in Athens. **Constantine Karamanlis** becomes Prime Minister and promises Greece a return to democracy. The Greek people vote overwhelmingly in favour of remaining a republic.

President Makarios returns to Cyprus but the Turks continue to occupy the northern part of the island.

In Portugal, 50 years of dictatorship are ended when **Dr Caetano** is ousted. The new government, headed first by **General Spinola** and later by **General Costa Gomes**, moves rapidly to give Portugal's African colonies—Guinea-Bissau, Mozambique and Angola—their independence.

The approach of African rule in Mozambique and Angola changes the balance of power in southern Africa, and, under pressure from **Mr Vorster,** the South African Prime Minister, Mr Ian Smith, the Rhodesian leader, releases two black leaders of the banned African Nationalist parties and allows them to fly to Lusaka in Zambia for talks with the leaders of other African states. Negotiations between the black and white leaders of Rhodesia soon become bogged down.

President Pompidou of France dies and **Giscard d'Estaing** is elected in his place.

Emperor Haile Selassie of Ethiopia is deposed by radical elements in his army.

Willy Brandt, West Germany's first Social Democratic Chancellor, resigns when it is revealed that an alleged East German spy has been working in his office. He is succeeded by a fellow Social Democrat, **Helmut Schmidt.**

President Peron of Argentina dies and is succeeded by his wife, **Isabelita.**

The IRA extends its terrorist activities to Britain.

1975 Sheik Mujibur Rahman, Prime Minister of Bangladesh, changes his country's constitution: makes himself President.

In a referendum to decide whether Britain is to stay in the European Economic Community, more than 17 million vote for staying in and more than 8 million against.

The British Government decides to halt work on the Channel Tunnel because of rapidly rising construction costs.

Mrs Margaret Thatcher is elected leader of the Conservative Party, replacing Edward Heath.

In Lebanon the Muslims become the largest community in the country, a position previously held by Christians. Fighting breaks out between extremist factions in the two communities. The situation is made worse by the presence in Lebanon of tens of thousands of Palestinian refugees, many of them members of the Palestinian Liberation Army. The country slides into civil war.

King Feisal of Saudi Arabia is assassinated.

Chiang Kai-Shek dies at the age of 87.

The deposed Emperor Haile Selassie dies in detention.

President Anwar Sadat re-opens Suez Canal and, with the agreement of Israel, the first ships pass through the Canal since its closure after the 1967 war.

In Helsinki, President Ford, Mr Brezhnev, Mr Wilson, Canada's **Mr Trudeau** and the leaders of 31 other countries sign a document intended to reduce tension between East and West. This is the result of three years work by the Conference on European Security and Co-operation. The document fails to receive universal acclaim, especially in the West. Peking is also very critical.

In Britain, the Government and the trade unions agree to a £6 limit on pay increases for the next 12 months.

In Nigeria General Gowon is removed as Head of State by a military coup.

In Indo-China, the longest war in the 20th century, lasting 30 years, comes to an end. In South Vietnam, Communist forces capture Saigon, the capital, and rename it Ho Chi Minh City. In Cambodia the Communist Khmer Rouge occupy the capital, Phnom Penh, and **Prince Sihanouk,** ousted in 1970, returns from exile as Head of State. Laos falls to the pro-Communist Pathet Lao after an almost bloodless coup.

In Portugal, the Armed Forces Movement removes its most dedicated pro-Communist members from positions of influence, and in both the Movement and the Government more moderate political elements begin to assert themselves.

In Mozambique, Portugal hands over power peacefully and smoothly; but in Angola, after 500 years of colonial rule, the last Commissioner-General can find no one to whom to hand over power. Three rival liberation movements are left fighting for control: the MPLA, supported by Russian arms and technicians and several thousand Cuban troops; the FNLA, supported by Communist China; and UNITA, supported by South African troops. The FNLA and UNITA join forces but, after early successes, give way to the MPLA. Attempts by President Ford and Dr Kissinger to send aid and arms to the forces fighting the MPLA are blocked by the U.S. Congress.

President Sheik Mujibur Rahman of Bangladesh and his family are assassinated in a military coup.

In Northern Ireland the number of civilians killed since 1969 passes the 1,000 mark. In Britain the IRA terror campaign is stepped up.

In Spain, General Franco dies at the age of 82, and **Prince Juan Carlos** is sworn in as King and Head of State.

In India, Mrs Indira Gandhi declares a state of emergency. Many opposition politicians are arrested, but her own Congress Party gives her full support.

British oil starts flowing ashore from the North Sea. The North Sea fields are expected to make Britain self-sufficient in oil by 1980.

1976 **Chou-En-Lai,** Chinese Prime Minister, Mao-Tse-Tung's right hand man for 40 years and the architect of China's policy of rapprochement towards the United States and the West, dies at the age of 77.

The world's first commercial passenger supersonic aircraft, the Anglo-French Concorde, goes into regular service.

Unemployment in Britain passes the 1½ million mark, and the pound falls below \$2 for the first time in history.

In Argentina President Isabelita Peron is deposed in a bloodless military coup and placed under arrest. **General Videla,** commander of the Army, becomes President.

Harold Wilson resigns as Prime Minister and **James Callaghan** takes his place.

In Portugal a moderate is elected President and in parliamentary elections the Socialists emerge as the largest single party but without an overall majority. Their leader, **Dr Mario Soares,** forms a minority government.

The Americans carry out man's deepest probe into space by launching two unmanned spacecraft, Viking I and Viking II, and landing them safely more than 200 million miles from earth, on Mars. The spacecraft beam back pictures, but the answer to the question, whether or not there is life on Mars, remains unsolved.

In Italy the Communists make substantial gains in the

parliamentary elections, but not enough to win a place in the newly-formed Government. At the same time, the Christian Democrat government, whose majority has been reduced, has to rely on the support of the Communists.

In Sweden, the Social Democrats lose power after 44 years and are replaced by a coalition of right-of-centre parties.

In West Germany **Helmut Schmidt,** the leader of the Social Democratic–Free Democrat (Liberal) Coalition Government, narrowly defeats the Christian Democrats.

The Canadian Prime Minister, Pierre Trudeau, and his Liberal Party suffer a severe set-back when the separatist Parti Québécois sweeps the Liberals out of government in provincial elections in Québec, Canada's second most important province.

The Cod War between Iceland and Britain ends and British trawlers withdraw from the 200-mile fishing limits declared by Iceland.

The European Economic Community, the U.S.A. and the Soviet Union declare 200-mile fishing zones around their respective territories.

Ian Smith agrees, under pressure from the South African Prime Minister, to proposals by Dr Kissinger, the U.S. Secretary of State, for majority rule within 2 years in Rhodesia. The British Government arranges a conference in Geneva between interested parties, but this adjourns without reaching agreement.

In South Africa, the independence of Transkei, the first of the Bantustans, the separate homelands for black South Africans, is proclaimed. The UN General Assembly refuses to recognise Transkei.

Chairman Mao Tse-tung dies and is succeeded as Chairman by the moderate **Hua Kuo-feng.** After a brief power struggle, Mao's widow and her alleged 'radical' supporters are arrested.

In Britain the Devolution Bill is laid before Parliament but is defeated by a vote in the House of Commons.

In Lebanon the Syrian army, with the approval of Egypt and Saudi Arabia, imposes a truce on the warring factions of Maronite Christians and Muslims after 19 months of civil war in which more than 50,000 people have been killed, four times as many maimed and injured and Beirut, once the business and financial centre of the Middle East, reduced to rubble.

1977 Jimmy Carter, Democrat, is installed as 39th President of the U.S.A.

The new Race Relations Bill in Britain strengthens the law on racial discrimination. Proof of intention to incite racial hatred is no longer necessary—only the likelihood of it.

In Rumania, an earthquake disaster, the heaviest recorded in Europe since 1940, causes nearly 13,000 casualties.

In an effort to stem the increasing pollution of the Mediterranean, fifteen of the eighteen nations bordering it meet to discuss a remedy.

The women of Liechtenstein vote for the first time.

The worst-ever civil air disaster occurs on the island of Teneriffe when two Boeing 747 Jumbo jets collide on the runway, killing 582.

The Conservatives in England and Wales make great gains in the County Council elections. The Labour Government is kept in power by the making of a formal pact between itself and the Liberals, under their leader, **David Steel.** The pact is under pressure during the year, but holds.

In Israel, Labour, the dominant party since 1948, is defeated, and **Menahem Begin** forms a coalition cabinet.

In Uganda, **Archbishop Luwum** and two Cabinet ministers are arrested; it is later reported that they have been killed in a road accident whilst trying to escape. This announcement is followed by world-wide condemnation of President Amin.

The Soviet Union and the U.S.A. reach agreement on cooperation in exploration and the use of outer space.

On June 7, a public holiday marks the Queen's silver Jubilee. There are celebrations throughout the year all over Britain and the Commonwealth, and the Queen tours extensively at home and abroad.

British proposals for an interim government leading to majority rule are rejected outright by Ian Smith, Rhodesia's Prime Minister, who wins a general election.

The Soviet Union celebrates the 60th anniversary of the Russian Revolution.

The European Parliament in Luxembourg approves a ban on herring fishing in the North Sea until the end of 1978.

Workers at the Grunwick film processing factory in North London remain on strike in demand of union recognition;

there are angry scenes on the picket lines: court actions fail to resolve the dispute.

Steve Biko, founder and first president of the South African Students Association, dies while under arrest, and the post mortem finds 'extensive brain damage'. Over 1,200 black students mourning his death are arrested on the campus near Durban, and at the inquiry, which follows world-wide expressions of horror, the police are exonerated from blame for Biko's death.

Laker Airways's Skytrain inaugurates the cheapest-ever flight from Gatwick to New York.

Three Baader-Meinhof terrorists commit suicide in Stammheim Prison, in West Germany, following the rescue of 86 hostages on board a hi-jacked Boeing 737.

20,000 people die after a cyclone hits the Indian state of Andhra Pradesh, and thousands of others are made homeless.

Concorde begins scheduled flights between Europe and New York.

Britain's unemployment figures hover round the 1,500,000 mark. The gold and foreign currency reserves rise to a record of 20,394 million dollars.

President Sadat, in an attempt to resolve the conflict in the Middle East, is the first Egyptian leader to visit Israel.

1978 Early in the New Year, gales and heavy storms sweep the east of England, causing heavy damage and floods. 39 people lose their lives.

After strong speeches in public from both sides, hopes of an early settlement between Egypt and Israel begin to fade.

Agreement is reached between Ian Smith and three black moderate parties on broad constitutional outlines for an interim Government for Rhodesia; but since it is achieved without the participation of the Patriotic Front, representing the guerillas, there are doubts about its acceptability.

Fort Sumter: the beginning of the American Civil War

An Index of Important Battles
mentioned in the Diary of World Events

Prestonpans, 1745
Pyramids, 1798
Ramillies, 1706
Quebec, 1759
Quiberon Bay, 1759
Salamanca, 1812
Salamis, 480 B.C.
St Albans, 1455
Saratoga, 1777
Sedan, 1870
Sedgemoor, 1685
Sevastopol, 1855
Shrewsbury, 1403
Sluys, 1340
Solferino, 1859
Southwold Bay, 1672
Stalingrad, 1942
Stirling, 1297

Talavera, 1809
Tannenberg, 1914
Tewkesbury, 1471
Thermopylae, 480 B.C.
Towton, 1461
Trafalgar, 1805
Trasimene, 217 B.C.
Vienna, 1529
Vienna, 1683
Vittoria, 1813
Wagram, 1809
Wakefield, 1460
Waterloo, 1815
Worcester, 1651
Yarmak, 643
Yorktown, 1781
Zama, 202 B.C.

List of Kings and Queens of Scotland

ALPINES

Kenneth I, 843–60
Donald I, 860–63
Constantine I, 863–77
Aedh, 877–78
Eocha, 878–89
Donald II, 889–900
Constantine II, 900–43
Malcolm I, 943–54
Indulf, 954–62
Duff, 962–67
Colin, 967–71
Kenneth II, 971–95
Constantine III, 995–97
Kenneth III, 997–1005
Malcolm II, 1005–34
Duncan I, 1034–40
Macbeth, 1040–57
Malcolm III, 1057–93
Donald Bane, 6 months in 1093
Duncan II, 6 months in 1094
Donald Bane again, 1094–97
Edgar, 1097–1107
Alexander I, 1107–24
David I, 1124–53
Malcolm IV (The Maiden), 1153–65

William I (The Lion), 1165–1214
Alexander II, 1214–49
Alexander III, 1249–86
Margaret, 1286–90
No king, 1290–92
John Baliol, 1292–96
No king, 1296–1306

BRUCES

Robert I, 1306–29
David II, 1329–71

STUARTS

Robert II, 1371–90
Robert III, 1390–1406
Regent Albany, 1406–19
Regent Murdoch, 1419–24
James I, 1424–37
James II, 1437–60
James III, 1460–88
James IV, 1488–1513
James V, 1513–42
Mary, 1542–67
James VI, 1567–1625

Until 1603 James VI reigned over Scotland only; in 1603 he became King of England and Ireland. From 1603 onwards the kings of Scotland are the same as the kings of England.

Historic Acts of Parliament

Act	Date	What it did
Catholic Emancipation Act	1829	Gave full civic rights to Catholics.
Combination Acts	1799 & 1800	Made trade unions and meetings of men to discuss wages and hours illegal. Repealed, 1824. Trade Unions made legal, 1871.
Conventicle Act	1664	Made it illegal for more than five people to meet for religious worship. An anti-Catholic measure.
Corn Laws	1815	Prohibited import of foreign corn till wheat reached famine prices. Repealed, 1846.
Corporation Act	1661	Required that anyone taking up a municipal office should receive communion according to the rites of the Anglican Church and should declare it unlawful on any grounds to take up arms against the king. An anti-Presbyterian measure.
Education Act	1870	Introduced elementary education for all.
Education Act	1944	Introduced secondary education for all.
Factory Acts	Throughout 19th century	Regulated conditions of work. The Act of 1833 provided for the appointment of factory inspectors; the Act of 1847 limited the working day to 10 hours.
Government, Act	1657	Made Cromwell's rule legal, and enabled him to name his successor.
Habeas Corpus	1679	Made it illegal to hold a man in prison without trial.

Act	*Date*	*What it did*
Heresy, Statute of	1401	Provided that all heretics (people whose beliefs were not those of the Church) were to be imprisoned and, if they refused to give up their heresy, to be burned alive. Repealed, 1548.
Indemnity, Bill of	1660	First measure passed after restoration of Charles II; pardoned all offences committed during the Cromwellian period.
Kilkenny, Statute of	1366	Forbade the mixing of the English in Ireland with the Irish people.
Labourers, Statute of	1349	Passed during the labour shortage that followed the Black Death; bound a labourer to serve under anyone requiring him to do so for wages current two years before the plague began.
Libel Act	1791	Made the decision as to what was libellous a matter for the jury and not the judge.
Mines Act	1842	Prohibited the employment in mines of women, girls and boys under 10.
National Insurance Act	1916	First introduced compulsory national health contributions and a scheme of insurance against unemployment.
Navigation Act	1652	Prohibited the importation in foreign ships of any but products of the countries to which the ships belonged. Aimed at the Dutch.
Old Age Pensions Act	1908	Introduced old age pensions for the first time.
Parliament Acts	1911 & 1949	Limited the powers of the House of Lords.
Poor Laws	1562–1601	Placed on local authorities the responsibility for settling and supporting the poor.
Poyning's Act	1494	Forbade the Parliament of the Pale in Ireland to deal with matters not first approved of by the English King and his Council. Repealed, 1779.
Public Health Act	1848	Set up the first Central Board of Health.

Act	Date	What it did
Reform Bill	1832	Took away the right to elect M.P.s from 56 'rotten boroughs', gave the seats to counties or large towns hitherto unrepresented in Parliament, and gave the vote to £10 householders. Followed by the Act of 1867, which extended the vote to working people in towns; the Act of 1884, which gave the vote to country labourers; and the Acts of 1918 and 1928, which gave the vote to women.
Rights, Bill of	1689	Established the right of the people, through their representatives in Parliament, to depose the King and set on the throne whomever they chose.
Security, Act of	1706	Required the sovereign to swear to support the Presbyterian Church.
Settlement, Act of	1701	Confined the succession to the throne to Protestants and settled it on the House of Hanover.
Six Articles, Act of the	1539	An anti-Protestant measure, establishing the celibacy of the clergy, monastic vows and private masses. Repealed, 1548.
Stamp Act	1765	Imposed a tax on all legal documents issued within the colonies. Repealed, 1766.
Succession, Act of	1534	Required an oath to be taken by all acknowledging that Henry VIII's marriage with Catharine of Aragon was invalid.
Supremacy, Act of	1534	Ordered that the king 'shall be taken, accepted and reputed the only supreme head on earth of the Church of England'.
Test Act	1563	First anti-Catholic Act, exacting from all office-holders an oath of allegiance to Queen Elizabeth and a declaration that the Pope had no authority. A similar act was passed in 1673, and set aside in 1686.

Act	Date	What it did
Toleration Act	1689	Established freedom of worship.
Treaty of Accession to European Communities, Act	1972	It made Britain a full member as from 1 Jan 1973, of the three European Communities, i.e. the Economic Community, the Coal and Steel Community and of Euratom.
Triennial Bill	1641	Enforced the assembly of the House of Commons every three years.
Uniformity, Act of	1559	Restored the English Prayer Book and enforced its use on the clergy.
Union, Act of	1707	United England and Scotland.
Union with Ireland, Act of	1800	United England and Ireland.
Winchester, Statute of	1285	Bound every man to serve the king in case of invasion or revolt and to pursue felons when the hue and cry was raised against them.

Explorations and Discoveries

Date	Explorer	Nationality	Exploration or Discovery
982	Eric the Red	Viking	Discovered Greenland
c. 1000	Leif Ericsson	Viking	Reached N. America
1255	Nicolo and Maffeo Polo	Venetian	Travelled to Peking
1271–94	Marco Polo	Venetian	Journeyed through China, India and other parts of Asia
14th century	João Zarco, Tristão Vas and others	Portuguese	Discovered Madeira and the Azores
1487–88	Bartholomew Diaz	Portuguese	Rounded Cape of Good Hope
1492	Christopher Columbus	Italian in Spanish service	Discovered San Salvador (now Watling Island), the Bahamas, Cuba and Haiti

Date	Explorer	Nationality	Exploration or Discovery
1493–96	Christopher Columbus	Italian in Spanish service	Discovered Guadeloupe, Montserrat, Antigua, Puerto Rico and Jamaica
1497	John Cabot	Genoese in English service	Discovered Cape Breton Island, Newfoundland and Nova Scotia
1497–1503	Amerigo Vespucci	Florentine	Explored Mexico, part of E. coast of America and S. American coast
1498	Vasco da Gama	Portuguese	Discovered sea-route from Europe to India
1498	Christopher Columbus	Italian in Spanish service	Landed on mainland of S. America
1501–16	Various	Portuguese	Discovered Ceylon, Goa, Malacca, Canton, Japan and E. Indies
1502–4	Christopher Columbus	Italian in Spanish service	Discovered Trinidad
1509	Sebastian Cabot	Genoese in English service	Explored American coast as far as Florida, Brazilian coast and mouth of R. Plate
1519–22	Ferdinand Magellan	Portuguese in Spanish service	First to sail round the world; discovered the Magellan Strait, reached the Philippines and named the Pacific
1534–36	Jacques Cartier	French	Discovered Canada, explored the St Lawrence and named Mount Royal (Montreal)
1539	De Soto	Spanish	Discovered Florida, Georgia and the R. Mississippi
1554	Sir Hugh Willoughby and Richard Chancellor	English	Discovered the White Sea and the ocean route to Russia

Date	Explorer	Nationality	Exploration or Discovery
1576	Martin Frobisher	English	Began search for N.W. Passage
	John Davis	English	Discovered Davis Strait between Atlantic and Arctic Oceans
1577–80	Sir Francis Drake	English	Sailed round the world in the *Golden Hind*
1606	William Janszoon	Dutch	Discovered Australia
1606	Capt. John Smith and a party of colonists	English	Explored Chesapeake Bay, discovered Potomac and Susquehannah
1611	Henry Hudson	English	Sought N.E. and N.W. Passages; discovered Hudson River, Strait and Bay
1642	Abel Tasman	Dutch	Discovered Tasmania, New Zealand, the Tonga and Fiji islands
1700	William Dampier	English	Explored W. Coast of Australia
1728	Vitus Bering	Danish in Russian service	Discovered Bering Strait between Asia and America
1740–44	George, Lord Anson	English	Sailed round the world in the *Centurion*
1767	Capt. Wallis	English	Discovered Tahiti
1768–71	Capt. James Cook	English	Sailed round the world in the *Endeavour*; charted New Zealand coasts and surveyed E. Coast of Australia, naming New South Wales and Botany Bay
1772	Capt. James Cook	English	Discovered Easter Island, New Caledonia and Norfolk Island
1776	Capt. James Cook	English	Discovered several of the Cook (or Hervey) islands. Rediscovered Sandwich (now Hawaiian) islands

Date	Explorer	Nationality	Exploration or Discovery
1776	Mungo Park	Scottish	Explored the course of R. Niger
1831	Sir James Clark Ross and Rear-Admiral Sir John Ross	English	Located the magnetic pole
1839–43	Sir James Clark Ross	English	Discovered Victoria Land, Mounts Erebus and Terror, the Ross ice barrier
1847	Rear-Admiral Sir John Franklin	English	Lost in Arctic Ocean while seeking N.W. Passage
1852–73	David Livingstone	Scottish	Discovered the course of the Zambesi, the Victoria Falls and Lake Nyasa
1856	Capt. John Speke	English	Discovered Lake Tanganyika
1858	Capt. John Speke	English	Discovered Lake Victoria Nyanza
1862	Capt. John Speke and Lt.-Col. J. A. Grant	English	Discovered source of White Nile
1901	Capt. R. F. Scott	English	Discovered King Edward VII Land
1903–6	Capt. Roald Amundsen	Norwegian	First navigation of the N.W. Passage
1908–9	Sir Ernest Shackleton	English	Reached within 100 miles of South Pole
1909	Rear-Admiral Robert Peary	American	Reached North Pole
1911	Capt. Roald Amundsen	Norwegian	First reached South Pole (December 14)
1912	Capt. R. F. Scott	English	Reached South Pole (January 18)
1929	Admiral R. Byrd	American	First flight over South Pole
1957–58	Sir Vivian Fuchs and Sir Edmund Hillary	English and New Zealander	First crossing of the Antarctic Continent

Date	Explorer	Nationality	Exploration or Discovery
1961–62	Major Yuri Gagarin, Major Gherman Titov, Commander Alan Shepard, Capt. Virgil Grissom and Col. John Glenn	Russian and American	First journeys into space
1963	Valentina Tereshkova	Russian	First woman in space
1965	Col. Leonov Major White	Russian and American	First men to 'walk' in space
1968	Frank Borman, Bill Anders, and Jim Lovell	American	First men to circle moon
1969	Neil Armstrong and Edwin Aldrin	American	First men to step on the moon
	Charles Conrad and Alan Bean	American	Second pair to step on the moon

British Prime Ministers

REIGN OF GEORGE I

Sir Robert Walpole (*Whig*)	1721–27

REIGN OF GEORGE II

Sir Robert Walpole (*Whig*)	1727–42
Earl of Wilmington (*Whig*)	1742–43
Henry Pelham (*Whig*)	1743–46
Henry Pelham (*Whig*)	1746–54
Duke of Newcastle (*Whig*)	1754–56
Duke of Devonshire (*Whig*)	1756–57
Duke of Newcastle (*Whig*)	1757–60

REIGN OF GEORGE III

Duke of Newcastle (*Whig*)	1760–62
Earl of Bute (*Tory*)	1762–63
George Grenville (*Whig*)	1763–65
Marquess of Rockingham (*Whig*)	1765–66
Earl of Chatham (*Whig*)	1766–67
Duke of Grafton (*Whig*)	1767–70
Lord North (*Tory*)	1770–82

Marquess of Rockingham (*Whig*)	1782
Earl of Shelburne (*Whig*)	1782–83
Duke of Portland (*Coalition*)	1783
William Pitt (*Tory*)	1783–1801
Henry Addington (*Tory*)	1801–4
William Pitt (*Tory*)	1804–6
Lord Grenville (*Whig*)	1806–7
Duke of Portland (*Tory*)	1807–9
Spencer Perceval (*Tory*)	1809–12
Earl of Liverpool (*Tory*)	1812–20

REIGN OF GEORGE IV

Earl of Liverpool (*Tory*)	1820–27
George Canning (*Tory*)	1827
Viscount Goderich (*Tory*)	1827–28
Duke of Wellington (*Tory*)	1828–30

REIGN OF WILLIAM IV

Earl Grey (*Whig*)	1830–34
Viscount Melbourne (*Whig*)	1834
Sir Robert Peel (*Tory*)	1834–35
Viscount Melbourne (*Whig*)	1835–37

REIGN OF VICTORIA

Viscount Melbourne (*Whig*)	1837–41
Sir Robert Peel (*Tory*)	1841–46
Lord John Russell (*Whig*)	1846–52
Earl of Derby (*Tory*)	1852
Earl of Aberdeen (*Peelite*)	1852–55
Viscount Palmerston (*Liberal*)	1855–58
Earl of Derby (*Conservative*)	1858
Viscount Palmerston (*Liberal*)	1858–65
Earl Russell (*Liberal*)	1865–66
Earl of Derby (*Conservative*)	1866–68
Benjamin Disraeli (*Conservative*)	1868
W. E. Gladstone (*Liberal*)	1868–74
Benjamin Disraeli (*Conservative*)	1874–80
W. E. Gladstone (*Liberal*)	1880–85
Marquess of Salisbury (*Conservative*)	1885–86
W. E. Gladstone (*Liberal*)	1886
Marquess of Salisbury (*Conservative*)	1886–92
W. E. Gladstone (*Liberal*)	1892–94
Earl of Rosebery (*Liberal*)	1894–95
Marquess of Salisbury (*Conservative*)	1895–1902

REIGN OF EDWARD VII

A. J. Balfour (*Conservative*)	1902–5
Sir Henry Campbell-Bannerman (*Liberal*)	1905–8
Herbert H. Asquith (*Liberal*)	1908–10

REIGN OF GEORGE V

H. H. Asquith (*Liberal*)	1910–15
H. H. Asquith (*Coalition*)	1915–16
D. Lloyd George (*Coalition*)	1916–22
A. Bonar Law (*Conservative*)	1922–23
Stanley Baldwin (*Conservative*)	1923–24
J. Ramsay MacDonald (*Labour*)	1924
Stanley Baldwin (*Conservative*)	1924–29
J. Ramsay MacDonald (*Labour*)	1929–31
J. Ramsay MacDonald (*National Government*)	1931–35
Stanley Baldwin (*National Government*)	1935–36

REIGN OF EDWARD VIII

Stanley Baldwin (*National Government*)	1936

REIGN OF GEORGE VI

Stanley Baldwin (*National Government*)	1936–37
Neville Chamberlain (*National Government*)	1937–40
Winston S. Churchill (*Coalition*)	1940–45
Clement R. Attlee (*Labour*)	1945–51
Winston S. Churchill (*Conservative*)	1951–52

REIGN OF ELIZABETH II

Sir Winston S. Churchill (*Conservative*)	1952–55
Sir Anthony Eden (*Conservative*)	1955–57
Harold Macmillan (*Conservative*)	1957–63
Sir Alec Douglas-Home (*Conservative*)	1963–64
Harold Wilson (*Labour*)	1964–70
Edward Heath (*Conservative*)	1970–74
Harold Wilson (*Labour*)	1974-76
James Callaghan (*Labour*)	1976–

The ENGLISH LINE of SUCCESSION

ALFRED the GREAT 871-901

EDWARD the ELDER 901-924

ATHELSTAN 924-940 — EDMUND the ELDER 940-946 — EDRED 946-955

EDWY 955-959 — EDGAR 959-975

EDWARD the MARTYR 975-978 — ETHELRED 978-1016 — CANUTE 1016-1035

EDWARD the CONFESSOR 1042-1066 — EDMUND IRONSIDE 1016 — HAROLD I 1035-1040

Edward — HARDICANUTE 1040-1042

Margaret m. Malcolm III of Scotland

WILLIAM the CONQUEROR 1066-1087 m. Matilda of Flanders

WILLIAM II 1087-1100   Adela   HENRY I 1101-1135 m. Matilda

STEPHEN 1135-1154   Matilda m. Geoffrey of Anjou

HENRY II 1154-1189 m. Eleanor of Aquitaine

RICHARD I 1189-1199   JOHN 1199-1216 m. Isabella of Angouleme

HENRY III 1216-1272 m. Eleanor of Provence

EDWARD I 1272-1307 m. Eleanor of Castille

EDWARD II 1307-1327 m. Isabella of France

EDWARD III 1327-1377 m. Philippa of Hainault

Edward the Black Prince | John of Gaunt m. 1 Blanche of Lancaster II Katherine Swynford | Edmund of York

RICHARD II 1377-1399 | HENRY IV 1399-1413 m. Mary Bohun | John Beaufort | Richard of York m. Anne Mortimer

HENRY V 1413-1422 m. Katherine of France | John Beaufort | Richard of York m. Cecily Neville

HENRY VI 1422-1461 | Margaret m. Edmund Tudor | EDWARD IV 1461-1483 m. Elizabeth Woodville   RICHARD III 1483-1485

HENRY VII 1485-1509 m. Elizabeth   EDWARD V 1483   m. Anne Nevi[lle]

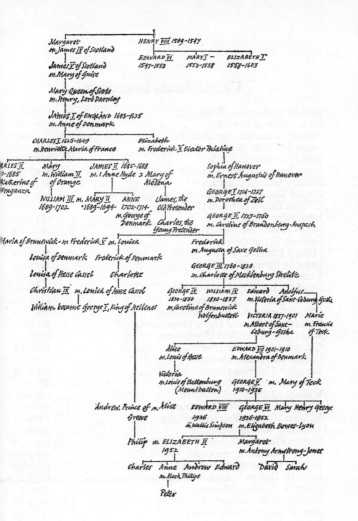

Margaret
m. James IV of Scotland

HENRY VIII 1509-1547

EDWARD VI · MARY I · ELIZABETH I
1547-1553 · 1553-1558 · 1558-1603

James V of Scotland
m. Mary of Guise

Mary Queen of Scots
m. Henry, Lord Darnley

JAMES I of ENGLAND 1603-1625
m. Anne of Denmark

CHARLES I 1625-1649
m. Henrietta Maria of France

Elizabeth
m. Frederick V Elector Palatine

CHARLES II
1660-1685
m. Katherine of
Braganza

Mary
m. William II
of Orange

JAMES II 1685-1688
m. 1 Anne Hyde 2 Mary of
Modena

Sophia of Hanover
m. Ernest Augustus of Hanover

WILLIAM III
1689-1702.

MARY II
1689-1694

ANNE
1702-1714
m. George of
Denmark

James, the
Old Pretender

GEORGE I 1714-1727
m. Dorothea of Zell

Charles, the
Young Pretender

GEORGE II 1727-1760
m. Caroline of Brandenburg-Anspach

Maria of Brunswick - m Frederick V m. Louisa

Frederick
m. Augusta of Saxe Gotha

Louisa of Denmark

Frederick of Denmark

Louisa of Hesse Cassel

Charlotte

GEORGE III 1760-1820
m. Charlotte of Mecklenburg Strelitz

Christian IX m. Louisa of Hesse Cassel

William became George I, King of Hellenes

GEORGE IV
1820-1830
m. Caroline of Brunswick
Wolfenbüttel

WILLIAM IV
1830-1837

Edward
m. Victoria of Saxe-Coburg-Gotha

Adolphus

Marie
m. Francis
of Teck

VICTORIA 1837-1901
m. Albert of Saxe-
Coburg-Gotha

Alice
m. Louis of Hesse

EDWARD VII 1901-1910
m. Alexandra of Denmark

Victoria
m. Louis of Battenburg
(Mountbatten)

GEORGE V
1910-1935

m. Mary of Teck

Andrew, Prince of m. Alice
Greece

EDWARD VIII
1936
m. Wallis Simpson

GEORGE VI
1936-1952
m. Elizabeth Bowes-Lyon

Mary Henry George

Philip m. ELIZABETH II
1952

Margaret
m. Antony Armstrong-Jones

Charles Anne Andrew Edward
m. Mark Phillips

David Sarah

Peter

United States Presidents

George Washington (*Federalist*) — 1789–97
John Adams (*Federalist*) — 1797–1801
Thomas Jefferson (*Republican*) — 1801–9
James Madison (*Republican*) — 1809–17
James Monroe (*Republican*) — 1817–25
John Quincy Adams (*Republican*) — 1825–29
Andrew Jackson (*Democrat*) — 1829–37
Martin Van Buren (*Democrat*) — 1837–41
William Henry Harrison (*Whig*) — 1841
John Tyler (*Whig*) — 1841–45
James Knox Polk (*Democrat*) — 1845–49
Zachary Taylor (*Whig*) — 1849–50
Millard Fillmore (*Whig*) — 1850–53
Franklin Pierce (*Democrat*) — 1853–57
James Buchanan (*Democrat*) — 1857–61
Abraham Lincoln (*Republican*) — 1861–65
Andrew Johnson (*Republican*) — 1865–69
Ulysses Simpson Grant (*Republican*) — 1869–77
Rutherford Birchard Hayes (*Republican*) — 1877–81
James Abram Garfield (*Republican*) — 1881
Chester Alan Arthur (*Republican*) — 1881–85
Grover Cleveland (*Democrat*) — 1885–89
Benjamin Harrison (*Republican*) — 1889–93
Grover Cleveland (*Democrat*) — 1893–97
William McKinley (*Republican*) — 1897–1901
Theodore Roosevelt (*Republican*) — 1901–9
William Howard Taft (*Republican*) — 1909–13
Woodrow Wilson (*Democrat*) — 1913–21
Warren Gamaliel Harding (*Republican*) — 1921–23
Calvin Coolidge (*Republican*) — 1923–29
Herbert C. Hoover (*Republican*) — 1929–33
Franklin Delano Roosevelt (*Democrat*) — 1933–45
Harry S. Truman (*Democrat*) — 1945–53
Dwight D. Eisenhower (*Republican*) — 1953–61
John F. Kennedy (*Democrat*) — 1961–63
Lyndon B. Johnson (*Democrat*) — 1963–69
Richard M. Nixon (*Republican*) — 1969–74
Gerald Ford (*Republican*) — 1974–77
Jimmy Carter (*Democrat*) — 1977–

A Glossary of Political Terms

Absolutism or Absolute Monarchy A system of government where the hereditary ruler, usually a king, has complete power to decide a country's internal and external policy without having to consult anyone. The French Revolution heralded the end of absolutism, and in the nineteenth century absolute monarchies everywhere gave place to constitutional monarchies or republics.

Amnesty An act granting forgiveness (literally, forgetfulness) to political and other offenders.

Anarchism Anarchists (from the Greek word *anarchia,* non-rule) believe that every form of government is evil. Towards the end of the last century anarchists assassinated Czar Alexander of Russia and other political leaders in order to draw attention to their theories. There was a strong anarchist movement in Spain during the 1930s.

Aristocracy From the Greek, meaning government by the best. It has come to mean the best by birth. The government of Britain can be said to have been aristocratic up to the Great Reform Bill of 1832 in the sense that both Houses of Parliament were virtually controlled by members of the great landed aristocratic families.

Autocracy Absolute rule by one man.

Authoritarian A term denoting a dictatorial system of government.

Autonomy A word of Greek origin meaning 'self-government'.

Balance of Payments The balance between the cost of a country's imports and the receipts for its exports. Britain is said to pass through a balance-of-payments crisis whenever the value of her imports exceeds the value of her exports.

Balance of Power The theory that the strength of one group of powers on the European continent should be equal to the strength of the other group, thus preventing any one group from becoming dominant.

Bi-partisan Foreign Policy A foreign policy on which both the government and opposition parties are agreed.

Bourgeoisie French for 'citizen class'. A term used by Marxist socialists to denote manufacturers, merchants and people with a business of their own, as opposed to the 'proletariat', who earn a living only by selling their labour.

Buffer State A small state established or preserved between two greater states to prevent direct clashes between them.

Common Market Term used to describe a group of countries that join together to remove all barriers on citizens of 'Market' members seeking jobs within the Market as well as to dismantle trade barriers among themselves, such as tariffs, customs duties, import and export restrictions, while retaining employment and trade limits against the rest of the world. The most ambitious attempt to create such an area is the European Common Market, set up in 1959 by France, West Germany, Italy, Holland, Belgium and Luxembourg and joined, in 1973, by Britain, Eire and Denmark.

Communism The theory, as expounded by Marx and Engels, which aims at the creation of a society in which the private ownership of land, factories, banks, trading houses, etc., is abolished, and everyone receives what he needs and works according to his capacity. Communists believe that revolution and the use of force are justified to bring about the creation of such a society.

Constitution Document or set of documents which set out how a country is to be governed. Britain is said to have an 'unwritten constitution' because, although there are many documents, such as the Great Reform Bill of 1832 or the Parliament Act of 1911, which deal with constitutional matters, there is no single document which sets out the constitutional machinery of Britain, and such written documents as the Great Reform Bill make sense only against the background of the unwritten customs and traditions which have grown up in Britain over the centuries. By contrast, countries such as the U.S.A., France and Germany are all said to have 'written constitutions' because there is a single document or set of documents to which one can refer.

Constitutional Monarchy A system of government where the king's political power is limited by the constitution: real power usually resting with an elected parliament.

Coup d'état A seizure of power and the machinery of government by force.

Democracy From Greek words meaning 'government by the people'. Democracy may be either direct, as practised in some city-states in Ancient Greece where all the adult citizens met in the market-place to discuss and decide on all questions of policy, or indirect, as practised in modern times when the people elect representatives to some kind of parliament. A democracy can be either a monarchy if its head of State is a king or queen as in Britain, or a republic if its head of State is a president as in the U.S.A. and France.

démarche a move or some procedure (especially diplomatic) to achieve some end.

detente This is a French word, meaning an easing of tensions between people or, in the political sense, between nations. The commonest use of the word at the moment is to describe the sequence of acts, events and negotiations designed to bring about less tense relations between the Soviet Union and the West. This has led to the partial nuclear test-ban treaty, signed in 1963 between Britain, the USA and the USSR: the 1967 treaty to prevent the spread of nuclear weapons; the seabed treaty of 1971, banning nuclear weapons from the seabed: the treaty of 1973 which banned the future production of biological weapons and required the destruction of existing stockpiles: the Helsinki agreement on human rights and co-operation in various fields: and the continuing Strategic Arms Limitation Talks (SALT), which began in 1969.

Dictatorship Rule by one man who, in deciding what to do about the internal or external affairs of the country he controls, does not have to consider or consult anyone but himself.

Fascism An authoritarian extreme right-wing nationalist movement which denies the individual all rights in his relations with the state. In Italy Fascism was led by Mussolini, who held power from 1922 to 1943, and there were strong Fascist movements in many other countries between the two world wars. The German version was Hitler's National Socialism. Fascism derives from the Latin word *fasces*, the name for the axe encased in a bundle of rods which was carried in procession before the chief magistrates in Ancient Rome as a symbol of their power over the life and liberty of ordinary citizens.

Federation A union of states or provinces under a common central government to which they surrender some but not all their powers of government. A federal form of government is usually found in countries which cover a vast area such as the

U.S.A., Canada and Australia, but in Europe Switzerland is a federation, and its component states, called cantons, enjoy a large measure of autonomy.

Free Trade A policy of allowing goods to move freely between countries without imposing tariffs or customs duties. Adam Smith in 1776 set out the classic case for Free Trade in his *Wealth of Nations*. Britain's superiority as a manufacturing country in the Victorian era made her favour Free Trade, but as other countries became industrialised towards the end of the nineteenth century and her superiority vanished, the demand for 'Protection', i.e. tariffs and customs duties to 'protect' goods manufactured in Britain from foreign competition, grew. All countries today are partially 'protected', but many countries, such as Britain and the U.S.A., are working towards making industrial trade as free as possible.

Imperialism In its original sense, the system of government by an emperor. It has come to be used of any policy of political, military or economic expansion carried out at the expense of weaker people. British imperialism saw its heyday in the latter part of the nineteenth century, its leading exponents being Disraeli, Lord Rosebery and Joseph Chamberlain; but since then the tendency within the British Commonwealth has been to give colonial people self-government and independence as soon as and wherever possible.

Industrial Revolution Term applied to the economic developments which between the 1750s and the 1830s transformed Britain from a primarily agricultural to a primarily industrial country.

Isolation A refusal to enter into firm commitments and alliances with other powers.

Laisser-Faire The theory that the state should refrain from all interference in economic affairs. From a phrase coined by eighteenth-century French economists, 'laisser-faire et laisser-passer', 'to let go and pass', i.e. to leave the individual alone and let commodities circulate freely. A reaction against laisser-faire set in in the nineteenth century, inspired by a revulsion against the social conditions created by the Industrial Revolution, and found expression, for example, in the Factory Acts regulating working conditions. The twentieth century has seen an ever-increasing degree of state intervention for social and economic reasons.

Liberalism The body of political and social ideas associated with the Liberal Party in Britain and similar parties elsewhere. The British Liberal Party, which developed out of the Whig Party in the nineteenth century, stood for parliamentary reform, individual liberty, freedom of speech, of the press and of worship, for laisser-faire, i.e. a minimum of state interference in economic affairs, and for international free trade. Towards the end of the century, the Liberal Party modified its views on laisser-faire to ensure minimum living standards for the working class, and, inspired by Lloyd George, the Liberal governments of 1906–14 laid the foundation of what we call today the Welfare State. Since the First World War the influence of the Liberals has declined everywhere, their place as the party of social reform being taken by the Socialists.

Nationalism Term for movements which aim at the strengthening of national feeling and at the unification of a nation or its liberation from foreign rule. Modern nationalism was born in the French Revolution, and under the impact of that event nationalism became a potent factor in European politics in the nineteenth century and helped to bring about the unification of Germany and Italy. In the twentieth century nationalism became a powerful force in Asia and Africa.

National Socialism A German authoritarian extreme right-wing nationalist movement which denied the individual all rights in his relations with the state, personified by Hitler as the Fuehrer ('Leader').

Neutral Term used to describe the condition of a country which in war refrains from hostilities and maintains a strictly impartial attitude towards the belligerents, and in peace stands aloof from the quarrels of other countries and refuses to enter into military alliances. Example: Switzerland and Sweden.

Neutralist Term which has come into use since the Second World War to describe countries which are unwilling to become involved in the Cold War disputes between the Communist and Western power blocs. Example: India.

Nuclear Test Ban Treaty The agreement signed by the Soviet Union, the U.S.A. and Britain in Moscow in July, 1963, by which the signatories bound themselves not to test nuclear weapons of any sort by exploding them either under water or in the atmosphere, including outer space. The purpose of the

Treaty was to stop the further pollution of the world by radio-active debris. The conclusion of the Treaty led to a dramatic lessening of tension (*détente*) between the Western and Communist powers.

Plebiscite A direct vote by the voters of a country or district on a specific question. In the usual election the people vote for or against the government on all the policies for which it stands; in a plebiscite or referendum they vote only on one particular question, as in Britain in 1975 when they were asked to vote on whether they wanted Britain to stay in the Common Market or not.

Radical A person seeking political, social or economic reform 'from the root'. Term used to describe the wing of the Liberal party which was most forward in its demands for reform. Radicalism lost much of its popular support with the rise of Socialism in this century.

Reactionary In politics, a person who wants to prevent or undo reforms.

Republic A country where the head of state is a president and not a king.

Responsible Government A country is said to have responsible government where the government is responsible to Parliament for everything it does, and where it must resign if it loses the 'confidence' of Parliament. In this sense Britain has responsible government, but the U.S.A. has not, because there the President, elected by the whole country for a term of four years, continues in office whether he has the approval of Congress (Parliament) or not. Both countries are, of course, democracies, despite this difference in their constitutions.

Socialism The political, social and economic theories which aim at the establishment of a classless society, through the substitution of common for private ownership of the means of production (land, factories), distribution (shops, transport), and exchange (banks). The Communists believe that all means, including revolution and oppression, are justified in the pursuit of their aims. The Socialists in Britain, Western Europe and most of the African and Asian countries of the Commonwealth are Social Democrats, i.e. they want to bring about a Socialist Society by means such as elections and through democratic institutions such as Parliament. Some Social Democrats want a '*mixed economy*', i.e. one in which not all the means of production, distribution and exchange pass into public ownership, but a large proportion remains in private hands.

Tory Name given to the forerunner of the present Conservative party. Traditionally the Tories were the party of the squire and the parson, as opposed to the *Whigs*, the forerunners of the Liberals, who, though led by a group of great land-owning families, drew their support mainly from the business classes and Nonconformists.

White House The official residence of the President of the U.S.A. in Washington. It was partially burnt when the British occupied Washington briefly during the 1812–14 war with the U.S.A., and afterwards painted white to hide the scars left by the fire. Hence the name. The term 'The White House' is often used to mean 'the American government', e.g. 'The White House reviews its Far Eastern policy.'

Government in Britain

1. National Affairs

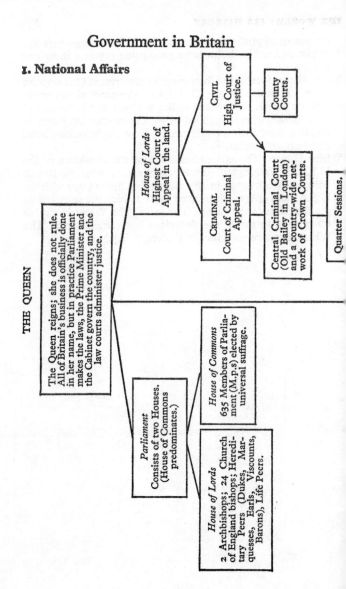

THE QUEEN

The Queen reigns; she does not rule. All of Britain's business is officially done in her name, but in practice Parliament makes the laws, the Prime Minister and the Cabinet govern the country, and the law courts administer justice.

Parliament
Consists of two Houses. (House of Commons predominates.)

House of Lords
2 Archbishops; 24 Church of England bishops; Hereditary Peers (Dukes, Marquesses, Earls, Viscounts, Barons), Life Peers.

House of Commons
635 Members of Parliament (M.p.s) elected by universal suffrage.

House of Lords
Highest Court of Appeal in the land.

CIVIL
High Court of Justice.

County Courts.

CRIMINAL
Court of Criminal Appeal.

Central Criminal Court (Old Bailey in London) and a country-wide network of Crown Courts.

Quarter Sessions.

Petty Sessions or Magistrates' Courts.

Prime Minister (who retains power only as long as he commands a majority in the House of Commons) and his fellow ministers the more important of whom belong to the Cabinet.

Lord Chancellor's Office

Treasury

Overseas Development

Chancellor of the Duchy of Lancaster

Foreign Office (incorporating Commonwealth Office)

Lord Privy Seal's Office

Royal Navy

Welsh Office

Prices & Consumer Protection

Defence

Army

Royal Air Force

Scottish Office

Lord President of the Council's Office

Civil Service Department

Northern Ireland

Home Office

Energy

Trade

Industry

Aerospace & Shipping

Industry

Industrial Development

Posts & Telecommunications

Paymaster-General's Office

Health & Social Security

Attorney-General Solicitor-General

Agriculture Fisheries & Food

Education and Science

Dept. of the Environment

Housing & Construction

Transport

Employment and Productivity

Planning & Local Government

2. Local affairs

The management of local affairs is left to local authorities subject to supervision—largely exercised through financial control—by the central Government in London. The administration of London which became the Greater London Council in place of the London County Council in the 1960's, continues as at present but outside London local government was drastically reorganised in 1974.

The 1,400 local authorities formerly existing in England and Wales (County Councils, County Borough Councils, Municipal Boroughs, Rural Districts, Urban Districts, Parish Councils and Meetings) were replaced by:

6 Metropolitan counties —large conurbations— West Midlands, Mersey-Side, West Yorkshire, South Yorkshire, Tyne and Wear, Greater Manchester—responsible for education and personal social services.	52 new counties responsible for planning, transport, education and personal social services.	some 375 new district authorities responsible for housing, refuse collection, play- and sports-grounds etc.

The 430 local authorities formerly existing in Scotland (counties, counties of cities, town councils and district councils) were in 1975 replaced by:

8 regional authorities responsible for major planning, transport, education and personal social services.	47 district authorities responsible for housing, refuse collection, parks and sports grounds.

The Commonwealth

The Commonwealth grew out of the British Empire. All the states, nations and territories which belong to it today were once governed by men sent out from England who received their orders from London.

The transformation from dependence to independent nationhood usually followed this broad pattern:

Once British power was firmly established, the British Governor would try to draw local notabilities into the business of running the country, consulting them on important matters, and even appointing them to be his official advisers; in due course he would set up a legislative Council or Parliament, but he would make certain of being able to get his way in the last resort by allowing only a minority of its members to be elected by the local population and by appointing the majority himself; later on he would gradually increase the number of locally elected members until in the end there would be no officially appointed members left; at that stage London would usually surrender its powers to run the affairs of the country concerned, the leader of the majority in the Legislative Council or Parliament would become Prime Minister, the Governor would cease to play an active part in politics and, like the Queen in Britain, would be able to act only as advised by the Prime Minister.

The first countries to reach the top of the ladder of self-government were those settled by people of British or European stock. They were known as 'Dominions', and in defining their relationship to one another and to Britain, the Imperial Conference of 1926 described them as 'autonomous communities within the British Empire, equal in status, in no way subordinate one to another in any aspect of their domestic or foreign affairs, though united by a common allegiance to the Crown, and freely associated as members of the British Commonwealth of Nations.'

They were—apart from Britain—five in number:

> Australia   Canada
> Newfoundland (after a referendum joined Canada as a Province in 1949 and ceased being an independent Dominion)
> New Zealand
> South Africa (left the Commonwealth in 1961).

After the Second World War the number of countries which attained independent nationhood increased rapidly and, since many of them had populations which were not predominantly of British or European descent, it became customary to refer to the Commonwealth and not the British Commonwealth.

In January 1977 the following were fully independent members of the Commonwealth, in addition to those listed above:

India	Tanzania[1]	Mauritius
Sri Lanka	Malawi[2]	Swaziland
Ghana	Malta	Tonga
Nigeria	Zambia[3]	Western Samoa
Cyprus	Gambia	Fiji
Sierra Leone	Singapore	Bangladesh
Jamaica	Guyana[4]	Nauru
Trinidad	Botswana[5]	Grenada
Uganda	Lesotho[6]	Papua New Guinea
Malaysia	The Bahamas	Seychelles
Kenya	Barbados	

Former Names: [1] Tanganyika and Zanzibar. [2] Nyasaland.
[3] N. Rhodesia. [4] Brit. Guiana. [5] Bechuanaland. [6] Basutoland.

(Burma became independent in 1948 but decided to leave the Commonwealth. Pakistan left the Commonwealth in January 1971.)

There are altogether 36 independent countries within the Commonwealth (including Britain). They form an association of countries. They are not a state or even a federation. There is no single parliament or government, no central defence force or executive power. They are no longer 'united by a common allegiance to the Crown'. For example, India, Ghana, Nigeria, Cyprus, Uganda, Kenya, Tanzania, Malawi and Zambia are republics although all recognise the Queen as Head of the Commonwealth. And there is no common foreign policy. Britain, Canada, Australia and New Zealand belong to military alliances designed to stop the spread of Communism; India, Ceylon, Ghana and Tanzania are 'uncommitted'.

The essence of the Commonwealth relationship is consultation, and the most important forms of consultation are the Commonwealth Prime Ministers' Conferences which, whenever possible, are held in London at least once every two years and now have a permanent home in Marlborough House, formerly the late Queen Mary's residence.

Other Commonwealth bonds:

> Constant consultation between the Commonwealth delegations at the United Nations in New York.
> Commercial ties and Imperial preferences.
> Language (Many Commonwealth leaders with multilingual populations find that English is the only language in which they can talk to all their people.)
> Common political traditions and habits of thought.

Education (Many Commonwealth universities are linked to British universities in order to ensure high academic standards. Moreover, many Commonwealth countries continue to have their doctors, scientists, engineers, administrators and soldiers trained in Britain.)

Sport (Cricket and cricketing language are familiar in countries like Britain, Australia, New Zealand and the West Indies, but hardly outside the Commonwealth.)

Despite the rapid increase since the end of the Second World War in the number of fully independent countries within the Commonwealth, there still remain, in almost every part of the world, territories which continue to be dependent on Britain. Some are well advanced in self-government; others are little more than small island communities, fortresses, anchorages or former coaling stations which may have difficulty in surviving as fully independent states. The still dependent territories include:

In Africa:

Rhodesia (illegally declared independent in 1965 by its then Prime Minister, Mr Smith, but no country in the world has recognised his claim to independence)

In the Atlantic:

Bermuda   Falkland Islands
St Helena

In the Caribbean:

Leeward Islands   Windward Islands

Four of the larger island units in these two groups—Antigua, Dominica, St Lucia and the island group of St Kitts, Nevis and Anguilla—have in 1967 been granted the new status of 'Associated States', i.e. complete self-government except in foreign and defence policy. St Vincent now also belongs to this group.

In the Mediterranean:

Gibraltar

In and around the Indian Ocean:

Aldabra Is.

In the Far East:

Brunei   Hong Kong

In the Pacific:
    British Solomon Islands   Pitcairn Islands
    Gilbert and Ellice Islands
    New Hebrides (under joint Anglo-French administration)

      Total population of the Commonwealth: about 1200 million.

The United Nations

The United Nations came into existence on October 24, 1945, and every year October 24 is celebrated as United Nations' Day throughout the world.

The aims of the United Nations are set out in its Charter in these words: 'to save succeeding generations from the scourge of war . . . to reaffirm faith in fundamental human rights, in the

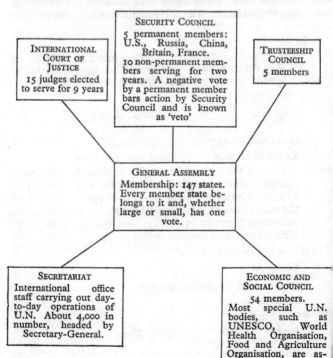

INTERNATIONAL COURT OF JUSTICE
15 judges elected to serve for 9 years

SECURITY COUNCIL
5 permanent members: U.S., Russia, China, Britain, France. 10 non-permanent members serving for two years. A negative vote by a permanent member bars action by Security Council and is known as 'veto'

TRUSTEESHIP COUNCIL
5 members

GENERAL ASSEMBLY
Membership: 147 states. Every member state belongs to it and, whether large or small, has one vote.

SECRETARIAT
International office staff carrying out day-to-day operations of U.N. About 4,000 in number, headed by Secretary-General.

ECONOMIC AND SOCIAL COUNCIL
54 members. Most special U.N. bodies, such as UNESCO, World Health Organisation, Food and Agriculture Organisation, are associated with it.

dignity and worth of the human person, in the equal rights of
men and women and of nations large and small, and to establish
conditions under which justice and respect for the obligations
arising from treaties and other sources of international law can be
maintained, and to employ international machinery for the promotion of the economic and social advancement of all peoples'.

Members of the U.N. in 1945: 51 countries
Members of the U.N. in 1977: 147 countries.

The principal organ of the U.N. is the General Assembly.
Around it are grouped the other five main organs of the U.N.:

General Assembly All other U.N. bodies report to it. It
controls the U.N. budget and assesses each country's contribution. It elects new members on the recommendation of the
Security Council. On 'important' questions, i.e., questions
affecting the world's peace and security or the election of new
members or the budget, a two-thirds majority of those
present and voting is essential before any action can be taken.
It meets every year in regular session beginning on the third
Tuesday in September.

Security Council It is primarily responsible for keeping international peace and security. Any nation—whether a member
of the U.N. or not—may bring a dispute or threat to peace
to its attention and ask it to take action. Any of the five permanent members can block action by voting 'No'. This is
known as the veto. Its ten non-permanent members are
elected by the General Assembly.

International Court of Justice Its 15 judges are elected by
the General Assembly on the recommendation of the Security
Council. They consider legal disputes brought before them by
nations which cannot agree between themselves. They also
give advice on international law when asked to by the General Assembly, the Security Council or other U.N. bodies.

Trusteeship Council It looks after the interests of non-self-
governing territories in different parts of the world which
have been placed under the trusteeship of the U.N. Its aim
is to help these territories towards full self-government as
quickly as possible.

Secretariat It consists of international civil servants who,
while they belong to it, must forget their national loyalties and
work only for the best interests of the U.N. The head of the
Secretariat is the Secretary-General, who is appointed by the

General Assembly on the recommendation of the Security Council, usually for a five-year term.

The U.N. has had four Secretaries-General:

1. Trygve Lie, of Norway (1945–1953).
2. Dag Hammarskjoeld, of Sweden (1953–1961. Killed in an air crash in Africa).
3. U Thant, of Burma (1961–1971).
4. Kurt Waldheim, of Austria (1972–).

Economic and Social Council (ECOSOC) Its aim is to establish lasting world peace by helping the poor, the sick, the hungry, the illiterate in all parts of the globe. It is responsible for assisting under-developed countries and promotes health and education schemes. In a broad sense it supervises the work of many special U.N. bodies like the U.N. Educational, Scientific and Cultural Organisation (UNESCO), the International Bank for Reconstruction and Development, the International Labour Organisation (I.L.O.), the Food and Agriculture Organisation (F.A.O.), the U.N. International Children's Emergency Fund (U.N.I.C.E.F.) and the International Atomic Energy Agency which seeks to help countries by encouraging and supporting the use of atomic energy for peaceful development purposes.

Location of U.N. Headquarters: New York.

Official languages in which the U.N. conducts its business: Chinese, English, French, Russian, Spanish.

FURTHER READING

The Making of Man, by I. W. Cornwall (Phoenix House)

Looking at History, by R. J. Unstead (A. & C. Black)

History: Civilisation from the Beginning (Macdonald Illustrated Library)

Larousse Encyclopaedia of Ancient and Medieval History and *Larousse Encyclopaedia of Modern History* (Paul Hamlyn)

The Story of Britain, by R. J. Unstead (A. & C. Black)

Boys and Girls of History, by Eileen and Rhoda Power (Dobson)

A History of Everyday Things in England, by Marjorie and C. H. B. Quennell (Carousel paperbacks)

The Story of the United Nations, by Katharine Savage (Bodley Head)

The World

2: ITS GEOGRAPHY
(*including Its Weather*)

GEOGRAPHY, which literally means 'writing about the earth', is the science of the physical world. It includes in its scope the earth's surface, land and sea, and the features and products of both of these. It deals with natural divisions, like continents or mountain ranges; and political divisions, like countries and towns. This brings it inside the borders of History. It deals with those factors, like the climate and surrounding atmosphere, which directly affect the earth and sea and their products. This introduces Meteorology and Physics. It deals with both natural and man-made products, which makes it an important part of Economics, and links it with Agriculture. It describes the influence of nature on man, and of man on nature. So that it overlaps Anthropology and Sociology.

THE EARTH: *some facts and figures*

The Earth is the fifth largest of the nine major planets (the others are Mercury, Venus, Mars, Jupiter, Saturn, Uranus, Neptune and Pluto) and the third in distance from the sun— about 93,000,000 miles. In shape, it is almost, but not quite, a sphere, being slightly flattened at the poles, as well as being rather pear-shaped, with the pear's stalk at the North Pole.

About seven tenths of the Earth's outer crust are covered with water, this water forming the four oceans and the seas. The other three tenths are land, and comprise the six continents and innumerable islands. The whole surface is blanketed by a layer of air known as the atmosphere. This air is formed of various gases, without which nothing on earth would be able to live. Changes and movements within the atmosphere, together with the rays from the sun, are responsible for our weather.

There are close on 4,000,000,000 people living on earth, of whom well over half live in the continent of Asia.

Polar diameter (i.e. from pole to pole through the earth's centre), 7,900 miles.

Equatorial diameter (between points on the equator exactly opposite one another), 7,926·5 miles.

Equatorial circumference, 24,901·8 miles.
Total surface area (estimated), 196,950,000 sq. miles.
Area of land, 57,312,000 sq. miles.
Area of sea, 139,638,000 sq. miles.
Total mass (weight), about 6,588,000,000,000,000,000,000
(i.e. 6,588 million million million) tons.

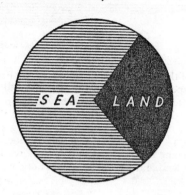

THE OCEANS AND SEAS

The four oceans together with the seas cover about seven-tenths of the earth's surface. All the oceans form one vast mass of water which is divided, for convenience, into the Pacific, the Atlantic, the Indian and the Arctic. *Seas* are smaller, more self-contained portions of the ocean, like the Mediterranean Sea, which is almost entirely surrounded by land. Some seas, like the Caspian, are completely surrounded, but the water is nevertheless salt, not fresh.

The greatest known ocean depth (36,198 ft., just off the Philippines), is about a mile more than the greatest land height (Mt. Everest, 29,028 ft.). The average depth of the ocean (12,451 ft.) is much greater than the average height of the land above sea-level (2,300 ft.).

The floor of the ocean, like the land, has many ridges and valleys. Where it adjoins the great land masses, on what is called the *Continental Shelf*, it is relatively shallow; but it soon plunges steeply down the *Continental Slope* into the *Deep-Sea*

Plain, which forms most of the ocean floor and varies in depth from 12,000 to 18,000 ft.; here and there dropping into enormous cracks and valleys known as the *Deep Trenches.*

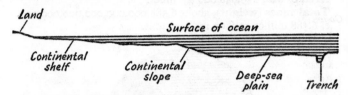

The origin of the Continental Shelf has not yet been explained. It might be expected that the abrupt Continental Slope would come at the water's edge, rather than anything up to a hundred miles out from the land. One possible reason is that the water level has risen, or the land level fallen, during the course of millions of years. Or it may be that the continental boundary did originally come at the slope, but that the sea has gradually worn away the land and left the original boundary far behind.

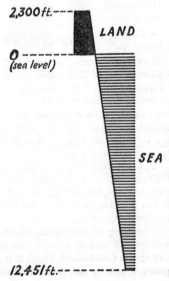

The Average Height of Land Compared with the Average Depth of Ocean

OCEANS AND MAIN SEAS: *Their Areas and Depths*

Ocean or sea	Area (sq. miles)	Average depth (ft.)	Greatest depth (ft.)
Oceans:			
Pacific	63,801,668	14,048	36,198
Atlantic	31,839,306	12,880	30,246
Indian	28,356,276	13,002	26,400
Arctic	5,440,197	3,953	17,850
Seas:			
Malay Sea	3,144,056	3,976	21,342
Caribbean Sea	1,063,340	8,172	23,748
Mediterranean Sea	966,757	4,878	14,435
Bering Sea	875,753	7,714	13,422
Gulf of Mexico	595,760	4,961	12,744
Sea of Okhotsk	589,807	2,749	11,154
East China Sea	482,317	617	10,500
Hudson Bay	475,762	420	1,500
Sea of Japan	389,074	4,429	12,276
Andaman Sea	307,954	2,854	12,392
North Sea	222,124	308	1,998
Black Sea	178,378	3,160	6,864
Red Sea	169,073	1,611	7,254
Baltic Sea	163,059	189	1,380

You won't find the Malay Sea on the map. It consists of the following seas: Sulu, Celebes, Molucca, Halmahera, Ceram, Banda, Arafura, Timor, Flores, Bali, Java, Savu and South China; the following gulfs: Thailand, Tomini and Boni; and the following straits: Malacca, Singapore and Macassar.

THE CONTINENTS

A continent is a large mass of land, not broken up by a large stretch of sea. The Earth's land surface is made up of six such continents, as well as a large number of islands. The continents and islands fit into four main divisions:

(1) an immense landmass, nearly all of it in the eastern hemisphere, consisting of the continents of *Europe*, *Asia* and *Africa*;

(2) a smaller landmass, the *Americas*, in the western hemisphere; this is sometimes divided into two continents, North America and South America;

(3) two large island continents in the southern hemisphere, *Australia* and *Antarctica*;

(4) a great number of islands.

Generally, islands are regarded as belonging to the nearest continent. The far-flung islands of the Pacific, however, are usually grouped with Australia, New Zealand and New Guinea in the continent of *Oceania*.

Although the ice that forms over it in winter makes it fairly solid, the Arctic is a sea, not a continent. The ice and snow covering the Antarctic, however, have formed above land which rises above sea level.

More than half of all the land in the world is uninhabitable—it is rock, desert, tundra, dense jungle, swamps or is covered with ice. Less than half of the remainder is suitable for cultivation.

Nearly one-half of the people in the world live on one-thirtieth of the total area of land. There are immense areas (like the Northern Territory of Australia and the North-West Territories of Canada) with only one inhabitant to every 25 or 50 square miles; and other areas (like East Pakistan and England) where more than 750 persons, on the average, are crowded into each square mile of land.

The total world population is about 3,782,000,000. At the beginning of the century it was about a third of that figure. This enormous increase in population makes many people anxious about overcrowding and possible shortage of food in the future. But many experts say that there is no real need to worry, since science is not only converting what was thought to be useless land (and even parts of the sea) into fertile soil, but is also constantly getting more nourishment from resources already available. There has also been anxiety that the world might run short of oil, before the full development of new sources for energy.

The Continents: Area and Population

Continent	Area (sq. miles)	Population
Europe	1,903,000	473,000,000
Asia *	10,661,000	2,256,000,000
U.S.S.R.	8,649,000	255,000,000
Africa	11,683,000	401,000,000
America	16,241,000	561,000,000
Oceania	3,286,000	21,000,000

Total World Population: 3,967,000,000

* Excluding figures for U.S.S.R. which are given separately and including European and Asiatic Turkey.

The Largest Islands

Island	Ocean	Continent	Area (sq. miles)
Australia	Indian–Pacific	Oceania	2,948,366
Greenland	Atlantic–Arctic	N. America	839,782
New Guinea	Pacific	Oceania	316,861
Borneo	Pacific	Asia	285,000
Baffin Is.	Arctic	N. America	236,000
Malagasy	Indian	Africa	227,737
Sumatra	Indian	Asia	161,612
Honshu	Pacific	Asia	88,919
Great Britain	Atlantic	Europe	84,186
Victoria Is.	Arctic	N. America	80,450
Celebes	Indian	Asia	73,160
South Island, N.Z.	Pacific	Oceania	58,093
Java	Indian	Asia	48,534
North Island, N.Z.	Pacific	Oceania	44,281
Cuba	Atlantic	N. America	44,206
Newfoundland	Atlantic	N. America	42,734
Ellesmere Is.	Arctic	N. America	41,000
Luzon	Pacific	Asia	40,420
Iceland	Atlantic	Europe	39,758
Mindanao	Pacific	Asia	36,537
Hokkaido	Pacific	Asia	34,276
Novaya Zemlya	Arctic	Asia	32,000
Ireland	Atlantic	Europe	31,839
Hispaniola	Atlantic	N. America	29,536
Tasmania	Pacific	Oceania	26,215

THE COUNTRIES OF THE WORLD BY CONTINENTS

The following tables tell you what the areas and populations of the countries are; the names of their capitals; and the populations of the capitals.

Of course, the number of people in any country is changing every day: so we have given approximate figures, based on the latest counts (or *censuses*).

Note: The Commonwealth is a free association of independent states, with a total area (excluding the United Kingdom) of 9,902,356.6 sq. miles. Member countries are:

United Kingdom	Malawi
Canada	Malaysia
Australia	Malta
New Zealand	Mauritius
Bahamas	Nauru
Bangladesh	Nigeria
Barbados	Papua New Guinea
Botswana	Seychelles
Cyprus	Sierra Leone
Fiji	Singapore
Gambia	Sri Lanka
Ghana	Swaziland
Grenada	Tanzania
Guyana	Tonga
India	Trinidad and Tobago
Jamaica	Uganda
Kenya	Western Samoa
Lesotho	Zambia

EUROPE AND THE MEDITERRANEAN

Country	Area (sq. miles)	Population	Capital	Population of Capital
Albania	10,700	2,432,000	Tirana	200,000
Andorra	180	30,000	Andorra La Vella	11,750
Austria	32,376	7,519,900	Vienna	1,593,000
Belgium	11,800	9,650,944	Brussels	1,075,000
Bulgaria	43,000	8,594,493	Sofia	965,728
Cyprus	3,500	634,000	Nicosia	235,000
Czechoslovakia	49,400	14,686,255	Prague	1,091,449
Denmark	17,000	5,065,313	Copenhagen	1,251,226
Finland	130,000	4,727,259	Helsinki	496,872
France	213,000	52,913,000	Paris	2,317,227
Germany				
West	95,980	61,442,000	Bonn	285,000
East	41,768	16,890,800	E. Berlin	1,094,147
Gibraltar	2	30,117	Gibraltar	20,000
Greece	51,200	8,768,641	Athens	2,540,241
Hungary	36,000	10,631,000	Budapest	2,055,646
Iceland	40,500	220,545	Reykjavik	84,334
Irish Republic	26,600	2,978,248	Dublin	567,866
Italy	131,000	56,024,000	Rome	2,842,616
Liechtenstein	65	24,257	Vaduz	4,632
Luxembourg	1,000	357,300	Luxembourg	78,300
Malta, Gozo	121	318,481	Valetta	14,152
Monaco	⅜	24,500	Monaco	2,422
Netherlands	13,500	13,815,838	Amsterdam	987,205
Norway	125,000	4,035,365	Oslo	462,732
Poland	121,000	34,186,000	Warsaw	1,436,100

Country	Area (sq. miles)	Population	Capital	Population of Capital
Portugal	34,500	9,260,000	Lisbon	783,000
Rumania	91,600	21,559,416	Bucharest	1,934,025
San Marino	23	21,000	San Marino	2,000
Spain	197,000	35,472,000	Madrid	3,146,071
Sweden	173,000	8,236,179	Stockholm	1,357,558
Switzerland	16,000	6,385,000	Berne	162,405
Turkey (in Europe)	9,200	3,772,705	see Asia	1,698,502
United Kingdom of Great Britain and Northern Ireland	93,026	55,521,534	London	7,379,014
U.S.S.R. (in Eur.)	1,707,000	134,650,000	Moscow	7,734,000
R.S.F.S.R. (Eur.)	252,000	49,870,000	Moscow	2,013,000
Ukraine	80,000	9,371,000	Kiev	1,189,000
Byelorussia	26,000	3,315,000	Minsk	447,000
Lithuania	25,000	2,497,000	Vilnius	806,000
Latvia	17,400	1,438,000	Riga	408,000
Estonia	14,000	3,850,000	Tallinn	471,000
Moldavia	109 acres	1,000	Kishinev	1,000
Vatican City	99,000	21,352,000	Vatican City	1,204,000
Yugoslavia			Belgrade	

ASIA

Country	Area (sq. miles)	Population	Capital	Population of Capital
Afghanistan	250,000	16,516,000	Kabul	500,000
Bahrain	231	216,000	Manama	89,608
Bangladesh	55,126	81,000,000	Dacca	1,730,250
Bhutan	18,000	1,010,000	Thimpu	—
Brunei	2,226	162,200	Bandan Seri Begawan	42,000
Burma	261,789	30,834,000	Rangoon	3,186,866
Cambodia	70,000	7,300,000	Phnom Penh	2,000,000
China Mainland	4,300,000	827,850,000	Peking	8,000,000
Taiwan (Formosa)	13,890	15,353,291	Taipei	1,921,736
Macau	5	248,316	Macau	157,175
Hong Kong	404	4,477,600	Victoria	767,000
India	1,262,000	606,000,000	Delhi	4,065,698
Indonesia	735,000	129,000,000	Djakarta	5,000,000
Iran (Persia)	628,060	28,448,000	Teheran	3,150,000
Iraq	172,000	11,500,000	Baghdad	2,696,000
Israel	8,000	3,230,000	Jerusalem	380,000
Japan	142,748	110,050,000	Tokyo	11,701,000
Jordan	37,700	2,660,000	Amman	691,000
Korea North	48,000	14,500,000	Pyongyang	286,000
South	38,500	35,900,000	Seoul	8,687,000
Kuwait	7,500	1,066,400	Kuwait	400,000

Country	Area (sq. miles)	Population	Capital	Population of Capital
Laos	90,000	3,000,000	Vientiane	120,000
Lebanon	4,300	2,645,000	Beirut	600,000
Malaysia	128,000	10,434,000	Kuala Lumpur	770,000
Johore	7,330	1,274,000	Johore Baru	....
Kedah	3,640	955,000	Alor Star	....
Kelantan	5,765	681,000	Kota Bahru	....
Malacca	640	404,000	Malacca	....
Negri Sembilem	2,570	479,600	Seremban	....
Pahang	13,900	503,000	Kuantan	....
Penang	400	777,000	George Town	234,930
Perak	8,100	1,563,000	Ipoh	125,776
Perlis	310	121,000	Kangar	....
Sabah	29,000	656,000	Kota Kinanalu	41,830
Sarawak	48,000	977,000	Kuching	63,491
Selangor	3,166	1,629,000	Kuala Lumpur	500,000
Trungganu	5,000	406,000	Kuala Triengganu	....
Maldive Islands	115	123,000	Malé	13,610
Mongolia (Outer)	600,000	1,500,000	Ulan Bator	400,000
Nepal	54,000	13,000,000	Katmandu	399,603
Oman	120,000	750,000	Muscat	7,000
Pakistan	310,403	73,400,000	Islamabad	235,000
Philippines	115,000	42,759,000	Manila	1,438,253
Qatar	4,000	180,000	Doha	180,000
Saudi Arabia	927,000	7,200,000	Riyadh	666,840
Singapore	226	2,278,200	Singapore	—
Sri Lanka	25,332	12,747,755	Colombo	563,705

Country	Area (sq. miles)	Population	Capital	Population of Capital
Syria	71,000	8,746,224	Damascus	1,655,804
Thailand (Siam)	198,000	42,000,000	Bangkok	4,300,000
Timor (East)	7,329	610,541	Dili	7,000
Turkey (in Asia)	285,000	36,423,964	Ankara	1,698,542
United Arab Emirates	32,000	655,937		
U.S.S.R. (in Asia)				
R.S.F.S.R. (in Asia)	4,887,000	*see Europe*		
Kazakhstan	1,065,000	14,337,000	Alma Ata	851,000
Turkmenistan	188,000	2,581,000	Ashkhabad	297,000
Uzbekistan	157,000	14,079,000	Tashkent	1,643,000
Kirghizia	777,000	3,368,000	Frunze	498,000
Tadzhikistan	54,000	3,486,000	Dushanbe	448,000
Georgia	27,000	4,594,000	Tbilisi	1,030,000
Azerbaijan	33,000	5,689,000	Baku	1,406,000
Armenia	11,000	2,834,000	Erevan	928,000
Vietnam	129,000	43,780,375	Hanoi	1,378,335
Yemen	75,000	6,500,000	Sana'a	135,000
Yemen P.D.R.	180,000	1,598,000	Aden	250,000

Notes

1. This map is drawn to Mercator's Projection, a convenient method for showing all the countries of the world, but also very misleading in some ways. See under **Projections,** page B48.

2. For an explanation of the International Date Line see page B4.

AFRICA

Country	Area (sq. miles)	Population	Capital	Population of Capital
Afars and Issas	9,000	81,200	Djibouti	62,000
Algeria	856,000	17,000,000	Algiers	2,000,000
Angola	488,000	5,748,000	Luanda	480,613
Benin	47,000	2,948,000	Porto Novo	85,000
Botswana	220,000	720,000	Gaborone	34,000
Burundi	10,700	3,475,000	Bujumbura	70,000
Cameroun	183,000	7,000,000	Yaounde	180,000
Cape Verde Islands	1,516	272,071	Praia	6,000
Central African Republic	234,000	3,220,000	Bangui	301,793
Chad	488,000	4,000,000	Ndjaména	150,000
Congo	129,960	2,100,000	Brazzaville	156,000
Egypt	385,000	34,000,000	Cairo	8,143,000
Equatorial Guinea	11,000	286,000	Malabo	9,000
Ethiopia	400,000	26,000,000	Addis Ababa	912,000
Gabon	101,400	500,000	Libreville	31,000
Gambia	4,000	493,499	Banjul	39,476
Ghana	92,100	8,545,561	Accra	851,614
Guinea	97,000	3,890,000	Conakry	120,000
Guinea Bissau	14,000	600,000	Bissau	6,000
Ivory Coast	127,000	5,400,000	Abidjan	1,100,000
Kenya	225,000	12,934,000	Nairobi	509,000
Lesotho	11,700	1,181,300	Maseru	30,000
Liberia	43,000	1,481,524	Monrovia	201,600
Libya	810,000	2,257,037	Tripoli	551,447
Madagascar	228,000	8,000,000	Tananarive	400,000

Country	Area (sq. miles)	Population	Capital	Population of Capital
Malawi	45,400	5,310,000	Lilongwe	102,000
Mali	465,000	6,308,000	Bamako	404,000
Mauritania	419,000	1,481,000	Nouakchott	135,900
Mauritius, etc.	805	894,750	Port Louis	139,400
Morocco	180,000	15,379,259	Rabat	565,000
Mozambique	298,000	10,000,000	Maputo	441,363
Niger	459,000	4,030,000	Niamey	100,000
Nigeria	357,000	79,760,000	Lagos	1,000,000
Réunion	1,000	445,500	St Denis	85,992
Rhodesia	151,000	6,310,000	Salisbury	503,000
Rwanda	10,169	4,000,000	Kigali	7,000
St Helena	47	5,058	Jamestown	1,475
Ascension Is.	38	1,131	Georgetown	—
Tristan da Cunha	45	292	Edinburgh	—
S. Tomé and Principé	372	74,500	São Tomé	3,187
Sénégal	78,000	5,000,000	Dakar	581,000
Seychelles	125	59,200	Victoria	13,736
Sierra Leone	28,000	3,002,426	Freetown	274,000
Somalia	246,000	3,200,000	Mogadishu	220,000
South Africa	472,000	24,920,000	Pretoria, Cape Town	563,384 1,107,764
S.W. Africa	318,000	746,328	Windhoek	61,260
Spanish Presidios:				
Ceuta	5	67,187	—	
Melilla	72	64,942	—	
Sahara	125,000	63,000	Villa Cisneros	250

Country	Area (sq. miles)	Population	Capital	Population of Capital
Sudan	967,000	19,500,000	Khartoum	194,000
Swaziland	6,700	493,728	Mbabane	21,500
Tanzania	363,000	13,968,000	Dar es Salaam	300,000
Togo	21,000	2,089,900	Lomé	214,200
Tunisia	63,380	5,600,000	Tunis	1,127,000
Uganda	91,000	10,400,000	Kampala	331,000
Upper Volta	100,000	5,514,000	Ouagadougou	125,000
Zaïre	905,000	21,637,000	Kinshasa	1,300,000
Zambia	291,000	4,696,000	Lusaka	483,000

NORTH AMERICA

Country	Area (sq. miles)	Population	Capital	Population of Capital
Bahamas	5,380	197,000	Nassau	112,000
Barbados	166	251,300	Bridgetown	18,789
Belize	8,900	140,000	Belmopan	4,000
Bermuda	21	53,000	Hamilton	3,000
Canada	3,560,000	22,493,000	Ottawa	693,000
Cayman Islands	100	10,652	George Town	3,000
Costa Rica	19,653	2,000,000	San José	481,630
Cuba	44,000	8,553,000	Havana	1,755,360

Country	Area (sq. miles)	Population	Capital	Population of Capital
Dominica	290	78,000	Roseau	10,157
Dominican Republic	19,300	4,012,000	Santo Domingo	817,000
El Salvador	7,700	4,210,000	San Salvador	685,000
Grenada	133	104,000	St. George's	8,600
Guadeloupe	688	323,000	Point à Pitre	39,000
Guatemala	42,000	5,400,000	Guatemala	1,200,000
Haiti	10,700	4,768,000	Pt.-au-Prince	400,000
Honduras	43,000	2,646,828	Tegucigalpa	305,387
Jamaica	4,400	2,060,300	Kingston	614,000
Leeward Is.				
Antigua and Barbuda	170	66,000	St Johns	22,000
Monserrat	39	12,905	Plymouth	1,300
St Kitts-Nevis	101	48,000	Basseterre	17,000
Anguilla	35	6,500	—	—
Virgin Is. (British)	59	10,030	Road Town	2,129
Martinique	400	332,000	Fort-de-France	60,600
Mexico	761,530	61,000,000	Mexico City	8,941,912
Netherlands Antilles	394	234,400	Willemstad	154,000
Nicaragua	57,000	2,400,000	Managua	400,000
Panama	31,900	1,678,000	Panama City	418,000
Panama Canal Zone	647	51,000	Balboa Heights	3,950
Puerto Rico	3,400	2,913,000	San Juan	851,247
St Pierre and Miquelon	93	5,000	St Pierre	3,500
Trinidad and Tobago	1,980	1,061,850	Port-of-Spain	100,000
Turks and Caicos Islands	193	7,000	Grand Turk	2,686
United States	3,536,855	215,892,000	Washington, D.C.	2,909,111

Country	Area (sq. miles)	Population	Capital	Population of Capital
Virgin Is. (U.S.)	133	90,000	Charlotte Amelie	11,000
Windward Is.				
St Lucia	238	112,500	Castries	47,000
St Vincent	150	100,000	Kingstown	23,000

SOUTH AMERICA

Country	Area (sq. miles)	Population	Capital	Population of Capital
Argentina	1,080,000	23,360,000	Buenos Aires	8,774,529
Bolivia	415,000	4,700,000	La Paz	654,700
Brazil	3,289,000	108,000,000	Brasilia	544,862
Chile	290,000	10,000,000	Santiago	4,000,000
Colombia	440,000	23,500,000	Bogotá	3,200,000
Ecuador	226,000	7,000,000	Quito	700,000
Falkland Is.	4,700	1,905	Stanley	1,079
Guiana, French	35,000	48,000	Cayenne	20,000
Guyana	83,000	714,233	Georgetown	168,000
Paraguay	157,000	2,500,000	Asuncion	437,000
Peru	531,000	14,121,564	Lima	3,600,000

Country	Area (sq. miles)	Population	Capital	Population of Capital
Surinam	54,000	480,000	Paramaribo	110,000
Uruguay	72,000	2,763,964	Montevideo	1,229,748
Venezuela	354,000	11,992,700	Caracas	2,183,935

OCEANIA

Country	Area (sq. miles)	Population	Capital	Population of Capital
Australia	2,968,000			
New South Wales	309,000	13,601,000	Canberra	208,000
Queensland	667,000	4,811,100	Sydney†	3,021,300
South Australia	380,000	1,015,100	Brisbane†	957,000
Tasmania	26,000	1,241,700	Adelaide	857,000
Victoria	88,000	409,000	Hobart†	132,000
Western Australia	976,000	3,688,200	Melbourne†	2,479,500
Northern Territory	520,280	1,138,300	Perth	805,700
Norfolk Island	13	96,300	Darwin†	47,000
Fiji	7,100	1,870	Kingston†	—
French Polynesia	2,500	560,000	Suva†	64,000
Gilbert Is.	264	119,200	Papeete†	15,220
Guam	209	48,000	Tarawa	17,000
Mariana, Caroline and		105,000	Agaña	—
Marshall Islands*	687	101,592	Saipan	
Nauru	8	6,970	Nauru†	—
New Caledonia	7,200	100,600	Noumea†	12,000
New Hebrides	5,700	89,931	Vila†	5,500

*Trust Territory of the Pacific Islands.   †Seaport

Country	Area (sq. miles)	Population	Capital	Population of Capital
New Zealand	104,000	3,125,600	Wellington†	349,600
Cook Islands }	200 {	18,937	Avarua	—
Niue		3,992	Alofi	956
Ross Dependency	175,000	—	—	—
Papua New Guinea	178,000	2,793,800	Port Moresby†	117,000
Samoa				
Eastern	76	28,000	Pago Pago†	1,251
Western	1,097	151,300	Apia†	35,000
Solomon Islands	11,500	196,708	Honiara	14,993
Tavalu	10	10,000	Funajuti	1,000
Tonga, etc.	270	90,120	Nuku'alofa†	18,396

† Seaport

ANTARCTICA

By the Treaty of Antarctica, signed in December 1959, the following countries agreed to freeze all their claims to Antarctic territory for thirty years, without giving them up: Argentina, Australia, Belgium, Chile, France, Great Britain, Japan, New Zealand, Norway, the Republic of South Africa, the U.S.A. and the U.S.S.R.

The aim of the treaty was to allow the research and peaceful co-operation that had started during the International Geophysical Year to continue in this scientifically important area.

The areas given here (except for the Australian and New Zealand claims) are only rough estimates.

Claimant country	Name of claim or area	Limits	Approx. area (sq. miles)
Australia	Australian Antarctic Territory	45° E.–160° E. from 60° S. to Pole (except Adelie Land)	2,472,000

Claimant country	Name of claim or area	Limits	Approx. area (sq. miles)
France	French Antarctica and Southern Lands (four groups of Is. in South Pacific Ocean; Adelie Land)	136° E.–142° E. from 60° S. to Pole	178,000
Great Britain	Falkland Is. Dependencies (S. Shetlands, S. Orkneys, S. Sandwich, minor is. and Graham's Land)	20° W.–80° W. from 58° S. to Pole (and 20° W.–50° W. from 50° S. to 58° S.)	590,000
New Zealand	Ross Dependency	160° E.–150° W. from 60° S. to Pole	160,000
Norway	Queen Maud Land	20° W.–45° E., from shore of continent to Pole	950,000
Argentina		25° W.–73° W. from 60° S. to Pole	
Chile		53° W.–90° W. from 60° S. to Pole	
Unclaimed	Ellsworth Highland, Marie Byrd Land	80° W.–150° W., shore of continent to Pole	750,000

THE WORLD'S LARGEST CITIES

City and Country	Population
Tokyo, Japan	11,701,899
*Shanghai, China	10,000,000
Mexico City, Mexico	8,941,912
Buenos Aires, Argentina	8,774,529
Seoul, Korea	8,684,000
Cairo, Egypt	8,143,000
Peking, China	8,000,000
*New York, U.S.A.	7,895,563
Moscow, U.S.S.R.	7,734,000
London, England	7,379,014
Tientsin, China	7,000,000
Chungking, China	6,000,000
Sao Paulo, Brazil	5,901,533
*Bombay, India	5,850,000
*Canton, China	5,000,000
*Jakarta, Indonesia	5,000,000
Shenyang, China	4,400,000
*Leningrad, U.S.S.R.	4,372,000
*Rio de Janeiro, Brazil	4,296,782
Luta, China	4,200,000
Delhi, India	4,065,698
Santiago, Chile	4,000,000
Lima, Peru	3,600,000
*Bangkok, Thailand	3,000,000

* Seaport

THE WORLD'S HIGHEST MOUNTAINS

Peak	Location	Height (ft.)
Everest	Nepal–Tibet	29,028
Godwin Austen (K2)	Karakoram (India)	28,250
Kanchenjunga	Nepal–Sikkim	28,146
Makalu	Nepal–Tibet	27,824
Dhaulagari	Nepal	26,811
Nanga Parbat	N. W. Kashmir	26,629
Nanda Devi	Tibet, nr. India	25,645
Kamet	India–Tibet	25,447
Minya Konka	Sinkiang (China)	24,900
Communist Peak	U.S.S.R.	24,590

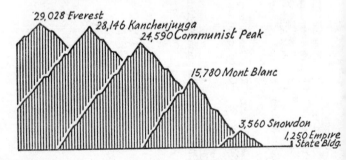

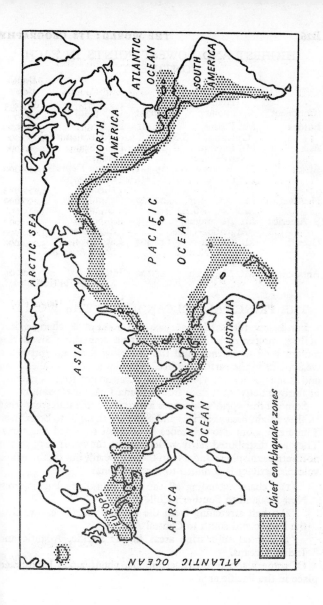

HIGHEST AND LOWEST POINTS IN EACH CONTINENT

Continent	Highest point	Height	Lowest point	Depth below sea-level (ft.)
Europe	Mt. Elbrus, Caucasus, U.S.S.R.	18,481	Polders, Netherlands (2)	12–15
Asia	Mt. Everest, Nepal–Tibet	29,028	Dead Sea, Jordan	1,286
Africa	Mt. Kilimanjaro (Kibo Peak), Tanzania	19,321	Qattara Depression, Egypt, U.A.R.	436
N. America	Mt. McKinley, Alaska, U.S.A.	20,320	Death Valley, U.S.A.	282
S. America	Mt. Aconcagua, Argentina–Chile	22,835	Rio Negro, Argentina	98
Oceania	Mt. Carstensz-toppen, New Guinea	16,404	Lake Eyre, South Australia	38
Antarctica	Mt. Markham	15,100	Interior	8,200 (ice-filled)

THE PRINCIPAL VOLCANOES OF THE WORLD

Far below the earth's surface the solid rock changes into boiling, molten rock. From time to time something causes this molten rock to expand, and thus to blow itself up through a weak point in the earth's surface. The liquid rock is called lava, and it may come out violently, as occasionally from Vesuvius, or fairly quietly, as it does from Mauna Loa, on Hawaii.

Some of the world's volcanoes are active, some quiescent (that is, they might *become* active) and some are thought to be extinct. There are about 430 volcanoes in all with recorded eruptions. They are distributed fairly widely about the earth (275 in the northern hemisphere and 155 in the southern), but on the whole volcanic activity is confined to three regions:

(1) a chain extending all the way round the Pacific from New Zealand to Southern Chile;

(2) a belt stretching from the Canary Islands eastward to the Pacific and south to Central Africa;

(3) isolated submarine areas in the Pacific, Atlantic and Indian Oceans.

Of some 2,500 recorded eruptions, about 2,000 have taken place in the Pacific area.

THE PRINCIPAL VOLCANOES OF THE WORLD

I. Active

Volcano	Height (ft.)
Cotopaxi (Ecuador)	19,613
Popocatapetl (Mexico)	17,887
Sangay (Ecuador)	17,749
Tungurahua (Ecuador)	16,512
Cotacachi (Ecuador)	16,197
Klyuchevskaya (U.S.S.R.)	15,912
Purace (Colombia)	15,604
Wrangell (Alaska, U.S.A.)	14,005
Tajmulco (Guatemala)	13,812
Mauna Loa (Hawaii, U.S.A.)	13,675
Cameroons (Nigeria)	13,350
Tacana (Guatemala)	13,333
Erebus (Antarctica)	13,200
Acatenango (Guatemala)	12,992
Colima (Mexico)	12,631
Fuego (Guatemala)	12,582
Kerintji (Indonesia)	12,484
Santa Maria (Guatemala)	12,362
Rindjani (Indonesia)	12,225
Semeru (Indonesia)	12,060
Ichinskaya (U.S.S.R.)	11,834
Atitlan (Guatemala)	11,565
Nyiregongo (Congo)	11,384
Irazu (Costa Rica)	11,260
Slamat (Indonesia)	11,247
Spurr (Alaska, U.S.A.)	11,070
Raung (Indonesia)	10,932
Etna (Sicily)	10,784

II. Quiescent

Volcano	Height (ft.)
Kilimanjaro (Tanzania)	19,321
Misti (Peru)	19,031
Pichincha (Ecuador)	15,712
Kronotskaya (U.S.S.R.)	12,328
Lassen (U.S.A.)	10,466
Welirang (Indonesia)	10,354
Sundoro (Indonesia)	10,285
Balbi (Solomon Is.)	10,171
Apo (Philippine Is.)	9,690
Marapi (Indonesia)	9,551
Tambora (Indonesia)	9,353
Paricutin (Mexico)	9,100

III. Believed Extinct

Volcano	Height (ft.)	Volcano	Height (ft.)
Aconcagua (Argentine–Chile)	22,835	Demavend (Iran)	17,604
Chimborazo (Ecuador)	20,610	Karisimbi (Congo)	15,020
Orizaba (Mexico)	18,701	Mikeno (Congo)	14,780
Elbrus (U.S.S.R.)	18,526	Fujiyama (Japan)	12,395

LAKES OF THE WORLD*

Lake	Location	Area (sq. miles)	Length (miles)	Salt or fresh
Caspian Sea¹	U.S.S.R.–Iran (Asia–Europe)	170,000	680	Salt
Superior	U.S.A.–Canada	31,820	383	Fresh
Victoria	Uganda–Kenya–Tanzania	26,200	200	Fresh
Aral Sea¹	Kazakhstan Republic, U.S.S.R.	26,166	265	Salt
Huron	U.S.A.–Canada	23,010	247	Fresh
Michigan	U.S.A.	22,400	307	Fresh
Baikal	U.S.S.R.	13,197	385	Fresh
Tanzania	Congo–Zambia, Tanzania–Burundi	12,700	420	Fresh
Great Bear	Canada	12,000	195	Fresh
Great Slave	Canada	11,170	325	Fresh
Nyasa	Malawi–Tanzania–Mozambique	11,000	350	Fresh
Erie	U.S.A.–Canada	9,940	241	Fresh
Winnipeg	Canada	9,398	260	Fresh
Ontario	U.S.A.–Canada	7,540	193	Fresh
Chad²	Niger–Chad–Cameroun–Nigeria	7,200	—	Fresh

¹ Classified as lakes, despite their names, as they are completely landlocked.
² In flood, Lake Chad becomes the world's largest fresh-water lake, covering 50,000 square miles.
* Some of these lakes are subject to seasonal variations in area.

PRINCIPAL RIVERS OF THE WORLD

River	Continent	Approx. length (miles)	Flow (cu. ft./sec.) where known	Outflow into:
Nile	Africa	4,150	420,000	Mediterranean Sea
Amazon	S. America	3,900	7,200,000	Atlantic Ocean
Missouri–Mississippi }	N. America	3,800	513,000	Gulf of Mexico
Yangtze Kiang	Asia	3,400	770,000	Pacific Ocean
Ob-Irtish	Asia	3,200	—	Gulf of Ob/Pacific
Hwang Ho (Yellow)	Asia	2,900	116,000	Yellow Sea (Pacific)
Congo	Africa	2,900	2,000,000	Atlantic Ocean
Amur	Asia	2,800	—	Gulf of Tartary
Lena	Asia	2,800	—	Arctic Ocean
Mekong	Asia	2,800	600,000	South China Sea
Niger	Africa	2,600	—	Atlantic Ocean
Yenisei	Asia	2,550	—	Arctic Ocean
MacKenzie	N. America	2,500	450,000	Arctic Ocean
La Plata Parana	S. America	2,300	2,800,000	Atlantic Ocean
Volga	Europe	2,300	350,000	Caspian Sea
Yukon	N. America	2,000	—	Bering Sea
St Lawrence	N. America	1,800	400,000	Atlantic Ocean
Rio Grande	N. America	1,800	5,180	Gulf of Mexico

THE WORLD'S GREAT WATERFALLS
In Order of Height (Single Leaps Only)

Waterfall	Country	River	Height (ft.)
Angel Falls	Venezuela	Tributary of Caroni River	3,212
Ribbon Falls	California, U.S.A.	Tributary of Yosemite River	1,612
King George VI	Guyana	Utshi River	1,600

Waterfall	Country	River	Height (ft.)
Upper Yosemite	California, U.S.A.	Yosemite Creek	1,430
Tugela (highest fall)	Natal, Republic of S. Africa	Tugela River	1,350
Gavarnie	Pyrenees, France	Gave de Pau	1,385
Wollomombi	New South Wales, Australia	Wollomombi River	1,100
Takakkaw	British Columbia, Canada	Tributary of Yoho River	1,000
Staubbach	Switzerland	Pletschen River	980
Mardola	Norway	Elkesdals Lake	974
Vettisfoss	Norway	Utla River	856
Chirombo	Zambia	Ieisa River	880
King Edward VIII	Guyana	Semang River	840
Gersoppa	India	Sharavati River	830
Sutherland	New Zealand	Arthur River	815

In Order of Volume

Waterfall	Country	River	Height (ft.)	Average annual flow (cu. ft./sec.)
Guaira or Sete Quedas	Brazil–Paraguay	Alto Parana River	130	470,000
Khon	Laos–Khmer	Mekong River	70	410,000
Niagara	U.S.A.–Canada	Niagara River	167	212,000
Paolo Afonse	Brazil	Sao Francisco River	192	100,000
Urubupunga	Brazil	Alto Parana River	40	97,000
Iguazu	Argentina–Brazil	Iguazu River	237	61,660
Patos–Maribondo	Brazil	Rio Grande	115	53,000
Victoria	Zambia and Rhodesia	Zambesi River	354	38,430
Grand	Labrador	Hamilton River	245	35,000
Kaieteur	Guyana	Potaro River	741	23,400

GREAT SHIP CANALS OF THE WORLD

Canal	Year opened	Length miles	Depth feet	Width feet
Amsterdam (Netherlands)	1876	16·5	23	88
Corinth (Greece)	1893	4	26.25	72
Elbe and Trave (Germany)	1900	41	10	72
Gota (Sweden)	1832	115	10	47
Kiel (Germany)	1895	61	45	150
Manchester (England)	1894	35·5	28–30	120
Panama (U.S.A.)	1914	50·5	45	300
Princess Juliana (Netherlands)	1935	20	16	52
Saulte Ste. Marie (U.S.A.)	1855	1·6	22	100
Saulte Ste. Marie (Canada)	1895	1·11	22–25	142
Suez (Egypt)	1869	100	34	197
Welland (Canada)	1887	26·75	25	200

PRINCIPAL LANGUAGES OF THE WORLD

There are probably over 2,000 languages spoken today. Nobody can say the exact number, since many are spoken only by small groups and tribes and have never been recorded on paper. About two thirds of the world's population speak twelve principal languages. The second twelve languages listed here account for about half the remaining population.

Language	Speakers (millions)	Language	Speakers (millions)
Mandarin (China)	493	Italian	58
English	291	Urdu (Pakistan and India)	54
Russian	167	Cantonese (China)	45
Hindi	162	Javanese (Indonesia)	42
Spanish	155	Ukrainian (mainly U.S.S.R.)	41
German	123	Telegu (India)	41
Japanese	98	Wu (China)	39
Bengali (India, Pakistan)	85	Tamil (India and Ceylon)	37
Arabic	82	Min (China)	36
Portuguese	80	Korean	35
French	73		
Malay	71		

DISTANCES BY AIR BETWEEN SOME OF THE WORLD'S CHIEF CITIES, IN MILES

	Amsterdam	Brussels	Buenos Aires	Cairo	Calcutta	Copenhagen
Amsterdam	—	98	7,124	2,041	4,731	393
Brussels	98	—	7,050	1,993	4,761	469
Buenos Aires	7,124	7,050	—	7,368	10,279	7,517
Cairo	2,041	1,993	7,368	—	3,533	1,986
Calcutta	4,731	4,761	10,279	3,533	—	4,390
Copenhagen	393	469	7,517	1,986	4,390	—
Dublin	467	487	6,853	2,473	5,160	770
Geneva	424	331	6,892	1,755	4,748	708
Johannesburg	5,614	5,528	5,028	3,908	5,263	5,736
Karachi	3,718	3,723	9,151	2,210	1,355	3,443
London	231	218	6,921	2,081	4,962	608
Madrid	908	818	6,268	2,081	5,319	1,280
Montreal	3,421	3,452	5,629	5,421	7,600	3,606
New York	3,635	3,657	5,305	5,003	7,918	3,845
Paris	253	162	6,892	1,997	4,877	630
Rome	812	737	6,947	1,321	4,482	955
Singapore	6,529	6,556	9,858	4,696	1,801	6,191
Stockholm	703	787	7,820	2,115	4,200	324
Sydney	10,349	10,399	7,311	8,949	5,678	9,967

	Dublin	Geneva	Johannesburg	Karachi	London	Madrid
Amsterdam	467	424	5,614	3,718	231	908
Brussels	487	331	5,528	3,723	218	818
Buenos Aires	6,853	6,892	5,028	9,151	6,921	6,268
Cairo	2,473	1,755	3,908	2,210	2,194	2,081
Calcutta	5,160	4,748	5,263	1,355	4,962	5,319
Copenhagen	770	708	5,736	3,443	608	1,280
Dublin	—	740	5,885	4,179	279	905

	Dublin	Geneva	Johannesburg	Karachi	London	Madrid
Johannesburg	5,885	5,201	—	4,393	5,650	5,045
Karachi	4,179	3,632	4,393	—	3,938	4,140
London	279	468	5,650	3,938	—	774
Madrid	905	627	5,045	4,140	774	—
Montreal	2,965	3,669	8,047	6,989	3,241	3,451
New York	3,171	3,853	7,976	7,260	3,443	3,581
Paris	486	254	5,439	3,808	215	655
Rome	1,184	444	4,812	3,297	908	844
Singapore	6,952	6,524	5,378	2,942	6,760	7,069
Stockholm	1,004	1,029	5,949	3,342	899	1,603
Sydney	10,695	10,425	6,845	6,841	10,575	10,980

	Montreal	New York	Paris	Rome	Singapore	Stockholm	Sydney
Amsterdam	3,421	3,635	253	812	6,529	703	10,349
Brussels	3,452	3,657	162	737	6,556	787	10,399
Buenos Aires	5,629	5,305	6,892	6,947	9,858	7,820	7,311
Cairo	5,424	5,603	1,997	1,321	4,696	2,115	8,949
Calcutta	7,600	7,918	4,877	4,482	1,801	4,200	5,678
Copenhagen	3,606	3,845	630	955	6,191	324	9,967
Dublin	2,965	3,171	486	1,184	6,962	1,004	10,695
Geneva	3,669	3,853	254	444	6,524	1,029	10,425
Johannesburg	8,047	7,976	5,439	4,812	5,378	5,949	6,845
Karachi	6,989	7,260	3,808	3,297	2,942	3,342	6,841
London	3,241	3,443	215	908	6,760	899	10,575
Madrid	3,451	3,581	655	844	7,069	1,603	10,980
Montreal	—	333	3,430	4,107	9,201	3,658	9,955
New York	333	—	3,621	4,282	9,534	3,919	9,949
Paris	3,430	3,621	—	697	6,667	949	10,534
Rome	4,107	4,282	697	—	6,224	1,234	10,136
Singapore	9,201	9,534	6,667	6,224	—	5,997	3,914
Stockholm	3,658	3,919	949	1,234	5,997	—	9,697
Sydney	9,955	9,949	10,534	10,136	3,914	9,697	—

Great Britain and Northern Ireland

THE COUNTIES: *Their Areas and Populations*

Note: The list that follows this note gives the new counties or shires, their areas and populations as they have been since April, 1974, when the provisions of the Local Government Act, 1972, came into force. This Act brought some old counties to an end, rearranged the area and boundaries of others, and introduced new counties and districts.

England is now divided into six metropolitan counties and districts: Greater Manchester, Merseyside, S. Yorkshire, Tyne and Wear, W. Midlands, W. Yorkshire. Besides these, there are 39 non-metropolitan counties: Avon, Bedfordshire, Berkshire, Buckinghamshire, Cambridgeshire, Cheshire, Cleveland, Cornwall, Cumbria, Derbyshire, Devon, Dorset, Durham, E. Sussex, Essex, Gloucestershire, Hampshire, Hereford and Worcester, Hertfordshire, Humberside, I. of Wight, Kent, Lancashire, Leicestershire, Lincolnshire, Norfolk, N. Yorkshire, Northamptonshire, Northumberland, Nottinghamshire, Oxfordshire, Salop, Somerset, Staffordshire, Suffolk, Surrey, Warwickshire, W. Sussex, Wiltshire.

In Wales, the local government areas are now: Clwyd, Dyfed, Gwent, Gwynedd, Mid Glamorgan, Powys, S. Glamorgan, W. Glamorgan.

England

National Capital: London

County or Shire	Administrative Headquarters	Area (acres)	Population
Avon	Bristol	332,596	919,600
Bedford	Bedford	305,094	493,800
Berkshire	Reading	310,179	658,700
Buckinghamshire	Aylesbury	465,019	501,800
Cambridgeshire	Cambridge	842,433	540,300
Cheshire	Chester	575,375	910,900
Cleveland	Middlesbrough	144,030	565,400
Cornwall	Truro	876,295	401,500
Cumbria	Carlisle	1,701,455	473,800
Derbyshire	Matlock	650,146	902,820
Devonshire	Exeter	1,658,278	936,300
Dorset	Dorchester	664,116	572,900
Durham	Durham	601,939	607,600
Essex	Chelmsford	907,849	1,411,000
Gloucester	Gloucester	652,741	487,600
Greater Manchester	Manchester	318,560	2,730,000
Hampshire	Winchester	932,468	1,434,000
Hereford & Worcester	Worcester	970,203	585,900

County or Shire	Administrative Headquarters	Area (acres)	Population
Hertford	Hertford	403,797	938,100
Humberside	Kingston-upon-Hull	867,784	848,200
Kent	Maidstone	922,196	1,445,400
Lancashire	Preston	751,063	1,369,200
Leicestershire	Leicester	630,842	836,500
Lincoln	Lincoln	1,454,273	521,900
Greater London	S.E.1.	390,302	7,111,500
Merseyside	Liverpool	159,750	1,588,400
Norfolk	Norwich	1,323,174	659,300
Northampton	Northampton	584,972	500,100
Northumberland	Newcastle-upon-Tyne	1,243,692	285,700
Nottinghamshire	Nottingham	534,735	982,700
Oxfordshire	Oxford	645,314	539,100
Salop	Shrewsbury	862,479	354,800
Somerset	Taunton	854,488	401,700
Staffordshire	Stafford	671,184	988,400
Suffolk	Ipswich	940,800	570,000
Surrey	Kingston-upon-Thames	414,922	1,000,700
Sussex, East	Lewes	443,627	657,300
Sussex West	Chichester	492,068	623,100
Tyne & Wear	Newcastle	133,390	1,192,600
Warwick	Warwick	489,405	471,800
West Midlands	Birmingham	222,254	2,777,500
Wight, Isle of	Newport I.O.W.	94,146	111,000
Wiltshire	Trowbridge	860,109	511,600
Yorkshire North	Northallerton	2,055,000	648,600
Yorkshire South	Barnsley	385,610	1,317,200
Yorkshire West	Wakefield	503,863	2,082,600

Wales
National Capital: Cardiff

Clwyd	Mold	599,481	374,000
Dyfed	Carmarthen	1,424,668	320,100
Gwent	Cwmbran	339,933	440,100
Gwynedd	Caernarvon	955,244	224,200
Mid Glamorgan	Cardiff	251,732	545,206
Powyss	Llandrindod Wells	1,254,656	100,800
South Glamorgan	Cardiff	102,807	391,100
West Glamorgan	Swansea	201,476	371,700

Scotland
National Capital: Edinburgh*

Borders	Newtown St. Boswells	1,154,288	99,105
Central	Stirling	622,080	270,000

County or Shire	Administrative Headquarters	Area (acres)	Population
Dumfries and Galloway	Dumfries	1,574,400	143,585
Fife	Cupar	322,560	337,690
Grampian	Aberdeen	2,151,000	450,000
Highlands	Inverness	6,280,320	182,044
Lothian	Edinburgh	433,920	755,293
Orkney	Kirkwall	240,848	17,748
Shetland	Lerwick	352,337	19,526
Strathclyde	Glasgow	3,422,520	2,515,002
Tayside	Dundee	1,894,080	401,987
Western Isles	Stornoway, Lewis	716,800	29,615

* Aberdeen, Edinburgh and Glasgow are the principal Scottish Cities. Their populations are estimated as: Aberdeen 212,237; Glasgow 856,000; Edinburgh 475,042.

Northern Ireland

National Capital: Belfast

Counties and County Boroughs	Area (sq. m.)
Antrim	1,099
Belfast County Borough	25
Armagh	489
Down	952
Fermanagh	657
Londonderry*	810
Londonderry City	3.4
Tyrone	1,218

* Excluding the City of Londonderry

Other British Isles

Island	Capital or chief town	Area (acres)	Population
Isle of Man	Douglas	145,325	60,496
Channel Islands:			
Jersey	St. Helier	28,717	72,532
Guernsey	St. Peter Port	15,654	51,620
Alderney	St. Anne's	1,962	1,785
Sark	—	1,274	604

BRITAIN'S LARGEST CITIES

City and Aerodromes[1]	Population
London (B.A.A.)	7,379,014
Birmingham (M)	1,058,800
Glasgow (M)	856,000
Leeds (M)	746,000
Sheffield —	558,800
Liverpool (M)	539,700
Manchester (M)	488,518
Edinburgh (B.A.A.)	475,042
Bradford (M. See Leeds)	460,000
Bristol (M)	416,300
Belfast (S)	363,000
Coventry (M)	337,000
Newcastle-upon-Tyne —	295,800
Leicester —	289,400
Cardiff —	287,000
Kingston-upon-Hull —	285,970
Nottingham —	280,300
Stoke-on-Trent —	256,200

[1] S: owned and operated by State; B.A.A.: operated by British Airports Authority; M: owned and operated by Municipal Authority.

BRITAIN'S HIGHEST MOUNTAINS AND LARGEST LAKES

Peak	County	Height (ft.)	Lake	County	Area (sq. miles)
		England			
Scafell Pike	Cumbria	3,210	Windermere	Westmorland–Lancs.	10
		Wales and Monmouthshire			
Snowdon	Gwynydd	3,560	Bala	Merioneth	4
		Scotland			
Ben Nevis	Inverness	4,406	Loch Lomond	Dunbarton–Stirling	27
		Northern Ireland			
Slieve Donard	Down	2,796	Lough Neagh	Antrim–Londonderry–Tyrone–Armagh	150

IMPORTANT RIVERS OF BRITAIN

River	Length (miles)	Rises in:	Flows to:
Severn	220	Plynlimmon, Dyfed	Bristol Channel
Thames	209	Cotswold Hills, nr. Cirencester	North Sea
Trent	170	N. Staffordshire	Joins Ouse to form R. Humber
Great Ouse	156	Northants.	The Wash
Wye	130	Plynlimmon	Severn, nr. Chepstow
Tay	117	Grampian Mts., N. Argyllshire	Firth of Tay
Spey	110	Grampian Mts., Inverness	Moray Firth
Clyde	106	S. Lanark (union of Daer and Potrail Water)	Firth of Clyde
Tweed	97	Tweedsmuir Hills, S. Peebles	North Sea, at Scot.-Eng. border
Dee	87	Cairngorm Mts., W. Aberdeenshire	North Sea (at Aberdeen)
Ribble	75	Pennine Chain, W. Yorkshire	Irish Sea (nr. Southport)
Dee	70	Merioneth, N. Wales	Irish Sea
Mersey	70	Pennine Chain (union of Goyt and Tame at Stockport)	Irish Sea (at Liverpool)
Tees	70	Cross Fell, Cumbria	North Sea
Forth	66	S. Perth	Firth of Forth
Towy	66	Hills between Cardigan and Radnor	Carmarthen Bay
Eden	65	Pennine Chain (Cumbria–Yorks.)	Solway Firth (Irish Sea)
Wear	65	Pennine Chain (W. Durham)	North Sea
Derwent	60	N. of the Peak (Derby)	Trent
Ouse	60	Yorks. (union of Swale and Ure)	Joins Trent to form R. Humber
Tamar	60	Devonian Hills	English Channel (at Plymouth)
Derwent	57	Yorkshire moors	Ouse (between Selby and Goole)
Exe	54	Exmoor (N. Devon)	English Channel (Exeter)
Teifi	53	Llyn Teifi, N.E. Dyfyd	Cardigan Bay (at Cardigan)
Tyne	45	Northumberland (union of N. and S. Tyne)	North Sea (at Tynemouth)

A Dictionary of Geographical Terms

Aborigines The earliest known inhabitants of a country.

Alluvium The fine sand or soil deposited in low places by running water.

Antipodes Two places precisely opposite one another on the earth, such as Barfleur in Normandy and Antipodes Island south-east of New Zealand. At antipodes the hours and seasons are reversed, so that when it is midnight in summer in Barfleur it is noon in winter on Antipodes.

Archipelago A group of islands.

Atoll A coral reef, typical of the Pacific Ocean, shaped like a ring or horseshoe round a lagoon.

Aurora borealis The Northern lights; an electrical discharge seen by night over the higher latitudes of the northern hemisphere.

Axis The imaginary line running from pole to pole through the centre of the earth.

Bar A collection of gravel, sand or mud at the mouth of a river.

Basin The area of land drained by a river and its tributaries.

Bayou A marshy creek or offshoot to a river or lake which remains swampy because of floods and lack of drainage.

Blowhole A hole in the roof of a seaside cave through which air and sometimes water are forced by the rising tide.

Beaches, Raised Line of former sea shore left dry through a rise in the land.

Bore or **Eagre** A tidal wave arising in the estuaries of certain rivers.

Butte A flat-topped hill, like a MESA but smaller.

Canyon A narrow, deep gorge, with steep sides, cut by a river through soft rock in a dry region. The biggest and best known is the Grand Canyon of the Colorado River, U.S.A.

Cape A headland or piece of land jutting out into the sea.

Cataract A large waterfall, or series of waterfalls.

Col A mountain pass or neck.

Continental drift The movement by which, according to one theory, the continents arrived at their present positions after breaking off from a single original mass of land. The main

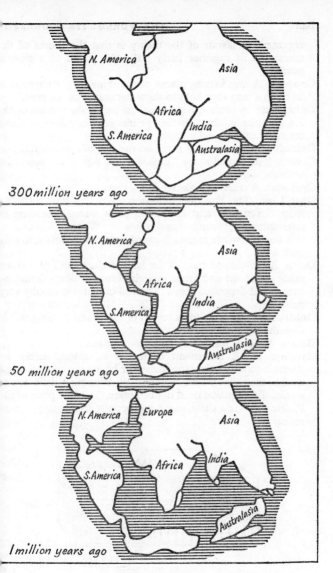

Continental Drift

argument in favour of the theory is that the shores of the
continents fit together fairly well, like pieces of a jig-saw
puzzle.

Contour A line joining places of the same height above sea-
level; in a map they help to show the shapes of the land.

Coral Reef A barrier, lying at or just below the surface of the
sea, built up of the skeletons of immense numbers of small
creatures called coral polyps.

Couloir A steep, narrow gorge on the side of a mountain.

Crater The funnel-shaped hollow at the top of the cone of a
volcano.

Crevasse A crack in a glacier or ice sheet.

Date Line The line that follows roughly the 180° meridian
from Greenwich, and marks the point where according to
international agreement the day begins. When a ship crosses
this line eastwards it goes forward a day; westwards, it goes
back a day.

Delta A fan-shaped tract of flat land at the mouth of a river,
made up of silt and other material brought down from up-
stream and deposited there. The soil of deltas is usually very
rich.

Doldrums The term for a region of calms and baffling winds
near the equator.

Dunes Mounds formed by wind-blown sand.

Earthquake A movement of the earth, caused either by
volcanic activity below the surface or by a large area of earth,
weaker than that which surrounds it, slipping a little downwards. Earthquakes need not be severe. In some parts of the
Pacific they are a daily, and not especially frightening, occur-
rence.

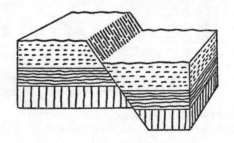

rosion The wearing away of the land by sun, wind, rain, frost, running water, moving ice and the sea.

ault A break in the earth's crust along which movement has taken place—usually, but not always, vertically—so that the layers (strata) of the two rock faces no longer match. It is often along a fault that earthquakes occur.

ord A long, narrow inlet of the sea, with steep sides, scooped out in ages past by glaciers. A fiord is usually very deep, becoming shallower towards its mouth.

öhn Wind A warm, dry wind blowing down the sides of mountains facing away from the prevailing wind. It is best known in the valleys of the northern Alps. Other föhn winds are the Chinook (the eastern side of the Rocky Mountains, Canada and the U.S.A.); the Nor'Wester (New Zealand) and the Samoon (Iran).

eysers Hot springs which shoot jets of hot water and steam into the air at regular or irregular intervals.

laciers Masses of ice that move very slowly down a valley towards the sea, propelled by gravity, carrying rock material with them.

orse Latitudes Regions of calms and variable winds between latitudes 25° and 40° N. and S.; so-called because becalmed sailors whose food was running out used to throw their horses overboard.

ebergs Masses of ice that have broken off from glaciers and are afloat in the sea. Only about one-ninth of an iceberg is above the surface.

ternational Date Line Generally, every country sets its time according to the rising and setting of the sun. So that anywhere in the world the sun is at its highest at about 12 o'clock midday, *local time*. But suppose you were to travel due west from London so fast that the sun stayed in the same relative position above you (many aeroplanes in fact do this) and that you went right on till you came round to London again. According to all the local times you passed through, time would have stood still. Yet in fact your journey would have taken twenty-four hours.

By international agreement, a line has been drawn down the meridian opposite that of Greenwich, and whenever anyone crosses this line East to West he adds on a day; or if from West to East, he takes off a day. The line does not quite keep

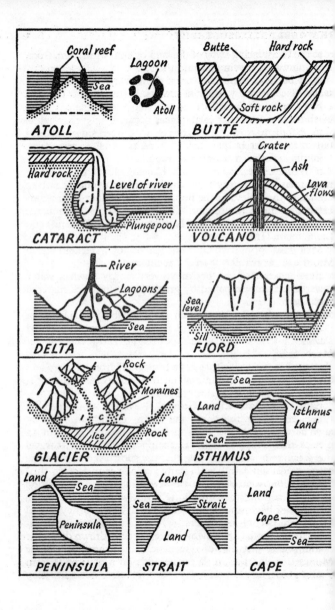

to the meridian. To avoid confusion it has been drawn round any lands or groups of islands where it might have upset the calendar too much. (See map on page B15.)

Isobars Lines on a map joining places of the same average barometric pressure.

Isotherms Lines on a map joining places of the same average temperature.

Isthmus A narrow strip of land joining two large land areas or joining a peninsula to the mainland. Examples: the isthmuses of Panama and Suez.

Latitude The distance of a place north or south from the equator, measured in degrees of the MERIDIAN.

Littoral The seashore, the land along the coast, or the land lying between the levels of high and low tide.

Longitude The distance of a place east or west of a given MERIDIAN.

Magnetic North The pole of the lines of magnetic force that run north and south through the earth. It changes its position slightly from year to year, but in general it is in an area north of Canada, roughly at longitude 97° W. and latitude 71° N.

Meridian An imaginary circle on the earth's surface passing through the two poles; on it all places have noon at the same time.

Mesa A flat, table-like mass with steep sides all round. Eventually, by wearing away, mesas becomes BUTTES.

Meteor or Shooting Star. A body of matter flying around in outer space which enters the earth's atmosphere. It usually travels so fast that the friction caused by passing through the atmosphere burns it up quickly. Some big ones, however, do survive the journey and reach the earth. These are called *meteorites*. One of the biggest fell in Arizona, blowing a crater a mile wide and 600 ft. deep.

Mirage An optical illusion, caused by the presence of layers of air of different density, in which the image of a sheet of water may appear over the desert, or images of ships and icebergs, upside-down, over polar waters.

Monsoons Winds of the Indian Ocean and nearby lands blowing from the north-east in October to March, and from the south-west in April to September.

Moraine A continuous line of rocks and gravel along the edges of a glacier.

Oasis An area in the desert made fertile by the presence o
water.
Pampas Dreary expanses of treeless, grassy plain and sal
marshes in Argentina.

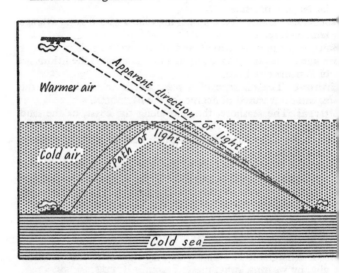

Peninsula A tract of land almost surrounded by water.
Pothole A hole worn in solid rock, usually at the foot of a water
fall, by the constant grinding of a stone, kept in motion b
the current.
Prairie The almost flat, mostly treeless grasslands of Nortl
America. Similar areas are the steppes of the U.S.S.R., th
pampas of Argentina and the veld of South Africa.
Projections Ways of representing the earth's surface on a maj
Because the earth is round, any map distorts the area
represents (just as flattening out an orange peel distorts it
original shape). Only a globe can be really accurate.
   Different types of projection have been worked out, eac
suited to a particular purpose. The two main ones are Conic:
and Cylindrical. The former shows each hemisphere as a con
which has been unrolled. A Cylindrical Projection shows th
earth as though it were an unrolled cylinder. Mercator'

projection, used on page B14, is cylindrical. Its main fault is that it makes the Equator out to be the same length as all other latitudes, even those near the Poles, which are really only a few miles long. Thus countries near the Poles appear far larger than they really are.

Roaring Forties The seaman's name for the steady north-west anti-trade winds between latitudes 40° and 60° S.

Sierra A mountain range.

Sirocco The hot, dry and sometimes dusty southerly wind blowing from the Sahara; it is experienced in North Africa, Sicily and southern Italy.

Stalactite A column of mineral matter, particularly calcium carbonate, hanging from the roof of a cave like a giant icicle.

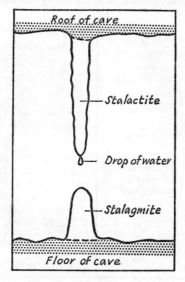

Stalagmite A column of calcium carbonate rising from the floor of a cave, formed by water containing the mineral falling from the roof or from a STALACTITE.

Strait A narrow band of sea connecting two large sea areas. Example: the Straits of Gibraltar, connecting the Atlantic and the Mediterranean.

Trade Winds Regular steady winds in the tropics, between latitudes 30° N. and 30° S., blowing to the equator.

Tropics The tropic of Cancer (line of latitude 23½ degrees North) and the Tropic of Capricorn (line of latitude 23½ degrees South) are, respectively, the northernmost and southernmost lines on which the sun's rays shine vertically.

Tsunami The correct name for what is often wrongly called a tidal wave, namely, a huge sea wave sometimes experienced along the coasts of the oceans (as in Japan and Chile in 1960) and caused by earthquakes on the ocean floor.

Typhoon A violent, destructive whirlwind blowing in the China Seas from August to October.

Whirlpool A circular eddy in the sea produced by the coming together of two currents, or in a river by the way the channel is formed.

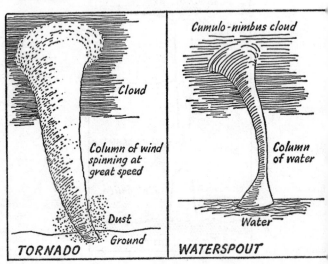

Weather

CLOUDS

There are three principal formations of cloud that can easily be recognised from the translations of their Latin names: **stratus**, a flat layer; **cumulus**, a heap, pile or pack; and **cirrus**, meaning a lock of curly hair. These often combine, as the list shows, in other formations. It may be helpful to remember that **alto** means high and **nimbo** or **nimbus** means rain.

TYPES OF CLOUD

Type	Usual range of height of base in feet	Description
Cumulus	1,000–1,500	Flat base, high rounded tops. Small, white, scattered puffs mean fair weather, but heavy, deep clouds often become cumulo-nimbus.
Stratus	Up to 500–2,000	Unbroken grey layer; looks like fog that has lifted from the ground.
Stratocumulus	1,000–4,500	Broad layer arranged in round masses or rolls, often so close together that their edges join.
Nimbostratus	Near surface to 20,000	Dark grey with a base that is the same throughout. Often gives continuous rain or snow; if these do not reach the ground the cloud appears to trail.
Cumulonimbus	Up to 2,000–5,000	Heavy, dark, very tall—as high as 3 miles. Tops often spread out in anvil-shape. Thunderstorm cloud; gives showers of rain, snow, hail, etc.
Altocumulus	6,500–20,000	Small, thin rounded patches, resembling cumulus, sometimes so close together their edges meet.

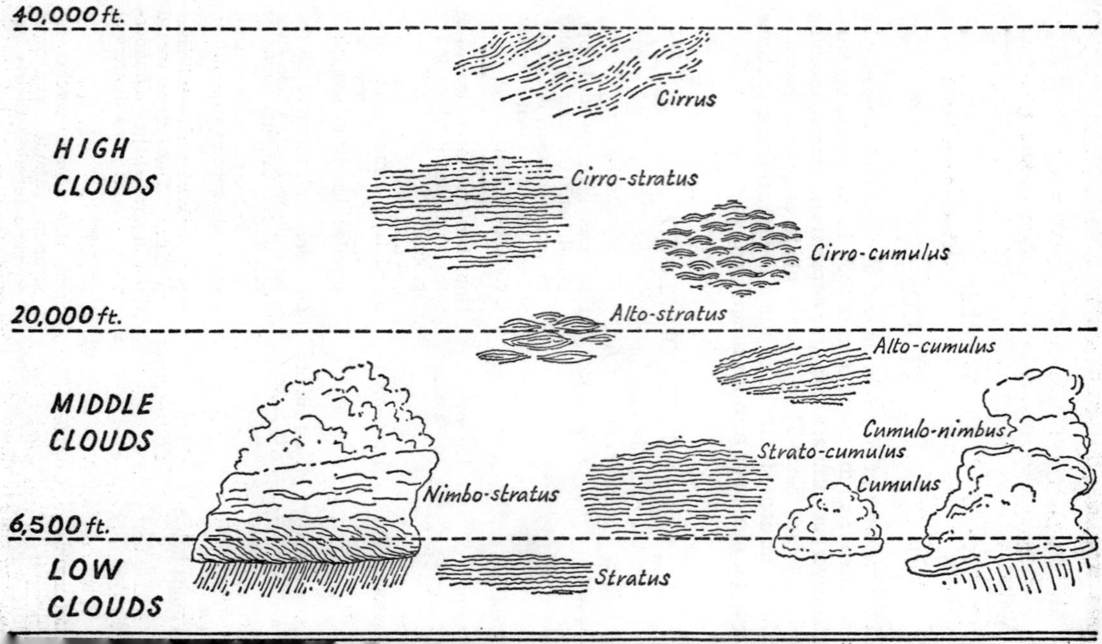

40,000 ft.

HIGH CLOUDS

Cirrus

Cirro-stratus

Cirro-cumulus

20,000 ft.

MIDDLE CLOUDS

Alto-stratus

Alto-cumulus

Cumulo-nimbus

Strato-cumulus

Cumulus

Nimbo-stratus

6,500 ft.

LOW CLOUDS

Stratus

Type	Usual range of height of base in feet	Description
Altostratus	6,580–20,000	Sheet or veil, sometimes thin, but sometimes so thick it blocks out the moon or even the sun, when it normally indicates continuous rain.
Cirrus	20,000–40,000	Detached pieces, delicate and feathery ('mares' tails').
Cirrocumulus	20,000–40,000	Small flakes or rolls in groups or lines ('mackerel sky'). Made up of ice crystals.
Cirrostratus	20,000–40,000	Thin, milky veil producing a ring of light round the moon.

OTHER INFLUENCES ON WEATHER

Rain is simply what happens when the water droplets that make up a cloud become too heavy to be supported by the upward-moving currents of air.

Snow occurs when the temperature of the atmosphere at cloud level is below freezing; it falls either as individual ice crystals

always with six sides) or as snowflakes composed of several crystals joined together.

Sleet is a mixture of snow and rain that occurs when the snow has been melting during its fall but has not melted completely.

Hail is produced during a thunderstorm, when moist air is drawn up particularly fast, forming hard pellets of ice in a cumulonimbus cloud. Hailstones grow larger as they pick up more water vapour which freezes around them. Sliced in half

Cross sections of hailstones

they can be seen to be made up of a varying number of coats or skins of ice built outwards from a centre.

Dew is what results when at night the ground releases the heat it has stored up during the day, and the air on or just above it becomes cooler. When the temperature falls below a certain point the water vapour on the ground or on nearby objects like blades of grass forms the drops of water we call dew.

Hoar Frost is frozen dew.

Fog is a thick mass of small water drops in the lower air, resulting from condensation. In cities the water drops are often mixed with particles of dust and smoke; when the mixture is really detestable it earns the name of *smog*.

Mist is simply a thinner version of fog.

Land fogs occur mainly in autumn and winter and **sea fogs** in spring and summer. This is because the sea takes in and gives off the sun's heat much more slowly than the land, and begins to lose the previous summer's heat (thus cooling the air above it and causing fog) only after the winter has passed.

Thunder is produced by the expansion of air due to the tremendous heat of lightning flashes.

Lightning is an electrical discharge from a thunder-cloud which generates electricity much as a power station does.

SOME VIOLENT KINDS OF WEATHER

Typhoons and **hurricanes** are caused by tropical cyclones. These cyclones occur where the pressure of the atmosphere has sunk very much lower than that of the surrounding air. Around its calm centre—known as the 'eye' of the storm—winds of hurricane force (that is, of speeds greater than 75 m.p.h.) blow continuously. Cyclones cause immense damage in the tropics. They occur most often in the seas off China (typhoons), but nearly as often in the West Indies (hurricanes).

Whirlwinds are like cyclones, having an area of low pressure at their centres, but they are very much smaller, consisting of columns of air whirling very rapidly round an axis that is vertical or nearly so. In the desert they can cause **sandstorms**.

A **tornado** is an extremely violent whirlwind.

A **waterspout** is a tornado occurring at sea; a portion of cloud looking like an upside-down cone reaches down from the base of a thunder-cloud to where it meets a cone of spray raised from the sea to form a continuous column or spout between sea and cloud. In the days of sailing-ships waterspouts were known to tear ships to pieces.

WORLD WEATHER RECORDS

Record	Degree or amount	Where recorded	When recorded
Highest shade temperature	57·8° C. (136° F.)	San Louis, Mexico	1933
Lowest temperature	−88·3° C. (−127° F.)	Vostok, Antarctica	1960
Maximum rainfall (24 hours)	870 mm. (73·62 in.)	Cilaos, Ile de Réunion	1952
Maximum rainfall (one month)	9,300 mm. (366·14 in.)	Cherrapunji, India	1861
Greatest annual total rainfall	22,900 mm. (905·12 in.)	also at Cherrapunji	1861

BRITISH WEATHER RECORDS

Highest temperature	100·5° F. (38·1° C.)	Tonbridge, Kent	1868
Lowest temperature	−17° F. (−27° C.)	Braemar, Scotland	1895
Maximum rainfall (24 hours)	11 in.	Martinstown, near Dorchester	1955
Maximum annual rainfall	6,528 mm (257 in.)	Sprinkling Tarn, Cumberland	1954

FURTHER READING

A Dictionary of Geography, by W. G. Moore (Penguin)
Standard Encyclopædia of the World's Oceans and Islands, ed
   Anthony Huxley (Weidenfeld & Nicolson)
The Observer's Book of The Weather (Warne)

The World

3: ITS FAMOUS PEOPLE
(*Actual and Mythical*)

In *A Dictionary of Famous People* are to be found short biographies of the great men and women of both the distant and the recent past. In *Names in the News* short notes are given about celebrated persons now living. Those in *A Dictionary of Mythology* were, of course, never alive at all, in any ordinary sense—they are the gods and goddesses found in the myths and legends of ancient peoples.

A Dictionary of Famous People

WHEN the story of a man's life, his biography, is told very briefly it is called a potted biography. The biographies in this section have been potted and then potted again. They are meant to answer the following questions: 'Who was he?' 'When did he live?' 'Where did he come from?' 'What did he do?' For fuller details you should, of course, consult either a separate biography of your man (or woman) or one of the big encyclopaedias that are devoted entirely to telling the stories of famous lives. (For famous Britishers the best source of all is the *Dictionary of National Biography*.)

Left out of this section are most of those people whose achievements are mentioned elsewhere; for example,

Kings and Queens of England and Scotland (HISTORY);
British writers (THE ENGLISH LANGUAGE);
Explorers and discoverers (HISTORY);
Painters, sculptors and architects (THE ARTS).

In the case of other historical figures, dates of birth and death are given and you are advised to 'see HISTORY'—which usually means the DIARY OF WORLD EVENTS. In some instances people who appear elsewhere in the book are treated fully here (e.g. Captain Scott); this is because there is something important to add that has not been said in the other section where the mention occurs.

The letter *c.* before a date (e.g. *c.* 450 B.C.) is short for the Latin *circa*, 'about', and means that the date is not certainly known.

Aeschylus (*c.* 525–456 B.C.), Greek tragic dramatist.
Akbar, Jalal-ud-din Mohammed (1542–1605), greatest of the Mogul emperors.
Alaric 1st (376–410), King of the Visigoths, who sacked Rome.
Alban, St, lived in the last part of the 3rd century; served as soldier in Rome, was converted to Christianity and, returning to Britain to preach, was martyrised.

Alcibiades (*c.* 450–404 B.C.), Athenian statesman and general, pupil of Socrates.

Alcott, Louisa May (1832–88), American writer, author of *Little Women*.

Alexander II (1818–81), Czar of Russia who emancipated the serfs; assassinated by Nihilists.

Alexander the Great (356–323 B.C.), see HISTORY.

Alfred the Great (849–99), see HISTORY.

Ampère, André Marie (1775–1836), French mathematician, the first to propound the electro-dynamic theory.

Andersen, Hans Christian (1805–75), Danish storyteller and poet; author of famous fairy tales.

Andrew, St, one of Jesus' disciples, and patron saint of Scotland; commemorated on 30 November.

Anselm, St (1033–1109), Archbishop of Canterbury; quarrelled with William Rufus about the authority of the Pope, but regained his position under Henry I.

Antonius Marcus (Mark Antony) (*c.* 83–30 B.C.), see HISTORY.

Aquinas, Thomas, St (*c.* 1225–74), Italian religious teacher and philosopher.

Archimedes (*c.* 287–212 B.C.), Greek mathematician, physicist and inventor; made many discoveries in mechanics (notably the lever) and invented the Archimedean screw. Killed during siege of Syracuse by Romans.

Aristophanes (*c.* 450–*c.* 385 B.C.), Greek comic dramatist.

Aristotle (384–322 B.C.), Greek philosopher and pupil of Plato; took the whole field of knowledge as his subject.

Arkwright, Sir Richard (1732–92), pioneer of British cotton industry.

Arne, Thomas (1710–78), English composer.

Arnold, Thomas (1795–1842), headmaster of Rugby; regarded as the creator of the modern Public School system. The original of the headmaster in *Tom Brown's Schooldays*.

Arthur (*c.* 600), Celtic warrior about whom a great deal of legend has collected.

Atatürk, Kemal (1881–1938), creator of modern Turkey.

Attila (*c.* 406–53), king of the Huns, see HISTORY.

Attlee, 1st Earl (1883–1967), Deputy Prime Minister, 1942–5; Prime Minister, 1945–51.

Augustine, St (354–430), religious philosopher and teacher.

Augustine, St, missionary monk sent to Britain in 597; first Archbishop of Canterbury. Died in 604.

Augustus Caesar (63 B.C.–A.D. 14), first Emperor of Rome; see HISTORY.

Bach, Johann Sebastian (1685–1750), great German composer.

Bacon, Francis, Lord Verulam (1561–1626), English philosopher and statesman; Attorney-General under Elizabeth, Lord Chancellor under James I; author of *Novum Organum* and *Essays*.

Bacon, Roger (*c.* 1214–94), Franciscan friar, the first man in modern times to insist on the importance of experiment in science.

Baden-Powell, Lord (1857–1941), famous for his defence of Mafeking during Boer War; founded Boy Scouts (1908) and Girl Guides (1910).

Baird, John Logie (1888–1946), pioneer of television.

Bakewell, Robert (1725–95), pioneer of modern agriculture.

Ball, John (d. 1381), English priest who was a leader of the Peasants' Revolt.

Balzac, Honoré de (1799–1850), great French novelist; author of 80 novels with the general title of *La Comédie Humaine*.

Banks, Sir Joseph (1744–1820), English botanist and 'father of Australia'.

Barnado, Dr Thomas (1845–1905), devoted his life to the welfare of homeless children; founder of the homes named after him.

Baudelaire, Charles (1821–67), French poet, whose work has had an immense influence on modern poetry.

Becket, St Thomas à (1118–70), see HISTORY.

Bede, 'The Venerable' (*c.* 673–735), monk and historian, 'the father of English history'.

Beethoven, Ludwig van (1770–1827), German composer.

Bell, Alexander Graham (1847–1922), inventor of the telephone.

Benedict, St (*c.* 480–544), founded the Order of Benedictine monks.

Bentham, Jeremy (1748–1832), radical writer and thinker; helped develop the Utilitarian philosophy that the aim of politics should be 'the greatest happiness of the greatest number'.

Berlioz, Hector (1803–69), French composer.

Bernard, St (923–1008), Cistercian monk, patron saint of mountaineers.

Bernhardt, Sarah (1845–1923), famous French tragic actress.

Bismarck, Prince Otto (1815–98), see HISTORY.

Blake, Robert (1599–1657), Parliamentary general in the Civil War; admiral in the wars against Holland and Spain.

Blériot, Louis (1872–1936), French inventor and aviator; first to fly the English Channel, 1909.

Blondin, Charles (1824–97), French tight-rope walker famous for his crossing of the Niagara Falls.

Boadicea (d. A.D. 62), see HISTORY.

Boccaccio, Giovanni (1313–75), Italian novelist and poet.

Bolivar, Simon (1783–1830), 'the Liberator'; revolutionary who broke Spanish power in South America; first president of Venezuela and Dictator of Peru.

Boone, Daniel (1734–1820), American explorer and settler.

Booth, William (1829–1912), founder and first general of the Salvation Army.

Borgia, Cesar (1476–1507), son of Pope Alexander VI, made himself ruler of Romagna by murdering those who stood in his way. Banished by Pope Julius II and died in the invasion of Castile.

Botha, General Louis (1862–1919), Boer general who became first Premier of South Africa.

Boyle, Robert (1627–91), English scientist; the first man to distinguish between a mixture and a compound. Author of Boyle's Law (see DICTIONARY OF SCIENCE AND MATHEMATICS).

Bragg, Sir William (1862–1942), English scientist who received the 1915 Nobel Prize with his son, **Sir Lawrence Bragg** (b. 1890), for their work on X-rays and crystal structures.

Brahms, Johannes (1833–97), German composer.

Brecht, Bertolt (1898–1959), German dramatist and poet.

Bright, John (1811–89), famous Radical statesman, one of those responsible for the introduction of Free Trade.

Britten, Benjamin (1913–1976), English composer.

Brown, Sir Arthur Whitten (1886–1948), made the first transatlantic flight in 1919 with Sir John Alcock.

Brown, John (1800–1859), fanatical opponent of slavery in America. He was hanged for having incited slaves to rebel, and his death was a signal for the outbreak of the Civil War.

Bruce, Robert (1274–1329), see HISTORY.

Brummell, George (1778–1840), 'Beau Brummell', leader of fashion in English society when George IV was Prince Regent.

Brunel, Isambard Kingdom (1806–59), engineer and steam-ship-designer: constructed Clifton Suspension Bridge and much of the G.W. Railway.

Brunel, Sir Mark Isambard (1769–1849), father of Isambard, and constructor of the Thames tunnel.

Brutus, Marcus (85–42 B.C.), see HISTORY.

Buddha (Sidharta Gautama), the founder of Buddhism in the 6th century B.C.

Burghley, William Cecil, Lord (1520–1598), principal adviser to Queen Elizabeth for 40 years.

Burke, Edmund (1729–97), political philosopher, statesman and orator: most famous for his attacks on the French Revolution.

Byrd, William (1543–1623), English composer.

Cabot, John (*c.* 1455–*c.* 1498), see EXPLORATIONS AND DISCOVERIES.

Cabot, Sebastian (*c.* 1493–1557), see EXPLORATIONS AND DISCOVERIES.

Caesar, Caius Julius (*c.* 101–44 B.C.), see HISTORY.

Calvin, John (1509–64), French religious reformer who preached his severe doctrine (Calvinism) in Geneva, where he created a Protestant republic.

Campbell, Sir Malcolm (1885–1948), racing driver who held land and water speed records.

Canute the Great (995–1035), see HISTORY

Carnegie, Andrew (1835–1919), son of poor Scottish weaver who became American multi-millionaire; gave away most of his money to benefit the public, especially by the founding of libraries.

Cartier, Jaques (1491–1557), see EXPLORATIONS AND DISCOVERIES.

Casabianca, Louis de (*c.* 1754–98), captain of a French war-ship at the Battle of the Nile; he and his 10-year-old son refused to leave the burning ship and died together.

Cassius, Caius (d. 42 B.C.), see HISTORY.

Catherine the Great (1729–96), Empress of Russia; came to the throne by deposing and murdering her husband, the weak

Peter; carried Russia's frontiers by conquest to the Black Sea and the borders of Germany.

Cato, Marcus Porcius (234–149 B.C.), Roman statesman, soldier and writer: opposed the luxurious living of his times.

Cavell, Edith (1865–1915), British nurse shot by the Germans for helping wounded British soldiers to escape from Belgium.

Cavour, Count Camillo de (1810–61), one of the founders of modern Italy.

Caxton, William (c. 1422–91), founder of the first English printing press.

Cecilia, Saint, the patron saint of music: martyrised c. A.D. 176.

Cervantes, Saavedra, Miguel de (1547–1616), Spanish novelist, author of *Don Quixote*.

Chaplin, Sir Charles Spencer (1889–1977), the most famous of all film comedians.

Charlemagne (742–814), see HISTORY.

Charles V (1510–58), Holy Roman Emperor who ruled Austria, the Netherlands and Spain.

Chatham, William Pitt, Earl of (1708–78), statesman and Parliamentarian, in control of English policy during Seven Years War.

Chekhov, Anton (1860–1904), great Russian dramatist and short-story writer; author of *The Cherry Orchard*, etc.

Chippendale, Thomas (c. 1717–79), famous furniture designer.

Chopin, Frédéric (1810–49), Polish composer and pianist.

Churchill, Sir Winston (1874–1965), British statesman and author: Prime Minister 1940–45 and 1951–55.

Cicero, Marcus Tullius (106–43 B.C.), most eloquent of the Roman orators.

Cierva, Juan de la (1895–1936), Spanish engineer who invented the autogiro.

Claudius I (10 B.C.–A.D. 54), Roman Emperor; erected many great buildings; visited Britain; murdered by his wife Agrippina.

Clemens, Samuel Langhorne ('Mark Twain') (1835–1910), American writer and humorist, author of *Tom Sawyer* and *Huckleberry Finn*.

Cleopatra (69–30 B.C.), see HISTORY.

Clive, Robert, Lord (1725–74), English general, victor of Plassey, who laid the foundations of the British empire in India.

Cobbett, William (1762–1835), politician, social reformer and writer, author of *Rural Rides*.

Cobden, Richard (1804–1865), statesman, economist and advocate of Free Trade.

Cody, Samuel (1861–1913), the first man to fly in Britain, 1908.

Cody, William (1846–1917), American plainsman and showman known as 'Buffalo Bill'.

Coke, Sir Edward (1552–1634), great English jurist.

Coke, Thomas William (1752–1842), pioneer of scientific farming.

Columbus, Christopher (1451–1506), see EXPLORATIONS AND DISCOVERIES.

Confucius (*c.* 551–479 B.C.), the most celebrated of the Chinese philosophers.

Cook, Capt. James (1728–79), see EXPLORATIONS AND DISCOVERIES.

Copernicus, Nicholas (1473–1543), Polish founder of modern astronomy; author of the Copernican theory that the planets revolve round the sun.

Corneille, Pierre (1606–84), French tragic dramatist.

Cortes, Hernando (1485–1547), Spanish conqueror of Mexico.

Cranmer, Thomas (1489–1556), first Protestant Archbishop of Canterbury; see HISTORY.

Crispin, St (3rd century), patron of shoemakers: commemorated on 25 October.

Croesus (d. *c.* 546 B.C.), last king of Lydia (part of modern Turkey), celebrated for his fabulous wealth.

Crockett, Davy (1786–1836), American frontiersman; fought in Congress for a fair deal for the Red Indians; killed at the Battle of Alamo.

Cromwell, Oliver (1599–1658), see HISTORY.

Cruikshank, George (1792–1878), famous book illustrator and caricaturist.

Cunard, Sir Samuel (1787–1861), founder of the shipping company which became the Cunard Line.

Curie, Pierre (1859–1906) and **Marie** (1867–1934), pioneers of the science of radioactivity, and first to isolate radium.

Daguerre, Louis (1789–1851), French inventor of the earliest photographic process (the daguerrotype).

Daimler, Gottlieb (1834–90), German inventor with N. A.

Otto of the Otto gas engine, and also of the motor-car named after him (see CARS).

alton, John (1766–1844), English scientist who discovered atomic theory.

amien, Father Joseph (1840–89), Belgian missionary who volunteered to look after lepers in Honolulu, and himself died of the disease.

ante Alighieri (1265–1321), greatest of the Italian poets, author of the *Divine Comedy*.

anton, Georges (1759–94), President of the Committee of Public Safety during the first French Revolution; supplanted by Robespierre and guillotined.

arius I (548–485 B.C.), see HISTORY.

arling, Grace (1815–42), English lighthouse-keeper's daughter famous for saving a shipwrecked crew by putting out with her father in a small boat.

arnley, Earl of (1545–67), Mary Queen of Scots' second husband, murdered after Mary had entered into an intrigue with Bothwell.

arwin, Charles (1809–82), English naturalist whose *Origin of the Species* first set out the theory of evolution by means of natural selection.

avid (1038–970 B.C.), king who united Israelites in Canaan.

avid, St (6th century), patron saint of Wales.

avis, Jefferson (1808–89), President of the Confederate States during the American Civil War.

avy, Sir Humphrey (1778–1829), scientist who invented miners' lamp.

ebussy, Claude (1862–1918), French composer.

e Gaulle, General Charles (1890–1970), led Free French in Second World War; President of France, 1958–69.

e Havilland, Sir Geoffrey (1882–1965), a pioneer of civil and military aviation.

emocritus (*c.* 460–357 B.C.), Greek philosopher to whom the conception of the atomic theory is attributed.

emosthenes (385–322 B.C.), most famous of the Athenian orators; he roused the Athenians to resist Philip of Macedon.

escartes, René (1596–1650), French philosopher and mathematician.

iaghilev, Sergei (1872–1929), Russian ballet impresario and founder of the Ballets Russes.

Diocletian (245–313), Roman Emperor under whom t
Christians were ruthlessly persecuted; see HISTORY.

Diogenes (412–322 B.C.), Greek philosopher who scorned weal
and social conventions and is said to have lived in a tub.

Disraeli, Benjamin (Earl of Beaconsfield) (1804–81), s
HISTORY.

Dominic, St (1170–1221), founder of the Order of Dominicar
or Black Friars.

Dostoeivsky, Feodor (1821–81), one of the greatest Russi
novelists, author of *Crime and Punishment*.

Drake, Sir Francis (*c.* 1540–96), see HISTORY.

Dumas, Alexandre (1802–70), prolific French novelist ar
dramatist, author of *The Count of Monte Cristo* and *The Thr
Musketeers*.

Dunstan, St (909–88), famous Abbot of Glastonbury and Arch
bishop of Canterbury, who lived through seven reigns.

Duval, Claude (1643–70), notorious French-born highwayma
hanged at Tyburn.

Dvorak, Antonin (1841–1904), Czech composer.

Edison, Thomas Alva (1847–1931), inventor of electric lightii
and the gramophone.

Eiffel, Alexandre (1832–1923), French engineer who built th
Eiffel Tower and the locks on the Panama Canal.

Einstein, Albert (1879–1955), German mathematical physici
and one of the greatest of all men of science; author of th
theory of relativity.

Elgar, Sir Edward (1857–1934), English composer.

Emmet, Robert (1778–1803), Irish patriot; he led a rebellic
in 1803, and was executed for high treason.

Empedocles (*c.* 500–*c.* 430 B.C.), Greek philosopher, founder
a school of medicine which regarded the heart as the seat of lif

Epicurus (342–270 B.C.), Greek philosopher who taught th
pleasure was the chief good of man and was to be attaine
through the practice of virtue.

Erasmus, Desiderius (1466–1536), Dutch scholar and phil
sopher, one of the great figures of the Renaissance.

Essex, Robert Devereux, Earl of (1567–1601), Queen Eliz
beth's favourite; he conspired against her and was execute

Euclid (*c.* 330–*c.* 260 B.C.), Greek mathematician who laid th
foundations of modern geometry.

Euripides (480–406 B.C.), great Athenian tragic dramatist.

velyn, John (1620–1706), famous for his diaries, and one of the founders of the Royal Society.

abius Maximus ('Cunctator') (d. 203 B.C.), the Roman dictator who saved Rome from Hannibal by deliberately avoiding battle. From this policy comes the term 'Fabian tactics'.

abre, Jean (1823–1915), French naturalist, life-long observer of the habits of insects.

ahrenheit, Gabriel (1686–1736), German physicist, inventor of the method of grading a thermometer which bears his name.

araday, Michael (1791–1867), English physicist and chemist, founder of the science of electro-magnetism.

awkes, Guy (1570–1606), a Yorkshire Catholic, one of the conspirators in the Gunpowder Plot; he was captured in the cellar of Parliament House, tried and executed.

erdinand of Spain (1452–1516) and Isabella (1451–1504), see HISTORY.

laubert, Gustave (1821–80), one of the greatest French novelists.

leming, Sir Alexander (1881–1955), discoverer of penicillin.

okker, Anthony (1860–1939), famous Dutch airman and aeronautical engineer.

ord, Henry (1863–1947), founder of the Ford Motor Co. and pioneer of the cheap motor-car.

orester, Cecil Scott (1899–1966), author, creator of Hornblower.

ox, Charles James (1749–1806), Whig statesman who favoured American independence and opposed the war with France.

ox, George (1624–91), founder of the Society of Friends (the Quakers).

rancis of Assisi, St (1182–1226), founder of the Franciscan Order of monks; lover of flowers, animals and birds.

ranco, General Don Francisco (1892–1975), Head of Spanish State, 1936–75.

ranklin, Benjamin (1706–90), American statesman, philosopher and scientist; played an important part in framing the constitution of the U.S.A.; invented the lightning conductor.

rederick I (c. 1123–90), Holy Roman Emperor and German national hero; drowned on his way to the Third Crusade.

rederick II (the Great) (1712–86), King of Prussia; see HISTORY.

Freud, Sigmund (1856–1939), Austrian psychiatrist an founder of psycho-analysis.

Frost, Robert (1874–1963), distinguished American poet.

Fry, Elizabeth (1780–1845), Quaker prison reformer.

Galen, Claudius (131–201), Greek physician, who made im portant discoveries in anatomy.

Galileo (1564–1642), great Italian mathematician, physicist an astronomer.

Galton, Sir Francis (1822–1911), founder of eugenics an inventor of the device of finger-print identification.

Galvani, Luigi (1737–98), Italian physicist and doctor, wh demonstrated the principle of animal electricity.

Gandhi, Mohandas Karamchand (1869–1948), great India patriot, social reformer and teacher, driving spirit of th movement for national independence.

Garibaldi, Giuseppe (1807–82), Italian patriot who fought fo the unification of Italy.

Garrick, David (1717–79), the leading tragic actor of his day

George, St, patron saint of England; believed to have been champion of Christianity during the days of Diocletian, an to have been martyrised in A.D. 303.

Gershwin, George (1898–1937), American jazz pianist an composer; wrote *Rhapsody in Blue* and the Negro opera, *Porg and Bess*.

Gibbons, Grinling (1648–1720), celebrated wood-carver an sculptor.

Gilbert, Sir William Schwenck (1836–1911), Englis humorist and playwright, best remembered for the famou Savoy operas, in which he collaborated with Sir Arthur Sulliva

Gladstone, William Ewart (1809–98), see HISTORY.

Glendower, Owen (1359–1415), Welsh chieftain who oppose Henry IV.

Gluck, Christoph von (1714–87), composer, born in Bohemi

Goethe, Johann Wolfgang von (1749–1832), the most cele brated German writer; novelist, poet, philosopher and scientis

Gordon, Charles, General (1833–85), see HISTORY.

Gordon, Lord George (1751–93), instigator of the Anti-Poper riots of 1780.

Gorki, Maxim (1868–1936), Russian novelist.

Grace, Dr William (1845–1915), famous cricketer wh dominated the game for over 40 years. Altogether he score

54,896 runs, including 126 centuries, and took 2,876 wickets.

rahame-White, Claude (1879–1959), the first Englishman to be granted a British certificate of proficiency in aviation, 1909.

rant, Ulysses Simpson (1822–85), the most famous American general of the Civil War; twice President of the U.S.A.

regory, St (257–336), founder of the Armenian Church; his festival is 9 March.

regory the Great, St (c. 540–604), one of the most important of the Popes, 590–604.

regory XIII (1502–85), Pope who introduced the Gregorian calendar.

renville, Sir Richard (1541–91), Elizabethan sea-captain who, with his one ship, the *Revenge*, fought a fleet of Spanish warships in 1591 and died on the deck of the *San Pablo*.

rieg, Edvard (c. 1843–1907), Norwegian composer.

rey, Lady Jane (1537–54), see HISTORY.

rimaldi, Joseph (1779–1837), great English clown.

rimm, the brothers **Jakob** (1785–1863) and **Wilhelm** (1786–1859), German philologists and folk-lorists who collected the famous fairy-tales.

ustavus Adolphus (1594–1632), King of Sweden; see HISTORY.

wynn, Nell (1650–87), the dancer and actress who became mistress to Charles II.

adrian (76–138), see HISTORY.

akluyt, Richard (c. 1552–1616), geographer; first of the English naval historians.

alley, Edmund (1656–1742), Astronomer Royal; made first magnetic survey of the oceans, and discovered the comet named after him.

ampden, John (1594–1643), one of the leaders in Parliament's quarrel with Charles I.

andel, George Frederick (1685–1759), composer.

annibal (247–183 B.C.), see HISTORY.

ardicanute (1019–42), son of Canute the Great, and the last Danish king of England; imposed the tax known as Danegeld.

ardie, James Keir (1856–1915), first Socialist M.P. (1892).

argreaves, James (d. 1778), inventor and pioneer of modern wool industry.

aroun-al-Rashid (763–809), the most famous Caliph of Baghdad; hero of the *Arabian Nights*.

Harris, Joel Chandler (1848–1908), American author of th Uncle Remus stories.

Harte, Francis Bret (1839–1902), American poet and autho famous for his stories of Californian mining life.

Harvey, William (1578–1657), English doctor who discovere circulation of the blood.

Hastings, Warren (1732–1818), first Governor-General India; impeached on charges of cruelty and corruption an acquitted after a trial stretching over 7 years.

Havelock, Sir Henry (1795–1857), hero of the relief of Cawr pore and Lucknow in the Indian Mutiny.

Hawke, Edward, Lord (1705–81), victorious admiral in th battle of Quiberon, fought against the French in a storm, 175

Hawkins, Sir John (1532–95), Elizabethan naval officer, vice admiral in the battle with the Spanish Armada.

Hawthorne, Nathaniel (1804–64), American novelist, auth of *The Scarlet Letter*.

Haydn, Franz Joseph (1732–1809), Austrian composer.

Heine, Heinrich (1797–1856), German lyric poet.

Hemingway, Ernest (1898–1961), American novelist, auth of *A Farewell to Arms* and *For Whom the Bell Tolls*.

Henry the Navigator (1394–1460), Portuguese prince who ir spired many voyages of exploration down the Atlantic coast Africa.

Hepplewhite, George (d. 1786), one of the four great 18t century cabinet-makers (the others were Chippendale, Robe Adam and Sheraton).

Hereward the Wake, the last of the Saxon chiefs to hold ou against the Normans.

Herod the Great (*c.* 73–4 B.C.), King of Judea under th Romans; to him is attributed the massacre of the innocents.

Herodotus (*c.* 485–425 B.C.), Greek historian, called 'the fath of history'.

Herschel, Sir John (1792–1871), celebrated astronomer.

Herschel, Sir William (1738–1822), father of the last-name discoverer of the planet Uranus and the satellites of Saturn

Hill, Sir Rowland (1795–1879), originator of the penny post

Hippocrates (*c.* 460–*c.* 370 B.C.), Greek physician: the 'father medicine'. Rules of conduct for doctors are still based on h Hippocratic Oath.

Hitler, Adolf (1889–1945), see HISTORY.

Hobbes, Thomas (1588–1679), English philosopher, advocate of strong government, author of *Leviathan*.

Homer (*c.* 700 B.C.), most famous of all epic poets, and regarded as the author of the *Iliad* and the *Odyssey*; seven Greek towns vie for the honour of having been his birthplace.

Hood, Samuel, Lord (1724–1816), British admiral who captured Toulon and Corsica, 1793.

Hopkins, Sir Frederick Gowland (1861–1947), English biochemist noted for his work on proteins and vitamins.

Horace (65–8 B.C.), great Roman satirist and poet.

Houdini, Harry (1873–1926), American locksmith who went on the stage as an expert in escaping from handcuffs, locked rooms, etc.

Howard, John (1726–90), prison reformer.

Howe, Richard, Earl (1726–99), British admiral who won a famous victory ('the Glorious First of June') over the French in 1794 off Brest.

Hugo, Victor (1802–85), great French poet, dramatist and novelist, author of *Les Misérables* and *The Hunchback of Notre Dame*.

Hume, David (1711–76), Scottish historian and philosopher.

Hunter, the brothers **William** (1718–83) and **John** (1728–93), both famous Scottish physicians, who made many discoveries in anatomy. John is regarded as the founder of modern surgery.

Huss, John (1369–1415), Bohemian religious reformer, whose death by burning alive led to a half century of civil war.

Huxley, Thomas Henry (1825–95), English naturalist and ardent supporter of the theory of evolution of Charles Darwin (*q.v.*).

Ibsen, Henrik (1828–1906), Norwegian writer, one of the world's greatest dramatists.

Innocent III (1160–1216), powerful Pope who initiated the 4th Crusade.

Irving, Sir Henry (1838–1905), great English actor, and the first to be knighted.

Ivan the Terrible (1530–84), first Czar of Russia, who earned his name by his cruel treatment of his subjects.

Jackson, Andrew (1767–1845), American general, twice President of the U.S.A.

Jackson, Thomas (1824–63), most successful general on the Southern side in the American Civil War; known as 'Stonewall' Jackson for the dogged fight he put up at the First Battl of Bull Run.

James, Henry (1843–1916), great Anglo-American novelist.

Jefferson, Thomas (1743–1826), drew up the American De claration of Independence; twice U.S. President.

Jeffreys, George, Lord (1648–89), judge notorious for his hars judgements, especially during the so-called 'Bloody Assize held to try the followers of the Duke of Monmouth who ha rebelled against James II.

Jenghiz Khan (1162–1227), Mogul ruler who twice conquere China and drove the Turks back into Europe.

Jenner, Edward (1749–1823), English country doctor who dis covered vaccination as a means of preventing smallpox.

Jerome, Jerome K. (1859–1927), humorous writer, author • *Three Men in a Boat*.

Jesus Christ (c. 4 B.C.–A.D. 30 or 33), the founder of Christ anity; born at Bethlehem, the first-born of His mother Mar According to Matthew, His birth was miraculous and Josep was His foster-father. He learned His father's trade of car pentry at Nazareth, and began His mission when He was abo thirty. A summary of His teaching is found in the Sermon c the Mount.

Joan of Arc, St (1412–31), see HISTORY.

John, St, the Baptist (executed A.D. 28), the forerunner of Jes Christ.

Johnson, Amy (1904–41), first woman aviator to fly solo fro England to Australia.

Jones, John Paul (1747–92), Scottish mariner who commande the American fleet during the War of Independence.

Josephine, Empress (1763–1814), wife of Napoleon I until l divorced her and married Marie-Louise.

Julian the Apostate (331–63), Roman Emperor who professe Christianity until the last two years of his life, when he trie to re-establish paganism.

Jung, Carl (1875–1961), Swiss psychiatrist.

Justinian I (c. 483–565), see HISTORY.

Kant, Immanuel (1724–1804), German scientist and phil sopher.

Kean, Edmund (1787–1833), one of the greatest English trag actors.

Kelvin, William Thomson, Lord (1824–1907), scientist an

inventor; made important discoveries in the field of thermo-dynamics (the branch of physics dealing with heat).

Kemble, Frances ('Fanny') (1809–93), noted actress, and member of a famous theatrical family, which included her father, **Charles Kemble** (1775–1854), her uncle **John Philip Kemble**, a famous tragic actor, and her aunt Mrs Siddons (*q.v.*).

Kennedy, John Fitzgerald (1917–63), President of the United States from 1961 until his assassination at Dallas, Texas, in November 1963.

Kepler, Johann (1571–1630), German astronomer who worked out the laws of planetary motion.

Khayyam, Omar (11th century), Persian poet and mathe-matician, whose *Rubaiyat* was translated by the English poet, Edward Fitzgerald.

Kidd, Captain William (*c.* 1645–1701), famous pirate whose crimes were committed under cover of the British flag. Hanged at Execution Dock in London.

Kitchener, Horatio, Lord (1850–1916), reconquered the Sudan (1897); Commander-in-Chief in the Boer War; Secretary of State for War, 1914–16. Drowned when the troopship *Hampshire* was sunk by a mine.

Knox, John (1505–72), see HISTORY.

Kruger, Paul (1825–1904), President of the Transvaal who was leader of the Boers in the bitter quarrel with the British that led to the Boer War.

Kruschev, Nikita Sergeyevich (1894–1971), Russian Prime Minister, 1958–64. See HISTORY.

Kublai Khan (1216–94), Mogul Emperor, grandson of Jenghiz Khan; he greatly extended the empire and lived in extra-ordinary splendour.

Lafayette, Marie-Joseph, Marquis de (1757–1834), French statesman and general, who took an active part in the American War of Independence.

La Fontaine, Jean de (1621–95), French poet and fablewriter.

Lamarck, Jean Baptiste, Chevalier de (1744–1829), French naturalist, author of a theory of the evolution of animals, known as Lamarckism.

Landseer, Sir Edwin (1802–73), most famous English animal painter of his day; designed the lions which are part of the Nelson Monument in Trafalgar Square.

Lanfranc (*c.* 1005–89), Archbishop of Canterbury in the time of William the Conqueror.

Langton, Stephen (1151–1228), Archbishop of Canterbury; one of the leaders of the group that compelled King John to sign the Magna Carta.

Lasker, Emmanuel (1868–1941), world chess champion, 1894–1921.

Latimer, Hugh (*c.* 1485–1555), Bishop of Worcester, one of the founders of English Protestantism; burned at the stake at Oxford.

Laud, William (1573–1645), Archbishop of Canterbury, favourite and chief minister of Charles I; tried for treason and executed under the Long Parliament.

Lavoisier, Antoine (1743–94), French chemist who gave oxygen its name and was the first to establish that combustion is a form of chemical action; guillotined during the French Revolution.

Laurence, John, Lord (1811–79), marched to the relief of Delhi in the Indian Mutiny.

Lawrence, Thomas Edward ('Lawrence of Arabia') (1888–1935), British soldier and archaeologist; led the Arabs against the Turks in the First World War; described his campaign in *Seven Pillars of Wisdom*.

Leacock, Stephen (1869–1944), Canadian economist and humorous writer.

Lee, Robert Edward (1807–70), Commander-in-Chief of the Southern forces in the American Civil War.

Leibnitz, Gottfried (1646–1716), discovered, independently of Newton, the differential calculus.

Leicester, Robert Dudley, Earl of (1531–88), favourite of Queen Elizabeth and leader of the English forces in the Low Countries, 1585–7.

Lenin, Vladimir Ilyich (1870–1924), see HISTORY.

Leonidas, King of Sparta when Greece was invaded by Xerxes, 480 B.C.; killed leading the defence of the Pass of Thermopylae.

Lesseps, Ferdinand, Vicomte de (1805–94), French engineer responsible for building the Suez Canal.

Lilburne, John (1614–57), English politician and pamphleteer; leader of the Levellers during the English Revolution.

Lincoln, Abraham (1809–65), President of the United States whose pronouncement against slavery led to the outbreak of the Civil War. Soon after the victory of the North, he was assassinated while at the theatre by a fanatical anti-abolitionist, John Wilkes Booth.

Linnaeus, Carl (1707–78), Swedish naturalist, founder of modern botany; he devised a system for naming and classifying plants and animals (see NATURAL HISTORY).

Lister, Joseph, Lord (1827–1912), English surgeon who first established the need for antiseptics in surgical operations.

Liszt, Franz (1811–86), Hungarian composer and pianist.

Livy (59 B.C.–A.D. 17), great Roman historian.

Lloyd George, David, Earl of Dwyfor (1865–1945), see HISTORY.

Locke, John (1632–1704), English philosopher and founder of empiricism, which is the doctrine that all knowledge is derived from experience.

London, John ('Jack') (1876–1916), American novelist, author of *White Fang*, *Call of the Wild*.

Longfellow, Henry Wadsworth (1807–82), American poet, author of *Hiawatha*.

Lonsdale, Earl of (1857–1944), distinguished sportsman who presented the Lonsdale belts for boxing.

Lope de Vega, Felix (1562–1615), Spanish dramatist and author of more than 2,000 plays.

Louis XIV (1638–1715), King of France for 72 years; called *le grand monarque* (the great king), he gave expression to the idea of absolute monarchy, in which the king claims complete power over his subjects. See HISTORY.

Louis XVI (1754–93), see HISTORY.

Loyola, St Ignatius (1491–1556), founder of the Order of Jesuits.

Luther, Martin (1483–1546), see HISTORY.

Macadam, John (1756–1836), inventor of the Macadam process of road-making.

Macaulay, Thomas Babington, Lord (1800–59), celebrated historian and poet, author of *History of England* and the *Lays of Ancient Rome*.

Macbeth, King of Scotland immortalised by Shakespeare; he reigned from 1040 to 1057.

Macdonald, Flora (1722–90), Scottish Jacobite who sheltered Prince Charles Edward after his defeat at Culloden Moor, 1746.

Machiavelli, Niccolo (1469–1527), Florentine statesman and historian; author of *The Prince*, which describes how a ruler may build up his power.

Macready, William Charles (1793–1873), the greatest tragic actor of his day.

Magellan, Ferdinand (c. 1480–1521), Portuguese navigator; see EXPLORATIONS AND DISCOVERIES.

Malory, Sir Thomas (c. 1430–70), compiled the *Morte D'Arthur*, which tells the story of King Arthur and his Knights of the Round Table.

Malthus, Thomas Robert (1766–1834), English economist, who regarded the growth of the population as a danger, and proposed that marriage should be discouraged.

Mao Tse-Tung (1893–1976), Chairman of the Chinese Communist Party from 1936 until his death.

Marat, Jean-Paul (1743–93), one of the leading figures in the Reign of Terror during the French Revolution; assassinated by Charlotte Corday.

Marconi, Guglielmo, Marchese (1874–1937), inventor of the first practical method of wireless telegraphy.

Marco Polo (see **Polo, Marco**).

Marcus Aurelius (121–180), Roman Emperor who drove off the barbarians, and was famous for his wisdom and his taste for philosophy and literature.

Maria Theresa (1717–80), Empress of Austria, Queen of Bohemia and Hungary; see HISTORY.

Marie Antoinette (1755–93), daughter of Maria Theresa, and wife of Louis XVI of France; see HISTORY.

Mark Antony (see **Antonius, Marcus**).

Marlborough, John Churchill, Duke of (1650–1722), perhaps the greatest of all British soldiers; see HISTORY.

Marx, Karl (1818–83), German philosopher and economist, on whose teaching and writings Communism is based.

Masaryk, Thomas (1850–1937), founder and first President of Czechoslovakia.

Maupassant, Guy de (1850–93), famous French novelist and short-story writer.

Maxim, Sir Hiram (1840–1916), inventor of the automatic quick-firing gun named after him.

Maxwell, James Clerk (1831–79), Scottish physicist who formulated the electro-magnetic theory of light; his work made wireless possible.

Mazzini, Giuseppe (1805–72), Italian patriot who worked for the independence and unification of his country.

Mendel, Gregor (1822–84), Austrian botanist and monk whose study of the common garden pea resulted in the law of heredity known as the Mendelian law.

Mendelssohn, Jakob Ludwig Felix (1809–47), German composer.

Mercator, Gerhardus (1512–94), Flemish geographer who simplified navigation by inventing a system of projection in which the longitudes are represented by equidistant parallel lines and the degrees of latitude by perpendicular lines parallel to the meridian.

Mesmer, Friedrich (1733–1815), German doctor who developed the system of animal magnetism known as 'mesmerism'.

Metternich, Prince (1773–1859), Austrian statesman who led the conservative resistance to the ideas of progress spread by the French Revolution.

Mill, John Stuart (1806–73), writer on politics, economics and philosophy, and one of the founders of modern liberalism.

Millikan, Robert Andrew (1868–1953), American physicist who discovered cosmic rays.

Miltiades (d. 489 B.C.), one of the leaders of the Athenians against the Persians at Marathon.

Mithridates (c. 132–63 B.C.), King of Pontius from 120 to 63 B.C., implacable enemy of the Romans; he spoke 22 languages and, surrounded by enemies, was said to have made himself immune from all poisons.

Mohammed (c. 570–632), the founder of the Moslem religion; see HISTORY.

Molière (Jean Baptiste Poquelin) (1622–73), the greatest of the French comic dramatists.

Monk, George, Duke of Albemarle (1608–69), general and admiral who fought in the Anglo-Dutch wars; having fought on Cromwell's side against the Royalists, he later helped to restore Charles II to the throne.

Montaigne, Michel de (1533–92), great French essayist.

Montcalm, General Louis, Marquis de (1712–59), French commander in Canada, defeated by Wolfe.

Monteverdi, Claudio (1568–1643), Italian composer.

Montezuma II (1466–1520), last Aztec ruler of Mexico, Emperor when Cortes invaded the country.

Montfort, Simon de, Earl of Leicester (1208–65), powerful baron who forced Henry III to grant the first English Parliament; see HISTORY.

Montgolfier, Joseph (1740–1810) and **Jaques** (1745–99), French brothers who made many ascents in balloons inflated by heated air.

Montrose, James Graham, Marquess of (1612–50), general who raised the Highlands in support of Charles I and II.

Moore, Sir John (1761–1809), British general killed during retreat to Corunna in the Peninsular War.

More, Sir Thomas (1478–1535), Lord Chancellor under Henry VIII who was executed for refusing to take the Oath of Supremacy; wrote *Utopia*.

Morgan, Sir Henry (c. 1635–88), Welsh buccaneer who preyed on the Spaniards in the Caribbean; captured Panama in 1671.

Mountevans, Admiral Lord (1881–1957), British sailor and explorer known as 'Evans of the Broke'; wrote *South with Scott*.

Mozart, Wolfgang Amadeus (1756–91), Austrian composer.

Mussolini, Benito (1883–1945), Fascist dictator of Italy, 1922–43; see HISTORY.

Nansen, Fridtjof (1862–1930), Norwegian explorer and organiser of relief for victims of the First World War.

Napoleon I (Bonaparte) (1769–1821), see HISTORY.

Nasser, Gamel Abdel (1918–70), President of the United Arab Republic, 1958–70.

Napoleon III (1808–73), see HISTORY.

Nelson, Horatio, Viscount (1758–1805), England's greatest naval commander; see HISTORY.

Nero, Claudius Caesar (37–68), Roman Emperor whose reign is notorious for his cruelty and wild living.

Newton, Sir Isaac (1642–1727), probably the greatest of all scientists; famous for his work on the nature of white light the calculus and gravitation; wrote the *Principia*.

Ney, Marshal (1769–1815), one of Napoleon's generals.

Nicholas II, Czar of Russia (1868–1918); shot with his family by the revolutionaries, 16 July 1918.

Nicholas, St (4th century), patron saint of Russia; associated (as Santa Claus) with Christmas.

Nietzsche, Friedrich (1844–1900), German philosopher, who believed that the mass of people must be led by the few Supermen.

Nightingale, Florence (1820–1910), creator of modern nursing and hospital reformer; the 'lady with the lamp' of the Crimean War.

Nijinsky, Vaslav (1890–1950), great Russian ballet dancer, Polish-born.

Nobel, Dr Alfred (1833–96), Swedish inventor of dynamite; in his will he left money for the annual prizes named after him (for work done for the benefit of mankind in physics, chemistry, physiology and medicine, literature and peace).

Northcliffe, Lord (1865–1922), pioneer of modern journalism.

Nostradamus (Michel de Notre Dame) (1503–66), French astrologer.

Nuffield, Lord, William Richard Morris (1877–1963), pioneer motor-car manufacturer and philanthropist.

Oates, Captain L. E. G. (1880–1912), British explorer who was in the sledge party that accompanied Captain Scott in his dash for the South Pole. On the return journey the party became storm-bound, and Oates, badly frostbitten, walked out to his death in a blizzard rather than be a burden to his comrades.

Oates, Titus (1649–1705), informer against Roman Catholics in Charles II's reign.

O'Casey, Sean (1883–1964), Irish dramatist, author of *Juno and the Paycock*.

Offa, King of Mercia, reigned from *c.* 757 to 796; built an embankment from the Dee to the Wye, called Offa's Dyke.

Ohm, Georg (1787–1854), discoverer of a law of electric current known as Ohm's Law; see SCIENCE.

Otto, Nikolaus (1832–91), German engineer, inventor of the four-stroke cycle named after him; see CARS.

Ovid (43 B.C.–A.D. 18), Roman poet.

Owen, Robert (1771–1858), social reformer and factory owner; inspired the earliest Factory Acts, trade unionism and co-operative trading.

Paganini, Niccolo (1782–1840), Italian violinist whose virtuosity has become a legend.

Paine, Thomas (1737–1809), English revolutionary writer; after the publication of his *Rights of Man* he was forced to flee to France.

Palestrina, Giovanni de (1525–94), Italian composer.

Palmerston, Viscount (1784–1865), Whig Foreign Secretary, 1830–46; supported liberal uprisings throughout Europe; twice Prime Minister.

Pancras, St (3rd century), patron saint of children; martyrised at the age of fourteen.

Pankhurst, Emmeline (1858–1928), leader of movement for votes for women with her daughters **Dame Christabel** and **Sylvia**.

Paracelsus, Philippus (1493–1541), Swiss mystic and al chemist.

Parnell, Charles Stewart (1846–91), leader of the Irish National Party.

Pascal, Blaise (1623–62), French philosopher and mathe matician; constructed the first calculating machine.

Pasteur, Louis (1822–95), French chemist and founder of th sciences of bacteriology and immunology; first to show tha infectious diseases are caused by germs; devised the process o pasteurisation by which milk can be prevented from going bad

Patrick, St (c. 389–c. 461), patron saint of Ireland.

Pavlov, Ivan (1849–1936), Russian physiologist; made man discoveries concerning the digestive system and the brain an nervous system.

Pavlova, Anna (1885–1931), great Russian ballet dancer.

Peel, Sir Robert (1788–1850), British statesman, founder o the modern police service; see HISTORY.

Penn, William (1644–1718), Quaker who founded Pennsyl vania.

Pepys, Samuel (1633–1703), naval administrator and famou diarist.

Pericles (c. 490–429 B.C.), greatest of the Athenian statesmen see HISTORY.

Pétain, Marshal Henri Philippe (1856–1951), hero of th defence of Verdun by the French in 1916; in 1940 signe armistice with the Germans, and in 1945 was condemned t death for treason; the sentence was commuted to life im prisonment.

Peter (the Great) (1672–1725), Czar of Russia who did muc to modernise his kingdom; founded St Petersburg (no Leningrad).

Peter the Hermit (d. 1115), French monk who raised the arm for the disastrous First Crusade.

Petrarch, Francesco (1304–74), Italian poet and schola creator of the sonnet.

Petrie, Sir Flinders (1853–1942), British Egyptologist.

Philip II of Macedonia (382–336 B.C.), conqueror of Greece and father of Alexander the Great; see HISTORY.

Philip II of Spain (1527–98), see HISTORY.

Piccard, August (1884–1962), Swiss physicist; ascended into stratosphere in a balloon, 1931 and 1932, and later explored the ocean in his bathysphere.

Pindar (522–443 B.C.), Greek lyric poet.

Pitman, Sir Isaac (1813–97), founder of the Pitman system of shorthand.

Pitt, William (1759–1806), British Prime Minister (at twenty-four, the youngest) throughout the period of the French Revolution and much of the war with France; see HISTORY.

Pizarro, Francisco (c. 1471–1541), Spaniard who conquered Peru with great cruelty; killed by his own soldiers.

Planck, Professor Max (1858–1947), German physicist whose law of radiation laid the foundation of the quantum theory.

Plato (427–347 B.C.), great Athenian philosopher, pupil of Socrates, teacher of Aristotle.

Plimsoll, Samuel (1824–96), M.P. who secured the passing of an Act of Parliament which defined a line (the Plimsoll Mark) above which the water must not rise when a ship is loaded. (See SHIPS.)

Plutarch (c. 46–120), Greek historian, author of *The Lives of Great Men of Greece and Rome.*

Poe, Edgar Allan (1809–49), American poet and short-story writer; wrote *Tales of Mystery and Imagination,* one of which, *The Murders in the Rue Morgue,* is among the earliest detective stories.

Polo, Marco (1254–1324), Venetian explorer; see EXPLORATIONS AND DISCOVERIES.

Pompey the Great (106–48 B.C.), Roman general; see HISTORY.

Priestley, Joseph (1733–1804), discovered and identified many of the common gases: discovered oxygen.

Proust, Marcel (1871–1922), French novelist; author of 15 novels with the general title, *A la Recherche du Temps Perdu* (*In Search of Lost Time*).

Ptolemy, Claudius (c. 90–168), Greek astronomer and geographer, born in Alexandria; according to the Ptolemaic system, the earth was the centre of the universe and the heavenly bodies revolved around it. (See COPERNICUS.)

Purcell, Henry (c. 1659–95), English composer.

Pushkin, Alexander (1799–1837), great Russian poet, autho of *Eugene Onegin*.

Pym, John (1584–1643), Puritan statesman who led the cam paign in the House of Commons against Charles I.

Pythagoras (c. 582–c. 507 B.C.), Greek scientist and mathe matician; to him is attributed the discovery of the multiplica tion table, the decimal system and the square on th hypotenuse.

Rabelais, François (c. 1494–1553), French monk and satiric writer, author of *Gargantua* and *Pantagruel*.

Rachmaninov, Serge (1873–1943), Russian composer.

Racine, Jean (1639–99), French tragic dramatist.

Raffles, Sir Thomas Stamford (1781–1826), founder • Singapore, 1819; also of the Zoological Society of London.

Raleigh, Sir Walter (1552–1618), English statesman, poe sailor and explorer; favourite of Queen Elizabeth; founded th colony of Virginia; was imprisoned in the Tower for 12 year and there wrote a *History of the World*. Set free in 1615 • lead an expedition to Guiana in search of gold, he was ur successful; and on his return was executed.

Rasputin, Grigori (1871–1916), Russian monk who becam all-powerful at the court of the last Russian Czar, Nicholas I

Réamur, René (1683–1757), French chemist; inventor of th thermometer that bears his name.

Rhodes, Cecil (1853–1902), see HISTORY.

Richelieu, Cardinal Duc de (1585–1642), one of the greate of French statesmen; Prime Minister to Louis XIII.

Ridley, Nicholas (1500–55), Bishop of London, burned at th stake with Latimer.

Rienzi, Cola di (1313–54), Roman patriot who led a popula rebellion in 1347.

Rilke, Rainer Marie (1872–1926), German lyric poet.

Rimbaud, Jean (1854–91), important modern French poe all his poems were written between his 16th and 19th years

Rizzio, David (c. 1540–66), Italian musician, favourite of Mar Queen of Scots; stabbed to death in her presence by th jealous Darnley.

Roberts, Field-Marshal Earl (1832–1914), English genera who distinguished himself in the Afghanistan campaign; le the campaign against the Boers.

Robespierre, Maximilien (1758–94), French lawyer who was president of the Committee of Public Safety during the Reign of Terror; sent many people to the guillotine, but was himself overthrown and guillotined.

Rob Roy (Robert McGregor) (1671–1734), Scottish highlander noted for his brigandage.

Rockefeller, John Davison (1839–1937), oil magnate who was said to have been the richest man in the world.

Rodney, Lord (1719–92), English admiral, victor in two great battles in the wars with France and Spain, 1780 and 1782.

Roland, Madame (1754–93), one of the leading figures of the French Revolution; she was guillotined, and died pronouncing the famous words, 'Oh liberty, what crimes are committed in thy name!'

Rommel, Field-Marshal (1891–1944), German general; see HISTORY.

Roosevelt, Franklin Delano (1882–1945), four times U.S. President; see HISTORY.

Ross, Sir Ronald (1857–1932), discoverer of the parasite that causes malaria.

Rouget de Lisle, Claude Joseph (1760–1836), French poet who wrote the words and music of the *Marseillaise*.

Rousseau, Jean-Jacques (1712–78), French writer who urged a return to nature and argued that man was naturally good; his ideas had a great influence on the events of his time.

Rupert, Prince (1619–82), Royalist admiral and general; fought for his uncle, Charles I, against Cromwell's troops, and at sea for Charles II against the Dutch.

Russell, Bertrand (Earl Russell) (1872–1970), English philosopher and mathematician.

Rutherford, Lord (1871–1937), New Zealand-born scientist, author of the nuclear theory of the atom and the first man to split the atom.

Saladin (1137–93), Sultan of Egypt and Syria and Moslem hero of the Third Crusade; see HISTORY.

Santos-Dumont, Alberto (1873–1932), famous Brazilian airman, one of the pioneers of modern aviation.

Sappho (*c.* 611–*c.* 592 B.C.), the most famous poetess of the ancient world; a native of the Greek island of Lesbos.

Savonarola, Girolamo (1452–98), Florentine friar who denounced the corruption of his day and was burned at the stake.

Schiller, Johann Friedrich von (1759–1805), one of the greatest German dramatists and poets.

Schliemann, Heinrich (1822–90), German archaeologist who discovered the ruins of ancient Troy.

Schubert, Franz (1797–1828), Austrian composer.

Schumann, Robert (1810–56), German composer.

Schweitzer, Albert (1875–1965), famous musician and organist who became a doctor of medicine in order to devote his life to the work of a medical missionary in Equatorial Africa.

Scipio, Publius (Scipio Africanus the Elder) (c. 232–183 B.C.), Roman general who distinguished himself in the Second Punic War.

Scott, Captain Robert Falcon (1868–1912), polar explorer who commanded the Antarctic expeditions of 1901–4 and 1910. With a small party he reached the South Pole on 18 January 1912, only to find that Amundsen had reached it before him. On the return journey the party were storm-bound, and all perished only 11 miles from their next depot.

Scott-Paine, Hubert (1891–1954), pioneer in the construction of flying-boats and high-speed motor-boats.

Selfridge, Harry Gordon (1858–1947), American whose famous shop in Oxford Street (opened in 1909) was the model for the modern British department store.

Shaftesbury, Anthony Ashley Cooper, Earl of (1801–85), the greatest social reformer of the 19th century; inspired changes in the treatment of lunatics, took part in the campaign against slavery and was largely responsible for the Factory Acts that forbade women and children to work underground in the mines and limited working hours.

Sheraton, Thomas (1751–1806), great English cabinet maker.

Sherman, General William (1820–91), great American soldier and leader of the famous 300-mile march across Georgia during the Civil War.

Shostakovich, Dmitri (1906–1975), Russian composer.

Sibelius, Jean (1865–1957), Finnish composer.

Siddons, Sarah (1755–1831), the greatest English tragic actress of her day.

Sidney, Sir Philip (1554–86), poet and soldier, one of Queen Elizabeth's favourites; killed fighting against the Spaniards at Zutphen.

Simpson, Sir James (1811–70), Scottish surgeon; first to use chloroform as an anaesthetic.

Smeaton, John (1724–92), rebuilder of the Eddystone lighthouse after its destruction by fire.

Smith, Adam (1723–90), political economist and first important advocate of free trade; author of *Wealth of Nations*.

Smuts, Field-Marshal Jan (1870–1950), South African soldier, who fought against the British in the Boer War, but afterwards worked for friendship with Britain. Prime Minister of South Africa, 1912–24 and 1939–48.

Sobieski, John (1629–96), King of Poland who freed Vienna from the Turks, 1683; see HISTORY.

Socrates (470–399 B.C.), Greek philosopher, whose teachings are known from the writings of his pupils, Xenophon and Plato. He taught people to think carefully and logically. Charged with corrupting the morals of the young, he was condemned to die by drinking hemlock.

Solomon (10th c. B.C.), son of David, ruler of Israel and Judah.

Solon (638–558 B.C.), great Athenian law-giver.

Somerset, Duke of (1506–52), Protector of England in early days of Edward VI's reign; later deposed and executed.

Sophocles (495–406 B.C.), popular Athenian dramatist; author of *Antigone, Electra, Oedipus*.

Soult, Marshal Nicolas (1769–1851), one of the most successful of Napoleon's marshals, and Wellington's opponent in the Peninsular War.

Spinoza, Benedict (1632–77), Dutch philosopher.

Stalin, Joseph (1879–1953), Soviet dictator from 1923 until his death; see HISTORY.

Stanley, Sir Henry Morton (1841–1904), explorer of Central Africa; in 1867, as a newspaper correspondent, he sought and found the missing David Livingstone.

Stendhal (Marie Henry Beyle) (1783–1842), French novelist.

Stephenson, George (1781–1848), English engineer, inventor of the first successful railway locomotive (see TRAINS).

Stevenson, Robert (1772–1850), lighthouse builder who invented the 'flashing' system of throwing light at sea.

Stowe, Harriet Beecher (1811–96), American author of *Uncle Tom's Cabin*, which helped to create strong feeling against slavery.

Stradivari, Antonio (1644–1730), Italian who was the greatest of all violin-makers.

Strafford, Thomas, Earl of (1593–1641), supporter of the authority of Charles I; abandoned by the King, he was impeached and executed.

Strauss, Johann (1825–99), Austrian composer.

Strauss, Richard (1864–1949), German composer.

Stravinsky, Igor (1882–1971), Russian-born American composer.

Strindberg, August (1849–1912), Swedish dramatist and novelist.

Sullivan, Sir Arthur (1842–1900), English composer; collaborator with W. S. Gilbert (*q.v.*) in the Savoy operas.

Sun Yat Sen, Dr (1867–1925), one of the leaders of the Chinese Revolution of 1911; President of the Chinese Republic, 1921–25.

Suvarov, Alexander (1730–1800), great Russian General.

Swedenborg, Emanuel (1688–1772), Swedish philosopher.

Tacitus, Caius (55–*c.* 120), Roman historian.

Tagore, Sir Rabindranath (1861–1941), Indian poet and philosopher.

Talleyrand-Périgord, Charles-Maurice de (1754–1838), Napoleon's Foreign Minister, 1797–1807.

Tamerlane (Timur the Lame) (1335–1405), founder of the Mogul dynasty in India; brutal conqueror of Turkestan, Persia and Syria.

Tarquin Superbus, the last king of Rome; banished 510 B.C.

Tasso, Torquato (1544–95), great Italian poet.

Telford, Thomas (1757–1834), Scottish road-maker and builder of canals and bridges, including the Menai Suspension Bridge.

Tell, William (14th century), legendary hero of the Swiss struggle for freedom against the Austrians.

Teresa, St (1515–82), Spanish nun famous for her austere life and her visions.

Terry, Dame Ellen (1848–1928), great English actress, long associated with Sir Henry Irving (*q.v.*).

Thales of Miletus (*c.* 624–565 B.C.), Greek philosopher who believed that water was the principal element.

Themistocles (*c.* 514–449 B.C.), Athenian soldier and statesman who defeated the Persian fleet at Salamis, 480 B.C.

Thomson, Sir Joseph (1856–1940), physicist and mathematician, discoverer of the electron.

Thoreau, Henry David (1817–62), nature-worshipping American philosopher; author of *Walden*.

Thucydides (*c.* 460–399 B.C.), greatest of the Greek historians.

Titus (40–81), Roman emperor, son of Vespasian; did much for the welfare of the Roman people, completed the Colosseum; see HISTORY.

Tolstoy, Count Leo (1828–1910), great Russian novelist; author of *War and Peace*, generally regarded as the greatest novel ever written.

Torquemada, Tomas de (1420–98), Inquisitor-General during Spanish Inquisition.

Toussaint L'Ouverture (1743–1803), Negro ex-slave who freed Santo Domingo (the Dominican Republic) from the French.

Trajan (*c.* 52–117), Roman emperor; did much to consolidate the Empire—work that was continued by his successor, Hadrian; see HISTORY.

Trotsky, Leon (1879–1940), one of the leaders of the Russian Revolution; in 1925 driven into exile in Mexico, where he was later assassinated.

Tschaikovsky, Peter Ilyitch (1840–93), Russian composer.

Turgenev, Ivan (1818–83), Russian novelist.

Tussaud, Madame Marie (1760–1850), Swiss who escaped from Paris at the time of the French Revolution and set up her exhibition of wax figures in London.

Tut-ankh-amen (*c.* 1350 B.C.), Egyptian Pharaoh whose tomb was discovered in 1922, with the mummy and the gold sarcophagus intact.

Twain, Mark (see Clemens, Samuel).

Tyler, Wat (d. 1381), leader of the Peasants' Revolt; see HISTORY.

Tyndale, William (*c.* 1492–1536), translator of the Bible; put to death for heresy.

Valentine, St, martyrised *c.* 273. The habit of sending Valentines is of pre-Christian origin, and is not connected with the saint.

Vaughan Williams, Ralph (1872–1958), English composer.

Verdi, Giuseppe (1813–1901), Italian composer.

Verlaine, Paul (1844–1896), French poet.

Verne, Jules (1828–1905), French writer of early science fiction, author of *Twenty Thousand Leagues under the Sea*, *Round the World in Eighty Days*.

Vernier, Pierre (1580–1637), inventor of the sliding scale.

Vespasian (A.D. 9–79), Roman emperor; at one time commander of the Roman Army in Britain.

Vespucci, Amerigo (1451–1512), Italian navigator; the first map-makers gave his name to America.

Villeneuve, Pierre (1763–1806), commanded the French fleet against Nelson at Trafalgar.

Villon, François (1431–*c*. 1489), French poet.

Virgil (Publius Vergilius Maro) (70–19 B.C.), great Roman epic poet, author of the *Aeneid*.

Vitus, St (4th century), Roman Catholic saint and martyr; the custom of dancing before his shrine on his commemoration day, 15 June, gave rise to the name, St Vitus Dance, given to a nervous ailment.

Voltaire, François-Marie Arouet de (1694–1778), great and influential French philosopher and writer, author of *Candide*.

Wagner, Richard (1813–83), German opera composer.

Wallace, Alfred Russel (1823–1913), English traveller and naturalist; one of the founders of zoological geography; author of *Travels on the Amazon*.

Wallace, Sir William (*c*. 1270–1305), Scottish patriot; see HISTORY.

Warbeck, Perkin (1474–99), Pretender to the English Crown; claimed to be one of the princes murdered in the Tower; provided with an army by the French and the Scots, he invaded England in 1497, but was defeated and hanged.

Warwick, Richard Neville, Earl of (*c*. 1428–71), 'the King-maker'; see HISTORY.

Washington, George (1732–99), first President of the American Republic, 1789; see HISTORY.

Watt, James (1736–1819), great British engineer, designer of first efficient steam-engine.

Wedgwood, Josiah (1730–95), most famous of the English potters.

Wellington, Arthur Wellesley, Duke of (1769–1852), 'the Iron Duke'; see HISTORY.

Wesley, Charles (1708–88), hymn-writer, brother of John.

Wesley, John (1703–91), founder of Methodism.

Whitman, Walt (1819–92), American poet, author of *Leaves of Grass*.

Whittington, Richard (*c.* 1358–*c.* 1423), London apprentice who became four times Lord Mayor of London.

Whymper, Edward (1840–1911), first mountaineer to reach the summit of the Matterhorn.

Wilberforce, William (1759–1833), leading spirit of the successful campaign against the Slave Trade.

Wilkes, John (1727–97), popular Whig politician; expelled from the House of Commons, he was three times elected M.P. for Middlesex, being again expelled each time. In the end his opponents gave way and he was able to take his seat.

William I of Prussia (1797–1888), first German Emperor; see HISTORY.

William II (1859–1941), Emperor of Germany; see HISTORY.

William the Silent (1533–80), Prince of Orange who attempted to free Holland from the grip of Spain; assassinated; see HISTORY.

Wingate, Major-General Orde (1903–44), leader of the Chindit forces that operated behind Japanese lines in Burma during the Second World War. Killed in air crash.

Wolfe, General James (1727–59), British commander at the siege of Quebec, in which he was killed.

Wolsey, Cardinal Thomas (1471–1530), Archbishop of York and Chancellor to Henry VIII; see HISTORY.

Wright, Sir Almroth (1861–1947), discovered the system of inoculation against typhoid.

Wycliff, John (*c.* 1324–84), religious reformer; translator of the Bible.

Xenophon (430–355 B.C.), Greek historian and general, pupil of Socrates.

Xerxes (*c.* 519–465 B.C.), King of Persia; see HISTORY.

Ximenes, Francisco (1436–1517), succeeded Torquemada (*q.v.*) as Inquisitor-General in the Spanish Inquisition.

Young, Brigham (1801–77), Mormon leader and head of the Latter Day Saints of Salt Lake City.

Zeppelin, Ferdinand, Graf von (1838–1917), German inventor of the airship bearing his name.

Zola, Emile (1840–1902), great French novelist.

Names in the News

AT any one moment, thousands of our fellow men and women are 'names in the news'—enjoying the secure fame of, say, a great living composer, or the fleeting celebrity of a popular actor or a sportsman at the height of his career. Out of these thousands we have picked two or three hundred that we believe might be of special interest to readers of JUNIOR PEARS.

Of most of them, we can safely say that they are actors, or musicians, or writers, or whatever it may be: but there is at least one field in which what a man or woman actually *does* may change overnight—making hundreds of encyclopaedias for the moment, and in this respect, out-of-date. This is the field of politics, where a general election can turn all the members of the Government into members of the Opposition, or a cabinet reshuffle can lose half a dozen Ministers their jobs. Foreign Presidents and Prime Ministers present the same difficulty. So we must say of all political figures mentioned here that the positions they are said to hold were those they held towards the beginning of 1978, when this book was prepared for the printer.

A number of British and Commonwealth politicians have the title 'Rt. Hon.' (short for Right Honourable). This title is given to members of the Privy Council, a body that gives advice to the Queen.

Aga Khan (IV) (b. 1936), Imam of the Ismaili Moslems.
Amin, Idi (b. 1926), President of Uganda.
Amis, Kingsley (b. 1922), poet and novelist.
Archer, Peter (b. 1926), Solicitor-General.
Ardizzone, Edward (b. 1900), artist and illustrator.
Arlott, John (b. 1914), writer and broadcaster on cricket.
Armstrong, Neil (b. 1930), US astronaut; first man to set foot on the moon.
Arnold, Malcolm (b. 1921), British composer.
Ayckbourn, Alan (b. 1940), British playwright.
Ashcroft, Dame Peggy (b. 1907), actress.
Ashton, Sir Frederick (b. 1906), principal choreographer Royal Ballet.

Attenborough, David (b. 1926), maker of zoological films.

Attenborough, Sir Richard (b. 1923), producer and actor.

Banda, Dr. Hastings (b. 1905), President of Malawi since 1966; Prime Minister, 1963–66.

Bannister, Dr. Roger (b. 1929), first man to run mile inside 4 minutes.

Barenboim, Daniel (b. 1942), pianist and conductor.

Barker, Ronnie (b. 1929), British comedian.

Beckett, Samuel (b. 1906), novelist and playwright.

Begin, Menachem (b. 1913), Prime Minister of Israel.

Benn, Rt. Hon. Anthony Wedgwood (b. 1925), Secretary of State for Energy.

Bennett, Richard Rodney (b. 1936), British composer.

Bergman, Ingrid (b. 1917), Swedish-born actress.

Betjeman, Sir John (b. 1906), Poet Laureate.

Bolt, Robert (b. 1924), dramatist.

Booth, Albert (b. 1929), Secretary of State for Employment.

Boult, Sir Adrian (b. 1889), orchestral conductor.

Bradman, Sir Donald (b. 1908), Australian cricketer who during his career (1927–48) scored 28,067 runs in 338 innings, with 117 centuries and an average of 95·14.

Brandt, Willy (b. 1913), Chancellor of W. Germany, 1969–74.

Brezhnev, Leonid Ilyich (b. 1906), First Secretary of the Communist Party of the Soviet Union Central Committee since 1964.

Brook, Peter (b. 1925), producer, co-director of the Royal Shakespeare Theatre.

Brzezinski, Zbigniew (b. 1929), National Security Adviser to President Carter.

Burton, Richard (b. 1925), actor.

Callaghan, Rt. Hon. James (b. 1912), Prime Minister since April, 1976.

Carter, James Earl (b. 1924), President of the United States since 1977.

Castro, Dr. Fidel (b. 1927), Prime Minister of Cuba since 1959.

Chadwick, Sir James (b. 1891), English physicist, discoverer of the neutron.

Cheshire, Group Captain Geoffrey, V.C. (b. 1917), famous pilot of Second World War; founder of Cheshire Homes for the Sick.

Clark, Lord (b. 1903), former Director, National Gallery; ar
critic and historian.

Cleese, John (b. 1939), comedian.

Cockerell, Christopher (b. 1910), inventor of the hovercraft

Coggan, Most Rev. and Rt. Hon. Donald (b. 1909), Arch
bishop of Canterbury since 1975.

Connery, Sean (b. 1930), actor.

Cook, Peter (b. 1937), comedian.

Cousteau, Jacques-Yves (b. 1910), French underwater ex
plorer.

Cowdrey, Colin (b. 1932), former England cricket captain.

Copland, Aaron (b. 1900), American composer.

Crawford, Michael (b. 1942), actor.

Dali, Salvador (b. 1904), Spanish surrealist painter.

Davis, Colin (b. 1927), Musical Director, Royal Opera House
Covent Garden.

Day, Robin (b. 1923), television commentator.

Dayan, Moshe (b. 1915), Foreign Minister of Israel.

Dell, Edmund (b. 1921), Secretary for Trade.

Dench, Judi (b. 1934), British actress.

Desai, Morarji (b. 1896), Prime Minister of India.

Dietrich, Marlene (b. 1904), German-born actress.

Du Maurier, Dame Daphne (b. 1907), author.

Elwyn Jones, Lord (b. 1910), Lord Chancellor.

Ennals, David (b. 1923), Secretary of State for Social Services

Ezra, Sir Derek (b. 1919), Chairman of National Coal Boar
since 1971.

Finney, Albert (b. 1936), British actor.

Fonteyn, Dame Margot (b. 1919), prima ballerina, Roya
Ballet.

Foot, Rt. Hon. Michael (b. 1913), Lord President of th
Council and Leader of the House of Commons.

Fraser, Lady Antonia (b. 1932), writer.

Fraser, Malcolm (b. 1922), Prime Minister of Australia.

Freeson, Reg (b. 1926), Minister of Housing and Construction

Fuchs, Sir Vivian (b. 1908), Director of British Antarcti
Survey, 1958–73: led Commonwealth Trans-Antarctic Ex
pedition, 1955–58.

Galbraith, John Kenneth (b. 1908), American economist.

Gandhi, Mrs Indira (b. 1917), Prime Minister of India, 1966-
77: daughter of Pandit Nehru, India's first Prime Minister.

Garbo, Greta (b. 1905), Swedish-born film actress.

Gielgud, Sir John (b. 1904), actor.

Giscard d'Estaing, Valery (b. 1926), President of France since 1974.

Gormley, Joseph (b. 1917), President, National Union of Mineworkers.

Grade, Sir Lew (b. 1906), chairman, Associated Television Corporation.

Greene, Graham (b. 1904), novelist.

Gromyko, Andrei (b. 1909), Foreign Minister, U.S.S.R.

Guinness, Sir Alec (b. 1914), actor.

Hailsham, Lord (b. 1907), Lord High Chancellor of Great Britain, 1970–74.

Hall, Sir Peter (b. 1930), Director of the National Theatre.

Harlech, Lord (b. 1918), President, British Board of Film Censors.

Harrison, Rex (b. 1908), actor.

Hart, Judith (b. 1946), Minister of State for Overseas Development.

Hartnell, Norman, Sir (b. 1901), dress designer.

Hattersley, Roy (b. 1932), Minister for Prices and Consumer Protection.

Healey, Rt. Hon. Denis (b. 1917), Chancellor of the Exchequer.

Heath, Rt. Hon. Edward (b. 1916), Leader of the Conservative Party, 1964–75; Prime Minister, 1970–74.

Helpmann, Sir Robert (b. 1909), dancer, choreographer, actor.

Heyerdahl, Thor (b. 1914), author and ethnologist, leader of Kon-Tiki expedition, 1947.

Hillary, Sir Edmund (b. 1919), mountaineer: with Sherpa Tensing, first to reach summit of Everest, 1953.

Hirohito (b. 1901), Emperor of Japan.

Hitchcock, Alfred (b. 1899), film producer and director.

Hoffman, Dustin (b. 1937), American film actor.

Home, Lord (b. 1903), Secretary of State for Foreign and Commonwealth Affairs, 1970–74; Prime Minister, 1963–64.

Howell, Denis (b. 1923), Minister for Sport.

Howerd, Frankie (b. 1921), comedian.

Hoyle, Professor Sir Fred (b. 1915), mathematician, astronomer and writer.

Hua Kuo Feng (b. 1922), Chairman of Communist Party of China.

Hume, Cardinal Basil (b. 1923), Archbishop of Westminster.

Hunt, Lord (b. 1910), soldier and mountaineer; leader of the successful 1953 Mt. Everest expedition.

Hussein Ibn Talal (b. 1935), King of Jordan.

Hutton, Sir Leonard (b. 1916), first professional cricketer to captain England.

Innes, Hammond (b. 1913), writer.

Jackson, Glenda (b. 1936), actress.

Jenkins, Rt. Hon. Roy (b. 1920), President, Common Market Commission.

Joseph, Rt. Hon. Sir Keith (b. 1918), Secretary of State for Social Services, 1970–74.

Juan Carlos I (b. 1938), King of Spain.

Kaunda, Kenneth (b. 1924), President of Zambia.

Kenyatta, Jomo, President of Kenya since 1964.

Khama, Sir Seretse (b. 1921), President of Botswana.

Kosygin, Alexei (b. 1904), Chairman of the Council of Ministers of the U.S.S.R. since 1964.

Kyprianou, Spyros (b. 1932), President of Cyprus.

Larkin, Philip (b. 1922), poet.

Lever, Rt. Hon. Harold (b. 1914), Chancellor of Duchy of Lancaster.

Lovell, Professor Sir Bernard (b. 1913), Director of Jodrell Bank Experimental Station, Cheshire.

Luns, Dr. Joseph (b. 1911), Secretary-General, N.A.T.O.

Lynch, John (b. 1917), Taoiseach (Head of Government) of Republic of Ireland.

Maclean, Alastair (b. 1922), novelist.

Macmillan, Rt. Hon. Harold (b. 1894), Prime Minister, 1957–63.

Mason, Rt. Hon. Roy (b. 1925), Secretary of State for Northern Ireland.

Matthews, Sir Stanley (b. 1915), former professional footballer: first played for England 1934.

McKellen, Ian (b. 1935), British actor.

Menuhin, Yehudi (b. 1916), American violinist.

Methven, Sir John (b. 1926), Director-General, Confederation of British Industry.

Miles, Sir Bernard (b. 1907), actor, founder of the Mermaid Theatre.

Millan, Bruce (b. 1928), Secretary of State for Scotland.

Milligan, Spike (b. 1919), comedian, writer.

Mills, John (b. 1908), actor and producer.

Mintoff, Dom (b. 1916), Prime Minister of Malta.

Moore, Dudley (b. 1935), British comedian.

Moore, Henry (b. 1898), sculptor.

Morecambe, Eric (b. 1926), comedian.

Morris, John (b. 1932), Secretary of State for Wales.

Mountbatten of Burma, 1st Earl (b. 1900), Chief of Combined Operations, 1942–43; Supreme Allied Commander, S.E. Asia, 1943–46; Viceroy of India, 1947; Chief of Defence Staff, 1959–65.

Muggeridge, Malcolm (b. 1903), journalist and broadcaster.

Muldoon, Robert (b. 1924), Prime Minister of New Zealand.

Murray, Lionel (Len) (b. 1922), General Secretary, Trade Union Congress since 1973.

Murdoch, Iris (b. 1919), novelist.

Nixon, Richard Milhous (b. 1913), President of the United States, 1969-74. See HISTORY.

Nunn, Trevor (b. 1936), Director, Royal Shakespeare Company.

Nureyev, Rudolf (b. 1939), ballet dancer.

Nyerere, Julius (b. 1922), President of Tanzania since 1964.

Olivier, Lord (Laurence Olivier) (b. 1907), actor, Director of the National Theatre, 1962–73, now Associate Director.

Orme, Stanley (b. 1923), Minister of State, Department of Health and Social Security.

Osborne, John (b. 1929), playwright and actor.

O'Toole, Peter (b. 1934), actor.

Owen, David (b. 1938), Foreign Secretary since 1977.

Packer, Kerry, Chairman of Channel Nine TV network, Sydney, Australia, and creator of the controversial 'cricket circus'.

Parker, Peter (b. 1925), Chairman, British Railways Board.

Paul VI, His Holiness Pope (b. 1897), elected Pope in 1963.

Pears, Sir Peter (b. 1910), singer.

Pinter, Harold (b. 1930), actor and playwright.

Podgorny, Nikolai (b. 1903), President of U.S.S.R.

Powell, Rt. Hon. Enoch (b. 1912), Minister of Health, 1960–63.

Previn, André (b. 1929), composer and conductor.

Priestley, John Boynton (b. 1894), author and playwright.

Ramphal, Shridath (b. 1928), Secretary-General of the Commonwealth.

Redgrave, Sir Michael (b. 1908), actor.

Redgrave, Vanessa (b. 1937), actress: daughter of Sir Michael Redgrave.

Rees, Rt. Hon. Merlyn (b. 1925), Home Secretary.

Richardson, Sir Ralph (b. 1902), actor.

Robson, Dame Flora (b. 1902), actress.

Rose, Sir Alec (b. 1908), sailed solo round the world, 1967–68.

Rubinstein, Artur (b. 1888), pianist.

Ryland, Sir William (b. 1913), Chairman, Post Office Corporation.

Ryle, Sir Martin (b. 1918), Astronomer Royal.

Sadat, Anwar (b. 1918), President of Egypt.

Sartre, Jean-Paul (b. 1905), French writer, philosopher and dramatist.

Schmidt, Helmut (b. 1918), Chancellor of W. Germany.

Schwarzkopf, Elisabeth (b. 1915), opera and concert singer.

Scofield, Paul (b. 1922), actor.

Scott, Sir Peter (b. 1909), artist, writer and naturalist; son of the explorer, Captain Scott.

Searle, Ronald (b. 1920), artist and cartoonist.

Secombe, Harry (b. 1921), singer and comedian.

Segovia, Andres (b. 1894), Spanish guitarist.

Sellers, Peter (b. 1925), actor.

Shepherd, Lord (b. 1919), Lord Privy Seal and Leader of the House of Lords.

Sheppard, Rt. Rev. David (b. 1929), Bishop of Liverpool: former English cricket captain.

Shore, Rt. Hon. Peter (b. 1925), Secretary of State for Environment.

Silkin, John (b. 1923), Minister for Planning and Local Government.

Silkin, Sam (b. 1918), Attorney-General.

Simenon, Georges (b. 1903), Belgian novelist, creator of the French detective, Maigret.

Sinatra, Frank (b. 1917), American singer and actor.

Smith, Ian (b. 1919), Prime Minister of S. Rhodesia from 1964 made illegal declaration of independence, November 1965.

Snow, Lord (b. 1905), author and scientist.

Solzhenitsyn, Alexander (b. 1918), Russian novelist.

Spender, Stephen (b. 1909), poet.

Steel, David (b. 1938), leader of the Liberal Party.

Stockhausen, Karlheinz (b. 1928), German composer.

Sutherland, Graham (b. 1903), artist.

Sutherland, Joan (b. 1926), Australian-born opera singer.

Swann, Sir Michael (b. 1920), Chairman, B.B.C.

Taylor, Alan John Percivale (b. 1906), historian.

Thatcher, Margaret (b. 1925), Leader of the Opposition; Secretary of State for Education and Science, 1970–74.

Thomas, George (b. 1909), Speaker of the House of Commons.

Thorpe, Rt. Hon. Jeremy (b. 1929), Leader of the Liberal Party, 1967–76.

Tippett, Sir Michael (b. 1905), composer.

Tito (Josip Broz) (b. 1892), President of Jugoslavia since 1953.

Trethowan, Ian (b. 1922), Director-General, B.B.C.

Trudeau, Pierre, (b. 1919), Prime Minister of Canada since 1968.

Ustinov, Peter (b. 1921), actor, dramatist, producer.

Vance, Cyrus (b. 1917), Secretary of State, U.S.A.

Varley, Eric (b. 1933), Secretary of State for Industry.

Vorster, Balthazar (b. 1915), Prime Minister of S. Africa.

Waldheim, Kurt (b. 1918), Secretary-General, United Nations since 1972.

Walton, Sir William (b. 1902), composer.

Wedgwood, Dame Cicely Veronica (b. 1910), historian.

Welles, Orson (b. 1915), American actor, writer and producer.

Whitelaw, Rt. Hon. William (b. 1918), Deputy leader, Conservative Party; Secretary of State for N. Ireland, 1972–3.

Whittle, Air Commodore Sir Frank (b. 1907), developed gas turbine for jet propulsion.

Widgery, Lord (b. 1911), Lord Chief Justice of England.

Williams, Mrs. Shirley (b. 1930), Secretary of State for Education and Science.

Williamson, Malcolm (b. 1931), composer and Master of the Queen's Musick.

Wilson, Rt. Hon. Sir Harold (b. 1916), Prime Minister, 1964–70; and from February 1974 until his resignation in April 1976. Led Labour Government, 1964–70.

Vise, Ernie (b. 1926), comedian.

Yamani, Shaikh Ahmad Zaki, Minister of Petroleum and Mineral Resources, Saudi Arabia.

Young, Brian (b. 1922), Director-General of the Independent Broadcasting Authority (I.B.A.).

A Dictionary of Mythology

The majority of the gods, goddesses and other mythological characters who appear in this list are Greek or Roman. Some, however, are Egyptian or Norse; and it is important to remember that, though the Greek and Roman myths are the most familiar to us, the Babylonians, the Hebrews, the Chinese, Japanese, Indians and many other peoples built mythical stories, and invented mythical characters, on the basis of their religious beliefs.

The fact that the Romans borrowed many of their myths from the Greeks, giving their own names to the gods, leads often to confusion. The following table shows, side by side, the Greek and Roman names of the principal gods and goddesses.

Greek	Roman
Aphrodite (goddess of love)	**Venus**
Apollo (god of light and the arts)	**Phoebus Apollo**
Ares (god of war)	**Mars**
Artemis (huntress)	**Diana**
Athene (goddess of wisdom)	**Minerva**
Cronus (father of Zeus)	**Saturn**
Demeter (goddess of corn)	**Ceres**
Dionysus (god of wine and revelry)	**Bacchus**
Eros (god of love)	**Cupid**
Hera (mother of the gods and goddess of marriage)	**Juno**
Hermes (messenger of the gods)	**Mercury**
Hestia (goddess of the hearth)	**Vesta**
Pan (god of the flocks)	**Faunus**
Poseidon (god of the sea)	**Neptune**
Zeus (father of the gods)	**Jupiter**

The printing of a name in small capital letters (e.g. VENUS) means that the mythical person named is the subject of a separate entry.

Achilles, King of the Myrmidons, most famous of the Greek heroes of the Trojan War.

Adonis, Greek god: a young man of great beauty, wounded by a boar and changed by APHRODITE into an anemone.

Aeneas, Trojan prince, hero of Virgil's *Aeneid*; the mythical ancestor of the Romans.

Aeolus, wind-god, who unchained the tempests.

Aesculapius, god of medicine.

Agamemnon, King of Mycenae, leader of the Greeks against Troy.

Ajax, Greek warrior at the siege of Troy.

Amazons, mythical race of war-like women.

Amphitrite, sea-goddess and wife of POSEIDON.

Ammon, Egyptian god.

Andromeda, daughter of the king of Ethiopia who, by claiming to be as beautiful as the NEREIDS, roused the anger of POSEIDON, and was condemned to be devoured by a sea monster. She was saved by PERSEUS, who married her.

Antigone, daughter of OEDIPUS. When the king of Thebes forbade the burial of her brother, Polynices, she defied his order, and was buried alive in a cave; there she hanged herself.

Aphrodite, Greek goddess of love; she was said to have sprung from the foam of the sea.

Apollo, Greek and Roman god of light, the arts and divination; also called Phoebus.

Aquilo, the north wind.

Ares, the Greek god of war.

Argonauts, the fifty Greek heroes who, with JASON, sought the Golden Fleece in their ship the *Argo.*

Ariadne, daughter of MINOS of Crete; gave THESEUS the thread which enabled him to find his way out of the Labyrinth.

Artemis, Greek goddess and huntress.

Atalanta, Greek princess who declared she would marry only the man who could beat her at running; she was outrun by Milanion, who dropped three golden apples one after another to tempt Atalanta and slow her down.

Athene or **Pallas,** Greek goddess of wisdom.

Atlas, King of Mauretania who, for warring against ZEUS, was condemned to support the sky on his shoulders.

Bacchus, Roman god of wine.

Baldur, most beautiful of the Norse gods.

Bellerophon, Greek hero who caught PEGASUS, the winged horse, and killed the CHIMAERA.

Boreas, the north wind.

Calypso, nymph who delayed ODYSSEUS for seven years on his way home from Troy.

Cassandra, Trojan princess; she had the gift of prophecy, but was fated never to be believed.

Castor and Pollux, sons of ZEUS and Leda; they were transported to the heavens and became the constellation known as the Twins.

Centaurs, creatures, half-horse and half-man, living on Mt Pelion in Thessaly.

Cerberus, three-headed dog who guarded the gates of HADES.

Ceres, Roman corn goddess.

Charon, boatman who ferried the dead across the STYX.

Chimaera, fire-breathing monster, a mixture of lion, dragon and goat; slain by BELLEROPHON.

Circe, enchantress who turned ODYSSEUS' companions into swine.

Cronus, Greek name for SATURN.

Cupid, Roman name for EROS, the god of love.

Cybele, the 'great mother', goddess of nature.

Cyclops, one-eyed giants who forged ZEUS'S thunderbolts.

Danae, daughter of the king of Argos, visited by ZEUS in a shower of gold; mother of PERSEUS.

Daphne, nymph who was changed into a laurel-bush to save her from APOLLO.

Demeter, Greek goddess of the corn.

Diana, Roman goddess and huntress.

Dido, mythical queen who founded Carthage.

Dionysus, Greek god of wine and revelry.

Dryads, Greek goddesses of the forest.

Echo, nymph who, having displeased HERA, was changed into a rock and condemned to repeat the last words of those who spoke to her.

Electra, sister of ORESTES.

Elysium, or the Elysian fields, the Greek and Roman paradise.

Endymion, beautiful youth who was loved by the moon.

Erebus, the dark subterranean region below which was HADES.

Eros, the god of love.

Euphrosyne, one of the three GRACES.

Eurydice, wife of ORPHEUS.

Eurus, the south-east wind.

Fates, the three goddesses, Clotho, Lachesis and Atropos, who were in charge of human destinies; they weaved the web of each man's life, which ended when Atropos cut the thread.

Fauns, Roman gods of the fields.

Flora, goddess of flowers and gardens.

Freya, Norse goddess of love.

Furies or **Eumenides,** goddesses whose mission was to punish human crimes.

Gorgons, three sisters, MEDUSA, Euryale and Stheno, who had the power to change into stone all who looked at them.

Graces, the three goddesses, EUPHROSYNE, Aglaia and Thalia, who were regarded as the bestowers of beauty and charm.

Hades, the Greek god of the infernal regions; also the infernal regions themselves.

Harpies, winged monsters with women's faces and long claws.

Hector, most valiant of the defenders of Troy: killed by ACHILLES.

Hecuba, wife of PRIAM, King of Troy; nineteen of her children were killed during the siege.

Helen, Greek princess of great beauty; her removal to Troy by PARIS was the cause of the Trojan War.

Helicon, Greek mountain consecrated to the MUSES.

Hera, wife of ZEUS and goddess of marriage.

Heracles, Greek demi-god.

Hercules, Roman name for HERACLES.

Hermes, Greek messenger of the gods.

Hesperides, daughters of ATLAS, guardians of the golden apples stolen by HERCULES.

Hestia, Greek goddess of the hearth, known to the Romans as Vesta.

Horus, falcon-headed Egyptian god.

Hygieia, Greek goddess of health.

Hymen, god of marriage.

Icarus, son of Daedalus; his father made for them both wings fastened with wax. Icarus flew too near the sun; the wax fastenings melted, and he fell into the sea and was drowned.

Irene, Greek goddess of peace.

Iris, the rainbow, a messenger of the gods.

Isis, Egyptian goddess of medicine, marriage and agriculture.

Ixion, thrown into Hell by ZEUS and condemned to be bound to a flaming wheel everlastingly revolving.

Janus, Roman god of beginnings (hence *Januarius,* the first month of the year); he was able to see both the future and the past and is always represented with two heads.

Jason, Greek hero and leader of the ARGONAUTS, who won the Golden Fleece.

Juno, wife of JUPITER and goddess of marriage.

Jupiter, Roman name for the father of the gods and king of heaven.

Lethe, one of the rivers of Hell; all who drank its waters became forgetful of the past.

Mars, Roman god of war.

Medea, witch who married JASON and, when he left her, took her revenge by devouring their children.

Medusa, one of the three GORGONS. She offended MINERVA, who turned her hair into serpents. PERSEUS cut off her head and carried it with him to turn his enemies into stone.

Menelaus, King of Sparta and husband of HELEN of Troy.

Mercury, messenger of the gods.

Midas, King of Phrygia to whom the favour was granted that everything he touched turned into gold. When this happened even to his food, he prayed for the power to be taken away.

Minerva, Roman goddess of wisdom and the arts.

Minos, King of Crete who demanded an annual tribute of young men and women from Athens; they were sent into the Labyrinth and devoured by the Minotaur.

Mnemosyne, goddess of memory and mother of the MUSES.

Muses, nine goddesses who presided over the arts: Clio (History), Euterpe (music), Thalia (comedy), Melpomene (tragedy), Terpsichore (dancing), Erata (elegaic poetry), Polymnia (lyric poetry), Urania (astronomy), Calliope (eloquence and epic poetry).

Naiads, nymphs presiding over rivers and springs.

Narcissus, beautiful youth who pined away for love of his own reflection and was turned into a flower.

Nemesis, Greek goddess of vengeance and retribution.

Neptune, Roman god of the sea.

Nereids, nymphs of the Mediterranean.

Notus, the south wind.

Oceanides, nymphs of the sea.

Oceanus, Greek god of the sea.

Odin, or **Wotan,** father of the Norse gods.

Odysseus, King of Ithaca, one of the heroes of the siege of Troy, whose many adventures on his return home are described in Homer's *Odyssey*. The Romans called him ULYSSES.

Oedipus, King of Thebes, who, discovering that he had un-wittingly killed his father and married his mother, blinded himself.

Orestes, son of AGAMEMNON and Clytemnestra. When Agamem-non was killed by Clytemnestra, Orestes was saved by his sister ELECTRA, who then drove him to kill his mother in revenge.

Orion, giant hunter; killed by ARTEMIS, he became one of the constellations.

Orpheus, great musician of Greek myth; went into Hades in search of his dead wife, EURYDICE, and so charmed the infernal spirits with his music that they returned Eurydice to him on condition that he should not look behind him until he had left the lower world. He broke this condition and was torn to pieces.

Osiris, Egyptian god, protector of the dead.

Pales, Roman goddess of flocks and shepherds.

Pan, goat-footed Greek god who presided over the flocks.

Pandora, the first woman to be created. ATHENE made her wise; ZEUS gave her a box full of evil things. On earth she married Epimetheus, the first man; then opened the box and so released all the ills from which men suffer.

Paris, Trojan prince who took HELEN from her husband and so caused the Trojan War. Appointed to choose the most beautiful of the three goddesses, HERA, ATHENE and APHRODITE, he chose the last, thus bringing down on Troy the hatred of the other two.

Parnassus, Greek mountain sacred to the MUSES.

Pegasus, winged horse that sprang from the blood of MEDUSA.

Penelope, wife of ODYSSEUS. During his long absence she was pressed to choose a new husband, and promised to do so when she had finished weaving a tapestry; but every night she un-did the work she had done that day.

Perseus, son of ZEUS and DANAE. He and his mother were cast adrift and came to the country of King Polydectes. The king hoping to get rid of Perseus, sent him to bring back MEDUSA' head.

Phaethon, son of the Sun-God, whose father allowed him to drive the sun-chariot for one day only; he was unable to manage the horses, and ZEUS, angered, struck him dead.

Pleiades, the seven daughters of ATLAS who killed themselve in despair and were turned into stars.

Pluto, King of HADES and god of the dead.

Polyphemus, the most famous of the CYCLOPS; he imprisoned ODYSSEUS, who escaped by blinding him.

Pomona, goddess of fruits and gardens.

Poseidon, god of the sea.

Priam, the last King of Troy, killed in the sack of the city.

Procrustes, robber who fitted his victims to a bed, stretching them or lopping their limbs to do so. Slain by THESEUS.

Prometheus, the god of fire. Having formed the first man of clay, he stole fire from heaven to bring him to life. ZEUS had him chained to a mountain, where his liver was devoured every day by a vulture, but grew again every night. He was freed by HERACLES.

Proserpina, wife of PLUTO and mother of the FURIES.

Proteus, sea god who could change his shape at will.

Psyche ('the soul'), beautiful maiden loved by CUPID.

Pygmalion, King of Cyprus who fell in love with a statue of a woman he had made himself.

Remus, brother of ROMULUS.

Romulus, thrown with his brother REMUS into the Tiber at birth; washed ashore and adopted by a she-wolf. Romulus founded Rome (the traditional date is 753 B.C.).

Saturn, husband of CYBELE and father of JUPITER. A promise made to Titan forced him to eat his children when they were born. Cybele saved Jupiter by putting a stone in his place. Jupiter dethroned his father and Saturn took refuge in Latium, where he showed men how to cultivate the land.

Satyrs, the companions of BACCHUS.

Sirens, monsters, half-woman and half-bird, who lived on the rocks between the isle of Capri and the coast of Italy. By the sweetness of their singing they lured sailors to destruction.

Sisyphus, founder of Corinth, who for his greed and dishonesty was condemned after death to roll a stone for ever uphill; as soon as it got to the top it rolled down again.

Styx, the river flowing round HADES, over which CHARON ferried the dead.

Tantalus, King of Lydia condemned for ever to hunger and thirst.

Tartarus, the lowest region of HADES.

Telemachus, son of ODYSSEUS who set out in search of his father.

Theseus, Greek hero who, among his many adventures, killed the Minotaur (see MINOS).

Themis, goddess of justice.

Thor, the Norse god of war.

Titans, sons of the Heaven and the Earth. Rebelling against the gods, they attempted to climb to Heaven by piling mountain upon mountain; but they were destroyed by JUPITER's thunderbolts.

Triton, one of the sea-gods.

Ulysses, Roman name for ODYSSEUS.

Venus, the Roman goddess of beauty and love.

Vulcan, Roman god of fire.

Zephyrus, the west wind.

Zeus, Greek name for the father of the gods.

A Dictionary of Science and Mathematics

Abacus A digital computing device of ancient origin consisting of counters strung on wires, one wire for each digital position.

Aberration Deviation from perfect image formation in an optical or equivalent system.

Absolute Temperature A temperature scale originally based on *Charles's Law* (q.v.) of the expansion of gases. This law suggests that if a gas could be cooled down to about $-273°$ C. it would occupy zero volume. In fact all gases liquefy before reaching such a low temperature, but there does exist a minimum possible temperature, $-273.15°$ C., below which matter cannot be cooled. This temperature is called *absolute zero* and is itself unattainable, although temperatures within one millionth of a degree of it have been reached using special cooling techniques. The Absolute (or Kelvin) Temperature scale measures temperatures from absolute zero in degrees kelvin, the degree kelvin being of the same magnitude as the degree centigrade. To convert an absolute temperature to a centigrade temperature it is necessary simply to add 273.15 (in the table the 0.15 has been omitted for simplicity). The importance of the absolute scale is that it is always absolute temperatures which appear in the equations of *thermodynamics* (q.v.) e.g. the *gas laws* (q.v.). See *thermometer*.

TEMPERATURE CONVERSIONS

Fahrenheit	Centigrade	Absolute or Kelvin (K.)
−459.4	−273.0	0
−148.0	−100.0	173
−112.0	−80.0	193
−76.0	−60.0	213
−40.0	−40.0	233
−4.0	−20.0	253
0	−17.8	255.2
32.0	0	273
50.0	10	283
68.0	20	293
86.0	30	303
104.0	40	313
122.0	50	323
140.0	60	333
158.0	70	343
176.0	80	353
194.0	90	363
212.0	100	373

Fahrenheit	Centigrade	*Absolute* or Kelvin (K.)
1,292·0	700	973
1,472·0	800	1,073
1,832	1,000	1,273
2,192	1,200	1,473
2,732	1,500	1,773

Acceleration The rate of change of velocity, expressed in metres per second per second, or feet per second per second, etc. Negative acceleration = retardation.

Accumulator A type of electric *cell* (q.v.) or battery that can be recharged. The commonest sort (as used for car batteries) has positive plates of lead peroxide and negative plates of spongy lead with dilute sulphuric acid as the electrolyte.

Acid Acids are a very important group of chemical compounds. Examples of inorganic acids are hydrochloric acid (HCl), nitric acid (HNO_3), and sulphuric acid (H_2SO_4). Organic acids such as acetic acid ($CH_3 \cdot COOH$) usually contain the *carboxyl* group, COOH. All acids contain *replaceable* (or *acidic*) hydrogen in their molecules (though in organic acids, only the hydrogen in COOH is acidic), and the most characteristic reaction of acids is for this hydrogen to be replaced by a metal to form a *salt* (q.v.). Some metals react directly with acids to give a salt and hydrogen gas while another example of this kind of reaction is the neutralisation of an acid by a *base* (q.v.) to give a salt and water. E.g. Potassium hydroxide (a base) reacts with dilute nitric acid to give potassium nitrate (a salt) and water. Here the potassium replaces the acidic hydrogen which goes into making the water. The reason why acids so readily lose their acidic hydrogen is that in solutions of acids to a great extent the hydrogen is already separate from the rest of the molecule in the form of positive hydrogen ions.

Acids have a sour taste and when concentrated can be very corrosive and dangerous to handle. *Indicators* (q.v.) can be used to test whether a solution is acidic or not: e.g. in the presence of an acid, blue litmus turns red.

Acoustics The study of *sound*. See RADIO AND TELEVISION.

Adsorption The taking-up of a gas by a solid in such a way that a layer of gas only one molecule thick is held firmly in the surface of the solid. Adsorption is an essential part of some chemical phenomena, including *catalysis* (q.v.).

Alkali A *base* (q.v.) that is soluble in water, e.g. the hydroxides of sodium and potassium (caustic soda and caustic potash). Alkalis can be identified in solution by means of *indicators* (q.v.).

Alpha Radiation (Alpha Rays, α-Rays) This is a stream of particles that are the nuclei of helium atoms. They are emitted from radioactive substances. Some emitters of alpha rays are: uranium, radium, plutonium. Alpha rays have such little penetrating power that a sheet of paper will stop them, but where they do penetrate they have intense effects.

Alternating Current See RADIO AND TELEVISION

Altimeter An instrument used to measure height above the Earth.

Amino-acid An organic compound of the form $H_2N-CHR-COOH$ where R represents a univalent side-chain. Glycine is the simplest amino-acid in which R is a hydrogen atom. A large number of different amino-acids are possible, but the 20 or so that are the building blocks for *proteins* (q.v.) are particularly important.

In proteins, amino-acids link together by forming a *peptide bond* between the carboxyl group (−COOH) of one amino-acid and the amino group (H_2N-) of the next, with the elimination of a water molecule. This process can be repeated to give chains of great length.

Ampere (A) The S.I. unit of electric *current* (q.v.).

Analog Computer A computer in which numerical quantities are represented by physical quantities, e.g. the numbers between 1 and 2 may be represented by the corresponding voltages between 1 volt and 2 volts. Another example of an analog computer is the slide rule in which numbers are represented by lengths.

Angle Formed when two lines meet at a point. If straight lines AB and BC meet at the point B, the angle so formed is denoted by $\angle ABC$ or $A\hat{B}C$. Alternatively, a particular angle may be referred to by a symbol, commonly a Greek letter such as θ (theta) or ϕ (phi). Angles are measured either (a) in degrees, there being 360 degrees (360°) to the full circle, or (b) in circular measure, in which case the unit is the *radian* (q.v.).

Angular Velocity The rate of motion through an angle about an axis. Measured in degrees, revolutions or *radians* (q.v.) per unit time. The angular velocity of a point in radians/unit time

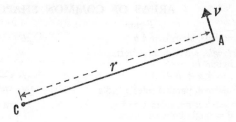

can be calculated by dividing its linear velocity perpendicular to the line joining it to the axis by the length of the line. In the diagram, the angular velocity of *A* (which has linear velocity *v*) about *C* is v/r radians/sec. *Angular acceleration* is the rate of change of angular velocity.

Angstrom (Å) Unit of length. 1 angstrom = 10^{-10} m = 10^{-8} cm = 3.9×10^{-9} inches. 1 inch = 2.54×10^8 Å. Used in atomic physics e.g. to measure the wavelengths of X-rays (0.1 Å to 10 Å) or the distance between atoms in molecules and crystals (the distance between neighbouring copper atoms in copper metal is 3.4 Å).

Anion A negatively charged atom or *radical* (q.v.).

Anode Positive electrode. See ELECTROLYSIS.

Anti-matter Particles like electrons, protons and neutrons all have corresponding anti-particles: anti-electrons (called *positrons*), anti-protons and anti-neutrons. It is possible that somewhere in the universe there exists anti-matter composed entirely of anti-particles (e.g. an anti-hydrogen atom would have an anti-proton as nucleus and one orbiting positron), but this has never been detected. If anti-matter were to meet ordinary matter both would be annihilated and much energy released.

Archimedes Principle This states that when a body is partially or totally immersed in a fluid (i.e. a liquid or gas) its apparent loss of weight is equal to the weight of fluid displaced: i.e. the body experiences an upthrust equal to the weight of fluid displaced.

Area The amount of space covered as a flat expanse, for the calculation of which two dimensions are necessary. Units are square metres, square inches (□), square yards, etc. Units for land measurement are the hectare (metric system) and acre.

AREAS OF COMMON SHAPES

Figure	Area
Rectangle, sides a and b	ab
Triangle, sides a, b, c, vertical height h.	$\frac{1}{2}bh$
$s = \frac{1}{2}(a + b + c)$	$\sqrt{s(s-a)(s-b)(s-c)}$
Trapezoid, parallel sides a and c	$\frac{1}{2}h(a + c)$
Parallelogram, sides x and y, θ = angle between sides	$xy \sin \theta$
Circle, radius r	πr^2
Sector of circle, radius r, θ = angle between radii boundaries	$\dfrac{r^2\theta}{2}$ (θ in radians)
Segment of circle	$\dfrac{r^2}{2}(\theta - \sin \theta)$ (θ in radians)
Ellipse, semi-axes a and b	πab
Surface of sphere, radius r	$4\pi r^2$
Surface of cylinder, height h, radius r	(1) $2\pi rh$ (curved surface only) (2) $2\pi r(h + r)$ (total surface)
Surface of cone, slant height l, radius r	(1) πrl (curved surface) (2) $\pi r(l + r)$ (total surface)

Arithmetical Progression Series of quantities in which each term differs from the preceding by a constant *common difference*. An A.P. in which the first term is a, the common difference d, the number of terms n and the sum of n terms S has:

$$S = a + (a + d) + (a + 2d) + (a + 3d) + \ldots + (a + (n - 1)d)$$
$$= \frac{n}{2}\{2a + (n - 1)d\}$$

Armature The coil or coils—usually rotating—of an electric motor or dynamo.

Atmosphere Normal or Standard. Unit of pressure = pressure which will support a column of mercury 760 mm. or 29·92 in. high at 0° C, sea-level at Lat. 45°. 1 Normal atmosphere = 1·0132 Bars = 14·72 lb./sq. in. = 101,320 N/sq.m.

Atom The smallest particle of an *element* (q.v.) still retaining the chemical properties of that element.

It consists of a positively charged heavy nucleus surrounded by negatively charged electrons, which move in orbits very similar to the way in which planets move round the sun. The

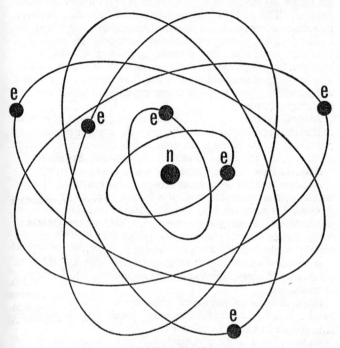

CARBON ATOM

Schematic diagram, 6 planetary electrons, 2 on inner orbits, 4 on outer orbits. These four are the valency electrons. The nucleus has 6 protons and 6 neutrons all very close together in the one body, which carries almost all the mass of the atom.

positive charge on the nucleus exactly balances the total negative charge of all the surrounding electrons when the atom is neutral.

The nucleus consists of two types of particle very strongly held together—protons and neutrons. A proton carries one unit of positive charge. A neutron has no charge. The mass of a neutron is very slightly more than the mass of a proton.

The chemical properties of the atom are determined by the electrons, which in number, of course, are equivalent to the proton charge in the nucleus. So if a proton is removed from (or added to) the nucleus of an atom it is no longer the same element. The addition or subtraction of neutrons, however, makes no difference to the chemical properties.

The number of protons (and the corresponding number of electrons) determines the element. An atom of carbon, for example, has six planetary electrons, an atom of copper twenty-nine, an atom of uranium ninety-two. The simplest atom is that of hydrogen, whose nucleus is one proton and which has one planetary electron.

Atomic Number A number that tells the number of protons in the nucleus of an atom and therefore the number of planetary electrons. A list of elements starts with hydrogen of atomic number 1 and continues in series 1, 2, 3, 4, etc. See *element*.

Atomic Pile Original name for a *nuclear reactor* (q.v.).

Atomic Weight A number showing how heavy the atom of an element is compared with the isotope carbon 12 taken as 12·0000. Owing to the facts that when atomic nuclei fuse to make another element energy is given out, and therefore mass lost, and many elements are mixtures of isotopes of different weights, the atomic weight is rarely a whole number.

Avogadro's Law Equal volumes of all gases under the same conditions of temperature and pressure contain equal numbers of molecules.

Base A chemical substance which reacts with an *acid* (q.v.) to give a *salt* (q.v.) and water only. Bases may be insoluble (e.g. copper II oxide) or soluble (see *alkali*).

Battery A number of electric *cells* (q.v.) joined together to give a bigger electromotive force. Thus three dry cells, each 1·5 V, in series give 4·5 V.

Beta Radiation (Beta Rays, β-Rays) A stream of very fast electrons emitted by some radioactive substances. These electrons come from the nucleus by breakdown of neutrons, not from the planetary electrons. Beta rays are more penetrating than *alpha rays* (q.v.), the most energetic of them being capable of penetrating 1 mm. of lead. Because of their penetrating power they are used for the measurement of thickness in industry, e.g. the thickness of the tin layer on iron in tinplate.

Big Bang Theory The currently favoured theory of the

origin of the universe. According to the theory, the universe originally existed in a state of extreme compression, sometimes called the primordial fireball. About ten billion ($10^{10} = 10,000,000,000$) years ago it exploded in a 'big bang', and since then has been continuously expanding at great speed. This expansion of the universe is observed today in the rapidity with which galaxies (distinct groups of many millions of stars) are flying apart from each other. It is possible that the expansion of the universe will slow down and change to a contraction in the future. The universe would then return to its fireball state. However, recent evidence supports the idea that the universe will continue to expand for ever.

Binary numbers A system of numbers in which the only digits used are 0 and 1. In the familiar decimal system the number 268 can be read as $2 \times 10^2 + 6 \times 10^1 + 8 \times 10^0 = 200 + 60 + 8 = 268$. In the binary system powers of 2 are used instead of powers of 10. Thus $1101 = 1 \times 2^3 + 1 \times 2^2 + 0 \times 2^1 + 1 \times 2^0 = 8 + 4 + 0 + 1 = 13$. The numbers up to 15 are:

1	0001	6	0110	11	1011
2	0010	7	0111	12	1100
3	0011	8	1000	13	1101
4	0100	9	1001	14	1110
5	0101	10	1010	15	1111

Binary numbers are used in digital computers since an electrical circuit can represent a 0 or a 1 depending on whether it is off or on.

Binomial Theorem One of the most important theorems in algebra, leading to many sorts of *series* (q.v.). It states that the expression $1 + x$ raised to the power of n (i.e. $(1 + x)^n$) can be written in the form $(1 + x)^n = 1 + nx + \dfrac{n(n-1)x^2}{1 \cdot 2} + \dfrac{n(n-1)(n-2)x^3}{1 \cdot 2 \cdot 3} + $ etc.

If **n** is a positive integer (i.e. a positive whole number) this expansion is valid for any **x**, and the series ends after **n + 1** terms. If **x** is between -1 and 1, the binomial expansion is valid for all **n** (positive or negative, integer or fraction). In this case the expansion is an infinite series which however adds up to a finite number.

Black hole The term used to describe immensely dense stars with gravitational fields so powerful that no radiation can escape from them.

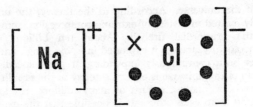

ELECTROVALENT BOND

The sodium, less one electron, is positive. The chlorine with an extra electron is negative.

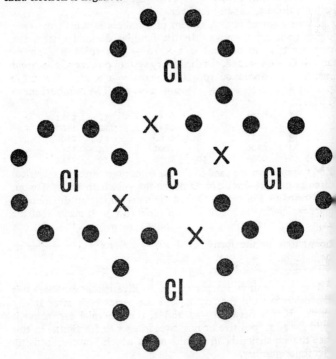

COVALENT BOND

The seven electrons of chlorine are shown as dots, the four electrons of carbon as x's.

Bond The method of binding together of atoms to form molecules. Three types of bond account for most compounds. They are:

(a) Electrovalent bond (ionic, polar);
(b) Covalent bond (non-polar, homopolar);
(c) Dative bond (co-ordinate, semipolar).

The *electrovalent bond* exists in simple compounds where one atom needs an electron and the other gives it. Thus a sodium ion is positively charged when giving an electron and a chlorine ion is negatively charged when it accepts an electron. In solution

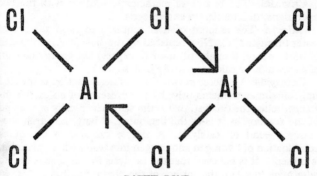

DATIVE BOND

The arrows indicate the giving of electrons by chlorine to alu-minium. These arrowed lines show dative bonds, the ordinary lines covalent bonds.

these ions exist separately, but in the solid the positive binds to the negative in a crystal structure.

The *covalent bond* works differently. It is created by the giving of an electron from each atom in such a way that each shares the pair of electrons thus formed. This accounts for the binding of atoms that are not ionised in solution and atoms that are the same. For example, it is a covalent bond that makes a molecule of hydrogen from two atoms. It is a covalent bond that holds together the two hydrogen atoms and one oxygen atom in a molecule of water.

The *dative bond* also depends on the sharing of a pair of electrons, but in this case one atom supplies both. This bond is that found in many complex compounds in which some of the atoms remain together as a group even when the compound itself is ionised in solution. For example, potassium ferrocyanide ionises in water to form positive potassium ions and negative 'ferrocyanide' ions.

Boyle's Law This states that if a fixed mass of gas is compressed or expanded without change in temperature the product of volume and pressure remains constant. If P is pressure and V is volume the law is usually expressed thus:

$$PV = K \text{ (where } K \text{ is a constant)}$$

Calculus The branch of mathematics dealing with the two operations, differentiation and integration.

Calorie The amount of heat required to raise 1 gram of water through 1° C. Now replaced by the *joule* (q.v.) as the unit of heat energy, though still used to express the energy content of foodstuffs. 1 calorie = 4·187 joules.

Catalysis A process in which a chemical reaction is speeded up, sometimes tremendously, by the presence of an extra substance, called the catalyst, that is the same chemically at the end of the reaction as it is at the beginning. Many industrial processes depend on catalysis. A simple example is the quick combination of hydrogen and oxygen into water where platinum is present. It is believed that the catalysis in this case is due to *adsorption* (q.v.) on the surface of the platinum.

Cation A positively charged atom or *radical* (q.v.).

Cell A source of *electromotive force* (q.v.) caused by chemical action. A primary cell is one that cannot be recharged once its electrolyte or electrodes are used up. A simple primary cell consists of zinc and copper in dilute sulphuric acid. The copper is the positive electrode and the zinc the negative. This is the simple voltaic cell. It is of no use for practical work. A dry cell of the normal type consists of zinc as the negative pole or electrode, in the form of the container, with a jelly of ammonium chloride as the electrolyte and a central carbon rod as the positive pole or electrode. This gives 1·5 V. Many other dry cells have been developed for use in rockets and satellites. A fuel cell is one in which primary fuels or derivatives of them are used. A solar cell is not really chemical. It consists of a special substance that generates electricity when light shines on it.

A secondary cell can be recharged. See ACCUMULATOR.

Centripetal force The force acting on a body constrained to move in a curved path. For a body of mass m travelling in a circle of radius r at velocity v the force is $m \cdot v^2/r$ and directed towards the centre of the circle.

Charles's Law The law that determines the effect of heat on a gas when the pressure is kept constant. It states that the volume of a gas (*any* gas) increases by a certain fixed amount ($\frac{1}{273}$ of its volume at $0°$ C.) for every degree Centigrade rise in temperature. Another way of stating this is to say that if the pressure is constant, the volume of a fixed mass of any gas is directly proportional to its *absolute temperature* (q.v.).

Coefficient In mathematics this means the number that indicates how many of a thing there are. For example, $2x$ means 2 of the thing called x, and 2 is the coefficient of x. In physics and technology the word coefficient is used to indicate a constant value of importance. For example, the coefficient of linear expansion for a material, the coefficient of friction between two chosen substances, etc.

Colloid A material that does not dissolve in a liquid is usually deposited on the bottom if the particles are big enough. If the particles are small enough, however, they remain in suspension though individually invisible, kept up by the random movements of the molecules of solvent. Particles as small as this are said to be colloidal, and the suspension they form is a colloidal solution. The range of size of colloidal particles is between 0·0000001 and 0·00005 cm. (between 1 and 500 nanometres).

Colour The sensation when the eye receives certain wavelengths of light. Ordinary 'white' light consists of electromagnetic radiation of many different wavelengths from about 4,000 Angstroms to about 7,000 Angstroms. If these are spread out as in a spectrum so that only a portion enters the eye at a time, then as the eye moved along the spectrum from the short-wavelength end to the long-wavelength end colour is seen, going from violet to red through a series usually given as seven, namely, violet, indigo, blue, green, yellow, orange, red. These are the colours of the rainbow. Actually this is a very rough-and-ready description. If tiny separate parts of the spectrum are exposed one at a time hundreds of different hues can be seen.

The colours of everyday objects are caused by selective absorption of parts of the spectrum of white light.

Complex Numbers Algebraic expressions such as $x + iy$ where x and y are real, and i is the square root of -1. The real part is x and iy is the imaginary part of the number. In equations involving complex numbers the real and imaginary parts are equated separately, otherwise operations are normal.

Compound A substance that consists of chemical elements bonded together. Examples: the elements sodium and chlorine when combined together chemically make sodium chloride (common salt), a compound.

Conductor An electrical conductor is a material that conducts electricity easily, such as the metals. The best conductor is silver and the next best copper.

Conversion Table

1 cm. = 0·3937 in.	1 yd. = 0·9144018 m.
1 m. = 39·37 in.	1 sq. in. = 6·451626 sq. cm.
1 sq. cm. = 0·1549997 sq. in.	1 sq. yd. = 0·8361307 sq. m.
1 sq. m. = 1·195985 sq. yd.	1 acre = 0·404687 hectare
1 hectare = 2·7104 acres	1 cu. yd. = 0·7645594 cu. m.
1 cu. m. = 1·3079428 cu. yd.	1 gal. = 4·5434 litres
1 litre = 0·22009 gal. or	1 quart = 1·1358 litres
0·88036 quarts	1 bushel = 36·37 litres
1 kg. = 2·204622341 lbs.,	1 lb., Avoirdupois =
Avoirdupois	0·4535924277 kg.
1 in. = 2·54005 cm.	

These figures are very exact. Quick, very rough answers can be obtained by the methods below:

To Turn

Metres into feet multiply by $3\frac{1}{4}$
Feet into metres multiply by 3 and divide by 10
Metres into yards add $\frac{1}{10}$
Yards into metres subtract $\frac{1}{10}$
Kilometres into miles multiply by 5 and divide by 8
Miles into kilometres add $\frac{3}{5}$ of the number of miles
Square metres into square yards add $\frac{1}{5}$
Square yards into square metres subtract $\frac{1}{5}$
Square kilometres into square miles multiply by 2 and divide by 5
Square miles into square kilometres multiply by $2\frac{3}{5}$
Cubic metres into cubic yards add $\frac{1}{3}$
Cubic yards into cubic metres subtract $\frac{1}{4}$
Kilogrammes into pounds (Avoirdupois) add $\frac{1}{10}$ and multiply by 2
Pounds into kilogrammes subtract $\frac{1}{10}$ and divide by 2
Litres into pints add $\frac{3}{4}$
Pints into litres multiply by 3 and divide by 5

Cosine In trigonometry the cosine of an angle (other than the right angle) in a right-angled triangle is the ratio of the side next to the angle to the hypotenuse. Cos 90° = 0, cos 60° = 0·5, cos 45° = 0·707, cos 30° = 0·866. See *trigonometry*.

Cosmic Rays are very energetic charged particles which penetrate the earth's atmosphere from outer space, although their ultimate origin is still uncertain. They consist chiefly of protons with some electrons, alpha-particles and heavier nuclei. Cosmic rays that collide with gas particles in the atmosphere can produce a variety of *elementary particles* (q.v.) which may be detected using equipment carried by balloons, rockets or satellites. Several elementary particles were first discovered in this way.

Cosmology The study of the origin, evolution and structure of the universe, nowadays carried out using satellite-borne X-ray and ultra-violet telescopes as well as earth-bound optical, infra-red and radio telescopes. See *Big Bang Theory*.

Cryogenics The science of producing and maintaining very low temperatures and the study of properties of matter at those temperatures. Modern cryogenics dates from 1908 when helium, the gas with the lowest boiling point at atmospheric pressure (− 269° C), was first liquefied. Since then many remarkable effects have been discovered: e.g. *superconductivity* (q.v.).

Crystallography The science which deals with the regular structure of crystals. Often investigated by *X-rays* (q.v.).

Current Electric current is the rate of flow of electric charge. In a metallic conductor this flow is due to electrons, which drift along between the metal atoms. As electrons are negatively charged, they are going in the opposite direction to the direction of current usually accepted. A current of 1 A is approximately 6 million billion electrons per second.

Decibel See RADIO AND TELEVISION.

RELATIVE DENSITIES OF COMMON SUBSTANCES

Metals			Liquids at 15° C.		
Steel	.	7·6–7·8	Acetone	.	0·79
Brass	.	8·4–8·7	Alcohol	.	0·79
Aluminium	.	2·70	Ether	.	0·74
Copper	.	8·89	Glycerine	.	1·26
Lead	.	11·34	Oil (lubricating)	.	0·9–0·92
Titanium	.	4·5	Turpentine	.	0·87
Mercury	.	13·6	Blood	.	1·04–1·067
			Water at 4° C.	.	1·00

Miscellaneous Solids			*Gases at N.T.P.*	
Celluloid	1·4	Air	0·00129
Glass	2·4–2·8	Argon	0·00178
Ice	0·92	Carbon dioxide	0·00198
Paraffin Wax	0·9	Helium	0·000179
Brick	2·1	Hydrogen	0·00009
Coal (soft)	1·3	Methane	0·000717
Diamond	3·5	Oxygen	0·00143
Rubber	0·97–0·99		
Balsa wood	0·12–0·2		
Ebony	1·19		
Lignum vitae	1·25		
Oak	0·74		
Boxwood	0·93		
Cork	0·24		

Density The mass per unit volume of a substance. It can be expressed in kilograms/cubic metre, tons/cubic yard, pounds/cubic foot, etc. The density of a substance varies with temperature. Often the *relative density* or *specific gravity* is used. This is the ratio of the density of a substance to that of water at 4° C. and is therefore simply a number. The density of water at 4° C. is 1000 kg./m^3 or 1 gm./c.c. The two densest substances are osmium and iridium.

Deoxyribonucleic acid (DNA) The molecule found in the nucleus of nearly all living cells which carries the genetic code responsible for determining the organism's structure. See *proteins*.

Digital computer Any device which performs calculations on numbers represented digitally.

Direct Current (D.C.) A current passing in the same direction all the time round a circuit. It can vary in size, but not in direction.

Dispersion The name given to the splitting-up of light into the spectrum by a prism or lens.

Dissociation The reversible splitting-up of a chemical compound into parts. *Thermal dissociation* may occur when a compound is heated: e.g. ammonium chloride dissociates into the gases ammonia and hydrogen chloride on heating. *Electrolytic dissociation* into charged ions may occur when a compound is dissolved in water: e.g. hydrogen chloride gas dissolves in water to give hydrochloric acid which is dissociated into positive hydrogen ions and negative chloride ions.

Dyne See FORCE and NEWTON.

Electrode The name given to the part by means of which electricity is led into or away from a gas or liquid. The negative electrode is the cathode and the positive one the anode.

Electrolyte A compound which, when molten or dissolved in solution, *dissociates* (q.v.) into oppositely charged *ions* (q.v.) and can thus carry an electric current.

Compounds formed by electrovalent *bonds* (q.v.), such as *salts* (q.v.), are commonly electrolytes. For example, sodium chloride consists of distinct Na^+ and Cl^- ions, but when solid the ions are held rigidly together in a crystal structure which does not conduct electricity. When molten or dissolved in water, the ions are not held together so strongly and are able to move under the influence of an electric potential. Thus an electrolyte can conduct electricity (see *electrolysis*).

Electrolysis The movement of ions to form an electric current in an electrolyte, usually as the result of an applied electric potential. Negative ions move towards the anode and positive ions towards the cathode. As a result, gases may be liberated or metal deposited. When metal is deposited on the cathode the process is called electroplating.

Electron Elementary particle with small mass and unit negative electric charge. Electrons orbit the nucleus of an atom much as the planets orbit the sun.

Electromagnetic Waves Waves that consist of varying electrical and magnetic quantities travelling along at the speed of light. Light, radio waves, X-rays, gamma rays, are all electro-magnetic radiation. (See RADIO AND TELEVISION.)

Electromotive Force (e.m.f.) The electrical pressure developed by a cell, battery or generator which enables them to produce an electric current in a circuit. Measured in volts.

Elements The chemical units of which compounds are made. There are 92 naturally occurring chemical elements, though some have never been prepared, and a number have been made artificially (transuranic elements) to extend the list to 103 or more.

THE ELEMENTS

Atomic number	Name	Symbol	Atomic weight	Relative densities (gases at N.T.P.)
1	Hydrogen	H	1·008	0·0000899
2	Helium	He	4·003	0·0001785
3	Lithium	Li	6·939	0·534
4	Beryllium	Be	9·012	1·85
5	Boron	B	10·811	2·34
6	Carbon	C	12·011	Diamond 3·52 { Graphite 2·25 Amorphous 0·5–1·0
7	Nitrogen	N	14·007	0·0012506
8	Oxygen	O	15·999	0·0014290
9	Fluorine	F	18·998	0·0016970
10	Neon	Ne	20·183	0·008999
11	Sodium	Na	22·990	0·97
12	Magnesium	Mg	24·312	1·75
13	Aluminium	Al	26·982	2·70
14	Silicon	Si	28·086	2·33
15	Phosphorus	P	30·974	{ Yellow 1·82 Red 2·20
16	Sulphur	S	32·064	{ Monoclinic 1·96 Rhombic 2·07
17	Chlorine	Cl	35·453	0·00321
18	Argon	A	39·948	0·0017837
19	Potassium	K	39·102	0·862
20	Calcium	Ca	40·08	1·55
21	Scandium	Sc	44·956	3·0
22	Titanium	Ti	47·90	4·54
23	Vanadium	V	50·94	6·11
24	Chromium	Cr	52·00	7·18
25	Manganese	Mn	54·94	7·21
26	Iron	Fe	55·85	7·87
27	Cobalt	Co	58·93	8·9
28	Nickel	Ni	58·71	8·9
29	Copper	Cu	63·54	8·95
30	Zinc	Zn	65·37	7·14
31	Gallium	Ga	69·72	5·90
32	Germanium	Ge	72·59	5·32
33	Arsenic	As	74·92	5·73
34	Selenium	Se	78·96	{ Red 4·45 Grey 4·80
35	Bromine	Br	79·909	3·12
36	Krypton	Kr	83·80	0·003733
37	Rubidium	Rb	85·47	1·53
38	Strontium	Sr	87·62	2·55
39	Yttrium	Y	88·905	4·46
40	Zirconium	Zr	91·22	6·5
41	Niobium	Nb	92·906	8·57
42	Molybdenum	Mo	95 94	10·2

Atomic number	Name	Symbol	Atomic weight	Relative densities (gases at N.T.P.)
43	Technetium	Tc	99	—
44	Ruthenium	Ru	101·07	12·2
45	Rhodium	Rh	102·91	12·4
46	Palladium	Pd	106·4	12·0
47	Silver	Ag	107·87	10·5
48	Cadmium	Cd	112·40	8·65
49	Indium	In	114·82	7·31
50	Tin	Sn	118·69	7·31
51	Antimony	Sb	121·75	6·69
52	Tellurium	Te	127·60	6·25
53	Iodine	I	126·904	4·94
54	Xenon	Xe	131·30	0·005887
55	Caesium	Cs	132·905	1·90
56	Barium	Ba	137·34	3·5
57	Lanthanum	La	138·91	6·15
58	Cerium	Ce	140·12	6·77
59	Praseodymium	Pr	140·907	6·77
60	Neodymium	Nd	144·24	7·00
61	Prometheum	Pm	147	—
62	Samarium	Sm	150·35	7·54
63	Europium	Eu	151·96	5·25
64	Gadolinium	Gd	157·25	7·90
65	Terbium	Tb	158·92	8·23
66	Dysprosium	Dy	162·50	8·54
67	Holnium	Ho	164·93	8·78
68	Erbium	Er	167·26	9·05
69	Thulium	Tm	168·93	9·31
70	Ytterbium	Yb	173·04	6·97
71	Lutecium	Lu	174·97	9·84
72	Hafmium	Hf	178·49	13·3
73	Tantalum	Ta	180·95	16·6
74	Wolfram	W	183·85	19·3
75	Rhenium	Re	186·2	21·0
76	Osmium	Os	190·2	22·5
77	Iridium	Ir	192·2	22·4
78	Platinum	Pt	195·09	21·4
79	Gold	Au	196·97	19·3
80	Mercury	Hg	200·59	13·55
81	Thallium	Tl	204·37	11·85
82	Lead	Pb	207·19	11·34
83	Bismuth	Bi	208·98	9·75
84	Polonium	Po	210	9·32
85	Astatine	At	211	—
86	Radon	Rn	222	0·009725
87	Francium	Fr	223	—
88	Radium	Ra	226·05	5·0
89	Actinium	Ac	227·05	—
90	Thorium	Th	232·12	11·7
91	Protactinium	Pa	231·05	15·37

Atomic number	Name	Symbol	Atomic weight	Relative densities (gases at N.T.P.)
92	Uranium	U	238·07	18·95
93 *	Neptunium	Np	237	20·25
94 *	Plutonium	Pu	239	19·84
95 *	Americium	Am	241	13·67
96 *	Curium	Cm	242	—
97 *	Berkelium	Bk	243–250	—
98 *	Californium	Cf	251	—
99 *	Einsteinium	Es	246, 247, 249, 251–256	—
100 *	Fermium	Fm	250, 252–256	—
101 *	Mendelevium	Md	256	—
102 *	Nobelium	No	254	—
103 *	Lawrencium	Lr	257	—
104 *	Kurchatovium(?)	Ku	—	—
105 *	Hahnium(?)	—	—	—

* These are called transuranic elements. They have all been artificially created, often in negligibly small amounts, by means of nuclear
reactors or machines such as cyclotrons.

Elementary Particle Electrons, protons and neutrons are
the familiar elementary particles that make up atoms and nuclei.
However, many other particles smaller than atoms are now
known to exist, though high energy *particle accelerators* (q.v.) are
usually needed to create them. Many of these fundamental or
elementary particles are very short-lived and decay into more
stable particles or gamma rays in a minute fraction of a second.
Examples of these elementary particles are the *neutrino* (a
particle with no mass and no charge), the π-*mesons* (which help
to explain how the protons and neutrons in a nucleus stay
together) and heavier particles like the Σ (*sigma*) and the Ω^-
(*omega minus*). The list of elementary particles keeps growing,
and surprises keep appearing. In 1974 two new particles (called
psi particles) were discovered which lived a thousand times
longer than any theory expected that they should.

Energy The capacity of a body or substance for doing work.
It can exist in a number of forms e.g. mechanical, potential, heat,
chemical, electrical, radiant and nuclear energy. The law of
conservation of energy states that energy is never lost or gained
but only changes from one form to another.

In driving a car to the top of a hill, work is done against the
force of gravity and the car gains *potential* energy. This is converted into *kinetic* energy of motion as the car freewheels down
the hill. Friction at the moving parts causes wastage of energy a

heat energy and the car would slow down without the engine which converts *chemical* energy stored in the petrol into kinetic energy.

Einstein showed that matter is a form of energy. In nuclear fission and fusion, matter is converted into energy according to the formula $E = m \cdot c^2$ (m = mass, c = speed of light). This is the origin of the energy released in nuclear bombs and in the sun. The sun's energy reaches the earth in the form of *radiant* energy (heat and light rays).

All forms of energy are now measured in *joules* (q.v.). Calories were formally used to measure heat energy. The c.g.s. unit of energy is the *erg* = 10^{-7} joules.

Useful formulae:

Kinetic energy = $m \cdot v^2/2$ (m = mass of body, v = velocity of body).

Change in potential energy = $m \cdot g \cdot h$ (m = mass, g = gravitational acceleration, h = change in vertical height).

Electrical energy = $V \cdot I \cdot t$ (V = voltage, I = current, t = time).

Change in heat content = $m \cdot s \cdot (T_2 - T_1)$ (m = mass, s = specific heat, T_2 = final temperature, T_1 = initial temperature).

Equivalent Weight The equivalent weight of an element is the number of units by weight of it that will combine with, or displace, 1 unit of hydrogen or 8 units of oxygen. It is therefore equal to the atomic weight divided by the valency. The equivalent weight of an acid is the weight of acid containing unit weight of replaceable hydrogen (see acid), and that of a base is the the weight of base required to neutralise the equivalent weight of an acid.

Erg See ENERGY.

Expansion Most substances expand on being heated, and each has its own capacity for such expansion. The coefficient of linear expansion is the figure that is used for finding how much a substance expands in one direction

$$l_2 = l_1 (1 + \alpha t)$$

Where l_1 is the length at the first temperature, t is the rise in temperature in degrees Centigrade, α is the coefficient of linear expansion and l_2 is the length at the second temperature.

A similar relationship exists for volume expansion. If $V_1 = $

volume at first temperature, $t =$ rise in temperature in degrees Centigrade, β is the coefficient of cubical expansion and $V_2 =$ the volume at the second temperature

$$V_2 = V_1 (1 + \beta t)$$

For solids $\beta = 3\alpha$ approximately.

Factorial The factorial of a positive whole number n is the product $n \times (n-1) \times (n-2) \times \ldots \times 2 \times 1$ and is written $n!$. E.g. $4! = 4 \times 3 \times 2 \times 1 = 24$.

Fission The splitting of a thing into two more or less equal parts. In nuclear fission, the nucleus of an atom splits into two parts accompanied by the release of nuclear energy and one or more neutrons. Fission may occur spontaneously or by the nucleus being hit by a neutron, but only occurs readily in certain *fissile* materials such as uranium 235 and plutonium 239. It is possible that the neutrons released during fission can hit other nuclei and bring about further fission. This process can be repeated and result in a runaway *chain reaction* with an enormous build up of energy. However, a chain reaction can only occur if the amount of fissile material is above a *critical size*, so that the number of neutrons continues to rise despite some escaping and some hitting nuclei without causing fission. Atomic bomb explosions are uncontrolled chain reactions of this kind. But nuclear fission can be controlled in *nuclear reactors* (q.v.) and used as a source of energy.

Fluorescence The property of some substances to absorb light of one wavelength and emit light of a longer wavelength: e.g. fluorescein, an organic compound whose solution in alkalis glows bright green due to fluorescence. In fluorescent lighting tubes, the electric current causes mercury vapour to emit ultra-violet light, which then excites fluorescent substances on the sides of the tube to emit visible light. Unlike *phosphorescence* (q.v.), fluorescence stops as soon as the original illumination stops.

Force That which makes a body change its state of rest or uniform motion in a straight line. Units are the newton (S.I. system), the dyne (c.g.s. system) and the poundal (f.p.s. system). Force (p), mass (m) and acceleration (f) are related by the equation $p = mf$ (Newton's second law of motion).

Formulae (not dealt with under separate entries, see AREA, VOLUME, BINOMIAL THEOREM, etc.).

Circumference of circle $= 2\pi r$ (or πd).

Mechanics
Falling bodies

Where g = gravity = $9 \cdot 8$ (in m. per sec. per sec.); u = initial velocity (in m. per sec.); v = final velocity (in m. per sec.); h = height (in m.); t = time (in sec.).

$$v = u + gt$$
$$h = \frac{u + v}{2} t$$
$$h = ut + \tfrac{1}{2} gt^2$$
$$g = \frac{v - u}{t}$$
$$2\,gh = v^2 - u^2$$

Time of swing of pendulum : $t = 2\pi \sqrt{\dfrac{l}{g}}$ where t = time of complete swing (once in each direction) (in sec.); l = length of pendulum (in m.); g = gravity.

Useful Factors

$$(a + b)^2 = a^2 + 2ab + b^2$$
$$(a - b)^2 = a^2 - 2ab + b^2$$
$$a^2 - b^2 = (a + b)(a - b)$$
$$a^3 + b^3 = (a + b)(a^2 - ab + b^2)$$
$$a^3 - b^3 = (a - b)(a^2 + ab + b^2)$$
$$x^4 + x^2 y^2 + y^4 = (x^2 + xy + y^2)(x^2 - xy + y^2)$$
$$a^3 + b^3 + c^3 - 3abc =$$
$$(a + b + c)(a^2 + b^2 + c^2 - ab - bc - ca)$$
$$a^2(b - c) + b^2(c - a) + c^2(a - b) =$$
$$-(a - b)(b - c)(c - a)$$
$$bc(b - c) + ca(c - a) + ab(a - b) =$$
$$-(a - b)(b - c)(c - a)$$
$$a(b^2 - c^2) + b(c^2 - a^2) + c(a^2 - b^2) =$$
$$(a - b)(b - c)(c - a)$$

Quadratic Equation

$$ax^2 + bx + c = 0. \quad \text{Solution:}$$
$$\frac{-b \pm \sqrt{b^2 - 4ac}}{2a}$$

Geometrical Progression

pth term $= ar^{p-1}$

Sum to n terms $= a\dfrac{r^n - 1}{r - 1}$ or $a\dfrac{1 - r^n}{1 - r}$

Sum to infinity when $-1 < r < 1 = \dfrac{a}{1 - r}$

Arithmetical Progression

Last term $= a + (n - 1)d$

Sum to n terms $= \dfrac{n}{2}[2a + (n - 1)d]$

Friction The force that resists the movement of one surface over another. It results from the fusing together of high points of contact between the surfaces. To overcome the fusion, force must be used. If F is the frictional force resisting the motion of one body over another and N is the normal force acting between the two bodies, then the coefficient of friction (μ) is given by F/N. Frictional forces always act to slow down a moving body by causing kinetic energy to be dissipated as heat. In many machines this is undesirable as it represents a waste of useful energy and also the heat produced may damage the surfaces in contact. To reduce friction between moving parts, lubricants are used as well as ball- and roller-bearings. Friction can however be extremely useful as in belt drives and brakes. The study of surfaces in contact and lubrication is known as *tribology*.

Fusion (i) The melting of a solid substance (used, for instance in the term 'latent heat of fusion').

(ii) *Nuclear fusion* is the joining together of the nuclei of two atoms to form a single heavier nucleus. Fusion occurs most readily between nuclei of the lighter elements (e.g. the isotopes of hydrogen—deuterium and tritium) but still requires exceedingly high temperatures (hundreds of millions of degrees before it can proceed. Fusion reactions are accompanied by vast release of energy and this is thought to be the source of the energy of the sun and other stars. On earth, uncontrolled fusion reactions occur in hydrogen bombs, but there is much current interest in the problem of controlling nuclear fusion and using it as a source of energy.

Gamma Radiation (**Gamma Rays**, γ-**Rays**) Radiation of the same nature as X-rays and light, i.e. electromagnetic radiation, but of much shorter wavelengths. It is emitted by some radioactive substances, e.g. cobalt 60, and is the most penetrating of all radiation.

Gas Laws The combination of *Boyle's Law* (q.v.) and *Charles's Law* (q.v.) into one equation:

$$PV = nRT$$

where P = pressure; V = volume; T = absolute temperature; R = gas constant = 8·314 joules per degree per mole; n = no. of *moles* (q.v.).

Gram–Atom The weight in grams equivalent to the *atomic weight* (q.v.). For example, the atomic weight of oxygen is 16, so a gram-atom of oxygen is 16 grams.

Gram-equivalent The weight in grams of a substance equal to the *equivalent weight* (q.v.).

Gram-molecule The weight in grams equal to the molecular weight of an element or compound. For example, the molecular weight of H_2SO_4 is 98, so a gram-molecule of H_2SO_4 is 98 gm.

Gravity Every object attracts every other object with a force directly proportional to the product of the masses of the objects and inversely as the square of the distance between them. If m_1 is the mass of one object, m_2 the mass of the other, d the distance between them, then the gravitational force $F = \dfrac{Gm_1m_2}{d^2}$, where G is a constant. G = 6·67 ... 10^{-11} Nm²kg⁻².

For objects on or near the earth, the mass of the earth is very much greater than an object, and so the gravitational force between them makes the object 'fall' towards the earth. The acceleration as it does this is called the acceleration due to gravity. At the Earth's surface this is 9·8 m. per sec. per sec. in the S.I. system and 32 ft. per sec. per sec. in the f.p.s. system.

Half-life The time for half the nuclei in a sample of radioactive material to decay. This ranges from a fraction of a second for some man-made radioisotopes to 4,510 million years for Uranium 238. (See ISOTOPE.)

Heat Energy possessed by a substance in the form of random motions of the atoms which make up the substance. In a red-hot piece of iron the atoms are vibrating back and forth very fast, and so the iron contains more heat than when it is cold and the atoms are moving much less fast. However, heat must not be confused with *temperature* (q.v.). The adding of heat to a substance usually causes a rise in temperature but the amount of this rise depends on the mass and *specific heat* (q.v.) of the substance. Adding heat to a substance may cause a *change of state* (e.g. a solid melting to a liquid) without a change in temperature (see *latent heat*). Measured in *joules* (q.v.).

Heavy water Water in which the hydrogen is replaced by the *isotope* (q.v.) deuterium and hence written as D_2O rather than H_2O. The nucleus of ordinary hydrogen is simply one proton, while that of deuterium is one proton and one neutron.

Hologram A photograph taken with the light from a laser which, when even a small part of it is illumined by laser light, reconstitutes the entire picture. The discovery of Professor Denis Gabor of Imperial College, London, for which he was awarded the 1971 Nobel prize for Physics.

Indicator A substance added in small quantities to a chemical reaction which shows when the reaction is complete by a sudden change of colour. The most familiar indicators change colour depending on whether a solution is acidic or alkaline: e.g. litmus is red in acids but blue in alkalis, and phenolphthalein is colourless in acids but purple in alkalis.

Infra-red Light *Electromagnetic waves* (q.v.) with wavelengths longer than those of visible light and in the range 7,500–100,000 Angstroms, or 0·75–10 micrometres. Infra-red radiation is invisible to the eye but has a heating effect and can be detected at great distances by modern crystal detectors. Every warm body emits infra-red radiation.

Insulator A material, such as glass, rubber, porcelain, plastics, that has no free electrons, and so will not allow electric current to pass when an e.m.f. is applied.

Interferometer A device in which the phenomenon of interference of light or radio waves is used as a tool in astronomy, metrology and spectroscopy.

Ionisation The process by which mobile *ions* (q.v.) are produced from atoms and molecules. This can occur when *electrolytes* (q.v.) become molten or dissolve to form solutions, or when gases are subjected to electrical discharges and become *plasmas* (q.v.).

Ion An atom or group of atoms that is electrically charged due to an excess or deficiency of electrons. Negatively charged ions are called *anions*; positive ions are called *cations*.

Isotope One of two or more forms of the same chemical

element, differing from other isotopes only in atomic weight. The difference is due entirely to the addition or subtraction of neutrons from the nucleus. Examples: The hydrogen atom has one proton and one planetary electron. Add a neutron to the nucleus and it becomes twice as heavy. It is heavy hydrogen or deuterium. Add another neutron and it becomes tritium, three times as heavy as the normal hydrogen. All three isotopes are hydrogen so far as the chemistry is concerned. Many elements have several stable isotopes (tin has ten). It is customary to give the mass number of an isotope after the name in order to indicate which isotope is present, e.g. uranium 238, uranium 235, plutonium 239, etc.

Every element can be made to have radioactive isotopes, called *radioisotopes*. Many of these are used in science and industry because they emit radiation (alpha, beta or gamma). A few elements have naturally occurring radioisotopes. Tritium is a radioisotope of hydrogen. See *half-life*.

FAMILIAR RADIOISOTOPES

Name	Type of radiation	Half-life
Carbon 14	beta	5,600 years
Phosphorus 32	beta	14·3 days
Cobalt 60	beta, gamma	5·3 years
Strontium 90	beta	28 years
Iodine 131	beta, gamma	8 days
Caesium 137	beta, gamma	30 years
Radium 226	alpha, gamma	1,620 years
Uranium 235	alpha	710 million years
Uranium 238	alpha	4,510 million years
Plutonium 239	alpha	24,400 years

Joule The S.I. unit of energy or work. It is the work done when 1 newton acts through 1 metre. Replaces the calorie as the unit of heat energy. 1 joule = 0·239 calories.

Laser A device for producing an intense, narrow beam of light, in which all the waves are in step. The atoms of some gases, if electrically excited, can be persuaded by a 'trigger' pulse of light of a certain wavelength to emit more light of the same wavelength. If such a gas is put into a tube with accurately parallel mirrors at each end, and triggered, the light waves will run up and down, getting stronger as they pass over and re-trigger the atoms of the gas. If some of the light is allowed to escape at one end it emerges in such a narrow beam that a laser can shine a spot only a mile or so across on the moon, and so intense it can burn through steel. An even more interesting possibility is the use of the laser in communications. Since a beam of light has an enormously higher frequency than the shortest radio wave, and since the amount of information a beam can carry is proportional to its frequency, a light beam, if it can be *modulated* (See RADIO AND TELEVISION: modulation), should be able to carry as many as a thousand television channels. (See Aircraft, Rockets and Missiles: SATELLITES, Communications.)

Latent heat The latent heat of fusion (vaporisation) is the amount of heat required to turn unit mass of a solid (liquid) into liquid (gas) at the same temperature. The latent heat of fusion of ice is 335 joules per gram; the latent heat of vaporisation of water is 2257 joules per gram.

Lens A piece of transparent material, usually glass, shaped and polished to have curved surfaces. The commonest are a double-convex lens and a double-concave lens. Every combination of two of the following surfaces is possible: convex, concave, plane.

A single lens like this is known as a thin lens, and simplified approximate formulae can be used. The principal focus is then the point where parallel rays parallel to the axis come to a point. The distance from the centre of the lens to the point image is called the focal length.

Lens are of two sorts whatever their surfaces. One sort makes rays of light *converge* when they pass through the lens; the other sort makes rays of light *diverge*.

The focal length of a convergent lens can be found very simply by getting an image of a distant object and the distance from lens to image is then the focal length.

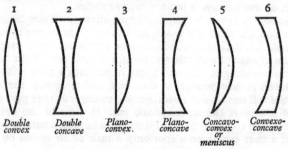

| 1 | 2 | 3 | 4 | 5 | 6 |

Double convex   Double concave   Plano-convex.   Plano-concave   Concavo-convex or meniscus   Convexo-concave

1, 3 and 5 are convergent; 2, 4 and 6 are divergent

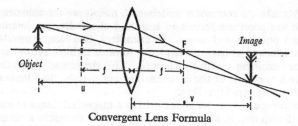

Convergent Lens Formula

The equation of a simple lens, where u = distance of object from centre of lens, v = distance of image from centre, f = focal length, and distances are considered positive when measured *against* the direction the light is travelling, is:

$$\frac{1}{v} - \frac{1}{u} = \frac{1}{f}$$

All measurements are positive when taken from lens to a *real* image or object.

Light Radiation that affects our eyes and we 'see'. It is electromagnetic, and the wavelengths of visible light extend from about 4,000 Angstroms (blue) to about 7,000 Angstroms (red). It is customary to speak of all electromagnetic radiation of near wave-lengths to these as 'light', even though it causes no sensation on the eye.

Magnifying Power The magnifying power of a single convex used with the eye as a magnifying glass equals 1 plus $\frac{25}{f}$, where f equals focal length in centimetres.

The magnifying power of an astronomical telescope or a Galileo-type telescope is the focal length of the objective divided by the focal length of the eyepiece.

Mass The mass of a body is proportional to the amount of matter in it. It is *not* the same as *weight* (q.v.), because $W = M \cdot g$ where g = acceleration due to gravity.

Mathematical Signs

Is equal to	=	Is approximately equal to	≑
Is not equal to	≠	Is identical to	≡
The difference between	∼	The sum of	Σ
Greater than	>	Varies as	∝
Not greater than	≯	Angle	∧
Less than	<	Infinity	∞
Not less than	≮		

Metals As commonly understood, metals are the substances that are good conductors of heat and electricity, are lustrous when polished and so on. In chemistry, however, a metal is characterised as having a tendency towards losing electrons and thus becoming positively charged. This definition means that only a very few of the elements are not metals. See Periodic Table on pages D34–D35.

Microscope A device for getting a magnified image of very small objects. A single magnifying glass is therefore a simple microscope.

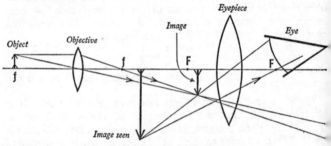

Geometrical Diagram of Microscope

A compound microscope consists of two lenses, one of short focal length, the objective, one of long focal length, the eyepiece. The object is placed in the plane of the principal focus.

The magnifying power is found by multiplying the power of the objective by that of the eyepiece. The power of the objective is the *optical tube length* divided by the focal length of the objective. The optical tube length is taken for modern microscopes as being 18 cm. So if, for example, the focal length of an objective is 0·5 cm., then the magnifying power is 36. An eyepiece with a magnification of 3 will then give a total magnification of 108.

The eyepiece and objective are complex lenses, not simple ones, in order to correct for the various errors that a simple lens inflicts on the image, errors that become more and more important as the magnification is increased.

Microscope, Electron A microscope which substitutes beams of electrons for beams of light to form a very greatly magnified image of an object. Electron microscopes are no available which are able to photograph living organisms, and to provide three-dimensional photographs.

Mole The amount of substance that contains as many elementary units as there are in 0·012 kg. of carbon 12. The number of such units is *Avogadro's number* = 6·023 × 10²³.

Molecule The smallest unit of a chemical compound to retain its identity. If split up, the results are the atoms of elements of which it is compounded. A single element can exist in molecular form. For example, hydrogen can be atomic or molecular. In the latter case two atoms of hydrogen are combined into a molecule.

Momentum The product of a body's mass and velocity.

Neutron One of the fundamental particles of nature. Its mass is slightly greater than that of a proton, but the neutron carries no electrical charge. Because of this it is not acted on by the electrical forces in an atom, and so can penetrate more easily. A neutron is therefore a good nuclear projectile. It is the causing agent in nuclear *fission* (q.v.). Neutrons are produced in immense numbers in a *nuclear reactor* (q.v.).

Newton (N) The S.I. unit of force. It is the force that would give a mass of 1 kg. an acceleration of 1 metre per second per second. The force of gravity on a mass of 1 kg. is 9·8N. Replaces the dyne as the unit of force. 1 N = 10⁵ dynes.

Normal Solution A solution of which 1 litre (1,000 c.c.) contains one *gram-equivalent* (q.v.) of a substance. Indicated by *N*, e.g. *N*-hydrochloric acid means normal hydrochloric acid solution in water. Used for quantitative analysis. A more dilute solution is one-tenth normal, shown by *N*/10.

Normal Temperature and Pressure (N.T.P.) Normal temperature is taken as 0° C., normal pressure as 76 cm. of mercury. These together give a standard set of conditions for comparing the behaviour of gases.

Nuclear Reactor An apparatus in which a nuclear fuel undergoes *fission* (q.v.) under controlled conditions. The essential parts of a nuclear reactor are: (a) the fuel, which is usually in the form of rods and may be plutonium, natural uranium or enriched uranium (uranium in which the proportion of fissile U-235 to non-fissile U-238 has been made higher than in natural uranium), (b) the *moderator*, which is placed between the fuel rods with the purpose of slowing down the fast neutrons produced during fission so that they produce further fission more readily (moderators commonly used are graphite or *heavy water* (q.v.)), (c) *control rods* (often of cadmium which absorb neutrons and slow down the rate of fission thus preventing a runaway chain reaction, (d) the *coolant*, which is a fluid (such as carbon dioxide gas or liquid sodium) that is pumped in pipes through the reactor core to remove the vast quantities of heat generated during fission (this heat may be used to generate electricity), (e) a very thick shield of concrete, steel and water to prevent dangerous radiation from escaping from the core. The *fast breeder reactor* is a reactor which 'breeds' more nuclear fuel at the same time as producing energy by fission. This is possible because a fast neutron produced by fission can be absorbed by a non-fissile U-238 nucleus giving a U-239 nucleus which then decays radioactively into fissile plutonium. The reactor at Dounreay, Scotland is of this type. Nuclear reactors will be a very important source of electricity in the future but an outstanding problem is what to do with the dangerous radioactive waste products.

Nucleus Means the centre part of anything. Used chiefly to mean the heavy centre part of an atom. Every atomic nucleus consists of protons and neutrons, with the exception of ordinary hydrogen, the nucleus of which is one proton. Examples: oxygen, 8 protons 8 neutrons; iron, 26 protons 30 neutrons; radium, 88 protons 138 neutrons.

Ohm (Ω) The S.I. unit of electrical resistance. It is defined by means of *Ohm's Law* (q.v.) i.e. if a conductor carries a current of I amps when the potential difference across it is V volts, then the resistance of the conductor is V/I ohms.

Ohm's Law This states that the current through a conductor is directly proportional to the potential difference across the conductor and inversely proportional to its resistance. Discovered by the German physicist, Georg Ohm, in 1827. See DICTIONARY OF RADIO AND TELEVISION.

Ozone (O_3) is a form of oxygen whose molecules consist of three atoms of oxygen instead of the usual two. It can be obtained by passing an electrical discharge through ordinary oxygen. Ozone occurs in large quantities in the ozone layer of the upper atmosphere, between heights of about 15 and 40 kilometres above the earth. Here it plays a vital role in absorbing a large proportion of the sun's *ultra-violet radiation* (q.v.) which would otherwise be damaging to life on the earth's surface.

Particle Accelerator A machine which accelerates *elementary particles* (q.v.) near to the speed of light by means of electric and magnetic fields. The resulting beams of high energy particles are allowed to hit stationary atomic targets or to meet other beams of particles head on. By observing the products of such collisions, much is learnt about elementary particles and the atomic nucleus.

Periodic Table A table grouping the elements so that certain chemical and physical properties are repeated at regular intervals. It is arranged in horizontal *periods* and vertical *groups*. Elements in one group have similar physical and chemical properties, e.g. fluorine, chlorine, bromine, iodine, all in sub-group *b* of group VII and called the *halogens*. See pages D34 to D35.

Phosphorescence Light emitted by some substances without heating, some as the result of irradiation with ultra-violet light or other light, some as the result of chemical action, e.g. phosphorescent organisms in sea-water and creatures like fireflies and glow-worms. See FLUORESCENCE.

Plasma A highly-ionised gas i.e. a gas consisting of charged particles, usually electrons and positive ions. It is the state of matter in which most of the universe exists. In extremely high temperature plasmas (as in the interiors of stars) nuclear *fusion* (q.v.) can occur. Plasma physics is therefore of great importance in the attempt to use controlled nuclear fusion as a source of energy.

Polymer A compound consisting of a chain of repeated molecular units. It is formed from the individual *monomer* units by the process of polymerisation. Natural polymers include rubber and *proteins* (q.v.), while synthetic polymers include many plastics (e.g. polythene) and artificial fibres (e.g. nylon).

Power The rate of doing work or using energy. The S.I. unit is the *watt*, equal to 1 joule per second. In electrical circuits the power in watts is found by multiplying the volts by the amperes. The horse-power was formally used in mechanics. 1 horse-power = 746 watts.

CONVERSION TABLE OF PRESSURES

Cm. of Hg	In. of Hg	Millibars	Kg./sq. m.	Lb./sq. in.
71·2	28	942	9,650	13·74
73·7	29	976	9,970	14·2
75·5	29·7	1,000	10,220	14·55
76·2	30	1,019	10,400	14·8
78·7	31	1,052	10,750	15·3

Group →	IA	IIA	IIIB	IVB	VB	VIB	VIIB	←
Period ↓	Alkali metals	Alka-line earth metals	← ——Transition metals——					→
1	1 ● H* 1.008							
2	3 Li 6.939	4 Be 9.012						
3	11 Na 22.990	12 Mg 24.312						
4	19 K 39.102	20 Ca 40.08	21 Sc 44.956	22 Ti 47.90	23 V 50.94	24 Cr 52.00	25 Mn 54.94	26 Fe 55.8
5	37 Rb 85.47	38 Sr 87.62	39 Y 88.905	40 Zr 91.22	41 Nb 92.906	42 Mo 95.94	43 Tc 99	44 Ru 101.
6	55 Cs 132.905	56 Ba 137.34	57 La** 138.91	72 Hf 178.49	73 Ta 180.95	74 W 183.85	75 Re 186.2	76 O. 190
7	87 Fr 223	88 Ra 226.05	89 Ac† 227.05					

◣	Metals
◉	Semiconductors
◉	Non-metals

** Lanthanides (rare earth me

58	59	60	61
Ce	Pr	Nd	P
140.12	140.907	144.24	1

† Actinides

90	91	92	93
Th	Pa	U	N
232.12	231.05	238.07	2

(showing atomic weights)

←VIII→			IB	IIB	IIIA	IVA	VA	VIA	VIIA	O
			Noble metals						Halo-gens	Inert gases
										2 He 4.003
					5 B 10.811	6 C 12.011	7 N 14.007	8 O 15.999	9 F 18.998	10 Ne 20.183
					13 Al 26.982	14 Si 28.086	15 P 30.974	16 S 32.064	17 Cl 35.453	18 Ar 39.948
28		29	30	31	32	33	34	35	36	
Ni		Cu	Zn	Ga	Ge	As	Se	Br	Kr	
58.71		63.54	65.37	69.72	72.59	74.92	78.96	79.909	83.80	

	28	29	30	31	32	33	34	35	36
Co	Ni	Cu	Zn	Ga	Ge	As	Se	Br	Kr
.93	58.71	63.54	65.37	69.72	72.59	74.92	78.96	79.909	83.80
	46	47	48	49	50	51	52	53	54
h	Pd	Ag	Cd	In	Sn	Sb	Te	I	Xe
.91	106.4	107.87	112.40	114.82	118.69	121.75	127.60	126.904	131.30
	78	79	80	81	82	83	84	85	86
	Pt	Au	Hg	Tl	Pb	Bi	Po	At	Ce
2.2	195.09	196.97	200.59	204.37	207.19	208.98	210	211	222

*Hydrogen is sometimes placed above fluorine at the head of group VIIA. It is not included in the alkali metals.

	63	64	65	66	67	68	69	70	71
n	Eu	Gd	Tb	Dy	Ho	Er	Tm	Yb	Lu
35	151.96	157.25	158.92	162.50	164.93	167.26	168.93	173.04	174.97

	95	96	97	98	99	100	101	102	103
a	Am	Cm	Bk	Cf	Es	Fm	Md	No	Lr,
9	241	242	247	251	254	253	256	254	257

Pressure The force or weight per unit area acting on a surface. Measured in newtons per square metre (S.I. units), kilograms per sq. m. or pounds per sq. in. etc. Atmospheric pressure, that is the weight of air in a column of unit cross-sectional area up to the top of the earth's atmosphere, is roughly 15 lb. per sq. in. Pressure in gases is also expressed as the height of mercury (or other liquid) that the gas will support. A pressure of 0·76 m. (760 mm. or 29·921 in.) of mercury is equivalent to 33·9 ft. of water. This is equivalent to 14·696 lb. per sq. in. or 10,332·3 kg. per sq. m. To turn kilograms weight to newtons multiply by 9·8, the gravitional acceleration in metres per sec. per sec. A *bar* is equivalent to 100,000 newtons per sq. m. High pressures, especially in gases, are measured in kilobars. A *torr* is equivalent to 1 mm. of mercury and is used to measure low pressures in gases.

Proteins An extremely important class of biological *polymer* (q.v.) which form a vital part of all living organisms.

Proteins consist of long chains formed by the polymerisation (i.e. linking together) of up to several hundred simpler compounds called *amino-acids* (q.v.). About 20 different amino-acids are found in proteins, different proteins varying in the number of each amino-acid they contain and the order in which they are arranged along the chain. Thus an extremely wide variety of protein structures is possible, each fulfilling a specific function; and, in fact, different organisms produce their own set of proteins. Proteins also vary widely in shape; in some the chain is extended, and in others it is folded into a complicated globular structure.

Many proteins are *enzymes*, that is biological *catalysts* (q.v.), which control the multitude of chemical reactions occurring in living organisms. Most enzymes remain inside the cells producing them, while others pass outside: e.g. the digestive enzymes of animals which are secreted into the alimentary canal to catalyse the breakdown of food into simpler compounds.

Other proteins fulfil the function of transporting substance within an organism: e.g. the protein haemoglobin (which contains iron) is found in red blood cells and transports oxygen from the lungs to all cells of the body. Still other proteins compose the muscles and are responsible for the ability of muscle to contract and produce movement. In bones, skin and tendons protein fibres (rather like lengths of string) play an essential role as building materials.

Proteins are synthesised (i.e. manufactured), when needed, from their component amino-acids inside all animal, plant and bacterial cells. Viruses, the simplest organisms, have to 'hijack' the protein-making machinery of more complicated cells in order to produce the proteins they need; this is what is happening when viruses *infect* animals and plants. The instructions for the production of each different protein are carried by means of the *genetic code* in the genetic material inside the nucleus of the cell (see *deoxyribonucleic acid* (DNA)). It is copies of these instructions which are passed on when new cells are formed by cell division, thus enabling the new cells to produce the proteins they require.

Projectile Body thrown or projected. If v is the initial velocity, a the angle of projection, g gravity, the projectile moves in a parabola. The following relationships are true:

$$\text{Total time of flight} = \frac{2v \sin a}{g}$$

$$\text{Maximum height} = \frac{v^2 \sin^2 a}{2g}$$

$$\text{Horizontal range} = \frac{v^2 \sin 2a}{g}$$

Proton The positive heavy particle of the nucleus of an atom; also the nucleus of a normal hydrogen atom.

Pulsar A type of radio star discovered in 1968 which gives out pulses of radio waves at very regular intervals. Believed to be composed of very densely packed neutrons.

Pythagoras Greek mathematician. The theorem of Pythagoras is the one that states that in a right-angled triangle the square on the hypotenuse is equal to the sum of the squares on the other two sides. See *Trigonometry*.

Theorem of Pythagoras:
$AB^2 = AC^2 + BC^2$

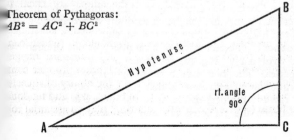

Quasar (or quasi-stellar source) Much the brightest and most distant type of giant star so far discovered.

Radian A unit of angular measure. One radian is the *angle* (q.v.) made at the centre, O, of any circle when the radius, r, of the circle is drawn round the circle's circumference (see diagram).

Since the circumference of a circle has length $2\pi r$, there are 2π radians to a full circle: i.e. 2π radians equals $360°$ or 1 radian equals $57\cdot3°$. A right-angle is equal to $90°$ or $\pi/4$ radians.

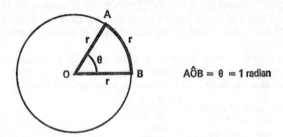

$A\hat{O}B = \theta = 1$ radian

Radical A group of atoms that stay together when a compound dissociates but yet not a stable group to qualify as a molecule, e.g. SO_4, NO_3, etc.

Radioactivity The spontaneous emission of radiation (alpha, beta or gamma) from a material, due to the break-up of the nuclei of the atoms. Materials that are abundantly radioactive are radium and uranium and some artificially made radioisotopes. Many materials, however, are known to have a tiny proportion of a radioactive isotope present, and these materials are everywhere—in food, plants, rocks, etc.

Reaction The correct name for what goes on when chemicals combine or split up.

Reagent Chemicals commonly used in chemical laboratories for experiments and analysis, such as dilute hydrochloric acid, ammonium hydroxide, dilute nitric acid, etc.

Reciprocal The reciprocal of a number y is one divided by y and is written $1/y$. E.g. the reciprocal of 4 is $1/4 = 0\cdot25$.

Reflection The 'bouncing back' of light rays, heat rays, etc. The simple law of reflection is that the angle between the incoming ray and the perpendicular to the surface is equal to the angle between the reflected ray and the same perpendicular.

This is expressed as: The angle of incidence = Angle of reflection. With flat or 'plane' mirrors the perpendicular is easy to draw in diagrams, but with curved reflecting surfaces the perpendiculars have to be arrived at by knowledge of the geometry of circles, parabolas, etc.

Such regular reflection is called mirror or specular reflection. At a roughened surface light is reflected in *all* directions and does not obey the above rules. This is called diffused or scattered reflection.

Refraction The sudden change of direction of light when passing from one transparent substance into another. A ray of light passing from air into water is bent towards the perpendicular, or normal.

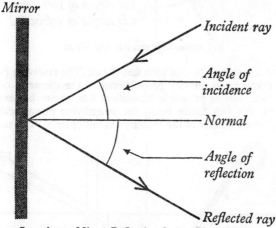

Specular or Mirror Reflection from a Plane Mirror

If the angle of incidence (i) is taken as that between the incident ray and the normal and the angle of refraction (r) as that between the refracted ray and the normal, then if the less-dense medium is a vacuum $\frac{\sin i}{\sin r} = \mu$, the *refractive index* of the substance. In ordinary experiments, as air is so little different from a vacuum for the passage of light, i is measured in air and r in the substance.

Resolving Power The power of an optical instrument or

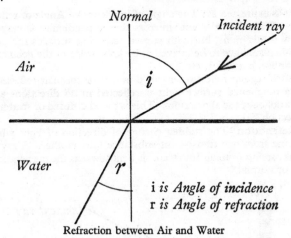

i *is Angle of* **incidence**
r *is Angle of* **refraction**

Refraction between Air and Water

any optical system to deal with fine detail. The resolving power of a telescope is directly proportional to the diameter of the objective. Hence prismatic binoculars 8 × 40 are better than 8 × 25, the first figure being the magnifying power and the second the diameter of the objective in millimetres. The second

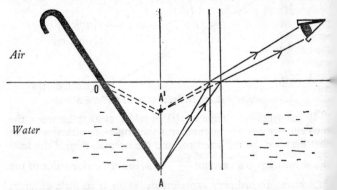

Apparent Bending of Walking-stick in Water Due to Refraction

The point *A* seems to be at A^1. Similarly with all points on *OA* so that the part immersed seems to be along OA^1.

binocular has the same magnifying power as the first but less resolving power, and so, though objects look just as big, the detail does not show up so well. The resolving power of the human eye is such that two point objects subtending an angle of about 1 minute at the eye can be seen separately, i.e. resolved.

Root This has two meanings in mathematics. (a) One of several equal factors of a number. Thus the square root $\sqrt{}$ or $^2\sqrt{}$ is one of two equal factors: e.g. $3 = \sqrt{9}$ (also written $9^{\frac{1}{2}}$) and $3 \times 3 = 9$. The cube root is one of three equal factors: e.g. $4 = {}^3\sqrt{64}$ (also written $64^{\frac{1}{3}}$) and $4 \times 4 \times 4 = 64$. (b) The root of an equation in an unknown x is a particular value of x that satisfies the equation.

Root-mean-square The average value of a quantity that takes positive and negative values equally (e.g. an alternating current) is zero. If the values are squared, the mean found, and then the square root taken, the non-zero result is called the root-mean-square value.

Salt A salt is the compound formed when the hydrogen in an *acid* (q.v.) is replaced by a metal. Examples of a salt are potassium nitrate and calcium sulphate. Sodium chloride ($NaCl$) is a salt in the chemical sense but is also called common salt in everyday use.

Series In mathematics a series is a sum of many terms each being of the same form so that a general expression can be given for the nth term: e.g. $1 + 1/2 + 1/4 + 1/8 + 1/16 + \ldots$ is a series whose nth term is $1/2^{(n-1)}$. *Infinite series* are series in which the number of terms is without limit. Despite having an infinite number of terms, some infinite series sum up to a limiting value. Such series are called *convergent* (e.g. the series given above if continued to infinity adds up to the value 2). Series which are not convergent are called *divergent*.

Set A set is a collection of objects or things that have at least one feature in common. A set may be described by listing all its members (called *elements*) or by specifying the properties that are necessary for membership of the set. To indicate that a, b, ... are elements of the set A, the usual notation is to write $A = \{a, b, c \ldots\}$. Sets may have finite or infinite numbers of elements. Examples: the set of all people who have reached the summit of Mount Everest, (a finite set); the set E of positive even whole numbers, i.e. $E = \{2, 4, 6, 8, \ldots\}$, (an infinite set).

Set Theory is an important branch of mathematics which deals with the relationships between sets.

Sine In trigonometry the sine of an angle (other than the right angle) in a right-angled triangle, is the ratio of the side opposite the angle to the hypotenuse. Sin 90° = 1, sin 60° = 0·866, sin 45° = 0·707, sin 30° = 0·5. See *Trigonometry*.

S.I. Units The internationally recommended system of *units* (q.v.) in which the base units are:

Quantity	Name of unit	Symbol
length	metre	m
mass	kilogram	kg
time	second	s
electric current	ampere	A
temperature	kelvin	K
amount of substance	mole	mol
luminous intensity	candela	cd

Other quantities are derived by combining these units e.g. the S.I. unit of volume is the cubic metre (m^3), that of velocity the metre per second ($m. s^{-1}$), that of energy the joule ($m.^2 kg. s^{-2}$) and that of electric charge the coulomb ($A. s$).

Specific Gravity See DENSITY.

Specific Heat The amount of heat in joules that must be added to unit mass of a substance to raise its temperature by 1° C. The table gives values for a gram of substance.

SPECIFIC HEATS OF COMMON SUBSTANCES

Aluminium	.	0·846	Alcohol	.	2·428
Brass	.	0·384	Chloroform	.	0·980
Copper	.	0·389	Air	.	1·009[1]
Iron	.	0·474	Carbon dioxide	.	0·846[1]
Rubber	.	1·675	Oxygen	.	0·911[1]
Wood	.	1·675	Water	.	4·187

[1] At constant pressure.

Spectroscope An apparatus in which light is dispersed by a triangular prism or diffracted by a diffraction grating to give bright vertical coloured lines on a dark background—the bright-line spectrum of the light. It consists normally of a rigid stand on which the prism is placed, a collimator, with a slit at one end to produce a beam of parallel light, and a telescope through which the spectrum is viewed. Telescope and collimator are rotatable on the graduated rigid prism table. By an arrangement of prisms in one special prism the spectrum comes through in the same straight line as the telescope and collimator. This is then a direct-vision spectroscope. There are many sorts of spectroscope, ranging from a small pocket-size direct-vision spectroscope to a piece of apparatus occupying a small room and used in industry for analysis. A spectrograph is a form of spectroscope in which the spectrum is photographed.

Squares, Cubes, Square Roots, Cube Roots and Reciprocals See *Root*.

N	N^2	N^3	$\sqrt{N}$	$\sqrt[3]{N}$	$\dfrac{1}{N}$
1	1	1	1·0	1·0	1·0
2	4	8	1·414	1·26	0·5
3	9	27	1·732	1·442	0·3333
4	16	64	2·0	1·587	0·25
5	25	125	2·236	1·71	0·2
6	36	216	2·449	1·817	0·1667
7	49	343	2·646	1·913	0·1429
8	64	512	2·828	2·0	0·125
9	81	729	3·0	2·08	0·1111
10	100	1,000	3·162	2·154	0·1
11	121	1,331	3·317	2·224	0·0909
12	144	1,728	3·464	2·289	0·0833
13	169	2,197	3·606	2·351	0·0769
14	196	2,744	3·742	2·41	0·0714
15	225	3,375	3·873	2·466	0·0667
16	256	4,096	4·0	2·52	0·0625
17	289	4,913	4·123	2·571	0·0588
18	324	5,832	4·243	2·621	0·0556
19	361	6,859	4·359	2·668	0·0526
20	400	8,000	4·472	2·714	0·05
21	441	9,261	4·583	2·759	0·0476
22	484	10,648	4·69	2·802	0·0455
23	529	12,167	4·796	2·844	0·0435
24	576	13,824	4·899	2·885	0·0417
25	625	15,625	5·0	2·924	0·04
26	676	17,576	5·099	2·962	0·0385
27	729	19,683	5·196	3·0	0·037
28	784	21,952	5·292	3·037	0·0357
29	841	24,389	5·385	3·072	0·0345
30	900	27,000	5·477	3·107	0·0333
31	961	29,791	5·568	3·141	0·0323
32	1,024	32,768	5·657	3·175	0·0313
33	1,089	35,937	5·745	3·208	0·0303
34	1,156	39,304	5·831	3·24	0 0294
35	1,225	42,875	5·916	3·271	0·0286
36	1,296	46,656	6·0	3·302	0·0278
37	1,369	50,653	6·083	3·332	0·027

N	N^2	N^3	$\sqrt{N}$	$\sqrt[3]{N}$	$\dfrac{1}{N}$
38	1,444	54,872	6·164	3·362	0·0263
39	1,521	59,319	6·245	3·391	0·0256
40	1,600	64,000	6·325	3·42	0·025
41	1,681	68,921	6·403	3·448	0·024
42	1,764	74,088	6·481	3·476	0·0238
43	1,849	79,507	6·557	3·503	0·0233
44	1,936	85,184	6·633	3·53	0·0227
45	2,025	91,125	6·708	3·557	0·0222
46	2,116	97,336	6·782	3·583	0·0217
47	2,209	103,823	6·856	3·609	0·0213
48	2,304	110,592	6·928	3·634	0·0208
49	2,401	117,649	7·0	3·659	0·0204
50	2,500	125,000	7·071	3·684	0·02

Superconductivity This is the remarkable property of many metals and alloys to lose all electrical resistance below a certain critical temperature (usually within 20° of absolute zero). This means that an electric current can flow in a loop of the metal indefinitely without generating heat or decreasing in strength. Because of the low temperatures required (the metal is usually bathed in liquid helium) superconductivity is expensive to use on a large scale. But superconducting magnets which can produce very high magnetic fields without vast consumption of electrical energy are now quite widely used.

Surface Tension A force acting in the surface of a fluid, whether the surface separates one liquid from another or a liquid from a gas such as air. The effect of the force is to make the liquid surface behave rather like a stretched elastic skin with a tendency to reduce its area. It is surface tension which causes water to climb up a narrow capillary tube and causes water surfaces to be meniscus-shaped. Surface tension also governs the formation and shape of liquid drops and bubbles.

Surface tension is measured in newtons per metre. It varies with the temperature. The surface tension of pure water at 20° C. is 0·07275 newtons per metre.

Tangent In geometry a straight line touching (not cutting) a curve at only one point. In trigonometry the tangent of an angle (other than the right angle) in a right-angled triangle is the ratio of the side opposite the angle to the other side that is not the hypotenuse. Tan 0° = 0, tan 30° = 0·577, tan 45° = 1·0, tan 60° = 1·732, tan 90° = ∞. See *Trigonometry*.

Telescope An optical device for getting an image of a distant object much bigger than the object appears seen with the naked eye. (The image obtained is really much smaller than the actual object.) There are two simple types: the astronomical telescope and the Galilean telescope. The astronomical telescope has a very long focus convergent lens as objective and a very short focus convergent lens (or system of lenses) as eyepiece. The magnifying power is the focal length of objective divided by the

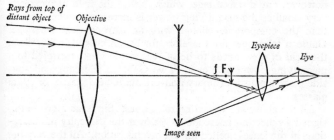

Geometrical Diagram of Astronomical Telescope

F is focus of objective
f is focus of eyepiece

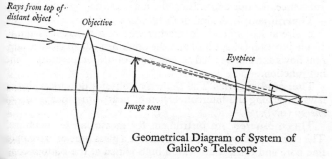

Geometrical Diagram of System of
Galileo's Telescope

focal length of eyepiece. The bigger the objective in diameter, the greater the resolving power. The image seen is inverted. Prisms can be inserted between the lenses to invert the image and at the same time make the light reflect along paths across and back and across and forward so that the length of the telescope can be short and the optical path long. The result is a prismatic monocular giving the image upright in relation to the object. Two of them make a pair of prismatic binoculars.

The Galilean telescope uses a long-focus convergent lens as objective and a short-focus divergent lens as eyepiece. The image is seen upright. The magnification is again the focal length of objective divided by the focal length of eyepiece, and as the eyepiece has to be placed within the focal length of the objective the length of the telescope is much less than that of the astronomical telescope for the same magnification. There is, however, one disadvantage, which is that the field of view gets very small as the magnifying power is increased, much more so than the comparable change with an astronomical telescope. Galilean telescopes are therefore for use in everyday life, when the field of view needs to be of reasonable size, restricted to a magnifying power of 2 or 3. Two Galilean telescopes side-by-side make a pair of ordinary non-prismatic field glasses or opera glasses.

All the above are refracting telescopes. Sir Isaac Newton designed a reflecting telescope to get over the difficulty of aberrations in the lenses needed for big magnification. All the very big observatory telescopes of today are reflecting ones.

Temperature The state of hotness or coldness of a body or substance. This is not the same as the heat energy of a body or substance, for this depends on the mass and the specific heat.

Thermocouple A kind of *thermometer* (q.v.) made by joining one wire at its two ends to another wire of a different material. If one junction is kept cool and the other heated, an electric current flows and can be used as a measure of the temperature of the hot junction.

Thermodynamics The branch of physics dealing with the laws governing the interconversion of heat with other forms of *energy* (q.v.).

Thermometer An instrument for measuring temperature. The commonest type of thermometer is a glass tube of extremely fine bore and thick walls with a bulb joined at the bottom containing mercury or some other liquid, which also reaches a certain distance up the tube. Warming makes the liquid expand up the tube; cooling makes it contract. A scale of numbers is arrived at by fixing two reference points, usually the melting point of ice and the boiling point of water.

Two temperature scales are in common use. One, called the Fahrenheit scale, has the melting point of ice at 32° and the boiling point of water at 212°. This is in general use in Britain and the U.S.A. The second scale is called **Centigrade** (Celsius in many European countries) and has the lower point at $0°$ and the upper at $100°$. It is in use generally in many countries, and is international for scientific measurement.

To convert Fahrenheit to Centigrade, first subtract 32 and then multiply the result by $\frac{5}{9}$.

To convert Centigrade to Fahrenheit multiply by $\frac{9}{5}$ and then add 32.

Examples:

(1) $59°$ F., convert to $°$ C.

$$59 - 32 = 27; \; 27 \times \tfrac{5}{9} = 15° \text{ C.}$$

(2) $20°$ C., convert to $°$ F.

$$20 \times \tfrac{9}{5} = 36; \; 36 + 32 = 68° \text{ F.}$$

To convert $°$C to the *absolute temperature* scale (q.v.) add $273 \cdot 15$.

Liquid-in-glass thermometers are limited. Mercury freezes at $-39°$C.; ethyl alcohol boils at $78 \cdot 3°$ C. So other devices must be used for very low and very high temperatures. For extreme temperatures a *thermo-couple* (q.v.) is frequently used, depending on the electricity generated when two dissimilar metals are joined and the junction heated or cooled. A platinum resistance-thermometer depends on the change of electrical resistance in platinum wire when it is heated. Modern materials called thermistors are also used. The resistance of such materials gets less as it is heated. So an electrical current increases.

Special thermometers of the liquid-in-glass sort are devised to read the minimum or the maximum temperature reached in a certain period of time. A clinical thermometer is a type of maximum thermometer in which the thread of mercury stays put at its highest because of a very narrow constriction at the base of the tube where it joins the mercury-supply bulb.

Trigonometry The branch of mathematics that deals with the properties of *angles* (q.v.). The usual starting-point for trigonometry is the definition of the *sine*, *cosine* and *tangent* of an angle (all q.v.).

In the diagram ABC is a right-angled triangle with $\angle ACB = 90°$ and the angle $\angle BAC$ denoted by θ. Sine θ, cosine θ, and tangent θ (commonly written $\sin \theta$, $\cos \theta$ and $\tan \theta$) are defined by the following ratios of lengths:

$$\sin \theta = \frac{BC}{AB}, \quad \cos \theta = \frac{AC}{AB}, \quad \tan \theta = \frac{BC}{AC} = \frac{\sin \theta}{\cos \theta}.$$

It is important to understand that these ratios are independent of the size of the triangle ABC and depend only on the magnitude of the angle θ. The numerical values of the sine, cosine and tangent of any angle can be found in books of mathematical tables. Other trigonometrical ratios are defined as follows:

Cosecant θ or cosec $\theta = \dfrac{1}{\sin \theta} = \dfrac{AB}{BC}$

Secant θ or sec $\theta = \dfrac{1}{\cos \theta} = \dfrac{AB}{AC}$

Cotangent θ cot $\theta = \dfrac{1}{\tan \theta} = \dfrac{AC}{BC}$

A useful relationship between $\sin \theta$ and $\cos \theta$ is derived by using *Pythagoras's theorem* (q.v.). According to this theorem, for the right-angled triangle ABC, $AB^2 = AC^2 + BC^2$ and therefore

$$\cos^2 \theta + \sin^2 \theta = \frac{AC^2 + BC^2}{AB^2} = 1.$$

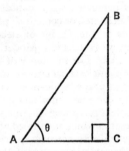

One common use of trigonometric ratios is the calculation of unknown sidelengths and angles of triangles (and other geometrical figures) when only some of them are originally given.

Ultra-violet Light Light that is invisible to human beings and of shorter wavelength than visible light. Sometimes called 'dark light'. It is very active in affecting chemicals and causing *fluorescence* (q.v.). It is present in the light from the sun, but much of it is filtered out by the earth's atmosphere. It is dangerous for the eyes. Range of wavelengths 1,800–4,200 Å. It is also present in mercury-vapour discharge light.

Units All physical quantities can be expressed in terms of five base units: mass (M), length (L), time (T), electric current and temperature. Thus volume = L . L . L, force = (M . L)/(T . T). The magnitude of the base units is set by convention. In the c.g.s. system the base units are the centimetre (L), gram (M) and second (T). In the f.p.s. system they are the foot (L), pound (M) and second (T). The currently accepted system is the Système International d'Unités (see S.I. UNITS).

Vacuum Space which contains no matter. In practice unobtainable since, whatever the walls of the container were made of, the container would evaporate slowly and so destroy the vacuum. Usually very low pressures of air or other gases are called vacuums.

Valency The valency of an element is a number that tells in what proportions the element combines with other elements, and so can be used to work out molecular formulae of compounds. Elements of valency 1 (monovalent elements) include hydrogen, chlorine, silver and sodium; of valency 2 (divalent elements) include oxygen, magnesium and calcium; of valency 3 (trivalent elements) include aluminium and nitrogen; and of valency 4 (tetravalent elements) include carbon.

Oxygen being divalent means that one atom of it will combine with two atoms of monovalent hydrogen (giving water H_2O), or with one atom of divalent magnesium (giving MgO, magnesium oxide), or with 'half' an atom of tetravalent carbon (giving carbon dioxide, CO_2). Three atoms of oxygen combine with two of aluminium to give aluminium oxide Al_2O_3.

Valency is closely related to the theory of the chemical *bond* (q.v.) and is not always as simple as above. Many elements can combine with each other in a number of different ways: e.g. nitrogen and oxygen can give the oxides N_2O, NO, N_2O_3, NO_2, and N_2O_5 and two oxides of copper exist, CuO and Cu_2O.

Vapour Pressure A liquid loses atoms or molecules into its gaseous surround, usually air. When the pressure of these evaporated atoms or molecules is such that as many are returning to the material as are leaving it the vapour is saturated and its pressure is called the vapour pressure of the liquid. It increases with a rise in temperature and depends only on that temperature and the nature of the liquid. A volatile liquid has a high vapour pressure at ordinary temperatures. A liquid that has a low vapour pressure does not evaporate easily. On heating a liquid there comes a temperature at which the vapour pressure equals atmospheric pressure. It then boils.

VAPOUR PRESSURES OF SOME LIQUIDS AT 20° C. IN MM. OF MERCURY

Water	.	.	17·5	Benzene . . .	74·6
Mercury	.	.	0·0013	Chloroform . . .	161
Acetone	.	.	185	Ether	440
Alcohol	.	.	44·5	Carbon Tetrachloride .	91

Velocity In everyday use the same as speed, but in science and mathematics having the extra quality of being negative or positive to show *direction* in relation to any problem.

If u is the starting velocity, f the acceleration, then the velocity v after time t is given by $v = u + ft$. The distance travelled is given by $s = ut + \frac{1}{2}ft^2$. From these can be derived the equation $v^2 = u^2 + 2fs$.

Viscosity The internal friction of fluids, i.e. resistance to flow of one part over another. Examples: treacle, a very viscous fluid; ether, a liquid of low viscosity. Viscosity decreases with rise in temperature.

Volt The S.I. unit of *electro motive force* (q.v.) (e.m.f.), potential difference or electrical pressure.

Volume The amount of space occupied by an object, expressed in cubic inches, cubic metres, cubic feet, etc.

VOLUMES OF COMMON SHAPES

Cube: l^3, where l = length of one side.

Rectangular prism: $l \times b \times d$, where l = length, b = breadth, d = depth.

Sphere: $\frac{4}{3}\pi r^3$, where r = radius.

Cylinder: $\pi r^2 l$, where r = radius of base, l = length of cylinder.

Cone: $\frac{1}{3}\pi r^2 h$, where r = radius of base, h = vertical height.

$\frac{1}{3}\pi r^2\sqrt{l^2 - r^2}$, where l = length of sloping side.

Pyramid: $\frac{1}{3}$ area of base $\times h$, where h = vertical height.

Waves Many kinds of disturbance travel from one point to another as waves, for example, ripples on a water surface.

pressure variations in air (sound) and electrical and magnetic disturbances (light). The important thing is that the disturbance varies periodically in both space and time. This can be understood by considering a water wave. If a water wave is photographed at one time it will look as in diagram (a) where the shape of the wave is repeated regularly and the distance, λ, between successive crests is called the *wavelength*. If the wave is travelling from left to right with velocity v, at a slightly later time the picture will look as in (b) which has the earlier wave shape dotted in (the crest at A having moved to A^1). Moreover if we remain fixed at B, we have to wait a time T equal to λ/v

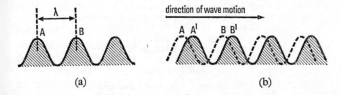

(a) (b)

before the crest originally at A reaches B. The time T between successive crests arriving at a given point is called the *period*. The reciprocal $1/T$ is the number of crests passing a point per second and is called the *frequency*, f. We have shown the important relationship

$$T = \lambda/v \text{ or } v = f.\lambda$$

which is true for all wave motions. It is important to note that it is the shape of the wave and the energy carried by it that moves from A to A' and not the water itself. The water molecules are actually moving backwards and forwards in the direction at right angles to the direction the wave is travelling. For this reason, water waves are examples of *transverse* waves. *Longitudinal* waves, by comparison, are waves in which the particles are moving back and forth in the same direction as that in which the wave is moving e.g. sound waves.

All kinds of waves show the characteristic properties of *reflection* (q.v.), *refraction* (q.v.) and *diffraction*.

Weight The force of attraction exerted on a body by gravity. See *Mass*.

Weights and Measures, Tables of

Avoirdupois Weight

16 drams (*dr.*)	=	1 ounce (*oz.*)
16 ounces	=	1 pound (*lb.*)
14 pounds	=	1 stone (*st.*)
28 pounds	=	1 quarter (*qr.*)
4 quarters	=	1 hundredweight (*cwt.*)
20 hundredweights	=	1 ton (*tn.*)
100 pounds	=	1 central, or short hundredweight
2,000 pounds	=	1 short ton
7,000 grains	=	1 pound

Linear Measure

12 inches (*in.*)	=	1 foot (*ft.*)
3 feet	=	1 yard (*yd.*)
5½ yards	=	1 rod, pole or perch
40 poles	=	1 furlong (*fur.*)
8 furlongs	=	1 mile (*mi.*)
3 miles	=	1 league (*l.*)

Land Measure

7·92 inches	=	1 link (*li.*)
25 links	=	1 rod (*rd.*)
4 rods or 100 links	=	1 chain (*ch.*)
80 chains	=	1 mile

Square Measure

144 square inches (*sq. in.*)	=	1 square foot (*sq. ft.*)
9 square feet	=	1 square yard (*sq. yd.*)
30¼ square yards	=	1 square rod, pole or perch
40 square poles	=	1 rood (*r.*)
4 roods	=	1 acre (*ac.*)
640 acres	=	1 square mile (*sq. mi.*)

Land Square Measure

625 square links	=	1 square rod
16 square rods	=	1 square chain
10 square chains	=	1 acre

Cubic or solid Measures

1,728 cubic inches (*cu. in.*)	=	1 cubic foot (*cu. ft.*)
27 cubic feet	=	1 cubic yard (*cu. yd.*)

Liquid Measure

4 gills	=	1 pint (*pt.*)
2 pints	=	1 quart (*qt.*)
4 quarts	=	1 gallon (*gal.*)

Dry Measure

2 pints	=	1 quart
4 quarts	=	1 gallon
2 gallons	=	1 peck (*pk.*)
4 pecks	=	1 bushel (*bush.*)
8 bushels	=	1 quarter (*qr.*)
36 bushels	=	1 chaldron (*chal.*)
5 quarters	=	1 wey
2 weys	=	1 last

Circular Measure

60 seconds (″)	= 1 minute (′)
60 minutes	= 1 degree (°)
90 degrees	= 1 quadrant (*quad.*)
4 quadrants or 360 degrees	= 1 circle (o)

Miscellaneous Measures

1 gal. of pure water weighs 10 lb.
The gramme is the weight of 1 c.c. of pure water.
The litre is 1,000 c.c. of pure water, and weighs 1 kg.
A hand (in measuring a horse) is 4 in.
The British Thermal Unit (B.T.U.) is the amount of heat required to raise 1 lb. of water by 1° F.
A Therm is 100,000 B.T.U.
One horse-power is the power needed to raise 550 lb. 1 ft. in 1 sec.
The kilowatt is the power needed to raise 737·6 lb. 1 ft. in 1 sec. (746 watts = 1 h.p.).

THE METRIC SYSTEM

Measures of Weight

10 milligrammes (*mg.*)	=	1 centigramme (*cg.*)
10 centigrammes	=	1 decigramme (*dg.*)
10 decigrammes	=	1 gramme (*g.*)
10 grammes	=	1 decagramme (*Dg.*)
10 decagrammes	=	1 hectogramme (*hg.*)
10 hectogrammes	=	1 kilogramme (*kg.*)

Linear Measure

10 millimetres (*mm.*)	=	1 centimetre (*cm.*)
10 centimetres	=	1 decimetre (*dm.*)
10 decimetres	=	1 metre (*m.*)
10 metres	=	1 decametre (*Dm.*)
10 decametres	=	1 hectometre (*hm.*)
10 hectametres	=	1 kilometre (*km.*)

Measures of Capacity

10 millilitres (*ml.*)	=	1 centilitre (*cl.*)
10 centilitres	=	1 decilitre (*dl.*)
10 decilitres	=	1 litre (*l.*)
10 litres	=	1 decolitre (*Dl.*)
10 decolitres	=	1 hectolitre (*hl.*)
10 hectolitres	=	1 kilolitre (*kl.*)

X-Rays Electromagnetic radiation of very short wavelength, ranging from a tenth of an Angstrom to 20 Angstroms. X-rays affect a photographic plate and cause fluorescence in some chemicals. They penetrate matter according to its density. They are used in medical practice for showing up growths, bone fractures, foreign bodies, etc., in the human body.

FURTHER READING

How Much and How Many: The Story of Weights and Measures, by Jeanne Bendick (Brockhampton Press)

Brains and Computers, by A. M. Andrew (Harrap)

The Second Book of Experiments, by Leonard de Vries (Murray)

Electricity, by Leslie Hunter (Burke)

Transistors Work Like This, by Egon Larsen (Phoenix)

The Young Scientist, ed. W. Abbott (Chatto & Windus)

The Magic of Electricity, by Sam Rosenfeld (Faber)

For the life stories of individual scientists: the *Immortals of Science* series (Chatto & Windus) and the *Lives to Remember* series (A. & C. Black)

The Atom, by Charles Hatcher (Macmillan)

Men who Changed the World: stories of invention and discovery, by Egon Larsen (Phoenix)

Science, ed. Dr J. Bronowski (Macdonald Illustrated Library)

The Double Helix, by James Watson (Weidenfeld and Nicolson and Penguin)

The Biological Time Bomb, by Gordon Rattray Taylor (Thames and Hudson)

The New Materials, by David Fishlock (Murray)

The Naked Ape, by Desmond Morris (Cape)

Modern Cosmology, by Jagjit Singh (Pelican)

Men of Mathematics (Vols 1 and 2), by E. T. Bell (Pelican)

Biographical Encyclopaedia of Science and Technology, by Isaac Asimov (Pan)

A Dictionary of Radio and Television

SOME of the terms used in discussing radio and television are general scientific terms (e.g. *ampere*, *ohm*) and if not found in this section should be looked for in the DICTIONARY OF SCIENCE AND MATHEMATICS.

Abbreviations

A—ampere
mA—milliampere (milliamp)
μA—microampere
V—volt
mV—millivolt
μV—microvolt
Ω—omega (capital) = ohm
MΩ—megohm
μΩ—microhm
F—farad
μF—microfarad

W—watt
kW—kilowatt
mW—milliwatt
H—henry
mH—millihenry
μH—microhenry
A.C.—alternating current
D.C.—direct current
e.m.f.—electromotive force
R.M.S.—root-mean-square

Note: The above abbreviations are in accordance with the ruling of the British Standards Institution.

L.F.—low frequency
H.F.—high frequency
V.H.F.—very high frequency
R.F.—radio frequency
A.F.—audio frequency
R.C.C.—resistance–capacity coupling
S.G.—screen grid
D.C.C.—double cotton covered
S.C.C.—single cotton covered
D.S.C.—double silk covered ⎱ synonymous terms
D.W.S.—double wound silk ⎰
S.W.G.—standard wire gauge
S. pole—south pole

N. pole—north pole
L.T.—low tension
H.T.—high tension
G.B.—grid bias
Q.P.P.—quiescent push–pull

Aerial (Antenna) A conductor that can either send out o- pick up radio waves and therefore can be the last stage of a trans- mitter or the first stage of a receiver. In its simplest form it is metallic rod or wire but efficient, directional aerials can be c- complicated design.

A transmitter operating on long or medium waves has a- aerial that is a high wire leading through the transmitter to th- ground. For waves as short as, or shorter than, those used f- television the antenna is free of any earth connection and th- length of rod forming the antenna is related to the wavelength- The commonest relationship is that the antenna is a half th- wavelength. The usual design is of two rods in line, each rojust under a quarter wavelength long, the two ends at the middle being where the line joining the antenna to the transmitter or receiver is placed. This is the *half-wave dipole* or Hertzian antenna.

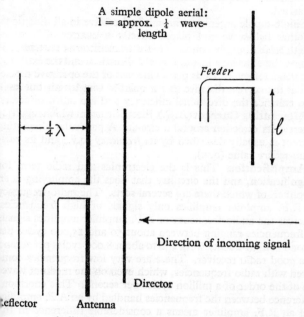

A simple dipole aerial:
l = approx. ¼ wavelength

Feeder

←—¼λ—→

Direction of incoming signal

Director

Reflector   Antenna

A dipole with one reflector and one director

The B.B.C. television video signal is transmitted in London on a wavelength of 6·67 m. or 21 ft. 10½ in. A half-wave antenna would therefore have a total length of 10 ft. 11¼ in. In practice, owing to end-effects, so that the effective length is slightly bigger than the physical length, the antenna would be about 10 ft. 5 in. long.

The audio signal for television is on a different wavelength from that of the video signal, so an aerial correctly designed for one will not be accurate for the other. In practice, a compromise is often made.

If the electrical component of the electromagnetic wave being transmitted or received is vertical, then the half-wave antenna is vertical. If the electrical component is horizontal the antenna is horizontal. Some of the B.B.C. regional television signals and all its V.H.F. frequency-modulation signals are horizontally polarised.

Single-dipole antennae transmit and receive in all directions. Another half-wave rod placed exactly a quarter of a wave-length *behind* but unconnected to the transmitter or receiver, enhances the efficiency in the forward direction, and the extra rod is called a reflector. Rods placed in *front* of the operative dipole, and at the correct distance (*not* a quarter wavelength but less), also enhance the directional efficiency and are called directors.

Alternating Current (A.C.) Electric current which regularly reverses its direction around a circuit. A particular alternating current is usually described by its *frequency* (q.v.) and its *root-mean-square* value (q.v.).

Amplification This is the electronics and radio term for magnification, and the circuitry that does the amplifying is an amplifier, of which there are several sorts. The radio-frequency or R.F. amplifier amplifies only signals of high frequencies, whereas the audio-frequency or A.F. amplifier amplifies signals of frequencies ranging between about 50 and 15,000 cycles per second in high-fidelity work and to about 8,000 cycles per second in a good radio receiver. These are very low frequencies compared with radio frequencies, which even on the medium wave are of the order of a million cycles per second. This enormous difference between the frequencies handled by an A.F. amplifier and an R.F. amplifier means a considerable difference in the circuits and valves used.

In radio and electronics and television, amplification involves the use of thermionic valves and transistors. Any one such valve or transistor with its associated circuit of resistors, capacitors and perhaps inductance, is called a *stage*. Each stage except the last in a radio receiver is designed as a voltage amplifier, but the final stage has to deliver power to a loudspeaker or the coils of a cathode-ray tube in a television receiver. This final stage is therefore a power amplifier.

The general principle of amplification is that an input alternating voltage, still at radio frequency if it is R.F. amplification, but at audio frequency if it is A.F. amplification, is applied be tween the grid and cathode of a thermionic valve. The output is then taken from the anode circuit. If a transistor is used the input is in most cases (i.e. using common emitter connections) applied between base and emitter and the output taken between collector and emitter. In each case what is taken out is bigger than what is put in. The ratio of output to imput is called the *stage gain*.

The stage gain depends on the *amplification factor*, μ (mu), of the valve, the A.C. resistance of the valve, Ra, the *load*, and the type of coupling between stages. See VALVE.

Amplitude Modulation The addition of an audio-frequency signal to a carrier in such a way that the carrier amplitude varies in response to the signal. See MODULATION.

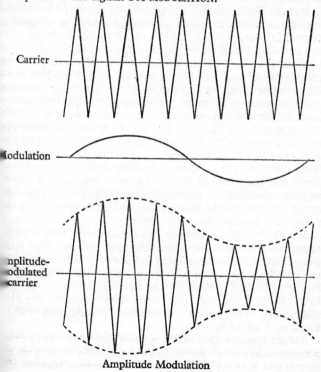

Carrier

Modulation

Amplitude-
modulated
carrier

Amplitude Modulation

Anode The positive electrode of an electrolytic cell or thermionic valve or discharge tube.

Audio Frequency (A.F.) This means a *frequency* (q.v.) within the range of sound wave frequencies audible to human ears. It can be taken as between 20 cycles per second and 20,000 cycles per second, though many people have a much smaller range than this. High-fidelity amplifiers are capable of reproducing from about 50 cycles per second to 15,000 cycles per second.

Automatic Gain Control A circuit device which automatically maintains the output of a stage almost constant, even though the input may be varying. It operates by the principle of *feedback* (q.v.), and is used in radio receivers to reduce the effect of *fading* (q.v.).

British Broadcasting Corporation The oldest broadcasting organisation in the world, developing out of a company first formed in 1922.

The B.B.C. broadcasts in sound to countries all over the world in forty languages beside English. It is organised into two parts, one for the home programmes, with headquarters in Broadcasting House in London, W.1, one for the programmes going overseas—the external services—with headquarters in Bush House, London, W.C.2.

The B.B.C. broadcasts in two television services, known as B.B.C.-1 and B.B.C.-2, and in four radio services known as Radio 1, 2, 3 and 4. B.B.C. Home radio was substantially re-organised from April 4th 1970. Radio 1 is the channel for pop music. Radio 2 is the principal channel for more traditional forms of popular music and for sport coverage. Radio 3 is a serious all music channel during the day but includes items on drama, poetry, the arts etc. during the evening. Radio 4 is the main channel for up-to-the-moment news and current affairs broadcasting and for plays, documentaries and discussions of more general interest than those found in Radio 3. The radio services are broadcast on medium or long waves, and on very high frequency (V.H.F.). Details of the wavelengths used are printed in the *Radio Times*, and fuller information is available from the Engineering Information Department, Broadcasting House, London, W1A 1AA.

Radio 1 is transmitted on 247 metres; Radio 2 on 1500 metres, 202 metres in parts of Scotland, and on V.H.F.; Radio 3 on 464 metres and V.H.F.; Radio 4 on various medium wavelengths and on V.H.F. Many of the V.H.F. programmes are transmitted in stereo. Radio 2 is to be found between 88–91 Mhz, Radio 3 between 90 and 93 and Radio 4 from 92–95 Mhz.

The External Services are mainly broadcast on short waves in the bands from 11–49 metres, but some of the services to Europe are broadcast on medium wavelengths and some of the short-wave programmes are relayed on medium wave from transmitters in Cyprus and various other parts of the world.

B.B.C.-1 television is transmitted on both the 405-line standard, and on the newer 625-line standard. B.B.C.-2 is transmitted only on 625 lines. The 405-line services are transmitted on V.H.F., the 625-line services on U.H.F., and in colour.

The B.B.C. has 20 local radio stations, all of which transmit on both V.H.F. and on medium-wave. They are as follows:

B.B.C. Radio Birmingham
(Pebble Mill Road, Birmingham B5 750)
B.B.C. Radio Blackburn
(King Street, Blackburn, Lancs. BB2 2EA)
B.B.C. Radio Brighton
(Marlborough Place, Brighton, Sussex BN1 1TU)
B.B.C. Radio Bristol
(3 Tyndalls Park Road, Bristol BS8 1PP)
B.B.C. Radio Carlisle
(Hilltop Heights, Carlisle, Cumberland)
B.B.C. Radio Derby
(56 St. Helens St., Derby DE1 3HY)
B.B.C. Radio Humberside
(9 Chapel St., Hull HU1 3NU)
B.B.C. Radio Leeds
(Merrion Centre, Leeds LS2 8NJ)
B.B.C. Radio Leicester
(Epic House, Charles St., Leicester LE1 3SH)
B.B.C. Radio London
(Harewood House, Hanover Sq., London W1R 0JD)
B.B.C. Radio Manchester
(33 Piccadilly, Manchester M60 7BB)
B.B.C. Radio Medway
(30 High St., Chatham, Kent ME4 4EZ)
B.B.C. Radio Merseyside
(Commerce House, 13/17 Sir Thomas St., Liverpool L16 BS)
B.B.C. Radio Newcastle
(Crestina House, Archbold Terrace, Newcastle-upon-Tyne NE2 1DZ)
B.B.C. Radio Nottingham,
(York House, Mansfield Road, Nottingham MG1 3JB)
B.B.C. Radio Oxford
(242/254 Banbury Road, Oxford OX2 7DW)

B.B.C. Radio Sheffield
(Ashdell Grove, 60 Westbourne Road, Sheffield S10 2QU)
B.B.C. Radio Solent
(South Western House, Canute Road, Southampton SO9 4PJ)
B.B.C. Radio Stoke-on-Trent
(Conway House, Cheapside, Hanley, Stoke-on-Trent, Staffs ST1
   1JJ)
B.B.C. Radio Teesside
(91/93 Linthorpe Road, Middlesbrough, Teesside TS1 5DG)

Capacitance This is the property of a *capacitor* (q.v.) to
store electric charge when a voltage is applied across the capacitor
plates. The unit of capacitance is the *farad* (F), and a capacitor
has a capacitance of one farad if it stores a charge of one coulomb
when there is a voltage of one volt across it. The farad is too
large for most practical purposes and it is normal to use the
microfarad, μF (one millionth of a farad), and the picofarad, pF
(one million millionth of a farad).

In understanding how a capacitor behaves in a circuit it is
important to remember that electric current is the flow of electric
charge. So whenever charge is moving into or out of a capacitor
(i.e. the capacitor is *charging* or *discharging*) a current must flow.
Also, the charge stored in a capacitor is always equal to the voltage
across it times its capacitance.

Suppose a capacitor is connected in a circuit with a battery,
a *resistor* (q.v.) and a switch. When the switch is open there is
no voltage across the capacitor and therefore no charge stored in
it. On closing the switch, current flows for a short time, charging
up the capacitor until the voltage across it is equal to that of the
battery. The insulating layer in the capacitor then prevents any
further current flow. If the battery is now removed from the
circuit, the capacitor discharges through the resistor and a current again flows for a short time (but in the opposite direction)
until there is no voltage across the capacitor. If the battery is now
reconnected, but with positive and negative reversed, the
capacitor will again charge up (in the opposite direction to before)
and current will again flow. Thus we can see that if we connec
a capacitor to an A.C. generator whose voltage is regularly
changing from positive to zero, zero to negative, and negative
through zero to positive again, the capacitor will regularly charg
up, discharge and recharge in the opposite direction. A
alternating current will therefore flow even though there is a

insulating layer in the capacitor. The A.C. is exactly of the same *frequency* (q.v.) as the voltage but the current maxima coincide with the voltage zeros: i.e. the voltage and current are 90° out of *phase* (q.v.). The magnitude of the current is given by V/X_C, where V is the voltage and X_c is called the *capacitive reactance*. For a capacitor of capacitance C farads and A.C. of frequency f, $X_c = 1/2\pi Cf$ ohms.

Capacitor A circuit component which has the property of *capacitance* (q.v.). The simplest form of capacitor is the parallel plate capacitor which consists of two plates of metal separated by an insulating material called a *dielectric*. The capacitance C is given by the formula

$$C = \frac{\varepsilon A}{d} \times \frac{10^{-9}}{36\pi} \text{ farads}$$

where A is the area of the overlapping plates, d is the distance between the plates and ε is a constant which depends on the dielectric used and is called the *dielectric constant*. For low values of capacitance the dielectric may be air (ε = 1). This is often the case for variable capacitors used in tuning radios. When the dial is turned, one set of plates interleaves with another set separated by air gaps and A in the above formula is increased or decreased. Higher value capacitors are made with ceramic, mica or paper dielectrics and may be rolled up for convenience.

Carrier Wave Electromagnetic waves of the frequencies of speech and music cannot be transmitted efficiently over long distances. So in telecommunications a wave of much higher frequency, the carrier wave, is used to 'carry' the desired signal by the technique of *modulation* (q.v.).

Cathode The negative electrode of an electrolytic cell or a thermionic valve or discharge tube.

Cathode-ray Tube This device is a glass envelope roughly conical in shape with a long neck in which a cathode emits electrons which travel towards a fluorescent screen on the large end of the envelope. A metal electrode in the neck is the anode to attract the electrons and speed them on their way to the screen. The cathode and focusing electrodes and anodes constitute the *electron gun*. When correctly designed a narrow intense beam of electrons travels to the screen and produces a tiny spot of light.

There are two main uses for a cathode-ray tube. One is with extra apparatus to make an oscilloscope, an apparatus that allows

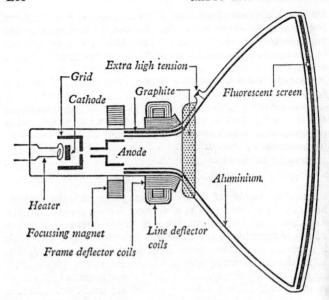

Grid

Cathode

Extra high tension

Graphite

Fluorescent screen

Anode

Aluminium.

Heater

Focussing magnet

Frame deflector coils

Line deflector coils

A **wide-angle** television cathode-ray tube showing only
electrodes for a triode assembly

waves and oscillations to be seen as visible traces and measured

The other use is in a television receiver. The electron beam is
forced to traverse the screen in lines, each successive line being
below the one before it, so that the whole of the working area of
the screen is *scanned*. In order to make the beam do this its movements are controlled by electromagnetic coils on the neck.

Circuit The name given to the arrangement of conductors
capacitors, inductances, valves, etc., that make up the theoretica
picture of an electronics device. All these components are show
in diagrams by conventional graphical symbols and the connect
ing wires by straight lines. The circuit diagram must be dis
tinguished from the wiring diagram, which shows the natura
disposition, soldering points, etc., of the real components. Th
circuit diagram merely tells the theory on which the behavio
of the apparatus is based and can be calculated.

Coil Conducting wire wound on a former and used in A.C

circuits as a source of *inductance* (q.v.). There may be many or few turns and the core may or may not be of a magnetic material, depending on the application. Coils are widely used in *tuning* (q.v.) circuits and as *chokes* when a high impedance to A.C. is required.

Colour Television The first British colour television broadcast was made on 2 July 1967, and the B.B.C.'s full colour service on B.B.C.2 opened on 2 December. Since then both B.B.C.1 and I.T.V. have begun transmitting a high proportion of colour programmes.

Condenser See CAPACITOR.

Crystal Detector An early form of rectifier consisting of a thin pointed wire (the 'cat's whisker') in contact with a *semi-conductor* (q.v.) crystal. Used as a detector for radio waves prior to the invention of diode valves and *p–n junction* (q.v.) diodes.

Decibel (dB) A unit which compares two levels of *power* (q.v.). To say that two power levels, P_2 and P_1, differ by n dB means that $n = 10 \times \log_{10} P_2/P_1$. Depending upon whether P_2 is greater or less than P_1, n may be positive or negative. If, for example, $P_2 = 2P_1$, then P_2 is $10\log_{10}2$ (about 3) dB up on P_1. In electronics, decibels are often used to compare the output power of a circuit with the input power i.e. to give a measure of the circuit gain or loss. A bel is ten decibels.

If it is required to give actual power levels instead of just relative power levels, the *decibel referred to one milliwatt* (dBm) is often used. In this case P_1 is fixed at a reference level of one milliwatt. The table below gives the correspondence between power levels measured in milliwatts and dBm.

DECIBEL TABLE
(Based on 1 milliwatt reference)

Milliwatts	Decibels	Milliwatts	Decibels
1	0	3·981	6
1·259	1	5·012	7
1·585	2	6·310	8
1·995	3	7·943	9
2·512	4	10·000	10
3·162	5	1 watt	30

Detection (Demodulation) The reverse process to *modulation* (q.v.): i.e. the separation of the original signal from the

modulated *carrier wave* (q.v.). This is usually done in radio and
television receivers (after changing from a frequency-modulated
signal to an amplitude-modulated signal if necessary) by rectify-
ing the high frequency signal to give a direct current varying at
audio frequencies. See RECTIFICATION.

Diagrams There are certain standard *graphical symbols* (q.v.)
used in electrical, electronic, radio and television circuit diagrams.
Straight lines indicate conducting connections (lengths of copper
wire when an amateur is wiring up a piece of apparatus).

Diode This means 'two electrodes' and refers to a component
that will allow the passage of an electric current in one direction
only and hence can be used for *rectification* (q.v.). The diode may
be a thermionic valve with only a cathode and an anode or a
semiconductor *p–n junction* (q.v.).

Doping The adding of small quantities of impurities to a
semiconductor (q.v.). Adding of antimony or arsenic to germanium gives *n-type* germanium. This has a higher conductivity
(see *resistivity*) than undoped germanium because the impurity
atoms bring extra electrons which are readily available for
carrying electricity. Adding aluminium or indium to germanium
gives *p-type* germanium. This also has an increased conductivity
but due to the presence of positively charged *holes* which, like
electrons, can carry electricity. See P–N JUNCTION and TRANSISTOR.

Early Bird The world's first commercial communications
satellite, launched by the United States in the spring of 1965.

Earth A term much used in radio and electronics. For
ordinary circuits, including telephone and distribution lines, the
earth, being a conductor of electricity, though a poor one, can be
used as the return wire to complete the circuit. For circuit
involving electromagnetic oscillations and waves the earth is the
conductor to which the transmitter or receiver is connected, the
antenna being the other. Thus when medium or long radio
waves are used the antenna system is a long, high wire or
system of wires and the earth connection is a system of wire
buried in the ground. For an ordinary receiver the water pipe
is a good enough earth. The word 'earth' is also used, however
to mean the common metallic connection to all the circuit
frequently the metal chassis on which everything is mounted
The advantage of an earth connection is that stray currents us
the earth as a 'sink' and in receiving weak signals on medium
and long waves the signal is increased. Modern receive

frequently need no earth connection at all. Transmission and reception of television signals and any others using dipole antennae make no use of an earth connection.

Electric Field An electric field is a region of space in which an electric charge experiences a force.

Electromagnetic Waves (EM waves). Waves (see DICTIONARY OF SCIENCE) consisting of both electric and magnetic quantities varying regularly in space and time and travelling together at the speed of light.

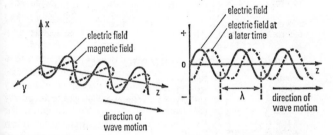

(a) Simplified diagram of an electromagnetic wave

(b) Diagram showing how the electric field varies

Diagram (a) gives an instantaneous picture of an EM wave. The *electric field* (q.v.) is in the *x*-direction and oscillates between +ve and −ve values as in diagram (b). The *magnetic field* (q.v.) is in the *y*-direction and varies in a similar way. The whole wave travels in the *z*-direction at the speed of light so that at a later time the electric field will vary as shown dotted in (b). The wavelength, λ, is the distance between one crest and the next. The frequency, f, is the number of oscillations per second at a given point. These are related to the speed of light, c, by the equation

$$c = f.\lambda$$

The value of c for EM waves in free space, c_0, is 3×10^8 m per sec. or 186,000 miles per sec. Note that EM waves do not need a medium through which to travel, unlike sound waves. EM waves do of course travel through other materials but at a velocity c_0/μ where μ is the refractive index of the material.

EM waves have very different properties depending on the wavelength. Different names are given to different ranges of wavelength, and these make up the *Electromagnetic Spectrum*. (see DICTIONARY OF SCIENCE for *Gamma rays, Ultra-violet light*, etc).

WAVELENGTHS AND FREQUENCIES

λ	n	λ	n
2,000 m.	150 kc/s	50 m.	6 Mc/s
1,000 m.	300 kc/s	10 m.	30 Mc/s
500 m.	600 kc/s	3 m.	100 Mc/s
300 m.	1,000 kc/s	1 m.	300 Mc/s
	(1 Mc/s)	10 cm.	3,000 Mc/s
200 m.	1,500 kc/s	3 cm.	10,000 Mc/s
100 m.	3,000 kc/s	1 cm.	30,000 Mc/s
	(3 Mc/s)	5 mm.	60,000 Mc/s

THE ELECTROMAGNETIC SPECTRUM

Wavelength	Frequency	Name
0·01 Å	3×10^{14} Mc/s	
0·1 Å	3×10^{13} Mc/s	Gamma rays and X-rays
10 Å	3×10^{11} Mc/s	
100 Å	3×10^{10} Mc/s	Ultra-violet light
4,000 Å	$7 \cdot 5 \times 10^8$ Mc/s	Visible light ⌐violet
		⌐red
7,500 Å	4×10^8 Mc/s	Infra-red light
1,000,000 Å	3×10^6 Mc/s	
(0·01 cm.)		
0·1 cm.	300,000 Mc/s	Radio waves from millimetre
1,000,000 cm.	30 kc/s	waves to long waves

Fading The variation in strength of a received radio signal. Medium waves suffer from this at night when the ground ray and the sky ray are received together and the sky ray is varying. Short waves suffer from it because of variations in the conditions of the reflecting ionosphere. It can be reduced in a receiver by *automatic gain control* (q.v.).

Farad The S.I. unit of *capacitance* (q.v.).

Feed Back This is the feeding back from a later part of a circuit to an earlier part. The feedback may be negative, in which case it stabilises, reduces amplification and, if it varies according to the input, provides automatic gain control. If the feedback is positive it can produce instability and even oscillation but increases amplification.

Ferrite A material made like a ceramic, i.e. by baking at a high temperature. It is made of a number of oxides, including iron oxide, and can be designed so that it has any magnetic properties desired. Moreover, it can be moulded into any shape. The magnetic coils used on the cathode-ray tubes of television receivers are wound on ferrite cores. A long rod of ferrite inside a coil constitutes a ferrite 'aerial' for a small radio receiver.

Filter A circuit device for passing oscillations of only certain desired frequencies, e.g. low-pass filter, high-pass filter, band-pass filter (for passing only a band of frequencies and cutting off everything of higher and lower frequencies).

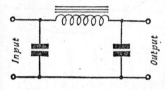

LOW-PASS FILTER: the higher the frequency of the input signal the more easily it is short-circuited. The lower the frequency the more easily it is passed on.

HIGH-PASS FILTER: the higher the frequency of the input signal the more easily it is passed on. The lower the frequency the more easily it is short-circuited.

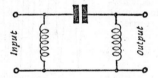

Frequency An alternating quantity (such as an alternating current or a radio wave) consists of repeated *cycles*, one cycle being the sequence of variation of the quantity from zero to maximum positive, from maximum positive through zero to maximum negative and then back to zero. The number of such cycles per second is called the frequency and is measured in *hertz* (one hertz is the same as one cycle per second).

Frequency Modulation (F.M.) A special way of making a *carrier wave* (q.v.) take an audio-frequency variation. Instead of the amplitude of the carrier being made to vary, the frequency is made to vary instead. It is done on V.H.F. transmissions by the B.B.C. to give a high-quality signal fairly free of interference by locally-made electrical noise. An F.M. receiver must have extra circuitry to transform the signal into an amplitude-modulated one for audio-frequency amplification in the usual way. The two stages needed are called the *limiter* and *discriminator*, usually combined into one stage called the *ratio detector*.

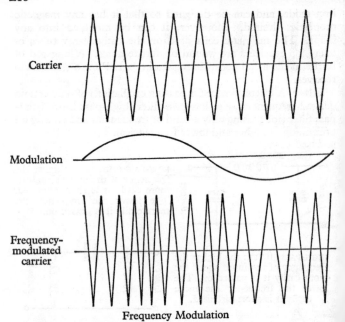

Frequency Modulation

Galvanometer An instrument which measures small electric currents.

Ganging The mechanical coupling of variable capacitors in order to tune two or more circuits with one dial.

Graphical Symbols There is a convention for representing in circuit diagrams the many sorts of components involved in electronics, radio and television. Most of these are now standardised, but some still have a few variations.

GRAPHICAL SYMBOLS

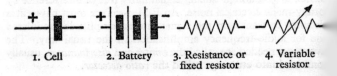

1. Cell   2. Battery   3. Resistance or   4. Variable
                                   fixed resistor   resistor

contd.

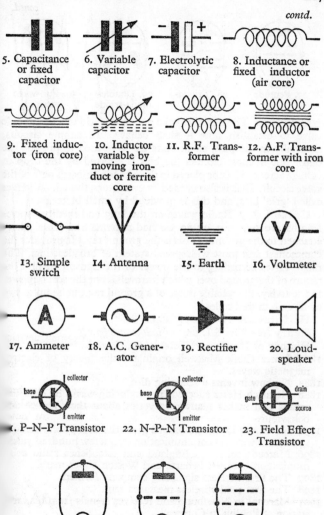

5. Capacitance or fixed capacitor **6. Variable capacitor** **7. Electrolytic capacitor** **8. Inductance or fixed inductor (air core)**

9. Fixed inductor (iron core) **10. Inductor variable by moving iron-duct or ferrite core** **11. R.F. Transformer** **12. A.F. Transformer with iron core**

13. Simple switch **14. Antenna** **15. Earth** **16. Voltmeter**

17. Ammeter **18. A.C. Generator** **19. Rectifier** **20. Loudspeaker**

21. P–N–P Transistor   **22. N–P–N Transistor**   **23. Field Effect Transistor**

24. Diode **25. Triode** **26. Tetrode**

27. Pentode   28. Triode-   29. Double-   30. Full-wave
                   hexode   diode-triode   rectifier

Grid Bias The negative volts put on the grid of a thermionic valve to establish how it shall behave. In simple circuits, especially in the past, small batteries were used to provide the bias. But in most circuits the bias is effected by the drop in voltage across a resistor placed in the cathode-to-earth part of the valve circuit. Bias is also needed by transistors, though no longer called 'grid' bias, and this is provided by small batteries.

Ground Ray Radio waves on the long and medium wavelengths are sent out by an earthed antenna and travel along attached to the ground. This is the ground ray. It provides the commonest and most widespread system of broadcasting. The range varies according to the power of the transmitter and the nature of the ground over which it travels. For the sort of power in use today, the reliable range of a ground ray can be up to two or three hundred miles.

Half-wave Aerial See AERIAL.

Henry (*H*) The S.I. unit of *inductance* (q.v.).

History of Radio and Television, *Some Important Dates*

1864 James Clerk Maxwell originates the theory of electromagnetic waves.

1884 Nipkow invents a scanning disc.

1888 Heinrich Hertz succeeds in producing waves by electric means and makes many discoveries about their nature and behaviour.

1894 Sir Oliver Lodge at Oxford gives the first public demonstration of wireless communication over a few hundred yards

1896 Marconi comes to England and establishes radio communication between Penarth and Weston-super-mare.

1897 The first wireless signalling company formed.

1898 The first paid wireless messages sent.

1901 Marconi in Newfoundland receives signals from his radio station at Poldhu in Cornwall.

1922 The British Broadcasting Company founded.

1926 Baird transmits moving pictures over a short distance.

1927 Transmission of pictures by wire over a distance of 250 miles in America.

1929 B.B.C. begins first experimental T.V. transmissions.

1936 Alexandra Palace station opened to give the world's first public high-definition T.V. service.

Hum Continuous, low frequency *noise* (q.v.) in audio equipment usually originating from the mains supply and caused, for example, by inadequate earthing or an unsmoothed power supply.

I.B.A. The Independent Broadcasting Authority (formerly the Independent Television Authority) was set up as the result of the Television Act 1954 to provide a service, additional to that of the B.B.C., for broadcasting entertainment, disseminating information, religious and educational programmes. The Authority receives no revenue through licence fees but derives its income through advertising. The first transmission started in September 1955.

Programmes are produced by 15 programme companies in 14 separate areas. National news bulletins for all areas are provided by Independent Television News, a non-profit-making company in which all the programme companies are shareholders. The programme companies under contract with the Authority for the six-year period from the end of July 1968 are:

Anglia Television (East of England); ATV Network (Midlands); Border Television (The Borders and Isle of Man); Channel Television (Channel Islands); Grampian Television (North-East Scotland); Granada Television (Lancashire); Harlech Television (Wales and West of England); London Weekend Television (London weekends from 7 p.m. Friday); Scottish Television (Central Scotland); Southern Independent Television (South of England); Thames Television (London weekdays to 7 p.m. Friday); Tyne Tees Television (North East England); Ulster Television (Northern Ireland); Westward Television (South-West England); and Yorkshire Television (Yorkshire).

Impedance (Z) The word used to represent for A.C. circuits the equivalent of *resistance* (q.v.) in a D.C. circuit. The impedance depends on the actual resistance and the *reactance* (q.v.) due to capacitance and inductance. Impedance has the same relationship to e.m.f. (E) and current (I) as resistance. So

$$I = \frac{E}{Z}$$

Inductance Whenever a coil has a varying magnetic field through it, an e.m.f. is set up in the coil causing a current to flow if the circuit is complete. This is known as *induction* and was discovered by Faraday. Whenever an electric current flows in a coil, a magnetic field is created through the coil. Therefore a varying current in a coil will produce a varying magnetic field through the coil and, by induction, will give rise to an induced current in the coil. However, the induced current is always in a direction which opposes the effect of the original current. This opposition to the passage of a varying current is called *inductive reactance* and depends on (a) the rate of change of current in the coil and (b) the *self inductance* (L) of the coil, which is a quantity that takes into account the diameter of the coil, the number of turns and the nature of the core. L is measured in *henries* and a coil has an inductance of one henry if a current varying at the rate of one ampere per second induces in the coil an e.m.f. of one volt. If A.C. of frequency f flows through a coil of inductance L, the inductive reactance (X_L) is $2\pi fL$ ohms, so that with an applied e.m.f. of V volts, the current will be $V/2\pi fL$ amps. By induction it is possible for a varying current in one coil to cause an induced current to flow in another coil. This is known as *mutual inductance* and is the basis of *transformers* (q.v.).

Inductance–Capacitance Circuit (*L–C* Circuit) In an A.C. circuit the voltage across an inductor leads the current through it by 90° (see PHASE), while that across a capacitor lags the current by 90°. This behaviour leads to interesting effects in both the series *L–C* circuit, in which an inductor is connected in series with a capacitor, and the parallel *L–C* circuit, in which an inductor is connected in parallel with a capacitor. In the series circuit, because the current through each component is the same, the voltage across the capacitor is 180° out of phase with that across the inductor. This means that the two voltages will cancel out if they are of the same magnitude. In the parallel circuit, because the voltage across each component is the same, the current through the capacitor is 180° out of phase with that through the inductor and the currents will tend to cancel each other out. The condition for complete cancellation is the same in each case, namely that the inductive reactance (X_L) equals the capacitive reactance (X_C), where both quantities depend on the frequency f of the electricity.

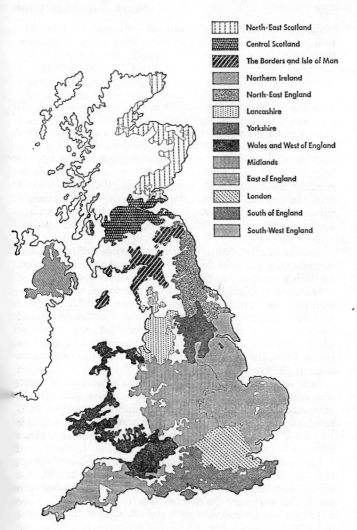

	North-East Scotland
	Central Scotland
	The Borders and Isle of Man
	Northern Ireland
	North-East England
	Lancashire
	Yorkshire
	Wales and West of England
	Midlands
	East of England
	London
	South of England
	South-West England

I.B.A. Television Transmission Areas

Now, $X_L = 2\pi fL$ and $X_c = 1/2\pi fC$
so if $X_L = X_c$
then, $2\pi fL = 1/2\pi fC$
                         $f^2 = 1/4\pi^2 LC$
                         $f = 1/2\pi\sqrt{LC}$

This special frequency is called the *resonant frequency*. At the resonant frequency in the series circuit, the combination of inductor and capacitor present no opposition to the current, though resistance in the wires does limit the current. The series *L–C* circuit is known as an acceptor circuit as, at the resonant frequency, the opposition to current is at a minimum. At the resonant frequency in the parallel circuit, the total current is zero. In practice, however, resistance in the wires means that the cancellation is not exact, but the circuit still has a maximum opposition to current at this frequency. It is therefore called a rejector circuit.

Because of this peculiar behaviour of series and parallel *L–C* circuits, they are used in *tuning* (q.v.) and other applications where it is necessary to pick out a particular frequency.

Integrated Circuit (I.C.) I.C.s are complete circuit elements (e.g. an amplifier), the individual components (transistors, capacitors and resistors) of which are all together on a single 'chip' of silicon. As individual containers for each component are not required and very little power is needed to make the circuit work, the chip can be made very small (up to 100 components per sq. mm.).

Intermediate Frequency (I.F.) This is the fixed frequency that results when an incoming signal is mixed with a locally generated oscillation. The I.F. in Britain for the *superhet* (q.v.) reception of long waves and medium waves is 470 kc/s. The I.F. for B.B.C. V.H.F. frequency modulation programmes is 10·7 Mc/s.

Ionosphere High above the earth's surface, starting at 70 miles or so, there are deep layers of gas electrified by the sun's rays. These electrified atoms and molecules affect radio waves and are known under the general term 'ionosphere'. The ionosphere varies daily and seasonally and according to the behaviour of the sun.

Medium waves are reflected from its lowest layers during the day and from higher layers at night (when the lowest layers have disappeared, this giving good intensity of reception some distance away). Short waves are reflected from the ionosphere and enable long-distance communication to take place. Very short waves penetrate the ionosphere and are lost.

Load The purpose of a circuit is to generate a signal or to modify an incoming signal and then to deliver the new signal into another apparatus known as the load. The load takes energy from the circuit that 'drives' it and the nature of the load (e.g. its impedance) alters the behaviour of the circuit. The load for an audio amplifier is usually a loudspeaker, and that for a radio transmitter is an *aerial* (q.v.).

Loudspeaker A device for turning electrical variations into variations of air pressure that reach the ears. There is commercially only one widely-used type—the moving-coil loudspeaker. In this a magnet, usually a permanent magnet, has an annular gap. On this gap floats a tiny light coil of fine wire. This moves according to the current flowing through it.

For an ordinary commercial loudspeaker the ability of the loudspeaker is usually restricted to about a range of 100–5,000 cycles per second. By special construction a loudspeaker can be made to cover a wider range than this, and a combination of loudspeakers can be made to cover from 30 to 15,000 cycles per second.

The loudspeaker is, of course, the final stage of a sound-radio receiver or the audio part of a television receiver.

Magnetic Field A region of space in which a magnet experiences a turning force (couple). Magnetic fields are produced by permanent magnets and electric currents.

Magnetometer An instrument for measuring the intensity of a magnetic field.

Maser A device for the amplification of electromagnetic waves. Used in radioastronomy for amplifying the very small signals received from distant radio galaxies, and for picking up the signals received from communications satellites.

Measuring Instruments To measure current an ammeter (milliammeter, microammeter) is used. For voltage (e.m.f., potential difference) a voltmeter is used. For resistance it is an ammeter that is required.

Microelectronics Microelectronics is concerned with the miniaturisation of electronic circuits. This is achieved by use of *integrated circuits* (q.v.) and *printed circuits* (q.v.), which enable complicated circuits (as in computers) to be kept to a very small size.

Microphone An apparatus for changing pressure waves in air (sound) into electrical variations. There are several sorts, such as the crystal microphone, the ribbon microphone, the moving-coil microphone, etc.

Microwave An electromagnetic wave with a wavelength between fifty and one-fiftieth of a centimetre.

Modulation This is the term for changing a carrier wave in such a way that it has with it the audio-frequency variations corresponding to speech or music. *Amplitude modulation* (q.v.) occurs when a carrier increases and decreases in amplitude. *Frequency modulation* (q.v.) occurs when a carrier varies in *frequency* according to the amplitude of the current from the microphone.

For reception of radio-telephony the modulation must be separated from the carrier. This is usually called *detection* (q.v.), but is sometimes called demodulation.

Molniyas The name given to the first series of Russian communications satellites.

Noise In electronic equipment, noise is unwanted hissing humming and crackling heard as a background to the wanted signal. Noise may be generated by the equipment itself (for instance due to the random thermal motions of electrons), and this is particularly troublesome in high frequency circuits carrying small signals. An important factor in such circuits is therefore the *signal-to-noise ratio* which needs to be large if the noise is not going to swamp the signal. Noise may also be picked up from outside sources, e.g. mains *hum* (q.v.) and 'atmospherics' in radio receivers.

Ohm's Law The most important law of simple electrical circuits. It states that the current through a conductor is directly proportional to the potential difference across the conductor and inversely proportional to its resistance. Ohm's Law is directly applicable to most simple DC circuits. By introducing the idea of *impedance* (q.v.), it can be generalised to AC circuits that include capacitors and inductors.

Oscillation An oscillation is one complete cycle of a regularly varying quantity. See *frequency*.

Oscillator An electronic circuit designed to generate continuous *oscillations* (q.v.). This is usually achieved by connecting

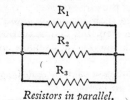

Resistors in parallel.

Total given by $\dfrac{1}{R} = \dfrac{1}{R_1} + \dfrac{1}{R_2} + \dfrac{1}{R_3}$

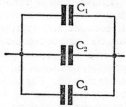

Capacitors in parallel.
Total $C = C_1 + C_2 + C_3$

an *inductance–capacitance circuit* (q.v.) to a valve or transistor amplifier and arranging positive *feedback* (q.v.) to keep the oscillations going. The *frequency* (q.v.) of the oscillations depends on the values of capacitance and inductance in the *L–C* circuit. Oscillators have numerous uses e.g. to generate the *carrier wave* (q.v.) needed to transmit radio signals.

Parallel A method of connecting circuit components. If components have ends ab, a_1b_1 a_2b_2, etc., then they are connected in parallel if all the a's are joined together and all the b's joined together. If electric cells of the same e.m.f. are joined in parallel, the total e.m.f. is that of any one of them but greater power is available from cells connected in this way. The diagram shows how to calculate the resultant resistance (or capacitance) when resistors (or capacitors) are connected in parallel. See *series*.

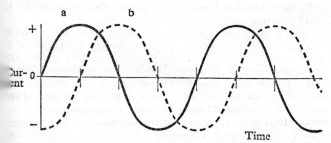

Two oscillations out of phase by 90° or one quarter of a cycle; (b) 'lags' on (a)

Phase This is a term which describes the time relationship of two oscillatory currents or waves of the same *frequency* (q.v.). If both are zero together, increase to their maximum positive together and subsequently remain in step, the two oscillations are said to be *in phase*. If, when oscillation (a) is at its maximum positive, oscillation (b) is zero, then (b) is said to be 90° *out of phase* with (a). The diagram shows the case of (b) *lagging* (a) by 90° (or equivalently (a) *leading* (b) by 90°) because when (a) is at its maximum positive, (b) is zero but increasing towards its maximum positive. If when (a) is at its maximum positive, (b) is at its maximum negative, then (a) and (b) are said to be *180° out of phase* and if combined would cancel each other out completely provided they were of the same magnitude. A phase difference of 360° means that the oscillations are again in phase as an oscillation merely repeats itself every 360°.

Piezoelectricity Electric current produced by mechanical stimulation of crystals.

p–n junction The boundary between a piece of *n*–type and a piece of *p*–type *semiconductor* (q.v.). (See *doping*). The *p–n* junction has the property of *rectification* (q.v.), and is therefore widely used in *diodes* (q.v.).

Power Power is the rate of doing work or using energy and is measured in *watts*. The rate of work done by an electrical apparatus in watts is equal to the voltage across it (in volts) multiplied by the current through it (in amps).

Prefixes Standard prefixes are:

p = 1 million-millionth = pica, e.g. 2 picafarads, 2 pF
n = 1 thousand millionth = nano, e.g. 4 nanoseconds, 4 ns
μ = 1 millionth = micro, e.g. 3 microamperes, 3μA
m = 1 thousandth = milli, e.g. 6 milliamperes, 6 mA
k = 1 thousand = kilo, e.g. 10 kilovolts, 10 kV
M = 1 million = mega, e.g. 10 megacycles, 10 Mc/s

Printed Circuit This is an insulating board with a layer of copper on one side. The copper is dissolved away except along protected paths which then act as connections between components mounted on the board. Photographic methods are often used to scale down the size of printed circuits.

Radio Receiver The simplest valve radio receiver consists of the valve and the associated tuning circuit and telephones. The commercial receiver is a *superhet* (q.v.). The controls are

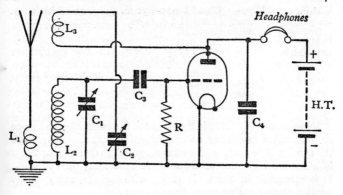

A one-valve receiver for medium-wave reception, using positive feed-back (reaction) *via* L_3 to increase the sensitivity. $C_1 = C_2 = 0.0005\mu F$ max; $C_3 = 0.0003\ \mu F$; $C_4 = 0.001\ \mu F$; $R = 2M\Omega$. Coils wound with No 28 D.C.C. wire on 2 in. diameter cylinder, $L_1 = 15$ turns, $L_2 = 75$ turns, $L_3 = 40$ turns. L_1 is spaced from L_2 with matchsticks and wound over it

normally: on-off, volume, tuning and (sometimes) tone. A wave-change switch is also usually included. The quality of a radio receiver depends, of course, on the circuitry.

The common way of building a receiver is to mount the components on and under a metal chassis, with the control spindles projecting from the front. Today the chassis technique is being replaced by a board on which connections are printed, i.e. a printed circuit (q.v.).

Radio Waves in Use

Names commonly used

Frequency	Wave-lengths	Wavelength range	Frequency range
Low frequency	Long waves	Above 600 m.	Below 500 kc/s
Medium frequency	Medium waves	200–600 m.	500–1,500 kc/s
High frequency	Short waves	10–80 m.	3,750 kc/s to 30 Mc/s

V.H.F.	Ultra-	Band I 4·41–7·32 m.	41–68 Mc/s
Very-high	short	Band II 3–3·43 m.	87·5–100 Mc/s
frequency	waves	Band III 1·39–1·72 m.	174–216 Mc/s
U.H.F.		Band IV 51–63 cm.	475–585 Mc/s
Ultra-high		Band V 31–49 cm.	610–960 Mc/s
frequency			
	Micro-	7·5 mm.–15 cm.	2,000–40,000 Mc/s
	waves	Divided into several	
		bands—S Band, X	
		Band, J Band, etc.	

Reactance (X) This is the term for the effect of capacitance or inductance in cutting down alternating current. It is given the symbol X, usually with suffixes L and C to denote whether it is inductive reactance or capacitive reactance, thus X_L, X_C. It is measured in ohms. It varies with the frequency of the applied alternating current. See *impedance*.

Rectification Alternating current reverses its direction every half cycle. Rectification is the process by which A.C. is converted to a direct current which always flows in the same direction.

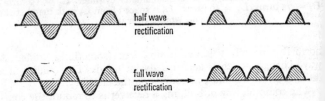

half wave rectification

full wave rectification

This is achieved by the use of rectifiers or *diodes* (q.v.) which allow current to pass through them in one direction only. In the *half wave* rectifier the $-ve$ half of the cycle is simply suppressed, while in the *full wave* rectifier, the $-ve$ half of the cycle is inverted so as to flow in the desired direction.

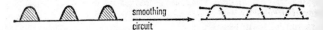

smoothing circuit

Rectification is very important because the mains supply A.C. while most electronic circuits need a D.C. supply. However to be suitable, the rectified supply has to be *smoothed* so that the voltage is nearly constant.

Resistance This is the tendency for all materials to oppo the flow of an electric current and to convert electrical energy into heat. It is measured in ohms and the resistance of a conductor depends, in simple cases, on the *resistivity* (q.v.) of the material and the dimensions of the conductor. A resistance of R ohms carrying a current of I amps converts electrical energy into heat at the rate of I^2R watts.

Resistivity This is the resistance (measured in microhms) of a cubic centimetre of material, and is a measure of how badly the material conducts electricity. The reciprocal of resistivity is *conductivity*, a measure of how well a material conducts electricity. Copper and other metals are good conductors, with a low resistivity which increases with temperature. Glass and plastics are insulators with a very high resistivity. Between these limits lie *semiconductors* (q.v.).

RESISTIVITIES

Resistivity in micro-ohm centimetres at room temperature

Aluminium	.	2·82	Amber . .	5×10^{16}
Brass .	.	About 8	Celluloid .	2×10^{10}
Copper	.	1·72	Germanium .	46×10^6
Iron	.	9·8	Graphite .	1,375
Magnesium	.	4·46	Mica (clear) .	4×10^{16}
Nichrome	.	About 100	Paraffin wax .	3×10^{18}
Nickel .	.	7·24	Plate glass .	2×10^{13}
Steel, hardened	.	About 45	Silicon . .	10
Tin . .	.	11·4	Sulphur .	2×10^{23}

Resistor An electronic component used in a circuit to provide known *resistance* (q.v.). Both fixed and variable resistors are very widely used.

Resonance When an *inductance–capacitance circuit* (q.v.) responds at a maximum to one frequency only, it is said to be in resonance with a signal of that frequency. *Tuning* (q.v.) consists of selecting the point of resonance.

Root-mean-square (R.M.S.) The average value of a quantity that takes positive and negative values equally (e.g. an alternating current) is zero. If the values are squared, the mean found and then the square root taken, the non-zero result is called the R.M.S. value. Because the heating effect of an electric current depends on the square of the current, the R.M.S. of an A.C. is equal to the constant D.C. needed to produce the same heating effect as the A.C. The peak value (or amplitude) of an A.C. is $\sqrt{2} = 1·414$ times the R.M.S. value.

Scanning The traversing of a scene or screen by a spot of light in an orderly fashion. It is scanning in successive lines in a very short time that allows a scene to be turned into electrical variations by a television camera and then into a pattern of light on a television-receiver screen.

Selectivity The ability of a radio receiver to tune to one radio station without interference from stations with nearby wavelengths.

Semiconductor A material whose *resistivity* (q.v.) is much higher than that of metals but much less than that of insulators. E.g. the elements germanium, silicon and selenium and the compounds copper oxide and indium antiminide. Semiconductors have three special electrical properties which make them very useful. (a) Unlike metals, the conductivity of semiconductors can be increased by the addition of small quantities of impurities. This is called *doping* (q.v.), and is the basis behind all modern semiconductor devices such as the *transistor* (q.v.). (b) Some semiconductors (notably selenium) increase their conductivity if light is shined on them. This is useful in photocells and in copying by the process of *xerography*. (c) Over some temperature ranges, semiconductors increase their conductivity very fast with increasing temperature, and can therefore be used where sensitivity to temperature is needed.

Series A method of connecting circuit components such that they are joined end to end. The current through each component is therefore the same, though the voltage across each will differ. The diagram shows how to work out the total resistance (capacitance) when resistors (capacitors) are connected in series. See *parallel*.

$$R_1 \qquad R_2 \qquad R_3$$

Resistors in series. Total $R = R_1 + R_2 + R_3$

$$C_1 \qquad C_2 \qquad C_3$$

Capacitors in series.

Total given by $\dfrac{1}{C} = \dfrac{1}{C_1} + \dfrac{1}{C_2} + \dfrac{1}{C_3}$

Sky Ray Radio waves going out into space and not following the ground.

Sound Sound is the sensation felt when our ears pick up pressure waves (i.e. sound waves) transmitted through a gas or other fluid from a vibrating source (e.g. a violin string). Sound waves through a gas consist of alternate compressions and rarefactions of the gas travelling along at the speed of sound. This is 332 metres per second or 760 miles an hour in air. The *pitch* of sound heard depends directly on the *frequency* (q.v.) of vibration of the source. Thus the note middle C corresponds to a frequency of vibration 256 cycles per second. The octave higher is always double the frequency.

Music and speech are built up from a large number of simple waves of different frequencies all mixed together. Even a single note played on a violin, say, consists of a lowest frequency which is called the *fundamental* (and corresponds to the pitch of the note), as well as a number of higher frequencies present in lesser strength. These are called *harmonics* and they determine the tone or quality of the note heard. This is why audio equipment sensitive to frequencies up to 15,000 cycles per second is needed for the faithful reproduction of sound.

Superhet The superheterodyne receiver. This is the common commercial type for sound and television. It enables high *selectivity* (q.v.) suitable for today's overcrowded air to be obtained without too much loss of quality.

The principle is to mix two oscillations together in a frequency-changer in such a way that no matter what the frequency of the incoming signal is, the outgoing frequency from the frequency-changer is always the same, the *intermediate frequency* (q.v.). At this fixed frequency it is comparatively easy to make satisfactory band-pass filters and transformers.

Symbols For the mathematical treatment of current, e.m.f., etc., symbols in the form of letters are used:

λ = lambda = wavelength	μ = mu = amplification factor of valve, sometimes written m.
n or f = frequency	
v = velocity	
R = resistance	g = mutual conductance of valve
I = current	
E = e.m.f.	L = inductance
R_a = A.C. resistance of valve	C = capacitance

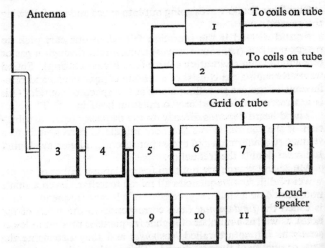

BLOCK DIAGRAM OF SUPERHET TELEVISION RECEIVER: 1. Frame Time Base. 2. Line Time Base. 3. R.F. Amplifier. 4. Frequency Changer. 5. I.F. Amplifier. 6. Video Detector. 7. Video Amplifier. 8. Sync. Separator. 9. I.F. Amplifier. 10. Audio Detector. 11. Audio Amplifier

Telstar The first television satellite, orbited by the United States.

Transformer A device for increasing or decreasing the magnitude of an alternating voltage. A step-up transformer consists of a primary coil of few turns and a secondary coil of a larger number of turns both wound on the same iron core but forming separate circuits. In a step-down transformer the primary has more turns than the secondary. The ratio of the voltage in the secondary to that in the primary is nearly equal to the ratio of the number of turns in the secondary to that in the primary. If the voltage is higher in the secondary than in the primary then the current in the secondary is proportionately lower than that in the primary, so that the power in each coil is the same. Transformers work by means of electromagnetic induction (see *inductance*). The A.C. in the primary produces a varying magnetic field through the secondary and so induces an e.m.f. in the secondary.

Transistor An electronic device consisting of three layers of *semiconductor* (q.v.). The *n–p–n* transistor has two layers of *n*-type semiconductor sandwiching a layer of *p*-type, and the *p–n–p* transistor has two layers of *p*-type sandwiching one of *n*-type (see DOPING). In either case, the middle layer is called the *base* and the outer layers are called the *collector* and *emitter*. The transistor is principally used as an amplifier, since a small current flowing in the base–emitter circuit can be used to control a much larger current in the emitter–collector circuit.

The transistor was invented in 1948 and since then has rapidly been replacing the *valve* (q.v.) in electronic circuits. The advantage of using transistors is that they can be made very small and reliable since they do not require the vacuum tube, the heater or the high voltage power supply necessary for valves.

Triode A thermionic valve with three electrodes—cathode, grid, anode.

Tuning In a radio receiver the frequency of the radio station heard is determined by the resonant frequency of an *inductance-capacitance circuit* (q.v.). By varying the capacitance in the circuit, the resonant frequency is changed and so different stations can be selected. See RESONANCE.

Valve (Thermionic Valve) This is an evacuated glass bulb containing a cathode, an anode and from zero to four other electrodes called grids. The cathode is heated (usually by a separate heating filament) and emits electrons. These electrons will only be attracted to the anode if it has a positive voltage with respect to the cathode, otherwise they will be repelled and no current will flow. Thus the simple two-electrode valve (the diode) can be used for *rectification* (q.v.). The triode valve has a perforated grid between the anode and cathode. The voltage applied to the grid now controls the electron flow between the cathode and anode. But because the grid is much closer to the cathode than the anode, small changes in the grid voltage bring about the same change in the cathode–anode current as much larger changes in the anode voltage. Hence amplification of voltages can be achieved, the amplification factor μ being the ratio of the change in anode voltage to the change in grid voltage to bring about the same change in cathode–anode current. More grids can be added to give tetrodes, pentodes etc. for special purposes. See GRID BIAS.

Video The word indicating the vision side of a television signal.

Watt (*W*) The S.I. unit of electrical *power* (q.v.).

FURTHER READING

A Dictionary of Electronics (Penguin)

Transistors Applied, by H. E. Kaden (Philips)

Electronic computers, by S. H. Hollingwood and G. C. Totill (Pelican)

Physics of Semi Conductors, by J. D. Suchet (Van Nostand)

The Annual Register of World Events (Longmans) (For information about progress in world-wide communications, year by year)

Radio Communication Handbook (The Radio Society of Great Britain)

A Dictionary of Aircraft, Rockets and Missiles

(with a section on Astronomy)

Abbreviations

A.P.U.	Auxiliary Power Unit
A.S.I.	Airspeed Indicator
A.T.C.	Air Traffic Control
C.A.A.	Civil Aviation Authority
D.F.	Direction Finder
E.A.S.	Equivalent Air Speed
F.A.A.	Federal Aviation Agency (U.S.A.)
F.A.I.	Fédération Aeronautique Internationale
I.A.S.	Indicated Air Speed
I.C.A.O.	International Civil Aviation Organisation
I.L.S.	Instrument Landing System
R.A.E.	Royal Aircraft Establishment
R.Ae.C.	Royal Aero Club
R. Ae.S.	Royal Aeronautical Society
R/T	Radio-telephony
S.B.A.C.	Society of British Aerospace Companies
T.A.S.	True Air Speed
V.F.R.	Visual Flight Rules
V.O.R.	V.H.F. Omni-range Beacon
V.T.O.L.	Vertical Take-off and Landing (q.v.)

Aerofoil The geometry of a section through a wing, roto
blade or tailplane so shaped that it can contribute lift.

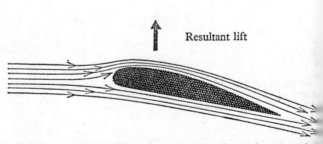

Resultant lift

Air flow over an aerofoil surface, caused by forward motion of t
aerofoil, results in a reduction of pressure above the upper surfa
and a slight increase of pressure beneath. Thus there is a resulta
lift at right-angles to the direction of the air flow.

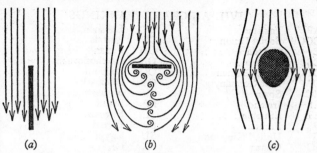

(a)   (b)   (c)

Air action on a flat plate and a stream-lined obstacle. In (a) the plate is edge-on and the air flows smoothly past. In (b) the plate is face-on and a large area of low pressure and turbulence is produced, slowing down the air. In (c) a crudely stream-lined object allows the air to flow round the surface.

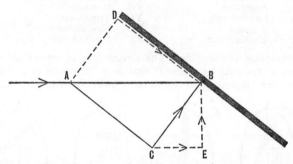

Action of air on a flat plate drawn forward. If the pressure due to the air is *AB*, this can be resolved into *CB*, at right-angles to the plate, and *DB* along the plate. *CB* can be resolved into *EB at right-angles to the air direction* and *CE* in the same direction as the air. *EB* represents the *lift*, and *CE* the *drag*.

In the same way, an aerofoil inclined at an angle of attack *DBA* to airflow in the direction *AB* will produce lift *EB* which will be additional to the lift already produced by its cambered upper surface.

Aircraft Markings All civil aircraft must be registered and carry their registration markings in prominent external positions. The markings consist of letters/numbers indicating country of origin followed by individual aircraft letters/numbers. Principal national markings are given in the table.

CIVIL AIRCRAFT MARKINGS

AP	Pakistan	OD	Lebanon
CCCP	Soviet Union	OE	Austria
C	Canada	OH	Finland
CS	Portugal	OK	Czechoslovakia
D	West Germany	OO	Belgium
DM	East Germany	OY	Denmark
EC	Spain	PH	Netherlands
EI	Ireland	PP	Brazil
ET	Ethiopia	SE	Sweden
F	France	SP	Poland
G	United Kingdom	SU	Egypt
9G	Ghana	SX	Greece
HA	Hungary	TC	Turkey
HB	Switzerland	TF	Iceland
HZ	Saudi Arabia	VH	Australia
I	Italy	VT	India
JA	Japan	XA	Mexico
LN	Norway	4X	Israel
LV	Argentine	YR	Romania
LX	Luxembourg	YU	Yugoslavia
LZ	Bulgaria	ZK	New Zealand
N	United States	ZS	South Africa

Airscrew (Propeller) The device that draws an aircraft through the air. Its action is similar to the action of a ship's propeller. It consists of two or more blades inclined at an angle

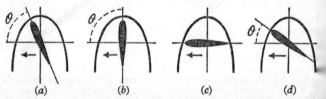

(a)   *(b)*   *(c)*   *(d)*

Section of propeller blade end-on, looking towards the hub. The angle between the line of the blade and the transverse axis of the hub is a measure of the pitch. The pitch is coarser in *(a)* than in *(d)*. In *(b)* it is coarsest and the propeller is said to be feathered. In *(c)* there is no pitch at all and the propeller achieves nothing. The arrow in each case indicates the direction in which the blade-section is supposed to be travelling for the hub to be going forward.

to the axis. In rotation the speed of the tip of a blade is greater than that of a part nearer the hub. This makes the resultant direction of air, due to the combination of forward aircraft speed and propeller rotation, change all the way along the blade. The remedy this to some extent the blade is twisted so that the tip is nearer position (c) in the diagram than the root, which may be in position (d).

As the forward speed of an aircraft changes so does the efficiency of the propeller. The higher the forward speed, the coarser should be the propeller pitch. Propellers are therefore made so that the pitch can be varied by the pilot to suit the conditions and are known as variable-pitch propellers.

Air-speed Indicator Speed through the air increases the pressure on the front. A small tube directed into the air, called a Pitot tube, can be used to direct the air-stream to a pressure-measuring device. At the same time a closed tube with holes in its sides can be used to measure the static atmospheric pressure. The difference between the two is an indication of air-speed.

Altimeter The normal height-measuring instrument is an aneroid barometer. As the atmospheric pressure decreases with height above the earth's surface, the decrease can be used as an indication of height. The drop is approximately 1 in. on the barometer for 1,000 ft. up to about 5,000 ft. Such an altimeter measures only height above sea-level, and the zero must be adjusted to suit prevailing conditions.

The radio altimeter relies on the reflection of radio signals to give the true height above the actual ground being flown over.

Artificial Horizon An instrument to assist a pilot flying blind to know when he is flying on an even keel. It depends on a gyroscope to maintain a picture of an aircraft in a horizontal position between two horizontal lines. As the aircraft changes its attitude so the picture changes.

Atmosphere The layer of gas round the earth. It consists chiefly of oxygen and nitrogen, but there are also small quantities of other gases, such as carbon dioxide, argon, helium, etc.

The pressure of the atmosphere is greatest at sea-level. It gets less and less the farther one goes away from the earth, but not in direct proportion to the height. The temperature also gets less with height up to about 36,000 ft., when it reaches $-57°$ C. and stays at this. This level is called the tropopause. Below it is the troposphere. Above it is the stratosphere.

The atmosphere is not a gas with constant characteristics. So standard atmosphere has been agreed on internationally. Figures for height records, etc., must be reduced to the standard conditions. The pressure at sea-level of this standard atmosphere is 14·7 lb./square in. or 29·75 in. of mercury. The temperature is taken as 59° F. or 15° C.

THE STANDARD ATMOSPHERE

Altitude (ft.)	Pressure (lb./in.²)	Temperature (° C.)
100,000	0·152	
90,000	0·245	
80,000	0·397	Ambient temperature
70,000	0·642	remains constant
60,000	1·038	above 36,000 ft.
50,000	1·679	
40,000	2·717	
35,000	3·455	−54·342
30,000	4·361	−44·436
25,000	5·450	−34·530
20,000	6·750	−24·624
15,000	8·291	−14·718
10,000	10·104	−4·812
8,000	10·913	−0·850
5,000	12·226	5·094
4,000	12·691	7·075
3,000	13·170	9·056
2,000	13·664	11·038
1,000	14·172	13·019
Sea-level	14·696	15·000

(lb./in² = pounds to the square inch)

Autogiro The trade name for a type of rotating-wing aircraft invented by Juan de la Cierva. The wing or rotor is not driven by an engine.

Automatic Pilot A device whereby an aircraft will fly automatically on an even keel on a prescribed course without the attention of the pilot. Any roll or yaw or pitch or change in direction is indicated by the instruments, and signals are sent by servo mechanisms to make the necessary change to rudder or elevator.

More elaborate automatic pilots can also maintain a rate of climb or descent or a constant height.

Ballistic Missiles See MISSILES.

Boundary Layer The layer of air close to the surface of an aerofoil. It is very thin. The airflow at the leading edge is usually laminar, i.e. parallel to the surface, but farther back it is broken up and the resulting turbulence produces drag. Several attempts have been made to avoid this, one important one being an arrangement for sucking in air through surface holes in the aerofoil.

British Aircraft Manufacturers

The organisations listed here are currently producing complete aircraft on a production basis. Amateur constructors and firms making kits of parts for home construction are not included.

AJEP Developments, Hertford.

British Aerospace, Aircraft Division, with factories at Bristol; Bitteswell; Brough; Chester; Hamble; Hatfield; Hurn; Kingston-upon-Thames; Preston; Prestwick; Weybridge; and Woodford.

Britten-Norman (Bembridge) Ltd, Bembridge, Isle-of-Wight.

Crosby Aviation Ltd, Knutsford, Cheshire.

W. H. Ekin (Engineering) Co Ltd, Crumlin, Co. Antrim, Northern Ireland.

Leisure Sport Ltd, Egham, Surrey.

NDN Aircraft Ltd, Goodwood, Sussex.

Short Brothers Ltd, Belfast, Northern Ireland.

Swales Sailplanes, Thirsk, North Yorkshire.

Vickers-Slingsby (A division of Vickers Ltd Offshore Engineering Group), Kirkbymoorside, York.

Wallis Autogyros Ltd, Rymerston Hall, Norfolk.

Westland Helicopters Ltd, Yeovil, Somerset.

Consol A long-range navigation aid developed in the 1940s, now largely replaced by more modern systems. Operating in the 900–1100 M (250–320 kHz) band, it has a useful range of around 700 miles over land by day. Radio waves of this type travel further at night and over the sea, giving a maximum range of 1,000–1,200 miles.

There are four stations—Bushmills (Northern Ireland), Lugo (Spain), Quimper (France) and Stavanger (Norway). These emit a series of Morse dots and dashes separated by a period of virtual silence called the equi-signal. By monitoring the number of dots and dashes heard between successive equi-signals the true bearing of the receiver from the station can be determined from published charts. In good reception, bearings accurate to about one degree can be attained. Given two or more signals, a number of bearing lines can be drawn, the intersection of which is the position of the receiver.

Decca Navigator A navigation system used by both ships and aircraft which was developed in the 1950s in Britain with the idea of making it world-wide in scope.

A Decca 'chain' consists of a master transmitter whose low-frequency transmissions (70–130 kHz) are closely related to those of three associated slave transmitters. These slaves transmit so that their signals are each in exact phase with that of the master. The receiver measures the phase of the received signal from each transmitter and displays the phase difference between the master signal and each slave. This can be presented in a number of ways: either numerically, by a coded light system or, in the more advanced receivers, directly on a map, thus giving a precise fix and track information. Each transmitter can be received over a distance of about 1,000 miles, and a number of chains cover most of Europe, the eastern seaboard of the United States and some other parts of the world, particularly in areas of heavy ship traffic. It is a very accurate aid, fixes of better than one mile accuracy are usual, and it is standard on a number of aircraft, such as many of those of British Airways and the larger helicopters used in North Sea oil exploration. Although it did not gain universal acceptance, it is still being developed and new chains are occasionally opened.

Delta Wing A wing planform which forms the shape of a triangle. It has many of the aerodynamic advantages of a swept-back wing but is structurally more efficient.

Dihedral Angle The angle between the wing and the horizontal, looking head-on at the aircraft. Most aircraft have some dihedral angle which tends to stabilise roll.

θ = dihedral angle

Drag The force resisting the motion of an aircraft through the air. It can be broken down into two parts: induced drag caused inevitably with lift (q.v.) by the pressure difference over the wing: and parasitic drag caused by turbulence (q.v.

due to roughness of the skin, interference of airflow round different parts of the aeroplane, projections such as aerials, radomes, cockpits.

Escape Velocity The velocity that a body must have to get away from the gravitational pull of earth. It is given by the equation

$$V = \sqrt{2gR}$$

where R = distance from centre of earth; g = acceleration due to gravity at distance R.

For ordinary purposes the escape velocity from the earth is taken as about 7 miles a second or 11·2 km. a second. At this velocity a projectile will follow a parabolic course and never return to earth.

Free Fall The state of non-resistance to a gravitational field. This happens with a body falling towards the earth before it enters the earth's atmosphere. It happens with a satellite in orbit. A passenger inside a vehicle in free fall has the sensation of being weightless, because the vehicle is not resisting the gravitational field. Anyone falling from a height towards the ground feels the air resistance and so is not exactly in free fall, though nearly so. In the 'weightless' condition a man jumping up will hit the ceiling. He will have no sense of balance. Men can experience this state for a few seconds only in an aircraft making a loop when the speed is enough for centrifugal force to balance the earth's gravitational force. Crews have now been weightless for long periods in manned space vehicles.

Fuels For rockets see under PROPELLANT.

Petrol is used in piston engines, but gas turbines (jet engines, turboprops, turbofans) burn a kerosene or paraffin-based fuel.

g The acceleration due to gravity, which on the surface of the earth is taken as roughly 32 ft. per sec. per sec. or 981 cm. per sec. per sec. It is also taken as a unit of acceleration for discussions of the forces acting on rockets and airmen and astronauts. An airman, for example, flying at 500 m.p.h. along a curved path of 1 mile radius would experience a centrifugal force equivalent to an acceleration of 5 g.

Gas Turbine See JET PROPULSION.

Gravity The force of attraction between bodies according to the law of gravitation, which states that any two bodies in the universe attract each other with a force that is directly proportional to the product of the masses and inversely proportional to the square of the distance between them. That is

$$\text{Force} = \frac{km_1m_2}{d^2}$$

k is the gravitational constant $= 6.67 \times 10^{-8}$ in c.g.s. units.

Calculation from this shows that the acceleration due to gravity (g) at the earth's surface is about 32 ft. per sec. per sec. This varies, however, with geographical position, and gets very much less with height above the earth's surface.

Guided Missiles See MISSILES.

Gyroscope Used in many navigational instruments in aircraft and ships. It consists essentially of a heavy wheel spun by an electric motor or a turbine and rotating at high speed. It has two properties: (i) if it is supported in frictionless gimbals so that it can rotate freely in all three dimensions, it will remain parallel to its original position, i.e. it has 'rigidity in space': (ii) if it is not supported in gimbals but is made to turn it will *precess* and exert a force proportional to the rate of turn—a measure of the force being a measure of the rate of turn. This is used, for example, to correct gunsights for the movement of the aircraft.

Both these properties can be combined: if a gyro is held in one direction in its gimbals so that it has to turn with the earth it will precess until it points North and the N–S axis of the earth's rotation is parallel to its own axis. It will then continue to point North, and can be used as a genuine compass.

Heat Barrier Currently a major problem in the advance of aircraft speeds. At sufficiently high speeds the kinetic energy of the air flowing past the aircraft is turned into appreciable heat energy, and the temperature of the aircraft skin at Mach 3 can reach the melting point of steel. Aircraft to travel at these speeds therefore must be made of heat-resisting materials, and the crew, passengers and electronic gear must be refrigerated. Spacecraft leave the atmosphere too quickly for kinetic heating to be a problem, but it becomes a major factor during re-entry.

Helicopter This is an aircraft that can rise vertically by the use of rotating wings. These wings, very long and narrow, are aerofoils, and constitute the rotor. When this is in action the lift provided by the passage of the blades through the air propels the

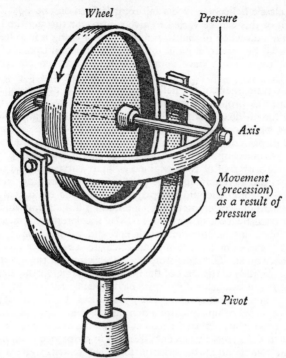

Wheel

Pressure

Axis

*Movement
(precession)
as a result of
pressure*

Pivot

A gyro in gimbals. Pressure on the axis makes the whole support move round. If this pressure is supplied by a weight that points towards the centre of the earth the axis will always point in the same direction in relation to the earth.

aircraft vertically. The engine-power has to be enough to provide lift for the whole weight of the aircraft.

For forward movement the plane of the rotor is tilted downward in front. This is achieved by altering the pitch of the rotor blades so that as each passes through the rear part of the rotation its pitch is increased and as it passes through the front part of the rotation its pitch is decreased. The unequal thrusts tilt the machine downwards and forwards.

As the helicopter body is free to rotate it tends to go round in the opposite direction to that of the rotor. To overcome this in the classic helicopter type a tail rotor is fixed on one side. The pitch of this can be varied to give control for turning the helicopter's direction of flight. Another way of doing it is to have a rotor at the rear rotating in the opposite direction to that of the front rotor, or to have counter-rotating rotors on concentric shafts.

A development of the helicopter is that using normal forward engines as propellers for forward flight, the rotor being used only for lifting. This was the method used in the Fairey Rotodyne, which could go from city-centre to city-centre carrying a load of passengers (the biggest of ordinary helicopters takes no more than a couple of dozen passengers) at a speed roughly comparable with that of twin-engined airliners current at that time.

Inertial Navigation The only type of airborne navigation which is automatic and independent of outside radio beacons. A system of accelerometers is mounted on a platform which is kept level by a set of gyroscopes. The accelerometers measure the forces in the fore-and-aft, lateral and vertical planes, and from these an onboard computer calculates speed, heading and distance gone. The crew simply tell the computer their latitude and longitude at the start of the flight, and thereafter the inertial system will automatically display navigational information about any required destination. The system can be linked to the autopilot for complete automation, and a wide range of output data is possible. Inertial becomes inaccurate due to mechanical drift in the gyros, but recent advances in gyroscope technology mean that after a transatlantic flight an inertial system will generally show a position within 5 n.m. of the true position. This is now virtually the standard long-range navigation system, and developments now being investigated will significantly reduce the present very small errors.

Jet Propulsion The pushing forward of a vehicle by the rapid backwards efflux of a mass of gas. In effect, a rocket is working by jet, but the expression is usually restricted to the gas turbine. The first jet engine was built by Sir Frank Whittle at the beginning of the last war, and flew in the Gloster E28/39 experimental jet aircraft in 1941.

The gas turbine works by sucking air in at the front, compressing it, mixing vaporised fuel—usually paraffin—with it, igniting the mixture, making the burning gases flow through turbine to drive the compressor by a shaft, and letting them

TABLE OF FAMOUS JET ENGINES

Makers	Name	Maximum thrust (lb.)
Rolls-Royce	Spey (military) RB.168–25R	12,250 (dry)
	RB.211–524	50,000
	Viper 600	3,750
	Olympus 593	37,700 (dry)
	Pegasus 11 Mk. 103	21,500
Pratt & Whitney	JT8D–17R	17,400
	JT9D–59A	53,000
	F100–PW100	23,810
U.S. General Electric	CF6–50A	49,000
	CF700–2D	4,250
U.S.S.R.	Kuznetsov NK–8–4	22,270
	Kuznetsov NK–144	28,660 (dry)
	Soloviev D–30KP	26,455

escape in a jet to drive the aircraft. In most large modern gas turbines the compressor and turbine are *axial*: that is, they consist of many small blades set on a drum moving in between stationary blades mounted on a closely-fitted casing. Small gas turbines have a centrifugal compressor. In a ramjet the forward motion of the engine is used to compress the incoming air sufficiently for combustion to take place. This can happen only at very high speeds—about three times the speed of sound.

Lift Vertical force due to the flow of air round an aerofoil. Three-quarters of it, roughly speaking, is composed of suction due to low pressure on the upper surface of the aerofoil: the other quarter is due to pressure underneath. The lift increases with the *angle of attack* (q.v.) until the aerofoil stalls.

Loran Loran is a navigation system which is broadly similar to Decca (q.v.), but the transmissions of master and slaves are not phase-, but time-linked. Each master and slave on a chain emits a short pulse at exactly the same time. The time between the arrival of the pulses from the master and from each of the slaves gives a position fix. Again, modern computing has taken much of the drudgery out of navigation, but Loran is being phased out of civilian use (although it is still being developed for military use).

Mach Number A number which relates the speed of an aircraft to the speed of sound in the same conditions. Mach 1, the speed of sound is taken as 1,094 ft. per sec. in air at NTP, so under the same conditions Mach 2 would be 2,188 ft. per sec. and Mach 3, 3,282 ft. per sec., and so on. Mach 1 is 761 m.p.h. at ground level but due to fall in pressure is only 660 m.p.h. at 36,000 ft. (tropopause).

Missiles Missiles are, of course, anything thrown, but today they almost invariably mean the powerful weapons that depend mainly on rocket-engines for their propulsion. They are classified into strategic and tactical; short, medium, intermediate or intercontinental in range; ballistic or guided; use, whether surface-to-air, air-to-air, etc.

Missiles as weapons are inextricably mixed up with space research, for the same basic missiles, without the warhead and modified electronically, serve to launch satellites.

Ballistic missiles are those that travel most of the way on a trajectory like that of any projectile. Guidance is used at first to set such a missile on course. Then the rocket burns out and the rest of the missile travels a natural course to target. They are classified as ICBM—intercontinental ballistic missile, and IRBM—intermediate-range ballistic missile.

Guided missiles are controlled for all or most of the way to their target. Some are guided all the way by radio signals from the ground. Others are steered by automatic celestial navigation, inertial systems or Doppler radio (which depends on a change of frequency when a source is approaching or receding) or radar. Missiles for short ranges at moving targets have homing devices, whether radar or the reception of radiation (radio or infra-red) from the target.

The number and naming of missiles has reached such a pitch that no list of missiles is worth giving, so soon are so many out of date. Mention may be made, however, of the U.S. Atlas, an ICBM of great range, the booster for several satellite launchings, and used for the first man-in-orbit scheme of the U.S.A.—Project Mercury, on February 20, 1962, when Colonel John H. Glenn completed three orbits and returned unharmed.

Navigation The method by which an object (ship, aircraft motor car) is steered towards a desired point. For aeronautica use either radio beacons, maps or inertial (*q.v.*) can be used while a magnetic compass, or more usually a gyroscopic com pass, is used to indicate heading. Radio beacons of types such as VOR or NDB are arranged so that the navigator can calculate a fix from differing bearings, while Decca (*q.v.*) uses phase-difference and Loran a time-difference between received signals. Inertial navigation uses self-contained sensors to determine position without outside reference.

For basic navigation *dead reckoning* and *astro* (star) navigation are used, as they were used by ancient sailors. The first depends on knowing wind speed and direction accurately so as to compensate the known heading, while the latter relies on tables of the angles of given stars at given times. Neither system is effective in fast-moving aircraft, and the modern computer has taken over most of the work.

Omega Omega is a very-low-frequency navigation aid (10 kHz) with eight beacons covering the entire earth. It is the system that is directly replacing the civilian Loran. With a wavelength of some 18 miles, once the on-board computer is told its present latitude and longitude, it simply 'counts' waves from each of the stations it receives and can calculate not only instantaneous position as the aircraft moves but also a wide range of navigational data just as inertial (q.v.) can. Omega can also be used by ships and submarines.

Orbit The name given to the closed path of a satellite round the earth or any body round any other. The earth is in orbit round the sun, the moon (and many artificial satellites) in orbit round the earth. Usually an orbit is an ellipse.

Propellant The name given to the materials used in rocket engines. They can be divided into two classes—liquid and solid, though the possibility of ionic propulsion and nuclear propulsion do not come into this division.

Liquid propellants consist mostly of a fuel and an oxidant. The fuel can be paraffin, petrol, alcohol, hydrazine, aniline or other liquid that can be oxidised to form enormous volumes of gas. The oxidant can be liquid oxygen, red fuming nitric acid, hydrogen peroxide, fluorine or any other yet to be announced. The V2 used on London during the Second World War was propelled by liquid oxygen and alcohol.

There are a few single liquid propellants, even though chemically they are mixtures.

There are also solid fuels. The simplest is, of course, gunpowder. There is also cordite. Other solid fuels include:

(a) J.P.N., a mixture of nitrocellulose, nitroglycerine, diethyl phthalate, carbamite, potassium sulphate, carbon and wax; (b) galcit, a mixture of potassium perchlorate and a fuel such as asphalt; (c) N.D.R.C., a mixture of ammonium picrate, sodium nitrate and resin.

Research continues for better and better fuels. Some are naturally kept secret even when discovered.

The 'goodness' of a propellant is measured as *specific impulse*, given by the equation

$$\text{Specific impulse} = \frac{\text{Thrust in pounds}}{\text{Rate of loss of mass in pounds}}$$

It is related to the exhaust velocity of gas by the equation

$$\text{Specific impulse} = \frac{\text{Exhaust velocity}}{\text{g}}$$

Propeller See AIRSCREW.

Radar Developed in Britain during the Second World War radar is an electronic system for determining the position of a target (usually airborne) from a ground station. A large radar aerial emits extremely high-frequency pulsed radio signals in a beam only about one degree wide. The aerial rotates at about 5-10 r.p.m., thus covering the whole sky with the beam.

Some tiny part of the radar beam may hit an aircraft and return to the aerial, where it is collected and the time taken for the two-way passage determined. From this, and the direction in which the beam was transmitted, a computer determines the position of the aircraft, which is then displayed on a cathode-ray tube as a fluorescent dot. Techniques have been evolved to eliminate returns from nearby buildings, or stationary object some distance away, such as masts. Modern computers can calculate such information as aircraft heading and speed from successive returns and display this information alongside the radar return on the tube.

Radar is used for many purposes. Virtually all air traffic controlled by radar, and its highly accurate position information means it can be used for long-range (up to 250 miles) or short range control. Around the airfield, aircraft are brought in land using either PAR (precision approach radar) or more commonly GCA (ground controlled approach) down to one-h mile or less from touchdown. Aircraft themselves can be equipped with radar for storm avoidance, when it is used for locating clouds (the beam reflects off the rain droplets). Secondary Surveillance Radar (SSR) is a development of ordinary (primary) radar, and is a back-up facility for air traffic control. The radar beam has a peculiar pulse pattern which triggers off a device called the transponder in an aircraft. But only such transponders as the air traffic controllers request will be 'on' (i.e. able to be triggered), and each will be set to one of 4,096 codes as the controller demands. Once triggered, a transponder emits a radio signal which is unique to its code. By very advanced computing techniques on the ground, this coded reply can be correlated with the primary reply, this giving positive information of each transponding return. Aircraft height also can be transponded, and the computer can convert transponder codes into aircraft call-signs and determine speed and heading.

Radio Beacons As well as the Decca, Consol and Loran (*q.v.*) beacon systems used for aerial navigation, all airways are defined by a different series of beacons. These basically fall into three types, VOR, NDB and DME.

A VOR (very-high-frequency omni-directional range) transmits in the range 108–118 MHz. An unmodulated reference tone which has the same phase regardless of direction has superimposed on it a second tone whose phase varies as the direction of transmission. A Morse-code identification is superimposed on the transmission. The airborne receiver simply picks up the signal, deciphers the phase of the varying signal and displays the associated bearing.

The older NDB (Non-directional beacon) transmits in the medium-wave band. A constant tone, with Morse-code identification, transmits uniformly in all directions. The airborne receiver interprets the direction from which the signal is coming (by rotating an aerial to give the strongest signal) and displays that relative bearing.

DME (Distance measuring equipment) and its military cousin Tacan (Tactical air-navigation) determine the time taken for a pulse to travel from the beacon to the aircraft; in the aircraft, this is converted into distance. Tacan also gives bearing information.

Records Records recognised officially have to be made according to certain fixed rules and all attempts are under the

control of the Fédération Aéronautique Internationale (F.A.I.).
Unofficially a number of aircraft have flown faster than the
official record shows, but not under the permissible conditions.

The official World Records correct to September, 1977, are:

Speed in straight line over 15 to 25 km. Capt. Eldon W.
Joersz and Maj. George T. Morgan, Jr., (U.S.A.F.) at
Beale Air Force Base, California, in a Lockheed SR-71A
on July 28, 1976, 2,193 m.p.h.

Altitude. Alexander Fedotov, U.S.S.R., in an E-266 (MiG-
25), 118,898 ft., on July 25, 1973.

Distance in a straight line. Major Clyde P. Evely, (U.S.A.F.),
in a Boeing B-52H Stratofortress, on January 10–11, 1962,
between Okinawa and Madrid, 12,532·3 miles.

Distance in a closed circuit. Captain William M. Stevenson,
(U.S.A.F.), in a Boeing B-52H Stratofortress, Seymour
Johnson Air Force Base–Bermuda–Sondrestrom (Green-
land)–Anchorage (Alaska)–March Air Force Base–Key
West–Seymour Johnson Air Force Base, June 6–7, 1962,
11,337 miles.

Altitude in sustained horizontal flight. Capt. Robert C. Helt
and Maj. Larry A. Elliott (U.S.A.F.) at Beale Air Force
Base, California, in a Lockheed SR-71A on July 28, 1976,
85,069 ft.

Speed in closed circuit. Maj. Adolphus H. Bledsoe, Jr., and
Maj. John T. Fuller (U.S.A.F.) at Beale Air Force Base,
California, in a Lockheed SR-71A over a 1,000 km circuit
on July 27, 1976, 2,092 m.p.h.

Re-entry This means re-entry into the earth's atmosphere.
All discussions of space travel depend on the solution of the
problem of how a vehicle in orbit at speeds of thousands of
miles an hour can get back to earth safely. This is the problem of
losing speed near the ground and of getting through the earth's
atmosphere without burning up.

The problem has been solved by the U.S.A. and Russia. Each
has brought space vehicles out of orbit and retrieved them.

The solution of the first stage, the entry into the atmosphere
at high speed, has been so far to have a fairly blunt-nosed
vehicle with an outer skin that burns up. In the few minutes of
travel such a burn-up of the outside can save the inside. The
solution of the final stage so far has been the use of parachutes.

released at a certain height, but the Space Shuttle will glide back to earth.

Reciprocating Engine Another name for piston engine, in which the rotation of a shaft is activated by the in-and-out action of pistons in cylinders. All early aero engines were piston engines.

Rocket A rocket is a vehicle driven by a type of engine that does not depend on air. It is therefore able to function in outer space.

In a rocket, fuels called propellants are burned to create intense volumes of gas, and this gas is shot out of the only opening in the rocket—the rear. The resultant pressure of the gases is therefore forward. So the rocket travels. The simplest rocket used in fireworks has gunpowder or similar fuel lit by a fuse when on the ground.

As the rocket travels upwards it loses the fuel that is being consumed. So the total weight gets less and the rocket acceler-

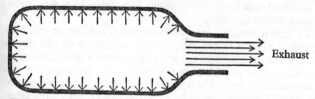

The propulsion system of a rocket. The fuel burns to form very quickly immense volumes of gas, which expand to press on the surroundings. The only outlet is at the rear. So the resultant pressure, shown by arrows, is forwards.

ates more and more until all the fuel is spent. The weight at starting must be great, because all the fuel is there. The ratio of this initial mass to the final mass when the fuel is gone is called the *mass ratio*. The velocity at the end is given by the equation

$$V = c \log_e R$$

where R = mass ratio; c = jet velocity.

Turned into common logarithms, this becomes

$$V = 2 \cdot 3 \, c \log_{10} R$$

The bigger the final velocity must be, the more fuel there must be and the bigger (and heavier) must be the casing and rocket-engine apparatus. Consequently the practice has become necessary, for space research, of using rockets in several stages. Then when the first stage, or booster, is burned out its heavy container can be automatically thrown away. The next rocket stage then starts to fire with all the advantages of height and speed reached with the help of the booster. So it can be smaller. Thus a composite rocket of several stages can be built up.

Rockets need an immense amount of engineering and electronics for the many controls needed if they are to achieve anything other than going up in smoke.

Largest known spacecraft launcher, the American Saturn V, weighs 3,000 tons at launch and is 365 ft. high. The five S1C stage Boeing F-1 kerosene engines produce $7\frac{1}{2}$ million pounds thrust, and the five S2 stage Rocket-dyne J-2 liquid hydrogen engines produce 1,000,000 lb. thrust.

Satellites Any body in orbit round a bigger body is a satellite. The moon is a satellite of the earth, and the earth can be described as a satellite of the sun.

Artificial satellites are man-made objects put into orbit, usually round the earth.

To get a satellite into orbit round the earth it must be launched parallel to the earth's surface, high above the earth's atmosphere, at sufficient speed. If the speed is too little the intended satellite will fall back to earth. If the speed is above the escape velocity (q.v.) it will fly off into space. Between a certain minimum velocity, depending on the height, and the escape velocity, there is a range of velocities that will take a satellite into orbit. This range at a height of 300 miles is from about 4·9 to 6·9 miles per sec., at 400 miles from 4·7 to 6·7 miles per sec. and at 1,000 miles from 4·45 to 6·3 miles per second. A vehicle launched at the lower speed would just orbit on a circular orbit, whereas one launched at exactly the higher speed would depart on a parabolic path.

If launched into orbit at a speed between these values (for the correct height) the vehicle would travel on an ellipse, being farthest away from the earth at one end and nearest at the opposite end.

The satellite must be launched more or less parallel to the earth. This is done by radioed instructions from the ground. Clearly, enormous rocket power is needed to get a satellite up to the launching height.

Since the successful orbital flight of the Russian Sputnik in October 1957, many thousand successful satellites have been launched; others have been launched secretly. Many of these have since come out of orbit; the time a satellite lasts depends on how deeply it dips into the earth's atmosphere. At 100 miles high a satellite might last a week before air resistance slowed it down and burnt it up; at 800 miles it could last indefinitely.

The amount of machinery in orbit is getting immense: as well as the existing satellites, there are the same number of last stage boosters, discarded fairings; one rocket blew up in orbit and produced no fewer than 200 fragments. The situation is also complicated by the chattering of the earlier satellites, which, although they have finished their missions, cannot be switched off, and their radio transmitters go on using valuable wavelengths.

Satellites serve several purposes; here is a short guide. (The unqualified type-names refer to U.S. machines.)

Physical Research—Designed to study electrical and magnetic fields at high altitudes, the emission of atomic particles and X-rays from the sun.

Navigation—Transit, Anna. The first named emits precisely timed radio signals as a navigational aid for Polaris submarines and other ships. The Anna series of satellites are used for surveying and mapping the positions of the continents on the globe.

Reconnaissance—Big Bird satellites carry cameras to watch military activity in hostile countries.

Communications—The first Telstar, launched in 1962, was a failure; but its successor allowed television viewers in Europe to see live events in America such as the Negro Freedom March on Washington, and President Kennedy's funeral. Satellites can pass on television, voice and telegraph channels at great distances; but at the moment it is uncertain how best to set up a world-wide satellite communications system. The difficulty is in choosing a height for the orbits. Low level repeaters like Telstar pass so quickly overhead that they are in range of stations on either side of the Atlantic for only about 20 minutes at a time. A considerable number would be necessary, and the ground stations would have to keep shifting their aim from one to the other. An alternative is a set of three satellites so high that they can see right round the globe to each other, and appear to stand still in the sky over the same three spots. This makes the tracking problem easier, but the relaying transmitters in the satellites must be more powerful to cope with the increased range. Another snag about the synchronous satellite (so called because it does one orbit in 24 hours, the time it takes the earth to rotate once) is that signals take an appreciable time to make the round trip, so it would be difficult to hold a telephone conversation.

Mancarrying—American and Russian satellites have carried men—and a woman—into orbit and safely back. This is the most spectacular feat in space, but from the scientific point of view probably the least valuable.

SATELLITES PLACED IN ORBIT DURING 1976–77

Satellite	Launcher	Weight lb.	Purpose	Country	Date
Cosmos 837	Vostok core	2,750	Comm.	U.S.S.R.	1.7.76
Cosmos 838	Scarp	?	Interceptor	U.S.S.R.	2.7.76
USAF Big Bird	Titan 3D	{ 30,000	Reconn.	U.S.A.	8.7.76
Capsule 65C		?	Pick-a-back		
Palapa 1	Thor Delta	1,265	Comm.	Indonesia	8.7.76
Cosmos 839	Skean	?	?	U.S.S.R.	8.7.76
Cosmos 840	Vostok core	9,000	Reconn.	U.S.S.R.	14.7.76
Cosmos 841	Skean	1,650	Military	U.S.S.R.	15.7.76
Cosmos 842	Skean	1,545	Nav.	U.S.S.R.	21.7.76
Cosmos 843	Scarp	?	Interceptor	U.S.S.R.	21.7.76
Cosmos 844	Vostok core	9,000	Reconn.	U.S.S.R.	22.7.76
Comstar 1B	Atlas-Centaur	3,350	Comm.	U.S.A.	22.7.76
Molniya 1AL	Vostok core	2,200	Comm.	U.S.S.R.	23.7.76
Cosmos 845	Skean	1,985	Military	U.S.S.R.	27.7.76
Intercosmos 16	Skean	1,200	Sc.	U.S.S.R.	27.7.76
NOAA-5 (ITOS-H)	Thor Delta	750	Weather	U.S.A.	29.7.76
Cosmos 846	Skean	1,545	Nav.	U.S.S.R.	29.7.7
Cosmos 847	Vostok core	9,000	Reconn.	U.S.S.R.	4.8.7
SDS 3	Titan 3B-Agena D	?	Sc.	U.S.A.	6.8.7
Cosmos 848	Vostok core	9,000	Reconn.	U.S.S.R.	12.8.7
Cosmos 849	Sandal	900	Military	U.S.S.R.	18.8.7
Cosmos 850	Sandal	900	Military	U.S.S.R.	26.8.7
Cosmos 851	Vostok core	5,600	Military	U.S.S.R.	27.8.7
Cosmos 852	Vostok core	9,000	Reconn.	U.S.S.R.	28.8.7
China 6	ICBM deriv.	595	Sc.	China	30.8.7
Cosmos 853	Vostok core	2,750	Comm.	U.S.S.R.	1.9.7
TIP 3	Scout	210	?	U.S.A.	1.9.7
Cosmos 854	Vostok core	9,000	Reconn.	U.S.S.R.	3.9.7
AMS 1	Thor-Burner 2	990	Weather	U.S.A.	11.9.
Statsionar 1B	Proton core	?	Comm.	U.S.S.R.	11.9.
USAF 94A	Titan 3B-Agena D	6,600	Military	U.S.A.	15.9.
Cosmos 855	Vostok core	9,000	Reconn.	U.S.S.R.	21.9.
Cosmos 856	Vostok core	9,000	Reconn.	U.S.S.R.	22.9.
Cosmos 857	Vostok core	9,000	Reconn.	U.S.S.R.	24.9.
Cosmos 858	Skean	1,650	Military	U.S.S.R.	29.9.
Cosmos 859	Vostok core	9,000	Reconn.	U.S.S.R.	10.10.
Marisat 3	Uprated Thor Delta	1,450	Comm.	U.S.A.	14.10.
Meteor 26	Vostok core	4,850	Weather	U.S.S.R.	15.10
Cosmos 860	?	?	?	U.S.S.R.	17.10.
Cosmos 861	?	?	?	U.S.S.R.	21.10
Cosmos 862	Vostok core	2,750	Comm.	U.S.S.R.	22.10
Cosmos 863	Vostok core	9,000	Reconn.	U.S.S.R.	25.10
Statsionar IC	Proton core	?	TV relay	U.S.S.R.	26.10
Cosmos 864	Skean	1,545	Nav.	U.S.S.R.	29.10
Cosmos 865	Vostok core	9,000	Reconn.	U.S.S.R.	1.11

Satellite	Launcher	Weight lb.	Purpose	Country	Date
Cosmos 866	Vostok core	9,000	Reconn.	U.S.S.R.	11.11.76
Cosmos 867	Vostok core	9,000	Reconn.	U.S.S.R.	23.11.76
Prognoz 5	Vostok core	2,050	Sc.	U.S.S.R.	25.11.76
Cosmos 868	Scarp	?	Interceptor	U.S.S.R.	26.11.76
Cosmos 869	Vostok core	14,500	?	U.S.S.R.	29.11.76
Cosmos 870	Skean	1,990	Military	U.S.S.R.	2.12.76
Molniya 2R	Vostok core	2,750	Comm.	U.S.S.R.	2.12.76
China 7	ICBM deriv.	2,650	Sc.	China	7.12.76
Cosmos 871	} Skean	90	Military	} U.S.S.R.	7.12.76
Cosmos 872		90	Military		
Cosmos 873		90	Military		
Cosmos 874		90	Military		
Cosmos 875		90	Military		
Cosmos 876		90	Military		
Cosmos 877		90	Military		
Cosmos 878		90	Military		
Cosmos 879	Vostok core	9,000	Reconn.	U.S.S.R.	9.12.76
Cosmos 880	Skean	?	?	U.S.S.R.	9.12.76
Cosmos 881	} ?	{ ?	? }	U.S.S.R.	9.12.76
Cosmos 882		{ ?	? }		
Cosmos 883	Skean	1,545	Nav.	U.S.S.R.	15.12.76
Cosmos 884	Vostok core	9,000	Reconn.	U.S.S.R.	15.12.76
Cosmos 885	Skean	?	?	U.S.S.R.	17.12.76
USAF Big Bird	} Titan 3D	{30,000	Reconn. }	U.S.A.	19.12.76
Capsule 125B		{ ?	Pick-a-back }		
Cosmos 886	Scarp	?	Interceptor	U.S.S.R.	27.12.76
Molniya 3F	Vostok core	3,300	Comm.	U.S.S.R.	28.12.76
Cosmos 887	Skean	1,545	Nav.	U.S.S.R.	28.12.76
Cosmos 888	Vostok core	9,000	Reconn.	U.S.S.R.	6.1.77
Meteor 2-02	Vostok core	6,050	Weather	U.S.S.R.	6.1.77
Cosmos 889	Vostok core	9,000	Reconn.	U.S.S.R.	20.1.77
Cosmos 890	Skean	1,545	Nav.	U.S.S.R.	20.1.77
NATO 3B	Uprated Thor Delta	1,545	Comm.	U.S.A.	28.1.77
Cosmos 891	Skean	?	?	U.S.S.R.	2.2.77
USAF 07A	Titan 3C	?	Military	U.S.A.	6.2.77
Cosmos 892	Vostok core	9,000	Reconn.	U.S.S.R.	9.2.77
Molniya 2S	Vostok core	2,750	Comm.	U.S.S.R.	11.2.77
Cosmos 893	Skean	1,215	?	U.S.S.R.	15.2.77
Tansei 3	Mu-3H	295	Sc.	Japan	19.2.77
Cosmos 894	Skean	1,545	Nav.	U.S.S.R.	21.2.77
Kiku 2(ETS-2)	Nu booster	285	Comm.	Japan	23.2.77
Cosmos 895	Vostok core	5,600	Military	U.S.S.R.	26.2.77
Cosmos 896	Vostok core	9,000	Reconn.	U.S.S.R.	3.3.77
Cosmos 897	Vostok core	9,000	Reconn.	U.S.S.R.	10.3.77
Palapa 2	Thor Delta	1,265	Comm.	Indonesia	10.3.77
USAF 19A	Titan 3B-Agena D	6,600	Military	U.S.A.	13.3.77
Cosmos 898	Vostok core	9,000	Reconn.	U.S.S.R.	17.3.77
Molniya 1AM	Vostok core	2,200	Comm.	U.S.S.R.	24.3.77
Cosmos 899	Skean	1,985	Military	U.S.S.R.	24.3.77
Cosmos 900	Skean	1,985	Military	U.S.S.R.	29.3.77
Meteor 27	Vostok core	4,850	Weather	U.S.S.R.	5.4.77
Cosmos 901	Sandal	900	Military	U.S.S.R.	5.4.77
Cosmos 902	Vostok core	9,000	Reconn.	U.S.S.R.	7.4.77
Cosmos 903	Vostok core	2,750	Comm.	U.S.S.R.	11.4.77
Cosmos 904	Vostok core	9,000	Reconn.	U.S.S.R.	20.4.77
ESA-GEOS	Thor Delta	1,265	Sc.	Europe	20.4.77
Cosmos 905	Vostok core	9,000	Reconn.	U.S.S.R.	26.4.77
Cosmos 906	Vostok core	6,050	?	U.S.S.R.	27.4.77
Molniya 3G	Vostok core	3,300	Comm.	U.S.S.R.	28.4.77
Cosmos 907	Vostok core	9,000	Reconn.	U.S.S.R.	5.5.77
SCS 7	} Titan 3C	{1,245	Comm. }	U.S.A.	12.5.77
SCS 8		{1,245	Comm. }		
Cosmos 908	Vostok core	9,000	Reconn.	U.S.S.R.	17.5.77
Cosmos 909	Skean	?	Target	U.S.S.R.	19.5.77
Cosmos 910	Scarp	?	Interceptor	U.S.S.R.	23.5.77
USAF 38A	Atlas-Agena D	1,545	Military	U.S.A.	23.5.77

Satellite	Launcher	Weight lb.	Purpose	Country	Date
Cosmos 911	Skean	1,545	Nav.	U.S.S.R.	25.5.77
Cosmos 912	Vostok core	9,000	Reconn.	U.S.S.R.	26.5.77
Intelsat 4A(F-4)	Atlas-Centaur	3,300	Comm.	U.S.A.	26.5.77
Cosmos 913	Skean	1,215	?	U.S.S.R.	30.5.77
Cosmos 914	Vostok core	9,000	Reconn.	U.S.S.R.	31.5.77
AMS 2	Thor Burner 2	990	Weather	U.S.A.	5.6.77
Cosmos 915	Vostok core	9,000	Reconn.	U.S.S.R	8.6.77
Cosmos 916	Vostok core	9,000	Reconn.	U.S.S.R.	10.6.77
Cosmos 917	Vostok core	2,750	Comm.	U.S.S.R.	16.6.77
GOES B	Uprated Thor Delta	1,380	Weather	U.S.A.	16.6.77
Signe 3	Skean	225	Sc.	Fr/USSR	17.6.77
Cosmos 918	Scarp	?	Interceptor	U.S.S.R.	17.6.77
Cosmos 919	Sandal	900	Military	U.S.S.R.	18.6.77
Cosmos 920	Vostok core	9,000	Reconn.	U.S.S.R.	22.6.77
NTS 2	?	650	?	?	23.6.77
Molniya 1AN	Vostok core	2,200	Comm.	U.S.S.R.	24.6.77
Cosmos 921	Skean	1,820	?	U.S.S.R.	24.6.77
USAF Big Bird	Titan 3D	30,000	Reconn.	U.S.A.	27.6.77
Meteor 28	Vostok core	4,850	Weather	U.S.S.R.	29.6.77
Cosmos 922	Vostok core	9,000	Reconn.	U.S.S.R.	30.6.77

Abbreviations: Sc—scientific, and includes a great variety of experiments in cosmic particles, meteorites, light, magnetism, etc.
Comm.—Communications, also abbreviated comsat.

The list above includes all Earth satellites known to have been launched successfully up to 30 June 1977. Details of satellite weight and purpose are often withheld for reasons of military security.

SPACE PROBES LAUNCHED TO JUNE 1977

Probe	Type	Country	Date
Pioneer 1	Lunar	U.S.A.	11.8.58
Pioneer 3	Space	U.S.A.	6.12.58
Lunik 1	Lunar	U.S.S.R.	2.1.59
Pioneer 4	Lunar	U.S.A.	3.3.59
Lunik 2	Lunar impact	U.S.S.R.	12.9.59
Lunik 3	Lunar orbit and photography of far side of moon	U.S.S.R.	4.10.59
Pioneer 5	Solar	U.S.A.	11.3.60
Venus Probe		U.S.S.R.	12.2.61
Ranger 1	Space	U.S.A.	23.8.61
Ranger 2	Space	U.S.A.	18.11.61
Ranger 3	Lunar	U.S.A.	26.1.62
Ranger 4	Lunar impact	U.S.A.	23.4.62
Mariner 2	Passed close to Venus 15.12.62 and radioed back much information	U.S.A.	27.8.62
Ranger 5	Moon photography and hard-land, but missed	U.S.A.	18.10.62
Mars 1	Mars study, failed	U.S.S.R.	1.11.62
Luna 4	Moon study	U.S.S.R.	2.4.63
Ranger 6	Moon photography and hard land; cameras failed	U.S.A.	2.2.64
Zond 1	Venus probe	U.S.S.R.	2.4.64
Ranger 7	As before: successful	U.S.A.	31.7.64
Ranger 8	As before: successful	U.S.A.	20.2.65
Ranger 9	As before: successful	U.S.A.	21.3.65
Luna 5	Moon photography: failed to make soft landing	U.S.S.R.	12.5.65

Probe	Type	Country	Date
Luna 6	Missed moon	U.S.S.R.	8.6.65
Zond 3	Photography of far side of moon	U.S.S.R.	15.7.65
Luna 7	Failed to make soft landing on moon	U.S.S.R.	4.10.65
Mariner 4	Photography of Mars	U.S.A.	28.10.64
Zond 4	Photography of Mars: cameras failed	U.S.S.R.	14.7.65
Luna 9	First soft landing on moon, pictures of lunar surface	U.S.S.R.	31.1.66
Luna 10	Lunar orbiter launched from earth orbiting platform	U.S.S.R.	31.2.66
Surveyor model	Failed to achieve simulated lunar trajectory	U.S.A.	8.4.66
Surveyor 1	First U.S. soft landing on moon, TV pictures transmitted	U.S.A.	30.5.66
Lunar Orbiter 1	To survey Apollo landing sites, crashed on moon surface	U.S.A.	10.8.66
Pioneer 7	Solar	U.S.A.	17.8.66
Luna 11	Second Soviet lunar satellite, scientific research	U.S.S.R.	24.8.66
Surveyor 2	Second U.S. attempt soft landing, crashed when vernier rocket failed	U.S.A.	20.9.66
Luna 12	Third Soviet in lunar orbit, radiation and photographs	U.S.S.R.	22.10.66
Surveyor model 3	Dummy launched on simulated lunar trajectory	U.S.A.	26.10.66
Lunar Orbiter 2	Fifth lunar satellite taking photographs	U.S.A.	6.11.66
Luna 13	Soft landing, transmitted TV pictures, forced rod into surface to test strength	U.S.S.R.	21.12.66
Lunar Orbiter 3	Sixth lunar satellite taking photographs. Weight 860 lb.	U.S.A.	5.2.67
Surveyor 3	Second U.S. lunar landing Ocean of Storms. TV pictures and soil samples. Weight 617 lb.	U.S.A. (on moon)	17.4.67 20.4.67
Lunar Orbiter 4	Seventh lunar satellite taking TV pictures	U.S.A.	4.5.67
Explorer 34	Interplanetary probe with radiation counters. Weight 163 lb.	U.S.A.	24.5.67
Venus 4	Interplanetary probe on undisclosed mission. 2,433 lb.	U.S.S.R.	12.6.67
Mariner 5	Probe passing Venus at 2,000 miles. Weight 540 lb.	U.S.A.	14.6.67
Surveyor 4	Lunar landing, failed by loss of contact	U.S.A.	14.7.67
Explorer 35	Eighth lunar satellite monitoring wind, magnetic field, particles. Weight 230 lb.	U.S.A.	19.7.67

Probe	Type	Country	Date
Lunar Orbiter 5	Ninth lunar satellite to map 'far side'. Weight 860 lb.	U.S.A.	1.8.67
Surveyor 5	Forced landing in Sea of Tranquillity. TV pictures and soil samples. Weight 616 lb.	U.S.A. (on moon)	8.9.67 11.9.67
Surveyor 6	Fourth U.S. lunar landing Sinus Medii. TV pictures. Moved on lunar surface. Weight 617 lb.	U.S.A. (on moon)	7.11.67 10.11.67
Pioneer 8	Solar flares study. Interplanetary orbit. Weight 145 lb.	U.S.A.	13.12.67
Surveyor	Fifth U.S. lunar landing Crater Tycho. TV pictures. Soil analysis. Weight 617 lb.	U.S.A. (on moon)	7.1.68 10.1.68
Zond 4	Launch from orbital platform on lunar related test	U.S.S.R.	2.3.68
Luna 14	Fourth Soviet in lunar orbit radiation and photographs	U.S.S.R.	7.4.68
Zond 5	Out and return moon probe. Photographs and biological experiments	U.S.S.R. (behind moon)	14.9.68 18.9.68
Pioneer 9	Interplanetary probe. Solar particles, radiation, cosmic rays. With TTS 2	U.S.A.	8.11.68
Zond 6	Out and return moon probe. Skip re-entry	U.S.S.R. (moon) return	10.11.68 14.11.68 17.11.68
Venus 5	Interplanetary probe of 2,490 lb. Launched from orbital platform	U.S.S.R. (on Venus)	5.1.69 16.5.69
Venus 6	Interplanetary probe of 2,490 lb.	U.S.S.R. (on Venus)	10.1.69 17.5.69
Mariner 6	Probe passing Mars at 2,000 miles. Weight 850 lb.	U.S.A. (near Mars)	25.2.69 31.7.69
Luna 15	Orbiting lander spacecraft. In moon orbit 17.7.69. Crashed Mare Cisium	U.S.S.R. (on moon)	13.7.69 21.7.69
Zond 7	Out and return moon probe. Skip re-entry. Weight 6,000 lb.	U.S.S.R. (moon) return	7.8.69 11.8.69 14.8.69
Venus 7	Interplanetary probe with improved heat and pressure shield	U.S.S.R. (near Venus)	17.8.70 15.12.70
Luna 16	Unmanned lunar spacecraft. Landed in Sea of Fertility. Brought back soil sample	U.S.S.R. (on moon) (relaunch) (recovery)	12.9.70 20.9.70 21.9.70 24.9.70
Zond 8	Unmanned test of manned. spacecraft. Free-return trajectory around moon. TV and photo equipment	U.S.S.R. (near moon) (recovery)	20.10.70 24.10.70 27.10.70
Luna 17	Unmanned lunar spacecraft Landed in Sea of Rains. Tests of 8-wheel Lunokhod-1 vehicle on surface	U.S.S.R. (on moon)	10.11.70 17.11.70

Probe	Type	Country	Date
Mars 2	Scientific tests on interplanetary medium en route to Mars	U.S.S.R.	19.5.71
Mars 3	Weight 10,250 lb, enough to enter Mars orbit and soft land 1,800 lb.	U.S.S.R.	28.5.71
Mariner 9	Octagon, 2,150 lb, attempt to survey Mars photographically	U.S.A.	30.5.71
Luna 18	Went into lunar orbit, but lunar landing was a failure.	U.S.S.R.	2.9.71
Luna 19	Lunar orbiting craft	U.S.S.R.	28.9.71
Luna 20	Lunar landing craft—relaunched from moon 22.2.72 with soil sample	U.S.S.R.	14.2.72
Pioneer 10	Jupiter probe due at planet December 1973, then escape from solar system	U.S.A.	3.3.72
Venus 8	Venus probe, parachute landing July	U.S.S.R.	27.3.72
Luna 21	Unmanned lunar spacecraft. Completed 40 orbits of moon. Carried mobile Lunokhod-2 vehicle	U.S.S.R. (on moon)	8.1.73 15.1.73
Pioneer 11	Second Jupiter probe, due at planet January 1975, then escape from Solar System	U.S.A.	6.4.73
Explorer 49	Radio astronomy Explorer B is a cylinder with four paddles and four aerials, with retro rocket	U.S.A. (moon orbit)	10.6.73 15.6.73
Mars 4	Similar to Mars 2 and Mars 3, but no landing capsule. Was 2,200 km. behind Mars on 10.2.74. Orbital engine failed	U.S.S.R.	21.7.73
Mars 5	Went into Mars orbit to act as data relay for Mars 6 and Mars 7 landers	U.S.S.R. (Mars orbit)	25.7.73 12.2.74
Mars 6	Mars landing probe; capsule launched 6.3.74 but failed to transmit data	U.S.S.R.	5.8.73
Mars 7	Mars landing probe; capsule launched 9.3.74 but missed planet by 13,000 km.	U.S.S.R.	9.8.73
Mariner 10	Dual purpose probe, flew past Venus 5.2.74 and due to pass Mercury 29.3.74	U.S.A.	3.11.73
Luna 22	Lunar orbiting craft, extending photographic mission of Luna 19 from 130 miles altitude	U.S.S.R.	29.5.74
Luna 23	Lunar landing craft, intended to collect soil sample but was damaged in landing Mare Crisium, 6.11.74	U.S.S.R.	28.10.74

Probe	Type	Country	Date
Helios 1	Solar probe intended to reach perihelion about 15.3.75	Germany	10.12.74
Venus 9	New generation Venus probe launched by Proton rocket. Landed on planet 22.10.75 and relayed pictures to Earth.	U.S.S.R.	8.6.75
Venus 10	Second of new Venus probes. Soft landing on planet 25.10.75. Also relayed pictures.	U.S.S.R.	14.6.75
Viking 1	Mars probe launched by Titan 3-Centaur. Entered Mars orbit 19.6.76 and Mars lander touchdown 20.7.76	U.S.A.	20.8.75
Viking 2	Mars probe launched by Titan 3-Centaur. Entered Mars orbit 7.8.76 and Mars lander touchdown in the Plain of Utopia 3.9.76.	U.S.A.	9.9.75
Helios 2	Solar and interplanetary probe launched by Titan 3-Centaur. Closest yet approach to Sun.	W. Germany	15 1.76
Luna 24	Lunar landing craft. Landing Mare Crisium 18.8.76. Collected 'generous sample' of lunar soil. Recovered 23.8.76	U.S.S.R.	9.8.76

MANNED SPACE VEHICLES LAUNCHED TO JUNE 1977

Name	Orbits or time	Country	Crew	Date
Vostok 1	1 orbit	U.S.S.R.	Gagarin	12.4.61
Freedom 7	No orbit	U.S.A.	Sheppard	5.5.61
Liberty Bell 7	No orbit	U.S.A.	Grissom	21.7.61
Vostok 2	17 orbits	U.S.S.R.	Titov	6.8.61
Friendship 7	3 orbits	U.S.A.	Glenn	20.2.62
Mercury Atlas 7	4 hr. 56 min.	U.S.A.	Carpenter	24.5.62
Vostok 3	3 days 22 hrs.	U.S.S.R.	Nikolayev	11.8.62
Vostok 4	2 days 22 hrs.	U.S.S.R.	Popovitch	12.8.62
Mercury Atlas 8	9 hrs. 13 min.	U.S.A.	Schirra	3.9.62
Sigma 7	22 orbits (manually controlled descent after instrument failure)	U.S.A.	Cooper	15.5.63
Vostok 5	81 orbits, 5 days	U.S.S.R.	Bykovsky	14.6.63
Vostok 6	48 orbits	U.S.S.R.	Valentina Tereshkova	15.6.63
Voskhod 1	16 orbits, 24 hrs. 17 mins.	U.S.S.R.	Komarov, Yegorov, Feoktikov	12.10.64

Name	Orbits or time	Country	Crew	Date
Voskhod 2	18 orbits	U.S.S.R.	Belyaev, Leonov[1]	18.3.65
Gemini 3[2]	3 orbits	U.S.A.	Grissom, Young	23.3.65
Gemini 4	62 orbits, 97 hrs. 50 mins.	U.S.A.	McDivitt, White[3]	3.6.65
Gemini 5	120 orbits, 190 hrs. 56 mins[4] (3,338,000 mls.)	U.S.A.	Cooper, Conrad	21.8.65
Gemini 6 &	26 hours	U.S.A.	Schirra, Stafford	15.12.65
Gemini 7[5]	206 orbits, 330 hrs. 25 mins. (5,716,000 mls.)	U.S.A.	Borman, Lovell	4.12.65
Gemini 8	4 orbits, 10 hrs. 18 mins.	U.S.A.	Armstrong, Scott	16.3.66
Gemini 9	48 orbits, 72 hrs. 21 mins.	U.S.A.	Stafford, Cernan	3.6.66
Gemini 10	44 orbits, 70 hrs. 48 mins.	U.S.A.	Young, Collins	18.7.66
Gemini 11[6]	48 orbits, 71 hrs. 18 mins.	U.S.A.	Conrad, Gordon	12.9.66
Gemini 12[7]	63 orbits, 94 hrs. 26 mins.	U.S.A.	Aldrin, Lovell	11.11.66
Soyuz 1	17 orbits, 24 hrs. 37 mins.	U.S.S.R.	Komarov[8]	23.4.67
Apollo 7	10 days 20 hrs. Live TV, rendezvous with booster	U.S.A.	Schirra, Eisele, Cunningham	11.10.68
Soyuz 3	3 days 23 hrs. Rendezvous with Soyuz 2, no docking	U.S.S.R.	Beregovoy	26.10.68
Apollo 8	6 days 3 hrs. First manned flight around moon	U.S.A.	Borman, Lovell, Anders	21.12.68
Soyuz 4	2 days 23 hrs. Docking target for Soyuz 5	U.S.S.R.	Shatalov	14.1.69
Soyuz 5	3 days 1 hr. Docked with Soyuz 4. Two cosmonauts transferred for re-entry.	U.S.S.R.	Volynov Khrunov Yeliseyev	15.1.69
Apollo 9	10 days 1 hr. LM manned flight for	U.S.A.	McDivitt Scott	3.3.69

[1] Leonov was the first man to leave a spaceship and float freely in outer space.
[2] Gemini 3 was a manoeuvrable spacecraft and changed its flight path three times.
[3] White was the second man and the first American to step out into space.
[4] The approximate time that would be required to fly to the moon, briefly explore and return to earth.
[5] These spacecraft carried out a successful rendezvous in orbit, approaching to within 6 feet of each other and flying in formation for more than 2 circuits of the earth.
[6] First orbit docking achieved.
[7] Decking achieved on third orbit.
[8] Komarov was first in-flight space fatality when parachute shroud lines became entangled.

Name	Orbits or time	Country	Crew	Date
	6 hrs. for lunar manoeuvres		Schweikart	
Apollo 10	8 days. LM manned flight for 8 hrs in 60 n.m. lunar orbit	U.S.A.	Stafford Young Cernan	18.5.69
Apollo 11	8 days. LM 'Eagle' vehicle for man's first landing on the moon, 20 and 21.7.69	U.S.A.	Armstrong Aldrin Collins	16.7.69
Soyuz 6	5 days. Rendezvous trials of three Soyuz craft in Earth orbit	U.S.S.R.	Shonin Kubasov	11.10.69
Soyuz 7	5 days. Rendezvous trials as above	U.S.S.R.	Filipchenko Volkov Gorbatko	12.10.69
Soyuz 8	5 days. Rendezvous trials as above	U.S.S.R.	Shatalov Yeliseyev	13.10.69
Apollo 12	10 days. LM 'Intrepid' vehicle on moon 19 and 20.11.69	U.S.A.	Conrad Gordon Bean	14.11.69
Apollo 13	6 days. LEM 'Aquarius' vehicle used as lifeboat for crippled service module	U.S.A.	Lovell Haise Swigert	11.4.70
Soyuz 9	17 days long-duration flight. Craft weighed 14,220 lb.	U.S.S.R.	Sevastyanov Nikolayev	1.6.70
Apollo 14	10 days. Landing in Fra Mauro highlands. Use of wheeled cart. Exploration of Cone Crater	U.S.A.	Shepard Mitchell Roosa	31.1.71
Soyuz 10	2 days. Docked with Salyut but trouble with hatch prevented transfer	U.S.S.R.	Rukavishnikov Shatalov Yeliseyev	22.4.71
Soyuz 11	24 days. Rendezvous with Salyut. Mission ended with death of cosmonauts	U.S.S.R.	Dobrovolski Volkov Patseyev	6.6.71
Apollo 15	12 days. Landing in Apennines. Use of Lunar Roving Vehicle. Exploration of Hadley Rille	U.S.A.	Scott Worden Irwin	26.7.71
Apollo 16	11 days. Landing in Descartes highlands 17 mile exploration in LVR2	U.S.A.	Young Duke Mattingly	16.4.72
Apollo 17	12 days. Landing in Taurus-Littrow	U.S.A.	Cernan Evans	7.12.72

Name	Orbits or time	Country	Crew	Date
	area LRV3—found volcanic evidence		Schmitt	
Skylab 2	First manned flight to Skylab space station (launched 14.5.73). Deployed sail to reduce temperature and released solar panel. Manned duration 28 days to 22.6.73	U.S.A.	Conrad, Kerwin, Weitz	25.5.73
Skylab 3	Second manned flight to Skylab space station. Record manned duration 59 days to 25.9.73	U.S.A.	Bean, Lousma Garriott	28.7.73
Soyuz 12	First Soviet manned flight for two years, tested improved Soyuz. Manned duration 2 days to 29.9.73	U.S.S.R.	Lazarev, Makarov	27.9.73
Skylab 4	Final flight to Skylab space station. Record manned duration 84 days to 8.2.74	U.S.A.	Carr, Pogue, Gibson	16.11.73
Soyuz 13	Verification of Soyuz modifications and for astronomy. Manned duration 8 days to 26.12.73	U.S.S.R.	Klimuk, Lebedev	18.12.73
Soyuz 14	Rendezvous and docking with Salyut 3 on 4.7.74. Manned duration 15 days to 19.7.74	U.S.S.R.	Popovich Artyukhin	3.7.74
Soyuz 15	Overshot Salyut 3 when booster overburned. Returned in 2 days.	U.S.S.R.	Sarafanov Demin	26.8.74
Soyuz 16	Successful rehearsal of ASTP mission. Manned duration 6 days to 8.12.74	U.S.S.R.	Filipchenko Rukavishnikov	2.12.74
Soyuz 17	Rendezvous and docking with Salyut 4 on 12.1.75. Manned duration 29½ days to 9.2.75	U.S.S.R.	Gubarev Grechko	10.1.75
(Undesignated)	Salyut 4 ferry flight failure. Mission would have been Soyuz 18. Immediate recovery	U.S.S.R.	Lazarev Makarov	5.4.75

Name	Orbits or time	Country	Crew	Date
	of cosmonauts successful			
Soyuz 18	Rendezvous and docking with Salyut 4 on 25.5.75. Manned duration 63 days to 26.7.75	U.S.S.R.	Klimuk Sevastianov	24.5.75
Soyuz 19	Apollo/Soyuz Test Project (ASTP). Docked with Apollo 18 17.7.75. Astronauts exchanged visits. Manned duration 6 days to 21.7.75	U.S.S.R.	Leonov Kubasov	15.7.75
Apollo 18	Apollo/Soyuz Test Project (ASTP). Docked with Soyuz 19 17.7.75. Astronauts exchanged visits. Manned duration 9 days to 24.7.75	U.S.A.	Stafford Slayton Brand	15.7.75
Soyuz 21	Rendezvous and docking with Salyut 5 on 7.7.76. Scientific and weather experiments. Manned duration 49 days to 24.8.76.	U.S.S.R.	Volynov Zholobov	6.7.76
Soyuz 22	Carried multi-spectral camera for East German geology survey. Watched Norway NATO exercise. Manned duration 8 days to 23.9.76.	U.S.S.R.	Bykovsky	15.9.76
Soyuz 23	Rendezvous with Salyut 5 on 15.10.76, failed to dock. Manned duration 2 days to 16.10.76.	U.S.S.R.	Vyacheslav Rozhdestvensky	14.10.76
Soyuz 24	Rendezvous and docking with Salyut 5 on 9.2.77. EVAs planned? Manned duration 18 days to 25.2.77.	U.S.S.R.	Gorbatko Glazhov	7.2.77

Shock Wave When air moves over an obstacle faster than the speed of sound it no longer has time to be pushed gradually out of the way. Instead it changes its direction of motion in jumps: the lines along which these jumps occur are called shock waves, and separate regions of different pressure. The boom of an aircraft passing through the sound barrier is simply its shock wave reaching one's ears: the sudden change of pressure is heard as an explosion, or frequently as a double bang.

Space Travel Exploration of other planets by man began in 1969 with the United States' Apollo 11 mission to the Moon. With its complete success the stage was set for other journeys to more remote planets and for more extensive exploration of the Moon itself.

During the remainder of the Project Apollo programme there were a further five successful landings on the Moon. The Lunar Modules carried in all 12 astronauts on to the lunar surface between 1969 and 1972.

Supersonic Flight Flight at speeds greater than Mach 1. It involves aerodynamic problems that are different from those of subsonic flight. No less troublesome are the problems of having to get from subsonic to supersonic speeds. Some of the adaptations already achieved are the sweptback wing with narrow section and small wing area. See SHOCK WAVE.

Turbofan Development of the jet engine in which a larger amount of air than is needed for combustion is taken in and mixed with the hot exhaust stream. The advantage is that the exhaust stream becomes heavier and slower so that it wastes less energy in turbulence (q.v.). Has better fuel consumption and has made possible the new generation of quieter jet engines.

Turbo-prop The driving of propellers by gas turbines. This system, vibrationless and powerful, has proved successful for civil airliners, notably the Viscounts and Britannias.

Turbulence Air moves in two states: laminar flow—that is, in orderly streams; or turbulent flow—that is, in a disorderly mass of small swirls. Under general conditions, whether the flow will be laminar or turbulent depends on the value of the *Reynold's number*—a dimensionless function of the size of the object, the viscosity and the velocity of flow. Turbulent flow absorbs much more energy than laminar flow, and therefore aircraft designers try to prevent it occurring. It begins in the *boundary layer*, a thin skin of relatively stationary air close to the

surface of the aeroplane. A promising system for preventing turbulence is to suck this layer away through fine holes in the
skin.

Types of Aircraft, Some Outstanding Modern
RUSSIA

An-22 Antheus Long-range heavy transport. Four NK-12MA
turboprops. Wing span 211 ft. Payload 80 tons.

Il-62M Long-range jet transport powered by four D-30KU
turbofans. Similar layout to VC10. Carries up to 186 passengers.
Capable of non-stop flight from Moscow to Havana, Cuba.

Il-68 Wide-body airbus powered by four NK-86 turbofans.
Wing span 157 ft. Carries up to 350 passengers.

MiG-25 (E-266) Twin jet all-weather fighter, NATO code
'Foxbat'. Two R-31 turbojets each rated at 24,250-lb. thrust
with afterburning.

Tu-134 A Medium-range transport with rear mounted D-30
turbofans of 14,990-lb. thrust. Seats for up to 80 passengers.

Tu-144 Supersonic transport powered by four Kuznetsov
NK-144 turbofans each rated at 44,090-lb. thrust with afterburning. Similar layout to Concorde. Carries up to 140
passengers. Max cruising speed Mach 2.35.

Tu-154 Medium/long-range transport powered by three
20,950-lb. thrust NK-8-2 turbofans. Carries up to 167 passengers.

Tu-28P 'Fiddler' Supersonic twin jet all-weather interceptor.
Carries two large 'Ash' delta wing air-to-air missiles under each
wing.

U.S.A.

Boeing 747 Four-jet heavy transport known as the 'Jumbo
Jet'. Powered by four JT9D, CF6 or RB.211 turbofans. Basic
accommodation for 385 passengers, but capable of carrying up
to 550 ten abreast.

Boeing 727-200 Short- to medium-range jet transport with
three rear-mounted JT8D turbofans. 163-189 seats.

General Dynamics F-16A Lightweight air combat fighter
One Pratt & Whitney F100-PW-100 turbofan. Mach 1.95.

Lockheed L-1011 TriStar High density transport powered by three Rolls-Royce RB.211 turbofans. Up to 400 passengers.

Lockheed C-5A Heavy logistics transport. Four U.S. General Electric TF39 turbofans each 41,000-lb. thrust. Span 222 ft. Carries 100 tons of payload. Used by U.S.A.F. Military Airlift Command.

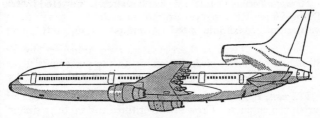

Lockheed Tristar

McDonnell Douglas F-4M Phantom R.A.F. version of multi-role supersonic fighter capable of more than Mach 2. Royal Navy Phantom is F-4K. Span 38 ft. 7½ in. Two Rolls-Royce Spey RB.168-25R Mk.201 turbofans, 12,500-lb. thrust each (dry), 70% afterburning.

McDonnell Douglas F-15 Eagle Air superiority fighter. Two Pratt & Whitney F100-PW-100 turbofans. More than Mach 2.5.

McDonnell Douglas DC-9 Twin turbofan short- to medium-range airliner. Seats for up to 139 tourist class passengers in Series 50 version.

McDonnell Douglas DC-10 High density transport powered by three U.S. General Electric CF6-6 turbofans. Up to 380 passengers.

UNITED KINGDOM

British Aerospace

Concorde Supersonic transport designed and produced in co-operation with Aerospatiale in France. Faster than Mach 2. Four Rolls-Royce Bristol Olympus 593 engines.

Lightning Supersonic fighter powered by two Rolls-Royce Avon 210 turbojets each of 14,430-lb. thrust. Armed with two 30-mm. Aden guns and two Firestreak missiles.

Jaguar GR Mk.1 Tactical support aircraft, powered by two Rolls-Royce Turbomíca Adour Mk.102 turbofans each of 7,305lb thrust with reheat. Maximum speed Mach 1.5 at 36,000 ft.

Panavia Tornado Multi-role combat aircraft, powered by two Turbo-Union RB.199-34R-2 turbofans each of 14,500 lb thrust with reheat. Maximum speed 1,320 m.p.h. at 36,000 ft.

One-Eleven Twin-jet short/medium range transport aircraft. Stretched 500 series aircraft seats up to 119 passengers. Rear-mounted Rolls-Royce Spey turbofans. 541 m.p.h.

Viscount Famous passenger airliner. Four Rolls-Royce Dart turboprop engines. Crew of two or three and up to 73 passengers. Range with maximum payload 1,725 miles. Maximum cruising speed 357 m.p.h.

Buccaneer Strike aircraft. Mk. 2B version powered by two 11,100-lb. thrust Rolls-Royce RB.168 Spey turbofans. Carries variety of weapons, including nuclear, in rotating bomb bay, plus Martel air-to-ground missiles on external pylons.

Comet First jet airliner ever to fly. Four Rolls-Royce Avon turbojets. Carries up to 101 passengers.

Harrier GR Mk. 3 V/STOL close support and armed reconnaissance aircraft. Uses two pairs of rotating nozzles which direct thrust downward for lift, or aft for propulsion. Rolls-Royce Bristol Pegasus 103 of 21,500-lb. thrust. Maximum level speed over 737 m.p.h.

Nimrod MR Mk. 2 Maritime reconnaissance aircraft developed from Comet. Four Rolls-Royce Spey Mk. 250 turbofans of 12,140-lb. thrust each.

Trident 3B Short/medium-haul three-jet airliner. Aft-mounted 11,960-lb. thrust Rolls-Royce Spey turbofans plus RB-162 booster. Tourist version has 152 seats.

Vulcan Four-jet medium bomber powered by 20,000-lb thrust Rolls-Royce Bristol Olympus 301 turbojets. Maximum cruising speed Mach 0·94.

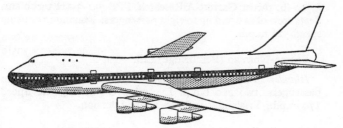

Boeing 747

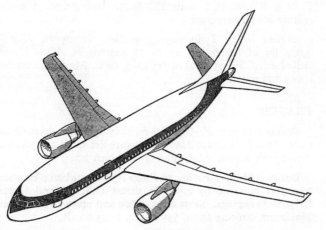

A300B European Airbus

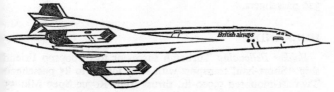

BAe/Aerospatiale Concorde

HS. 125 Srs 700 Twin-jet executive transport powered by 3,700-lb. thrust Garrett-AiResearch TFE 731-3-1H turbofans. Seats crew of two and up to eight passengers. Maximum cruising speed 522 m.p.h.

Britten-Norman (Bembridge) Ltd.

Islander Twin-engined light transport carrying up to ten passengers, two 260 b.h.p. Lycoming O-540 engines. Speed 170 m.p.h. Trislander is three-engined version.

Short Brothers Ltd.

Shorts 330 Widebody commuter airliner. Two 1,120-shp Pratt & Witney of Canada PT6A-45A turboprops. Standard seating for 30 passengers.

Skyvan Srs 3 Twin turboprop light transport. Carries 4,600 lb. of freight or up to 19 passengers. Two Garrett AiResearch TPE 331-201 of 715 s.h.p. each. Maximum cruising speed 203 m.p.h.

FRANCE

Dassault Mirage F1-C multi-mission fighter and attack aircraft. One SNECMA Atar 9K-50 turbojet rated at 15,873-lb. thrust with reheat. Maximum speed Mach 2.2.

Dassault Mystère-Falcon 20 Series F Twin turbofan executive transport powered by 4,500-lb. thrust U.S. General Electric CF700-2D engines. Seats crew of two and up to 14 passengers. Maximum cruising speed 536 m.p.h. at 25,000 ft.

Airbus A300B2 Wide-bodied short/medium range airliner. Two U.S. General Electric CF-6-50C turbofans. Seats up to 320 passengers.

HOLLAND

Fokker Fellowship Turbofan successor to turboprop Friendship. Short-haul transport with seats for up to 85 passengers. Two aft-mounted 9,900-lb. thrust Rolls-Royce Spey Mk. 55 engines. Maximum cruising speed 523 m.p.h.

Vertical Take-off and Landing (V.T.O.L.) A helicopter is a V.T.O.L. aircraft. The expression also includes newer devices concerned chiefly with getting fighters quickly off the ground without a long runway. There are several ways of getting vertical lift from jet engines. One is to direct the jets down for take-off and horizontally when airborne as in the Hawker Siddeley Harrier. Another way, used in the Short SC-1, was to have separate engines for the vertical and horizontal thrusts. Designers in several countries are at work on their own ways of solving the problem of V.T.O.L.

Wind Tunnel An experimental device in which a wind is created by fans, and aerofoils and aircraft made accurately to scale are suspended in the wind. Instruments attached to the models measure lift, drag and other parameters at varying wind speeds. Modern high-speed wind tunnels can achieve speeds as high as Mach 3 or Mach 4 in their working sections, but normally run for only a few seconds and depend on the rapid expansion of compressed air.

Astronomy

Astronomical Measures The nearest star (Bungula in Centaurus) is 25,000,000,000,000 miles away. Measurements as huge as this become meaningless when given in miles, so stellar distances (distances between stars) were expressed until a short time ago in light-years. A light-year is the distance light travels in one year. The speed of light is 186,000 miles per second, so a light-year represents some 6,000,000,000,000 miles.

A newer astronomical measure of distance is the *parsec*, which is the distance at which the mean radius of the Earth's orbit would subtend an angle of 1 second. A parsec is rather more than 19,000,000,000,000 miles—or, roughly, 3¼ light-years.

Constellations On a cloudless night between 2,000 and 3,000 stars are visible to the unaided eye. With the help of one of the great astronomical telescopes (like the one on Mount Wilson in California) this number is increased to some 50,000,000.

The observable stars are divided into groups or constellations (a word that means 'star-groups').

THE CONSTELLATIONS

Those in capital letters are invisible from Great Britain

Scientific name	English name
Andromeda	The Chained Lady
ANTLIA	The Pump
APUS	The Bird of Paradise
Aquarius	The Water-Pourer
Aquila	The Eagle
ARA	The Altar
ARGO	Jason's Ship Argo
Aries	The Ram
Auriga	The Charioteer
Bootes	The Herdsman
Caelum	The Graving Tool
Camelopardalis	The Giraffe
Cancer	The Crab

Scientific name	*English name*
Canes Venatici	The Hunting Dogs
Canis Major	The Great Dog
Canis Minor	The Little Dog
Capricornus	The Horned Goat
Cassiopeia	The Lady in the Chair
CENTAURUS	The Centaur
Cepheus	Cassiopeia's Consort
Cetus	The Sea Monster
CHAMAELEON	The Chamaeleon
CIRCINUS	The Pair of Compasses
Columba	The Dove
Coma Berenices	Berenice's Hair
CORONA AUSTRALIS	The Southern Crown
Corona Borealis	The Northern Crown
Corvus	The Crow
Crater	The Cup
CRUX	The Southern Cross
Cygnus	The Swan
Delphinus	The Dolphin
DORADO	The Goldfish
Draco	The Dragon
Equuleus	The Little Horse
ERIDANUS	The River
Fornax	The Furnace
Gemini	The Twins
GRUS	The Crane
Hercules	The Legendary Strong Man
HOROLOGIUM	The Clock
Hydra	The Sea Serpent
HYDRUS	The Water Snake
INDUS	The Indian
Lacerta	The Lizard
Leo	The Lion
Leo Minor	The Little Lion
Lepus	The Hare
Libra	The Balance
LUPUS	The Wolf
Lynx	The Lynx
Lyra	The Lyre
MENSA	The Table Mountain
MICROSCOPIUM	The Microscope
Monoceros	The Unicorn
MUSCA	The Fly
NORMA	The Square
OCTANS	The Octant
Ophiuchus	The Serpent
Orion	The Giant Hunter
PAVO	The Peacock

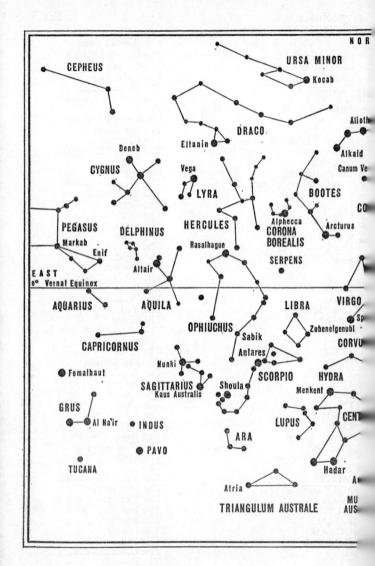

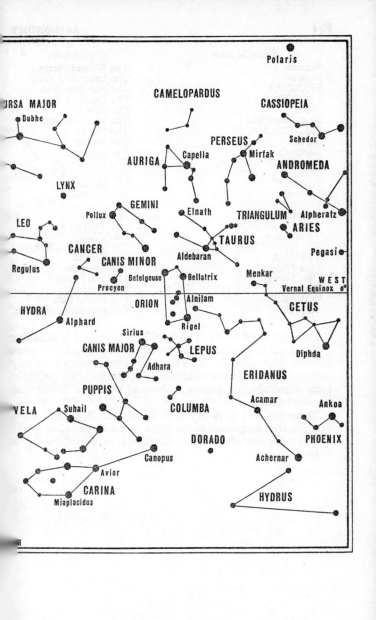

Scientific name	*English name*
Pegasus	The Winged Horse
Perseus	The Legendary Hero
PHOENIX	The Phoenix
PICTOR	The Painter's Easel
Pisces	The Fishes
Piscis Austrinus	The Southern Fish
RETICULUM	The Net
Sagitta	The Arrow
Sagittarius	The Archer
Scorpius	The Scorpion
Sculptor	The Sculptor's Workshop
Scutum	The Shield
Serpens	The Serpent
Sextans	The Sextant
Taurus	The Bull
TELESCOPIUM	The Telescope
Trinagulum	The Triangle
TRIANGULUM AUSTRALE	The Southern Triangle
TUCANA	The Toucan
Ursa Major	The Great Bear
Ursa Minor	The Little Bear
Virgo	The Maiden
VOLANS	The Flying Fish
Vulpecula	The Fox with the Goose

Magnitude of Stars The classification of stars is according to their brightness as seen from the earth. The unit of brightness is called the *magnitude*. Stars that can be seen without the help of telescopes are of magnitude 0–6. Magnitude 0 is the brightest each magnitude that follows is about $2\frac{1}{2}$ times less bright than the one before it.

There are four stars (given in the list on F43) that, being brighter than magnitude 0, are given minus magnitudes.

The brightness of the Sun in this scale is −26·7; of the Moon −11·2.

THE TWENTY BRIGHTEST STARS

Star	Constellation	Magnitude
Sirius	Great Dog	−1·43
CANOPUS	Jason's Ship Argo	−0·73
RIGIL KENTAURUS	Centaur	−0·27
Arcturus	Herdsman	−0·06
Vega	Lyre	0·04
Capella	Charioteer	0·09
Rigel	The Giant Hunter	0·15
Procyon	Little Dog	0·37
ACHERNAR	The River Eridanus	0·53
Betelgeuse	The Giant Hunter	0·90
AGENA	Centaur	0·66
Altair	Eagle	0·80
Aldebaran	Bull	0·85
ACRUX	Southern Cross	0·87
Antares	Scorpion	0·98
Spica	Maiden	1·00
Fomalhaut	Southern Fish	1·16
Pollux	Twins	1·16
Deneb	Swan	1·26
BETA CRUCIS	Southern Cross	1·31

The Solar System The centre of the Solar System is the Sun, our Earth being one of the planets revolving round it.

THE SUN

Diameter, miles	864,000
Mass, reckoning the Earth as 1	330,000
Density, reckoning the Earth as 1	0·25
Volume, reckoning the Earth as 1	1,300,000
Force of gravity on the surface, reckoning the Earth as 1	27·7
Period of rotation on its axis	25·38 days
Speed of rotation at its equator	4,407 m.p.h.
Surface area	12,000 times that of Earth
Volume	339,300,000,000,000,000 cu. miles
Mass	1,998,000,000,000,000,000,000,000,000,000 tons
Temperature	c. 10,000° F.
Height of biggest flames from the surface	286,000 miles

THE MOON

Diameter, miles	2,163
Surface area	14,660,000 sq. miles
Volume	5,300,000,000 cu. miles
Mass	78,000,000,000,000,000,000 tons
Speed in its orbit	2,288 m.p.h.
Estimated temperature, day	+214° F.
Estimated temperature, night	−250° F.
Force of gravity at surface, reckoning the Earth as 1	4/25
Time of revolution round the Earth	27 days 7 hr. 43 min. 11 sec.
Number of visible craters	30,000

THE PLANETS

	Average distance from the Sun (in miles)	Time taken to revolve round Sun	Diameter (in miles)
Mercury	36,000,000	88 days	3,100
Venus	67,200,000	224¾ days	7,700
Earth	93,000,000	365¼ days	7,927
Mars	141,500,000	687 days	4,200
Jupiter	483,300,000	11·86 years	88,700
Saturn	886,100,000	29·46 years	75,100
Uranus	1,783,000,000	84·01 years	29,300
Neptune	2,793,000,000	164·79 years	27,700
Pluto	3,666,000,000	248·43 years	3,600

Relative Gravitational Pull If the Earth's gravitational pull is reckoned as 100 the relative pull on the surface of the Sun and the other planets is:

Sun	.	.	.	.	2770	Jupiter	.	.	.	26
Mercury	.	.	.	38	Saturn	.	.	.	11
Venus	.	.	.	86	Uranus	.	.	.	8
Mars	.	.	.	38	Neptune	.	.	.	11

Motor Cars

Motorcycles, Lightweights, mopeds and 3-wheelers

HISTORY AND DEVELOPMENT

1876 is perhaps the birth year of the motor car of today. It was then that the internal-combustion engine was developed to a workable form by Otto.

But the dream of the self-propelled carriage is a very old one. As far back as the sixteenth century, Johann Hautach made a vehicle propelled by coiled springs—a clockwork car. Steam carriages were also developed. The Frenchman Cugnot constructed a workable steam carriage in 1770—a three wheeler.

Cugnot Steam Carriage

Murdock, Dallery, Symington, Gurney and others all achieved a varying degree of success with steam-propelled carriages during the next fifty years (see models and drawings at the Science Museum). Gurney's steamer could climb Highgate Hill—a long, steep ascent—and in 1831 a Gurney coach ran regularly between Cheltenham and Gloucester at speeds up to 12 m.p.h. At the same time, Ogle and Summers built a car which achieved no less than 35 m.p.h. on the rough roads of that time—a speed greater than Stephenson's 'Rocket' locomotive of the same period, which had the advantage of running on rails.

But on the whole, these were triumphs that led nowhere. Opposition to any new kind of road vehicle was intense, and these early cars were constantly under attack from the highly organised horse-drawn coaching systems. Even more important, the first cars coincided with the almost fantastically rapid growth of Britain's railway systems: men with money chose to invest in railways, not horseless carriages.

Thus when Otto made a workable internal-combustion engine of the sort used in cars today, his achievement was of very little interest to Britain. Cars continued to be thought of as dangerous and unpleasant toys until the turn of the century. In France, however, Panhard and Levassor built a car round the new engine. There was activity in America, too, with petrol-driven cars such as the Duryea. In Germany, Benz constructed a petrol-engined three-wheeler (1885). Daimler made a two-cylinder V engine in 1889. Incidentally, the names Panhard and Daimler are still seen on motors today. Meanwhile in Britain what few cars there were had to proceed at walking pace behind a man carrying a red warning flag!

Prescott Steamer, 1903   Benz, 1885

In 1896 this ridiculous law was repealed (the London–Brighton run for Veteran cars celebrates the event each year) and motoring began to be taken more seriously in Britain.

At the turn of the century motorists had a choice of three sorts of self-propelled vehicle: steam, petrol-driven and electric. Electric cars were silent and very easy to manage, but useful only as town carriages. They could not go far without having their batteries recharged—a problem still to be solved.

Steam cars were very numerous. Serpollet, White, Stanley and other manufacturers produced silent, fast and powerful vehicles with hill-climbing power that the petrol cars of the time could not approach. In addition, they involved none of the noisy and difficult gear-changing inseparable from the early petrol-engined cars. An American Stanley Steamer held the world speed record in 1906 at no less than $127\frac{1}{2}$ m.p.h.—an extraordinary speed, for petrol-driven road cars of the same date were not expected to reach more than 30 or 40 m.p.h.

But steam cars had their disadvantages. They were difficult to run. They used a lot of water. They could be very dirty. And it took up to 20 minutes to get steam up.

While the design of the steam car remained static and unchanging, the petrol car developed very rapidly indeed. Britain had an extremely advanced design in the Lanchester, a car that was many years before its time. A host of famous car makes, many of them still familiar, came into being—Peugeot, Singer, Sunbeam, Riley, Fiat and Rover among them.

Most important of all, petrol cars were developed that rivalled steam cars in speed and silence—and beat them in ease of operation and cost. The first Rolls-Royces (1905–10) in particular set an entirely new standard of refinement, luxury and (from the owner's point of view) simplicity. They were an example to all other makers of petrol cars and a clear indication that the days of the steam car were numbered. Another nail in the steam coffin was the self-starter—an American invention—which gave the petrol car an additional lead over the hard-to-start steamers.

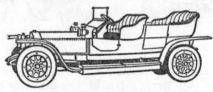

Rolls-Royce Silver Ghost

The Rolls-Royce was a craftsman-built car, individually made In America Henry Ford started to build cars by mass-production that is, in batches of thousands of cars, all made from interchangeable parts and assembled by largely unskilled labour Ford's contribution to motoring development, although very different from that of the Rolls-Royce, was just as important While Rolls-Royce set a new standard of perfection, Ford made cars available to people the world over. Motoring for the masses began with Ford.

By 1914 the car had settled into a pattern that has not change very greatly. The engine was a multi-cylinder unit fed wit controlled amounts of petrol and air by means of a jet car burettor (the earliest cars had a wick carburettor). The rea

wheels drove the car and the front wheels steered it. Steering
was effected by a wheel (earlier cars often had tillers) and braking
by internal expanding hub brakes—though only on the rear
wheels. Electricity was generally responsible for starting and
lighting the most modern cars—and almost invariably responsible
for engine ignition. The car's body and chassis were separate,
although the first all-steel, 'unit construction' chassis bodies so
common today had been produced. Early troubles of quick tyre
wear and constant puncturing had been largely overcome.

During the First World War car design was neglected. Engine
design advanced rapidly, however. In particular, many new and
better metals were developed that allowed higher speeds within
the engine and greater power development. It became apparent
that the huge, thundering racing cars powered by massive engines
were not necessarily the fastest; the comparatively tiny feather-
weight racing cars of Ettore Bugatti—an immortal name—were
beginning to steal the thunder. Smaller, lighter cars of fairly
good performance and refinement began to appear. The Peugeot
Bébé, designed by Bugatti, was a very early arrival. And in 1923
the first Austin 7 appeared. The Austin 7 and cars like it brought
motoring for the masses to Europe just as the Model T Ford
brought it to America. Motoring now became world-wide.

Model T Ford, 1927

Peugeot Bébé, 1913

Austin 7, 1926

By 1925 steam and electric cars had virtually disappeared from the scene. More and more saloon cars were being made. Economy cars of various sorts were successfully produced in huge numbers. Mass-production methods inevitably superseded hand fitting. Motoring was beginning to change people's habits and to expand their horizons.

Morris Cowley

During the next fifteen years the car finally overthrew the old order. For hundreds of years people had lived their lives within an area of a few square miles. A villager stayed in his village. But now the motor bus took him to other towns, other districts. Charabancs brought visitors to his village. More and more people could afford cars. Road networks covered whole countries and continents. The motor car that had started as a toy had become a near-necessity.

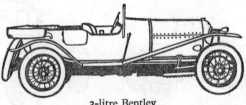

3-litre Bentley

Car development was comparatively undramatic during th period 1925–40. Family cars became much cheaper and shoddie Sports cars increased their power and speed, but not violentl Racing became a nationally subsidised affair as well as a spo for rich amateurs. Luxury cars were smoother in outline b little else. Towards the end of the period, streamlining mac an uneasy appearance as a styling feature, but had little effe on car performance. Citröen, the giant French manufacture developed a unit-built car with front-wheel drive that was

Riley Falcon   Fiat 500, 1937

remain ahead of its time for twenty years. Other leaders in
design were Riley (small, comfortable, fast sports saloons from
1930 on); Lancia of Italy (small saloons of very advanced design,
including independent suspension for all four wheels—1937 on);
BMW of Germany (tubular backbone chassis frames, unusually
powerful engines); Fiat of Italy (the tiny 500-c.c. 'Topolino',
1937, the first miniature car to behave like a full-size model);
and MG (the sort of small and inexpensive sports car for which
Britain still finds world markets).

Racing cars saw their peak development in the Mercedes-Benz
and Auto Union machines of Germany, which developed more
than 600 B.H.P.—a power that would take some beating today.

Mercedes-Benz Grand Prix racing car, 1937

American cars developed almost exclusively along the lines of
size, comfort and silence. Problems of more power from less
fuel—or of getting more passenger space in a compact vehicle—
were of little interest to American car-owners, who could get all
the petrol (and therefore power) they needed at very low prices.

Which brings the story to World War Two.

WORLD WAR TWO TO TODAY

After the Second World War, car production was at first resumed on pre-war lines. At first slowly, the designers and makers explored and incorporated new developments. The most important concerned suspension systems (q.v. this section), brakes (particularly discs, q.v.), tyres, luxuries such as radios and heaters, automatic transmissions, better fuels and tyres—and new layouts for cars. Another very important development was the rapid rise of the Japanese motor industry.

Today there is no such thing as a typical car. The family motorist can choose between rear-engine, rear-wheel-drive cars; front-engine, front-wheel-drive cars; front-engine, rear-wheel-drive cars. It is generally true to say that present-day cars offer more space, convenience and comforts, performance, mechanical reliability and fuel economy than old models, at the expense of greater complication, shorter life (the modern welded-up integral body/chassis rusts far too quickly) and more difficult, expensive, 'only-the-garage-can-do-it' servicing.

Particularly in this and other technically advanced countries, cars seem suddenly to have become too popular—too 'necessary' —too demanding. The worries facing the present-day motorist include the thousands upon thousands of other cars that threaten to bring him to a standstill; the rapidly increasing costs of running and maintenance (yet family life so often depends on the car); and the sudden realisation, all over the world, that the materials needed to construct and fuel a car are running dangerously short.

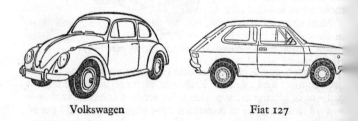

Volkswagen   Fiat 127

HOW CARS WORK

ENGINE

The Otto cycle (see History, above) is the name given to the four-stroke cycle of operation by which most car engines work. A very few cars use two-stroke engines.

With a four-stroke engine each cylinder is fired once during each two revolutions of the crankshaft. With a two-stroke engine, a cylinder fires at every revolution. Four-stroke engines use mechanically timed and driven valves to regulate the entrance and exit of gases into the cylinder. Two-stroke engines need no valves, and the flow of gases in and out of the cylinder is brought about by pressures within the engine itself.

Four-strokes are generally smoother at low speed, more economical and capable of developing greater power from a given capacity without the polluting emissions of two-strokes.

Both engines work on a similar principle. One part of petrol is mixed with about 20 parts of air in a carburettor. This highly inflammable mixture is compressed by a piston rising within a cylinder. The piston has springy rings to ensure a gastight seal. When the mixture is exploded by the spark plug, the piston is driven down. (A few cars have Diesel engines, which don't need spark plugs.) The piston is attached to a connecting-rod, in turn attached to a journal of the crankshaft. Thus the explosion drives the crankshaft round, and this movement is carried to the driving wheels (see Transmission). The action of the engine is therefore comparable to that of a man's arm cranking a car; the straight, up-and-down movement of his arm (his shoulder is the piston, his arm the connecting-rod) becomes a rotary or circular movement when applied to the crank.

Most European cars, both medium-sized and large, have four- or six-cylinder four-stroke engines with cylinders in line. Some 'baby' cars have fewer cylinders—the Fiat 126 has two. Big cars with six, eight or twelve cylinders may have V engines; if they did not, the engines might be too long or their crankshafts too flexible. Some engines have opposing cylinders laid flat—a very space-saving arrangement.

All the engines described so far are Reciprocating engines—that is, they contain parts that go up and down, driving other parts that go round and round. Many attempts have been and

TWO STROKE CYCLE

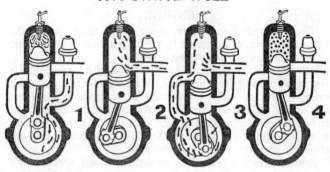

1. Ignition, induction.   2. Exhaust, crankcase charge compressed.
3. Exhaust, fresh charge enters cylinder.   4. Compression, partial
vacuum in crankcase.

are being made to construct engines with parts that all spin
(Rover long ago made a gas-turbine engine, for example). The
spinning, rotary engine should, in theory, be smoother and less
wasteful.

FOUR STROKE CYCLE

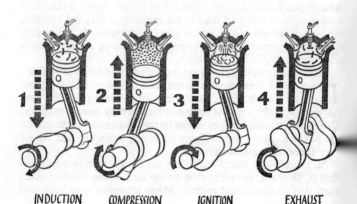

INDUCTION   COMPRESSION   IGNITION   EXHAUST

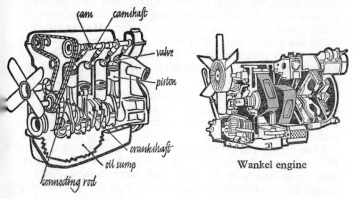

Four-cylinder, four-
stroke engine with
cylinders in line

Wankel engine

In fact, the Wankel engine is the only rotary design in international production. The drawing below shows the Wankel
operating cycle. The lobes (shown *a*, *b*, *c* below) describe
patterns within the casing of the engine that cause pressure/
suction areas for the mixture and exhaust. The advantages of
the Wankel engine include astonishing smoothness, but no
manufacturer has yet achieved fuel economy comparable with
the piston engines'.

Lubrication Two-stroke engines may be lubricated by a
small amount of oil added direct to the petrol. As the mixture
must pass through the crankcase as well as to the cylinder, the

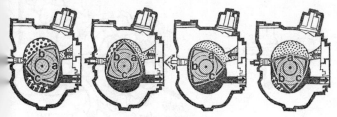

Wankel cycle

oil vapour provides enough lubrication for every part. However, modern engines have a positive oil supply from a separate oil tank.

Four-stroke engines are elaborately lubricated from a reservoir called the sump. Pure oil is drawn from the sump by an oil pump which passes it under high pressure through channels drilled through such components as the crankshaft, connecting-rods and valve gear.

Cooling Car engines develop great heat, not only through the explosions within the cylinder but also through friction of the moving parts. This heat must be got rid of, either by cooling with water or air.

Most car engines are *water-cooled*. The cylinder-head, where the explosions take place, and also the cylinder block that contains the cylinders, are channelled with water passages. Water is passed through these passages, generally with the aid of a pump driven by the engine itself.

The constantly flowing water in the engine is cooled by the radiator, a grille of small water tubes supported by a lattice of fins. This is joined to the top and bottom of the engine by short lengths of rubber hose so that a loop circuit is formed. The radiator is exposed to the outside air, and may be further cooled by an engine-driven fan. Hot liquids always tend to rise above cool: so the hottest part of the radiator is the top, and the coolest the bottom. The flow of cooling water is thus from bottom to top of the engine and from top to bottom of the radiator.

Air Cooling The cylinders of an air-cooled car are covered with fins (as on a motor-cycle engine) which present a large area of coolable metal to the passing air. The fins are generally

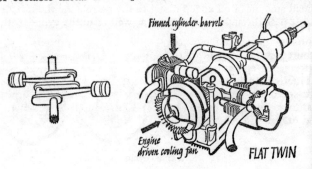

Finned cylinder barrels

Engine driven cooling fan

FLAT TWIN

supplemented by a powerful engine-driven fan to make sure of a good supply of cooling air even when the car is in heavy traffic.

Air-cooled engines need no cooling water, of course, and this is an advantage, as water may leak or freeze or cause corrosion. Air-cooling disadvantages include extra noise (water is a good sound damper) and the large amount of engine power needed to drive an adequate fan.

Surplus heat from either a water-cooled or air-cooled engine is generally used to warm the car interior.

Engine Power and Capacity *The size* of a car engine is described in terms of the amount of water that would be needed to fill all cylinders, with pistons down. In Europe we describe this amount in cubic centimetres (c.c.) or litres—thus 'Austin Maxi 1750', in which the engine is of approximately 1,750 c.c. capacity: or 'Riley 1½ litre', which was about 1,500 c.c. in capacity. 1,000 c.c. = 1 litre.

The power that an engine develops is described in Brake Horse Power or B.H.P. 'Austin A60' was so called because its engine developed approximately 60 B.H.P.

Capacity and power should not be confused. A racing-car engine of small capacity will develop considerable B.H.P.—probably four or five times as much as a family saloon of the same engine size. Both c.c. and B.H.P. must be known to get an idea of a particular engine.

Engine power depends on the rate at which it can digest fuel and get rid of the exhaust. Thus, the faster an engine can be made to turn—the more gulps of fuel it can consume—the more power it will deliver. Modern family-car engines often exceed 5,000 revolutions per minute. Modern racing-car engines may turn at 10,000 r.p.m. or even more.

To feed a family car with fuel, one carburettor may be enough. Sports and racing engines demand more fuel and therefore more carburettors to mix and deliver it. In the most modern high-performance engines, fuel injectors replace the carburettors. Yet more fuel may be given to the engine by a supercharger—a high-speed fan that forcibly feeds air to the carburettor (or mixture to the engine) under pressure. Supercharging is seldom used in cars you see on the road.

TRANSMISSION

The power developed by a car's engine must be transmitted
to its driving wheels through the clutch, gearbox, various drive
shafts and a differential. All these parts are transmission parts.

The Clutch is used to join or separate the engine from the
rest of the transmission. In starting a car from rest the clutch is
'let in' with a pedal so that the rapidly-turning engine can
gradually start the driving wheels turning without damage to
other transmission parts. Use of clutch also simplifies gear
changing.

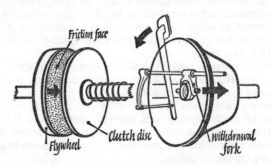

The clutch is made up of three disc-like plates, two joined t
the engine and one to the transmission. When the clutch ped
is pushed the plates are separated. When the pedal is release
the plates are pushed together by springs so that they join an
become one. The plates are lined on their meeting faces wi
a friction material so that they can tolerate gradual engag
ment.

The Gearbox allows the driver to match the speed and pow
of the engine to the road conditions. Car engines work efficient
only when they are turning fast: thus a car with only top ge
(highest) working would be unable to climb a hill, as the engi
would steadily lose its speed and therefore its power. Exac
the same is true of a small child attempting to climb a steep h
on an adult's bicycle.

Most cars have four gears. A number have five. First is t
lowest, used for starting the car from rest or for climbing ste

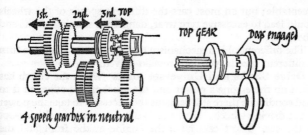

1st. 2nd. 3rd. TOP

TOP GEAR   Dogs engaged

4 speed gearbox in neutral

hills. Top is used for easy cruising conditions and for maximum speed. Some cars today are fitted with—

Overdrive, in effect a separate gearbox that gives a very high gear. This allows high-speed cruising under easy conditions with the engine turning over slower than it would in normal 'top'.

The majority of cars still make use of a gearbox containing trains of gear-wheels that are engaged by a lever: the clutch helps the operation. But there have always been many other kinds of gearboxes, and recently more and more cars have—

Automatic Gears A car with a fully automatic gearbox has no clutch pedal, and the driver need only set a lever to select the *conditions* under which the car is to be operated. If he selects 'normal driving' he need do nothing further except brake or accelerate. The car itself will do whatever gear-changing is necessary. But although automatic gearboxes simplify driving, they themselves are inevitably complicated, as the basic gearbox must be controlled by electric, hydraulic and vacuum systems that relate engine conditions to the car's needs.

Other kinds of gearing include epicyclic *'preselectors'*, in which the next gear wanted is 'dialled' for in advance; and the *variable-pulley* gearbox, in which belts are driven by two pulleys which change in relative size, and so give the most suitable of an infinite range of gears automatically, as in the Volvo/Daf.

The Freewheel is a device that allows clutchless gear changing and also lets the car run free, as if de-clutched, when the throttle is closed. When the engine is accelerated the drive is taken up again.

Differential When a car turns a corner the inner of the two driven wheels travels a lesser distance than the outer, and therefore turns slower. On a very small and light car this might be acceptable; but on most cars the different speeds of the wheels would lead to excessive tyre wear, dangerous steering effects and wheel slip.

The differential is a mechanism that allows two wheels to turn at different speeds, yet both remain driven.

Drive Shafts and Universal Joints When the clutch has taken up the engine's power and the gearbox has adjusted it to road conditions there still remains the necessity to take the power to the driving wheels. How this is done depends on the lay-out of the car. Most cars have the engine at the front and the driving wheels at the back: in this case power is led to the differential, and thence to the driving wheels, through the *propeller shaft*. Generally, this shaft is a simple tube with a universal joint at either end. It may, however, be an enclosed unit in another tube which is joined to the rear axle.

Morris Marina 1.8 showing propeller shaft

Two other shafts, called half-shafts, must then carry power from either side of the differential to each driving wheel. These may be enclosed in a rigid casing. If the car has independent rear suspension (described later) each shaft must have universal joints.

If the car is front-engined and front-wheel driven, or rear-engined and rear-wheel driven, then a propeller shaft is unnecessary. The drive can be taken from the differential straight to the rear wheels by two short shafts, each with universal joints.

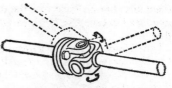

A Universal Joint

Universal Joints allow a stiff shaft to transmit power through an angle, or through constantly changing angles.

They must be fitted to a propeller shaft because the rear axle moves up and down on its springs while the gearbox remains stationary.

If the driving wheels are driven direct by shafts from the differential, then universal joints must be provided to allow for the wheels' up-and-down movements.

The three most commonly used universal joints are the flexible coupling, a rubber disc; the Hardy-Spicer type, which is comparable to gimbals; and the constant-velocity type, which uses metal balls running within tracks cut into two half-spheres, one cupping another.

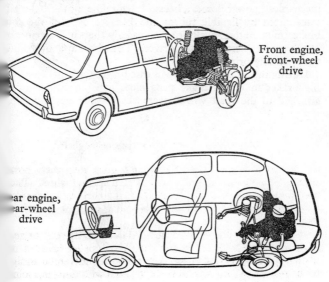

Front engine,
front-wheel
drive

Rear engine,
rear-wheel
drive

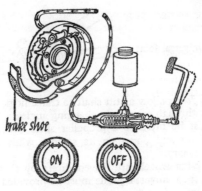

BRAKES

By the end of the Second World War, the majority of the world's cars were braked on all four wheels by internal expanding hub brakes operated by hydraulic power. Hydraulic systems are preferred to mechanical systems because there are no mechanical power losses; because hydraulic power is easily transmitted by flexible tubes; and because each of the four brakes must automatically receive exactly the same proportion of the power exerted by the driver. The diagram above shows the operating principles.

During the Second World War disc brakes (external contracting brakes in which brake pads close like pincers on a disc attached to the road wheel) were successfully developed for

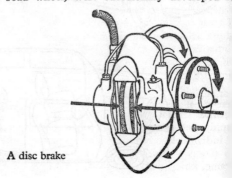

A disc brake

aircraft and have since been applied with great success to motor cars. Disc brakes are complementing or supplanting drum brakes.

Whatever system is used, an additional and separate braking system must also be supplied. This is called the 'parking brake' or 'hand-brake', and is used only to hold the car when at rest or to stop the car in the event of a failure of the main braking system. Hand-brakes are normally mechanically applied to one pair of wheels only.

BODY AND CHASSIS

The chassis of a car is the framework that supports the body, engine and other components. This 'skeleton' is often visible in old sporting cars. However, the majority of present-day mass-

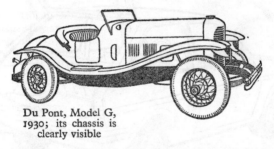

Du Pont, Model G,
1930; its chassis is
clearly visible

produced cars use the body itself as a chassis. The 'Unit Construction' modern car body is an all-metal welded box structure of great rigidity, and no separate chassis is needed. Sometimes additional local strength is given by a small chassis-like structure. Sometimes the engine and perhaps the transmission and driving wheels are mounted on a small separate chassis that may be removed from the body very quickly and easily for servicing.

Although 'Unit Construction' is general, it is not the only method in use. Triumph mass-produced small cars with a separate chassis frame. Luxury-car makers must be able to supply a chassis on which various specialist coach-builders can individual bodywork. Sports and racing cars are often built round a complicated arrangement of tubes called a Space frame, which gives great rigidity with minimum weight; or with a chassis taking the form of a massive spine with outriggers to hold bodywork, engine, suspension and other components.

Sheet steel is the raw material of bodies for mass-produced cars. It can be formed in huge presses with great speed and economy. Sheet aluminium may also be used for parts that are not highly stressed (boot lids, for example).

Plastics bodies (fibreglass) are popular with small-production makers. The time and space needed to produce the bodies forbid large-scale production.

Ford Fiesta

STEERING

Cars are steered by their front wheels: other lay-outs have been tried, but have never been successful.

A typical steering linkage consists of a steering wheel, whose motion is translated through the steering box to push the drop arm. This is connected by a drag link so that it steers one road wheel. The other road wheel is connected to the first by the track rod.

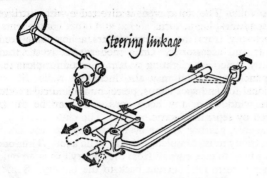

Steering linkage

ELECTRICAL SYSTEM

The equipment of a car includes a complete electrical generating system, a storage battery to hold the electricity and a variety of systems and mechanisms that use it.

Electric power is supplied by dynamo or alternator, which is usually driven by belt from a pulley on the engine's crankshaft. The output of the dynamo or alternator charges the battery (usually 12-volt, but sometimes 6). A voltage regulator or cut-out keeps the output at a suitable level.

The battery stores electric power and passes it on demand. The greatest demand is that of the self-starter motor, which makes the battery supply enough power to turn over the engine quicker and for longer than a man could.

The petrol/air mixture within the cylinders is fired by sparking-plugs. These are supplied by the ignition coil with current stepped up in voltage from the battery's 6 or 12 volts to 6,000–

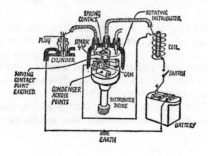

12,000 volts. The coil current is directed by the distributor to each sparking-plug in turn.

Electricity from the battery powers a host of other components and accessories. On a modern family car they will certainly include the lighting system, direction indicators, horn and panel lights; and may also include a radio, heater fan, additional fog and spot lamps, petrol pump and cigar lighter.

The windows or the hood—or both—may be raised and lowered by separate electric motors. The clutch, various panel instruments, gearbox and/or overdrive may also use electricity.

Electricity must complete a circuit to do a job. Thus one wire may be used to take current from the battery to a lamp bulb, and another wire to take current back to the battery. Sometimes, however, the car itself is used as a conductor of current, thus halving the considerable amount of wiring.

SUSPENSION

Suspension is the word used to describe those parts of the car that join the road wheels to the chassis or body.

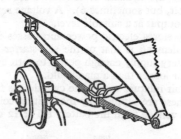

The traditional method of suspension was by leaf spring supporting an axle, and this method is still in common use for the rear axle.

Almost invariably today, the front wheels have independent front suspension (i.f.s.): with i.f.s., each wheel is free to behave independently of the other.

Independent rear suspension (i.r.s.) is also becoming increasingly common and is in any case necessary with a rear engined car.

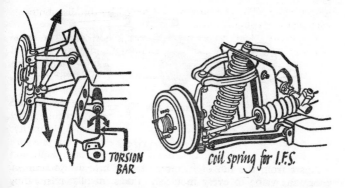

TORSION BAR

coil spring for I.F.S.

Springs may be in the form of leaves, coils, compressed liquids or torsion bars (bars twisted along their length). Citroën introduced inert gas as a springing medium—rather as if the car were suspended on four interlinked footballs. Others followed.

Ride Controllers and Shock Absorbers If a car were suspended only on springs it would meet a bump, bounce over it and keep on bouncing. So-called shock absorbers or dampers let the spring do its work but prevent it from bouncing. They control the ride of the car and keep it steady.

With most cars, this control is the result of keeping each wheel steady. But ideally, it would be better to control the ride of the car as a whole: Citroën have gone a long way towards achieving this by linking each inert-gas suspension unit to the other by means of a hydraulic mechanism so that the behaviour of any one road wheel affects the behaviour of the others. The car is in fact self-levelling. Some Leyland Cars vehicles have front and rear wheels collectively sprung by liquid-filled tubes ('Hydrolastic').

Anti-roll Bars are used to link the behaviour of one road wheel to another. Thus on heavy cornering the heavily loaded outside wheels transfer some of their load to the inside wheels and the car remains more nearly level.

Tyres, while not part of the suspension, will affect its behaviour. Over- or under-inflation has drastic effects both on the way a car feels and how it behaves. Attempts have been and are being made to design tyres having renewable treads; and there are now tyres that can be run flat for limited distances.

Lotus Formula 1 racing car

RACING CARS

Apart from the fun of it, motor racing has always been of enormous value to every motorist. Fuels, metals, oils, tyres, brakes—in fact, nearly every part of the ordinary car—all gain from the high-pressure testing and development that racing gives.

Grand Prix track racing is undertaken only by thorough-bred, out-and-out racing machines. The World Championship is decided by Grand Prix events. British cars and drivers have been consistently successful in the Grand Prix races of the last few years on circuits all over the world.

Track Racing also includes events for production cars, sports cars, Vintage and Veteran cars.

Road Racing includes the classic Le Mans—a race open to all kinds of sports/racing cars driven over a closed road circuit

Rallies are typified by the classic, all-Europe Monte Carlo and by the Lombard/RAC Rally of Great Britain—a five-day 2000+ miles event incorporating speed trials and forest stages. The winners of the various classes are those who lose the fewest number of points. Motoring clubs throughout Britain hold Rallies.

Time Trials, Sprints, Hill Climbs, Rallycross, etc., are events that pit the driver 'against the clock'. The winners are those who cover a given distance, climb a certain hill or complete a number of circuits in the shortest time. Many such events are held throughout Britain.

Trials are winter events held over deserted country roads in muddy fields and up hills. Often no one can complete the course, in which case the team that gets farthest wins. Special cars and skills are needed.

Club Racing takes place all over Britain and the world.

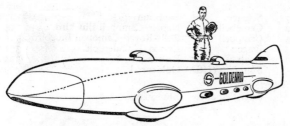

'Goldenrod' (USA)—fastest wheel-driven car (409·69 mph.)

Britain such races are the proving grounds for new drivers. Cars range from true racing machines to Vintage Sports Cars.

Drag Racing. An American motor sport that has invaded Europe. Aim: to achieve the highest speed in a straight line over a short distance.

Formula Track Racing Cars True racing cars are defined by Formulae arrived at by international agreement. At present these are in force:

Formula 1—3-litres unsupercharged or $1\frac{1}{2}$-litres supercharged engines in single-seater bodies. 12 cyls max.

Formula 2—Racing cars with single-seater bodies. Engine capacity up to 2,000 c.c. Carburettor or injector, but not supercharger. 6 cyls max.

Formula 3—2 litre. Limited modifications to engines from cars produced in units of 5,000 or more. There are other such Formulae, mostly aimed at producing cars based on standard components, such as *Formulae Ford* (racing cars based on Ford engines) and *Formula 5000* (big cars, big engines); and classes for production motor vehicles, such as *Gran Turismo* (fast touring) and *Saloon* cars; also *Sports* cars. The popular *Group 1* is for standard production saloons.

LAND SPEED RECORD

Some important figures (wheel-driven cars):

			m.p.h.
925	Campbell	Sunbeam	150.9
926	Thomas	Higham Special	171.1

			m.p.h.
1927	Segrave	Sunbeam	203·8
1932	Campbell	Napier–Campbell Bluebird	254
1935	Campbell	Rolls-Royce–Campbell Bluebird	301·1
1938	Eyston	Eyston Thunderbolt	357·5
1947	Cobb	Railton	394·2
1965	Summers (USA)	Goldenrod	409·6

Not wheel-driven:

1970	Gary Gabelich	Blue Flame	622·4

Lagonda

IDENTIFYING CARS

Cars are identified and described in various ways. Engine capacity and power have already been discussed (see Engine). Descriptions such as saloon, convertible or station wagon are well known to you.

But every car also carries a variety of identity marks:

Registration Letters and Numbers (number plates) which are allotted to each new car by the County Council concerned. The same letters and numbers appear in the car's 'log book'— the official Registration Book. However many owners the car may have, its number plate never changes.

Chassis and Engine Numbers are among other details appearing in the log book. These are permanently stamped on cars of every nationality.

Panther Lima

Jaguar XJ-S

Fiat X1-9

VW Golf and Polo

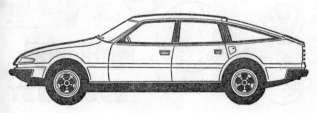

Rover 3500

Mercedes-Benz

Moskvich

Peugeot

Renault

Rover

POLSKI FIAT

Volga

Sunbeam

Skoda

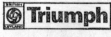
Triumph

VOLVO

Gordon Keeble

WOLSELEY

International Registration Letters appear on a separate plaque fixed to the rear of a car when it is taken abroad. Among the most frequently seen are:

A	Austria	MC	Monaco
AUS	Australia, Norfolk Islands	MEX	Mexico
B	Belgium	N	Norway
BR	Brazil	NA	Netherlands (Antilles)
BRG	British Guiana	NL	Netherlands (Holland)
BS	Bahamas	NZ	New Zealand
BUR	Burma	P	Portugal
C	Cuba	PA	Panama
CDN	Canada	PAK	Pakistan
CH	Switzerland	PL	Poland
CL	Ceylon	PTM	Malaya
CY	Cyprus	RA	Argentina
D	Germany	RNR	Zambia
	(Federal Republic)	RSR	Rhodesia
DK	Denmark, Faroe Islands	S	Sweden
E	Spain, Canary Islands	SF	Finland
EAK	Kenya	SGP	Singapore
EAT	Tanganyika	SK	Sarawak
EIR	Republic of Ireland	SU	U.S.S.R.
ET	Egypt	SWA	South-West Africa
F	France	SYR	Syria
FL	Liechtenstein	T	Thailand
GB	Great Britain and	TN	Tunisia
	Northern Ireland	TR	Turkey
	(and GBA, Alderney;	TT	Trinidad and Tobago
	GBG, Guernsey; GBJ,	U	Uruguay
	Jersey; GBM, Isle of	USA	U.S.A.
	Man)	V	Vatican City
GR	Greece	WAG	Gambia
HK	Hong Kong	WAL	Sierra Leone
I	Italy, Sardinia, Sicily	WAN	Nigeria, British
IND	India		Cameroons
IR	Iran	WD, WG, WL, WV	
IRQ	Iraq		Windward Islands
IS	Iceland	YU	Yugoslavia
JA	Jamaica	YV	Venezuela
L	Luxembourg	ZA	Union of South Africa

Toyota Corolla

Opel Manta

GROUP MANUFACTURERS

Many individual makers are members of a group of manufacturers. General Motors of the U.S.A., for instance, produces
various makes of cars not only in America but throughout the
world: Vauxhall in England and Opel in Germany are part of
the General Motors Group.

In Britain many old names have been brought under group
control:

Leyland Cars	*Chrysler, United Kingdom*
Austin	Hillman
MG	Humber
Morris	Chrysler
Wolseley	Sunbeam
Triumph	
Rover	
Jaguar	
Daimler	

'Hatchback'
—Renault 5

Audi Avant 1.6

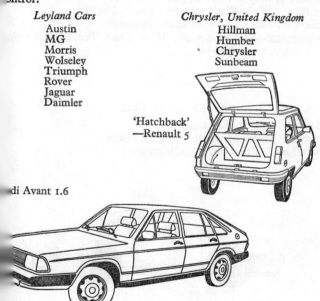

Leyland Cars 'Princess'

FURTHER READING

Autocar Handbook, *Motor Manual*—and these magazines'
annual Road Test compilations
The Observer's Book of Automobiles
Picture History of Motoring, L. T. C. Rolt
A History of the World's Sports Cars, R. Hough
About a Motor Car, Puffin Book (Penguin)
MAGAZINES—*Motor, Autocar, Motor Sport, Practical Motorist,
Car, Motor Cycle*, etc.

PLACES TO VISIT

Science Museum, Kensington
National Motor Museum, Beaulieu, Hants
Stratford Motor Museum, Gloucester

Porsche Turbo

Motorcycles, 3-wheelers, scooters and mopeds

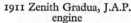

1911 Zenith Gradua, J.A.P.   1922 Matchless twin
        engine

HISTORY

The history of the motorcycle begins, like that of the motor
car, with the internal combustion engine. Gottlieb Daimler,
pioneer of cars, can perhaps be credited with the first motorcycle
(1885) although an Englishman, Edward Butler, produced a
motor tricycle a year before.

Whatever its origins, the motorcycle took some time to
establish itself. The bicycling craze of the 1890's submerged
whatever interest there might have been in motorcycles. At the
turn of the century, however, social conditions changed radically
in every way. Times were ripe for motorisation of any sort—
bicycles included.

And indeed the first motorcycles were very similar to the
powered bicycles—the mopeds—of today. Like mopeds, they
were power-*assisted* vehicles. You pedalled when the motor
needed help. Later and more powerful machines remained as
simple as mopeds. They had no gears, or only two; there was no
kick-starter—you pedalled or ran alongside the machine to get it
going. Transmission was by belt (as it still is with certain
scooters and mopeds). Lighting was by acetylene—a romantic
but smelly and time-consuming method.

Suddenly, though, the motorcycle caught on. From 1910 on,
design developed fast. During the First World War, the motorcycle came into its own: motorcycle dispatch riders were popular
heroes and machines like theirs were greatly coveted when the
war ended.

In the 1920's, no fewer than 200 firms produced motorcycles.
The pattern of these machines did not change greatly for 20
years. Spring front-forks, electric lighting, greater power, the
kick-starter, three or four gears, a pillion—all these features were
adopted as standard.

The motorcycle thus emerged as an international form of transport, appealing particularly to those who enjoyed transport for its own sake (and there is still no more exhilarating way of getting about): and to those who wanted personal transport at rock-bottom prices.

1930 Scott Squirrel, water-
cooled 2-stroke

1928 Coventry Victor twin

As we have said, the motorcycle began as a moped. Oddly enough this form of the motorcycle more or less disappeared from the scene—and the scooter, although it was invented soon after the First World War, was never commercially developed either. Three-wheelers, blending both motorcycle and car features, did make some progress. But the standard motorcycle was the most-used vehicle.

Harley Davidson

FROM WORLD WAR TWO TO TODAY

Wars leave nations poor. After the Second World War, every one wanted personal transport and few could afford it. Two wheelers became popular. The Moped, the minimal motorcycle was developed to such a high standard of simplicity and reliability that it became, and remains, a permanent part of the world transport scene.

Italian companies invented the Motor Scooter, whose advantages included weather protection, a soft ride and simple controls. Perhaps it was the scooter craze that led manufacturers (particularly in Japan) to re-think the motorcycle and produce today's stylish, colourful, fully-sprung, lively yet docile machines, particularly in capacities from 100–300 c.c. Such machines killed off the scooter fashion.

The bigger machines have changed too. A liquid-cooled, multi-cylinder motorcycle is today a common sight—and a very handsome one. Common too are imaginative finishes, luggage carriers, self-starters and the sort of attention to the details of engineering that make broken cables and messy, oily engines seem very old-fashioned.

The new crises in fuel, money, materials, parking space and public transport have lead to much greater use of all kinds of two-wheelers. Young people may stick to motor-cycles instead of turning to cars. Commuters may find it necessary to keep a two-wheeler handy. And big machines—'Superbikes'—are now a cult.

HOW MOTORCYCLES WORK

The Frame The wheels, engine and other parts of the machine are mounted in or on the frame—typically, a double loop of steel tubing (the 'duplex' frame). Single steel tubes like a bicycle's are sometimes used; so are steel pressings. The engine is sometimes used as part of the frame. All those parts of the motorcycle that help it to roll or steer are called 'cycle' parts and are associated with the frame. The forks that hold the wheels are mounted on the frame—at the front, to the steering head, and at the rear by various methods (see **Suspension**).

The frame needs little or no attention other than polishing. But it is wise to go each week over all the nuts and bolts that hold components to it.

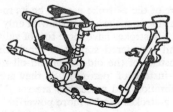

Duplex cradle frame

Engine Motorcycles and motor cars are very closely related mechanically. To avoid wasting space, we refer you back to the section on **Motor Cars** when talking about common features. Each reference is given like this—(G25)—which means, turn back to that page in the Cars section.

Like cars, motorcycles have either 2-stroke or 4-stroke engines (G9, 10). Several manufacturers produce Wankel-engined machines (G11) but it is too early yet to say how important these are.

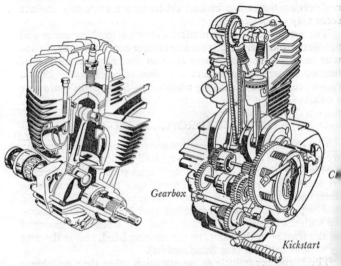

Gearbox

Kickstart

Above left: 2-stroke single-cylinder engine
Above right: Honda 125 overhead-cam 4-stroke engine and gearbox

The advantage of the 2-stroke used to be its mechanical simplicity—it is possible to make a 2-stroke with only three working parts. But today's 2-strokes have some sort of valve to admit the fuel mixture and a metered supply of lubricating oil from a separate tank instead of the old petrol-and-oil mix in the fuel tank ('posilube' instead of 'petroil'). So they are complex. In performance, vibration and noise they are roughly comparable with 4-strokes. 2-strokes can be more powerful.

The important advantages of the 4-stroke are considerable

better fuel economy; less annoyance from fouled plugs and exhaust systems; and a clean exhaust. As anti-pollution laws increase, the present trend to 4-stroke, will, presumably, continue.

Most motorcycle engines are air-cooled (G11, 12) and have fins outside the cylinders. Some 'superbikes' have liquid cooling —look for the radiator. Engine capacity varies from less than 50 c.c. for moped and beginners' machines to over 1,000 c.c. on machines for the important American market. The vast majority of motorcycles have one or two cylinders, but multi-cylinder machines are on the increase.

Motorcycle engines can be made to develop astonishing power for their size. 100 B.H.P. per litre is not uncommon (G13) which means that some of the 500 c.c. motorcycles you see on the road can develop as much power as a small car. A multi-cylinder 250 c.c. racing motorcycle may give as much as 180 B.H.P. per litre. Some racing engines reach 12,000 r.p.m. (G13).

Gearboxes Power from the engine is taken via a multi-plate clutch (G14) to a gearbox working in much the same way as a car's (G15) and for the same reasons (G14). Four or five gear ratios are usual, but six-speed boxes are not uncommon. A footchange—a lever rocked down by the toe for downward changes, and by toe or heel for changes up—is usual. Automatic and infinitely variable gearboxes (G15) have been used on motorcycles and are not unusual on scooters and mopeds.

Final drive Almost always, the drive from engine to gearbox—the 'primary' drive—is by chain. So too is the final drive—although belts have been used in the past and may be again in the lightweights of the future in conjunction with automatic, scooter-type transmissions. A few makers use shaft-drive on expensive and luxurious machines, but chain drive is the rule.

Ignition and Lighting Larger motorcycles and an increasing number of scooters use car-type electrical equipment (G21).

A simpler and cheaper system for ignition and lighting is supplied by the Alternator or the Magneto—machines rotated by the engine. They deliver high-tension current—the current wanted at the sparking plug.

On smaller, simpler motorcycles, scooters and mopeds, the magneto is within the flywheel of the engine and the current it produces is used both for ignition and lighting.

Brakes Drum brakes (G18), mechanically operated by rods or cables, were general, but today front and rear discs are seen.

Suspension The majority of motorcycles have telescopically-sprung front forks with dampers (G23) incorporated. The rear wheel is mounted in a sprung pivoted fork with a suspension system like a stubby version of the telescopic front fork.

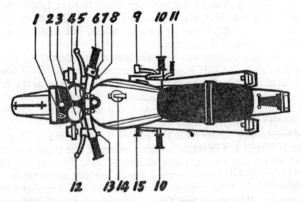

1 Headlight control switch	**9** Rear brake pedal
2 High beam indicator light	**10** Foot rests
3 Speedometer	**11** Kick starter pedal
4 Tachometer (engine r.p.m.)	**12** Clutch lever
5 Front brake lever	**13** Turn signal switch
6 Throttle grip	Horn button (below)
7 Emergency switch	**14** Fuel tank cap
8 Headlight control switch (above)	**15** Gear change pedal
Starter button (below)	

Controls Here is a typical enough layout of the control found on a modern motorcycle. British machines often hav some reversed controls—the gear-change is on the left, and so on Some machines have rocking, heel-and-toe gear-change lever Most motorcycles have steering-column locks and quite number have lockable petrol-tank fillers. Old motorcycles ha controls not shown here; decompressors to help startin steering-head adjusters (still used on some motorcycles) and on. All machines, old or new, have a petrol tap (not show which almost always has a position for 'reserve'.

Suzuki RGA 500 (4-cylinder)

MOTORCYCLE SPORT

Grand Prix Racing International events—the World Championship Series (controlled by the FIM)—in a dozen European countries and Venezuela. 6 classes from 50 c.c. to 500 c.c. Also Sidecars.

Circuit racing (controlled by the ACU) Club, national, and international. Formulae variable—designed to attract entries. F750, for basically roadster machines of 750 c.c., is internationally important and has World Championship status.

Amateurs and club members are more likely to start with *Motocross* (125, 250 and 500 c.c.—also sidecar events) which is virtually the same thing as a *Scramble*—a race over rough territory; *Trials* (mixed territory, observed sections, competitors lose marks for each failure); or *Grass track racing* under ACU rules. All these events (and similar events for sidecar machines) are open to anyone who can get his entry accepted at Club, Local, National or International level. *Speedway* schools are held at many venues throughout Great Britain. *Drag racing* events are 'against the clock' straight-line speed competitions. *Schoolboy Sport* covers most of these activities up to age 16.

Trials machine

LIGHTWEIGHTS, SCOOTERS

The scooter represents a successful attempt to 'civilize' the motorcycle (see **History**, this section). Everything in the design should lead to comfort, silence, convenience, minimum maintenance, maximum enclosure. The ideal scooter is the one that demands least from its owner—often a girl.

Suzuki GT 185

Not so long ago, scooters were seen everywhere. Today their place seems to have been taken by mainly Japanese machines of the sort shown above—a lightweight offering no weather protection, but with safe handling and braking, five gears and considerable performance. Or perhaps the scooter rider of yesterday might choose a fun bike by Honda or Suzuki; an about-town vehicle that can pack into an estate car or 'hatchback' (G31) small car. For strictly local use, there are today's excellent and reliable mopeds.

The little Suzuki shown opposite boasts a 5-speed gearbox and a 50 c.c. 2-stroke engine that is claimed to develop 4.9 B.H.P and give a top speed of 60-plus mph!

Perhaps the nearest equivalent to the scooter is the commuter Honda 50 (there are larger-engined models) with quiet 4-stroke engine, soft springing and some weather protection.

The typical scooter had an engine capacity of something between 125 and 200 c.c. Within or even well below these capacities, today's lightweights offer you a choice of 'masculine or 'feminine' characteristics, suited to anything from Moto-Cro

Rickman Kawasaki
Z1-R 1000

to shopping trips ... big or small wheels, fat or thin tyres ...
and either scooter-type or motorcycle-type controls.

Suzuki AP 50

MOPEDS

The moped ('motor + pedal') is basically a motorised bicycle
—and the simplest machines are adequately described in this
way. The more advanced mopeds, however, may have automatic, variable gears (or a 2, 3 or even 4-speed gearbox)—
excellent brakes—and springing front and rear.

Puch Maxi S

Legally, a moped is a machine of 50 c.c. or less *with pedals*. Without the pedals, motorcycle licensing restrictions about age apply. The Yamaha Sixteener is legally a moped, but the rather similar Suzuki 50 is not.

THREE-WHEELERS

The aim of the 3-wheeler has always been to give the advantages of the light car with further advantages in terms of tax, fuel economy, first cost and 'garageability'. In this country, however, the importance of these advantages has lessened over the last few years. First cost is too near that of the cheapest four-wheeled cars (which have also increased their operating and economy efficiencies). Three-wheelers do not keep their value well—secondhand prices are low. There can be no doubt that the modern miniature car scores over the 3-wheeler in terms of quietness, comfort, carrying capacity, and, all too often, reliability. On the other hand, the 3-wheeler offers the motorcyclist one enormous advantage: he or she need not pass the car driving test to drive certain 3-wheelers. A motorcycle licence suffices.

There is no 'typical' 3-wheeler. It could be said that there are two main classes—those derived from motorcycles and those derived from motor cars—but even then, there is a great deal of overlap. The 'car' type of 3-wheeler is typified by the Reliant 'Robin' with its water-cooled 4-cylinder engine, or by the dashing little Bond 'Bug'. Both are virtually cars with a wheel missing. The Trojan, Messerschmidt, Peel and many others exemplify the other school—they could be called motorcycles or scooters with a wheel (and bodywork) added.

Bond 'Bug'

Railways

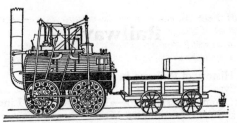

Locomotion No. 1

A SHORT HISTORY OF RAILWAYS IN BRITAIN

How Railways Began (1800–1850) Nobody knows when the first railway was built. The first mention of one, in which a special track of wooden rails was used, is found in the sixteenth century. Men had discovered that a cart or wagon ran more easily on a track than on the rough roads of the time. The earliest railways were purely local lines, no more than a few hundred yards long; with the coming of iron works and coal mines, they were used to help move wagonloads of material. The wagons were pulled by men or horses. One of the oldest mineral railways in the world, the Middleton Railway at Leeds, can trace its origin back to 1758; it survives today and is operated as a private line for freight by students of Leeds University.

The first railways to carry merchandise from one town to another were built early in the 1800s. The Surrey Iron Railway, from Wandsworth to Croydon, was approved by Parliament in 1801 and opened, for goods only, in 1804; while the first passenger-carrying railway in the world, the Oystermouth Railway from Swansea to Oystermouth (closed as recently as 1959) was opened in 1806. Both lines employed horses to pull the wagons or passenger trucks.

The Stockton & Darlington Railway was opened in 1825, followed in 1830 by the Liverpool & Manchester and Canterbury & Whitstable Railways.

At the time that these first railways were being built engineers were experimenting with steam locomotives—at first with little success. Richard Trevithick's road steam locomotive, one of the first effective models, was patented in 1802. It was followed a year later by his first rail steam locomotive, which ran at the Coalbrookdale Iron Works tramway in Shropshire. It was now that George Stephenson, one of the greatest railway engineers of them all, came upon the scene. At the time he was employed at Killingworth Colliery, Northumberland, and by 1815 he had built a type known as the 'Killingworth' locomotive, used on a number of colliery lines. A development of this type was built in 1825 for the Stockton & Darlington Railway by the newly founded firm of R. Stephenson & Co. This was the famous *Locomotion No. 1*, still in existence today.

The Stockton & Darlington was the first public railway in the world to use steam locomotives—though they were used only with goods trains. This line, regarded as the start of the present BR network, celebrated its 150th anniversary in 1975. In quest of suitable locomotives the Liverpool & Manchester Railway held trials in 1829 at Rainhill; the most successful entry was the *Rocket*, built by R. Stephenson & Co.

The Rocket

George Stephenson not only built locomotives but also sur-eyed, planned and engineered many railway routes.

The first trunk line was the London & Birmingham Railway, ngineered by Robert Stephenson, George's son and partner, nd completed in 1838. In the same year the Great Western ailway completed the first section of its line between London nd Bristol. Railway schemes were now introduced by the undred. All had to be submitted to Parliament for approval. any were rejected; but many were approved.

The Battle of the Gauges From the beginning George ephenson had had the foresight to realise that lines then only nnecting neighbouring towns would one day be joined to form eat trunk routes. He therefore standardised a gauge (the stance between the inner edges of the running rails) of 4 ft.

8½ in. for all the railways with which he was connected. This was a familiar gauge to Stephenson, since it was used on some colliery lines in the north-east. Other engineers, however, had their own ideas as to what the gauge should be. Isambard Kingdom Brunel, for example, engineer of the Great Western Railway, adopted a gauge of 7 ft. 0¼ in. for the line from London to Bristol, and many lines between London and the West of England and West Midlands were built to this 'Broad Gauge'. Very soon the immense disadvantages of using different gauges for neighbouring lines became obvious. At junction stations where standard and broad tracks met, passengers and goods had to be transferred from one train to another. In the end Parliament decreed that the standard gauge should be used for all main-line railways; and in 1868 the Great Western began to convert its tracks. During the period of change mixed-gauge tracks were used—these having three rails, one of which was common and the other two set to standard and broad gauge respectively; but broad-gauge tracks on the main line from London to Penzance remained until 1892, when the last stretch was converted in one week-end to standard gauge.

1850–1900 Gradually the pattern of railway routes became the one we know today. Small local companies soon realised the advantages of amalgamating with adjacent local lines and forming larger companies. Two of these amalgamations produced the Midland Railway in 1844 and the London & North Western Railway in 1846.

Meanwhile, more and more railways were built, many of them competing with other railways already in existence. Some companies were on friendly terms with their neighbours, but others were keen rivals and built railways simply in a spirit of competition. This explains why, today, some towns have more than one route to London or other big cities.

During the second half of the nineteenth century locomotives began to look less like the *Rocket*; boilers were made larger, chimneys shorter and cabs began to appear. By 1870 the locomotive had taken the shape familiar to our eyes today, and coaches had lost their resemblance to wagons.

1900–1970s By 1900 the main-line railway map was almost complete. The last main line to be built was the Great Central route to London from Nottingham and Leicester, opened 1899. Apart from underground lines in London and one or t

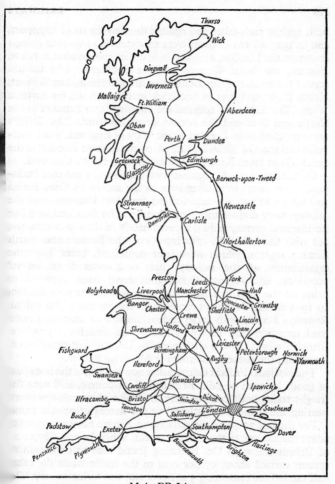

Main BR Lines

cal lines built as late as the 1930s, building of new railways had
en almost ceased. In fact, it was at this time that com-
tition from road transport began to take traffic from the rail-
ay; first came the electric trams and, later, cars, lorries and
ses. Railway companies could no longer afford to compete

both against each other and against the new forms of transport, and in 1923 all 123 of them were amalgamated into four groups known as the London, Midland & Scottish, the London & North Eastern, the Great Western and the Southern. The L.M.S. served the country from London to the Midlands, North West, North Wales and part of Scotland, reaching to the far north at Wick. The L.N.E.R. covered the country from London to the North and East and the remainder of Scotland. The G.W.'s area stretched from London to the West of England, West Midlands and most of Wales. The S.R. operated from London to the South Coast from Kent to Devonshire and North Cornwall.

On January 1, 1948, together with canals and some road transport, the railways were taken over by the nation. A Commission was set up to run the nationalised transport industry, and the railways were divided into six regions, one for Scotland, and five for England corresponding approximately to the old companies, but with the L.N.E.R. split into two—the Eastern and North Eastern regions, which were later combined. Since 1948 the organisation of the railways has been altered on several occasions, and regional boundaries have been changed to bring all the lines in a particular area within one organisation. In 1963 Britain's railways came under the control of the British Railways Board, with independent boards to manage canals, road transport and transport hotels and catering. The first British Railways Board chairman was Dr. Richard (later Lord) Beeching; the present chairman is Mr Peter Parker.

The National Freight Corporation now organises the transport of goods by road or rail. British Rail, of course, still runs the freight trains itself but you may see trains of container wagons bearing the name 'Freightliner' or the names of private firms.

For the last 20 years the railways of Britain have struggled to adapt themselves to the modern world. When he was Chairman of British Railways Dr. Beeching found that half the railway system carried about 95 per cent of the traffic while the other half carried the remaining 5 per cent and was losing money. The Beeching Plan, therefore, called for the closure of a large number of little-used lines, with passenger services taken over by buses. Many branch lines were closed and so, too, were some main lines. In some areas rail services provide a much better form of transport than buses, even though the trains are making a loss; during 1969 a system of payments was started in which the

Government helps to off-set some of the losses by paying British Railways to continue the services. More recently the Government has made payments towards the building of new trains, for resignalling schemes and for track improvements.

During the ten years from 1960 to 1970 the British railway system changed considerably. As we shall see later, steam locomotives finally gave way to diesels and electrics in 1968, train speeds were higher than ever before and 100 m.p.h. became common, new types of signalling were brought into use on a large scale, and new operating methods introduced. In 1974 BR completed the electrification at 25,000 volts a.c. of the West Coast main line over the 401 miles between Euston and Glasgow. From 1976, new High Speed Trains started regular 125 m.p.h. services.

LOCOMOTIVES

But for the steam locomotive, railways could not have been built on a large scale in mid-Victorian years. Steam locomotives reigned supreme on the railways of Britain for over a century until, at last, in the face of more modern forms of traction powered by diesel engines or electricity, the last steam locomotive was withdrawn from BR's main lines in August 1968.

Steam: Some Classic Locomotives of the past.

Steam locomotives were classified according to the 'Whyte' table of wheel arrangements (see H9). In the days when there were 123 different companies the number of locomotive designs ran into hundreds. Yet the same wheel arrangements were adopted by many companies for locomotives on the same type of work. In late Victorian times 2–4–0 and 4–4–0 locomotives were used for passenger duties and 0–6–0 locomotives for goods trains and for shunting. In the first years of the present century locomotive designers began to think in terms of larger locomotives than had been used until then. Some railways built 4–4–2 (Atlantic) locomotives for express duties and others had 4–6–0s. The Great Western built a solitary 4–6–2 (Pacific) locomotive, but it was not very successful and was later rebuilt as a 4–6–0. After the grouping in 1923 designs were standardised and express passenger trains were built right up to the maximum size and weight that the British loading gauge permitted. Some of the most famous express locomotives built during this period were the Great Western 'King' class 4–6–0, most powerful of all 4–6–0

Streamlined A4 Class ex-L.N.E.R.

Coronation Class ex-L.M.S.

designs; the L.N.E.R. streamlined 'A4' 4–6–2; the L.M.S. 'Coronation' class 4–6–2, which began as a streamlined engine; and the S.R. 'Merchant Navy' 4–6–2, a design which appeared in 1941 and was originally partly streamlined.

BR Types After nationalisation British Railways introduced twelve standard classes of steam locomotives. They were: three types of 4–6–2, for express passenger duties; two types of 4–6–0 for lighter express and intermediate passenger or freight working; three types of 2–6–0 for main-line and branch passenger or freight duties; a 2–6–4 tank for suburban passenger trains; two types of 2–6–2 tank for branch passenger and freight; and a 2–10–0 for heavy express or ordinary freight. Many BR and earlier steam locomotives have been preserved.

The Last of the Line The very last locomotive built specially for express passenger work, No. 71000 *Duke of Gloucester*, was completed in 1954; but even this engine was withdrawn after a life of only eight years. The last steam locomotive of all, a class '9' 2–10–0 freight engine, No. 92220, was built at Swindon Works for the Western Region in 1960. This engine did not carry the last number, since another

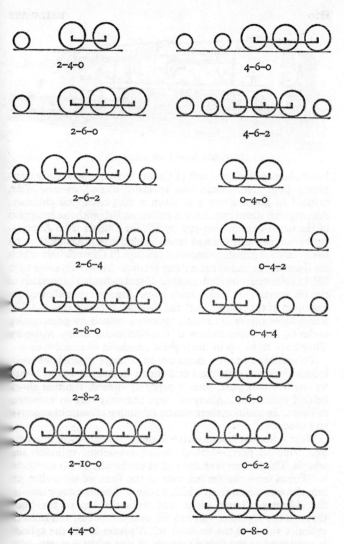

WHYTE CLASSIFICATION OF STEAM LOCOMOTIVE WHEEL ARRANGEMENTS

Modified Merchant Navy Class.

batch, Nos. 92221–50, built at Crewe Works, was actually completed first. No. 92220 was specially named *Evening Star*, painted in green livery and given a copper-capped chimney. Although no steam locomotives are left on BR (with the exception of the narrow gauge line run by BR for tourists from Aberystwyth) you can still see and travel behind steam locomotives on the numerous privately-operated railways in Great Britain which are listed at the end of the railway section. Moreover, since 1972 BR has allowed a limited number of steam-hauled excursions to run on selected secondary main lines. Among types allowed are examples of the 'King', 'A4' and 'Merchant Navy' classes. The steam locomotives are mostly privately-owned by preservation societies, but some belong to the National Railway Museum. They have to be up to the highest standards of maintenance.

To mark the 150th anniversary of railways a parade of steam locomotives was organised at Shildon in August 1975. Nearly 30 engines took part, mostly privately owned, running slowly behind each other. Many of them normally run on preserved railways. In addition there was an exhibition of static locomotives and coaches.

How a Steam Locomotive Works A steam locomotive has five principal parts—firebox, boiler, smokebox, cylinders and wheels. The firebox is at one end of the boiler, which surrounds it. Tubes from the firebox pass to the front of the boiler and into the smokebox, from which smoke and gases escape through the chimney. Steam pipes lead from the top of the boiler through the regulator valve to the cylinder valves, and from the cylinder valves to the smoke-box. A piston inside the cylinder is connected to the driving wheels so that when it moves backwards and forwards the connecting-rods to the driving wheels

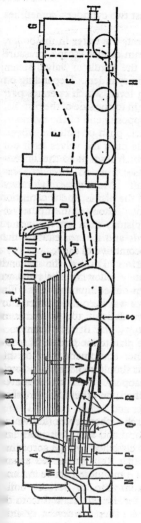

Simplified Diagram of British Railways 4–6–2 Express Steam Locomotive

A Smokebox
B Boiler
C Firebox
D Cab
E Coal space
F Water space
G Water tank filler
H Water pick up scoop for taking water at speed from troughs
I Firebox stays
J Safety valves
K Regulator valve operated by rodding from regulator lever in cab
L Steam pipe taking 'live' steam to cylinders

M Blast pipe for exhausting used steam from the cylinders out of the chimney
N Valve chest
O Piston
P Cylinder
Q Valve gear
R Connecting rod
S Coupling rod
T Brick arch
U Tubes carrying superheater elements. 'Wet' steam on its way from the regulator to cylinders passes through the superheater to dry it and make it more efficient
v Tubes to carry exhaust gases from firebox to smoke-box

make them turn. Engines have at least two cylinders, sometimes three or even four.

Coal is burnt in the firebox and heats the water in the boiler, turning it to steam. Because the steam cannot escape, pressure builds up. When the driver opens the regulator valve, steam passes through the pipe leading to the cylinders. Depending on the position of the driver's reversing lever, which operates part of the valve gear, the valves admit steam to one side of the pistons. The steam forces the piston to the opposite end of the cylinder, and the connecting-rods to the wheels push or pull the wheels round. When the steam has made its push the valves let it out of the cylinder into another pipe which leads it to the smoke-box. Here, with the smoke and gases from the fire, it is ex-hausted out of the chimney as a 'puff'. Meanwhile, the valves let in more steam to the other side of the piston, and this pushes the piston back again. So a continuous action is built up, steam pushing first on one side of the piston, then on the other, propelling it backwards and forwards and in turn causing the driving wheels to revolve and the locomotive to move.

Locomotives and Modernisation During the Second World War and the years immediately following, the railways were not able to replace old and worn-out equipment. Coal of a quality suitable for steam locomotives was becoming difficult to obtain and horribly expensive. It was difficult, too, to find men to train as firemen. So when, in 1955, the British Transport Commission announced an immense plan to modernise its loco-motives, coaches, signalling and other equipment, part of the plan was that diesel and electric trains should replace steam loco-motives, which would gradually disappear. Some trunk routes and suburban lines would be electrified; on others, diesel loco-motives would haul express passenger and freight trains. Trains with diesel engines built on the coaches themselves (known as multiple-units) would be used for local and semi-fast journeys

Diesel locomotives were originally classified by type according to horsepower but during 1968 British Rail introduced a new classification code in which each class is numbered between 1 and 56. Electric locomotive classes run from 70 to 87. Several manu-facturers built diesel locomotives for British Rail (including British Rail themselves), and this means there are several designs for each power type. At the beginning of 1978 there were, in service, 16 basic main line diesel classes of all types, with a grand

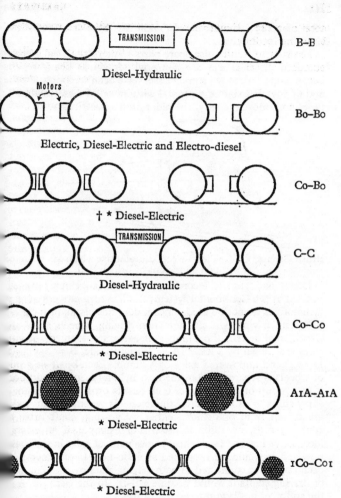

B–B

Diesel-Hydraulic

Motors

Bo–Bo

Electric, Diesel-Electric and Electro-diesel

Co–Bo

† * Diesel-Electric

TRANSMISSION

C–C

Diesel-Hydraulic

Co–Co

* Diesel-Electric

A1A–A1A

* Diesel-Electric

1Co–Co1

* Diesel-Electric

Powered Axles   Non-powered Axles   *No electric version on BR
† This type now obsolete

CLASSIFICATION OF DIESEL AND ELECTRIC LOCOMOTIVE
WHEEL ARRANGEMENTS

total of 2,283 locomotives. In addition, there are 1,007 diesel shunting locomotives.

In order to standardise spare parts some of the smaller non-standard diesel classes are being withdrawn as heavy repairs become due. Already several classes have been scrapped. At the end of 1971 BR started a general withdrawal of diesel-hydraulic types and, more recently, the older diesel-electric types.

Brush Class 47 Co-Co diesel-electric locomotive which can be found at work on all regions of British Rail.

Diesel and electric locomotive wheel arrangements are expressed by the Continental system; the Whyte notation for steam locomotives cannot be used, since it does not distinguish clearly between driving wheels and non-driving wheels. In the Continental system the number of axles are counted; driving axles are shown by a letter (A = 1 driving axle, B = 2, C = 3, D = 4) and unpowered axles by a figure. Each bogie or group of wheels is separated from the next by a hyphen. In addition, if in a group of driving axles each has its own driving motor a small suffix 'o' is added after the letter. If several driving axles are driven from one source either by gearing, shaft drive or coupling rods, no suffix is used. For example, if an electric locomotive has two four-wheel bogies with all axles individually powered it would be described as a Bo-Bo. If one motor on each bogie was connected to both driving axles by coupling rods or driving shafts it would become a B-B. In the last year or so the suffix 'o' has begun to go out of use.

How a Diesel Locomotive Works The diesel locomotive (or multiple-unit) power equipment is in two parts; the engine and the device for connecting the power output from the engine to the wheels, called the transmission.

The principle of the engine is the same for locomotives and multiple-units, but it is in the methods of transmission that variations occur. There are three of these: mechanical, hydraulic and electric.

The cylinders are the most important part of a diesel engine. There may be as few as four or as many as sixteen. Each has a piston sliding up and down inside it, connected to a crankshaft. Sometimes the pistons from two banks of cylinders drive a single crankshaft; in others, a cylinder may be open at both ends and have two pistons opposing each other, driving separate crankshafts connected by gearing. The diesel engine works by compression ignition. As the piston moves into the cylinder it compresses the air in the cylinder to a high pressure and to a very high temperature. Just before the piston stroke is completed a minute amount of fuel oil is injected into the cylinder by fuel pump, and the high temperature causes the fuel to ignite and explode, forcing the piston back. Several cylinders and pistons are arranged so that each fires in turn and, as one piston is rising to compress the air, the next will just be firing, the next driven half-way down, another at the end of its power stroke waiting to return to compress the air again. Generally four-stroke engines are used, in which the pistons make two strokes up and down for every one firing movement. The intermediate stroke cleans out the exhaust gas from the previous firing stroke and draws in fresh air for the next one.

The mechanical form of transmission employs a clutch and gearbox to transmit the drive from the output shaft of the engine to the wheels, just as in a motor-car. Its use in this country is limited to engines of less than about 400 h.p., and on British rail is confined to some small shunting locomotives and to the multiple-unit rail-car sets, nearly all of which are equipped with this form of transmission.

The hydraulic system of transmission uses what is called a hydraulic torque converter. This consists of a cylindrical container filled with oil. Inside are two turbine wheels, one connected to the output shaft of the engine, the other to the shaft that drives the axles. They are mounted in such a way that when one turbine wheel (the impeller, driven by the engine) revolves, its blades force the oil into the blades of the second wheel and cause it to revolve and drive the locomotive wheels. Sometimes a locomotive may have more than one torque convèrter covering several speed ranges, or even an automatic gear-box in addition. Hydraulic transmission is used on a few BR rail-car sets, and also, until recently, on some shunters and some Western Region main-line diesel classes.

In the third system of transmission the diesel engine drives an electric generator which feeds current to electric motors

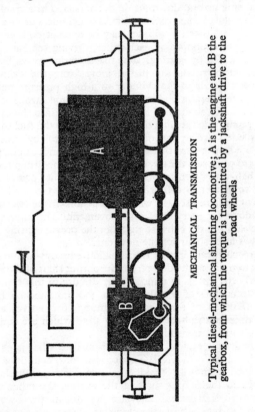

MECHANICAL TRANSMISSION

Typical diesel-mechanical shunting locomotive; A is the engine and B the gearbox, from which the torque is transmitted by a jackshaft drive to the road wheels

mounted on the locomotive axles. This is the most common system used on British Rail locomotives, and it is also in use on some Southern Region diesel multiple-unit trains.

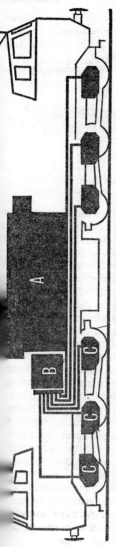

ELECTRIC TRANSMISSION

A typical diesel-electric locomotive; A is the diesel engine, which drives the generator, B, that provides current for C, the electric traction motors

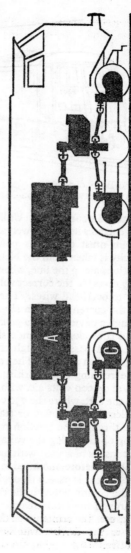

HYDRAULIC TRANSMISSION

A typical main-line diesel-hydraulic locomotive; A is the diesel engine, B the torque converter, from which the drive is transmitted by cardan shafts to C, the final axle drives

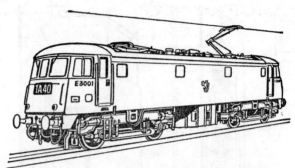

Bo-Bo 25,000 volt a.c. 3,200 h.p. electric locomotive for
services between Euston–Manchester/Liverpool/Glasgow

Electric Locomotives Unlike a steam or diesel locomotive,
which generates its own power, an electric locomotive or multiple
unit train must obtain its power from some outside source.
Electricity is taken from the National Grid and passed to railway
sub-stations along the line, where it is transformed (and rectified
in many cases) to the correct voltage and fed either to conductor
rails or to overhead wires. The electric locomotives and train
collect the current through *shoes* running on the conductor rail
or through a device called a *pantograph* which is mounted on the
roof and rubs along the underside of the conductor wire. The
current then passes through the control system and into the
electric traction motors. The return current is generally passed
into the running rails. British Rail have standardised electrification at 25,000 volts a.c. with overhead current collection except on the S.R. where the 750 volts d.c. third rail system is used.

An electric locomotive or train works by passing an electric
current through the traction motors. Speed can be varied by
reducing or increasing the voltage. In simple terms the traction
motor consists of a shaft with many coils of wire wound round it
called the armature, mounted inside an electromagnet. When an
electric current is passed through contacts on the armature shaft
called the commutator, to the coils of wire in the armature, and
thus through the electromagnet, a magnetic attraction is set up
which causes the armature shaft to revolve. And as this shaft is
geared to the driving wheels, the whole process moves the
locomotive.

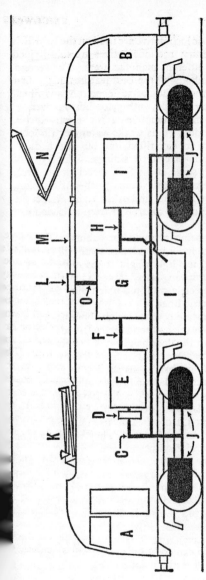

Simplified Diagram of British Rail Main Line Bo-Bo Electric Locomotive Operating on 25,000 Volts Alternating Current from Overhead Contact Wire

A Cab No. 1
B Cab No. 2
C Relatively low voltage direct current (about 1900 volts)
D Control equipment
E Main rectifier
F Relatively low voltage alternating current (about 2000 volts)
G Main transformer
H Low voltage alternating current (240 volts)
I Other equipment, such as compressor and ejector motors

for train brakes, and air-operated control apparatus, lighting on locomotive, train heating and control equipment
J Traction motors
K Second pantograph not in use (most locomotives have only one pantograph)
L Circuit breaker
M Supply from pantograph
N Pantograph collecting electricity from overhead wire
O High voltage alternating current (25,000 volts)

Seven types of a.c. electric locomotive are used on the L.M.R.'s electrified main lines; the first 100 locomotives are sub-divided into five classes built by different manufacturers. The second 100 are of all one class embodying the best features of the first 100 locomotives. The seventh class of 36 locomotives is much more powerful than the earlier 200, with 5,100 horse power.

Another type of modern locomotive is the electro-diesel, used on the Southern Region. This works as an electric loco-motive when running on an electrified line but has a diesel engine for running on non-electrified sidings. This type of locomotive, together with some of the S.R. diesel locomotives, can work certain Southern express trains push–pull fashion, that is with the locomotive at either end of the train. When the locomotive is pushing the driver controls it from a driving cab in the leading coach.

More electrification is being planned for suburban lines in cities. Some lines will run underground, and some will be rapid transit systems which will use lightweight trains more like the trams found in some European cities, rather than the tradi-tional, somewhat heavy electric multiple-unit trains found on existing BR suburban electric lines.

Coaches Modern main-line coaches weigh about 32–34 tons each, are 64 ft. 6 in. long over the body ends and 9 ft. wide over the body (9 ft. 3 in. if you count the door handles). Corridor coaches seat 48 or 64 second-class passengers or 42 first-class passengers. The latest coaches are of 'integral' construction in which the coach body is self-supporting without a heavy underframe. For the last 12 years all new second class coaches have been of the open pattern, with pairs of seats on each side of a central pas-sageway. BR's latest Mark III coaches, in use on HST trains and on certain other lines, are 75 ft. long. They weigh 32 tons and seat 48 first or 72 second class passengers.

In 1971 BR made history by introducing trains with fully air-conditioned coaches on ordinary services; until then they had been used for only a few special luxury expresses on which supplementary fares were charged. On air-conditioned coaches the windows do not open and the air is filtered and heated or cooled before being circulated inside the coach.

Brakes If you want to stop a train it's not much good turning off the power alone; a train can coast for several miles, particu-larly if it is running downhill, without appreciably slowing down.

A train's brakes usually consist of blocks which, when applied, press hard on the treads of the wheels. Latest freight wagons and a few electric multiple-units have disc brakes—special brake pads which press against discs on the axle. The means of applying and releasing them is by variations in air pressure. There are two systems in use: one employing a vacuum to hold the brakes off, and opening it to the atmosphere to apply them; and the other using compressed air to do the same thing.

The *vacuum brake* has been standardised on locomotive-hauled trains on BR until recent years. Throughout every passenger train and many freight trains runs an air-tight pipe flexibly connected between coaches and to the locomotive itself. Connected to this 'train pipe' by a branch pipe on each coach is a cylinder containing a piston. The piston is connected by rodding to the brake blocks. A vacuum pump or ejector on the locomotive draws air out of the system which releases the brake; admission of air to the train pipe by the driver's brake valve applies the brakes. The difference in air pressure above and below the piston causes it to move up or down and in turn the brake blocks press against the wheels or move away when released.

If a passenger operates the alarm signal or a train becomes uncoupled accidentally and breaks the flexible train pipe between the coaches, air enters the brake system automatically and applies the brakes.

The *compressed-air brake* is more complicated, but works on the principle that the release of compressed air will apply the brakes. All electric trains in Great Britain use the air brake and on most multiple-units this is applied and released electrically—a much quicker process—although there is still automatic application in case of emergency. Air brakes are used on 'Freightliner' goods trains and are gradually being adopted as the new standard type on locomotive-hauled passenger trains. The brake system on these trains uses two pipes running throughout the train, one to apply the brakes when the compressed air is let out through the driver's brake valve, the other full of high pressure compressed air to recharge the system to release them.

Track The rails used on early railways were of cast iron; but for very many years now the track has been made of steel. Until the 1950s *bull-head* was used almost exclusively on British railways and is still in use on many lines. This has a cross-section rather like a figure 8. It is laid in cast-iron *chairs* and held by wooden blocks or 'keys' wedged between the rail and the side of the chair. The chairs are bolted to wooden sleepers, and the sleepers themselves are held in position by granite ballast.

Since about 1946 the place of bull-head as a standard rail has been taken by what is called *flat-bottomed rail*. This, as its name suggests, has a flat base and is capable of standing upright without support. It is held in position by *baseplates*, and the rail and baseplates are spiked, clipped or bolted to the sleeper.

Rails are normally 60 ft. long and are supported by 24 sleepers to a length: there are 2,112 sleepers in one mile of track. Each length is joined to the next by *fishplates*—lengths of steel plate about 2 ft. long bolted through the rail ends with four bolts. When new track is laid, small gaps are left between rail ends to allow for expansion in hot weather. The holes through which the fishplate bolts pass are oval, to allow the rail to expand slightly.

Welded track is now used extensively in Britain. In this type of track the 60ft lengths of rail are welded together into one piece, often $\frac{1}{2}$ mile or even one mile in length without a break. In the previous paragraph we mentioned that gaps allow for the rails to expand in hot weather. If special measures are not taken, continuously-welded rail would be badly distorted when it expands in very hot weather. To overcome this difficulty welded rail is nearly always carried on concrete sleepers which are so heavy that the rail is held tightly in position. The sleepers are spaced slightly closer at about 26 for every 60 ft. Moreover, soon after it is laid the rail is heated artificially to average summertime temperatures, starting at one end and working through to the far end. As the rail is heated it expands, and is fastened down tightly in its expanded form. In subsequent hot weather, therefore, it cannot expand any more; in cold weather it tries to contract but since it is rigidly held it is unable to do so. In some ways it is like a piece of elastic which has been pulled tight and stretched a little. The engineers responsible for heating the rail try to fix it in position at a temperature about halfway between the extremes of cold in winter and heat in summer.

A new form of track in which sleepers and ballast are replaced by a solid bed of reinforced concrete paving to which the rail are attached is being tried out experimentally by British Railways for possible use on future high speed lines.

Signalling First, the signals themselves. *Semaphore signals*, with an arm about 5 ft long, are still used on many lines. *Stop* signals have a red arm with a white vertical stripe near the left end, and at night show a red light for danger and green for clear. *Distant* signals have a yellow arm with a vee notch cut from the left-hand end and a black vee stripe near the end. At night they show a yellow light at caution and green for clear. These signals give the driver an advanced indication of the next stop signals ahead. All semaphore signals have the arm horizontal for danger or caution. Some signals, nearly all on the Western Region, have the arm lowered at about 45 degrees to show clear, but most semaphore signal arms are inclined 45 degrees above horizontal for clear. Most main lines now have *colour-light signals* without arms, in which the indications are given by coloured lights—red, danger; yellow, caution; double-yellow, preliminary caution; and green, clear.

All passenger lines on British Rail are worked on the 'absolute block' system of signalling. In this, each line is divided into sections ('block sections'); where mechanical signalling is used, there is usually a signal box wherever sections meet.

The principle is that there shall never be more than one train in a block section on one line at a time. The signal boxes are equipped with 'block instruments' and bells for each line, so that signalmen in neighbouring boxes can keep each other fully informed about the passage of a train through the sections they control. The block instrument has a dial resembling a clock face but without any figures. The dial is marked with three panels; one says 'line blocked', another 'line clear' and the third 'train on line'. The indications are given by a needle pivoted in the centre. Normally the needle is vertical and pointing to the 'line blocked' panel. When deflected to the right ('twenty minutes to two' position) it points to the 'line clear' indication; to the left ('twenty minutes past ten') it points to 'train on line'. The needle is operated by an electro-magnet when the signalman turns a switch on the block instrument to the appropriate position. The indication is electrically repeated by the block instrument applying to the same section in the signal box at the other end of the section.

When a signalman wants to signal a train he must carry out

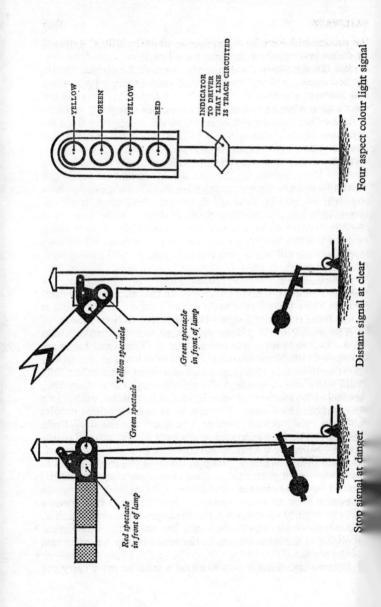

YELLOW

GREEN

YELLOW

RED

INDICATOR TO DRIVER THAT LINE IS TRACK CIRCUITED

Four aspect colour light signal

Yellow spectacle

Green spectacle

Green spectacle in front of lamp

Distant signal at clear

Green spectacle

Red spectacle in front of lamp

Stop signal at danger

the routine laid down by regulations in which he 'offers' the train by coded bell signals to the next signalbox ahead and if the line is clear the signalman there 'accepts' the train by a repetition of the bell signal. Bell signals are exchanged when the train enters and leaves the section of line between the two boxes and indicators show whether the section is clear or occupied by a train.

At one time the safety of trains depended solely on the correct operation of the block system by the signalmen: but today, lines carrying fast, frequent services are equipped with additional safeguards to prevent a signalman from forgetting a train. Many of these devices are worked by the trains themselves from what are known as *track circuits*. A track circuit is an electrically-insulated section of line which has a weak electric current passed through the running rails and connected to an electro-magnetic relay at one end of the section. As a train passes over the line, its wheels short-circuit the current, which is cut off from the relay. The relay arm therefore falls away from the magnet and makes contact with other electrical circuits, which can be used to operate such equipment as locks on signal and point levers and can prevent a signalman from pulling a signal lever to clear a signal when a train is standing on a track circuit ahead of it.

The track circuit is in fact the basis of all modern signalling, because it allows the signalman to 'see' trains several miles away. In mechanical signalling, where the signalman works points and signals from levers which operate rods or wires, Government regulations limit the mechanical operation of points to no more than 350 yds from the signal box. Thus, at big junctions, several signal boxes are often needed to control the layout. But with electric operation of points and signals there is no limit, and signal cabins can be arranged to work points and signals several miles away. Track circuits are used to show the signalman the positions of trains by lights on a track diagram in the signal cabin. Track circuits are also used to initiate the operation of barriers at level crossings, the ones in which barriers automatically lower across half the road when a train is coming. This type of crossing, which also has flashing lights to stop cars and pedestrians when a train is approaching, is gradually replacing the old type with swing gates. By the way, NEVER try to pass over a crossing when the barriers are down.

Modern signal cabins have been introduced on many sections of British Rail as part of the modernisation plan. In some, the signals and points are controlled from banks of thumb-switches. But in the most recent cabins the controlling miniature push-buttons or thumb-switches are placed in their appropriate positions on a diagram which consists of a replica of the track layout. The buttons usually work on the route-setting principle; that is, the operation of two buttons will set up a complete route from signal to signal—the equipment checking first that no other train is on the line concerned, then changing the points needed for the route and finally clearing the signal.

Illustrated opposite is part of a modern signalling panel. To set up a route the signalman turns the thumb-switch at the entrance to a signal section and presses a button at the end of it. When the route is set, white lights are illuminated on his diagram along the track concerned so that he can see the path the train will take. As the train passes along the route, the lights change from white to red to show the signalman the position of the train. After the train has passed the signalman restores the thumb-switch to its normal position until it is needed again and the white lights are extinguished. Where there is a junction, the button he presses determines the route that is set. For example, in the illustration, if he wants to send a train on the up relief line into the up goods lines he will turn switch 4 and press button D. That sets the route from signal 4 to signal 6. He then turns switch 6 and presses button F. The points will be set, signal 6 will clear and the white diagram lights will show the route set as far as signal 8. If instead the train was to continue straight up the relief line he would still turn switch 6 but press button E. Three routes are shown set up in the illustration—up relief to up goods; up main to up relief (switch 2 button E) and down main (switch 1 button A).

The signalmen in these modern cabins advise each other of approaching trains by the train describer. Usually the describer displays a code of figures and letters indicating the train's classification, its destination area and its number. The code is set up on the describer by the signalman who dials the code on a telephone-type dial or operates push buttons. The code description automatically moves from aperture to aperture along the track diagram in step with the train, so the signalman can see its description at a glance. When the train continues on its way towards the next signal cabin its description is automatically passed to the describer there so that the signalman knows what

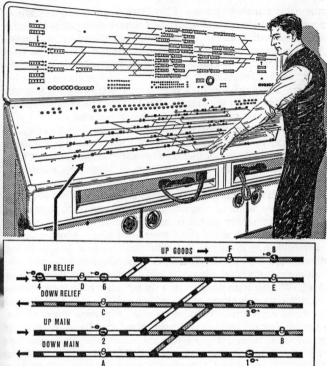

rain is approaching him. He can watch its progress, too, from
his track circuit diagram. Usually there are several automatic
signal sections controlled solely by track circuits between the
areas worked by the push-button panels. Colour-light signals
are installed throughout the 401 miles between Euston and
Glasgow, as part of electrification, mostly controlled from
centralised power signalboxes supervising long sections of line.
There are only 6 signalboxes between Euston and Nuneaton—a
distance of 97 miles, and over the 220 miles from the Warring-
ton area to Glasgow only five signal boxes. One of the latest signal
boxes, at Edinburgh, will control more than 200 route miles.

Most British Rail main lines, whether equipped with
semaphore or colour light signals, are fitted with 'A.W.S.'—the

automatic warning system. This device, situated at all semaphore distant signals and nearly all colour-light signals, gives the
driver an audible advice of the indication shown by the signal.
A bell rings in the cab if the signal is clear; if it is at caution a
horn sounds and the brakes are applied automatically unless the
driver acknowledges the warning.

More advanced than AWS is a new sophisticated form of
signalling in which the signals ahead (if indeed lineside signals
are retained) or the condition of the line ahead and the safe
running speed are displayed continuously in the driver's cab.
This form of signalling is used in some countries for high
speed running over 125 m.p.h. On other railways, Holland for
example, cab signalling is being tried on lower speed lines. It
can be achieved by pairs of wires laid along the centre of the
track which transmit signalling codes to a train passing above by
induction—a form of magnetism. If the wires are crossed at,
say, 100 metre intervals the transmitted code operates a counter
on the train which shows the distance travelled. Another means
of transmitting details of line conditions on to a display in the
driver's cab is by transponders. These are packages of electronic
equipment which are placed between the rails and are normally
dead. When a train passes over a transponder an inducted signal
from the train is aimed at the transponder, which is energised
by it and replies with coded details of its location (for example,
distance from London, and such fixed details as permanent
speed restrictions or other operating information that applies at
that place) for display to the driver. They are being installed
between London and Glasgow in connection with Advanced
Passenger Train trials (see page H31).

The next stage beyond that is the introduction of automatic
speed control. Automatic trains which drive themselves after
the train operator has pressed the start button are at work on
London's Victoria Line underground route.

Freight Services. Until the 1970s goods wagons on British
Rail did not change very much in size from the early days of
railways, 100 years or so ago. The normal open wagon or covered
goods van was still a four-wheeler of about 16 ft. in length. One
reason for the continuity in size has been the limitation of some
goods stations where short loading platforms were designed for
only one wagon at a time, and sidings in some places could only
be reached by short turntables or traversers.

But these small wagons are not suited to today's high speeds and the new operating methods now being adopted by the railways. Until a few years ago the normal British goods train was slow moving, with each wagon or group of wagons starting from different stations and terminating at different stations. There were several thousand goods stations which handled all the different types of freight traffic. Very often a wagon would pass through two, three or even more marshalling yards on its journey. The basic division of a goods train was a single wagon. But under Dr. Beeching new methods of operation were investigated. Many small stations and goods yards were closed and freight trains were reorganised to run between main centres without remarshalling. Lorries collect and deliver freight from factories and shops to the main goods stations.

British Rail developed the Freightliner train for carrying goods. These consist of long flat bogie wagons, able to travel at up to 75 m.p.h., for carrying containers. They run as block trains, that is without intermediate remarshalling. Containers are loaded in the factory or warehouse, then taken by lorry to the goods station where the container is lifted on to one of the railway wagons. One wagon can often carry up to three containers. When loaded the train sets off on its journey. At the other end the containers are again taken by road to their destination. While they are being unloaded at the warehouse, other containers are being put on the train for its next journey.

Coal in special hopper wagons and oil in tank wagons is often taken in block loads, from a colliery or port to a power station or oil storage depot. For today's freight services BR has been developing new types of wagon, longer and carrying heavier loads than the old types. Some are four-wheelers but others, particularly oil and chemical tank wagons, are large bogie types weighing 100 tons fully loaded. Some coal trains between collieries and power stations are loaded and unloaded while moving slowly at each end of their journey. They are called merry-go-round trains.

Underground railways. In many cities of the world underground electric railways for many years have helped to move passengers quickly and to avoid street congestion. London underground railways were among the earliest, in the last century, with most of the system built between 1900 and 1910. Now new lines are being built, not only in London with the

Fleet Line, but also in rapid transit form—a cross between a tram and a train—in Newcastle and in other world cities. In Newcastle, which is the first railway of its type in Britain, the trains will be lightweight, articulated, two-car electric units, which can be coupled to make six-car formations. They have open saloon interiors, with plenty of room for standing, and sliding doors. They will work from overhead catenary at 1,500 volts d.c. New tunnels are being built under Newcastle city centre, and a new bridge across the River Tyne will link existing suburban railways to Whitley Bay and South Shields which will be served by the new Tyne & Wear Metro. In Liverpool, new underground lines are being built to extend existing BR electric services across the city.

Railway Speeds *The Record-Holders*

Railway speeds in the last few years have increased, but until 1976 British trains did not normally exceed 100 m.p.h., with averages of 80–90 m.p.h. The first 100 m.p.h. run by rail ever was claimed for the Great Western's 4-4-0 *City of Truro*, which was said to have reached 102·3 m.p.h. on May 9, 1904, with a Plymouth to London mail. This has since been disputed, and L.N.E.R. 4472 *Flying Scotsman* made the first authentic 100 m.p.h. run in 1934.

The world's speed record for steam locomotives is held by Great Britain's No. 60022 *Mallard*, which, in July 1938, reached 126 m.p.h. with a test train between Stoke and Peterborough on the L.N.E.R. main line. The world's rail-speed record for any form of traction is 205 m.p.h., achieved in March, 1955, by the French electric locomotives Nos. BB–9004 and CC–7107 between Bordeaux and Dax. For some years the Japanese have gone beyond the 100 m.p.h. speeds at one time thought to be the practicable limit for trains in daily service, with regular speed of up to 130 m.p.h. on the New Tokaido line between Tokyo and Osaka, built specially for high-speed running and opened in 1964. During 1972 the Japanese opened a second high-speed railway, the New San Yo line on which trains also run regularly up to 130 m.p.h. and more of these *Shinkansen* high speed railways are being built. On some, trains run every 15 min through the day on journeys of 300 miles or more.

In recent years, experiments have been taking place in Britain, France, Germany and Italy with trains running at 125 m.p.h., and even higher, on existing tracks. French Railway have also been testing a gas-turbine train designed to run at up to 300 km/hr (186 m.p.h.) as part of trials in readiness for a new high-speed electric line between Paris and Lyon with an eventual top speed of 300 km/hr, and due to open in 1981. In Italy a new line between Rome and Florence is being opened in sections and has a maximum speed of 250 km/hr (155 m.p.h.).

In Britain new high-speed railways are not considered to be worth the large amount of money they would cost, and British

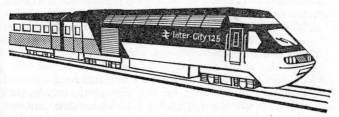

British Railways new production High Speed Train, 'Inter-City 125.

Rail has been experimenting with 125 and 150 m.p.h. trains designed to run on existing track. It has been found that by making certain curves less sharp and banking other curves with more superelevation, several Inter-city main lines can take trains of normal construction at up to 125 m.p.h. on certain sections. This has allowed the development of the High Speed Train (HST), which consists of fixed formation units of seven Mark III passenger coaches with two 2250-h.p. diesel-electric streamlined power cars, one at each end, so that there is no locomotive shunting at terminals. The prototype unit set up the world's speed record for diesel traction by reaching 141 m.p.h. between York and Northallerton in June 1973. Production units, known as 'Inter-City 125' trains, are now running from London to Bristol and South Wales, and on the East Coast route between London and Edinburgh.

The train designed for running in Britain at 150 m.p.h. on existing track is known as the Advanced Passenger Train (APT). Practically everything about it is new. The coach bodies will tilt as trains go round curves, and it will have special braking and suspension. The first experimental unit, which has been on trial for several years, is powered by gas turbines; on August 3, 1975, it raised the British rail speed record to 151 m.p.h. on a test run between Reading and Didcot. The first of three proto-type electric APT units are to start trials in 1978 and may enter commercial service a year later on the West Coast route between London and Glasgow. They will be 12-coach formations, including one power car in the centre; but in passenger service they are to be limited to 125 m.p.h., although trials are to be undertaken with two power cars in 14-car formations at the full 150 m.p.h. Production trains are expected in the early 1980s.

British Rail and French Railways are at present neck and neck in running the fastest trains in Europe, some at *average* speeds of 94 m.p.h. and top speeds of 125 m.p.h. The French achieve this over the 361 miles between Paris and Bordeaux with their Etendard and Aquitaine expresses, while BR runs many ser-vices each day at these speeds with Inter-City 125 units over the London–Bristol–South Wales and Edinburgh routes.

Locomotive numbering on BR BR diesel and electric locomotives are numbered in a series in which the class number forms the first two figures of the complete number. Shunting locomotives are numbered in classes 01 to 13, main line diesel locomotives in classes 20 to 56 and electric locomotives from 71 to 87 though with gaps as some classes have been withdrawn. The first locomotive in each class will be numbered 001. Thus the lowest numbered locomotive is a shunter 01.001, the high-powered Deltic locomotives which haul the expresses on the East Coast main line are 55.001 to 55.022, and the latest electric locomotives on the Euston-Glasgow line 87.001—87.035. The HST power cars are in class 253 and 254 as part of the multiple-unit classes in the series 100 to 254. In 1977 BR resumed loco-motive naming with classes 50 and 87.

Preservation Although British Rail no longer runs regular steam locomotives on main lines, steam locomotives are by no means extinct in Britain. Over the last few years as steam engines have been withdrawn many have been sold to private owners for preservation. Some are not in working order and can be seen only as static exhibits at museums. Others, including several large express locomotives, are kept in working order ready to run on BR main line special trips.

Numerous smaller tank and tender engines can be seen run-ning on standard gauge lines operated by preservation societies or private companies. These branches are all in private owner-ship and new railway companies have been formed to operate services mainly as tourist attractions. Most employ volunteer railway enthusiasts to help run and maintain the line under the guidance of a few professional engineers and other staff.

In September 1975, the new National railway museum was opened at York. It houses the state collection of locomotives, coaches and other relics.

Lines run by private railway companies with steam locomotives.

Standard gauge

Name	Location
Bluebell	Horsted Keynes–Sheffield Park
Dart Valley	{ Buckfastleigh { Paignton–Kingswear
Keighley & Worth Valley	Keighley–Oxenhope
Middleton	Leeds
Severn Valley	Bridgnorth–Hampton Loade– Bewdley
Lakeside	Windermere Lakeside–Haverthwaite
North Yorkshire Moors	Grosmont–Pickering
Kent & East Sussex	Tenterden–Bodiam
West Somerset	Minehead–Williton
Nene Valley	Yarwell Jct–Orton Mere (Peterborough)
North Norfolk	Sheringham–Weybourne
Gwili	Bronwydd Arms–Cwmdwyfran
Mid-Hants	Alresford–Ropley

Narrow gauge

Name	Location
Festiniog	Porthmadog–Llyn Ystradau (Blaenau Festiniog)
Talyllyn	Tywyn–Nant Gwernol
Welshpool & Llanfair	Llanfair Caereinion–Sylfaen
Ravenglass & Eskdale	Ravenglass–Dalegarth
Romney, Hythe & Dymchurch	Hythe–Dungeness
Sittingbourne & Kemsley	Sittingbourne
Fairbourne	Fairbourne
Llanberis Lake	Llanberis
Snowdon Mountain	Llanberis
Bala Lake	Llanuwchllyn
Vale of Rheidol (BR)	Aberystwyth–Devils Bridge

NOTE: Some other lines are attempting to complete arrangements to resume services as this edition closed for press. There are also numerous other narrow gauge and miniature railways.

SOME BRITISH RAILWAYS FACTS AND FIGURES

Largest station area: Clapham Junction, 27¾ acres
Largest number of platforms: Waterloo, 21
Busiest railway junction: Clapham Junction, 2,500 trains each 24 hours
Steepest Main-line Gradients:

Lickey Incline, 1 in 37·7 (nearly 2 miles)
Exeter (St David's, Central), 1 in 31·3 (7½ chains)
Dainton Bank (near summit), 1 in 37 (12 chains)

Highest altitude: Druimuachdar, 1,484 ft. above sea-level
Longest Bridge: Tay Bridge, 2 miles 364 yd.
Longest Tunnel: Severn Tunnel, 4 miles 628 yd.
Total number of locomotives in service (November 1977):

Diesel, 3,290
Electric, 320
Narrow gauge steam, 3

British Rail route mileage open for traffic at the beginning of 1977 (the latest date for which figures are available): 11,189
Route mileage electrified: 2,321
Total track mileage: 28,700

WORLD RAILWAYS

Facts and Figures

The total mileage of the world's railway routes is nearly 700,000, of which over 200,000 is in the U.S.A.

The country with the longest individual railway is Canada. The Canadian National Railways have over 20,000 miles of line. The USSR railways total over 75,000 route miles.

The journey between Moscow and Vladivostok, on the Trans-Siberian Railway (nearly 6,000 miles, taking 9 days) is the longest that can be taken without changing trains.

The longest stretch of perfectly straight line in the world runs for 328 miles across the Nullarbor Plain, Australia.

The highest railway station in Europe is 11,333 ft. above sea-level, on the Jungfrau Railway in Switzerland.

The highest railway stations in the world are in Chile (15,817 ft.) and Peru (15,806 ft.).

The world's longest tunnel (other than underground systems) is the Simplon No. 2 opened in 1921, 12 miles 559 yards long. It will be exceeded in 1982 by the new Seikan Tunnel linking the Japanese Islands of Honshu and Hokkaido which will be nearly 33 miles long.

Ships

SAILING SHIPS

What Is a Ship? An odd question? Well, strictly speaking the word applies only to vessels with three or more masts, all of them *square-rigged*. And a vessel is square-rigged when its main sails are square and are stretched by yards suspended by the middle at right angles to the mast. The other kind of rigging is *fore-and-aft*—that is, the sails are turned so that they run lengthwise of a ship. Look at the picture of sailing-ships: you'll see that one rigged fore-and-aft on the mizzen mast (the mast at the back) is a *barque*. Rig her fore-and-aft on the main mast, too, with only the foremast square-rigged, and she is a *barquentine*. A two-masted vessel with a square rig on both masts and a boom mainsail (you'll see what that is in the picture) is a *brig*; rig the main mast fore-and-aft, and she's a *brigantine*. A vessel rigged entirely fore-and-aft is a *schooner*; give her a square top sail and she's a *topsail schooner*.

Note: Despite what we've said about the strict meaning of the word 'ship', we shall use it in this section, as everyone in practice does, to mean any sea-going vessel.

SHIP'S FLAGS AND SIGNALS

The International Code On the sea, with its traffic of ships from all parts of the world, there must be no barriers of language. The International Code enables ships to communicate with one another no matter what tongue is spoken on board.

A set of signal flags consists of 26 alphabetical flags, 10 numeral pennants (a pennant is a flag that's triangular instead of rectangular), 3 substitutes and the answering, or code, pennant.

Now, every ship at sea has signal letters assigned to it. There are four of these in every case, the first letter or first two letters indicating the nationality of the ship. (For example, British ships' signal letters begin with G or M.)

If you want to signal to a particular ship you first hoist the flags that make that ship's signal letters. If you don't do this,

Fore-and-aft Schooner

Topsail Schooner

Brig

Brigantine

Barque

Barquentine

Cutter

will be understood that you are addressing all ships within signalling distance.

Ships receiving a signal have to hoist their answering pennant *at the dip* (that is, about half-way up) when they see each flag hoisted, and *close up* (that is, as high as it will go) when they have understood it. The ship sending the message hoists its own answering pennant to show that the message is completed.

The substitutes are used to repeat a letter. If, for example, one wanted to use the letter A three times in a single group of flags, one would clearly need three complete sets of flags to do it, were it not possible to use the substitutes.

All the signal flags have special meanings when flown alone. For example:

> A—Flown by man-of-war when on full-speed trial.
> B—'I am taking on or discharging explosives.'
> G—'Pilot wanted.'
> H—'Pilot on board.'
> P—Departure flag.
> Q over L—'Infectious disease on board.'
> W—'Medical assistance required.'
> Y—'I am carrying mails.'
> N and C together—SOS.
> C—'Yes.'
> N—'No.'

Sirens One short blast on a ship's siren means that she is directing her course to starboard, two short blasts to port, three short blasts for engines full-speed astern. In fog one long blast at intervals not longer than two minutes means a ship is under way, two long blasts that she is under way but not moving through the water.

Distress Signals (*a*) A gun or other explosive signal fired at intervals of about a minute.

(*b*) A continuous sounding of any fog-signal apparatus.

(*c*) Rockets or shells throwing red stars fired one at a time at short intervals.

(*d*) A signal by radio or any other method consisting of the letters SOS in Morse Code.

(*e*) A signal sent by radio consisting of the spoken word 'Mayday' (from the French *m'aidez*, meaning 'help me').

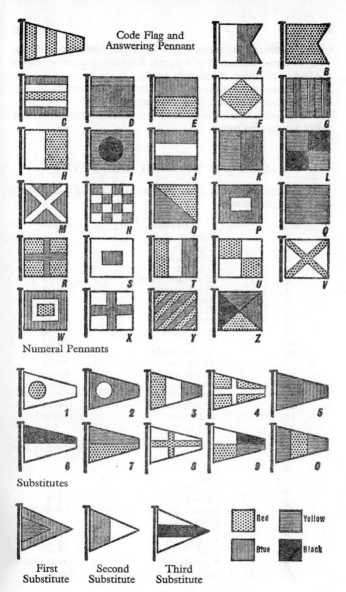

Code Flag and
Answering Pennant

Numeral Pennants

Substitutes

First Substitute   Second Substitute   Third Substitute

Red   Yellow
Blue   Black

International Code of Signals

(*f*) Hoisting of the signal flags NC in the International Code.

(*g*) A signal consisting of a square flag having above or below it a ball or anything resembling a ball.

(*h*) Flames on the ship (as from a burning tar barrel).

(*i*) A rocket parachute flare showing a red light.

The ensign hoisted upside down is generally understood as an unofficial distress signal.

MEASURES OF WIND AND WAVE

The **Beaufort Scale** for measuring the force of winds at sea is used internationally.

Scale No.	Wind force	M.p.h.
0	Calm	1
1	Light air	1–3
2	Light breeze	4–7
3	Gentle breeze	8–12
4	Moderate breeze	13–18
5	Fresh breeze	19–24
6	Strong breeze	25–31
7	Near gale	32–38
8	Gale	39–46
9	Strong gale	47–54
10	Storm	55–63
11	Violent storm	64–72
12	Hurricane	73–82
13	Hurricane	83–92
14	Hurricane	93–103
15	Hurricane	104–114
16	Hurricane	115–125
17	Hurricane	126–136

Wave Scale

		Height of waves, crest to trough (ft)
0	Calm	
1	Calm	$\frac{1}{4}$
2	Smooth	$\frac{1}{2}$–1
3	Smooth	2–3
4	Slight	3–5
5	Moderate	6–8
6	Rough	9–13
7	Very rough	13–19
8	High	18–25
9	Very High	23–32
10	Very High	29–41

		Height of waves, crest to trough (ft)
11	Phenomenal	37–52
12	Phenomenal	45 and over

Note: The highest sea in the Bay of Biscay is 27 ft. In mid-Atlantic the waves will sometimes top 40 ft.

THE WORLD'S BIGGEST SHIPS

	Flag	Tons	Length (feet)	Built
Oil Tankers:				
Bellamya	French	275,276	1,359·0	1976
Batillus	French	273,550	1,358·9	1976
Nissei Maru	Japanese	238,517	1,243·4	1975
Globtik Tokyo	British	238,252	1,243·0	1973
Globtik London	British	238,207	1,243·0	1973
Berge Empress	Norwegian	211,360	1,252·6	1976
Berge Emperor	Norwegian	211,360	1,285·5	1975
Aiko Maru	Japanese	209,788	1,200·3	1976
Jinko Maru	Japanese	209,787	1,200·3	1976
Al Rekkah	Kuwait	207,000	1,200·3	1977
Passenger Liners:				
France	French	66,348	1,035·0	1961
Queen Elizabeth II	British	65,863	963·0	1969
United States	U.S.A.	50,524	990·0	1952
Canberra	British	45,733	818·5	1961
Oriana	British	41,915	804·0	1960
Rotterdam	Netherlands	37,783	748·6	1959
Nieuw Amsterdam	Netherlands	36,982	758·5	1938

THE OBSERVER SINGLE-HANDED TRANSATLANTIC RACE

1976 Winner: Eric Tabarly, from France, in *Penduick VI*.

FASTEST ATLANTIC CROSSINGS BEFORE 1900

Date	Port	Ship	Time
1862	Queenstown	*Scotia*	9 days
1869	Queenstown	*City of Brussels*	8 days
1882	Queenstown	*Alaska*	7 days
1889	Queenstown	*City of Paris*	6 days
1894	Queenstown	*Lucania*	5½ days
1897	Southampton	*Kaiser Wilhelm*	6 days

THE BLUE RIBAND: RECORD ATLANTIC CROSSINGS BY SCREW STEAMSHIPS SINCE 1900

Westward

Date	Ship	European port	d.	Time h.	m.*	Speed (knots)	Sea miles
1900–1	Deutschland (G)	Southampton	5	11	54	23·15	3,044
1907 } 1910 }	Lusitania (B)	Queenstown	{ — 4	— 11	— 40	24·00 25·88	— —
1908 } 1911 }	Mauretania (B)	Queenstown	4	10	41	26·06	—
1929	Mauretania (B)	Cherbourg	4	21	44	26·9	3,162
1929	Bremen (G)	Cherbourg	4	17	42	27·83	—
1930	Europa (G)	Cherbourg	4	17	06	27·91	3,157
1933	Rex (It.)	Gibraltar	4	13	58	28·92	3,181
1935	Normandie (F)	Bishop's Rock	4	3	02	29·98	3,015
1936 } 1938 }	Queen Mary (B)	Bishop's Rock	{ 4 3	0 21	27 48	30·14 30·99	2,939 2,907
1952	United States (U.S.)	Bishop's Rock	3	12	12	34·51	2,906

* Days, hours, minutes.

Eastward

Date	Ship	European port	d.	Time h.	m.*	Speed (knots)	Sea miles
1900–1	Deutschland (G)	Eddystone Light	5	7	38	23·51	3,082
1904	Kaiser Wilhelm II (G)	Eddystone Light	5	8	16	23·58	—
1907 } 1910 }	Lusitania (B)	Queenstown	{ — 4	— 15	— 50	23·61 25·57	— —
1908 } 1911 }	Mauretania (B)	Queenstown	4	13	41	25·89	—
1924	Mauretania (B)	Cherbourg	5	1	49	26·25	3,198
1929	Mauretania (B)	Plymouth	4	17	50	27·22	3,098
1929 } 1933 } 1933 }	Bremen (G)	Cherbourg	{ 4 4 4	14 17 16	30 43 15	27·91 28·14 28·51	3,084 — 3,199
1935 } 1937 }	Normandie (F)	Bishop's Rock	{ 4 4	3 0	25 06	30·35 30·99	— 2,978
1936 } 1938 }	Queen Mary (B)	Bishop's Rock	{ 3 3	23 20	57 42	30·63 31·69	— 2,938
1952	United States (U.S.)	Bishop's Rock	3	10	40	35·59	3,144

Note: G = Germany; B = Britain; It. = Italy; F = France; U.S. = United States.

NAVAL VESSELS

In general Warships are usually painted grey, except in wartime when they are 'dazzle-painted' in patches of colour (grey, brown, blue) as a form of camouflage. Unlike a merchant ship, a warship has no raised deck at the stern. Propulsion is usually either by steam turbine or oil-fired water-tube boilers: some have diesel engines and a few have gas turbines. Nuclear power has been mainly confined to submarines, with such exceptions as the Soviet Union's ice-breaker *Lenin* and the U.S. passenger-freighter *Savannah*, both government-owned ships. The larger warships have an elaborate system of bulkheads (running the length and breadth of the ship) to enable them to continue floating after accidents or direct hits. The aircraft carrier and the cruiser are armoured (the latter having three or four inches of armour with about two inches of deck plating): smaller ships have no armour, relying on their speed and manoeuvrability. A warship's *standard displacement* is a measurement made when it is ready for sea with ammunition and stores, but omitting fuel and reserve feed water. *Load displacement* refers to the ship ready for sea with all stores, fuel and ammunition.

Aircraft Carrier. *Ark Royal*, 1955. 808 ft

Main Types: The Aircraft Carrier No attacking guns: usually 4.5-in. or 40 mm. guns and some A.A. guns for self-defence. Latest developments include steam catapults and rocket assistance for take-off: the Deck Landing Projector Sight, which is an aid to landing: non-skid decks. The largest carriers are American (the *Enterprise* has a load displacement of 83,350 tons). The only remaining British carrier (which will continue as a fixed-wing carrier until the late 1970's) is the *Ark Royal* standard displacement, 43,000 tons: 808 ft long: speed, 31 knots: over 40 aircraft).

Cruiser. *Blake*, 1961. 565ft

The Cruiser A general-purpose warship, fast and heavily armed. The largest are American. The two ships of the *Tiger* class are the last big all-gunned ships: the place of guns will be taken in future by guided missiles. The Royal Navy has 2 cruisers in the Operational Fleet, *Tiger* and *Blake*, which have both been converted for helicopter-carrying.

Destroyer. County Class 520ft

The Destroyer A small warship, very fast and man-oeuvrable. Used on general duties and also as mine-layers, radar pickets and on anti-submarine patrols. Destroyers are organised in flotillas, the leader having a black band round the top of the forward funnel. The Royal Navy has eight guided missile destroyers, the largest destroyers in the Fleet (standard displacement, 5,000 tons: 520 ft long: speed, 32 knots: armed with 4 4.5-in. guns and guided missile launchers). Two Type 4 destroyers are under construction.

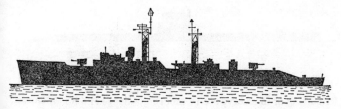

Frigate.   Leopard class, 1957.   Diesel.   340 ft

The Frigate A term used of a great variety of ships of 1,000 to 2,300 tons. Used on anti-submarine patrols and as escorts to merchant ships. Some of the latest are designed to act as anti-aircraft ships in the protection of convoys. The Royal Navy has 56 frigates in the Operational Fleet or engaged on trials and training.

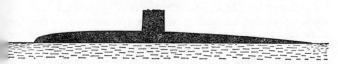

Submarine.   *Dreadnought*, nuclear propelled.   266 ft

The Submarine Underwater warship, long pressurised hull and small superstructure consisting of the bridge and conning tower. In conventional submarines diesel engines are used on the surface, electric motors when submerged. The Royal Navy has 31 submarines in the Operational Fleet, including four Polaris submarines (*Resolution, Repulse, Revenge and Renown*) and ten Fleet submarines (*Dreadnought, Churchill, Conqueror, Courageous, Swiftsure, Valiant, Warspite and Sovereign*). The Fleet submarines have a standard displacement of 3,500 tons, an American pressurised water-type reactor driving steam turbines, a length of 285 ft and a speed of about 30 knots. Four Fleet submarines are under construction.

Other ships in the Operational Fleet include the Royal Navy's two assault ships, which can carry an Army battalion and brigade group H.Q., landing craft, and R.A.F. as well as R.N. helicopters. There are also 2 commando ships, 1 ice patrol ship and 42 ships which constitute the Mine Counter-measure Force.

Submarine.   Porpoise class, 1958.   295 ft

Refitting or in reserve are 17 mooring, salvage and boom vessels, 2 seaward defence boats, 2 fleet maintenance ships, 1 submarine depot ship, 1 royal yacht/hospital ship.   There are also 84 fleet support and auxiliary vessels, ranging from minesweeper support ships to fleet replenishment tankers.

THE HOVERCRAFT

The most striking first applications of the hovercraft principle —developed by Christopher Cockerell in 1955—have been on water rather than on land.   The hovercraft travels on a cushion of air created between the underside of the vessel and the water or land.   The world's first commercial hovercraft service was established in 1962 when British United Airways began carrying passengers over the 19 miles of water between Wallasey and Rhyl.   The craft used, a Vickers VA-3, covers the distance with 24 passengers at a speed of about 60 knots.   One of the world's biggest hovercraft, the **Mountbatten,** weighing 165 tons, owned by British Rail and carrying 254 passengers and 30 cars, began flying (a journey by hovercraft is called a 'flight') between Dover and Boulogne in August, 1968.   It can make the crossing in 35 minutes.   The first hydrofoil passenger service was started on Lake Maggiore, between Switzerland and Italy, in 1953.

FURTHER READING
All About Ships and Shipping, ed. E. P. Harnack (Faber)
Boy's Book of World-Famous Liners (Hughes)
Ships and Aircraft of the Royal Navy. H.M.S.O. C.P. 38
   available at R.N. Recruitment Centres

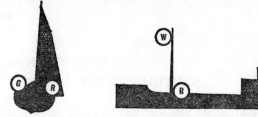

Sailing vessel under way

Steam vessel, less than 150 ft long, under way

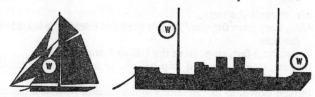

Sailing vessel or steam vessel under 150 ft long, at anchor

Vessel over 150 ft long, at anchor

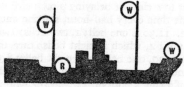

Lights at sea:
G—Green
R—Red
W—White

Steam vessel, over 150 ft under way

Small pulling boat under way

A vessel not under command

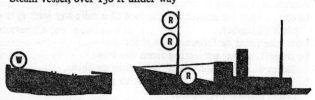

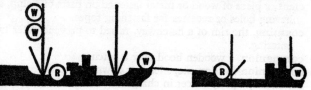

Vessel towing another

NAUTICAL TERMS

abaft, behind.

abeam, opposite the centre of the ship's side.

admiral, from the Arabic *Amir-al-Bahr*, Commander of the Seas.

aft, towards the stern.

alee, away from the wind; to put the helm over to the lee side of the boat.

avast, hold fast, stop; from the Italian *basta*, enough.

ballast, weight put in a ship or boat to help keep her stable; nowadays, usually sea-water.

batten down, to fix tarpaulins to the hatches with iron battens and wedges.

beam, the width of a ship at her widest part.

belay, to make a rope fast to a cleat or belaying pin.

bells are struck to give the time every half-hour, starting anew at each change of watch. 12.30 is one bell; 1, two bells; 1.30, three bells; and so on until 4, which is eight bells; then the pattern is repeated from 4.30, one bell, to 8, eight bells; 8.30 being one bell again, and 12 noon and midnight, eight bells.

bilge, the broadest part of a ship's bottom.

binnacle, the case in which the compass is housed.

boom, a spar for stretching the foot of a sail; any long spar or piece of timber.

bow, the front or forepart of a ship.

bowsprit, a spar projecting from the bow.

bulkhead, a partition dividing a cabin or hold.

bulwark, a ledge round the deck to prevent things falling or being washed overboard.

cable, a sea measure of 100 fathoms.

cleat, a piece of wood or metal fastened on parts of a ship, and having holes or recesses for fastening ropes.

coaming, the rim of a hatchway, raised to prevent water from entering.

companion, a wooden hood over a hatch.

companion-ladder, steps leading down to a cabin.

coxswain, a petty officer in charge of a boat and crew (a 'cock' was a small rowing boat).

davits, iron fittings that project over a ship's side for hoisting a boat.

Davy Jones' locker, the bottom of the sea. There are three possible explanations for this term:

> 1. Davy Jones was a noted pirate, given to putting his victims over the side.
> 2. In Negro language 'duffy' or 'davy' is a ghost, and 'Jones' means 'Jonah'.
> 3. The Hindu goddess of death is called Deva Lokka.

deadlights, a storm-shutter for a cabin window.

displacement, the quantity of water displaced by a boat afloat.

dog watch, a division of the usual four hour's watch, to make a change of watches; from 4 to 6 and 6 to 8 p.m.

draught, the depth to which a ship sinks in the water.

fathom, a nautical measure of 6 ft.

fender, a buffer made of bundles of rope, cork or other material, to prevent a ship from scraping against a pier when moored.

fid, a wooden tool used for separating the strands of a hemp or nylon fibre rope in splicing.

first watch, 8 p.m. till midnight.

flukes, the part of an anchor that hooks into the sea bed.

fore-and-aft, lengthwise of a ship.

forecastle (fo'c'sle), the forepart of the ship under the main-deck, the crew's quarters. The term is a survival from the old days when high wooden castles were built on each end of a fighting ship. The *aftercastle* is a term no longer used, but it is interesting to note that the cleaning gear for the after parts of ships in the Royal Navy is still stamped AX, the old sign for 'aftercastle'.

galley, a ship's kitchen.

grapnel, a small anchor with several claws or arms.

halyards, ropes by which sails are hoisted.

hatch, the cover for a hatchway.

hatchway, the opening in a ship's deck into the hold, or from one deck to another.

hawse, the bows or forward end of a ship.

hawser, a small cable; a large rope.

Jacob's ladder, a ladder with rope sides and wooden treads.

knot, one nautical mile per hour; 6.80 ft.

lanyard, a short rope used for fastening or stretching.

larboard, the port side: the term was officially banned in 1844, and 'port' substituted, to avoid confusion with 'starboard'.

lee, the sheltered side of a ship.

leeway, the distance a ship is driven to leeward of her true course.

marline spike, an iron tool used for separating the strands of a rope in splicing.

middle watch, from midnight till 4 a.m.

nautical, or sea mile, one-sixtieth of a degree measured at the equator.

night watch, 4 p.m. to 8 p.m.

offing, to seawards; towards the horizon.

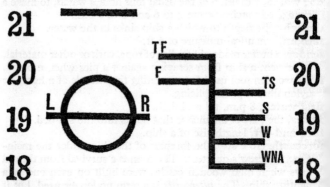

The line and the circle are the original Plimsoll Mark. The top line is the Deck Line. TF = Tropical Fresh Water. F = Fresh Water. TS = Tropical Summer. S = Summer. W = Winter. WNA = Winter North Atlantic. LR = Lloyd's Register. The figures show the amount of water the ship is drawing. They are 6 in. high and the bottom of the figure represents the foot.

Plimsoll line, a line 18 in. long running through a ring painted on both sides of a merchant ship. A ship may be safely loaded until this line is awash. It is named after Samuel Plimsoll, who was responsible for bringing it into use.

poop, the raised after-part of a ship.

port, the left side of a ship looking forward.

quarter, a ship's sides near the stern.

quarter-deck, the after end of the upper deck.

ratlines, the rope steps placed across the shrouds to enable sailors to go aloft.

scuppers, holes in a ship's sides for draining water from the decks.

shrouds, very strong wire ropes which support the masts on both sides.

splicing, joining two ropes by weaving together the untwisted strands.

starboard, the right side of a ship looking forward.

stay, a rope supporting the mast or a spar.

stern, the rear end of a ship.

superstructure, the parts of a ship built above the upper deck.

taffrail, the rail on the counter, or projecting stern, of a ship.

tonnage: The gross and net tonnage of a ship are measures of space, not of weight. Gross tonnage is the number of tons enclosed in a ship, 100 cu. ft counting as 1 ton. Net tonnage is the amount of space devoted to passengers and cargo. Dead-weight tonnage is the number of tons weight that a ship can carry.

topside (or **freeboard**), the part of a ship that is out of the water.

trick, a turn or spell of duty at sea. A trick at the wheel or as look-out lasts for two hours.

truck, the circular cap at the top of a mast.

waist, amidships.

warp, to haul a ship into position with a hawser.

watches, divisions of a ship's crew into two or three sections, one set having charge of the vessel while the others rest. Day and night are divided into watches of four hours each, except the period from 4 p.m. to 8 p.m., which is divided into two dog-watches of two hours each. Men not included in the watches are known as 'Daymen'.

weather side, the side of a ship on which the wind is blowing.

weigh, to heave up the anchor.

yawing, the swinging of a ship's head first in one direction and then in another, due to bad steering or to a high sea.

NAUTICAL MEASURES

6 ft	= 1 fathom
600 ft	= 1 cable
6,080 ft or 2,026·6 yd	= 1 nautical mil
3 nautical miles	= 1 league

The English Language

SOME OF THE TECHNICAL TERMS OF LANGUAGE

THESE are a few of the terms you will meet, and need, when you are thinking or talking about language. It is largely for the sake of those of you who are studying foreign and classical languages that we have included terms like *inflexion*, *gender* and *case*. They are now of little concern to the ordinary user of English; and for this we have to thank William the Conqueror. He brought with him to England not only his capacity for castle-building and strong government but also the French language. This became the official language of England for nearly 300 years. The result was that English for that period escaped from the hands of writers and teachers, who tend to fix a language in all its formality, and passed into the care of the ordinary people, who, by the time it got back into official use, had gaily lopped off nearly all the difficult word-endings, inflexions and marks of gender and case.

affix, a syllable, not a word in itself, which can be added to an existing word in order to change its meaning. See PREFIX and SUFFIX.

alliteration, the use in a phrase or sentence of words that begin with, or contain, the same letter or sound: e.g.

> Lord *L*undy from his ear*l*iest years
> Was *f*ar too *f*reely moved to tears.

anagram, a re-arrangement of the letters of a word or phrase which produces another word or phrase: e.g. 'Florence Nightingale' becomes, 'Flit on, cheering angel'.

antecedent, a word which determines the form of another word coming later in the sentence: e.g. in 'Few boys would say that they enjoy washing behind their ears', *boys* is the antecedent of the pronoun *they*, which therefore must be in the plural.

antithesis, words arranged to stress a contrast: e.g. 'To err is human, to forgive divine.'

antonym, a word whose meaning is directly opposite to that of another word: e.g. *light* and *dark*, *large* and *small*, *clean* and *dirty*.

apposition, a second description of a person or thing placed side by side with the first, the second having grammatically the same value as the first: e.g. 'Jones, *captain of Wales*, scored the final try.'

auxiliary verb, a verb that has no meaning itself but helps to make the meaning of another verb: e.g. *will* in 'I will go', *do* in 'I do see what you mean'.

case, the grammatical function of a noun or pronoun: i.e. whether it is subject, object, genitive, etc. Case has almost vanished from the English language, but it is worth remembering that the *subject* is said to be *nominative*; the *object*, *accusative*; the *indirect object*, *dative*; and the *apostrophe form of the word* (Jean's, Jim's), *genitive*.

clause, a group of words containing subject and predicate but not expressing a complete idea: e.g. 'A marshal *who can rid the town of rustlers*—that's what we want.'

complement, a noun or adjective forming the predicate of a verb that cannot govern a direct object: e.g. 'He is *silly*', 'He became *captain*.'

conjugation, the inflexion (*q.v.*) of verbs.

declension, the inflexion (*q.v.*) of nouns or adjectives.

diaresis, the pronouncing of two successive vowels as separate sounds, often marked by the sign (¨) over the second: e.g. Chloë, aërated.

epigram, a short poem, especially one with a witty twist in it; any sharp, memorable saying.

epithet, an adjective.

etymology, the study of the origin of words.

euphemism, disguising a nasty fact with a nice name: e.g. saying 'he is putting on weight' when you mean 'he's getting fat'.

gender, the distinction of nouns according to sex. (As far as their own language is concerned, lucky Englishmen hardly have to bother about this.)

gerund, a noun formed from a verb by adding *-ing*: e.g. '*Walking* is good for you', '*Parking* is forbidden.'

homonym, a word that looks the same as another word but has a different meaning: e.g. *bear*, meaning 'carry' and 'a shaggy animal'; *peer*, meaning 'a lord' and 'peep'.

hyperbole, use of exaggerated terms for emphasis, as in 'a thousand thanks', 'he's got tons of money'.

indirect object, the person or thing towards whom an action is directed: e.g. 'I gave *him* a penny.'

inflexion, the change made in the form of words to show what grammatical part they play in a sentence: e.g. *him* is formed by inflexion from *he*.

litotes, deliberate understatement for effect: e.g. saying *not a few* when you mean *a great many*.

malapropism, named after Mrs Malaprop in Sheridan's play, *The Rivals*. 'She's as headstrong as an *allegory* on the banks of the Nile,' said Mrs Malaprop, meaning *alligator*. That is a malapropism: an attempt to use a difficult word and getting it wrong.

meiosis, general understatement—the opposite of hyperbole: e.g. 'Golly, this is *some* game' (meaning it's a terrific game), 'I *didn't half* enjoy it' (meaning you enjoyed it immensely).

metaphor, a telescoped simile (*q.v.*)—instead of saying something is like something else, you say it *is* that other thing. E.g. not 'Sir Jasper is like a fox', but 'Sir Jasper is a fox'. Language is full of metaphors: the *spine* of a book, a *blind* alley, saw-*teeth*, etc.

metonymy, naming something not by its own name, but by something closely associated with it: e.g. 'The Crown' for 'the Government'.

mixed metaphor, using together metaphors that don't match, with ridiculous results: e.g. 'Well, he's a dark horse, and he can paddle his own canoe.'

onomatopœia, the forming of a word so that it resembles the sound of the thing of which it is the name: e.g. *click*, *cuckoo* *babble*.

oratio obliqua, indirect or reported speech: e.g. a friend says '. am grateful' and you report this as: 'He said he was grateful.

oxymoron, using together in one expression words that are contradictory: e.g. *bitter-sweet*, or 'he was a *happy pessimist*'

palindrome, a word or sentence that reads the same backwards or forwards: e.g. 'Madam, I'm Adam.'

periphrasis, presenting an idea in a roundabout, wordy way.

phrase, any group of words, usually without a predicate.

predicate, the part of a sentence that tells you about, or describes, the subject.

prefix, an affix attached to the beginning of words: e.g. *dis-, un-, in-* in the words 'disappeared', 'uninterested', 'invaluable'.

prosody, the technique of verse—its rhyme, metre, etc.

pun, a play on words, different in meaning but the same in sound, so as to produce an amusing effect: e.g. Tom Hood's

> A cannon-ball took off his legs,
> So he laid down his arms.

(*Note*: A pun can be used seriously; there are several examples in Shakespeare.)

rhetorical question, a question that isn't asked in order to obtain an answer, but as a striking way of suggesting that the answer is obvious: e.g. 'Did you ever see such a rotten bowler as Smith?'

simile, likening one thing to another: e.g. 'The ice was like iron', 'He ran like the wind.'

spoonerism, getting the initial letters of words mixed up: e.g. the statement of the famous Dr Spooner (after whom this error was named) that an undergraduate had 'hissed all his mystery lectures'.

split infinitive, putting a word between the parts of the infinitive: e.g. 'to quickly run', 'to suddenly fall down'. A safe rule is to avoid it if it sounds clumsy, but not if it is the sharpest and neatest way of saying what you want to say.

suffix, an affix attached to the end of a word: e.g. *-ness, -ship, -able* in the words 'thinness', 'scholarship', 'bearable'.

syllepsis, e.g. 'He was kicking the football with determination and his left foot', 'She lost her spectacles and her temper'.

synecdoche, naming a part when you mean the whole: e.g. 'a fleet of a hundred sail' (meaning ships).

synonyms, words that are much the same in meaning and use: e.g. beautiful, handsome, good-looking; breakable, fragile, frail.

syntax, the part of grammar that deals with the way words are arranged in sentences.

tautology, unnecessary repetition: e.g. 'I have been *all alone by myself* for hours.'

AN EMERGENCY GUIDE TO PUNCTUATION

If you want to feel in a really dangerous, exposed position, sit down to write a simple, brief guide to punctuation—knowing that H. G. Fowler, in his *Modern English Usage*, devoted 1,000 worried words to the comma alone, and that punctuation is always to some extent an individual matter. However, this section, as warily as possible, sets down such rules as it is safe to pass on. It is meant as a simple, rough-and-ready guide for emergencies.

Remember: punctuation is only a way of helping your reader to understand the sense of what you write. In speech you make your meaning clear by your pauses and by the way your voice rises and falls (e.g. the listener knows when you're asking a question from the way your voice rises at the end of the sentence). Punctuation is simply a collection of devices for getting these pauses and these rises and falls of voice on to paper. (E.g. your rising voice at the end of a question is suggested by the question-mark.)

A. To mark where a sentence ends we use one of three stops:

    (i) a **full stop** (.) where the sentence is a statement;
    (ii) a **question mark** (?) where the sentence asks a question;
    (iii) an **exclamation mark** (!) where the sentence is an exclamation.

B. The **comma** (,) is the stop that stands for the little pauses after single words or groups of words. Read the following sentence aloud (it comes from *Huckleberry Finn*) and note how the commas mark the pauses and the ups and downs of your voice:

> *We went to a clump of bushes, and Tom made everybody swea*
> *to keep the secret, and then showed them a hole in the hill, righ*
> *in the thickest part of the bushes.*

Warning. Alas, it's not always as easy as this. If you've go tangled up in one of the comma's trickier uses, try pp. 96–9 in Eric Partridge's *You Have a Point There.*

C. A more definite pause in the sentence is marked by a **semicolon** (;). For example, you might write:

There was no football this afternoon; the weather was far too wet.

You could say there are two sentences here; but (as has happened in the sentence you're now reading) the sense of each is so closely connected with the sense of the other that they gain from not being separated completely.

D. The **colon** (:) is generally used before a list of things or a quotation. E.g.

He told us what he had brought with him: a penknife, a fishing-rod, his lunch and half a pound of worms.

or

Shakespeare wrote: 'To be or not to be, that is the question.'

But *be warned*: some writers like to use the colon (as we have done in this sentence) where others would use a semi-colon.

E. **Inverted commas** or **quotation marks** (" ") are used (i) to mark off the actual words of a speaker where it is *those actual words* that you are writing down, e.g.

"Oh Lord," groaned the reader, "punctuation does seem difficult."

or (ii) to mark off a quotation that comes inside a sentence: e.g.

When he got to "See how they run" he made little running movements with his fingers.

Note: punctuation marks that don't belong to the quotation come outside the quotation marks. E.g.

Did I hear you recite "There was an old man of Kilkenny"? (not *"There was an old man of Kilkenny?"*).

Warning: There are two kinds of inverted commas, (" ") and (' '). It doesn't matter which you use; but note the following:

Tom said, "Did I hear you recite 'There was an old man of Kilkenny'?"

Where—as here—there's a quotation inside a quotation, use

your chosen mark for the main quotation and the other mark for the quotation inside it.

F. **Dashes** (—) or **brackets** ( ) are used to enclose things that are really said *aside*—in other words, they don't belong to the main structure of the sentence. If I say:

> *He's a good boy and—as I was saying to his mother yesterday —his work has been excellent,*

my main sentence is *He's a good boy and his work has been excellent. As I was saying to his mother yesterday* is said aside, and goes either between dashes or between brackets.

G. The **apostrophe** (') is not so difficult as some people make it (we knew a desperate little boy who'd grasped only that it often accompanies the letter 's', and so put it in front of every letter 's' he wrote, even in the middle of a word). There are two main uses of the apostrophe:

> (i) to show possession: *George's book, Mr Davis's Jaguar*;
> (ii) to mark a missing letter: e.g. *don't* (*do not*), *it's* (*it is*). (Of course, in *shan't* the apostrophe marks several missing letters. In the eighteenth century it was written *sha'n't*.)

H. An important use of the **hyphen** (-) is to join words where failing to join them would falsify one's meaning. E.g. a *gold nibbed pen* is a pen made of gold with a nib in it; a *gold-nibbed pen* is a pen (of whatever material) that has a gold nib.

Further Reading

You Have a Point There, by Eric Partridge
Mind Your Language! by Ivor Brown (Bodley Head)
Words! Words! Words! by Andrew Scotland (Cassell)
Modern English Usage, by H. G. Fowler (Oxford)
Roget's Thesaurus of English Words and Phrases (Penguin) is a very useful book (as well as an entertaining one) for the situation where you want to find a synonym (see L5). As an example, you want another word for 'beautiful': you look it up in the index, are directed to a numbered section, and there find: 'Beautiful, beauteous, handsome, fine, pretty, lovely, graceful, elegant, delicate, refined, fair, personable, comely, seemly, bonny . . . . .'

A DICTIONARY OF FOREIGN PHRASES AND CLASSICAL QUOTATIONS

It may seem odd to have a collection of words and phrases from other tongues in the middle of a section on THE ENGLISH LANGUAGE. But, rich though our own language is, we still find that certain things have been expressed most strikingly by the old Greeks or Romans or by modern Frenchmen. In some cases it is not simply that other nations have found a better way of saying something, but that there is a sort of historical flavour about a phrase that disappears if it is translated into English. 'Life is short, art is long' is somehow not quite the same thing as 'Vita brevis, ars longa'. Here, anyway, is a list of such phrases as are still in general use.

Abbreviations: Fr., French; Gr., Greek; Ger., German; It., Italian; L., Latin; Sp., Spanish.

à bas (Fr.), down, down with
ab extra (L.), from without
ab initio (L.), from the beginning
à bon marché (Fr.), good bargain, cheap
ab ovo (L.), from the egg
absit omen (L.), may there be no ill omen
ab uno disce omnes (L.), from one example you may judge the rest
ab urbe condita (L.), from the founding of the city: i.e. Rome, 753 B.C.
à cheval (Fr.), on horseback
à compte (Fr.), on account; in part payment
ad astra (L.), to the stars
ad Calendas Graecas (L.), at the Greek Calends—i.e. never, since the Greek had no Calends
à demi (Fr.), by halves, half
Deo et rege (L.), from God and the king
à deux (Fr.), of two, between two, two-handed
ad finem (L.), to the end, towards the end

ad hoc (L.), for this purpose

ad hominem (L.), to the man, personal

a die (L.), from that day

ad infinitum (L.), to infinity

ad libitum (L.), at pleasure

ad majorem Dei gloriam (L.), for the greater glory of God

ad nauseam (L.), to the point where one becomes disgusted

ad rem (L.), to the point

ad valorem (L.), according to value

advocatus diaboli (L.), devil's advocate

aetatis suae (L.), of his (or her) age

affaire de coeur (Fr.), an affair of the heart

affaire d'honneur (Fr.), an affair of honour

a fortiori (L.), with stronger reason

à haute voix (Fr.), aloud

à jamais (Fr.), for ever

à la bonne heure (Fr.), in good time; all right; as you please

à la mode (Fr.), in fashion

à la mort (Fr.), to the death

al fresco (It.), in the open air

allez vous en! (Fr.), away with you!

alma mater (L.), benign mother—applied by old students to their university

alter ego (L.), one's second self

à merveille (Fr.), wonderfully

à moitié (Fr.), half, by halves

amor vincit omnia (L.), love conquers all

ancien régime (Fr.), the old order of things

anno Domini (L.), in the year of our Lord

anno mundi (L.), in the year of the world

annus mirabilis (L.), year of wonders

ante bellum (L.), before the war

ante meridiem (L.), before noon

à outrance (Fr.), to the bitter end

à pied (Fr.), on foot

à propos de bottes (Fr.), apropos of boots—i.e. beside the point

à propos de rien (Fr.), apropos of nothing

aqua vitae (L.), water of life

à quoi bon? (Fr.), what's the good of it?

arrière pensée (Fr.), a mental reservation
ars est celare artem (L.), true art is to conceal art
ars longa, vita brevis (L.), art is long, life is short
à tout prix (Fr.), at any price
au contraire (Fr.), on the contrary
au courant (Fr.), fully acquainted with
audi alterem partem (L.), hear the other side
au fait (Fr.), well acquainted with; expert
au fond (Fr.), at bottom
au grand sérieux (Fr.), in all seriousness
au naturel (Fr.), in the natural state
au pied de la lettre (Fr.), close to the letter; quite literally
au revoir (Fr.), goodbye; till we meet again
autres temps, autres moeurs (Fr.), other times, other manners
aux armes! (Fr.), to arms!
ave atque vale (L.), hail and farewell
à volonté (Fr.), at pleasure
basta! (It.), enough!
beau monde (Fr.), the world of fashion
bête noire (Fr.), a bugbear; your favourite hate
bien entendu (Fr.), of course; to be sure
bis (L.), twice; encore
bon diable (Fr.), good-natured fellow
bon goût (Fr.), good taste
bona fides (L.), good faith
bon mot (Fr.), a witty saying
bonne bouche (Fr.), a tasty morsel
bon ton (Fr.), the height of fashion
bon vivant (Fr.), one who lives well
bon voyage! (Fr.), a good journey to you!
caput (Ger.), utterly beaten, done for
carpe diem (L.), enjoy the present day
casus belli (L.), that which causes or justifies war
cause célèbre (Fr.), a notable trial
caveat emptor (L.), let the buyer beware
cave canem (L.), beware of the dog
cela va sans dire (Fr.), that goes without saying
c'est-à-dire (Fr.), that is to say
ceteris paribus (L.), other things being equal
chacun son goût (Fr.), every one to his taste

cherchez la femme! (Fr.), look for the woman; there's a woman at the bottom of it!

çi-devant (Fr.), before this; former

comme il faut (Fr.), as it should be; correct

compos mentis (L.), of sound mind; sane

compte rendu (Fr.), an account rendered; a report

coram populo (L.), in the presence of the public

cordon sanitaire (Fr.), a line of guards posted to keep contagious disease within a certain area

corpus delicti (L.), the substance of the crime or offence

coup d'état (Fr.), a sudden decisive blow in politics

coûte que coûte (Fr.), cost what it may

crême de la crême (Fr.), cream of the cream; the very best

cui bono? (L.), to whose advantage is it? who is the gainer?

cum grano salis (L.), with a grain of salt

de bonne grace (Fr.), with good grace; willingly

de facto (L.), from the fact; actual or actually

de gustibus non est disputandum (L.), there is no arguing about tastes

de haut en bas (Fr.), from top to bottom

dei gratia (L.), by the grace of God

de jure (L.), in law; by right

de mal en pis (Fr.), from bad to worse

de minimis non curat lex (L.), the law does not concern itself with very small matters

de mortuis nil nisi bonum (L.), speak nothing but good of the dead

de novo (L.), anew

deo volente (L.), God willing

de pis en pis (Fr.), worse and worse

de profundis (L.), out of the depths

de rigueur (Fr.), compulsory; indispensable

desunt cetera (L.), the rest is missing

de trop (Fr.), too much, or too many; superfluous

deus ex machina (L.), a god out of the machine; one who puts things right at a critical moment

dies irae (L.), day of wrath; the day of judgement

Dieu et mon droit (Fr.), God and my right

dolce far niente (It.), sweet-doing-nothing; pleasant idleness

Domine dirige nos! (L.), Lord, direct us!

Dominus illuminatio mea (L.), the Lord is my enlightening

double entendre (Fr.), a double meaning; a play on words

dramatis personae (L.), characters of the play

ecce! (L.), behold!

eheu fugaces . . . labuntur anni (L.), alas! the fleeting years slip away!

ejusdem generis (L.), of the same kind

embarras de richesses (Fr.), an embarassment of riches

en avant! (Fr.), forward!

en déshabillé (Fr.), in undress

en famille (Fr.), with one's family

enfant terrible (Fr.), a terrible child; a little terror

en fête (Fr.), festive; keeping holiday

en masse (Fr.), in a body; all together

en passant (Fr.), in passing; by the way

en plein jour (Fr.), in broad day

en rapport (Fr.), in agreement; in sympathy with

en règle (Fr.), in order; according to rules

en route (Fr.), on the way

entente cordiale (Fr.), cordial understanding

en tout cas (Fr.), in any case, at all events

en train (Fr.), in progress

entre nous (Fr.), between ourselves

e pluribus unum (L.), one out of many

errare est humanum (L.), to err is human

esprit de corps (Fr.), the animating spirit of a collective body, such as a regiment, school, etc.

et tu, Brute! (L.), and you, too, Brutus! (said to be Julius Caesar's last words)

Eureka! (Gr.), I have found it!

ex cathedra (L.), from the chair of office

ex curia (L.), out of court

exempli gratia (L.), by way of example

ex gratia (L.), as an act of grace

ex libris (L.), from the books

ex officio (L.), by virtue of his office

experientia docet (L.), experience teaches

experto crede (L.), trust one who has tried

ex post facto (L.), after the deed is done; retrospective

façon de parler (Fr.), way of speaking

fait accompli (Fr.), a thing already done

far niente (It.), doing nothing

faute de mieux (Fr.), for want of better

faux pas (Fr.), a false step; a slip in behaviour

favete linguis (L.), favour me with your tongues, i.e. be silent

felo de se (L.), a suicide

festina lente (L.), hurry slowly

fiat justitia, ruat coelum (L.), let justice be done, though the heavens fall

fiat lux (L.), let there be light

fidei defensor (L.), defender of the faith

flagrante delicto (L.), in the very act

floreat (L.), let it flourish!

fons et origo (L.), the source and origin

force majeure (Fr.), superior power; a force one cannot resist

fortiter in re, suaviter in modo (L.), forcibly in deed, gently in manner

gaudeamus igitur (L.), so let us rejoice!

gloria in excelsis (L.), glory to God in the highest

hic et ubique (L.), here and everywhere

hic jacet (L.), here lies

hinc illae lacrimae (L.), hence (come) those tears

hoc genus omne (L.), and all that sort (of people)

hoi polloi (Gr.), the many; the rabble

homme d'affaires (Fr.), a man of business

homme du monde (Fr.), a man of the world

honi soit qui mal y pense (Fr.), evil to him who evil thinks

honoris causa (L.), for the sake of honour; honorary

hors de combat (Fr.), unfit to fight

hors concours (Fr.), outside the competition

ich dien (Ger.), I serve

idée fixe (Fr.), a fixed idea

idem (L.), the same

id est (L.), that is

in camera (L.), in a (judge's private) room; in secret

index expurgatorius (L.), a list of forbidden books

in excelsis (L.), in the highest

in extenso (L.), at full length

in extremis (L.), at the point of death

infra dignitatem (L.), below one's dignity

in medias res (L.), in the midst of things

in memoriam (L.), in memory; to the memory of

in re (L.), in the matter of

in situ (L.), in its original position

in statu pupillari (L.), in the state of being a ward

integer vitae (L.), blameless of life

inter alia (L.), among other things

in toto (L.), entirely

in vino veritas (L.), there is truth in wine; truth is told by him who has drunk wine

ipse dixit (L.), he himself said it

ipsissima verba (L.), the very words

ipso facto (L.), in the fact itself; by this very fact

je ne sais quoi (Fr.), I know not what

laborare est orare (L.), work is prayer

lapsus linguae (L.), a slip of the tongue

lares et penates (L.), household gods

laudator temporis acti (L.), one who praises past times

laus Deo (L.), praise to God

lèse-majesté (Fr.), high treason

lettre de cachet (Fr.), a sealed letter; a royal warrant for arrest or imprisonment

lex talionis (L.), the law of retaliation

locum tenens (L.), a deputy

magnum opus (L.), a great work

male fide (L.), with bad faith; treacherously

mal à propos (Fr.), ill-timed

mariage de convenance (Fr.), marriage for advantage rather than love

mauvaise honte (Fr.), false modesty

mauvais sujet (Fr.), a worthless fellow

mea culpa (L.), by my own fault

memento mori (L.), remember that you must die

mens sana in corpore sano (L.), a sound mind in a sound body

meo periculo (L.), at my own risk

meum et tuum (L.), mine and thine

modus operandi (L.), plan of working

modus vivendi (L.), a way of living

mot juste (Fr.), exactly the right word

multum in parvo (L.), much in little

mutatis mutandis (L.), with necessary changes

nemo me impune lacessit (L.), no one hurts me with impunity

ne plus ultra (L.), nothing further; perfection

nil admirari (L.), to admire nothing, to be superior and self-satisfied

nil desperandum (L.), never despair

noblesse oblige (Fr.), rank imposes obligations; much is expected from people in high positions

nolens volens (L.), whether he will or not

noli me tangere (L.), don't touch me

nolle prosequi (L.), to be unwilling to prosecute

nom de guerre (Fr.), an assumed name

nom de plume (Fr.), a pen name

non compos mentis (L.), not of sound mind

nosce teipsum (L.), know thyself

nota bene (L.), mark well

nouveaux riches (Fr.), persons who have only recently become rich; upstarts

nulli secundus (L.), second to none

obiit (L.), he, or she, died

obiter dictum (L.), a thing said by the way

ora pro nobis (L.), pray for us

O sancta simplicitas! (L.), O sacred simplicity!

O! si sic omnia! (L.), Oh, would that all (had been done or said) thus!

O tempora! O mores! (L.), O the times! O the manners!

pace (L.), by leave of

panem et circenses (L.), (give us) bread and circuses! (the cry of the Roman populace)

par excellence (Fr.), eminently, by way of ideal

par exemple (Fr.), for example

pari passu (L.), with equal pace; together

peccavi (L.), I have sinned

pièce de résistance (Fr.), the best item

pied-à-terre (Fr.), temporary lodging

pinxit (L.), (he) painted (this)

pis aller (Fr.), the last or worst shift

poste restante (Fr.), to remain in the Post Office till called for

post hoc, propter hoc (L.), after this, therefore because of this (a false reasoning)

post mortem (L.), after death

prima facie (L.), on the first view

primus inter pares (L.), first among equals

proxime accessit (L.), he came next

quis custodiet ipsos custodes? (L.), who will watch the watchers?

qui s'excuse s'accuse (Fr.), he who excuses himself, accuses himself

quod erat demonstrandum (L.), which was to be proved

quod erat faciendum (L.), which was to be done

quot homines, tot sententiae (L.), so many men, so many opinions

rara avis (L.), a rare bird

reculer pour mieux sauter (Fr.), to draw back to take a better leap

reductio ad absurdum (L.), the reducing of a position to a logical absurdity

répondez, s'il vous plait (Fr.), reply, please

requiescat in pace (L.), may he (or she) rest in peace

revenons à nos moutons (Fr.), let us return to our sheep; let us return to our subject

ruat coelum (L.), let the heavens fall

rus in urbe (L.), the country in the town

sans peur et sans reproche (Fr.), without fear and without reproach

sans souci (Fr.), without care

satis verborum (L.), enough of words

sauve qui peut (Fr.), save himself who can

semper idem (L.), always the same

sic transit gloria mundi (L.), so passes away earthly glory

sic vis pacem, para bellum (L.), if you want peace, prepare war

sine die (L.), without a day being appointed

sine qua non (L.), without which, not; an indispensable condition

sotto voce (It.), in an undertone

status quo (L.), the state in which: things as they now are

stet (L.), let it stand; do not delete

sub judice (L.), under consideration

sub poena (L.), under a penalty

sub rosa (L.), under the rose; privately

sub specie (L.), under the appearance of

succès d'estime (Fr.), a success of esteem or approval (if not profit)

suggestio falsi (L.), a suggestion of something false

sui generis (L.), of its own kind; peculiar

summum bonum (L.), the chief good

sursum corda (L.), lift up your hearts

tabula rasa (L.), a blank tablet

tant mieux (Fr.), so much the better

tant pis (Fr.), so much the worse

tempora mutantur, nos et mutamur in illis (L.), the times are changing and we with them

tempus fugit (L.), time flies

terra incognita (L.), an unknown land

tertium quid (L.), a third something

tête-à-tête (F.), a private interview, a confidential conversation

tour de force (Fr.), a feat of strength or skill

tout à fait (Fr.), entirely

tout à l'heure (Fr.), instantly

tout de suite (Fr.), immediately

tu quoque (L.), you too

ubique (L.), everywhere

ultima Thule (L.), the utmost limit

ultra vires (L.), beyond one's powers

veni, vidi, vici (L.), I came, I saw, I conquered

verbum sat sapienti (L.), a word is enough for a wise man

via media (L.), a middle course

vice versa (L.), the terms being reversed

videlicet (L.), that is to say; namely

vi et armis (L.), by force and arms

virginibus puerisque (L.), for girls and boys

vis-à-vis (Fr.), opposite

viva voce (L.), by the living voice; orally

vogue la galère! (Fr.), come what may!

voilà tout (Fr.), that's all

vox et praeterea nihil (L.), a voice and nothing more

vox populi, vox Dei (L.), the voice of the people is the voice of God

A SHORT LIST OF AMERICAN WORDS AND PHRASES

The Americans, of course, speak English. But their English is no longer quite the English that is spoken in the British Isles: and sometimes the differences between the two can cause great puzzlement—especially when (as in *biscuit*) the word is the same but the meanings no longer match. This is a list of common words and phrases that are most likely to give rise to difficulties. Some of them, of course, find their way across the Atlantic every year; and it might be interesting to guess which ones, as they become familiar, will have to come out of this list in later editions.

aluminum, aluminium
attorney, lawyer
baggage-check, luggage-ticket
barkeep, barman
baseball park, a baseball playing-field
battery, the pitcher and catcher together in a baseball team
bill, banknote
billboard, hoarding
billion, 1,000,000,000 (as compared with the English billion, which is 1,000,000,000,000. This is said to be the only example of something bigger in English than in American)
cracker, biscuit
biscuit, a soft cake rather like a scone, never sweet, and served hot with butter
bit, 12½ cents
bone up, to swot up
boner, a howler
bootlegger, an illicit seller of liquor
bouncer, chucker-out
box, the rectangular space in which the pitcher stands at baseball
boxcar, a freight-car on the railway, enclosed and covered
brakeman, guard on a freight train
bug, any insect

L19

bully, first-rate

bumper, railway buffers

bureau, dressing-table

buzz saw, circular saw

caboose, brake van on a goods train

cage, the special enclosure in which batting practice for baseball is carried on

cake, cake; but in the plural (**cakes**) it always means a kind of pancake

candy, sweets

candy-store, confectioners

car, a railway carriage or coach; sometimes the cage of a lift

cars (the), a train

carousel, roundabout

casket, coffin

check, cheque

check-room, cloakroom

checkers, draughts

chuckwagon, a wagon carrying food supplies for cowboys, pioneers, etc

clerk, sometimes a shop assistant

comfort station, public convenience

composition book, exercise book

conductor, guard on a passenger train

construction gang, gang of navvies on the railway

davenport, couch

depot, railway station (this use is now dying out)

derby (pronounced as spelt), a bowler hat

diamond, baseball field

dinner-pail, the container for a workman's or a schoolchild's midday meal

dirt wagon, dust cart

district attorney, public prosecutor

dooryard, backyard or back garden

doughboy, an infantry soldier

dove, dived

downtown, the business district in an American city (see **up-town**)

dresser, chest of drawers or dressing table

drug store, chemist's shop (soft drinks are sold there, too)

dry goods, articles of drapery, haberdashery, etc

duster, light overcoat or wrap

El, the elevated railway

engineer, engine driver

faucet, tap

fender, bumper of a car

first floor, ground floor

fixings, the garnishings of a meal

fraternity, an organisation of male students, usually designated by two or more Greek letters (e.g. the Phi Beta Kappa). See **sorority**

garbage can, dustbin

gas (short for **gasoline**), petrol

get next to, get wise to

given name, Christian name

gondola, railway wagon without sides or with very low sides

grab bag, lucky dip

grade, a division in American schools, similar to the English 'year'; also a mark in examinations

greenbacks, paper money

gridiron, a football field

guard, prison warder

haberdashery, articles for men's wear

hard sledding, a difficult task

hayseed, a yokel

highball, whisky and soda with broken ice in a tall glass

high-toned, stylish, superior

hogpen, a pig sty

home plate, base at first corner of the diamond in baseball; also the base at which the batter stands to bat

home run, or **homer,** a hit that allows the batter in baseball to make a circuit of all the bases without an error being made in handling the ball

homely, plain, ugly

homestead, a piece of land allotted under an Act of 1862 which gave possession of the land to any head of family who had lived on it for five years and had paid a small fee

homesteader, owner of a homestead

hood, the bonnet of a car

hundredweight, 100 lbs.

inaugural, the address made by a new President of the US on the day he takes office (**inauguration day**)

in short order, in no time, immediately

intermission, a school break

intersection, a street crossing

jag, a load (especially a load of liquor, more than the drinker can carry)

jail delivery, a mass escape from prison

janitor, a caretaker

jay, a simpleton

jug-handled, one-sided, unfair

jumping-rope, a skipping rope

keyman, a telegraphist

knock, to find fault with

line, a queue, a boundary

log-rolling, an agreement among politicians each to vote for some item of legislation desired by the others

longshoreman, a docker

lot, a plot of ground

luggage, empty baggage

lunch, a light snack taken at any time in the day

major, to specialise in a subject: an American student is said to major in the subject or subjects to which he gives most of his attention

make out, get along, manage

mean, seedy ('I feel mean tonight'): troublesome, inconvenient, unpleasant ('It was a mean, dirty job')

monkeyshines, capers

mortician, an undertaker

muslin, calico

name for, name after ('John was named for his uncle, Senator John Smith')

newsy, newsboy

night robes, night clothes

night stick, a policeman's truncheon

nine, a baseball team (compare the English 'cricket **eleven**')

nip and tuck, neck and neck, a close thing

notion department, the haberdashery section of an American department store

of, used in American in the sense of **before** a particular hour e.g. 'At ten minutes of seven I got up'

Old Colony, Massachusetts

Old Dominion, Virginia

Old Glory, the American flag

overly, excessively

owl train, a train running in the small hours of the night

paddle, to spank, to smack

panhandle, a narrow strip of land within the boundaries of a state but projecting from the main body of that state. (Look at West Virginia in the atlas: this is called **the Panhandle State**)

pass up, to refuse, decline

patrolman, a policeman

patrol wagon, a prison van, Black Maria

pavement, roadway

pay dirt, the earth in which a miner finds gold

peek-a-boo, hide and seek

penny, a one-cent piece

pie, tart. (The English **pie** is sometimes called in America a deep pie.)

pilot, a cowcatcher on a train

pint, 16 fl. oz. (as compared with the English pint of 20 fl. oz.)

pitcher, the player in baseball who throws the ball to the batter; he tries to 'strike' the batter out, or to 'fan' him, i.e. to cause him to fail in three attempts to hit the ball

platform, one of the projecting ends of a railway car on which passengers step when entering a train. (American railway stations usually have no platforms in the English sense of the word.)

plug-hat, a silk hat

pocket-book, a purse

point, a nib

porch, a verandah on a house

porch climber, a cat burglar

precinct, a division of a city for police or electoral purposes

prison warden, a prison governor

push-pin, a drawing pin

pussyfoot, to attempt to achieve one's aims by concealing what one is up to

quarter, a 25-cent piece

quitter, a shirker

railroad, to get something done in a rush

realtor, an estate agent

river, this word in American is always behind the name of the river, never in front (e.g. Hudson River, Mississippi River)

robin, a red-breasted thrush

rock, a stone of any size

root for, to encourage a team by cheering it on

round-trip ticket, return ticket

roundabout, a short jacket worn by a boy

roundsman, a policeman

rubber, to crane one's neck in order to see or hear

rubberneck, someone standing and staring

rubbers, overshoes

sand, courage, grit

schedule, timetable (the **ch** is pronounced as a **k**)

scratch-pad, scribbling block

section, district of a town or city

sedan, a saloon car

sherbet, a kind of water ice

shingle, the signboard of a professional man

shower party, a party at which the hostess is showered with presents from her friends

sidewalk, a pavement

side-wheeler, a paddle-boat

slingshot, a catapult

sociable, a social gathering

socialize, to get together socially

sorority, an organisation of female students (see **fraternity**)

sourdough, a person who has spent one or more winters in Alaska

spark guard, a fire guard

spat, a slight quarrel

speakeasy, an illegal drinking-place

spool, a cotton reel

spur line, a branch railway line

stand, a witness box

stand pat, to sit tight

station agent, a stationmaster

station house, a police station

stem-winder, a keyless watch

stock-holder, shareholder

stoop, the platform at the top of a flight of steps leading to the front door of a house

stop over, to break a journey

street car, a tram

string, a shoelace

subway, an underground railway

sulky, a light two-wheeled one-horse carriage for one person

suspenders, braces

switch-tower, a signal-box

switchyard, a shunting yard

tag day, a flag day

tape needle, a bodkin

Thanksgiving dinner, a dinner eaten on Thanksgiving Day,
the last Thursday in November. (Thanksgiving originated
among the early American settlers, as an expression of their
gratitude for their preservation.)

through; 'Monday through Friday', means from Monday to
Friday inclusive

thumb tack, drawing pin

tightwad, a miser

ton, 20 cwt. but 2,000 lb.

toss and catch, pitch and toss

towerman, a railway signalman

truck, a lorry or van

tube, a wireless valve

uptown, the residential district in an American city (see **downtown**)

vest, waistcoat

vestibule train, a corridor train

vine, any creeping plant

wad, a sheaf of bank notes

waist, a blouse

washroom, a lavatory

wash rag, a face flannel

way station, an unimportant railway station

well-fixed, well-to-do

windshield, a wind screen

World Series, the most important series of competitions among
American baseball teams

A DICTIONARY OF BRITISH WRITERS

This is a list of only the most famous of our writers, giving their dates, saying for which kind of writing they are most famous (as poet, novelist, dramatist or whatever it may be) and giving the name of their best-known work. The list was compiled by someone who would greatly have enjoyed saying more. ('Don't miss the *Canterbury Tales*. They're warm, funny, grave, full of unforgettable people and phrases, and, though it's worth getting used to the not-too-difficult Middle English of the original, there's a good modern translation published as a Penguin by Nevil Coghill.' That sort of thing.) But this is a list purely for reference—by, the compiler hopes, readers who are busy acquiring for themselves the desire to say more about a writer than that his dates were this or that, and his best-known work was that or this.

Addison, Joseph (1672–1719), essayist and dramatist.

Arnold, Matthew (1822–88), poet and critic. *The Scholar Gipsy*.

Auden, W. H. (1907–1973), poet.

Austen, Jane (1775–1817), novelist. *Pride and Prejudice*.

Bacon, Francis (1561–1621), essayist.

Barrie, Sir J. M. (1860–1937), novelist and playwright. *Peter Pan*.

Beaumont, Francis (1584–1616), dramatist, collaborated with John Fletcher (1579–1625). *Knight of the Burning Pestle*.

Beerbohm, Sir Max (1872–1956), essayist and critic.

Belloc, Hilaire (1870–1953), poet, essayist, historian and novelist. *Cautionary Tales*.

Bennett, Arnold (1867–1931), novelist. *Old Wives' Tale*.

Blake, William (1757–1828), poet. *Songs of Innocence and Songs of Experience*.

Borrow, George (1803–81), chronicler of gipsy life. *Lavengro*.

Boswell, James (1740–95), biographer, diarist. *Life of Dr Johnson*

Bridges, Robert (1844–1930), poet. *Testament of Beauty*.

Brontë, Charlotte (1816–55), novelist. *Jane Eyre*.

Brontë, Emily (1818–48), novelist. *Wuthering Heights*.

Browne, Sir Thomas (1605–82), essayist. *Religio Medici*.

Browning, Robert (1812–89), poet. *The Ring and the Book.*

Browning, Elizabeth Barrett (1806–61), poet. *Sonnets from the Portuguese.*

Buchan, John (1875–1940), novelist and historian. *Thirty Nine Steps.*

Bunyan, John (1628–88), author of *Pilgrim's Progress.*

Burns, Robert (1759–96), poet.

Butler, Samuel (1612–80), poet. *Hudibras.*

Butler, Samuel (1835–1902), novelist. *The Way of All Flesh.*

Byron, Lord (1788–1824), poet. *Don Juan.*

Campion, Thomas (1567?–1619), poet.

Carlyle, Thomas (1795–1881), historian and essayist. *The French Revolution.*

Carroll, Lewis (Charles Lutwidge Dodgson) (1832–98), author of *Alice in Wonderland.*

Chaucer, Geoffrey (1340?–1400), poet. *Canterbury Tales.*

Chesterton, G. K. (1874–1936), poet, essayist and novelist. The *Father Brown* stories.

Clare, John (1793–1864), poet.

Cobbett, William (1762–1835), essayist and social critic. *Rural Rides.*

Coleridge, Samuel Taylor (1772–1834), poet and critic. *Rime of the Ancient Mariner.*

Collins, Wilkie (1824–89), novelist. *The Moonstone.*

Collins, William (1721–59), poet.

Congreve, William (1670–1729), dramatist. *Way of the World.*

Conrad, Joseph (1857–1924), novelist. *Lord Jim.*

Cowley, Abraham (1618–67), poet.

Cowper, William (1731–1800), poet. *The Task.*

Crabbe, George (1754–1832), poet. *The Borough.*

Davies, W. H. (1870–1940), poet. *Autobiography of a Super-Tramp.*

Defoe, Daniel (1661?–1731), novelist. *Robinson Crusoe.*

Dekker, Thomas (1570?–1641?), dramatist.

De la Mare, Walter (1873–1956), poet and novelist.

De Quincey, Thomas (1785–1859), essayist and critic. *Confessions of an Opium-Eater.*

Dickens, Charles (1812–70), novelist. *David Copperfield.*

Donne, John (1573–1631), poet.

Doyle, Sir A. Conan (1859–1930), novelist. *Hound of the Baskervilles.*

Drayton, Michael (1563–1631), poet. *The Ballad of Agincourt.*

Dryden, John (1631–1700), poet and dramatist. *Absalom and Achitophel.*

Eliot, George (Mary Ann Evans) (1819–80), novelist. *Mill on the Floss.*

Eliot, T. S. (1888–1965), poet. *The Waste Land.*

Evelyn, John (1620–1706), diarist.

Fielding, Henry (1707–54), dramatist and novelist. *Tom Jones.*

Fitzgerald, Edward (1809–83), poet. *Rubaiyat of Omar Khayyam.*

Forster, E. M. (1879–1970), novelist. *Passage to India.*

Galsworthy, John (1869–1933), novelist. *The Forsyte Saga.*

Gaskell, Elizabeth Cleghorn (1810–65), novelist. *Cranford.*

Gay, John (1685–1732), poet. *The Beggar's Opera.*

Gibbon, Edward (1737–94), historian. *Decline and Fall of the Roman Empire.*

Gilbert, Sir W. S. (1837–1911), playwright and humorous poet. *The Bab Ballads.*

Gissing, George (1857–1903), novelist. *The Private Papers of Henry Ryecroft.*

Goldsmith, Oliver (1728–74), poet, essayist and playwright. *Vicar of Wakefield.*

Graves, Robert (b. 1895), poet and novelist.

Gray, Thomas (1716–71), poet. *Elegy in a Country Churchyard.*

Hardy, Thomas (1840–1928), poet and novelist. *Tess of the D'Urbervilles.*

Hazlitt, William (1778–1830), critic and essayist.

Herbert, George (1593–1633), poet.

Herrick, Robert (1591–1674), poet.

Hobbes, Thomas (1588–1679), philosopher. *Leviathan.*

Hood, Thomas (1799–1845), poet. *Song of a Shirt.*

Hopkins, Gerard Manley (1844–89), poet.

Housman, A. E. (1859–1936), poet. *A Shropshire Lad.*

Hudson, W. H. (1841–1922), novelist and naturalist. *Green Mansions.*

Hunt, Leigh (1784–1859), poet and essayist.

Jacobs, W. W. (1863–1943), novelist and short-story writer.

James, Henry (1843–1916), novelist. *Daisy Miller.*

Jefferies, Richard (1848–87), essayist and novelist. *Bevis.*

Johnson, Dr Samuel (1709–84), poet, critic and dictionary-maker. *Vanity of Human Wishes.*

Jonson, Ben (1573?-1637), poet and dramatist. *The Alchemist.*

Keats, John (1795-1821), poet. *Endymion.*

Kingsley, Charles (1819-75), novelist. *The Water Babies.*

Kipling, Rudyard (1865-1936), poet and novelist. *Jungle Tales.*

Lamb, Charles ('Elia') (1775-1834), essayist.

Landor, Walter Savage (1775-1864), poet.

Langland, William (1330?-1400?), poet. *Piers Plowman.*

Lawrence, D. H. (1885-1930), poet and novelist. *Sons and Lovers.*

Lear, Edward (1812-88), poet. *The Owl and the Pussycat.*

Lovelace, Richard (1618-58), poet.

Lytton, Lord (1831-91), novelist. *Last Days of Pompeii.*

Macaulay, T. B. (1800-59), historian. *History of England.*

Malory, Sir Thomas (*c.* 1470), author of *Morte d'Arthur.*

Marlowe, Christopher (1564-93), poet and dramatist. *Dr Faustus.*

Marryat, Frederick (1792-1848), novelist. *Children of the New Forest.*

Marvell, Andrew (1621-78), poet.

Masefield, John (1876-1967), poet and novelist. *Dauber.*

Massinger, Philip (1583-1640), dramatist. *New Way to Pay Old Debts.*

Meredith, George (1828-1909), novelist. *The Egoist.*

Milton, John (1608-74), poet. *Paradise Lost.*

Moore, George (1857-1933), novelist. *Esther Waters.*

Moore, Thomas (1779-1852), poet.

More, Sir Thomas (1478-1535), author of *Utopia.*

Morris, William (1834-96), poet. *The Earthly Paradise.*

O'Casey, Sean (1883-1964), dramatist. *Juno and the Paycock.*

Orwell, George (1903-50), essayist and novelist. *Animal Farm.*

Peacock, Thomas Love (1785-1866), poet and novelist.

Pepys, Samuel (1633-1703), diarist.

Pope, Alexander (1688-1744), poet. *Rape of the Lock.*

Raleigh, Sir Walter (1552-1618), poet.

Reade, Charles (1814-84), novelist. *Cloister on the Hearth.*

Richardson, Samuel (1689-1761), novelist. *Clarissa Harlowe.*

Rossetti, Christina (1830-94), poet. *Goblin Market.*

Rossetti, Dante Gabriel (1828-82), poet.

Ruskin, John (1819-1900), writer on art. *Stones of Venice.*

Scott, Sir Walter (1771-1832), poet and novelist. The *Waverley* novels.

Shakespeare, William (1564–1616), poet and dramatist. *Hamlet*.

Shaw, George Bernard (1856–1950), dramatist and critic. *St Joan*.

Shelley, Percy Bysshe (1792–1822), poet. *The Revolt of Islam*.

Sheridan, Richard Brinsley (1751–1816), dramatist. *The Rivals*.

Sidney, Sir Philip (1554–86), poet.

Skelton, John (1460?–1529), poet.

Smollett, Tobias (1721–71), novelist. *Roderick Random*.

Southey, Robert (1774–1843), poet and historian. *Life of Nelson*.

Spenser, Edmund (1552?–1599), poet. *Faerie Queene*.

Steele, Sir Richard (1672–1729), essayist.

Sterne, Laurence (1713–68), novelist. *A Sentimental Journey*.

Stevenson, Robert Louis (1850–94), poet and novelist. *Treasure Island*.

Suckling, Sir John (1609–42), poet.

Swift, Jonathan (1667–1745), author of *Gulliver's Travels*.

Swinburne, Algernon Charles (1837–1909), poet.

Synge, J. M. (1871–1909), dramatist. *Playboy of the Western World*.

Tennyson, Alfred, Lord (1809–92), poet. *Idylls of the King*.

Thackeray, William Makepiece (1811–63), novelist. *Vanity Fair*.

Thomas, Dylan (1914–53), poet. *Under Milk Wood*.

Thompson, Francis (1859–1907), poet. *The Hound of Heaven*.

Thomson, James (1700–48), poet. *The Seasons*.

Trollope, Anthony (1815–82), novelist. *The Warden*.

Vaughan, Henry (1622–95), poet.

Webster, John (1580?–1625?), dramatist. *Duchess of Malfi*.

Wells, H. G. (1866–1946), novelist. *Kipps*.

White, Gilbert (1720–93), naturalist. *Natural History of Selborne*.

Wilde, Oscar (1856–1900), poet, critic and dramatist. *Importance of Being Earnest*.

Wordsworth, William (1770–1850), poet. *Lyrical Ballads*.

Wycherley, William (1640?–1716), dramatist. *The Country Wife*.

Yeats, William Butler (1865–1939), poet.

Music and the Arts

Music

VERY probably, music is historically the first of all the arts. After all, one often hears of babies who sing before they say their first word and who beat out rhythms before they sing. So it is easy to imagine a caveman grunting out some sort of music in an age when even speech—let alone writing—was unknown, and before the first cave paintings adorned the walls of his home.

There is another way in which music can claim to be the first of the arts. One writer put it this way: 'all other arts aspire to the condition of music'. By this, the writer meant that music is the freest of the arts. A writer must say what he means in precise words; a painter must make us a picture of something we recognise; a sculptor must present us with a form that has meaning. Or so it was until very recently. The musician, though, has never had to follow these rules because music has no meaning. He plays a fast tune on a trumpet and we all find it 'lively' or 'stirring'. He plays a slow tune on a violin and we all find it 'melancholy' or 'sad'. We even talk of 'pastoral' music—music that suggests green fields and blue skies. Yet music (as the musician would agree) has no meaning other than the meaning we agree to give it. The astonishing thing is that we all agree about its meaning!

Music, then, is free of the rules that bind the other arts. But there are several rules that apply to music. For instance: the basic recipe for all music includes Melody, Harmony and Rhythm.

Rhythm is the cornerstone of music. To prove this, try humming a very well-known tune (*Pop Goes The Weasel* will do in a way that has all the notes of the melody in the right order but with the rhythm deliberately distorted. Most people will find it impossible to recognise the tune. It will have lost its identity with its rhythm. Just the same thing happens when you break up the rhythm of a sentence. For example, you can take these words:

'*To let a firework off, blue paper must be lit*'

and by altering the rhythm, change their sense into:

'*To let: a firework. Off-blue paper. Must be lit.*'

Melody is the tune. Some melodies—*Greensleeves*, for instance—are so powerful that even drastic rhythm changes cannot conceal them.

Harmony is the structure of notes and chords that fill out the melody and add to its meaning. You could call harmonies the adjectives and adverbs of music. So if the melody is the noun 'cat', it is the harmonies that make the cat happy or sad, black or tortoiseshell.

Most tunes can be given a variety of harmonies. Yet musically gifted people generally agree on what is the right set of harmonies for a given tune—and they will certainly agree in disliking any wrong harmony or false chord they hear.

All the music we hear contains some—usually all—of the elements of rhythm, melody and harmony. One way of classifying musical instruments is to arrange them under the headings of Rhythm, Melody, Harmony. For instance, a drum is a Rhythm instrument; a flute is a Melody instrument; a guitar is a Harmony instrument because it plays chords. Put these three instruments together and you would have a band that could play many kinds of music.

If you are thinking of taking up a musical instrument, you will be wise to find out which sort suits your natural talents best —Melody, Harmony or Rhythm.

MUSIC HISTORY

Wherever history is recorded it is usual to find some record of music. A mural in the tomb of Rameses (about 1150 B.C.) shows players with large, elaborate harps. Another mural in Thebes shows a girl lute player. There is an Assyrian relief in the British Museum picturing a mixed orchestra of players.

All these random examples take us well back before the birth of Christ.

Going further afield and still further back to 2500 B.C., we know of a Chinese scholar called Ling Lun who codified the five tones of oriental music then in use and named each tone. Some tones, according to Ling Lun, were upper class and even royal; others were mere peasants! Oddly enough, this idea of naming tones by social qualities, degrees of nobility and so on, is found quite frequently in various periods and countries.

Moving nearer to our own age, there are endless references in fact and fiction establishing the unchanging importance of music throughout history. Everyone knows about David playing his harp to Saul—about the Pied Piper of Hamelin—about Red Indian war chants. Not everyone knows that the rich Romans had water organs; when people came to dinner, the water organ (*hydraulus*) played. Some people hated the noise and wrote peevish comments about it. Rather the same thing happens today with record players!

The tragedy is that although we know that there has always been music, we cannot hear the music itself. We know exactly how the Egyptians, say, looked and dressed. We can read their writings, study their religions, see their own models and paintings and tools in the museums. But we cannot know how their music *sounded*. In fact we can make no sense at all even of some of the earliest written music. We can roughly trace a melodic thread, but we do not know the rhythms or tones; or harmonies, if any. Ancient music is a mystery without a key.

Because of the lack of clearly written music, we can go back only comparatively few centuries to recapture the sound of old music. True, some melodies heard today are truly ancient, even ageless—the chants of Jewish temples, certain Indian pieces and the Catholic Church's Gregorian chants—but our sort of music is possibly an invention of the middle ages.

Written Music Our music is in the main based on the Diatonic scale which can be sung as Doh, Re, Mi, Fa, Sol, La, Ti, Doh. The notes are each a tone apart excepting Mi-Fa and Ti-Doh, which are a semitone (half tone) apart. Doh is the Tonic or 'home' note defining the music's key. Countless simple tunes (e.g., *Three Blind Mice*) employ only the 'natural' tones of the major Diatonic scale (there are minor scales too). Semitones enlarge the scale to 12 notes. Music not restricted to a key may be expressed by the Chromatic scale of 12 semi-tones.

Several ways of naming notes and writing music have been tried, of course. The simplest were based on sketching a tune like this:

Sing this sketch and with luck you will hear *God Save the Queen*.

To reduce the luck element, notes were named from A to G. Four or more 'stave' lines were added to align the written notes (today we use five, as shown below). This system was developed to its present-day form—an unsatisfactory form, incidentally, for our music uses 12 notes and five into twelve won't go.

A glance above will show you the result of this bad division. The middle C is the only note the two clefs have in common. If you look for any other note—A, for instance—it will occupy one position in the treble clef and a different position in the bass clef.

This system also forces us to use a variety of complicated correction signs. As you can see, our alphabet of notes runs only from A to G—which makes seven notes; but as already pointed out, ours is a 12-note music. To insert the other five notes in written music, we have to make use of signs for sharps— ♯, flats—♭ and naturals—♮. But even then it does not work out. Our scale includes notes that could be called either sharp or flat! Here is an octave of notes from a piano:

* Is this note both B and C flat? † Is the black note F sharp or G flat? And for that matter, is there any real difference between D sharp and E flat? There is not on the piano, naturally. But is there on a violin?

Fortunately we can ask the questions without answering them here. It is enough to say that we live with our musical notation because the cure—introducing a new system—would be worse than the disease! Musicians are used to it, just as typists are used to their typewriter keyboard's layout.

Music's Development From now on we almost ignore all forms of music but our own European and American kinds— that is, the 12-note forms played in various arrangements of melody, harmony and rhythm.

As far as we know (we cannot be sure) this music first took a wide hold of Europe from, say, the tenth century A.D. on Hucbald, a monk who lived until A.D. 930, describes a raw-sounding two-voice harmony running in fifths (such as C and G, D and A, etc). The effect of playing only in fifths is very crude indeed.

John Cotton (A.D. 1130) wrote of music 'by at least two singers in such a manner that, while one sounds the main melody, the other colours it with other tones'. This suggests that polyphonic (many-voiced) music was only just beginning. Otherwise why did Cotton bother to explain it?

Polyphonic music developed fairly rapidly. By the fifteenth

and sixteenth centuries, minstrels' chants freed music of strict, almost mathematical forms and modes. New rhythms became acceptable. Harmonies were used for emotional as well as formal effects. Opera was reborn in Italy in about 1600. Instruments developed fast. Music schools were established. *Some important composers of the period: Monteverdi (opera) Byrd, Palestrina.*

In the seventeenth century, music almost began again with Bach, who developed past forms to an excellence that is still unsurpassed and also reached forward into the future both with his music and instruments (he virtually re-designed the organ, for example). Bach's impact on music is comparable with that of photography on graphic art—but Bach was also the age's supreme artist as well! *Important composers: Purcell, Handel, Bach.*

In the late eighteenth century, the modern symphony orchestra and its music came into being. Music began to move from so-called 'Classical' forms (that is, formal, variations-on-a-set-theme forms) into more free and spacious 'Romantic' forms. In our century, painting has received a very similar liberation: the painter of today need no longer draw to an academic formula—he can make his own rules and effects. *Typical 'classical' composers: Mozart, Gluck, Haydn.*

The rest of the story is probably best told by the names of nineteenth-century composers such as Beethoven, Mendelssohn, Berlioz, Schubert, Tchaikovsky, Brahms and others. All these are 'Romantic' composers in that they exploited and developed all that had gone before along their own individual lines; and also constantly strove to enlarge the range of effects and feelings that music and musical instruments convey. The restrictions put upon them, if any, were all self-imposed. They did not follow the Rules of the Game that existed in earlier centuries. They tried rather to change the game.

In our century, music has yet again started afresh. The very nature of 12-note music is in question. Why not a limitless scale? Or a number of different scales? Why follow any recognised form? Why accept the instruments of the orchestra as the only instruments—could not music be made electronically, without human instrumentalists?

Like painting, music need no longer be representational; it need no longer attempt to establish definite mind-pictures, as it generally did 60 years ago. Anything and everything that the listener agrees to accept as music—including arrangements of electronic noises—is now within the composer's scope.

Jazz When Pepys, the diarist, invited friends to his house for a musical evening 300 years ago, music was still at its formal stage. The Rules of the Game were known and followed. Thus the evening's music could be improvised on a formal theme understood by all the players present.

As music became more complicated, improvisation became less likely and less satisfactory. The written notes offered a more assured performance of more exciting and advanced music. Improvisation therefore slowly died.

It was revived by jazz players early in this century. The jazz player takes as his basis a set of harmonies that he and the others are familiar with—the chord structure of *Tea for Two*, for instance—and improvises melodies and counter melodies that fit those chords. Almost invariably, the improvisation is solidly supported by a firm and unchanging rhythm that locks the players together as they perform. This basis of firm harmonies and solid rhythm leaves the jazzman an enormous amount of freedom: and he makes the most of it. He plays round the melody. He adopts new instruments or alters old ones to fit his needs. He welcomes new sounds and ideas—indeed he will go out of his way to surprise his listeners.

The effect of jazz on other musical forms is already felt and felt strongly. Many modern 'classical' composers introduce jazz phrases and passages but seldom with success (the attempts of jazz musicians to use 'classical' forms and methods are equally poor). However, the sheer vitality, inventiveness and virtuosity of the best jazz musicians are heavily infectious. It is very probable that the jazz and 'classical' compositions of the future will move along tracks that meet here and there; and already both schools are making similar experiments for similar purposes.

Popular Music Dance, 'pop', 'rock' and most other forms of popular music owe a lot to jazz. 'Folk' music, for instance, often given jazz elements. However, pop is finding its own unique 'voices' as the range of (particularly electronic) instruments and sound sources increases. Again, pop musicians are discarding the old recipes for making a tune and reaching out for new freedoms. A pop song of the 1930's had 32 bars, the modern pop song has any number.

No one can predict the future of popular music—but then, the whole idea of pop is that it should please now, this moment.

THE INSTRUMENTS

Instruments can be split into families and groups in various ways, most of them a little vague. For instance, the Flute is a Woodwind instrument—but most modern flutes are made of metal. However, here are some customary groupings:

STRINGS

Bowed The violin family, particularly the violin—viola—cello—string bass. But also the viols, which have frets.

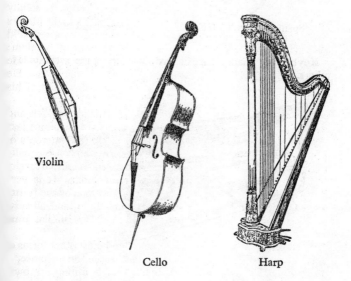

Violin

Cello

Harp

Hand or Plucked The harp. The guitar family—guitar in its 'classical' form with gut or nylon strings plucked with the fingers; or with steel strings plucked with a plectrum. Also banjo, ukelele, lute and many other fretted instruments.

Spanish ('Classic') Guitar   Venetian Lute

Keyboard Piano, harpsichord, klavier, spinet and many others.

Spinettina: Augsburg, 17th century

WIND

Flute family—flute, piccolo and others, all blown transversely
—that is, across a hole.

Recorder family. The various recorders, small and large;
and many other instruments that you blown *down*, including
the flageolet—a superior penny whistle—and various pipes.

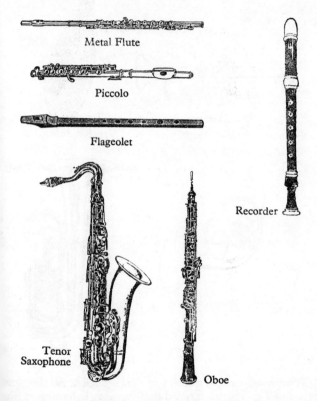

Metal Flute

Piccolo

Flageolet

Recorder

Tenor
Saxophone

Oboe

Bagpipes are wind instruments. They consist of a number of
pipes blown by the player and also by an air reservoir, the bag.
o there is some slight similarity with the—

Organ, which is an arrangement of various kinds of pipes and other sound producers fed air from a chamber that is kept filled by an air pump.

Reed instruments may have double reeds—oboes and bassoons—or, more commonly, single reeds, as in clarinets, saxophones.

BRASS WIND INSTRUMENTS

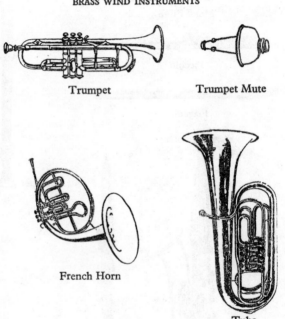

Trumpet

Trumpet Mute

French Horn

Tuba

Trumpets, cornets, horns, trombones, bugles. All these ca be called **Lip** instruments because the note is formed by th player's lips—not by a reed, or whistle.

All lip instruments are, at heart, a posthorn to which somethin has been added. A bugle is a simple horn wound into coil

A trumpet is a bugle with valves added to increase the number of notes obtainable. The French horn is a posthorn wound in circles and with valves to increase its range. The trombone literally shortens or lengthens itself (thus changing its pitch) when the player operates the slide. Naturally, there are many other differences and the posthorn idea is an oversimplification; but the fact remains that a trumpet with stuck valves or a trombone with a stuck slide reverts to the instrument that founded its family—and that basic instrument is a tapering tube with a mouthpiece, from which about five notes can be produced.

PERCUSSION INSTRUMENTS

Jazz Drum Kit

This family includes drums, cymbals, bells and other rhythm instruments—including the tunable kettle drums of the symphony orchestra, the jazz drummer's outfit, and the huge selection used by a Latin-American band.

Once again, the classification is a little vague. One could call a piano a percussion instrument—after all, its strings are hit by hammers.

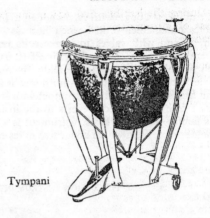

Tympani

From the instruments described so far, one could form anything from a symphony orchestra to a folk group. Throughout history and in every country, instruments have always been basically what they are today. Walt Disney once made a short film about the development of music called TOOT, WHISTLE, PLUNK & BOOM (suggest that they show it at your school) which made this point very well. There is really no *basic* difference between a panpipes and a recorder, or a lyre and ukelele. The differences lie only in additions, subtractions and modifications made over many centuries.

Vibes

During the last hundred years, though, a completely new class of instruments has appeared. So let us have a new heading:

Electric, Electronic instruments (sometimes called Electrophones) produce their sounds either by amplifying sounds produced by ordinary instruments—the electric guitar is the best example—or by creating original sounds electrically, as in the electric organ and Moog Synthesizer. Your local church organ is probably partly electric; its action and air pump may be worked by electricity. But if it is a new instrument, then it is very probably 'electronic'. Its notes and tones have nothing to do with wind and pipes and everything to do with electronic tone generators, electric amplifiers and so on.

The future of such instruments is limitless. Most of the pop and beat music heard today would be almost inaudible if there were a power failure—most of the sound is made, and all of it amplified, by electric devices. The modern church organ, obviously, would be struck dumb if its power supply were cut. And many musicians are experimenting with *musique concrète*—music actually manufactured from sounds of electronic origin.

Electric Guitar   Small Electric Organ

SOME MUSICAL TERMS

Many people are not clear about what is meant by the word 'Pitch', what the Conductor actually does and so on. Here are explanations of a few of these puzzles.

Ballad A song, often sentimental, that tells a story.

Bar Written music is divided into Bars by upright lines. Each bar contains so many beats. Count the beats and you will know the rhythm of the music. See MEASURE.

Beat Rhythmic pulse. A waltz has three beats to each bar.

Chamber Music Music for small instrumental groups—music that is best heard in a room, not a hall.

Conductor His function is not simply to make the orchestra play together, but rather to dictate *how* the music should be played. Two separate conductors will produce very different renderings of the same music from an orchestra.

Counterpoint, Contrapuntal Counterpoint is the combining of two or more melodies, played simultaneously. *Contrapuntal* is the adjective.

Fugue A contrapuntal composition for several parts—that is, instruments or voices.

Key Most music is written in the key of the composer's choice. The KEY SIGNATURE indicates to the player which key has been chosen. If the player sees F sharp written at the beginning of the music, he knows that his 'home key' is G—because the major scale of G is distinguished by possessing an F sharp. As the piece may not stick to its 'home key' of G, the composer will have to insert other sharps, flats and naturals as they occur. These are called Accidentals.

Measure A division of music in terms of beats. If there are three beats to the bar, then the writer will draw vertical lines at three-beat intervals and so divide his composition into Measures.

Notation To write a note filling a whole measure, you write a semi-breve, ○. A minim, ♭, is worth half the time value of the semi-breve and the crotchet, ♩, worth half that. And so on to quaver, semi-quaver and demi-semi-quaver, etc.

Pitch The highness or lowness of a musical sound. Middle A is internationally agreed to have a frequency of 440. A note at the top of the piano, well above middle C, has a high pitch. People with 'absolute pitch' are able to hear a note and name it correctly.

The Arts

IMAGINE a lucky dip of humanity—a pot filled with cavemen and car-workers, ancient-Egyptian washerwomen and Red Indian warriors. You dip your hand in and take out an SP—a Sample Person. You provide it with the basics of life—the materials for food, shelter and clothing. What will the SP do once settled?

It will first provide itself with the practical things it needs (a bird or beetle would do as much). But later it will do something that few, if any, other creatures do. It will add to what it needs something it doesn't need—an individual and personal touch of Art. The latest water-pot will be made in an improved shape and given colour and decoration; fringes will be cut in the edges of sleeves; the home will be decorated.

If your particular SP does none of these things you have chanced on a dull and lifeless specimen. Return it to the lucky dip and try again. You are unlikely to have to make too many tries. Mankind has always produced arts and artists. There were cavemen artists and Victorian ladies who painted flower pictures. There were Eskimos carving walrus tusks and Navajo Indians weaving blankets and rugs. Great artists have sprung from primitive peoples: wicked men have produced work of undying beauty: feeble men have shown huge artistic power.

Ah, but wait. What is all this about 'great' art—'beauty'—'power'? The *Mona Lisa* is only so much rotting pigment. St Paul's Cathedral is simply a large people-container with a useless dome on top. The SP's decorated water-pot holds water no better than the plain one. You can add up the pebbles in a bucketful and get a sure answer—but how do you add up art? Power, beauty, greatness—who says so? How are judgements possible?

One answer is this: you know artistic judgements are possible because you constantly make them yourself. You spend loving

Prototype for a tank (Leonardo da Vinci)

hours painting a kit model or getting a garment just right: you become angry with yourself if your achievement falls short of your intention. That is an artistic judgement. You prefer this poster to that—artistic judgement again. Perhaps you are becoming bored with this piece of writing? Then you are making an artistic judgement. There is nothing wrong with the printing or the paper.

How *is* art truly judged? The answer seems to be—time. Quite obviously 'great' art may stem from unusual human powers and mighty themes. But, then, you can see the 'greatness' of an artist in small things. **Leonardo da Vinci**, for example, did

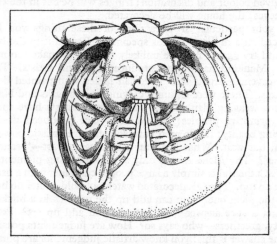

19th-century ivory netsuke

working sketches of machines and practice sketches of animals rolling in the grass. There is a quality about the drawings that says, 'The man who made these was a great artist.' There are very small carvings, *netsuke*, made by Japanese craftsmen. Netsuke were merely permanent, solid knots to hold the strings of a purse or pouch together, so no grand intentions or soarings of the spirit were needed in their production: yet in some of these little carvings you may find not only superb craftsmanship but also the work of considerable artists. Time—and the considered opinions of informed and enthusiastic minds—is needed to sort such matters out.

But you have no time. So let us think about—

YOUR JUDGEMENT

'Beauty is in the eye of the beholder.' In other words, you like it, I loathe it, on first sight.

Nevertheless, instant like/loathe decisions are generally worthless. You take the trouble to read the instructions that come with a power tool or dress pattern—to understand how the thing is *meant* to work. The same trouble should be taken with a work of art.

What do you need to know? First, how the thing fits into—or escapes from—its period. What were other artists producing at the time? What were the times like? What rules and conventions governed the artist and his art? Was the artist trying to please himself, or a patron, a customer?

The last question is important. There is a belief that artists are 'free'—they do their own thing, they need satisfy only themselves. This is nonsense, of course. Most artists, including those with the greatest and most revered names, worked to please a patron—the state, the Church, a rich man, a gallery, an agent, a market. Studies, experiments and innovations were private matters. Some artists rebelled against patronage: you may like to look up the fascinating story of James McNeill Whistler. In 1877, he was called a coxcomb who asked 200 guineas 'for flinging a pot of paint in the public's face'. Other artists had to appear in court to speak for or against him. The court awarded Whistler 'Damages one farthing'. So art *could* be added up then—but the addition did not hold. Today, Whistler is probably considered a 'great' painter. The farthing —or the 200 guineas—must now be multiplied by thousands and hundreds. Yet his work will not surprise *you*, a person living a hundred years later. You will be puzzled by the scandal and outrage caused by an artist determined to please himself.

Once you have understood the motives, methods and 'provenance' (place, time, pedigree) of a work of art, you are in a position to make a judgement. Having made it, look up other judgements, by notable critics. You will probably find that they have seen much more than you have seen.

You will also find that one critic disagrees with another. So you could well be right.

A HISTORY

If, as Henry Ford said, 'History is bunk,' then Art History is double bunk, because though most artists are conditioned by the times they live in, many ignore or flout their times yet still emerge as 'significant artists of the period'.

So when you read here that the arts of, say, Ancient Greece were thus-and-thus, take it with a pinch of salt. Imagine, if you like, an Ancient Greek reading the words and saying, 'Well! All I can say is, this writer ought to meet that crazy artist down the road!'

Another point. To avoid getting lost, go back to the first pages of this encyclopaedia—THE WORLD, ITS HISTORY.

Third and most important: there are countless excellently illustrated books about the arts. When something here stirs your curiosity, go to the library and look at the books.

Ancient Times Farming, home-building, community Man seems to have started around 7000 B.C. These people left artifacts (things made with tools) and art works all over the world. If you imagine a man of these times to be a shaggy brute with a club for hitting other shaggy brutes, you are probably right: nevertheless, his (or her) cave-drawings are vivid, accomplished and sure. Some we know to be very accurate—for example, we can compare the deer we see today with the deer drawings done all those thousands of years ago and say, 'He got it right.'

For wall and ceiling paintings, all kinds of techniques were used—charcoal sticks, scratchings, shallow relief and so on, often with colour. Frequently the irregularities of the surface

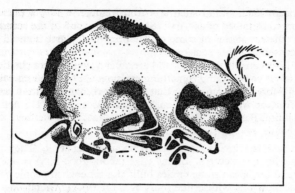

Prehistoric cave painting (from Altamira, Spain)

were picked up to show the shape of the subject. A protruding lump could be the flank of a beast, for example.

Primitive/Savage/Ethnic Art It is difficult today to know who are the 'savages'—ourselves, the tool-using technocrats so worried by our knowledge: or them, the primitive peoples, who live close to Nature because they must. The same difficulty strikes us in judging their art. It is only fairly recently that

Benin bronze

African, Eskimo and such arts from remote, wild places have come to be talked of as 'Art'. Similarly, it is only quite recently that the savageries of some of our present-day artists could be discussed in polite society.

Please consult the books and arrive at your own conclusions. At worst you will find something exciting. At best you may find a half-forgotten something that you will recognise with delight, or fear, or wonder. See books about Lascaux, the Dordogne, Altamira, Bardal, Willendorf, etc.

Neolithic/Megalithic Structures The ancient men carved and sculpted figures from rock, bone, anything at all. They also made huge structures. Stonehenge (about 2000 B.C.) is one of several European stone circles built at a time when people lived in shallow pits with crude roofs over them. Yet Stonehenge is massive. There are various theories about the purpose of Stonehenge (and obelisks, menhirs, dolmens and other great stone structures). Whatever the truth—probably to do with sun worship—Stonehenge is a staggering example of architecture for a purpose.

China China has 3,000 years of recorded history. Her influence pervaded the whole Far East—Japan, Korea, Tibet, Mongolia, Annam. A thousand years before Christ was born, the Chinese took for granted sophisticated and beautiful personal possessions—jade, lacquer, bronze, silk, strange stones and crystals marvellously worked, paintings and porcelain (invented 4th–5th centuries A.D.).

All other Chinese crafts and arts were secondary to painting and calligraphy—partly because of the supreme elegance of Chinese writing, but also because the brush strokes could be

Chinese calligraphic characters

used to express the manner and spirit of the writer and his message. Thus 'Dear Sir' can be written as an insult or compliment.

Look through books on Chinese art and you will find a strange conflict of simplicity (porcelain, scroll painting, calligraphy, etc.) and outrageous embellishment (certain buildings, fabrics and interior decorations). But invariably you find supreme, sometimes almost unbelievable, skill.

Wood was the material used for Chinese architecture—thus few ancient buildings survive. Intricate systems of interlinking keys supported the curved, tiled roofs.

A word about dynasties: 'Sun', 'Yuan', 'T'ang' are simply the names of ruling families, used to describe the period of a work much as we use 'Georgian' or 'Victorian'.

Japan From the 7th century A.D. the Japanese adopted China's arts and crafts. From 10th century A.D. on, when China's civilisation was falling apart, the Japanese went their own way, developing unrivalled skills with lacquer, ivory, pottery, glass and almost any other material—particularly multi-plate colour printing from wood blocks. See books showing *suzuribake* (writing cabinets), *netsuke* (drawstring toggles), *inrō* (little boxes for pills, etc.)—and even bamboo, which was and is the material for anything from plumbing systems to the most delicate craft objects. Sword-making was regarded as a fine art for very good reasons.

Architecture: look up the many Buddhist temples; and Shōsōin (the Imperial Treasure House, 8th century A.D.). The traditional Japanese domestic interior is particularly interesting in its refinement and simplicity.

India Great styles of art and architecture had flowered before the birth of Christ. Monasteries, sanctuaries, temples were covered with figures representing innumerable deities. India was, and is, a continent of many faiths and nations—and with an artistic history extending over some 2,000 years. Enough here to say that the golden age of Buddhist art lasted some 300 years, until about A.D. 600 (consult books for examples); that sculpture and architecture are wonderfully mixed—the buildings seem to writhe with figures; and that over the centuries, exquisite works in all materials were produced by artists who found, in their religions, fantastic sources.

Egypt The ancient Egyptian civilisations date from about 3000 B.C. The reigning Pharaoh, or king, was regarded as divine. The main function of the artist and architect was to immortalise him—to record his deeds, to preserve his body and possessions, for all time. Thus architecture and sculpture were monumental (the Pyramids—the Sphinx—the temple of Abu Simbel) and carried out on a staggering scale.

About 2250 B.C., the God/King concept was replaced by that of a heavenly being, Osiris. Now ordinary people could have monumental tombstones and memorials. Because of the Egyptian obsession with death and afterlife, those who could

Queen Nefertiti (Egypt, 1360 B.C.)

afford it were embalmed, mummified and securely entombed. Today, discoveries are still reported of arts and crafts from the distant past—of works in ivory, wood, glass, gold, precious stones; and, of course, portraiture to commemorate the dead. The painter or stone-carver used his art to report and record as literally as possible—but within certain conventions: an important person was shown large, a less important person small; the side and front of the face could be shown simultaneously; se postures and gestures denoted agreed characteristics and power (similarly, in Christian art, a halo denoted divine characteristics)

The influence of Egyptian architecture is still to be seen i anything from cinemas to railway bridges and factories. Loo up the Egyptian swollen columns and lotus-flower capitals, etc and see how many echoes you can spot in your district buildings.

Islam The Islamic world included Arab, Persian, Syrian an Egyptian peoples who followed the Moslem faith. Islamic a is distinct in that no human and animal figures are represented. The arts were centred on weaving, calligraphy (copying the Koran was a virtuous act), work in precious metals, often inlaid; and in pottery, glass, bronze, enamels. It was largely decorative art: plant forms and geometrical patterns, piercings and curlicues. Thus the term 'arabesque', meaning a curlicue or interlinked decoration.

An Arabesque

About a thousand years ago Islam became disunited. Eventually Moslem and Hindu worked together to evolve Mogul art.

The Taj Mahal

Architecture: Look up in books the Alhambra of Caliph Abdel-Walid (14th century); mosques, particularly Suleimaniyeh (1550); the Taj Mahal. The pointed arch—from which we derive our Gothic arches and vaulting—were Islamic innovations.

Ancient Greece Rhythm, discipline, order, humanity, harmony, balance—these seem to be the themes of Greek art and architecture. Quite certainly we still follow Greek traditions and find echoes of the Greek in every age that followed. We still describe as 'Classical' (meaning Greek) certain European painters of recent centuries. And we still like to see ideal representations of the human body. We feel at home in public buildings on the Greek scale, with classical Greek decorations.

Greek vase

The Greek tradition is probably only a bus ride distant from you as you read.

Greek artists and sculptors tried to express, through the human body, a concept of beauty: see the *Discobolos* (Discus Thrower) by **Myron,** 480–445 B.C. Greek architects sought logical rules and harmonies that could shape a disciplined structure: see for example the Parthenon.

The Greeks were masters of pottery, both in form and decoration; of monumental sculpture in stone and bronze; and of perspective and light-and-shade drawing (q.v.). The Grecian

The Parthenon (restored)

civilisations lasted more than a thousand years and were affected by various religions, scientific advances and philosophies. In the end, it could be said that their greatest achievements were humanistic; for most certainly their art was.

Roman The Greek civilisation gave way to the all-conquering Romans, who respected and adopted Greek artistic thinking and methods. But the Romans were not Greeks: thrusting, practical, empire-minded and brilliant engineers, their ideas were less 'human' and their ambitions more grandiose. They enjoyed dreams of glory and their art and architecture showed it. The Pantheon (A.D. 120) and the Colosseum (A.D. 70) are vast structures. A bronze statue of Emperor Nero stood 34 metres high. Their temples, unlike the Greeks', held great congregations. Their villas were centrally heated, lavishly furnished and decorated with wall paintings, mosaic floors and

The Pont Du Gard Aqueduct

The Colosseum (restored)

works of art and craft from any corner of their world (which
was the whole known world, excluding only China and the Far
East). You will find it very easy to discover more in libraries, by
visiting the Roman Palace at Fishbourne, Sussex, or simply by
reading newspaper stories about Pompeii, the latest 'finds', and
so on.

Etruscan art is often linked with Roman. The Etruscans once
dominated Italy and were eventually absorbed by the Romans.

European Art Western art—the art of Europe, of Europeans
in the United States of America and like-minded civilisations—
took the forms familiar to us in a comparatively short time: less
than a thousand years. When Rome was sacked, Constantinople
became the centre of Imperial Roman and Christian culture in
northern Europe. A distinct pattern of thought emerged between A.D. 1100 and 1500—the *Gothic* period; you can capture
the flavour of this time by visiting Westminster Abbey, the
cathedrals of Lincoln and Salisbury and the Keep of the Tower
of London. In York Minster you can follow a whole progression
of architectural styles and building methods. There are
fragments of Roman times, and demonstrations of 'Norman'
'Early English', 'Decorated', 'Perpendicular' developments in
the handling of windows, buttresses, vaultings, structures and
surfaces. Putting it briefly: what started as massive, thick and
round-arched ended as lofty, delicate, airy and filigree. The
changes took place over some 300 years.

A section of the Bayeux tapestry

St Sophia

You can also find traces (here we are working backwards) of the arts and sciences of the 'Dark Ages' and Mediaeval times. You can see how the simple pointed arch or the ribbed vault was developed, enlarged and elaborated. You can even see—for instance in the Bayeux tapestry or in stained-glass windows—how people living in the 11th century (the time of William the Conqueror) saw themselves; and judge how important Church and State were in the choice of the subjects the artist might draw from.

Gothic Art was mainly northern European. In the Byzantine Empire (the Christian, Near East area of Constantinople), great underground burial places, the catacombs, were decorated with paintings on the ceilings and elsewhere. The paintings—like the decorations on lamps and glass objects—were almost always simple representations of Christian doctrines and figures. Great basilicas with lavishly decorated domes were built (Hagia Sophia,

Section of an illuminated Saxon manuscript

Stained-glass window (York Minster)

Istanbul, A.D. 530). Fine work was done in mosaics, ivories, books, jewellery, enamel and wire-work.

RENAISSANCE The word means Rebirth. The new beginning spread through Italy, eventually to affect the whole of Europe, during the 14th–16th centuries. The works of such artists as **Giotto, Martini** and **Andrea Pisano** hint clearly enough at what was to come.

The Renaissance was one result of a chain-explosion of events, possibilities and attitudes. Links in the chain include the conquest of Constantinople by the Turks (which sent many Greek scholars to Italy); scientific research; voyages of exploration; the spread of printing; the nature of Italy itself—it was then a conglomeration of small city-states ruled by sophisticated families; and perhaps above all, a feeling of personal freedom very different from that which produced the often strait-jacketed figures seen in, say, old stained-glass windows and sacred statues.

In this climate, the artist could find new aims and bring science to aid his eye and craft. Talent found recognition and genius, acclaim. Sculptured figures came alive. Painted figures appeared to have roundness and flesh—and to inhabit landscapes painted in depth (see *Perspective*, *Modelling* below). The very buildings, while keeping the symmetries of ancient Greece, became ornate, colourful, even frivolous—like the new clothes.

Madonna and child, Bruges cathedral (Michelangelo)

Melencolia I (Dürer)

The Italian sun slowly thawed even the northern parts of Europe (though here and there, there were dark matters of church and state to keep out the light). By the end of the period, as later artists complained, the Italians seemed to have accomplished everything: colour, perspective, landscape, the use of human figures to express emotion, 'classical' symmetry, 'modern' adventurousness. Looking at the works of **Botticelli, Michelangelo, Giorgione, Titian** and the architect **Palladio**, you say to yourself, 'Only a superb mind could have thought of that. And only a superb hand could have done it!' (e.g., *The Creation of Adam*, a detail from **Michelangelo's** ceiling for the Sistine Chapel. Or **Giorgione's** *Fête Champêtre*. Or **Ghiberti's** bronze doors for the Baptistery, Florence. But really, such lists are pointless because the achievements were endless.)

In countries north of the Alps, the effects of the Renaissance were felt a century later. During the 15th century, a particularly brilliant school of painting arose in the Netherlands (**Hubert** and **Jan van Eyck, van der Weyden, Memling** and others). French architects adopted Italian manners in their architecture and sculpture. England was undergoing the Reformation and the effects of the Renaissance were minor. Germany, too, had other matters to deal with. Yet, throughout Europe, the Renaissance 'took', if only in terms of buildings, clothes,

Supper at Emmaus (Caravaggio)

ornaments, furnishings—and a new sense of possibility. **Dürer** of Germany, for example, travelled extensively: he was a supreme master in his own ways—but must have seen and been influenced by the mastery of the very different minds and hands he encountered.

PERSPECTIVE AND MODELLING Western people take it for granted that a two-dimensional work can suggest, 'This thing is near, that thing is distant' (perspective); and 'This thing is rounded, that thing is flat' (modelling).

In Eastern and many other cultures, these effects are not necessarily attempted. No doubt the problems of achieving 'reality' through perspective and modelling have always been recognized by artists of all places and periods: but generally, the problems were sidestepped by the adoption of conventions. For example, a Chinese scroll must be unrolled and viewed bit by bit, from bottom (Near things) to top (Distant things). Again, while the ancient Egyptians gave incised flat surfaces (a rock-face, say) an added drama and interest by using bas-relief—shallow modelling—for the figures, they did not bother with perspective. Yet again, you can see 'parallel perspective' in many eastern

Perspective joke drawing (after Hogarth)

Head of Venus (Botticelli)

drawings and paintings. The effect is faintly comical to us, as if the whole scene were slipping off the surface.

In the West, the huge importance of the problem seems always to have been recognised. You see it solved in Ancient Roman times and earlier. It was not until some 500 years ago, however, that a general onslaught was made by such masters as **Uccello, Masaccio, Jan van Eyck, Dürer** and **da Vinci**. They found, formalised and set down the answers we have accepted ever since. (The illustration on page M34 shows what happens if you don't accept them!) With the mysteries solved, western art could and did stride forward and enter new realms of 'reality'.

PRINTING, REPRODUCTION To western eyes, there is a respectability and importance in 'oil painting' that may seem to diminish the mere graphic arts of drawing, etching, wood engraving, etc. Yet master drawings (see books with such titles) are masterpieces in their own right—and have always been thought so in China and Japan.

In the east, basically linear works embellished with colour have been hand-printed from blocks for centuries. In the west, printing by mechanical presses began much later and has only recently found techniques that satisfactorily render colour; so superb drawings by great masters could lie neglected because there were no means of reproducing them, or because the drawings were regarded as only a step towards the 'serious' work, the oil painting.

Yet many great artists and great works were and are linear at heart (see **Botticelli's** *Birth of Venus*) and today it is accepted that a fine artist may be a draughtsman rather than a colourist. See **Brian Steadman's** present-day illustrations for *Alice in Wonderland/Alice Through the Looking Glass*; book illustrations, Victorian and later, by **Rackham, Harry Clarke, Edmund J. Sullivan, Beardsley, Joan Hassall**; 18th century cartoons and illustrations by **Rowlandson, Gillray**; and the numerous works of **Hokusai** (Japan, 19th century). See also the supreme drawings of such masters as **Michelangelo, Titian, Raphael, da Vinci, Dürer**, etc., who will lead you on to, say, **Ingres** (19th century), a 'classical' draughtsman—and so to the experimentalists of later periods and today.

AFTER THE RENAISSANCE many artists found rich patrons. The royal courts of France and Spain and the Catholic Church, for instance, constantly demanded allegorical, religious and portrait works. The Renaissance skills endured—but not always the conviction, as you may feel when you look at *The Toilet of Venus* (**Guido Reni**). Architects loaded basically classical structures with ornament, statues, pillars, pediments, sweeping stairways. The grandiose styles of, particularly, 17th-century Italy are called *Baroque*. Later, Baroque merged with the still more extravagant *Rococo* manner. The sugar-cake exercises of early 18th-century Rococo are often breath-taking: there may be too much of everything, but how beautifully everything is done! (See paintings by **Bernini, Lanfranco, Pozzo, Fragonard, Watteau**. But better—enjoy complete buildings and structures; the Palace of Versailles in France, the Trevi Fountain and much else in Rome. And look at exhibits in the Wallace Collection, London.)

British architects went their own way. They developed a style blended from Classical, Palladian and Renaissance. A very few, like **Inigo Jones**, could be called 'undiluted Classical' (Whitehall, or the Queen's House, Greenwich). **Sir Christopher Wren** and his disciples, however, made endless variations and combinations of classical and baroque themes (e.g., London and City churches, St Paul's Cathedral). Wren's inventiveness and sparkle was, fortunately, echoed by several contemporaries. A great deal of their work stands, though some is hidden or dwarfed by the efforts of present-day architects. St Paul's, for instance, is almost obscured by mean yet massive 20th-century office buildings.

Several 17th-century artists did not follow the trends of the time. **Velasquez** (Spanish) was coolly powerful, darkly dignified. **Rubens** (Flemish) was only incidentally a vivid Baroque

St Paul's Cathedral

painter. The calm, small, glowing interiors of **Jan Vermeer** (Dutch) seem intensely private, where so much painting of the time was public. And of course there was Holland's **Rembrandt**, who would have been considered a giant at any time—among painters.

Eventually the grandeurs and fripperies of Baroque and Rococo were swept away by the French Revolution. Educated tastes now preferred the drier, more severe style of *Neo-Classicism* (at heart, Greek/Roman) typified by the drawings and paintings of, say, **Ingres**—which contrast with the very different

approach of the *Romantics*, such as **Delacroix**. In England,
Reynolds (1723–92) argued a return to the 'Grand Style' of the
Renaissance (see his work, and that of his rival, **Gainsborough**).
In the Netherlands landscape painting had been highly regarded
since the 17th century and in Britain, too, this kind of work
found popularity (**Cox**, father and son, watercolourists of
18th–19th centuries; **Constable**, 18th–19th centuries).

Constable represents one of the accepted forms of painting
taken to its logical conclusion. There seemed nothing more to
say. But then **Turner** (1775–1851) produced—as one of his
critics said—'pictures of nothing, and very like'. His stormy
handling of paint and extraordinary success in apparently manufacturing light from paint upset the Fine Arts applecart and
perhaps led to *Impressionism*. Perhaps not. Certainly his light
still shines.

For some time after the French Revolution, artists could
depend on the rich, the Church and the State for patronage.
From 1800 onwards, most could not. They found themselves
in a free market—free to invent, to compete and even to starve.
Those painters who did not experiment followed Neo-Classical
trends in the main. They produced carefully finished 'painterly'
work, obviously worth hard cash. They added a zest and zing by
making their work sexier, or more dramatic, or more story-
telling, than of old (see the later paintings of **Greuze** (French),
a forerunner of the super-sentimentalists of the Victorian age).

In Britain, the architects flourished. During the 18th and
early 19th century, they produced some of the most delightful
buildings we know. Wren's innovations, it was found, could be
adapted to small structures: thus the fine 'Queen Anne' houses,
in which various Classical motifs were carried out in brick. The
Industrial Revolution was under way—people were moving
into the new, crowded towns—whole strings and squares of
housing had to be supplied: even this was done successfully,
with a grace that can be admired in cities and towns throughout
the country (Edinburgh's New Town, Bath, and in London, see
Bedford Square and the other Georgian squares and streets
near by). The severely Classical, Inigo Jones manner was
carried on by such architects as **Nash**, who not only built, but
planned whole areas of cities (go to Regent's Park in London).

Queen Anne, Georgian and Regency styles are at heart
ornamented Classical—that is, Ancient Greek/Roman/Palladian,

Italian. There were other styles. There was a craze for the 'Gothic Taste', an amazing mixture of castellations, church-y pointed windows, rustic ironwork and twisted chimneys. The craze lasted some seventy years: look for late-Gothic railway stations, lodges, cottages, schools, in your neighbourhood. The date may be shown in bright bricks and will probably be *c.* 1850.

The Prince Regent (later George IV) gave his name to Regency architecture. But his personal interest was in exotic styles—Chinese and Indian and anything else from the East all mixed together. He built Brighton Pavilion. You can go inside this amazing pleasure palace. At the same time (1800 on) the light-hearted yet formal seafront buildings of Brighton and other seaside resorts and country towns were being built in the Regency style.

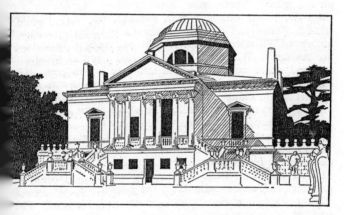

Chiswick House

ᴠɪᴄᴛᴏʀɪᴀɴ In the period 1840–1900 industrialisation, the railways and machines brought changes to all and vast wealth to some, particularly in Britain, the rich and powerful pace-setter. Artists from abroad came to England: native artists prospered. 'Finish'—perfect execution—was one way to the favour of rich patrons. Another was to cram the picture or sculpture with detail and to make it tell a story ('Look, master has died and the dog is sad! See how his eyes glisten!').

Such works were laughed at when the new century arrived—or at any rate, after the First World War. The laughter only recently died down. Victorian craftsmanship was remarkable; and as works of Art—but judge for yourself from, say, *Too early* (**Tissot**); *The Lament for Icarus* (**Draper**); *Derby Day* (**Frith**); *April Love* (**Hughes**). See also the flaming luxury of some of **Lord Leighton's** work; *Pegwell Bay* by **Dyce**; the super-reality of *The Stonebreaker* (**Brett**); and the book illustrations of the period.

There were endless revolts against the fundamentally commercial values of the time. The *pre-Raphaelite Brotherhood* sought to rediscover the purity and truth-to-Nature of an earlier golden age. **Grimshaw** (*Liverpool Quay by Moonlight*) achieved effects that might astonish a present-day colour photographer. There were social realists (*Application for Admission to the Casual Ward*), **Fildes**; and Fairy Painters (**Dadd, Paton** and others). Works from China and Japan influenced **Whistler** the impressionist, and **Aubrey Beardsley** the line artist. **William Morris** founded a sort of Mediaeval arts and crafts workshop whose influence is still seen. The French-inspired *Aesthetic Movement* inspired one, as G. S. Gilbert said mockingly, to 'stroll down Piccadilly/With a poppy or a lily/In my mediaeval hand'. (Get a book about *Art Nouveau* to see what happened later on.)

In France the major revolution brewed. *Modern Art* (q.v.) was starting with the realism of **Courbet**, the rapid emotional effects of the *Impressionists*, the deliberately unclassical nudes of **Manet**, the lushness and freedom of **Renoir**, the posters and paintings of **Toulouse-Lautrec**, the painters of light such as **Monet**. *Post-impressionists* like **Cézanne** and **van Gogh** added strength to the new art.

The Victorians loved to display their wealth. A town house or a sideboard had to be florid, 'important', completely covered with decoration. So much Victorian architecture survives that your own eyes are a sufficient guide. Enough here to say that every conceivable style, ornament and tradition of the past were used, sometimes simultaneously, sometimes disastrously, often delightfully. See St Pancras Station, Big Ben, Balmoral, perhaps your own local railway station or town hall or old public house—anything. Look particularly for uses of cast-iron, a key material of the period.

MODERN ART Until the arrival of the French Impressionists of
the 19th century, the art of painting had been based on Nature
in some form or other. 'Those who take as their standard
anything other than Nature,' **da Vinci** wrote, 'weary themselves
in vain.' **Whistler**, three centuries later, said much the same
thing: the job of the painter was 'to pick and choose, as the
musician gathers notes and chords,' from Nature.

But then came the Instant-Nature reproducer, the camera—
and various machines that appeared more than human in their
cleverness and power—and above all a belief that Man could
dominate Nature. So the 20th-century architect talked of
houses as 'machines for living', the sculptor turned to mechanisms such as mobiles, and the painter to abstract, theoretical,
non-representational pictures—and to Isms. Surrealism,
vorticism, pointillism, dadaism, expressionism, cubism, futur-
ism . . .

Time has already been unkind to most of the Isms. There is
nothing so dated as a 1930s book about Modern Art unless it is
a pre-World War One Futurist Manifesto ('HURRAH for motors!
HURRAH for speed! HURRAH for draughts!')

Recently, soiled nappies have been displayed in the name of
Art—and even naughtier, more shocking articles. 'I admit it's
ugly, but is it Art?' is the question we so often have to answer
today.

Time will give the answers—and decide which of our present-
day artists are truly important, even great. In all periods,
innovators have been derided and attacked. Contrariwise, for
every old name still remembered, there are a hundred or a
thousand forgotten. We wait and see.

Some names: innovators and experimenters who bred modern
art include **Cézanne, Matisse, Rouault** and the Impressionists
Monet, Renoir, Toulouse-Lautrec and **Degas**. All worked
in France, as did **Picasso** (Spanish), the most diverse and prolific of all. Whatever Isms or classifications these artists chose
to apply to themselves from time to time, their works are distinct
and personal. The same is true of **Paul Klee** (Swiss), **Kandinski**
(Russian), **Brancusi** (Rumanian), **Magritte** (Belgian), **Jackson
Pollock** (American) and **Henry Moore** or **Graham Sutherland** (English). All are moderns, all produced paintings or
sculptures or both that belong to this century and no other. But
this is usually their only link.

Younger, present-day artists of note include **Bridget Riley** (fascinating visual conjuring tricks of the Op Art School), **David Hockney** and **Francis Bacon**. A current American school of interest produces super-real paintings—probably a spinoff from *Pop Art*; you may know, from posters, the work of Pop-artist **Roy Lichtenstein** (blow-ups of frames from strip cartoons) and of artists who paint super-real tubes of toothpaste, etc.

Artists who defy classification include **L. S. Lowry** ('naive' industrial landscapes with figures) and an endless list of commercial artists who are coming to be regarded as Fine Artists. But then, the distinction between Fine Arts in a gallery and commercial art on, say, a plastic food pack is becoming blurred.

Sculpture is equally diverse. **Reg Butler's** skeletal structures, **Jacob Epstein's** brutal and massive pieces, the abstract forms of **Barbara Hepworth**, the elongated delicacy of **Giacometti**— all are regarded as important, but so are stacks of bricks and junked cars.

In architecture, in this century, new materials—particularly steel-reinforced concrete—have changed the very nature of buildings and, seemingly, have often directed the architect's hand. Concrete and steel lend themselves to modular production of parts that can be endlessly repeated: thus the massive tower blocks and office complexes that dominate our town and city skylines.

Architecture is the functional art. It provides containers for things or people. The functional worth of modern high-rise buildings designed to house humans is under continuous and heavy attack, as is their 'art' element. It seems that the architects and planners of today's familiar, commonplace buildings and centres will be judged harshly tomorrow.

Adventurous and exciting buildings in the modern idioms exist, of course; see the cathedrals of Liverpool and Coventry various small buildings—aviary, elephant house, giraffe house— in Regent's Park Zoo, London; buildings for the universities of Essex, Southampton, Leicester.

The pioneers of present-day architecture include **Frank Lloyd Wright** of America, **le Corbusier** of France, **Pier Luigi Nervi** of Italy—and **Walter Gropius** of Germany, founder of the *Bauhaus*, a German institution that influenced the design of houses and household objects after World War and through the 1930s.

Photography Much of present-day art is wild, provocative and formless. One of many reasons why is—photography, which was already flourishing a hundred years ago.

Picture a successful Victorian artist. He has spent his adult life mastering his craft and art. A photographer sets up his camera beside the artist's easel. The one goes 'click' and the other paints on. Later they compare results. Perspective, modelling, detail, light and shade, 'truth'—the photograph is as perfect as the painting in everything but colour (and that is soon to come!). What should the artist do? Burn his canvases and buy a camera? Or change the very nature of his art?

The problem was and is a real one. The camera cannot eliminate the unwanted or invent the wanted—but the able photographer can find ways to over-ride these difficulties and produce the effect he desires. He can use the camera 'creatively', choose his subjects and settings 'artistically'. There are already Old Masters of photography.

One effect on the non-photographic artist was to make him tackle his art from a different starting point. The camera can show every leaf and twig? Right, then the artist will become an impressionist. Or he will put a frame round a single leaf and call his picture, *Forest*.

In short—the wilder schools of *modern art* (q.v.) would most probably have emerged anyhow. But photography made quite sure that they did emerge.

EXCEPTIONS AND REBELS In our history—we warned you at the outset—we may have made it appear that in each period, art and artists followed the general patterns of that period. Probably most artists did just that, just as you talk of television or tennis, not of tatting or tipcat. But there were always exceptions: artists who didn't, wouldn't or couldn't 'belong'. Please look up: the English painters **Turner, Samuel Palmer, William Blake, Lowry**; the works of **Fuseli, Hokusai, Bosch, Henri Rousseau, Pieter Breughel, el Greco**; the architects **Gaudi, Mackintosh**. This short list (you may enjoy extending it) is of artists who have nothing in common but their uncommonness.

ART AND CRAFT What are they? When does one become the other? A craft can be defined as a high human skill: Art might be defined as a message designed to appeal to the highest human sensibilities. But why cannot a craft object make this appeal?

Is a superb pocket watch by **Breguet** craft, or art? Can a pile of bricks (displayed in a recent Art exhibition) truly be art? Is the *Cutty Sark* both a work of art and craft? Can a photograph be art?—and if not, why not?

There are no answers to these old questions. But you must ask them, constantly.

REMARKABLE BOOKS

There are today endless books about the Arts. Anything you want can be found in libraries and bookshops. Some books, however, are things apart. Right at the top of your list put:

Homes Sweet Homes; *Pillar to Post*; *Progress at Pelvis Bay*, all by Sir Osbert Lancaster. Architecture, furnishing, period feeling, in words-and-pictures nutshells. Very funny. There are paper-back editions, but try to get new or secondhand hardbacks.

First and Last Loves by Sir John Betjeman. Random opinions, enthusiasms, invaluable snippets. Illustrated. And many other works by this author.

Particular Pleasures by J. B. Priestley, containing the author's reflections on certain paintings.

Architecture by W. R. Dalzell.

One Hundred Details from Pictures in the National Gallery by Sir Kenneth Clark. Also *The Nude* and other works by this author.

Autobiography of Cellini, describing the work of a 16th-century artist/craftsman.

Drawings and Notebooks of Leonardo da Vinci (1452–1519)—thoughts, sketches, theories of a genius.

The Saturday Book, editor John Hadfield, was a handsome gift annual for grown-ups. It appeared for more than twenty years. Many beautiful things, expert texts.

Pears Encyclopaedia of Myths and Legends vols 1–4 by Sheila Savill. Magnificently illustrated with the art of cultures from all over the world.

Sport

AT the beginning of this section, sports are arranged alphabetically; under each heading are given details of governing bodies, championships and records. These are followed by a list of those results of the 1976 Olympics not recorded under particular sports. Finally, under 'Personalities', brief notes are given on some of the sportsmen and women who have made the greatest impression on the British scene in 1977–78.

Archery

Governing body: Grand National Archery Society, National Agricultural Centre, Stoneleigh, Kenilworth, Warks., CV8 2LG.

Olympic Games 1976

Men	D. Pace (U.S.A.)	2,571 pts.
Women	L. Ryon (U.S.A.)	2,499 pts.

29th World Target Archery Championships 1977

Men (individual)	R. McKinney (U.S.A.)
Men (team)	U.S.A.
Women (individual)	Miss L. Ryon (U.S.A.)
Women (team)	U.S.A.

British Target Championships 1977

Men	M. Deacon (London)
Women	Miss P. M. Edwards (Kent)

Association Football

The Football Association was founded in 1863; the F.A. Cup competition was first held in 1871/72; official international matches have been played since 1872.

Governing bodies: Football Association (England), 16 Lancaster Gate, London, W2 3LW; Football Association (Scotland), 6 Park Gardens, Glasgow, G3 7YE; Football Association (Irish), 20 Windsor Avenue, Belfast, BT9 6EG; Football Association (Eire), 80 Merrion Square South, Dublin, 2; Football Association (Wales), 3 Fairy Road, Wrexham, LL13 7PS.

LEAGUE CHAMPIONS

1889	Preston North End	1897	Aston Villa
1890	Preston North End	1898	Sheffield United
1891	Everton	1899	Aston Villa
1892	Sunderland	1900	Aston Villa
1893	Sunderland	1901	Liverpool
1894	Aston Villa	1902	Sunderland
1895	Sunderland	1903	Sheffield Wednesday
1896	Aston Villa	1904	Sheffield Wednesday

1905	Newcastle United	1949	Portsmouth
1906	Liverpool	1950	Portsmouth
1907	Newcastle United	1951	Tottenham Hotspur
1908	Manchester United	1952	Manchester United
1909	Newcastle United	1953	Arsenal
1910	Aston Villa	1954	Wolverhampton Wanderers
1911	Manchester United		
1912	Blackburn Rovers	1955	Chelsea
1913	Sunderland	1956	Manchester United
1914	Blackburn Rovers	1957	Manchester United
1915	Everton	1958	Wolverhampton Wanderers
1920	West Bromwich Albion		
1921	Burnley	1959	Wolverhampton Wanderers
1922	Liverpool		
1923	Liverpool	1960	Burnley
1924	Huddersfield Town	1961	Tottenham Hotspur
1925	Huddersfield Town	1962	Ipswich Town
1926	Huddersfield Town	1963	Everton
1927	Newcastle United	1964	Liverpool
1928	Everton	1965	Manchester United
1929	Sheffield Wednesday	1966	Liverpool
1930	Sheffield Wednesday	1967	Manchester United
1931	Arsenal	1968	Manchester City
1932	Everton	1969	Leeds United
1933	Arsenal	1970	Everton
1934	Arsenal	1971	Arsenal
1935	Arsenal	1972	Derby County
1936	Sunderland	1973	Liverpool
1937	Manchester City	1974	Leeds United
1938	Arsenal	1975	Derby County
1939	Everton	1976	Liverpool
1947	Liverpool	1977	Liverpool
1948	Arsenal	1978	Nottingham Forest

F.A. CUP WINNERS

1872	Wanderers	1886	Blackburn Rovers
1873	Wanderers	1887	Aston Villa
1874	Oxford University	1888	West Bromwich Albion
1875	Royal Engineers	1889	Preston North End
1876	Wanderers	1890	Blackburn Rovers
1877	Wanderers	1891	Blackburn Rovers
1878	Wanderers	1892	West Bromwich Albion
1879	Old Etonians	1893	Wolverhampton Wanderers
1880	Clapham Rovers		
1881	Old Carthusians	1894	Notts County
1882	Old Etonians	1895	Aston Villa
1883	Blackburn Olympic	1896	Sheffield Wednesday
1884	Blackburn Rovers	1897	Aston Villa
1885	Blackburn Rovers	1898	Nottingham Forest

1899	Sheffield United	1939	Portsmouth
1900	Bury	1946	Derby County
1901	Tottenham Hotspur	1947	Charlton Athletic
1902	Sheffield United	1948	Manchester United
1903	Bury	1949	Wolverhampton
1904	Manchester City		Wanderers
1905	Aston Villa	1950	Arsenal
1906	Everton	1951	Newcastle United
1907	Sheffield Wednesday	1952	Newcastle United
1908	Wolverhampton	1953	Blackpool
	Wanderers	1954	West Bromwich Albion
1909	Manchester United	1955	Newcastle United
1910	Newcastle United	1956	Manchester City
1911	Bradford City	1957	Aston Villa
1912	Barnsley	1958	Bolton Wanderers
1913	Aston Villa	1959	Nottingham Forest
1914	Burnley	1960	Wolverhampton
1915	Sheffield United		Wanderers
1920	Aston Villa	1961	Tottenham Hotspur
1921	Tottenham Hotspur	1962	Tottenham Hotspur
1922	Huddersfield Town	1963	Manchester United
1923	Bolton Wanderers	1964	West Ham
1924	Newcastle United	1965	Liverpool
1925	Sheffield United	1966	Everton
1926	Bolton Wanderers	1967	Tottenham Hotspur
1927	Cardiff City	1968	West Bromwich Albion
1928	Blackburn Rovers	1969	Manchester City
1929	Bolton Wanderers	1970	Chelsea
1930	Arsenal	1971	Arsenal
1931	West Bromwich Albion	1972	Leeds United
1932	Newcastle United	1973	Sunderland
1933	Everton	1974	Liverpool
1934	Manchester City	1975	West Ham
1935	Sheffield Wednesday	1976	Southampton
1936	Arsenal	1977	Manchester United
1937	Sunderland	1978	Ipswich
1938	Preston North End		

FOOTBALL LEAGUE CUP WINNERS

1961	Aston Villa	1971	Tottenham Hotspur
1962	Norwich City	1972	Stoke City
1963	Birmingham City	1973	Tottenham Hotspur
1964	Leicester City	1974	Wolverhampton
1965	Chelsea		Wanderers
1966	West Bromwich Albion	1975	Aston Villa
1967	Queen's Park Rangers	1976	Manchester City
1968	Leeds United	1977	Aston Villa
1969	Swindon Town	1978	Nottingham Forest
1970	Manchester City		

SCOTTISH CUP WINNERS

1951	Celtic	1965	Celtic
1952	Motherwell	1966	Rangers
1953	Rangers	1967	Celtic
1954	Celtic	1968	Dunfermline
1955	Clyde	1969	Celtic
1956	Heart of Midlothian	1970	Aberdeen
1957	Falkirk	1971	Celtic
1958	Clyde	1972	Celtic
1959	St Mirren	1973	Rangers
1960	Rangers	1974	Celtic
1961	Dunfermline	1975	Celtic
1962	Rangers	1976	Rangers
1963	Rangers	1977	Celtic
1964	Rangers	1978	Rangers

EUROPEAN CUP WINNERS

1958	Real Madrid	1969	A.C. Milan
1959	Real Madrid	1970	Feyenoord
1960	Real Madrid	1971	Ajax
1961	Benfica	1972	Ajax
1962	Benfica	1973	Ajax
1963	A.C. Milan	1974	Bayern Munich
1964	Inter Milan	1975	Bayern Munich
1965	Inter Milan	1976	Bayern Munich
1966	Real Madrid	1977	Liverpool
1967	Celtic	1978	Liverpool
1968	Manchester United		

WORLD CUP WINNERS

1930	Uruguay	1958	Brazil
1934	Italy	1962	Brazil
1938	Italy	1966	England
1950	Uruguay	1970	Brazil
1954	West Germany	1974	West Germany

OLYMPIC GAMES WINNERS

1908	United Kingdom	1952	Hungary
1912	United Kingdom	1956	U.S.S.R.
1920	Belgium	1960	Yugoslavia
1924	Uruguay	1964	Hungary
1928	Uruguay	1968	Hungary
1932	No competition	1972	Poland
1936	Italy	1976	East Germany
1948	Sweden		

RECORDS

Championship wins: Liverpool ten times; Arsenal eight times; Everton and Manchester United seven times; Aston Villa and Sunderland six times

Highest score in F.A. Cup: Preston North End 26, Hyde o (1887)

Highest score in Cup Final: Bury 6, Derby County o (1903)

Highest score by one man in League game: 10 goals, J. Payne for Luton Town v. Bristol Rovers (1936)

Highest score by one man in Division I: 7 goals, E. Drake for Arsenal v. Aston Villa (1935)

Highest score by one man in a full international: 6 goals, G. J. Bambrick for Ireland v. Wales (1930)

Most goals during career: 550, by James McGrory (Glasgow Celtic), 1922–38. **English record:** 434, by A. Rowley (West Bromwich Albion, Fulham, Leicester City and Shrewsbury Town)

Most caps won by amateur: 62, by R. Haider (Kingstonian and Hendon), 1966–73

Most caps won by a professional: Bobby Moore (West Ham United), 108 for England

Most Welsh caps: I. Allchurch (Newcastle United, Cardiff City and Swansea Town), 1950–66, 68

Most Scottish caps: D. Law (Huddersfield Town, Manchester City and Manchester United), 1958–74, 55

Most Irish caps: P. Jennings (Watford and Tottenham Hotspur), 1963–77, 63

Athletics

Governing bodies: Amateur Athletic Association, 70 Brompton Road, London, SW3 1EE; Women's Amateur Athletic Association, 70 Brompton Road, London, S.W.3.

WORLD AND UNITED KINGDOM RECORDS

(The records given here are those that have been officially ratified as at 31st December 1977; they are for fully-automatic timing for distances up to and including 400 metres)

	Men	
	World	*United Kingdom*
100 metres	9·95 sec.	10·29 sec.
	J. Hines (U.S.A.)	P. Radford

	World	*United Kingdom*
200 metres	19·83 sec. T. Smith (U.S.A.)	20·66 sec. R. Steane D. Jenkins
400 metres	43·86 sec. L. Evans (U.S.A.)	45·45 sec. D. Jenkins
800 metres	1 min. 43·4 sec. A. Juantorena (Cuba)	1 min. 45·8 sec. S. Ovett
1,000 metres	2 min. 13·9 sec. R. Wolhunter (U.S.A.)	2 min. 18·2 sec. J. Boulter
1,500 metres	3 min. 32·2 sec. F. Bayi (Tanzania)	3 min. 34·5 sec. S. Ovett
1 mile	3 min. 49·4 sec. J. Walker (New Zealand)	3 min. 55·0 sec. S. Ovett
2 kilometres	4 min. 51·4 sec. J. Walker (New Zealand)	5 min. 2·9. sec. B. Foster
3 kilometres	7 min. 35·2 sec. B. Foster (G.B.)	7 min. 35·2 sec. B. Foster
2 miles	8 min. 13·7 sec. B. Foster (G.B.)	8 min. 13·7 sec. B. Foster
3 miles	12 min. 47·8 sec. E. Puttemans (Belgium)	12 min. 58·2 sec. D. Bedford
5 kilometres	13 min. 12·9 sec. D. Quax (New Zealand)	13 min. 14·6 sec. B. Foster
10 kilometres	27 min. 30·5 sec. S. Kimobwa (Kenya)	27 min. 30·8 sec. D. Bedford
20 kilometres	57 min. 24·2 sec. J. Hermans (Holland)	58 min. 39·0 sec. R. Hill
30 kilometres	1 hr. 31 min. 30·4 sec. J. Alder (G.B.)	1 hr. 31 min. 30·4 sec. J. Alder
1 hour	20,944 metres J. Hermans (Holland)	20,472 metres R. Hill
110 metres hurdles	13·21 sec. A. Casanas (Cuba)	13·69 sec. B. Price
200 metres hurdles	22·5 sec. M. Lauer (W. Germany) G. Davis (U.S.A.)	23·0 sec. A. Pascoe
400 metres hurdles	47·45 sec. E. Moses (U.S.A.)	48·12 sec. D. Hemery

	World	*United Kingdom*
3,000 metres steeplechase	8 min. 8·0 sec. A. Garderud (Sweden)	8 min. 19·0 sec. D. Coates
High jump	2·33 metres V. Yashchenko (U.S.S.R.)	2·18 metres M. Naylor
Long jump	8·90 metres R. Beamon (U.S.A.)	8·23 metres L. Davies
Triple jump	17·89 metres J. de Oliveria (Brazil)	16·54 metres K. Connor
Pole vault	5·70 metres D. Roberts (U.S.A.)	5·40 metres B. Hooper
Shot-put	22·00 metres A. Baryshnikov (U.S.S.R.)	21·55 metres G. Capes
Discus-throw	70·86 metres M. Wilkins (U.S.A.)	64·94 metres W. Tancred
Hammer-throw	79·30 metres W. Schmidt (West Germany)	64·14 metres I. Chipchase
Javelin-throw	94·58 metres M. Nemeth (Hungary)	84·92 metres C. Clover
Decathlon (10 events)	8,617 pts. B. Jenner (U.S.A.)	8,124 pts. D. Thompson

Women

60 metres	7·2 sec. B. Cuthbert (Australia) I. Turova-Bochkaryeva (U.S.S.R.) L. Alaerts (Belgium) A. Lynch (G.B.)	7·2 sec. A. Lynch
100 metres	10·88 sec. M. Oelsner (East Germany)	11·16 sec. A. Lynch
200 metres	22·21 sec. I. Szewinska (Poland)	22·81 sec. S. Lannaman
400 metres	49·28 sec. I. Szewinska (Poland)	51·28 sec. D. Murray
800 metres	1 min. 54·9 sec. T. Kazankina (U.S.S.R.)	2 min. 0·2 sec. R. Wright
1,500 metres	3 min. 56·0 sec. T. Kazankina (U.S.S.R.)	4 min. 4·8 sec. S. Carey

	World	*United Kingdom*
3 kilometres	8 min. 27·1 sec. L. Bragina (U.S.S.R.)	8 min. 52·8 sec. A. Ford
1 mile	4 min. 23·8 sec. N. Marasescu (Rumania)	4 min. 36·1 sec. M. Stewart
100 metres hurdles	12·59 sec. A. Ehrhardt (East Germany)	13·11 sec. S. Colyear
400 metres hurdles	55·63 sec. K. Rossley (East Germany)	57·59 sec. E. Sutherland
High jump	2·00 metres R. Ackermann (East Germany)	1·87 metres B. Lawton
Long jump	6·99 metres S. Siegl (East Germany)	6·76 metres M. Rand
Shot put	22·32 metres H. Fibingerova (Czechoslovakia)	16·31 metres M. Peters
Discus-throw	60·50 metres F. Melnyk (U.S.S.R.)	59·88 metres M. Ritchie
Javelin	60·32 metres K. Schmidt (U.S.A.)	67·20 metres T. Sanderson
Pentathlon	4,839 pts. N. Tkachenko (U.S.S.R.)	4,385 pts. S. Longden

THE MILE RECORD

1884	George (G.B.)	4 min. 12·75 sec.
1915	Taber (U.S.A.)	4 min. 12·6 sec.
1923	Nurmi (Finland)	4 min. 10·4 sec.
1931	Ladoumègue (France)	4 min. 9·2 sec.
1933	Lovelock (New Zealand)	4 min. 7·6 sec.
1934	Cunningham (U.S.A.)	4 min. 6·8 sec.
1937	Wooderson (G.B.)	4 min. 6·4 sec.
1942	Hägg (Sweden)	4 min. 6·2 sec.
1942	Andersson (Sweden)	4 min. 6·2 sec.
1942	Hägg (Sweden)	4 min. 4·6 sec.
1943	Andersson (Sweden)	4 min. 2·6 sec.
1944	Andersson (Sweden)	4 min. 1·6 sec.
1945	Hägg (Sweden)	4 min. 1·3 sec.
1954	Bannister (G.B.)	3 min. 59·4 sec.
1954	Landy (Australia)	3 min. 57·9 sec.
1957	Ibbotson (G.B.)	3 min. 57·2 sec.
1958	Elliott (Australia)	3 min. 54·5 sec.
1962	Snell (New Zealand)	3 min. 54·4 sec.
1964	Snell (New Zealand)	3 min. 54·1 sec.

1965	Jazy (France)	3 min. 53·6 sec.
1966	Ryun (U.S.A.)	3 min. 51·3 sec.
1967	Ryun (U.S.A.)	3 min. 51·1 sec.
1975	Bayi (Tanzania)	3 min 51·0 sec.
1975	Walker (New Zealand)	3 min. 49·4 sec

THE XXIst OLYMPIC GAMES WINNERS

(Montreal, 1976)

Men

100 metres	H. Crawford (Trinidad)	10·06 sec.
200 metres	D. Quarrie (Jamaica)	20·23 sec.
400 metres	A. Juantorena (Cuba)	44·26 sec.
800 metres	A. Juantorena (Cuba)	1 min. 43·5 sec. (world record)
1,500 metres	J. Walker (New Zealand)	3 min. 39·2 sec.
5,000 metres	L. Viren (Finland)	13 min. 24·8 sec.
10,000 metres	L. Viren (Finland)	27 min. 40·4 sec.
Steeplechase 3,000 metres	A. Garderud (Sweden)	8 min. 8·0 sec. (world record)
Marathon	W. Cierpinski (E. Germany)	2 hr. 9 min. 55·0 sec. (Olympic record)
110 metres hurdles	G. Drut (France)	13·30 sec.
400 metres hurdles	E. Moses (U.S.A.)	47·64 sec. (world record)
4 × 100 metres relay	U.S.A. (Glance, Jones, Hampton, Riddick)	38·33 sec.
4 × 400 metres relay	U.S.A. (Frazier, Brown, Newhouse, Parks)	2 min. 58·7 sec.
High jump	J. Wszola (Poland)	7 ft. 4½ in. (Olympic record)
Pole vault	T. Slujarski (Poland)	18 ft. 0½ in. (equals Olympic record)
Long jump	A. Robinson (U.S.A.)	27 ft. 4¾ in.
Triple jump	V. Saneyev (U.S.S.R.)	56 ft. 8¾ in.
Shot-put	U. Beyer (E. Germany)	69 ft. 0¾ in.
Discus-throw	M. Wilkins (U.S.A.)	221 ft. 5 in.
Hammer-throw	Y. Sedykh (U.S.S.R.)	254 ft. 4 in. (Olympic record)
Javelin-throw	M. Nemeth (Hungary)	310 ft. 4 in. (world record)

| 20 kilometres walk | D. Bautista (Mexico) | 1 hr. 24 min. 40·6 sec. (Olympic record) |
| Decathlon | B. Jenner (U.S.A.) | 8,618 pts. (world record) |

Women

100 metres	A. Richter (W. Germany)	11·08 sec.
200 metres	B. Eckert (E. Germany)	22·37 sec. (Olympic record)
400 metres	I. Szewinska (Poland)	49·29 sec. (world record)
800 metres	T. Kazankina (U.S.S.R.)	1 min. 54·9 sec. (world record)
1,500 metres	T. Kazankina (U.S.S.R.)	4 min. 05·5 sec.
100 metres hurdles	J. Schaller (E. Germany)	12·77 sec.
4 × 110 metres relay	E. Germany (Oelsner, Stecher, Bodendorf, Eckert)	42·55 sec. (Olympic record)
4 × 400 metres relay	E. Germany (Maletzki, Rohde, Streidt, Brehmer)	3 min. 19·2 sec. (world record)
High jump	R. Ackermann (E. Germany)	6 ft. 4 in. (Olympic record)
Long jump	A. Voigt (E. Germany)	22 ft. 0¾ in.
Shot-put	I. Khristova (Bulgaria)	69 ft. 5¼ in. (Olympic record)
Discus-throw	E. Schlaak (E. Germany)	226 ft. 4 in. (Olympic record)
Javelin-throw	R. Fuchs (E. Germany)	216 ft. 4 in. (Olympic record)
Pentathlon	S. Siegl (E. Germany)	4,745 pts.

Badminton

Governing body: Badminton Association of England, 44/45 Palace Road, Bromley, Kent, BR1 3JU.

THOMAS CUP
(Men's International Championship)

		Venue
1961	Indonesia beat Thailand	Djakarta
1964	Indonesia beat Denmark	Tokyo
1967	Malaysia beat Indonesia	Djakarta
1970	Indonesia beat Malaysia	Kuala Lumpur
1973	Indonesia beat Denmark	Djakarta
1976	Indonesia beat Malaysia	Djakarta

ALL-ENGLAND CHAMPIONSHIPS
(Men's singles)

1960	Erland Kops	1970	R. Hartono
1961	Erland Kops	1971	R. Hartono
1962	Erland Kops	1972	R. Hartono
1963	Erland Kops	1973	R. Hartono
1964	K. A. Nielsen	1974	R. Hartono
1965	Erland Kops	1975	S. Pri
1966	T. Huang	1976	R. Hartono
1967	Erland Kops	1977	F. Delfs
1968	R. Hartono	1978	Lim Swie-king
1969	R. Hartono		

UBER CUP
(Women's International Championship)

		Venue
1960	U.S.A. beat Denmark	Philadelphia
1963	U.S.A. beat England	Wilmington
1966	Japan beat U.S.A.	Wellington
1969	Japan beat Indonesia	Tokyo
1972	Japan beat Indonesia	Tokyo
1975	Indonesia beat Japan	Djakarta

ALL-ENGLAND CHAMPIONSHIPS
(Women's singles)

1960	J. Devlin	1970	E. Takenaka
1961	Mrs. G. C. K. Hashman	1971	Mrs. E. Twedberg
1962	Mrs. G. C. K. Hashman	1972	Mrs. N. Nakayama
1963	Mrs. G. C. K. Hashman	1973	M. Beck
1964	Mrs. G. C. K. Hashman	1974	H. Yuki
1965	U. Smith	1975	H. Yuki
1966	Mrs. G. C. K. Hashman	1976	G. Gilks
1967	Mrs. G. C. K. Hashman	1977	H. Yuki
1968	Mrs. E. Twedberg	1978	Mrs. G. Gilks
1969	H. Yuki		

INTER-COUNTY CHAMPIONSHIP

1960	Kent	1970	Surrey
1961	Surrey	1971	Surrey
1962	Surrey	1972	Surrey
1963	Surrey	1973	Surrey
1964	Essex	1974	Surrey
1965	Surrey	1975	Surrey
1966	Surrey	1976	Lancashire
1967	Surrey	1977	Essex
1968	Surrey	1978	Hampshire
1969	Surrey		

Basket Ball

Governing body: English Basket Ball Association, Calomax House, Lupton Avenue, Leeds LS9 7EE.

OLYMPIC GAMES, 1976

Men	**Women**
U.S.A.	U.S.S.R.

NATIONAL CUP

1960	Central Y.M.C.A.	1970	Liverpool & Bootle Police
1961	London University	1971	Manchester University
1962	Central Y.M.C.A.	1972	Avenue (Chingford)
1963	Central Y.M.C.A.	1973	London Latvian SK
1964	Central Y.M.C.A.	1974	Sutton
1965	Aldershot Warriors	1975	Embassy All-Stars
1966	Oxford University	1976	Cinzano SCP
1967	Central Y.M.C.A.	1977	Cinzano SCP
1968	Oxford University	1978	Cinzano SCP
1969	Central Y.M.C.A.		

Boxing

Governing bodies: British Boxing Board of Control, Ramillies Buildings, Hill's Place, London, W.1; Amateur Boxing Association, 70 Brompton Road, London, SW3 1HA.

OLYMPIC GAMES WINNERS 1976

Heavyweight	T. Stevenson (Cuba)
Light Heavyweight	L. Spinks (U.S.A.)
Middleweight	M. Spinks (U.S.A.)
Light Middleweight	J. Rybicki (Poland)
Welterweight	J. Bachfeld (E. Germany)
Light Welterweight	R. Leonard (U.S.A.)
Lightweight	H. Davis (U.S.A.)
Featherweight	A. Herrera (Cuba)
Bantamweight	Y. Jo Gu (N. Korea)
Flyweight	L. Randolph (U.S.A.)
Light Flyweight	J. Hernandez (Cuba)

WORLD PROFESSIONAL CHAMPIONS

Weight	*as at 31/12/75*	*as at 31/12/76*	*as at 31/12/77*
Heavy	M. Ali (U.S.A.)	M. Ali (U.S.A.)	M. Ali (U.S.A.)
Light Heavy	J. Conteh (Great Britain)	J. Conteh (Great Britain)	M. Cuello (Argentina)
Middle	R. Valdez (Columbia)	C. Monzon (Argentine)	R. Valdez (Columbia)
Light Middle	E. Obed (Bahamas)	E. Dagge (W. Germany)	R. Mattioli (Australia)
Welter	J. Stracey (Great Britain)	C. Palomino (U.S.A.)	C. Palomino (U.S.A.)
Light Welter	S. Muansurim (Thailand)	S. Muansurim (Thailand)	S. Muangsurin (Thailand)
Light	G. Ishimatsu (Japan)	E. de Jesus (Puerto Rico)	E. de Jesus (Puerto Rico)
Junior Light	A. Escalera (Puerto Rico)	A. Escalera (Puerto Rico)	A. Escalera (Puerto Rico)
Feather	D. Kotey (Ghana)	D. Lopez (U.S.A.)	D. Lopez (U.S.A.)
Bantam	R. Martinez (Mexico)	C. Zarate (Mexico)	C. Zarate (Mexico)
Fly	L. Estaba (Venezuela)	M. Canto (Mexico)	M. Canto (Mexico)

WORLD HEAVYWEIGHT CHAMPIONS

1892	James J. Corbett (U.S.A.)	1949	Ezzard Charles (U.S.A.)
1897	Bob Fitzsimmons (Britain)	1951	Jersey Joe Walcott (U.S.A.)
1899	James J. Jefferies (U.S.A.)		
1905	Marvin Hart (U.S.A.)	1952	Rocky Marciano (U.S.A.
1906	Tommy Burns (Canada)	1956	Floyd Patterson (U.S.A.)
1908	Jack Johnson (U.S.A.)	1959	Ingemar Johansson (Sweden)
1915	Jess Willard (U.S.A.)		
1919	Jack Dempsey (U.S.A.)	1960	Floyd Patterson (U.S.A.
1926	Gene Tunney (U.S.A.)	1962	Sonny Liston (U.S.A.)
1930	Max Schmeling (Germany)	1964	Cassius Clay (U.S.A.)
1932	Jack Sharkey (U.S.A.)	1970	Joe Frazier (U.S.A.)
1933	Primo Carnera (Italy)	1973	George Foreman (U.S.A
1934	Max Baer (U.S.A.)	1974	Muhammad Ali (U.S.A
1935	James Braddock (U.S.A.)	1978	Leon Spinks (U.S.A.)
1937	Joe Louis (U.S.A.)		

BRITISH PROFESSIONAL CHAMPIONS
as at 31/12/77

Weight		*Weight*	
Heavy	——	Light Welter	C. Powers
Light Heavy	B. Johnson	Light	J. Watt
Middle	A. Minter	Feather	A. Richardson
Light Middle	J. Batten	Bantam	J. Owen
Welter	H. Rhiney	Fly	C. Magri

BRITISH AMATEUR CHAMPIONS 1977

Weight		*Weight*	
Heavy	J. Awome	Light	T. Marsh
Light Heavy	V. Smith	Feather	M. O'Brien
Middle	H. Graham	Bantam	J. W. Turner
Light Middle	E. Henderson	Fly	F. Nickels
Welter	E. Byrne	Light Fly	J. Dawson
Light Welter	D. Williams		

RECORDS

Longest reigning world champion: Joe Louis
(22nd June 1937—1st March 1949)

Longest reigning British heavyweight champion:
Henry Cooper (12th January 1959—13th June 1970)

Cricket

Governing bodies: The Cricket Council, Lord's Ground,
London, NW8 8QN; Women's Cricket Association, 70 Brompton
Road, London, SW3 1HA.

TEST MATCHES

England v. Australia 1876-77 to April 1977

The leading records of the series of matches are as follows:

Highest innings totals

3-7 dec.   By England at the Oval, 1938
9-6 dec.   By Australia at Lord's, 1930

Lowest innings totals

   By Australia at Birmingham, 1902
   By England at Sydney, 1886-87

Highest individual innings

364   L. Hutton for England at the Oval, 1938
334   D. G. Bradman for Australia at Leeds, 1930
311   R. B. Simpson for Australia at Manchester, 1964
307   R. M. Cowper for Australia at Melbourne, 1965–66
304   D. G. Bradman for Australia at Leeds, 1934
287   R. E. Foster for England at Sydney, 1903–4
270   D. G. Bradman for Australia at Melbourne, 1936–37

Most runs for a batsman in one rubber

England in England, 562 (av. 62·44) by D. C. S. Compton, 1948
England in Australia, 905 (av. 113·12) by W. R. Hammond, 1928–29
Australia in England, 974 (av. 139·14) by D. G. Bradman, 1930
Australia in Australia, 810 (av. 90·0) by D. G. Bradman, 1936–37

Batsmen scoring two centuries in a match

136 and 130   W. Bardsley for Australia at the Oval, 1909
176 and 127   H. Sutcliffe for England at Melbourne, 1924–25
119 n.o. and 177   W. R. Hammond for England at Adelaide. 1928–29
147 and 103 n.o.   D. C. S. Compton for England at Adelaide,
                                                           1946–47
122 and 124 n.o.   A. R. Morris for Australia at Adelaide, 1946–47

Bowlers taking nine or ten wickets in an innings

10 for 53   J. C. Laker for England at Manchester (2nd inns.), 1956
 9 for 37   J. C. Laker for England at Manchester (1st inns.), 1956
 9 for 121 A. A. Mailey for Australia at Melbourne, 1920–21

Bowlers taking fourteen or more wickets in a match

19 for 90   J. C. Laker for England at Manchester, 1956
16 for 137   R. A. L. Massie for Australia at Lord's, 1972
15 for 104   H. Verity for England at Lord's, 1934
15 for 124   W. Rhodes for England at Melbourne, 1903–4
14 for 90   F. R. Spofforth for Australia at the Oval, 1882
14 for 99   A. V. Bedser for England at Nottingham, 1953

Hat-tricks

For England   W. Bates at Melbourne, 1882–83
                J. Briggs at Sydney, 1891–92
                J. T. Hearne at Leeds, 1899

For Australia   F. R. Spofforth at Melbourne, 1878–79
                H. Trumble at Melbourne, 1901–2
                H. Trumble at Melbourne, 1903–4

Most wickets taken by a bowler in one rubber

England in England, 46 (av. 9·60) by J. C. Laker, 1956
England in Australia, 38 (av. 23·18) by M. W. Tate, 1924–25
Australia in England, 31 (av. 17·67) by D. K. Lillee, 1972
Australia in Australia, 36 (av. 26·27) by A. A. Mailey, 1920–21

Record wicket partnerships by England batsmen

1st	323	J. B. Hobbs and W. Rhodes at Melbourne, 1911–12
2nd	382	L. Hutton and M. Leyland at the Oval, 1938
3rd	262	W. R. Hammond and D. R. Jardine at Adelaide, 1928–29
4th	222	W. R. Hammond and E. Paynter at Lord's, 1938
5th	206	E. Paynter and D. C. S. Compton at Nottingham, 1938
6th	215	L. Hutton and J. Hardstaff, jr., at the Oval 1938
	215	G. Boycott and A. P. E. Knott at Nottingham 1977
7th	143	F. E. Woolley and J. Vine at Sydney, 1911–12
8th	124	E. Hendren and H. Larwood at Brisbane, 1928–29
9th	151	W. H. Scotton and W. W. Read at the Oval, 1884
10th	130	R. E. Foster and W. Rhodes at Sydney, 1903–4

Record wicket partnerships by Australian batsmen

1st	244	R. B. Simpson and W. M. Lawry at Adelaide, 1965–66
2nd	451	W. H. Ponsford and D. G. Bradman at the Oval, 1934
3rd	276	D. G. Bradman and A. L. Hassett at Brisbane, 1946–47
4th	388	W. H. Ponsford and D. G. Bradman at Leeds, 1934
5th	405	S. G. Barnes and D. G. Bradman at Sydney, 1946–47
6th	346	J. H. Fingleton and D. G. Bradman at Melbourne, 1936–37
7th	165	C. Hill and H. Trumble at Melbourne, 1897–98
8th	243	C. Hill and R. J. Hartigan at Adelaide, 1907–8
9th	154	S. E. Gregory and J. McC. Blackham at Sydney, 1894–95
10th	127	J. M. Taylor and A. A. Mailey at Sydney, 1924–25

TEST CRICKET, 1877–1978

Summarised results (as at February 3, 1978)

	W.	D.	L.		W.	D.	L.
ENGLAND v.				**WEST INDIES v.**			
Australia	74	68	88	England	22	28	21
South Africa	46	38	18	Australia	7	10	24
West Indies	21	28	22	New Zealand	5	7	2
New Zealand	23	24	0	India	17	16	4
India	25	21	7	Pakistan	6	5	4
Pakistan	9	20	1				
Rest of the World	1	0	4	**NEW ZEALAND v.**			
				England	0	24	23
AUSTRALIA v.				Australia	1	3	5
England	88	68	74	South Africa	2	6	9
South Africa	29	13	11	West Indies	2	7	5
West Indies	24	10	7	India	3	9	10
New Zealand	5	3	1	Pakistan	1	10	7
India	19	6	5				
Pakistan	6	4	2	**INDIA v.**			
				England	7	21	25
SOUTH AFRICA v.				Australia	5	6	19
England	18	38	46	West Indies	4	16	17
Australia	11	13	29	New Zealand	10	9	3
New Zealand	9	6	2	Pakistan	2	12	1

	W.	D.	L.			W.	D.	L.
PAKISTAN *v.*				PAKISTAN *v.*				
England	1	20	9	New Zealand	.	7	10	1
Australia	2	4	6	India .	.	1	12	2
West Indies	4	5	6					

Greatest number of appearances in Test Cricket (as at February 3, 1978)

ENGLAND

M. C. Cowdrey	118
A. P. E. Knott	94
T. G. Evans	91
W. R. Hammond	85
K. F. Barrington	82
J. H. Edrich	79
T. W. Graveney	79
L. Hutton	79
D. C. S. Compton	78
D. L. Underwood	77
G. Boycott	71
J. B. Statham	70
F. S. Trueman	67
R. Illingworth	66
P. B. H. May	66
F. E. Woolley	64
E. R. Dexter	62
T. E. Bailey	61
A. W. Greig	61
J. B. Hobbs	61
W. Rhodes	58
K. W. R. Fletcher	56
J. A. Snow	54
H. Sutcliffe	54
F. J. Titmus	53
D. L. Amiss	51
A. V. Bedser	51
E. Hendren	51
M. J. K. Smith	50
G. A. R. Lock	49
B. L. d'Oliveira	48
L. E. G. Ames	47
J. C. Laker	46
J. M. Parks	46
M. Leyland	41
H. Verity	40
R. E. S. Wyatt	40

AUSTRALIA

R. N. Harvey	79

AUSTRALIA (*contd.*)

I. M. Chappell	72
K. D. Walters	68
W. M. Lawry	67
I. R. Redpath	66
R. Benaud	63
R. R. Lindwall	61
G. D. McKenzie	60
S. E. Gregory	58
R. B. Simpson	57
K. R. Miller	55
W. A. Oldfield	54
D. G. Bradman	52
R. W. Marsh	52
G. S. Chappell	51
A. T. W. Grout	51
W. W. Armstrong	50
C. Hill	49
V. Trumper	48
C. C. McDonald	47
A. R. Morris	46
I. W. Johnson	45
A. K. Davidson	44
A. L. Hassett	43
K. R. Stackpole	43
P. J. Burge	42
M. A. Noble	42
N. C. O'Neill	42
W. Bardsley	41
W. A. Johnston	40

SOUTH AFRICA

J. H. B. Waite	50
A. D. Nourse, sen.	4
B. Mitchell	4
H. W. Taylor	4
T. L. Goddard	4
R. A. McLean	4
H. J. Tayfield	3
D. J. McGlew	3
A. D. Nourse, jun.	3

NEW ZEALAND				PAKISTAN			
J. R. Reid	.	.	58	Hanif Mohammad	.	.	55
B. E. Congdon	.	.	55	Mushtaq Mohammad	.	49
B. Sutcliffe	.	.	42	Intikhab Alam	.	.	47
G. T. Dowling	.	.	39	Asif Iqbal	.	.	45
G. M. Turner	.	.	39	Imtiaz Ahmed	.	.	41
M. G. Burgess	.	.	38	Saeed Ahmed	.	.	41
K. J. Wadsworth	.	.	33	Majid J. Khan	.	.	37
R. C. Motz	.	.	32	Wasim Bari	.	.	36
V. Pollard	.	.	32	Fazal Mahmood	.	.	34

WEST INDIES				INDIA			
G. Sobers	.	.	93	P. R. Umrigar	.	.	59
L. R. Gibbs	.	.	79	B. S. Bedi	.	.	58
R. B. Kanhai	.	.	79	C. G. Borde	.	.	55
C. H. Lloyd	.	.	63	V. L. Manjrekar	.	.	55
R. C. Fredericks	.	.	59	B. S. Chandrasekhar	.	50
W. W. Hall	.	.	58	E. A. S. Prasanna	.	.	47
F. M. Worrell	.	.	51	F. M. Engineer	.	.	46
D. L. Murray	.	.	49	Mansur Ali Khan	.	.	46
E. D. Weekes	.	.	48	V. Mankad	.	.	44
B. F. Butcher	.	.	44	P. Roy	.	.	43
C. C. Hunte	.	.	44	G. R. Viswanth	.	.	43
C. L. Walcott	.	.	44	R. G. Nadkarni	.	.	41

COUNTY CHAMPIONS

Since 1920

1920	Middlesex	1947	Middlesex
1921	Middlesex	1948	Glamorgan
1922	Yorkshire	1949	Middlesex & Yorks, tie
1923	Yorkshire	1950	Lancs & Surrey, tie
1924	Yorkshire	1951	Warwickshire
1925	Yorkshire	1952	Surrey
1926	Lancashire	1953	Surrey
1927	Lancashire	1954	Surrey
1928	Lancashire	1955	Surrey
1929	Nottinghamshire	1956	Surrey
1930	Lancashire	1957	Surrey
1931	Yorkshire	1958	Surrey
1932	Yorkshire	1959	Yorkshire
1933	Yorkshire	1960	Yorkshire
1934	Lancashire	1961	Hampshire
1935	Yorkshire	1962	Yorkshire
1936	Derbyshire	1963	Yorkshire
1937	Yorkshire	1964	Worcestershire
1938	Yorkshire	1965	Worcestershire
1939	Yorkshire	1966	Yorkshire
1946	Yorkshire	1967	Yorkshire

1968	Yorkshire	1973	Hampshire
1969	Glamorgan	1974	Worcestershire
1970	Kent	1975	Leicestershire
1971	Surrey	1976	Middlesex
1972	Warwickshire	1977	Middlesex & Kent, tie

Since 1864 the title has been won outright by Yorkshire 31 times, Surrey 18, Nottinghamshire 12, Lancashire 8, Middlesex 6, Gloucestershire 3, Warwickshire 3, Worcestershire 3, Glamorgan 2, Hampshire 2, Derbyshire 1, Leicestershire 1. Seven times it has been shared by Nottinghamshire 5, Lancashire 4, Surrey 2, Yorkshire 2, Gloucestershire 1, Middlesex 1.

RECORDS

Highest scores in first-class cricket: 499, Hanif Mohammed, for Karachi, 1958–59; 452 (not out), D. G. Bradman, for N.S.W., 1929–30; 443 (not out), B. B. Nimbalkar, for Maharashtra, 1948–49. Highest score in England 424, A. C. MacLaren, for Lancashire, *v.* Somerset at Taunton in 1895

Highest scores in Test cricket: 365 (not out), by G. Sobers for W. Indies, 1958. 364, by L. Hutton for England, 1938

Most runs in first-class cricket: 61,237, between 1905 and 1934, by J. B. Hobbs

Highest team innings: Australia, Victoria 1,107 *v.* N.S.W., 1926–27; England, England 903 (for 7 dec.) *v.* Australia, 1938

Most runs in a day: Australians *v.* Essex, 1948, 721

Highest batting partnership: 577, by V. S. Hazare and Gu' Mohammed, in India (1946–47)

Most runs in a season: 3,816, by Denis Compton (1947)

Most wickets in a season: 304, by A. P. Freeman (1928)

Highest number of wickets in a match: 19, by J. C. Laker, fo' England *v.* Australia at Old Trafford (1956)

Most wickets during career: 4,187, by W. Rhodes, between 189' and 1930

The only tie in Test Match history: West Indies 453 and 28 Australia 505 and 232, Brisbane, December 1960. Australia starte' the last possible over needing 6 runs with 3 wickets left.

Biggest win: Pakistan Western Railways beat Dera Ismail Khan b' an innings and 851 runs, 1964–65

Most centuries in one season: D. C. S. Compton, 18 (1947)

Fastest scoring: P. G. H. Fender for Surrey *v.* Northamptonshire ' 1920, 100 runs in 35 min.

Highest batting average in England: D. G. Bradman, 115·' (1938). By an Englishman: G. Boycott, 100·12 (1971). In firs' class games (1927–49) Bradman's figures were 338 inns., 117 ce' turies, 43 not outs, 28,067 runs, 95·14 average

Cross-Country Running

Governing bodies: English Cross-Country Union, 121 Derwent Close, Cambridge; Women's Cross-Country & Race Walking Association, 10 Anderton Close, Bury, Lancs.

ENGLISH CHAMPIONSHIP

Men

	Individual	*Team*
1971	D. Bedford (Shaftesbury H.)	Shettleston Harriers
1972	M. Thomas (Thames Valley)	Tipton Harriers
1973	D. Bedford (Shaftesbury H.)	Gateshead A.C.
1974	D. Black (Small Heath)	Derby & County
1975	T. Simmons (Luton Utd.)	Gateshead Harriers
1976	B. Ford (Aldershot/Farnham)	Gateshead Harriers
1977	B. Foster (Gateshead)	Gateshead Harriers
1978	B. Ford (Aldershot/Farnham)	Tipton Harriers

Women

	Individual	*Team*
1971	Mrs. R. Ridley (Essex L.A.C.)	Coventry Godiva
1972	Mrs. R. Ridley (Essex L.A.C.)	Cambridge Harriers
1973	Mrs J. Smith (Barnet and District A.C.)	Cambridge Harriers
1974	Mrs. R. Ridley (Essex L.A.C.)	Barnet & District A.C.
1975	Mrs D. Nagle (Guinness A.C.)	Cambridge Harriers
1976	A. Ford (Feltham A.C.)	London Olympiades
1977	G. Penny (Cambridge Harriers)	Sale A.C.
1978	M. Stewart (Birchfield)	Sale A.C.

INTERNATIONAL CHAMPIONSHIP

Men

	Individual	*Team*	*Venue*
1971	D. Bedford (England)	England	San Sebastian
1972	G. Roelants (Belgium)	England	Cambridge
1973	P. Paivarinta (Finland)	Belgium	Waregem
1974	E. de Berk (Belgium)	Belgium	Monza
1975	I. Stewart (Scotland)	New Zealand	Rabat
1976	C. Lopes (Portugal)	England	Chepstow
1977	L. Schots (Belgium)	Belgium	Dusseldorf
1978	J. Tracey (Ireland)	France	Glasgow

Women

1971	Mrs D. Brown (U.S.A.)	England	San Sebastian
1972	J. Smith (England)	England	Cambridge
1973	P. Pigni Cacchi (Italy)	England	Waregem
1974	P. Pigni Cacchi (Italy)	England	Monza
1975	J. Brown (U.S.A.)	U.S.A.	Rabat
1976	C. Valero (Spain)	U.S.S.R.	Chepstow
1977	C. Valero (Spain)	U.S.S.R.	Dusseldorf
1978	G. Wairtz (Norway)	Rumania	Glasgow

Cycling

Governing body: British Cycling Federation, 70 Brompton Rd, London, SW3 1EN.

1976 OLYMPIC GAMES WINNERS

1,000 m. sprint	A. Tkac (Czechoslovakia)
1,000 m. T.T.	K. J. Grunke (E. Germany)
4,000 m. pursuit	G. Braun (W. Germany)
4,000 m. team pursuit	West Germany
Individual road race	B. Johanssen (Sweden)
Road team T.T.	U.S.S.R.

1975–76 WORLD CHAMPIONS

Men

Professional road race	F. Moser (Italy)
Amateur road race	C. Corti (Italy)
Professional sprint	K. Nakano (Japan)
Amateur sprint	H. Geschke (E. Germany)
Professional 5,000 m. pursuit	G. Braun (W. Germany)
Amateur 4,000 m. pursuit	N. Durpisch (E. Germany)
Professional 100 km. motor-paced	C. Stam (Holland)
Amateur hour paced	G. Minneboo (Holland)
Amateur tandem sprint	L. Vackar/M. Vymazel (Czechoslovakia)
Amateur kilometre T.T.	L. Thomas (E. Germany)
Amateur 100 km. team T.T.	Russia
Amateur 4,000 m. team pursuit	E. Germany

Women (all amateur)

Road race	J. Bost (France)
Sprint	G. Tsareva (Russia)
Pursuit	V. Kuznetsova (Russia)

RECORDS

Men's professional motor-paced 1 hour record: 78 km. 809 m.,
W. Avogardi in Italy, 1975
Men's professional unpaced standing start 1 hour record: 49 km.
431·957 m., E. Merckx in Mexico, 1972
Men's amateur unpaced flying start 1 kilometre: 1 min. 1·1 sec.,
L. Borghetti in Mexico, 1967

Equestrian

Governing bodies: British Horse Society and British Show
Jumping Association, National Equestrian Centre, Stoneleigh,
Kenilworth, Warwickshire, CV8 2LR.

SHOW JUMPING

Olympic Games, 1976: Individual—A. Schockemohle (W. Germany)
Team—France (H Parot, M. Rozier, M. Roche, M. Roguet)
World Championships, 1974: Men—Hartwig Steenken (W. Germany)
Ladies—Janou Tissot (France)
European Championships, 1977: J. Heins (Holland)
President's Cup, 1977: Great Britain
B.S.J.A. National Championship, 1977: Caroline Bradley on *Bernar*
Ladies' National Championship, 1977: Amanda Rooney on *S. M. S.
Barbarella*

HORSE TRIALS

Olympic Games, 1976: Individual—T. Coffin (U.S.A.)
Team—U.S.A. (T. Coffin, M. Plumb, B. Davidson, M. Tauskey)
World Championships, 1974: Individual—Bruce Davidson (U.S.A.)
Team—U.S.A.
European Championships, 1977: Individual—Lucinda Prior-Palmer
(Great Britain) Team—G.B.
Badminton Horse Trials, 1978: Mrs. J. Holderness-Roddam on
Warrior

DRESSAGE

Olympic Games, 1976: Individual—C. Stuckelberger (Switzerland)
Team—West Germany (H. Boldt, R. Klimke, G. Grille)
Advanced Dressage Championship 1977: Jennie Loristol-Clarke on
Dutch Courage
Dressage Horse of the Year, 1977: *Dutch Courage*

Fencing

Governing body: Amateur Fencing Association, The de Beaumont Centre, 83 Perham Road, London, W14 9SY.

1976 OLYMPIC CHAMPIONS, MEN

Foil	F. dal Zoto (Italy)
Team Foil	West Germany
Epee	A. Pusch (W. Germany)
Team Epee	Sweden
Sabre	V. Krovopovskov (U.S.S.R.)
Team Sabre	U.S.S.R.

WOMEN

Foil	I. Schwarzenberger (Hungary)
Team Foil	U.S.S.R.

1977 ENGLISH CHAMPIONS

Men's foil	N. Bell (Thames)
Men's foil team	Salle Paul
Ladies' foil	Miss H. Cawthorne (Allen F.C.)
Ladies' foil team	Polytechnic
Men's epee	E. Bourne (Salle Boston)
Men's epee team	Salle Boston
Men's sabre	J. Philbin (Polytechnic)
Men's sabre team	Polytechnic

Gliding

Governing body: British Gliding Association, Kimberley House, Vaughan Way, Leicester.

World Records—Solo

Distance	1,460·8 km.	H. W. Grosse (W. Germany)	1972
Height	12,894 m.	P. Bikle (U.S.A.)	1961
Speed	(100 km. triangle) 165·35 km/h.	K. Briegleb (U.S.A.)	1974

Golf

Governing bodies: Royal and Ancient Golf Club, St Andrews, Fife, KY16 9JD; Ladies' Golf Union, 11 The Links, St Andrews, Fife.

OPEN CHAMPIONS
Since 1946

1946	Sam Snead (U.S.A.)	1959	G. Player (South Africa)
1947	Fred Daly (Balmoral)	1960	Kel Nagle (Australia)
1948	Henry Cotton (Royal Mid-Surrey)	1961	A. Palmer (U.S.A.)
		1962	A. Palmer (U.S.A.)
1949	Bobby Locke (South Africa)	1963	Bob Charles (N.Z.)
		1964	A. Lema (U.S.A.)
1950	Bobby Locke (South Africa)	1965	P. Thomson (Australia)
		1966	J. Nicklaus (U.S.A.)
1951	Max Faulkner (un-attached)	1967	R. de Vicenzo (Argentine)
		1968	G. Player (South Africa)
1952	Bobby Locke (South Africa)	1969	A. Jacklin (Potters Bar)
		1970	J. Nicklaus (U.S.A.)
1953	Ben Hogan (U.S.A.)	1971	L. Trevino (U.S.A.)
1954	P. Thomson (Australia)	1972	L. Trevino (U.S.A.)
1955	P. Thomson (Australia)	1973	T. Weiskopf (U.S.A.)
1956	P. Thomson (Australia)	1974	G. Player (South Africa)
1957	Bobby Locke (South Africa)	1975	T. Watson (U.S.A.)
		1976	J. Miller (U.S.A.)
1958	P. Thomson (Australia)	1977	T. Watson (U.S.A.)

RYDER CUP

1953	U.S.A.	1963	U.S.A.	1973	U.S.A.
1955	U.S.A.	1965	U.S.A.	1975	U.S.A.
1957	Great Britain	1967	U.S.A.	1977	U.S.A.
1959	U.S.A.	1969	Tie		
1961	U.S.A.	1971	U.S.A.		

WALKER CUP

1953	U.S.A.	1963	U.S.A.	1973	U.S.A.
1955	U.S.A.	1965	Tie.	1975	U.S.A.
1957	U.S.A.	1967	U.S.A.	1977	U.S.A.
1959	U.S.A.	1969	U.S.A.		
1961	U.S.A.	1971	Great Britain		

CURTIS CUP

1954	U.S.A.	1962	U.S.A.	1970	U.S.A.
1956	Great Britain	1964	U.S.A.	1972	U.S.A.
1958	Great Britain	1966	U.S.A.	1974	U.S.A.
1960	U.S.A.	1968	U.S.A.	1976	U.S.A.

WORLD CUP

1960	U.S.A.	1966	U.S.A.	1972	Taiwan
1961	U.S.A.	1967	U.S.A	1973	U.S.A.
1962	U.S.A.	1968	Canada	1974	U.S.A.
1963	U.S.A.	1969	U.S.A.	1975	U.S.A.
1964	U.S.A.	1970	Australia	1976	Spain
1965	South Africa	1971	U.S.A.	1977	Spain

LADIES' BRITISH OPEN CHAMPIONSHIPS 1977

Amateur   **Professional**
Mrs A. Uzielli   Miss V. Saunders

LADIES' CLOSE AMATEUR CHAMPIONSHIPS 1977

England: Miss V. Marvin
Ireland: Miss M. McKenna
Scotland: Miss C. Lugton
Wales: Miss T. Perkins

Hockey

Governing bodies: Hockey Association of England, 70 Brompton Road, London SW3 1HB; All-England Women's Hockey Association, 160 Great Portland Street, London, W1N 5TB.

OLYMPIC WINNERS

1920	England	1956	India
1924	No competitition	1960	Pakistan
1928	India	1964	India
1932	India	1968	Pakistan
1936	India	1972	W. Germany
1948	India	1976	New Zealand
1952	India		

COUNTY CHAMPIONSHIP

	MEN		WOMEN
1971	Staffordshire	1971	Herts. drew with Lancs.
1972	Wiltshire	1972	Essex
1973	Surrey	1973	Lancashire
1974	Hertfordshire	1974	Lancashire
1975	Kent	1975	Leics. drew with Surrey
1976	Hertfordshire	1976	Lancashire
1977	Middlesex	1977	Lancashire
1978	Lancashire	1978	Hertfordshire

Ice Hockey

Governing body: International Ice Hockey Federation, Prinz Eugenstrasse 12, A 1040 Wien, Austria.

WORLD CHAMPIONSHIPS

		Venue
1970	U.S.S.R.	Stockholm
1971	U.S.S.R.	Geneva
1972	Czechoslovakia	Prague
1973	U.S.S.R.	Moscow
1974	U.S.S.R.	Helsinki
1975	U.S.S.R.	Dusseldorf
1976	Czechoslovakia	Katowice
1977	Czechoslovakia	Vienna
1978	U.S.S.R.	Prague

1976 OLYMPIC WINNERS (INNSBRUCK)
U.S.S.R.

Ice Skating

Governing body: National Skating Association of Great Britain, Charterhouse, London, EC1M 6AT.

WORLD RECORDS (*as at 31/12/77*)

Men

500 metres	E. Kulikov (U.S.S.R.)	37·00 sec.	1975
1,000 metres	E. Kulikov (U.S.S.R.)	1 min. 15·33 sec.	1977
1,500 metres	J. Storholt (Norway)	1 min. 51·18 sec.	1977
3,000 metres	A. Schenk (Netherlands)	4 min. 8·30 sec.	1972
5,000 metres	K. Stenshjemmet (Norway)	6 min. 56·90 sec.	1977
10,000 metres	V. Leskin (U.S.S.R.)	14 min. 34·33 sec.	1977

Ladies

500 metres	S. Young (U.S.A.)	40·68 sec.	1976
1,000 metres	T. Averina (U.S.S.R.)	1 min. 23·46 sec.	1975
1,500 metres	T. Averina (U.S.S.R.)	2 min. 9·90 sec.	1975
3,000 metres	G. Stepanskaya (U.S.S.R.)	4 min. 31·00 sec.	1976

1976 OLYMPIC WINNERS (INNSBRUCK)

Figure Skating

Men	J. Curry (Great Britain)
Women	D. Hamill (U.S.A.)
Pairs	I. Rodnina and A. Zaitsev (U.S.S.R.)
Ice Dancing	L. Pakhomova and A. Gorshkov (U.S.S.R.)

Speed Events

Men's 500 metres	E. Kulikov (U.S.S.R.)
Men's 1,000 metres	P. Mueller (U.S.A.)
Men's 1,500 metres	J. E. Storholt (Norway)
Men's 5,000 metres	S. Stenson (Norway)
Men's 10,000 metres	S. Stenson (Norway)
Ladies' 500 metres	S. Young (U.S.A.)
Ladies' 1,000 metres	T. Averina (U.S.S.R.)
Ladies' 1,500 metres	G. Stepanskaya (U.S.S.R.)
Ladies' 3,000 metres	T. Averina (U.S.S.R.)

Lacrosse

Governing bodies: English Lacrosse Union, 64 Broad Walk, Hockley, Essex, SS5 5DF; All-England Ladies' Lacrosse Association, 70 Brompton Road, London S.W.3.

IROQUOIS CUP

1960	Heaton Mersey	1971	S. Manchester & Wythenshawe
1961	Boardman and Eccles		
1962	Old Hulmeians	1972	S. Manchester & Wythenshawe
1963	Mellor		
1964	Old Hulmeians	1973	S. Manchester & Wythenshawe
1965	Mellor		
1966	S. Manchester & Wythenshawe	1974	Urmston
		1975	S. Manchester & Wythenshawe
1967	Mellor		
1968	Old Hulmeians	1976	Hampstead
1969	Mellor	1977	Sheffield University
1970	Lee		

Lawn Tennis

Governing body: Lawn Tennis Association, Barons Court, London, W14 9EG.

WIMBLEDON CHAMPIONS

Since 1920

Men's Singles

1920	W. T. Tilden	1926	J. Borotra
1921	W. T. Tilden	1927	H. Cochet
1922	G. L. Patterson	1928	R. Lacoste
1923	W. M. Johnston	1929	H. Cochet
1924	J. Borotra	1930	W. T. Tilden
1925	R. Lacoste	1931	S. B. Wood

1932	H. E. Vines	1958	A. J. Cooper
1933	J. H. Crawford	1959	A. Olmedo
1934	F. J. Perry	1960	N. Fraser
1935	F. J. Perry	1961	R. Laver
1936	F. J. Perry	1962	R. Laver
1937	J. D. Budge	1963	E. McKinley
1938	J. D. Budge	1964	R. Emerson
1939	R. L. Riggs	1965	R. Emerson
1946	Y. Petra	1966	M. Santana
1947	J. A. Kramer	1967	J. Newcombe
1948	R. Falkenburg	1968	R. Laver
1949	F. R. Schroeder	1969	R. Laver
1950	J. E. Patty	1970	J. Newcombe
1951	R. Savitt	1971	J. Newcombe
1952	F. A. Sedgman	1972	S. Smith
1953	E. V. Seixas	1973	J. Kodes
1954	J. Drobny	1974	J. Connors
1955	M. A. Trabert	1975	A. Ashe
1956	L. A. Hoad	1976	B. Borg
1957	L. A. Hoad	1977	B. Borg

Women's Singles

1920	Mlle S. Lenglen	1952	Miss M. Connolly
1921	Mlle S. Lenglen	1953	Miss M. Connolly
1922	Mlle S. Lenglen	1954	Miss M. Connolly
1923	Mlle S. Lenglen	1955	Miss A. Brough
1924	Miss K. McKane	1956	Miss S. Fry
1925	Mlle S. Lenglen	1957	Miss A. Gibson
1926	Mrs. L. Godfree	1958	Miss A. Gibson
1927	Miss H. Wills	1959	Miss M. Bueno
1928	Miss H. Wills	1960	Miss M. Bueno
1929	Miss H. Wills	1961	Miss A. Mortimer
1930	Mrs. F. Moody	1962	Miss K. Susman
1931	Frl C. Aussem	1963	Miss M. Smith
1932	Mrs. F. Moody	1964	Miss M. Bueno
1933	Mrs. F. Moody	1965	Miss M. Smith
1934	Miss D. Round	1966	Mrs. L. W. King
1935	Mrs F. Moody	1967	Mrs. L. W. King
1936	Miss H. Jacobs	1968	Mrs. L. W. King
1937	Miss D. Round	1969	Mrs. P. F. Jones
1938	Mrs. F. Moody	1970	Mrs. B. M. Court
1939	Miss A. Marble	1971	Miss E. Goolagong
1946	Miss P. Betz	1972	Mrs. L. W. King
1947	Miss M. Osborne	1973	Mrs. L. W. King
1948	Miss A. Brough	1974	Miss C. Evert
1949	Miss A. Brough	1975	Mrs. L. W. King
1950	Miss A. Brough	1976	Miss C. Evert
1951	Miss D. Hart	1977	Miss V. Wade

DAVIS CUP

1950	Australia	1964	Australia
1951	Australia	1965	Australia
1952	Australia	1966	Australia
1953	Australia	1967	Australia
1954	U.S.A.	1968	U.S.A.
1955	Australia	1969	U.S.A.
1956	Australia	1970	U.S.A.
1957	Australia	1971	U.S.A.
1958	U.S.A.	1972	U.S.A.
1959	Australia	1973	Australia
1960	Australia	1974	South Africa
1961	Australia	1975	Sweden
1962	Australia	1976	Italy
1963	U.S.A.	1977	Australia

WIGHTMAN CUP

1950	U.S.A.	1964	U.S.A.
1951	U.S.A.	1965	U.S.A.
1952	U.S.A.	1966	U.S.A.
1953	U.S.A.	1967	U.S.A.
1954	U.S.A.	1968	Great Britain
1955	U.S.A.	1969	U.S.A.
1956	U.S.A.	1970	U.S.A.
1957	U.S.A.	1971	U.S.A.
1958	Great Britain	1972	U.S.A.
1959	U.S.A.	1973	U.S.A.
1960	Great Britain	1974	Great Britain
1961	U.S.A.	1975	Great Britain
1962	U.S.A.	1976	U.S.A.
1963	U.S.A.	1977	U.S.A.

RECORDS

Longest match: M. Cox and R. Wilson (G.B.) beat C. Pasarell and R. Holmberg (U.S.A.) at Salisbury, Maryland, in the American Indoor Championships, 1968, after 6 hr. 23 min. playing time: 26–24, 17–19, 30–28

Largest number of games in Davis Cup singles: 86 in 1970; A. Ashe (U.S.A.) beat C. Kuhnke (W. Germany) 6–8, 10–12, 9–7, 13–11, 6–4

Largest number of games in a Wimbledon singles: 112, when R. Gonzales (U.S.A.) beat C. Pasarell (U.S.A.), 22–24, 1–6, 16–14, 6–3, 11–9 in 1969

Longest Wimbledon match: 5¼ hours, when Gonzales beat Pasarell

Greatest number of Wimbledon wins: William C. Renshaw (G.B.), 7 singles titles (1881-2-3-4-5-6-9) and 7 doubles (1880-1-4-5-6-8-9). Mrs. Helen Wills-Moody (U.S.A.) won the women's singles eight times

Greatest number of wins: Miss Elizabeth Ryan (U.S.A.), 19 titles (1914–34); Mrs. L. W. King (U.S.A.), 19 titles (1961–75)

Motor Cycling

Governing body: Auto-Cycle Union, 31 Belgrave Square, London, SW1X 8QQ.

WORLD CHAMPIONS

	1975	*1976*	*1977*
	Road Racing		
50 c.c.	A. Nieto (Kreidler)	A. Nieto (Bultaco)	A. Nieto (Bultaco)
125 c.c.	P. Pilleri (Morbidelli)	P. Bianchi (Morbidelli)	P. Bianchi (Morbidelli)
250 c.c.	W. Villa (Harley Davidson)	W. Villa (Harley Davidson)	M. Lega (Morbidelli)
350 c.c.	J. Cecotto (Yamaha)	W. Villa (Harley Davidson)	T. Katayama (Yamaha)
500 c.c.	G. Agostini (Yamaha)	B. Sheene (Suzuki)	B. Sheene (Suzuki)
Sidecar	R. Steinhausen (Konig)	R. Steinhausen (Konig)	G. O'Dell (Yamaha)
	Moto Cross		
125 c.c.	——	G. Rahier (Suzuki)	G. Rahier (Suzuki)
250 c.c.	H. Everts (Puch)	H. Mikkola (Husqvarna)	G. Moisseev (KTM)
500 c.c.	R. de Coster (Suzuki)	R. de Coster (Suzuki)	H. Mikkola (Yamaha)
	Speedway		
	O. Olsen (Jawa)	P. Collins (Weslake)	I. Mauger (Jawa)
	Trials		
	M. Lampkin (Bultaco)	Y. Vesterinen (Bultaco)	Y. Vesterinen (Bultaco)

BRITISH CHAMPIONS
Road Racing

	1975	*1976*	*1977*
Solo	R. Marshall (Yamaha)	S. Parrish (Suzuki & Yamaha)	R. Marshall (Yahama)
Three-wheeler	M. Hobson (Yamaha)	R. Greasley (Yamaha)	B. Hodgkins (Yamaha)

	1975	*1976*	*1977*

Moto Cross

Solo	J. V. Allan (Bultaco)	G. Noyce (Maico)	G. Noyce (Maico)
Three-Wheeler	N. Thompson (Heanes Norton)	T. Good (Yamaha Wasp)	J. Elliot (Norton Wasp)

Speedway

	J. Louis (Weslake)	M. Simmons (Weslake)	M. Lee (Weslake)

Trials

	M. Rathmell (Montesa)	M. Rathmell (Montesa)	R. Shepherd (Honda)

RECORD

Winner of most World Championships: Giacomo Agostini (15, in 1966–75)

Motor Racing

Governing body: R.A.C. (Motor Sport Division), 31 Belgrave Square, London, SW1 8QH.

World Driving Championship 1977	N. Lauda (Austria), *Ferrari*
British Grand Prix 1977	J. Hunt (G.B.), *McLaren*
Le Mans 24-hrs. 1977	J. Ickx, J. Barth, P. Gregg, H. Haywood, *Porsche*
R.A.C. Rally 1977	B. Waldegard and H. Thorszelius, *Ford RS Rally*
Monte Carlo Rally 1977	S. Munari and S. Maiga (Italy), *Lancia Stratos*

RECORDS

Winner of most World Championships: Juan Manuel Fangio (five, in 1951, 1954, 1955, 1956, 1957)

Winner of most Grand Prix: Jackie Stewart (26)

Winner of most Grand Prix in one year: Jim Clarke (seven, in 1963)

Netball

Governing body: All-England Netball Association, 70 Brompton Road, London, SW3 1HD.

WORLD CHAMPIONS

1963	Australia beat New Zealand
1967	New Zealand beat Australia
1971	Australia beat New Zealand
1975	Australia beat England

INTER-COUNTY CHAMPIONSHIP

1970	Kent	1973	Kent	1976	Essex
1971	Kent	1974	Kent	1977	Essex
1972	Kent	1975	Essex	1978	Essex

NATIONAL CLUBS TOURNAMENT

1972	Aquila	1974	Aquila	1976	Downs
1973	Sudbury	1975	Aquila	1977	Aquila

Rackets

Governing body: Tennis and Rackets Association, 7 Orchard Gate, Esher, Surrey KT10 8HY.

BRITISH ISLES OPEN CHAMPIONSHIP

1929	J. Simpson	1960	J. Dear
1932	Lord Aberdare	1962	G. Atkins
1933	I. Akers-Douglas	1968	J. Leonard
1934	A. Cooper	1970	C. J. Swallow
1936	D. Milford	1971	M. G. M. Smith
1946	J. Dear	1972	H. R. Angus
1954	G. Atkins	1977	J. A. R. Prenn
1959	J. Thompson		

WORLD CHAMPIONSHIP

1903	J. Jamsetjhi (India)	1947	J. Dear (Queen's)
1911	C. Williams (Harrow)	1954	G. Atkins (Queen's)
1914	J. Soutar (U.S.A.)	1972	W. Surtees (U.S.A.)
1928	C. Williams (U.S.A.)	1973	H. R. Angus (Queen's)
1937	D. Milford	1974	W. Surtees (U.S.A.)
	(Marlborough)		

Rowing

Governing body: Amateur Rowing Association, 6 Lower Mall, London, W6 9DJ.

THE GRAND CHALLENGE CUP

Between 1839 and 1929 the Cup was won 21 times by Leander, 12 times by London B.C., 7 times by Oxford University B.C., 4 times by Magdalen College, Oxford, 3 times by Thames R.C. and once each by Sydney R.C. and Harvard Athletic Association B.C. The winners since 1930 have been:

1930	London R.C.
1931	London R.C.
1932	Leander Club
1933	London R.C.
1934	Leander Club
1935	Pembroke College, Cambridge
1936	F.C. Zurich R.C., Switzerland
1937	R. Wiking, Germany
1938	London R.C.
1939	Harvard University, U.S.A.
1946	Leander Club
1947	Jesus College, Cambridge
1948	Thames R.C.
1949	Leander Club
1950	Harvard University, U.S.A.
1951	Lady Margaret B.C., Cambridge
1952	Leander Club
1953	Leander Club
1954	Club Krylia Sovetov, U.S.S.R.
1955	University of Pennsylvania, U.S.A.
1956	Centre Sportif des Forces de l'Armée, France
1957	Cornell University, U.S.A.
1958	Trud Club, Leningrad, U.S.S.R.
1959	Harvard University, U.S.A.
1960	Molesey B.C.
1961	U.S.S.R. Navy
1962	U.S.S.R. Navy
1963	London University
1964	U.S.S.R.
1965	Ratzeburger, W. Germany
1966	T.S.C. Berlin, E. Germany
1967	S. C. Wissenschaft DH f K, Leipzig
1968	London University B.C.
1969	S. C. Einheit, Dresden
1970	A. S. K. Vorwärts, Rostock
1971	Tideway Scullers School
1972	W.M.F. Moscow, U.S.S.R.
1973	Trud Kolomna, U.S.S.R.
1974	Trud Kolomna, U.S.S.R.
1975	Leander Club and Thames Tradesmen's R.C.
1976	Thames Tradesmen's R.C.
1977	University of Washington R.C., U.S.A.

DIAMOND SCULLS

First rowed 1844. Winners since 1950:

1950	A. D. Rowe (Leander)
1951	T. A. Fox (Pembroke)
1952	M. T. Wood (Australia)
1953	T. A. Fox (London)
1954	P. Vlasic (Jugoslavia)
1955	T. Kocerka (Poland)
1956	T. Kocerka (Poland)
1957	S. A. Mackenzie (Australia)
1958	S. A. Mackenzie (Australia)
1959	S. A. Mackenzie (Australia)
1960	S. A. Mackenzie (Australia)
1961	S. A. Mackenzie (Australia)
1962	S. A. Mackenzie (Australia)
1963	G. Kottman (Switzerland)
1964	S. Cromwell (U.S.A.)
1965	D. M. Spero (U.S.A.)
1966	A. Hill (Germany)
1967	M. Studach (Switzerland)
1968	H. A. Wardell-Yerburgh (Eton Vikings)

1969	H.-J. Böhmer (D.D.R.)	1973	S. Drea (Eire)
1970	J. Meissner (W. Germany)	1974	S. Drea (Eire)
1971	A. Demiddi (Argentina)	1975	S. Drea (Eire)
1972	A. Timoschinin	1976	E. O. Hale (Australia)
	(U.S.S.R.)	1977	T. J. Crooks (Leander)

UNIVERSITY BOAT RACE

Rowed on the river Thames between Putney and Mortlake: 4 miles, 374 yards.

1829	Oxford	1883	Oxford
1836	Cambridge	1884	Cambridge
1839	Cambridge	1885	Oxford
1840	Cambridge	1886	Cambridge
1841	Cambridge	1887	Cambridge
1842	Oxford	1888	Cambridge
1845	Cambridge	1889	Cambridge
1846	Cambridge	1890	Oxford
1849	Cambridge	1891	Oxford
1849	Oxford	1892	Oxford
1852	Oxford	1893	Oxford
1854	Oxford	1894	Oxford
1856	Cambridge	1895	Oxford
1857	Oxford	1896	Oxford
1858	Cambridge	1897	Oxford
1859	Oxford	1898	Oxford
1860	Cambridge	1899	Cambridge
1861	Oxford	1900	Cambridge
1862	Oxford	1901	Oxford
1863	Oxford	1902	Cambridge
1864	Oxford	1903	Cambridge
1865	Oxford	1904	Cambridge
1866	Oxford	1905	Oxford
1867	Oxford	1906	Cambridge
1868	Oxford	1907	Cambridge
1869	Oxford	1908	Cambridge
1870	Cambridge	1909	Oxford
1871	Cambridge	1910	Oxford
1872	Cambridge	1911	Oxford
1873	Cambridge	1912	Oxford
1874	Cambridge	1913	Oxford
1875	Oxford	1914	Cambridge
1876	Cambridge	1920	Cambridge
1877	Dead heat	1921	Cambridge
1878	Oxford	1922	Cambridge
1879	Cambridge	1923	Oxford
1880	Oxford	1924	Cambridge
1881	Oxford	1925	Cambridge
1882	Oxford	1926	Cambridge

1927	Cambridge	1956	Cambridge
1928	Cambridge	1957	Cambridge
1929	Cambridge	1958	Cambridge
1930	Cambridge	1959	Oxford
1931	Cambridge	1960	Oxford
1932	Cambridge	1961	Cambridge
1933	Cambridge	1962	Cambridge
1934	Cambridge	1963	Oxford
1935	Cambridge	1964	Cambridge
1936	Cambridge	1965	Oxford
1937	Oxford	1966	Oxford
1938	Oxford	1967	Oxford
1939	Cambridge	1968	Cambridge
1946	Oxford	1969	Cambridge
1947	Cambridge	1970	Cambridge
1948	Cambridge	1971	Cambridge
1949	Cambridge	1972	Cambridge
1950	Cambridge	1973	Cambridge
1951	Cambridge	1974	Oxford
1952	Oxford	1975	Cambridge
1953	Cambridge	1976	Oxford
1954	Oxford	1977	Oxford
1955	Cambridge	1978	Oxford

Cambridge have won 68 times, Oxford 55 times.

OLYMPIC GAMES, 1976
Men

Single sculls	P. Karppinen (Finland)
Double sculls	Norway
Coxless quadruple sculls	E. Germany
Coxless pairs	E. Germany
Coxed pairs	E. Germany
Coxless fours	E. Germany
Coxed fours	U.S.S.R.
Eights	E. Germany

Women

Single sculls	C. Scheiblich (E. Germany)
Double sculls	Bulgaria
Coxless pairs	Bulgaria
Coxed quadruple sculls	E. Germany
Coxed fours	E. Germany
Eights	E. Germany

RECORDS

Jack Beresford, Junior, won the Wingfield Sculls 7 times, 1920–2
and won medals in 5 successive Olympics
World professional titles record: W. Beach (Australia), 1884–87

Rugby League Football

Governing body: The Rugby Football League, 180 Chapeltown Road, Leeds, LS7 4HT.

WORLD CUP

1954	Great Britain	1970	Australia
1957	Australia	1972	Great Britain
1960	Great Britain	1975	Australia
1968	Australia	1977	Australia

CHALLENGE CUP COMPETITION

since 1950

1950	Warrington	1965	Wigan
1951	Wigan	1966	St. Helens
1952	Workington Town	1967	Featherstone Rovers
1953	Huddersfield	1968	Leeds
1954	Warrington	1969	Castleford
1955	Barrow	1970	Castleford
1956	St. Helens	1971	Leigh
1957	Leeds	1972	St. Helens
1958	Wigan	1973	Featherstone Rovers
1959	Wigan	1974	Warrington
1960	Wakefield Trinity	1975	Widnes
1961	St. Helens	1976	St. Helens
1962	Wakefield Trinity	1977	Leeds
1963	Wakefield Trinity	1978	Leeds
1964	Widnes		

Rugby Union Football

Governing body: Rugby Football Union, Twickenham, Middlesex, TW2 7RQ.

INTERNATIONAL CHAMPIONSHIP

since 1920

1920	England, Scotland and Wales, tie	1931	Wales
1921	England	1932	England, Wales and Ireland, tie
1922	Wales	1933	Scotland
1923	England	1934	England
1924	England	1935	Ireland
1925	Scotland	1936	Wales
1926	Ireland and Scotland, tie	1937	England
1927	Ireland and Scotland, tie	1938	Scotland
1928	England	1939	England, Wales and Ireland, tie
1929	Scotland		
1930	England	1947	Wales and England, tie

1948	Ireland	1963	England
1949	Ireland	1964	Scotland and Wales, tie
1950	Wales	1965	Wales
1951	Ireland	1966	Wales
1952	Wales	1967	France
1953	England	1968	France
1954	England, France and Wales, tie	1969	Wales
		1970	France and Wales, tie
1955	Wales and France, tie	1971	Wales
1956	Wales	1972	series not completed
1957	England	1973	5-way tie
1958	England	1974	Ireland
1959	France	1975	Wales
1960	England and France, tie	1976	Wales
1961	France	1977	France
1962	France	1978	Wales

COUNTY CHAMPIONSHIP

since 1960

1960	Warwickshire	1970	Staffordshire
1961	Cheshire	1971	Surrey
1962	Warwickshire	1972	Gloucestershire
1963	Warwickshire	1973	Lancashire
1964	Warwickshire	1974	Gloucestershire
1965	Warwickshire	1975	Gloucestershire
1966	Middlesex	1976	Gloucestershire
1967	Surrey and Durham	1977	Lancashire
1968	Middlesex	1978	North Midlands
1969	Lancashire		

VARSITY MATCH

since 1960

1960	Cambridge	1969	Cambridge
1961	Cambridge	1970	Oxford
1962	Cambridge	1971	Oxford
1963	Cambridge	1972	Cambridge
1964	Oxford	1973	Cambridge
1965	Drawn	1974	Cambridge
1966	Oxford	1975	Cambridge
1967	Cambridge	1976	Cambridge
1968	Cambridge	1977	Oxford

MIDDLESEX SEVEN-A-SIDE TOURNAMENT

since 1951

1951	Richmond II	1956	London Welsh I
1952	Wasps	1957	St. Luke's College, Exete
1953	Richmond I	1958	Blackheath
1954	Rosslyn Park I	1959	Loughborough College
1955	Richmond I	1960	London Scottish

1961	London Scottish I	1970	Loughborough Colleges I
1962	London Scottish I	1971	London Welsh I
1963	London Scottish I	1972	London Welsh I
1964	Loughborough Colleges I	1973	London Welsh I
1965	London Scottish I	1974	Richmond I
1966	Loughborough Colleges I	1975	Richmond I
1967	Harlequins I	1976	Loughborough Colleges I
1968	London Welsh I	1977	Richmond I
1969	St. Luke's, Exeter I	1978	Harlequins I

RECORDS (*as at 28/2/78*)

Most Caps: W. J. McBride (Ireland), 63; G. Edwards (Wales) 49; A. B. Carmichael (Scotland) 49; J. Pullen (England), 42

Highest international score: Wales beat France 49–14, 1910

Greatest winning margin: S. Africa beat France 55–6, 1906

Place kick record: 100 yd., at Richmond Athletic Ground, 1906, by D. F. T. Morkel in an unsuccessful kick for S. Africa v. Middlesex. 67 yd., successful by Don Clarke in a club match at Roturua

Longest dropped goal: 90 yd. at Twickenham in 1932, by G. Brand for South Africa v. England

Shooting

Governing bodies: National Rifle Association, Bisley Camp, Brookwood, Woking, Surrey, GU24 OPB; National Smallbore Rifle Association, Codrington House, Southwark Street, London, S.E.1.

QUEEN'S PRIZE

1965	Capt. J. Allen (Royal Marines)
1966	Major R. W. Hampton (Canada)
1967	J. Powell (Sussex R.A.)
1968	Capt. A. A. Parks (Canada)
1969	Major F. G. Little (Dean R.C.)
1970	G. F. Arnold (Dorking & District R.C.)
1971	R. M. Stevens (Ricochets R.C.)
1972	R. P. Rosling (City R.C.)
1973	Keith Pilcher (Surrey)
1974	Capt. F. O. Harriss (North London R.C.)
1975	C. M. Y. Trotter (Guernsey R.C.)
1976	Major W. H. Magnay (North London R.C.)
1977	D. A. Friend (Hurstpierpoint)

OLYMPIC GAMES, 1976

free pistol	U. Potteck (E. Germany)	573 pts.
small bore rifle, prone	K. Smieszek (W. Germany)	599 pts.
small bore rifle, three positions	L. Bassham (U.S.A.)	1,162 pts.
rapid fire pistol	N. Klaar (E. Germany)	597 pts.

Clay pigeon: Trap	D. Haldeman (U.S.A.)	190 pts.
Skeet	J. Panacek (Czechoslovakia)	198 pts.
Running game	A. Gazov (U.S.S.R.)	579 pts.

Ski-ing

Governing body: National Ski Federation of Great Britain, 118 Eaton Square, London, SW1W 9AF.

1976 OLYMPIC GAMES (INNSBRUCK)
Alpine

Men's downhill	F. Klammer (Austria)
Men's slalom	P. Gros (Italy)
Men's giant slalom	H. Hemmi (Switzerland)
Women's downhill	R. Mittermaier (W. Germany)
Women's slalom	R. Mittermaier (W. Germany)
Women's giant slalom	K. Kreiner (Canada)

Ski jumping

90 metres	K. Schnabl (Austria)
70 metres	H.-G. Aschenbach (E. Germany)

Biathlon

Individual	N. Kruglov (U.S.S.R.)
4 × 7·5 km. relay	U.S.S.R.

Nordic

Men's 15 km.	N. Bajukov (U.S.S.R.)
Men's 30 km.	S. Saveliev (U.S.S.R.)
Men's 50 km.	I. Formo (Norway)
Men's 4 × 10 km. relay	Finland
Combined event	U. Wehling (E. Germany)
Women's 5 km.	H. Takalo (Finland)
Women's 10 km.	R. Smetanina (U.S.S.R.)
Women's 4 × 5 km. relay	U.S.S.R.

BRITISH NATIONAL ALPINE CHAMPIONSHIPS

	Men	Women
1970	J. Vesey	G. Hathorn
1971	S. Varley	V. Sturge
1972	I. Penz	O. Chalvin
1973	S. Fitzsimmons	H. Carmichael
1974	K. Bartelski	T. Wallis
1975	S. Fitzsimmons	V. Iliffe
1976	S. Fitzsimmons	V. Iliffe
1977	P. Fuchs	H. Hutcheon
1978	Q. Byrne-Sutton	L. Holmes

Squash Rackets

Governing bodies: Squash Rackets Association, 70 Brompton Road, London SW3 10X; Women's Squash Rackets Association, 345 Upper Richmond Road, Sheen, London SW14 8QN.

OPEN CHAMPIONSHIP

1950	Hashim Khan (Pakistan)	1964	Abu Taleb (Egypt)
1951	Hashim Khan (Pakistan)	1965	Abu Taleb (Egypt)
1952	Hashim Khan (Pakistan)	1966	J. Barrington (amateur)
1953	Hashim Khan (Pakistan)	1967	J. Barrington (amateur)
1954	Hashim Khan (Pakistan)	1968	G. Hunt (Australia)
1955	Hashim Khan (Pakistan)	1969	J. Barrington (Ireland)
1956	Roshan Khan (Pakistan)	1970	J. Barrington (Ireland)
1957	Hashim Khan (Pakistan)	1971	J. Barrington (Ireland)
1958	Azam Khan (Pakistan)	1972	J. Barrington (Ireland)
1959	Azam Khan (Pakistan)	1973	G. Hunt (Australia)
1960	Azam Khan (Pakistan)	1974	Qamar Zaman (Pakistan)
1961	Azam Khan (Pakistan)	1975	G. Hunt (Australia)
1962	Mohibullah Khan (Pakistan)	1976	G. Hunt (Australia)
		1977	G. Hunt (Australia)
1963	Abu Taleb (Egypt)		

AMATEUR CHAMPIONSHIP

1970	G. Allaudin (Pakistan)
1971	G. Allaudin (Pakistan)
1972	C. Nancarrow (Australia)
1973	M. Khan (Pakistan)
1974	J. Leslie (Great Britain)
1975	K. Shawcross (Australia)
1976	B. Brownlee (New Zealand)
1977	B. Brownlee (New Zealand)

WOMEN'S CHAMPIONSHIP

1949–58	Miss J. Morgan
1959	Mrs H. G. Macintosh
1960	Mrs G. E. Marshall
1961–64	Miss H. Blundell (Australia)
1965–77	Mrs B. McKay (Australia)

Swimming

Governing bodies: Amateur Swimming Association, Harold ern House, Derby Square, Loughborough, Leicestershire, E11 OAL; Channel Swimming Association, 'The Moorings', lkham Valley Road, Hawkinge, Nr. Folkestone, Kent.

Men
WORLD AND UNITED KINGDOM RECORDS
(as at 31st December 1977)

	World	British
Freestyle		
100 metres	49·44 sec. J. Skinner (S. Africa)	52·30 sec. B. Brinkley
200 metres	1 min. 50·29 sec. B. Furniss (U.S.A.)	1 min. 52·47 sec. G. Downie
400 metres	3 min. 51·56 sec. B. Goodell (U.S.A.)	3 min. 59·98 sec. S. Gray
800 metres	8 min. 1·54 sec. R. Hackett (U.S.A.)	8 min. 23·45 sec. D. Parker
1,500 metres	15 min. 2·40 sec. B. Goodell (U.S.A.)	15 min. 42·55 sec. D. Parker
Breaststroke		
100 metres	1 min 2·86 sec. G. Moerken (W. Germany)	1 min. 3·43 sec. D. Wilkie
200 metres	2 min. 15·11 sec. D. Wilkie (G.B.)	2 min. 15·11 sec. D. Wilkie
Butterfly		
100 metres	54·18 sec. J. Bottom (U.S.A.)	55·98 sec. J. Mills
200 metres	1 min. 59·23 sec. M. Bruner (U.S.A.)	2 min. 1·49 sec. B. Brinkley
Backstroke		
100 metres	55·49 sec. J. Naber (U.S.A.)	59·60 sec. J. Carter
200 metres	1 min. 59·19 sec. J Naber (U.S.A.)	2 min. 6·87 sec. J. Carter
Individual medley		
200 metres	2 min. 5·31 sec. G. Smith (Canada)	2 min. 6·25 sec. D. Wilkie
400 metres	4 min. 23·68 sec. R. Strachan (U.S.A.)	4 min. 33·56 sec. A. McClatchey
Freestyle relay		
4 × 100 metres	3 min. 21·11 sec. U.S.A. National Team	3 min. 32·17 sec. British National Team

	World	British
4 × 200 metres	7 min. 23·22 sec. U.S.A. National Team	7 min. 32·11 sec. British National Team
Medley relay 4 × 100 metres	3 min. 42·22 sec. U.S.A. National Team	3 min. 49·56 sec. British National Team

EUROPEAN RECORDS (*as at 31st December, 1977*)

Freestyle

100 metres	51·25 sec. M. Guarducci	Italy
200 metres	1 min. 50·73 sec. A. Krylov	U.S.S.R.
400 metres	3 min. 54·83 sec. S. Rusin	U.S.S.R.
800 metres	8 min. 6·40 sec. V. Salnikov	U.S.S.R.
1,500 metres	15 min. 16·45 sec. V. Salnikov	U.S.S.R.

Breaststroke

100 metres	1 min. 2·86 sec. G. Moerken	W. Germany
200 metres	2 min. 15·11 sec. D. Wilkie	Great Britain

Butterfly

100 metres	54·75 sec. R. Pyttel	E. Germany
200 metres	1 min. 59·73 sec. R. Pyttel	E. Germany

Backstroke

100 metres	56·30 sec. R. Matthes	E. Germany
200 metres	2 min. 1·87 sec. R. Matthes	E. Germany

Individual medley

200 metres	2 min. 6·25 sec. D. Wilkie	Great Britain

| 400 metres | 4 min. 25·37 sec. | |
| | S. Fesenko | U.S.S.R. |

Freestyle relay

4 × 100 metres	3 min. 26·57 sec.	
	National Team	W. Germany
4 × 200 metres	7 min. 27·97 sec.	
	National Team	U.S.S.R.

Medley relay

| 4 × 100 metres | 3 min. 47·29 sec. | |
| | National Team | W. Germany |

Women
WORLD AND UNITED KINGDOM RECORDS

(as at 31st December, 1977)

	World	British
Freestyle		
100 metres	55·65 sec.	57·50 sec.
	K. Ender (E. Germany)	C. Brazendale
200 metres	1 min. 59·26 sec.	2 min. 4·40 sec.
	K. Ender (E. Germany)	C. Brazendale
400 metres	4 min. 8·91 sec.	4 min. 22·11 sec.
	P. Thumer	C. Brazendale
	(E. Germany)	
800 metres	8 min. 35·04 sec.	9 min. 2·87 sec.
	P. Thumer	L. Heggie
	(E. Germany)	
1,500 metres	16 min. 24·60 sec.	18 min. 14·4 sec.
	A. Browne (U.S.A.)	M. Verth
Breaststroke		
100 metres	1 min. 10·86 sec.	1 min. 13·50 sec.
	H. Anke (E. Germany)	M. Kelly
200 metres	2 min. 33·35 sec.	2 min. 38·26 sec.
	M. Koshevaia	D. Rudd
	(U.S.S.R.)	
Butterfly		
100 metres	59·78 sec.	1 min. 3·69 sec.
	C. Knacke (E. Germany)	S. Jenner
200 metres	2 min. 11·22 sec.	2 min. 15·45 sec.
	R. Gabriel	S. Jenner
	(E. Germany)	

	World	British
Backstroke		
100 metres	I min. I·51 sec. U. Richter (E. Germany)	I min. 6·09 sec. J. Beasley
200 metres	2 min. 12·47 sec. B. Treiber (E. Germany)	2 min. 21·18 sec. S. Davies
Individual Medley		
200 metres	2 min. 15·85 sec. U. Tauber (E. Germany)	2 min. 21·57 sec. S. Davies
400 metres	4 min. 42·77 sec. U. Tauber (E. Germany)	4 min. 54·95 sec. S. Davies
Freestyle relay		
4 × 100 metres	3 min. 44·82 sec. U.S.A. National Team	3 min. 55·77 sec. British National Team
Medley relay		
4 × 100 metres	4 min. 7·95 sec. E. German National Team	4 min. 21·07 sec. English National Team

EUROPEAN RECORDS (*as at 31st December, 1977*)

Freestyle		
100 metres	55·65 sec. K. Ender	E. Germany
200 metres	I min. 59·26 sec. K. Ender	E. Germany
400 metres	4 min. 8·91 sec. P. Thumer	E. Germany
800 metres	8 min. 35·04 sec. P. Thumer	E. Germany
1,500 metres	16 min. 47·11 sec. A. Maas	Holland
Breaststroke		
100 metres	I min. 10·86 sec. H. Anke	E. Germany
200 metres	2 min. 33·35 sec. M. Koshevaia	U.S.S.R.

Butterfly

100 metres	59·78 sec. C. Knacke	E. Germany
200 metres	2 min. 11·22 sec. R Gabriel	E. Germany

Backstroke

100 metres	1 min. 1·51 sec. U. Richter	E. Germany
200 metres	2 min. 12·47 sec. B. Treiber	E. Germany

Individual medley

200 metres	2 min. 15·85 sec. U. Tauber	E. Germany
400 metres	4 min. 42·77 sec. U. Tauber	E. Germany

Freestyle relay

4 × 100 metres	3 min. 45·50 sec. National Team	E. Germany

Medley race

4 × 100 metres	4 min. 7·95 sec. National Team	E. Germany

OLYMPIC WINNERS, 1976
Men

100 m. freestyle	J. Montgomery (U.S.A.)	49·99 sec. *W.R.*
200 m. freestyle	B. Furniss (U.S.A.)	1 min. 50·29 sec. *W.R.*
400 m. freestyle	B. Goodell (U.S.A.)	3 min. 51·93 sec. *W.R.*
1,500 m. freestyle	B. Goodell (U.S.A.)	15 min. 02·40 sec. *W.R.*
100 m. backstroke	J. Naber (U.S.A.)	55·49 sec. *W.R.*
200 m. backstroke	J. Naber (U.S.A.)	1 min. 59·19 sec. *W.R.*
100 m. breaststroke	J. Hencken (U.S.A.)	1 min. 03·11 sec. *W.R.*
200 m. breaststroke	D. Wilkie (G.B.)	2 min. 15·11 sec. *W.R.*
100 m. butterfly	M Vogel (U.S.A.)	54·35 sec.
200 m. butterfly	M. Bruner (U.S.A.)	1 min. 59·23 sec. *W.R.*

400 m. individual medley	R. Strachan (U.S.A.)	4 min. 23·68 sec. *W.R.*
4 × 100 m. medley relay	U.S.A. National Team (Naber, Hencken, Vogel, Montgomery)	3 min. 42·22 sec. *W.R.*
4 × 200 m. freestyle relay	U.S.A. National Team (Bruner, Furniss, Naber, Montgomery)	7 min. 23·22 sec. *W.R.*
Springboard diving	P. Boggs (U.S.A.)	619·05 pts.
Highboard diving	K. Dibiasi (Italy)	600·51 pts.

Women

100 m. freestyle	K. Ender (E. Germany)	55·65 sec. *W.R.*
200 m. freestyle	K. Ender (E. Germany)	1 min. 59·26 sec. *W.R.*
400 m. freestyle	P. Thumer (E. Germany)	4 min. 09·89 sec. *W.R.*
800 m. freestyle	P. Thumer (E. Germany)	8 min. 37·14 sec. *W.R.*
100 m. backstroke	U. Richter (E. Germany)	1 min. 01·83 sec. *O.R.*
200 m. backstroke	U. Richter (E. Germany)	2 min. 13·43 sec. *O.R.*
100 m. breaststroke	H. Anke (E. Germany)	1 min. 10·86 sec.
200 m. breaststroke	M. Koshevaya (U.S.S.R.)	2 min. 33·35 sec. *O.R.*
100 m. butterfly	K. Ender (E. Germany)	1 min. 00·13 sec. *W.R.*
200 m. butterfly	A. Pollack (E. Germany)	2 min. 11·41 sec. *O.R.*
400 m. individual medley	U. Tauber (E. Germany)	4 min. 42·77 sec. *W.R.*
4 × 100 m. medley relay	E. German National Team (Richter, Anke, Pollack, Ender)	4 min. 07·95 sec. *W.R.*
4 × 100 m. freestyle relay	U.S.A. National Team (Peyton, Boglioli, Sterkel, Babashoff)	3 min. 44·82 sec. *W.R.*
Springboard diving	J. Chandler (U.S.A.)	506·19 pts.
Highboard diving	E. Vaytsekhovskaya (U.S.S.R.)	406·59 pts.

Table Tennis

Governing body: English Table Tennis Association, 21 Claremont, Hastings, Sussex.

WORLD CHAMPIONSHIP

Men's Singles

1950	R. Bergmann (England)	1963	Chuang Tse-Tung (China)
1951	J. Leach (England)		
1952	H. Satoh (Japan)	1965	Chuang Tse-Tung (China)
1953	F. Sido (Hungary)		
1954	I. Ogimura (Japan)	1967	N. Hasegawa (Japan)
1955	T. Tanaka (Japan)	1969	S. Ito (Japan)
1956	I. Ogimura (Japan)	1971	S. Bengtsson (Sweden)
1957	T. Tanaka (Japan)	1973	H. En-tinh (China)
1959	Jung Kuo-Tuan (China)	1975	I. Jonyer (Hungary)
1961	Chuang Tse-Tung (China)	1977	M. Kohno (Japan)

Women's Singles

1950	A. Rozeanu (Rumania)	1961	Chiu Chung-Hui (China)
1951	A. Rozeanu (Rumania)	1963	K. Matsuzaki (Japan)
1952	A. Rozeanu (Rumania)	1965	N. Fukazu (Japan)
1953	A. Rozeanu (Rumania)	1967	S. Morisawa (Japan)
1954	A. Rozeanu (Rumania)	1969	T. Kowada (Japan)
1955	A. Rozeanu (Rumania)	1971	Lin Hui-Ching (China)
1956	T. Okawa (Japan)	1973	H. Yu-lan (China)
1957	F. Eguchi (Japan)	1975	Yung Sun Kim (N. Korea)
1959	K. Matsuzaki (Japan)	1977	P. Yung Sun (N. Korea)

SWAYTHLING CUP

1950	Czechoslovakia	1961	China
1951	Czechoslovakia	1963	China
1952	Hungary	1965	China
1953	England	1967	Japan
1954	Japan	1969	Japan
1955	Japan	1971	China
1956	Japan	1973	Sweden
1957	Japan	1975	China
1959	Japan	1977	China

CORBILLON CUP

1934	Germany	1938	Czechoslovakia
1935	Czechoslovakia	1939	Germany
1936	Czechoslovakia	1947	England
1937	U.S.A.	1948	England

1949	U.S.A.	1961	Japan
1950	Rumania	1963	Japan
1951	Rumania	1965	China
1952	Japan	1967	Japan
1953	Rumania	1969	U.S.S.R.
1954	Japan	1971	Japan
1955	Rumania	1973	S. Korea
1956	Rumania	1975	China
1957	Japan	1977	China
1959	Japan		

ENGLISH OPEN CHAMPIONSHIPS

Men's Singles

1970	S. Kollarovits (Czechoslovakia)
1971	T. Klamper (Hungary)
1972	S. Bengtsson (Sweden)
1973	S. Bengtsson (Sweden)
1974	K. Johansson (Sweden)
1975	A. Strokatov (U.S.S.R.)
1976	S. Bengtsson (Sweden)
1977	S. Gomozkov (U.S.S.R.)
1978	Li Chen-shih (China)

Women's Singles

1970	Mrs. M. Alexandru (Rumania)
1971	Mrs. M. Alexandru (Rumania)
1972	Mrs. M. Alexandru (Rumania)
1973	Mrs. B. Radberg (Sweden)
1974	Mrs. M. Alexandru (Rumania)
1975	Miss E. Antonian (U.S.S.R.)
1976	Mrs. J. Hammersley (Great Britain)
1977	Miss C. Knight (Great Britain)
1978	Chu Hsiang-yum (China)

Volley Ball

Governing body: English Volleyball Association, 17 Merton Close, Oldbury, Warley, Worcs.

OLYMPIC WINNERS

Men		Women	
1964	U.S.S.R.	1964	Japan
1968	U.S.S.R.	1968	U.S.S.R.
1972	Japan	1972	U.S.S.R.
1976	Poland	1976	Japan

Walking

Governing body: Race Walking Association, 112 Lennard Road, Beckenham, Kent.

WORLD RECORDS

20,000 metres	1 hr. 23 m. 32 s.	D. Bautisca (Mexico)	1977
2 hours	27,154 metres	B. Kannenberg (W. Germany)	1974
30,000 metres	2 hr. 12 m. 58 s.	B. Kannenberg (W. Germany)	1974
20 miles	2 hr. 27 m. 38 s.	V. Visini (Italy)	1975
30 miles	3 hr. 48 m. 23·4 s.	B. Kannenberg (W. Germany)	1975
50,000 metres	3 hr. 56 m. 38 s.	E. Vera (Mexico)	1977

OTHER BEST PERFORMANCES

3,000 metres	11 min. 51·2 sec.	P. Nihill (G.B.)	1971
2 miles	12 min. 45 sec.	W. Hardmo (Sweden)	1945
5,000 metres	19 min. 37 sec.	P. Stadtmuller (E. Germany)	1975
5 miles	33 min. 43 sec.	P. Embleton (G.B.)	1971
10,000 metres	41 min. 29·2 sec.	C. Stan (Rumania)	1973
7 miles	47 min. 49 sec.	P. Frenkel (E. Germany)	1972
1 hour	14,241 metres	B. Kannenberg (W. Germany)	1974
15,000 metres	1 hr. 3 m. 18 s.	B. Kannenberg (W. Germany)	1974
10 miles	1 hr. 8 m. 0·4 s.	B. Kannenberg (W. Germany)	1974

Water Polo

Governing body: Amateur Swimming Association, Harold Fern House, Derby Square, Loughborough, Leicestershire, LE11 0AL.

OLYMPIC WINNERS

1900	Great Britain	1948	Italy
1904	U.S.A.	1952	Hungary
1908	Great Britain	1956	Hungary
1912	Great Britain	1960	Italy
1920	Great Britain	1964	Hungary
1924	France	1968	Yugoslavia
1928	Germany	1972	U.S.S.R.
1932	Hungary	1976	Hungary
1936	Hungary		

Yachting

Governing body: Royal Yachting Association, 5 Buckingham Gate, London, SW1E 6JT.

OLYMPIC GAMES, 1976

Soling	P. R. H. Jansen, V. Bandolowski, E. Hansen (Denmark)
Tempest	J. Albrechtson, I. Hansson (Sweden)
Flying Dutchman	J. Diesch, E. Diesch (W. Germany)
470 class	F. Hubner, H. Bode (W. Germany)
Finn	J. Schumann (E. Germany)
Tornado	R. White, J. Osborn (G.B.)

THE AMERICA'S CUP

Shamrock I lost to *Columbia* in 1899
Shamrock II lost to *Columbia* in 1901
Shamrock III lost to *Reliance* in 1903
Shamrock IV lost to *Resolute* in 1920
Shamrock V lost to *Enterprise* in 1930
Endeavour lost to *Rainbow* in 1934
Endeavour II lost to *Ranger* in 1937
Sceptre lost to *Columbia* in 1958
Gretel lost to *Weatherley* in 1962
Sovereign lost to *Constellation* in 1964
Dame Pattie lost to *Intrepid* in 1967
Gretel II lost to *Intrepid* in 1970
Southern Cross lost to *Courageous* in 1974
Australia lost to *Courageous* in 1977

THE ADMIRAL'S CUP

1969	U.S.A.
1971	Great Britain
1973	Germany
1975	Great Britain
1977	Great Britain

Olympic Games, 1976
(Montreal)

(A list of winners not already noted under particular games or sports)

Gymnastics

Governing body: British Amateur Gymnastic Association, 23A High Street, Slough, SL1 1DY.

Men

Combined exercises, individual	N. Andrianov (U.S.S.R.)
Combined exercises, team	Japan
Floor exercises	N. Andrianov (U.S.S.R.)
Pommel horse	Z. Magyar (Hungary)
Rings	N. Andrianov (U.S.S.R.)
Vault	N. Andrianov (U.S.S.R.)
Parallel bars	S. Kato (Japan)
Horizontal bars	M. Tsukahara (Japan)

Women

Combined exercises, individual	N. Comaneci (Romania)
Combined exercises, team	U.S.S.R.
Vault	N. Kim (U.S.S.R.)
Asymmetric bars	N. Comaneci (Romania)
Beam	N. Comaneci (Romania)
Floor exercises	N. Kim (U.S.S.R.)

Modern Pentathlon

Individual	J. Pyciak-Peciak (Poland)
Team	Great Britain

Weightlifting

Governing body: British Amateur Weight Lifters' Association, 3 Iffley Turn, Oxford.

Flyweight	A. Voronin (U.S.S.R.)	534·25 lb.
Bantamweight	N. Nurikyan (Bulgaria)	578·5 lb. *O.R.*
Featherweight	G. Todorov (Bulgaria)	633·5 lb. *O.R.*
Lightweight	V. Peusner (U.S.S.R.)	694·25 lb.
Middleweight	Y. Mitkov (Bulgaria)	760·25 lb. *O.R.*
Light-heavyweight	P. Stojczev (Bulgaria)	820·75 lb. *O.R.*
Middle-heavyweight	D. Rigert (U.S.S.R.)	881·5 lb. *O.R.*
Heavyweight	V. Khristov (Bulgaria)	920·0 lb. *O.R.*
Super-heavyweight	V. Alexeyev (U.S.S.R.)	975·25 lb. *O.R.*

Wrestling

Governing body: British Amateur Wrestling Association 60 Calabria Road, London, N.5.

Freestyle

Light-Flyweight	K. Issaev (Bulgaria)
Flyweight	Y. Takada (Japan)
Bantamweight	V. Umin (U.S.S.R.)
Featherweight	J.-M. Yang (S. Korea)
Lightweight	P. Pinigin (U.S.S.R.)
Welterweight	J. Date (Japan)
Middleweight	J. Peterson (U.S.A.)
Light-Heavyweight	L. Tediashvili (U.S.S.R.)
Heavyweight	I. Yarygin (U.S.S.R.)
Extra-Heavyweight	S. Andiev (U.S.S.R.)

Graeco-Roman

Light-Flyweight	A. Shumakov (U.S.S.R.)
Flyweight	V. Konstantinov (U.S.S.R.)
Bantamweight	P. Ukkola (Finland)
Featherweight	K. Lipien (Poland)
Lightweight	S. Nalbandyan (U.S.S.R.)
Welterweight	A. Bsov (U.S.S.R.)
Middleweight	M. Petkovic (Yugoslavia)
Light-Heavyweight	Y. Rezantsev (U.S.S.R.)
Heavyweight	N. Bolboshin (U.S.S.R.)
Extra-Heavyweight	A. Kolchinski (U.S.S.R.)

Canoeing

Governing body: The British Canoe Union, 70 Brompton Road, London, SW3 1DT.

Men

Kayak singles 500 m.	V. Diba (Romania)
Kayak singles 1,000 m.	R. Helm (E. Germany)
Kayak pairs 500 m.	East Germany
Kayak pairs 1,000 m.	U.S.S.R.
Kayak fours 1,000 m.	U.S.S.R.
Canadian singles 500 m.	A. Rogov (U.S.S.R.)
Canadian singles 1,000 m.	M. Ljubak (Yugoslavia)
Canadian pairs 500 m.	U.S.S.R.
Canadian pairs 1,000 m.	U.S.S.R.

Women

Kayak singles 500 m.   C. Zirzow (E. Germany)
Kayak pairs 500 m.   U.S.S.R.

Handball

Men

U.S.S.R.

Women

U.S.S.R.

Judo

Governing body: The British Judo Association, 70 Brompton Road, London, SW3 1DR.

Heavyweight   S. Novikov (U.S.S.R.)
Light-heavyweight   K. Ninomiya (Japan)
Middleweight   I. Sonada (Japan)
Welterweight   V. Nevzorov (U.S.S.R.)
Lightweight   H. Rodriguez (Cuba)
Open class   H. Uemura (Japan)

Winter Olympics 1976 (Innsbruck)

Bobsleigh

Two-man   E. Germany
Four-man   E. Germany

Tobogganing

Men   D. Guenther (E. Germany)
Two-man   H. Rinn and N. Hahn (E. Germany)
Women   M. Schumann (E. Germany)

Personalities

Jim Batten: James Cornelius Batten was born on 7 November 1955 in Bow, London. He is 5 ft. 9 in. tall, has brown hair and brown eyes. He now lives in the London suburb of Milwall with his wife and two sons. Before turning professional at the age of 18 Jim won 3 national schoolboy titles, two A.B.A. national titles and the N.A.B.C. title. His manager is Terry Lawless and under his guidance he won, at the age of 21, the British Light Middle Weight title and he has since defended his title against Larry Paul. Since turning professional he has sparred with Carlos Palomino, Welter Weight Champion of the World. Jim hopes to slim down to Welter Weight. He is also a good footballer and was at one time on the books of Milwall F.C.

Caroline Bradley: Caroline Frances Bradley was born on 4 April 1946. She is single and lives in the Warwickshire village of Priors Marston and is 5 ft. 5 in. tall and has brown hair and green eyes. She took up show jumping seriously after she left school at the age of 18. She has ridden some very good and well-known horses amongst which have been *Franco, Acrobat, Marius* and *Bernar*. In 1977 she won the Leading Show Jumper of the Year Award riding *Marius*. In the same year she also won the British Show Jumping Association National Championship when she was riding *Bernar*.

Mike Brearley: John Michael Brearley was born at Harrow, Middlesex, on 28 April 1942. He is married and lives in London. He has black hair, hazel eyes and is 5 ft. 11 in. tall. He was previously a university lecturer, but now does counselling work with adolescents. He was a Cambridge blue in 1961–64 and was captain in 1963–64. He played his first game for Middlesex in 1961 and was capped in 1964. For a time he was out of full-time cricket, but he returned to it in 1971 when he was awarded the Middlesex captaincy. Honours in the period of his captaincy include Gillette Cup and Benson and Hedges Cup finalists in 1975; County Champions in 1976; Joint County Champions in 1977; Gillette Cup Winners 1977. He won his first England cap in 1976 when he made two appearances against the West Indies. He was captain of the England team which regained the Ashes in 1977. His right wrist was broken while he captained England in Pakistan in 1977–78.

Desmond Douglas: Born in Jamaica on 20 July 1955 and now living in Birmingham. He is 5 ft. 9 in. tall and has black hair and brown eyes. His career in table tennis began when he played for his school. He played for his first club when he was 15 and a year later he represented the England Juniors. In 1973 he represented England Seniors in the World Championships in Yugoslavia and since then he has been a regular member of the team. He is ranked number 1 in England, number 9 in Europe and number 25 in the World. In 1978 he is English Open Doubles Champion and Welsh Open Singles Champion and also Welsh Open Mixed Doubles Champion.

Brendan Foster: Born 12 January 1948 in Hebburn, Co. Durham, Brendan Foster is 5 ft. 10½ in. tall, with brown hair and grey eyes, and is married with no children. He lives in Gateshead, where he is Sports and Recreation Manager of Gateshead M.B.C. He started running at 14 and first represented England in the 1970 Commonwealth Games, where he won a bronze for the 1,500 metres, as he did in the 1971 European Games. In the 1972 Olympic Games he finished fifth over the same distance. In 1973 he moved up to 5,000 metres, winning the European Championships in 1974 and the Europa Cup for the second time in succession in 1975. He has held world records for 2 miles and 3,000 metres. In January 1976 he was awarded the M.B.E. and in the 1976 Olympic Games in Montreal he won a bronze medal in the 10,000 metres. In 1977 he won the English cross-country championship for the first time.

Gerry Francis: Gerald Charles James Francis was born on 6 December 1951 in the London suburb of Hammersmith and now lives in Bagshot, Surrey. He is 5 ft. 10 in. tall, with dark brown hair and blue eyes, is single and is the director of his own two companies. Queen's Park Rangers signed him on as an apprentice in 1968, and he played his first game for them as a substitute in a First Division match when he was still 16. His full debut, however, came against Portsmouth in the Second Division, when he scored in his team's 3–1 victory. Since then he has played over 250 games for Rangers, many of them as their captain, and scored over 50 goals. In 1975 he was made Captain of England, after only four full caps. An unfortunate injury in 1976 put him out of the game for some time, but 1977 saw him back on top form.

Alistair Hignell: Alistair James Hignell was born in Cambridge on 4 September 1955. He is single, 5 ft. 8 in. tall, has brown hair and blue eyes. He is a student teacher and his home is in Bristol. He played rugby for Eastern Counties and England Schools (under 19) in 1973 and 1974. In 1973 he also played cricket for Public Schools and England Schools (under 19) and in the following year he played for England Young Cricketers. In 1973 he was voted the 'most promising young cricketer'. He went up to Fitzwilliam College, Cambridge, in 1974 and was a rugby blue in 1974, 1975, 1976, 1977 (as captain), and he has been re-elected captain for 1978. He gained his first rugby international cap on the England tour of Australia in 1975. He is also a county cricketer and made his debut for Gloucestershire in 1974. In 1976 and 1977 he scored 1,000 runs in a season.

James Hunt: Born on 29 August 1947, in Sutton, Surrey, James Simon Wallis Hunt is 6 ft. 2 in. tall, with blond hair and blue eyes, is single, and lives in Marbella in Spain. While at Wellington College he achieved success in cross-country running, squash rackets and tennis—he qualified to play for Junior Wimbledon—but he has since concentrated on racing driving. His first international win in Formula 3 came in 1970, and in 1973 he entered his first Grand Prix, driving for Lord Hesketh. He finished the year eighth in the World Championship. The following year he had his first Formula 1 win, and in 1975 he won his first Grand Prix and ended the year fourth in the Championship. In 1976 he had six Grand Prix wins and, after running neck-and-neck with Nikki Lauda for most of the season, won the World Championship when he finished third in the Japanese Grand Prix. In 1977 he won the British Grand Prix.

John Lloyd: John Michael Lloyd was born in Leigh-on-Sea, Essex, on 27 August 1954. He is 6 ft tall, has fair hair and blue eyes and lives in London. He is the middle of three tennis-playing brothers. At present he is ranked number 2 in Britain and number 33 in the world. In 1970 he was the National Under-16 Champion and in 1972 he was British Junior Covered Courts Champion. Since 1975 he has been a British Davis Cup and King's Cup player. In 1977 he reached the finals of three Grand Prix tournaments. His elder brother, David, is nationally ranked number 8 and is also Davis Cup and King's Cup player. Tony, his younger brother, is nationally ranked number 13. John Lloyd is the only British player to have a fan club, and his official earnings from tournament play in 1977 were U.S. $78,676.

Douglas Morgan: Douglas Waugh Morgan was born in Edinburgh on 9 March 1947. He is married with one daughter and lives in Edinburgh where he works as a chiropodist. He has fair hair, blue eyes and is 5 ft. 9 in. tall. When he was at school at Melville College he played for three years in the rugby, cricket and hockey first teams. In 1968 he played rugby for Edinburgh and has been captain of Edinburgh since 1972. He was first capped for Scotland in 1973 and he now has 20 caps. He has played for the Barbarians and has made several overseas tours. In 1974 he toured Bermuda with the Penguins, New Zealand in 1975 with Scotland and in 1977 New Zealand and Fiji with the British Lions. He is at present captain of Scotland. As well as his rugby career he has also been twelfth man in the Scottish cricket team.

Lucinda Prior-Palmer: Lucinda Jane Prior-Palmer, born 7 November 1953 in London, is 5 ft. 8½ in. tall and has fair hair and blue eyes. She is single and lives near Andover. Her riding career started in the Pony Club, where she never actually won an event. Then on her fifteenth birthday she was given *Be Fair*, and the two progressed together from Novice One-Day Events to International Three-Day Events. In 1971 she was a member of the British Junior Three-Day Event team which won the European Championship, and in 1972 was short-listed for the Munich Olympics. In 1973 she and *Be Fair* won the Badminton Horse Trials, while in 1974 only an unlucky fall prevented her from being placed. In 1975 she was winner of the European Horse Trials Championship. In 1976 she won Badminton again, riding *Wideawake*, who tragically collapsed and died during their lap of honour; and in 1977 won the event for a third time, riding *George*. She also won the European Championship at Burleigh on *George* in 1977.

Derek Randall: Derek William Randall was born at Retford in Nottinghamshire on 24 February 1951. He is a qualified draughtsman. His cricket career began in the back garden at home. He played his first game in the Bassetlaw League when he was fifteen. By the time he was 18 he was a regular player with the Nottinghamshire second team. In the Centenary Test at Melbourne in March 1977 his 174 in the England second innings was the masterpiece of the occasion. In his seven years in big circket he has scored over 7,000 runs, with 204 not out against Somerset at Trent Bridge in 1976 his highest innings.

Barry Sheene: Born on 11 September 1950 in central London, Barry Stephen Frank Sheene is 5 ft. 10½ in. tall, has brown hair and blue eyes, and is unmarried. He lives in Putney and runs his own business. He has been interested in motor bikes since he was four; his first road bike was a Ducati 75 and he first raced at Brands Hatch, when he was 18, riding a Bultaco. He has since raced in many European countries; his first big win was the Belgian Grand Prix, in 1971. During his career he has suffered 34 broken bones and he was very lucky not to be killed at Daytona in 1975. Nevertheless, he has won the Motor Cycle News 'Superbike' championship three times and in 1976 won five international Grand Prix, to give him the 500 c.c. world championship which he also won in 1977. He was awarded the M.B.E. in 1978 and is no. 1 rider for Team Suzuki GB in the 1978 season.

Virginia Wade: Sarah Virginia Wade was born on 10 July 1945 in Bournemouth. She is 5 ft. 7 in. tall, with brown hair and blue eyes, is unmarried and lives in London. She has represented Great Britain in the Wightman Cup since 1965 and the Federation Cup since 1967, and has captained both teams since 1973. Her championship wins include the U.S. Open (1968), the Italian Open (1971) and three Italian doubles championships, the Australian Open (1973) and the French and U.S. doubles championships in 1973, as well as four British Hard Court Championships (1967, 1968, 1973 and 1974). She recently turned professional and has since been very successful on the Virginia Slims tournament circuit, as well as winning the Dewar Cup five times (most recently in the Albert Hall, in November 1976). Her home title which had so long eluded her became the splendid achievement when she won the Women's Singles title in 1977. She is currently ranked number one in Great Britain.

The Women's Movement

It is often—and sometimes as if it were nothing more than a joke—referred to as Women's Lib. As the author of this section suggests, a better and truer term for it is the Women's Movement. It is bringing about one of those great gradual changes in old-established attitudes that make the time we live in so remarkable. It has already achieved enough to ensure that in a great many ways the world you grow up in will be very different from the world in which your parents grew up. Among other things, the ideas and changes of outlook on which it draws have made possible an event that only twenty or thirty years ago would have seemed, at least, highly improbable: that in the near future the British Government, of whatever party, might be led by a woman.

This section, in our annual series of special sections on topics of urgent interest, sets out to explain from the inside the background to one of the most extraordinary (and, obviously, one of the most important) movements of our time.

THE WOMEN'S MOVEMENT

'Women hold up half the sky,' said Mao Tse-Tung, the great Chinese leader who died, as you will see if you turn to the section on World History in this encyclopaedia, in 1976. Now read through that section again with Mao's saying in mind. Does it look to you as if women have been holding up *half* the sky throughout the last 6,000 years?

How many women's names can you find? There's Cleopatra (41 BC), Boadicea (AD 61) and a handful of others with Margaret Thatcher as the last entrant in 1975—among more than 300 men. Not a very impressive display of women's contribution to our civilisation! What were they *doing* all those years? Sitting at home minding the kids while the men went off to explore, to invent and to fight?

Whenever you read about history you are seeing the past through the eyes of historians. What they saw and recorded was not all that happened. They gleaned their information from other sources, often from the works of previous historians. They have made decisions about which events, which aspects of life and which personalities, they should write down for posterity. Most historians have been men working in societies where men were firmly in control, both politically and economically. It is therefore not surprising that they developed a particular view of history which was not the whole story. Try to imagine what your school history books might tell you if they had been written by women who had drawn upon the observations of other women who had passed down stories about their lives from generation to generation. That, too, would be a lop-sided view of what happened, but it might provide the other half of the picture.

In 1973 Sheila Rowbotham wrote a book called *Hidden from History*. It was an attempt to search through various records of life in England from the 16th century to the present and pick out enough clues to trace the activities of women. It makes fascinating reading, not least because it hints at how little we know. 'I am turning over the topsoil,' she explained, 'in the hope that others will dig deeper.'

Sheila Rowbotham's book is an important part of a movement which developed in the late 1960s and early 1970s. It has been called 'Women's Lib', but that's a rather meaningless phrase coined by the popular press. Let's call it the 'Women's Movement'. What happened was that women began to reconstruct their past, reconsider their lives and rediscover themselves.

How it began

To understand the Women's movement and why it began when it did, we must look back over the 19th and 20th centuries to see what changes took place in women's lives.

In the early 19th century, women in Britain were technically the chattels of their menfolk. They had no rights over anything —not their wages, nor any money or property they inherited from relatives, nor even over their own children. Women could not vote in elections. Those who received an education (who were very few) were taught to embroider and play the piano and behave like 'young ladies'. Those who went out to work were in the lowest-paid jobs with no prospect of bettering themselves.

They were not allowed to be politicians, lawyers, soldiers or doctors. It was virtually impossible for them to become scientists or philosophers because of the limits on their education and the restraints on their personal lives. They were seldom taken seriously as artists or writers. When the Brontë sisters wrote their novels they used masculine names, Currer, Ellis and Acton Bell, because they guessed publishers would reject their work if they knew it was written by women. Mary Ann Evans, author of *The Mill on the Floss*, did the same and called herself George Eliot. No doubt there were countless women whose achievements were considerable, about whom we shall never know— either because they disguised themselves as men and were not found out, or because their actions are still hidden in history.

Meanwhile, most women were performing a very important function which we *do* know about. They were feeding and clothing and caring for their husbands and children. They were making it possible for men to go out to earn a living for their families. They were raising future generations of workers. In other words, if they hadn't been holding up their half of the sky, the whole lot would have fallen down. But historians, in the main, didn't set much store by that.

One of the first attempts to improve the legal position of

women came in 1867 when the second Reform Bill was going through Parliament. The philosopher John Stuart Mill moved an amendment to replace the word 'man' with 'person' in order to give women the vote on the same terms as men. He failed. In 1874 Emma Paterson organised the Women's Protective and Provident League—the beginning of women's trade unions. In 1882 the Married Women's Property Act won for married women the right to own property and deal with it as they pleased. Gradually, things were beginning to move.

In 1886 the Guardianship of Infants Act gave mothers certain rights over their children. 1888 saw the famous match girls' strike: women were beginning to realise they could fight for a better deal and win.

The Battle for the Vote

In 1903 the Women's Social and Political Union was formed at the home of the Pankhursts in Manchester. The battle for the vote was on. So great was the opposition to the idea of women taking part in the democratic process of election that when peaceful tactics failed, the suffragettes resorted to militancy. They broke windows, hurled stones at Cabinet Ministers, set fire to letter boxes and disrupted meetings. They were ignored, ridiculed and eventually imprisoned. When they refused food in protest they were forcibly fed by the hideously painful process of pushing rubber tubing down their throats. In 1910 came Black Friday when the suffragettes held a mass lobby of parliament which ended in a long savage battle with the police; 119 were arrested and several were seriously injured, of whom two later died. Still the men in Parliament refused to grant women the vote.

During the First World War half a million women went to work in munitions factories and in thousands of other jobs which men had vacated when they went off to fight. Only after that, in 1918, were women allowed to vote—as long as they were over thirty. When men came back from the war most women lost their jobs and returned to their homes to carry on working as housewives and mothers. Ostensibly nothing had changed but under the surface ideas and traditions were shifting. Women had proved they could step into men's shoes and do the same work no less competently. Ten years later, in 1928, they were accorded the right to vote on the same basis as men.

The Second World War—and a lull

In 1931 the Civil Service opened its doors to women, employ-ing them on condition that they resigned on marriage. When the Second World War broke out in 1939 women were once again called upon to keep the factories running while the men fought in Europe. This time the Government provided hundreds of nurseries so that their children would be adequately cared for when they went out to work. But when the War ended and the men returned to their jobs, women were once again sent back to domesticity. The nurseries were closed. Now women were told their children would suffer 'maternal deprivation' unless they stayed at home to look after them.

From the late 1940s to the mid-1960s there was a lull. Women seemed to be settling into more passive, subordinate roles. They were encouraged to see themselves as objects of beauty, fashioned for the delight of men. They bleached and dyed and curled and straightened and back-combed and sprayed their hair. They slept in big uncomfortable rollers. They plucked their eyebrows, wore mud-packs, worried themselves sick about teenage spots and then about ageing lines. They curled their eyelashes, added false ones, painted their eyelids, put cream and powder on their faces, rouge on their cheeks, lipstick on their lips. They took scented bubble-baths, shaved their legs and armpits, applied body lotion, deodorant, talcum powder and perfume. They grew their nails long and varnished them. They wore padded bras, tight girdles, narrow skirts and high-heeled shoes. They dieted as if their lives depended on it and strove to keep up with the latest fashions. Manufacturers of cosmetics, underwear and other aids to beauty enjoyed un-precedented commercial success as advertisements in magazines and on television told women that only if they bought *this* product or *that* would they feel like a *real* woman, get their man and live happily ever after.

They were homemakers, too. Advertisements and magazine features instructed them how to buy and cook the tastiest foods, to hang the whitest washing on the line, to keep their kitchens sparkling and their carpets spotless. 'The best Mum in the world' or the 'perfect wife' was the one who remembered to buy *his* brand instead of brand X.

The seeds are sown

While women's role as diligent and contented housewives was being idealised by the mass media, their work in the home was actually getting easier. New domestic appliances—mixers, liquidisers, vacuum cleaners, freezers, washing machines, dryers, dishwashers—were taking some of the drudgery out of housework. So were foods which came in cans and ready-mix packets. With instant coffee, TV dinners, frozen peas and fish fingers, women had more time on their hands to consider whether life ought to hold more for them. The seeds of the women's movement were being sown.

The most important single influence, however, was the Pill. Introduced in the early 1960s, the Pill provided the first means of contraception which was almost 100 per cent reliable. Women could now plan their families with some certainty. They could decide when to stop work and when to stop having children. The Pill gave them a kind of freedom they had never enjoyed before. They could plan their own lives.

The 1960s were years of relative prosperity. People in Britain (and elsewhere in the West) believed the 'affluent society' was here to stay. There was time to leave off worrying about how to earn a living and start experimenting with new ideas and new lifestyles. The 'Swinging Sixties' was the era of 'flower power', student rebellion and the 'alternative society'. Each flourished briefly and left some lasting impressions. Then, as the 1960s turned into the 1970s, the women's movement came to Britain.

Most of the ideas which formed the basis of women's liberation originated in the United States. Betty Friedan wrote a book called *The Feminine Mystique* in which she identified the first rumblings of discontent:

> The problem lay buried, unspoken for many years in the minds of American women. It was a strange stirring, a sense of dissatisfaction, a yearning that women suffered in the middle of the twentieth century in the United States. Each suburban wife struggled with it alone. As she made the beds, shopped for groceries, matched slip cover material, ate peanut butter sandwiches, chauffeured Cub Scouts and Brownies, lay beside her husband at night, she was afraid to ask even of herself the silent question: 'Is this all?'

American women began to meet together to exchange ideas and sound out their feelings. Some formed small, informal 'consciousness-raising' groups to examine what it was like to be female and discover what experiences and problems they had in common. Others joined the fast-growing National Organisation of Women (NOW), of which Betty Friedan was a founder-member, to campaign for practical changes such as equal rights under the law and better employment conditions.

Ideas cross the Atlantic

It did not take long for the message to cross the Atlantic. In 1969 the Women's Liberation Workshop emerged in London as a co-ordinating centre for the first crop of women's groups which had sprouted in London and a few other towns. The first outward signs were small square stickers attached to certain advertisements in London's underground. The stickers suggested it was an insult to women to use their bodies to sell products. There was a demonstration at the 1970 Miss World Contest, where feminists expressed their disgust at the way in which women were paraded and measured and compared and judged—as though their looks were all that mattered and their minds and abilities counted for nothing. The same year, 600 women attended the first conference of the British women's liberation movement in Oxford.

The first big rally was held in London in March 1971 on International Women's Day. A campaign was launched for four basic demands: equal pay; equal education and job opportunities; free abortion and contraception on demand; and comprehensive childcare facilities. More and more groups sprang up, some devoted to 'consciousness-raising', some to action and campaigning for the four demands, and some to specialist interests such as women's history, sexuality, education and art. Rallies and conferences became regular events; several feminist publications were launched, including the magazine Spare Rib. In 1974 the movement adopted two more demands: financial and legal independence, and 'the right to a self-defined sexuality' (which meant, briefly, that women themselves should be the ones to determine how, when, why and with whom they had sexual relations, rather than conforming as a matter of course to the traditional expectations of men).

The activities mentioned so far were identified with a rather small, élite sector of the female population in Britain: urban, intellectual, young middle-class women. In fact the women's movement was far broader. For while all this was going on, thousands of working-class women were beginning to realise that they were getting a raw deal and it was time they did something about it.

Some of them felt the campaigns carried out in the name of 'women's liberation' were a little too extreme, or misunderstood them because of the way they were reported in the newspapers. Many others were simply unaware of what was going on because they moved in such different circles. Nevertheless, they too wanted equal pay and equal opportunities.

In 1968 a group of women seat-cover sewers at the Ford motor factory in Dagenham went on strike because the company refused to give them equal pay with men who had equivalent skills. The men in their union supported them and they brought the whole plant to a standstill. They won equal pay. Like the matchgirls' strike, this was an important milestone on the road towards equality because it showed how much women could achieve if they fought together for a just cause.

The success of the Ford strike helped build up pressure within Parliament for a law to give women the right to equal pay. In 1970 the Equal Pay Act was passed, although a five-year interval was allowed to elapse before it came into force.

In 1972 May Hobbs led a campaign to improve the lot of women like herself who cleaned offices at night. 'All the night cleaners are women who cannot do day work because they have families,' she wrote:

They don't do night jobs for the benefit of their health or because they want to get away from their husbands and children. They go out to work because they need the money desperately—for little luxuries like food, rent and clothes for their kids.

The office workers aren't the cleanest people in the world. They slop their tea and coffee in the waste bins while the actual waste paper's usually at the side of the bin, so you have to crawl on your hands and knees to get that straightened out. The average office cleaner does about fifty to sixty offices per night. For that they have to empty all the waste-paper bins around 300–400, sweep all the offices, then you have hoover, you have to dust, you have to clean the toilets, lifts, then the backstairs, then the front stairs. You have to do all that in an eight-hour shift and if you don't get it done then you have to stay until you do. And because these women need the money so desperately they will bow to anything and that is the reason that you have to have this industry organised.

May Hobbs's aim was to get night cleaners to join the Transport and General Workers' Union as a first step towards negotiating better pay and conditions. Within the union, they formed the Cleaners Action Group and drew up a set of demands, some of which they won. It was the first of many campaigns around which the two main elements of the women's movement joined forces. May Hobbs drew support from many women's liberation groups who helped recruit night cleaners to the union.

The emergence of the women's movement caused new flurries of activity among the older-established women's organisations. Many of these, including the Fawcett Society and the Six Point Group, had their roots in the early part of the 20th century when women were fighting for the vote. They had continued to hold meetings and lobby Parliament for greater equality in a quiet, dignified manner, but they had ceased to make much impact. The upsurge of interest in feminist issues gave them a new lease of life.

The early and mid-1970s were the years in which the women's movement was most influential. New groups and campaigns and women's centres mushroomed in cities and towns throughout Britain. Scores of books were published about women's rights, about the theories of women's liberation, about aspects of women's lives, about women's history, anthropology, sexuality, literature and art. Hundreds of television and radio programmes were devoted to the 'problems' of women. Even popular newspapers such as the *Daily Mirror* began to give serious coverage to some (though not all) of the issues.

In 1972 Erin Pizzey set up the first refuge for battered wives in Chiswick, West London. It suddenly came to light that thousands of women were regularly beaten black and blue by the men they lived with. What was truly remarkable was that this had never before been brought to the public notice. It had been going on for centuries, yet until now there seemed to have been a conspiracy of silence about it. Perhaps it took the women's

movement to convince battered wives they were right to be out-
raged and to convince the public at large that violence of this
kind was not merely a 'natural' by-product of marriage.

Women flocked to Chiswick from all over the country to
escape their belligerent menfolk. Soon more refuges had to be
opened. By 1976 there were 75 in Britain, and the Women's
Aid Federation which linked them became an important part of
the broader women's movement.

There had been a series of unsuccessful attempts, beginning
in 1968, to persuade Parliament to pass a law against sex discrimination—a law, that is, which said women should not be
treated less favourably than men but should have equal opportunities. The first Anti-Discrimination Bill, presented to
Parliament by Joyce Butler MP, was received with contempt by
most other Members of Parliament. What—give women the
right to equal treatment? Enshrine equality in the law? How
absurd! Women were more suited to certain types of work,
they insisted. Women couldn't cope with big pieces of machinery. They were no good in positions of authority. And girls
had to be educated differently in order to fit them for a future as
wives and mothers. . . .

In seven years the climate of opinion changed quite dramati-
cally—largely as a result of vigorous campaigning by members
of the women's movement. In 1975 the great majority of MPs
were able to agree that women ought (in theory at least) to be
treated as men's equals. They passed the Sex Discrimination
Act which made it illegal to treat women less favourably than
men in education, training, employment, housing and the
provision of 'goods, facilities and services' (which covered
things like mortgages, hire purchase, being served in restaurant
and pubs, etc.). It came into force on 29 December 1975 along
with the Equal Pay Act. At the same time the government set
up the Equal Opportunities Commission to ensure the new
laws were enforced and to promote equality generally. Another
law passed in 1975 gave working women the right to maternity
leave: if they had been with the same employer for two years and
fulfilled certain other conditions, they were entitled to six weeks
paid maternity leave and reinstatement in their job 29 weeks
after the baby's birth.

Developments like these were not confined to Britain. Laws
bringing similar changes were passed in other European

countries as well as in the United States and Canada. The
United Nations designated 1975 as International Women's
Year, and women from almost every nation in the world met at
a massive conference in Mexico. From lunatic fringe to international respectability: the women's movement had come of
age. But it had scarcely begun to achieve its objectives.

What are the aims?

Women in the movement are not concerned simply to get
statutes enacted by Parliament, to march through cities and
to pass noble sentiments from one small group of like-minded
people to another. They want to challenge conventional ideas
and change the way in which society is organised.

One of their prime targets is education—not just what happens in schools, but all the influences which form children's
attitudes to themselves and the world. Toys, for instance: boys
play with model trains, aeroplanes and space ships, gamma-ray
guns, chemistry sets and skateboards, while girls have dolls,
dolls' houses, tea-sets, craft kits for making small, pretty things,
vacuum cleaners, washing machines, cosmetic sets and other
toys designed to make them 'just like Mummy'. The books and
comics boys read are about adventure, science fiction, fighting
and dare-devil stunts, while girls read mainly about personal
dramas which take place at home and at school, and about boys,
romance, jealousy, heartache and living happily ever after with
Mr Right. So boys' interests are directed outside the home
towards things mechanical and scientific, towards exploration
and towards an image of themselves as 'tough', concerned with
action rather than reflection, with thought rather than emotion.
Girls' interests are directed inwards to the home, towards household duties, love, marriage and babies.

Books used in schools present a similarly one-sided view of the
world. Here are just a few examples, taken from *Women's
Rights: A Practical Guide*:

1. The Oxford Children's Reference Library book, *Science*,
shows 107 males in its illustrations and seventeen females.
The males are engaged in a variety of active and scientific
pursuits, while almost all the females are engaged in passive and typically feminine pursuits such as combing hair,
vacuuming and mixing a pudding. School children who read

the book might gain the impression that science is mainly for boys; and it could add to other influences which discourage girls from studying science or aiming for jobs in the fields of science and engineering.

2. A book called *Famous Writers* in the Macdonald Junior Reference Library mentions thirty-four men and not one woman. This could lead children to believe that women have achieved little or nothing in the literary field; and girls may underrate their own abilities if they have no role models of their own sex.

3. The Ladybird reading books—even the new 'modernised' editions—often show the main characters, Jane and Peter, in stereotypical roles. One illustration in *Things We Like* shows a group of boys playing ball while Jane cheers them in the background:

> Peter has a red ball.
> He plays with the boys with the red ball.
> Jane looks on.
> That was good, Peter, says Jane.

This is just one of the many passages in the Ladybird reading scheme which show male characters playing active or leading roles while female characters are passive or supportive. Each passage adds to a general picture of the world which is passed on to children at a most impressionable age.

4. *Tudor Britain* in the series *History Topics and Models* (Evans Brothers) has a chapter 'Tudors at Work'. In three pages of text, there are only these three references to women:

> Behind the workroom was the family's living-room; here the master, his wife, family and apprentices had their meals.
> Work began at about six-thirty every morning when the master and his wife made sure that the boys were up and busy in the shop and workroom.
> The merchant's wife had some pottery and pewter for special occasions.

Women are described in terms of their relationships to men and never as individuals in their own right. *Their* work (preparing food, making clothes, child rearing, etc.) though no less important, is not discussed at all.

It is not surprising that when it comes to thinking about the future and choosing which exams to take, girls tend to set their sights lower than boys. They have sensed that life has certain departments which 'belong' to boys and are out-of-bounds to girls. The Sex Discrimination Act makes it illegal to treat girls less favourably than boys at school (and vice versa). What happens in *your* school? Do equal numbers of boys and girls do needlework? Cookery? Woodwork? Maths? Physics? Do equal numbers of boys and girls take A levels and go on to college or university? If not, why not? Are there some sections in this Encyclopaedia which seem to you to be more for boys than for girls? If so, why do you get that impression?

It is not the aim of the women's movement to force all girls to read Captain Marvel comics, play Cowboys-and-Indians and take A level physics. Of course, some girls will find they are better suited to sewing and cooking and looking after children than climbing Mount Everest or fixing motor cars—no matter what toys or books they've been brought up with. The point is that girls should be free to explore *all* the possibilities. They should have just as much chance to find out whether they are as good at science as domestic science. And then they should be free to move in whichever direction is best suited to their abilities. So should boys.

The Sex Discrimination Act has had very little impact on education. In the first two years after it came into force, not a single complaint of discrimination in education was brought to court, although girls and boys continued to receive unequal treatment in many schools. Why? The procedure for making a complaint under the Act is very long and complicated: parents and children have been reluctant to embark on it. The Act outlaws only the most obvious, direct forms of discrimination. There are many subtler forms which cannot be combated in the courts.

Young people learn a lot more at school than the subjects which are included in the timetable. They form certain attitudes and develop ideas. As they do so, they take the first vital steps towards determining what they will be when they grow up. If a girl has gained the impression that the most important thing she will do in future will be to get married and have children, she may not care very much what job she does until the 'Big Day' arrives. She may not want a job which requires a long

training. She may look through careers leaflets and decide
certain jobs are not suitable because all the pictures are of boys—
or because she knows of no other girls who have tried them. She
may have limited her choice already by specialising in arts
rather than science subjects. She may not realise that even if she
starts a family in her early twenties and stays at home until she
is 35 or 40, she still has a long working life ahead of her and
plenty of time to build an interesting career.

The women's movement is concerned that girls and boys
should have equal access to *all* jobs. Real equality of access must
include an equal chance to find out about each job, equal
opportunity to become interested in it and equal encouragement
to apply.

What happens in fact is that the great majority of girls go
into unskilled or semi-skilled factory jobs, or else become shop
assistants, waitresses, clerks, typists, secretaries, hairdressers,
nurses or teachers. They rarely become car mechanics, elec-
tricians, plumbers, lorry drivers, train drivers, engineers,
nuclear physicists, accountants, lawyers, airline pilots, business
executives, surgeons, politicians, photographers, university
lecturers . . . (this list is endless!). The jobs girls go into are
usually poorly paid with few opportunities for promotion. In
1977, well over a year after the Equal Pay Act came into force,
women's average gross earnings were £51 a week and men's
were £78.60.

Even when they are not confined to typically female jobs,
women are less likely than men to rise to senior levels. Employers often assume they are less able to wield authority or
carry responsibility; that their family commitments will interfere
with their career; or that men will resent women being promoted
over their heads. Some women are reluctant to seek promotion.
They've been told for so long that the female sex is weaker, less
capable and better suited to supportive roles, that they have
come to believe it of themselves!

Very often, they find they are obliged to stay in less demanding,
lower-paid jobs because—unlike their male colleagues—they
have a second job to do at home. Nearly 50 per cent of married
women go out to work. Like May Hobbs's cleaning ladies, they
work not for fun or for 'pin money' but because they need a
regular income to help support their families. In addition, they
do most (if not all) of the cleaning, washing, shopping and

cooking for their husbands and children. When their children are too young to go to school they may have to take a part-time job or stop work altogether for a few years. If their children are ill it falls to them, not their husbands, to stay away from work to look after them.

It is very rare for married men to take days off work for 'family reasons' or to interrupt their employment for a spell to look after their children. If they tried, their employers might not take too kindly to it, having grown accustomed to the idea that men have wives to keep things running smoothly at home. In the vast majority of households where husband and wife both have full-time jobs, it is the wife who does most of the housework. Her husband may help her, but *helping* is a far cry from carrying an equal share of the responsibility or doing 50 per cent of the work.

More use has been made of the new laws to tackle inequality in the employment field than in education. For example, there were 161 equal pay claims in the first ten months of 1976, of which 74 were successful. However, the Equal Pay and Sex Discrimination Acts have not made a great deal of difference to most working women. If a woman wants to claim equal pay or complain of sex discrimination at work, she must take her case to an industrial tribunal. If she is not in a trade union she will probably have to do this on her own without expert help—which may put her at a disadvantage if she is pitting her wits against an employer who can afford to hire a solicitor or barrister to represent him on the occasion. There are lots of loopholes in the laws: employers who want to give men preferential treatment can get round them quite easily. A woman cannot claim equal pay unless there is a man at her workplace doing a job which is the same or similar to hers. She cannot claim she is a victim of sex discrimination unless she can point to the man whom the employer has treated more favourably. Most women work in jobs where there are no men with whom they can compare themselves, so the laws can't help them at all. And then, of course, laws cannot change people's attitudes or habits—and these are often the main source of discrimination.

It is the aim of the women's movement to gain genuine equality of opportunity for women and men at work. This doesn't mean all women are supposed to put their jobs before their homes and families, or that women who stay at home as full-time mothers and housewives are somehow letting the side down. The idea is that women who *want* to combine full-time work with raising a family should have the same range of opportunities as men, while men who prefer to devote more time to their families should have more freedom to do so. This would require some fairly fundamental changes which can only be brought about by legislation—for instance:

1. *Special training schemes* to bring more women into jobs traditionally done by men. In 1976 the Engineering Industry Training Board launched a scheme for training girls as technicians in electronics and light mechanical engineering. It gave scholarships to 25 school-leavers in Birmingham and 25 in the Kingston–Croydon area of Surrey. Its two main aims were to demonstrate to industry that girls could do engineering just as well as boys and to change teachers' attitudes so that more girls would be encouraged to consider engineering as a career and to study appropriate subjects at school. Once the girls had been recruited they turned out to be of an unusually high calibre— thus proving the EITB's point. More schemes of this kind would help to bring girls into other areas of work.

2. *Part-time jobs and parental leave* should be as widely available and acceptable for men as for women. This would enable more couples to exchange roles and for the father to stay at home while the mother goes out to work, at least for some of the time while their children are young—if they wish to arrange their lives that way.

3. *Equal participation in trade unions by women and men.* Trade unions are the most common means by which working people negotiate for higher pay and better conditions. Since the early 1970s women have been joining them at a much faster rate than men—twice as fast, in fact. By 1978 there were almost four million women among a total of $11\frac{1}{2}$ million trade union members. However, unions still seem to be male institutions. Union meetings are dominated by male speakers and their executive committees rarely include more than one or two women. The result is that men shape union policy. If women had more say unions might have different priorities—for instance, they might devote more energy to campaigning for equal pay, better training, improved maternity and paternity leave and more nurseries. Why are women so poorly represented in the unions? One

reason is that meetings are usually held after work when most women have to rush off to do the shopping and cook an evening meal for their families. Another is that a lot of women lack confidence to speak out in a room or conference hall which is full of men, because of the way they have been brought up: they have not been encouraged—as boys often are—to think of themselves as organisers or leaders. A third reason is that men have run the unions since they were first set up more than 100 years ago, and some of them still seem reluctant to share power with women.

If women are to play a more active role, unions will have to make special efforts to encourage them. Some unions are beginning to do so by holding conferences and training courses for women, by appointing women's organisers and running campaigns on issues such as equal pay. Others pay lip service to the ideal of equality, while ensuring that their male members remain firmly in control.

4. *Well-equipped, properly staffed nurseries* available for all pre-school-age children of working parents, plus special arrangements for looking after children of school age during holidays and the hours after school when their parents are still at work. The law provides working women with maternity leave, but that only lasts until the seventh month after the baby's birth. Who is to look after the child when the mother takes up her legal right to return to work?

Most local authorities run day nurseries, but there are so few places that they are usually restricted to children of single parents and those from 'deprived backgrounds' (e.g. whose mothers are ill, or who live in especially poor housing conditions). The official attitude is summed up in the Plowden Report, which was published as long ago as 1967, but still forms the basis of government policy:

We do not believe that full-time nursery places should be provided, even for children who might tolerate separation without harm, except for exceptionally good reasons. We have no reason to suppose that working mothers as a group care any less about the well-being of their children than mothers who do not work . . . but some mothers who are not obliged to work may work full time regardless of their children's welfare. It is no business of the educational service to encourage these mothers to do so. It is true, unfortunately, that the refusal of full-time nursery places for their children may prompt some mothers to make unsuitable arrangements for their children's care during working hours. All the same, we consider that mothers who cannot satisfy the authorities that they have exceptionally good reasons for working should have a low priority for full-time nurseries for their children.

The policy of the women's movement differs from the views stated in the Plowden Report on two counts. First, it maintains that when a child is past the breast-feeding stage, it may be cared for equally well by its father or by another responsible adult. There is no evidence that mothers are *naturally* better suited to look after their children. Some men are better at it than some women, and vice versa. It depends on the personality, not the gender, of the individual.

Second, the idea that children will suffer if they are looked after in nurseries rather than in their own homes has no foundation in fact. What counts is the *quality* of the care they receive, wherever they may be. A child may be harmed by spending all day at home, if home is cramped, dirty or isolated. On the other hand, if a nursery is warm, well-ventilated, clean, spacious, full of playmates, toys and books, set in pleasant grounds and run by well-trained, enthusiastic nurses and teachers, a child may be better off there than at home. This raises the question of money: should more government funds be spent on child care? The women's movement maintains that it should—for the sake of women who want or need to work full-time, for the sake of children and for the sake of a more equal society. Meanwhile, mothers *and* fathers who want to stay at home to look after their children should be given equal encouragement and support by employers, neighbours and the government.

It will be a long time before the ideas behind these aims of the women's movement are widely accepted and longer still before they are actually achieved—if, indeed, they ever are. The same is true of many of its other objectives.

Despite all the new Women's Aid Centres and the Domestic Violence Act of 1976, which sought to improve legal protection for battered women, men continue to assault their wives. The fundamental causes of violence in the home have yet to be identified, let alone removed.

Newspapers, magazines and television programmes still

present a distorted image of women. Popular newspapers use photographs of scantily covered women to help increase their sales, while giving even scantier coverage to women's more serious activities! Next time you read a newspaper or watch the news on television, count how many stories are about men only, and how many refer to women. What are the most common reasons for mentioning women? Look at the adjectives used to describe women and compare them with those used to describe men. We know that more men hold positions of power and therefore do 'newsworthy' things, but is there not an imbalance nevertheless? Here is a report from the *Chelmsford Newsman Herald*, published in 1976, about the appointment of a new town councillor:

Things are stirring among Chelmsford's new district councillors. Temperatures are sent rising at committee meetings by the eagerly-awaited entrance of delicious Wendy Seely, newly elected member for Waltham ward. The sexy ex-actress seems to be the petite object of many an admiring glance from the usually sober elder statesmen on the council. On occasions she has attended council appointments recently she has looked quite a dish, wearing bright coloured bandanas round her lovely white neck, beautiful golden ringed hair tumbling down her shoulders, black tights. Any other business?

What does it tell you about the new councillor's political opinions? What does it tell you about the attitude of the reporter? As far as popular journalism goes, it seems women are expected to conform to roles which are almost as restricted today as they were in the 1950s. They are still presented as 'objects of beauty fashioned for the delight of men' or as 'homemakers'. Little serious attention is paid to what they do, think or feel beyond these narrow limits. The women's movement aims to right the imbalance.

If there is still so much to be done, what has the women's movement achieved in the last ten years?

Most people now accept the principle that women and men should have equal rights under the law. The need to improve women's lives and give them greater opportunities is generally recognised. People are beginning to get used to the idea that women can be television newscasters, plumbers and even

Prime Ministers. Women have won greater self-esteem. The notion that they should choose how to lead their lives is now a respectable one. It is hard to imagine that things will ever be quite the same again.

Acknowledgment

The extract from *Woman's Rights: A Practical Guide* (pp. 297–8 of the 1977 revised edition) by Anna Coote and Tessa Gill is reprinted by permission of Penguin Books Ltd.

Something to Join

A Section on Youth Organisations,
with notes on the Morse Code, Semaphore, Compass
and Knots.

ORGANISATIONS TO JOIN
(including some courses to apply for)

THIS is a list of some of the organisations that are either entirely for young people or have sections open to the young. A few of them provide courses only for those who have been specially recommended by their schools or other authorities. Take particular note of the age limits for membership, which are given in most cases. Note also that, in present conditions, subscriptions might well have increased in the months between preparation and publication of this edition.

Air Training Corps A national organisation sponsored by the Ministry of Defence (R.A.F.) with the aim of promoting and encouraging in young men a practical interest in aviation and the R.A.F., providing training useful both in Service and civilian life, and developing, through the promotion of sports and pastimes in healthy rivalry, the qualities of leadership and good citizenship.

Amateur Athletic Association Controls athletics in England and Wales, with affiliated clubs throughout the country. Details of clubs, membership open to boys of 11 and over, and of training facilities, instructional booklets and coaching schemes from 70 Brompton Road, London SW3 1EE. This is also the address of the Women's Amateur Athletic Association.

Army Cadet Force The British Army's own voluntary youth organisation. Open to boys between the ages of 13 and 18. 58 Buckingham Gate, SW1E 6AN.

Boys' Brigade Object: 'The advancement of Christ's Kingdom among boys.' Juniors, 8–12 years; Company, 11–17; Seniors, 16–19.

Brathay Exploration Group A group of young people who travel, explore and carry out work and study projects in this country and overseas. Each year the Group organises about twenty expeditions, and in recent years has visited Iceland, Norway, Greenland, Canada, Poland, Turkey, Tunisia, Corsica, Kenya and Uganda as well as the remoter parts of Scotland and Ireland. Membership is open to anyone, keen for adventure, who is at least 16 years old. To qualify for overseas and certain expeditions in the British Isles, previous expedition experience is necessary.

The Brathay Field Study Centre organises one-week courses for boys and girls studying for G.C.E. 'A' level in Geography or

Biology. Good library and laboratory facilities and opportunities for carrying out individual study projects in the Lake District.

Further details from The Principal, Brathay Hall, Ambleside, Cumbria.

British Red Cross Society Membership of the Junior Red Cross is open to boys and girls from 5 years to school-leaving age. Training is offered in first aid, nursing, child care, hygiene, accident prevention, camping, etc. Members help at holidays for handicapped children and undertake a variety of service activities within their community. They are encouraged to make contact with Junior Red Cross members abroad and to take part in the Society's international work by knitting blankets and raising money towards specific overseas projects. Headquarters: 9 Grosvenor Crescent, London SW1X 7EJ.

British Sub-Aqua Club Devoted to underwater exploration, science and sport. Has over 700 branches in Great Britain. Minimum age: 15, but special Snorkeller Award Scheme for juniors. Applications to Director, British Sub Aqua Club, 70 Brompton Road, London, SW3 1HA.

British Trust for Ornithology A national society for all birdwatchers: invites members to take part in varied field investigations into bird biology and distribution, with emphasis on the interactions between man and birds: the common birds census, nest record scheme, Birds of Estuaries Enquiry, bird ringing (by special permit only after considerable training and practice), moult enquiry and other special enquiries including regular censuses of species such as the heron. Services to members include the quarterly journal 'Bird Study', the newsletter 'BTO News', national conferences—both general and specialist—regional conferences, local meetings in co-operation with local bird clubs, specialist courses in modern techniques, use of the lending library and the extensive reference library at Tring, and grants and awards for research. Annual subscription £5 p.a. (£2 p.a. for members under 21 or up to 25 if in receipt of full-time education). Applications to the Membership Secretary, B.T.O., Beech Grove, Tring, Hertfordshire, Tel: Tring 3461.

Camping Club Youth Junior section of the Camping Club of Great Britain. Open to young people aged 12 to 17 inclusive. Annual subscription, £1 including entrance fee and V.A.T. Camping at home and abroad. Instruction given. 11 Lower Grosvenor Place, London, SW1W 0EY.

Concordia Youth Service Volunteers Runs international working camps to help with fruit picking and market gardening in Britain; also with the wine harvest, forestry and construction work on the Continent. Age limits for camps abroad: 18–30. Volunteers pay their own travel expenses. The age limit in British camps is 16–30, and the booking fee is £14. Applications to the Recruitment Secretary, Concordia, 11a Albemarle Street, London, W1x 4BE.

Council for British Archaeology Issues a *Calendar of Excavations* monthly from March until November with a final issue in January which enables anyone wishing to take part in excavations to get in touch with directors requiring voluntary helpers. For the over-16s only. Annual subscription to the *Calendar*: £3. C.B.A., 112 Kennington Road, London, SE11 6RE.

Cyclists' Touring Club A national organisation, founded 1878 to protect and promote the interests of cyclists. Personal benefits include legal aid, third-party insurance, illustrated travel magazine and handbook, local cycle runs, clubrooms, social events, organised holiday tours. Junior membership (under 18): £2 a year including VAT. 69 Meadrow, Godalming, Surrey.

Field Studies Council Has ten Field Centres distributed over England and Wales. Courses, usually lasting a week, are organised from March to late October and include field work in archaeology, botany, geography, zoology and art. Junior members (under 16) may attend only Family Courses or in groups with their teachers; young people over 16 may join suitable courses individually or in groups. Minimum annual subscription: £1. Applications to Information Office, Preston Montford, Montford Bridge, Shrewsbury SY4 1HW.

Girls' Brigade An international uniformed movement for girls of all ages from five upwards. It has a varied programme with a wide range of activities. The Brigade is a Church-based movement with the motto: 'Seek, serve and follow Christ'. National and International Headquarters: Brigade House, 8 Parsons Green, London SW6 4TH.

Girl Guides Association Parallel organisation with the Scouts; U.K. membership of over three quarters of a million, world membership of over 7·3 million in 94 countries. Commonwealth Headquarters: 17–19 Buckingham Palace Road, London, SW1W 0PT.

Junior Astronomical Society Aims to encourage people of all ages interested in astronomy and space. A quarterly journal, *Hermes*, includes articles on all aspects of astronomy and space-flight. Regular meetings are held in London. There are special sections to help observers. Subscription: £2·50 a year. Secretary: V. L. Tibbott, 58 Vaughan Gardens, Ilford, Essex, IG1 3PD.

Mountaineering Association Now amalgamated with the Youth Hostels Association (see page R7) which organises the mountaineering courses previously run by the Mountaineering Association.

National Council of YMCAs A world-wide organisation represented in 86 countries in 10,000 YMCAs with some 23 million people, mainly young, men and women, participating in a wide variety of programmes guided by trained leaders. There are some 250 centres in the U.K. Headquarters: 640, Forest Road, London, E17 3DZ.

National Federation of Young Farmers' Clubs Open to all young people between the ages of 10 and 26 who are interested in farming and the countryside. Headquarters: Y.F.C. Centre, National Agricultural Centre, Kenilworth, Warwickshire, CV8 2LG. Coventry 56131.

Outward Bound Trust Holds training courses at Aberdovey, Eskdale, Burghead, Ullswater and Ashburton to equip boys to face hazards and emergencies on the mountains and at sea. Also modified courses for girls. Applicants must be sponsored by employers, education authorities, youth organisations, etc., who may sometimes help financially. Courses last 26 days. Fees: juniors, £31·50; seniors, £35. The Trust now has facilities for training 4,000 boys and 500 girls a year. Age limits: boys, 14½–19½; girls, 16–20.

Quaker Work Camps, Friends Service Council Organises work camps in Britain and Ireland from July to mid-September lasting from 2 to 6 weeks each, and one or two short camps at Easter (1 to 2 weeks). Wide variety of work from manual, decorating, construction and conservation projects to running summer play schemes, residential holidays for mentally handicapped children, and work and study camps. Mixed international teams of 8–20 people. Minimum age 16, although this is raised to 18 or 19 in some cases. Handicapped participants are welcome. Volunteers pay their own travel expenses and pocket money, and those from Britain and Ireland are asked to contribute towards their maintenance if able to do so. Volunteers who have taken part in Quaker Work Camps or related Quaker activities can be sent to work camps abroad. Applications from Britain and Ireland to Quaker Work Camps Committee, Friends Service Council, Friends House, Euston Road, London, NW1 2BJ. Volunteers from other countries should apply through a work camp organisation in their own country.

Ramblers' Association Works with the support of some 450 rambling clubs and over 100 local groups throughout the country; publishes *Rucksack* three times a year and *Bed, Breakfast and Bus Guide* annually, supplying these free of charge to members. Loans 1/50,000 Ordnance Survey maps for small charge to members. Special rates for juniors and full-time students. Details from 1/4 Crawford Mews, York Street, London, W1H 1PT.

Partner organisation, **Ramblers' Holidays Ltd.**, organises walking and mountaineering holidays on the Continent: details from 13 Longcroft House, Fretherne Road, Welwyn Garden City, Herts.

St John Ambulance Association and Brigade The Association Branch organises training courses in first aid and nursing, while the Brigade Branch is a uniformed organisation that encourages the study not only of first aid and nursing but also a variety of other subjects: among them, fire-fighting, sea- and boat-training, canoeing, camping, cooking, swimming and lifesaving. Summer training camps are held in most counties. Age limits: boys (ambulance-cadets) and girls (nursing cadets), 8–18. Registrar, L. E. Hawes, HQ, St John Ambulance, 1 Grosvenor Crescent, London, SW1X 7EF.

Scout Association This firmly established youth movement offers a progressive and interesting system of character training for boys and young men. The movement embraces the following sections: Cub Scouts (8–11), Scouts (11–16) and Venture Scouts (16–20). In addition to camping and other normal Scouting activities, a wide range of specialist subjects is made available . . . sailing, gliding, pot holing, climbing, underwater swimming, etc. Scouting exists in some 150 countries with a world membership of over 13 million. Headquarters: Baden-Powell House, Queen's Gate, London, SW7 5JS.

Sea Cadet Corps A voluntary youth organisation for boys between 12 and 18. Through its discipline and sea training the

Corps sets out to help those who are considering a seafaring career. Although it is not a pre-service organisation and no cadet is obliged to become a sailor, the Corps is recognised as providing excellent training for boys who subsequently join the Royal Navy, one of its Reserves, the Merchant Navy or the Fishing Fleet. Headquarters: Broadway House, Broadway, Wimbledon, London, SW19 1RL.

White Hall Centre for Open Country Pursuits Courses run by the Derbyshire Education Committee in outdoor education, hillcraft, rock climbing, caving, camping, canoeing and mountain leadership. Open throughout the year. Minimum age: 14. Details from the Principal, White Hall Centre, Long Hill, Buxton, Derbyshire SK17 6SX.

Young Explorers' Trust (The Association of British Youth Exploration Societies) Seeks to promote and support expeditions for young people. Membership is open to groups and societies, however small, who are setting out to organise expeditions involving a significant element of exploration and discovery. The Trust offers an information service for expedition organisers, and meetings, study groups and training facilities are arranged. Overseas expeditions may apply for the Trust's approval, and grants are made annually to expeditions that reach the appropriate standard of organisation, safety and field tasks. Details from the Administrative Secretary, Young Explorers' Trust, at the Royal Geographical Society, 1 Kensington Gore, London, SW7 2AR. 01-589-9724.

Young Ornithologists' Club Run by the Royal Society for the Protection of Birds for boys and girls up to 15. Runs courses, holds meetings, organises projects and encourages field work: publishes its bi-monthly magazine *Bird Life*. Subscriptions: individual £2; family, £2·45; also group membership for schools and clubs. Applications to The Lodge, Sandy, Beds. SG19 2DL.

Youth Hostels Associations These organisations have the object of helping young people on walking or cycling tours. In Britain and Ireland alone they maintain some 400 hostels where members are provided with beds and meals at very low rates. A number of Adventure Holidays are now arranged as introductions to new activities such as pony trekking, sailing, skin-diving, etc. Subscription (England and Wales): 5–15, 85p a year; 16–20, £7·50; 21 and over, £2·50. Headquarters: *England and Wales*, Trevelyan House, St. Albans, Herts. *Scotland,*

7 Glebe Crescent, Stirling. *Northern Ireland*, 93 Dublin Road, Belfast, BT2 7HF.

Altogether in the 50 countries where the Youth Hostel movement flourishes there are over 4,000 hostels.

A British membership card (with photograph) is accepted in all countries affiliated to the International Youth Hostel Federation. The Y.H.A.'s sales department at 14 Southampton Street, London, WC2E 7HY, sells rucksacks, sleeping bags, tents, camping equipment, climbing kit, maps and guides.

Y.W.C.A. of Great Britain Affiliated to the World Y.W.C.A., active in over 80 countries. Services in U.K. include accommodation for single young people and older women; clubs and community centres; opportunities to serve others; detached youth work and courses for school leavers and fifth and sixth formers. Headquarters: 2 Weymouth Street, London, W1N 4AX.

THE MORSE CODE

The Morse code consists of groups of dots and dashes ('shorts' and 'longs'), each group representing a letter or number. You can communicate in Morse by flashing a light, by sound (the imprisoned hero in a book, you remember, always taps it out with his shoe on the wall of his cell) or by using a flag. The dots should be made as short as possible, and the dashes should be three times as long as the dots.

The Morse Alphabet The letters that occur most often in English are given the shortest symbols. The words placed against the letters are used so that mistakes shall not arise because letters have similar sounds. (For instance, 'm' spoken sounds very like 'n', 'b' very like 'd' and so on.)

A for	Alfa	· —		L for	Lima	· — · ·
B	Bravo	— · · ·		M	Mike	— —
C	Charlie	— · — ·		N	November	— ·
D	Delta	— · ·		O	Oscar	— — —
E	Echo	·		P	Papa	· — — ·
F	Foxtrot	· · — ·		Q	Quebec	— — · —
G	Golf	— — ·		R	Romeo	· — ·
H	Hotel	· · · ·		S	Sierra	· · ·
I	India	· ·		T	Tango	—
J	Juliett	· — — —		U	Uniform	· · —
K	Kilo	— · —		V	Victor	· · · —

W for Whiskey	· — —	Y	Yankee	— · — —
X	X-ray	— · · —	Z	Zulu	— — · ·

Numerals

1	· — — — —		6	— · · · ·
2	· · — — —		7	— — · · ·
3	· · · — —		8	— — — · ·
4	· · · · —		9	— — — — ·
5	· · · · ·		10	— — — — —

Full stop (AAA) · — · — · —
Apostrophe · — — — — ·
Oblique stroke — · · — ·
Brackets (KK) — · — — · —
Short break · · · ·
Beginning (CT) — · — · —
Hyphen — · · · · —
Inverted commas (RR) · — · · — ·
Underline (UK) · · — — · —
Question (IMI) · · — — · ·
Long break (BT) — · · · —
Ending (AR) · — · — ·
Finish of transmission for indefinite period (VA)· · · — · —

SEMAPHORE

It is immensely important in semaphore signalling that the angles should be clear and the arm and the wrist in a straight line. To ensure this, always press the first finger along the stick of the flag. Choose a position where you can be easily seen and a background that is as far away as possible—the sky being obviously the best.

Rules for Semaphoring At the end of each word you should drop the arms straight down in front of you—this is known as the 'ready' position—and pause. Should you make a mistake, give the 'annul' sign and begin the word again. ('Annul' means 'rub out', 'cancel'.) Before a number give the 'numeral' sign, and if you are going back to letters give the 'alphabet' sign before you do so.

When you are reading a message, acknowledge each word by making the letter 'A' (the 'general answer' sign). If you are

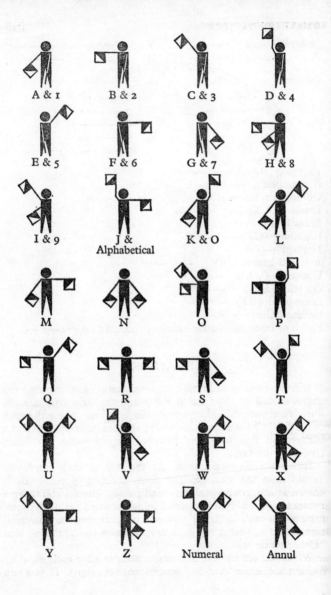

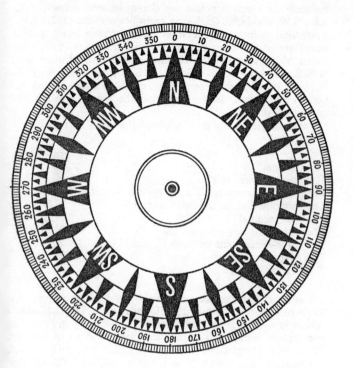

uncertain about a word, make no sign, and the sender will then repeat the word.

THE COMPASS

The magnetic compass is an instrument that enables navigators to steer in any direction required, and also shows the direction of any visible object. It is divided into points, quarter points and degrees.

The Points The compass circle is divided into thirty-two named points. The four main (or cardinal points, N., E., S. and W.), divide the card into four quadrants or quarters. Half-way between the cardinal points are the quadrantal points, N.E., S.E., S.W. and N.W. Half-way again between the cardinal and quadrantal points are the intermediate (three-letter) points, which are named from the cardinal and quadrantal points between which they lie, the cardinal points being named first; N.N.E., E.N.E., E.S.E., S.S.E., S.S.W., W.S.W., W.N.W., N.N.W. Between all these points are sixteen others (called 'by' points) which take their names from the nearest cardinal and quadrantal points.

For example, in the first quadrant (between N. and E.) the points are:

The cardinal	N.
The by-point next to it	N. by E.
The three-letter point half-way between N. and E.	N.N.E.
The by-point next to the half cardinal	N.E. by N.
The half cardinal	N.E.
The by-point	N.E. by E.
The three-letter point between E. and N.E.	E.N.E.
The by-point	E. by N.
The cardinal point	E.

Degrees The compass circle is also divided into degrees; it is in degrees (by what is called the **Quadrantal Notation**) that a course is usually given and steered. The card is divided into 360°, but is marked 0° at North and South and 90° at East and West. So N.E. would be given as N. 45° E. Gyro compass cards are marked right round from north through 90° (East), 180° (South), 270° (West) and 360° (North). This is called **Circular Notation**. Gyro compasses are carried in addition to magnetic compasses by most warships and many large merchant and passenger ships. The gyro, controlled by the earth's rotation, consists of a wheel turned at great speed by an electric motor. The points, with their equivalents in circular and quadrantal notation, are shown below.

Point	Circular	Quadrantal	Point	Circular	Quadrantal
N.	0	N.	N.E. by E.	56¼	N. 56¼ E.
N. by E.	11¼	N. 11¼ E.	E.N.E.	67½	N. 67½ E.
N.N.E.	22½	N. 22½ E.	E. by N.	78¾	N. 78¾ E.
N.E. by N.	33¾	N. 33¾ E.	E.	90	E.
N.E.	45	N. 45 E.	E. by S.	101¼	S. 78¾ E.

Point	Circular	Quadrantal	Point	Circular	Quadrantal
E.S.E.	112½	S. 67½ E.	S.W. by W.	236¼	S. 56¼ W.
S.E. by E.	123¾	S. 56¼ E.	W.S.W.	247½	S. 67½ W.
S.E.	135	S. 45 E.	W. by S.	258¾	S. 78¾ W.
S.E. by S.	146¼	S. 33¾ E.	W.	270	W.
S.S.E.	157½	S. 22½ E.	W. by N.	281¼	N. 78¾ W.
S. by E.	168¾	S. 11¼ E.	W.N.W.	292½	N. 67½ W.
S.	180	S.	N.W. by W.	303¾	N. 56¼ W.
S. by W.	191¼	S. 11¼ W.	N.W.	315	N. 45 W.
S.S.W.	202½	S. 22½ W.	N.W. by N.	326¼	N. 33¾ W.
S.W. by S.	213¾	S. 33¾ W.	N.N.W.	337½	N. 22½ W.
S.W.	225	S. 45 W.	N. by W.	348¾	N. 11¼ W.

KNOTS

The **Reef Knot** is both the firmest of knots and the quickest to untie. It is used for tying two ropes together.

The **Sheet Bend** is the best knot for tying together ropes of differing thickness. If the end is passed round again the knot becomes a **Double Sheet Bend,** which will neither stick nor jerk undone.

The **Clove Hitch** (an easy knot to make, as the picture shows) is used to make one rope fast to a larger one. When fastened to a pole or another rope it will neither slip up nor down.

The **Bowline** (used at sea for making a loop on a rope's end) makes a fixed loop that will never slip after the first grip. It can be safely used for making a halter for leading an animal.

The **Sheepshank** is used for temporarily shortening a rope.

The **Figure of Eight** is used at sea to prevent a rope un-reeving through a block.

The **Half-hitch** is used to tie ropes to poles.

The **Round Turn and Two Half-hitches** is used for securing a rope to a ring or a post.

The **Timber Hitch** is used for dragging timber along the ground.

The **Wall Knot** is a way of whipping, or finishing off, a rope that is unravelling. Take strand A and loop it back across the front of the rope; then take strand B and loop it over the end of strand A; finally looping strand C over the end of strand B and tucking its end into the loop formed by strand A. Finish by working the knot tight.

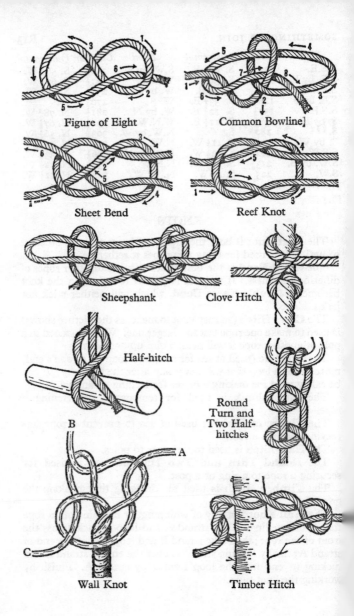

Figure of Eight

Common Bowline

Sheet Bend

Reef Knot

Sheepshank

Clove Hitch

Half-hitch

B

Round Turn and Two Half-hitches

A

C

Wall Knot

Timber Hitch

The Armed Services, The Police and Fire Brigades

The Armed Services

The present integrated Ministry of Defence was created on April 1, 1964, combining the four separate ministries previously responsible for armed service matters—The War Office, Admiralty and Air Ministry, and the former small administrative Ministry of Defence. The head of the Ministry is the Secretary of State for Defence, who is also chairman of the Defence Council—the permanent committee of military and civilian chiefs who determine defence policy.

THE ARMY

The man responsible for the detailed running of the Army is the Under-Secretary of State for the Army, a Member of Parliament, who in turn is responsible to the Secretary of State for Defence. The Under-Secretary controls the Army through the Army Board of the Defence Council and obtains expert military advice from the Chief of the General Staff (C.G.S.), who is the senior military member of the Board.

PRINCIPAL BRANCHES OF THE ARMY

The **Royal Armoured Corps** (R.A.C.), formed in 1939 by amalgamating the Cavalry and the Royal Tank Corps.

The **Royal Artillery** (R.A.) (the 'Gunners') who man both guns and missiles in Field, Anti-Tank and Air Defence roles.

The **Royal Engineers** (R.E.) (called the 'Sappers' from the days when they dug 'saps'—that is, trenches or mines that enabled the troops to advance towards the enemy). In general their job is to help the Army to move. They make paths through minefields, provide means of crossing obstacles and carry ou any necessary demolition and lay minefields in a withdrawal They compile and print maps for the Army and the R.A.F. an operate the Army Postal Service.

The **Royal Corps of Signals** (R. Sigs.) is responsible fc the Army's communications.

The **Infantry** is the fighting core of the Army and include the Foot Guards, the Parachute Regiment and the Special Air Service Regiment.

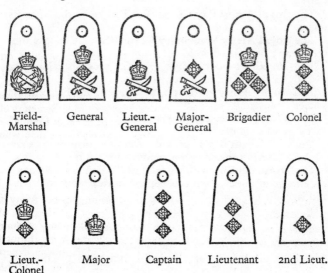

| Field-Marshal | General | Lieut.-General | Major-General | Brigadier | Colonel |

| Lieut.-Colonel | Major | Captain | Lieutenant | 2nd Lieut. |

The **Royal Corps of Transport** (R.C.T.) replaced the Royal Army Service Corps in 1965.

The **Royal Army Medical Corps** (R.A.M.C.) came into being in 1857, after the Crimean War, as the Army Hospital Corps. Took its present name in 1898.

The **Royal Army Ordnance Corps** (R.A.O.C.) is responsible for providing the Army with food, equipment and stores—vehicles, clothing, ammunition, explosives, etc. Also provides clerical staff and mobile bath and laundry units on active service.

The **Royal Electrical and Mechanical Engineers** (R.E.M.E.) was formed in 1942 to meet the needs of mechanical warfare. Looks after and maintains tanks, vehicles, guns, radar, radios, instruments, etc.

The **Intelligence Corps** is a small branch consisting of men trained to collect intelligence (that is, largely information about an enemy or possible enemy).

The **Corps of Royal Military Police** (R.M.P.), the 'Red Caps'.

The **Royal Army Pay Corps** (R.A.P.C.) pays the Army its wages.

The **Royal Army Veterinary Corps** (R.A.V.C.) looks after the Army's horses and dogs.

The **Royal Pioneer Corps** (R.P.C.) provides labour for road-building, unloading stores, etc.

The **Royal Army Educational Corps** is in charge of the soldier's education.

The **Army Catering Corps** (A.C.C.), from which the Army's cooks are drawn.

Queen Alexandra's Royal Army Nursing Corps (Q.A.R.A.N.C.) provides women nurses for military hospitals.

The **Women's Royal Army Corps** (W.R.A.C.), covering a wide range of duties, from cooking and clerical work to driving and signalling.

HOW THE ARMY IS DIVIDED

The standard formation in the modern Army is the division. In wartime the divisions are grouped to form corps (two divisions

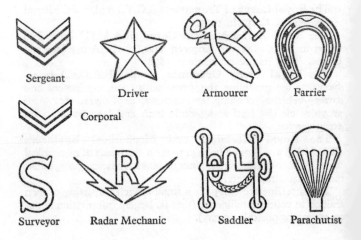

Sergeant

Driver   Armourer   Farrier

Corporal

Surveyor   Radar Mechanic   Saddler   Parachutist

Signaller   Sniper

Second Glider Pilot

or more), armies (two corps or more) and army groups (two armies or more).

The fighting infantry unit of the Army is the battalion. Nearly 800 strong, it is divided into a Headquarters, Headquarters' Company and four Rifle Companies.

THE ROYAL NAVY [1]

The official head of the Navy (senior of the three Armed Services) is the Under-Secretary of State for the Royal Navy. Before the creation of the unified Ministry of Defence, the title of the department head was First Lord of the Admiralty. The senior naval member of the Navy Board is the Chief of Naval Staff and First Sea Lord.

HOW THE NAVY IS ORGANISED

Outside the Ministry of Defence, the Navy is under the command of two Commanders in Chief: Commander in Chief Fleet,

[1] For an account of naval vessels, see the section on *Ships*.

who is responsible for all the Navy's ships, and Commander in Chief Naval Home Command, who is responsible for all the Navy's shore establishments, units ashore and the training of officers and ratings.

Ships and some submarines are based at four Base Ports, Portsmouth, Plymouth and Chatham in England and Rosyth in Scotland. The fleet is divided into two flotillas commanded by admirals; submarines are commanded by Flag Officer, Submarines; all are responsible to the Commander in Chief Fleet.

Under Commander in Chief Naval Home Command, establishments in the country are divided into regions which are commanded by admirals located at the four Base Ports and known as Flag Officers Portsmouth, Plymouth, Medway (Chatham), and Scotland and Northern Ireland (Rosyth).

The administration and training of the Fleet Air Arm come under the command of the Flag Officer, Naval Air Command.

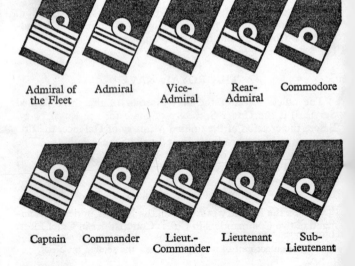

Admiral of the Fleet   Admiral   Vice-Admiral   Rear-Admiral   Commodore

Captain   Commander   Lieut.-Commander   Lieutenant   Sub-Lieutenant

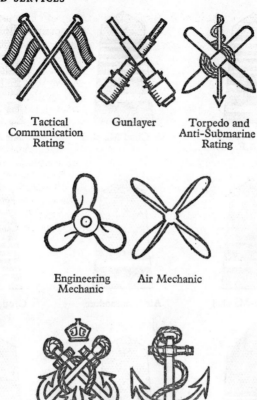

Tactical
Communication
Rating

Gunlayer

Torpedo and
Anti-Submarine
Rating

Engineering
Mechanic

Air Mechanic

Petty Officer

Leading Rating

The Corps of Royal Marines was founded in 1664 to serve on sea and land. Today they provide four commando units. Apart from serving in warships, the Marines are also drawn upon for the crews of landing craft and for other amphibious operations (that is, those carried out partly on sea and partly on land).

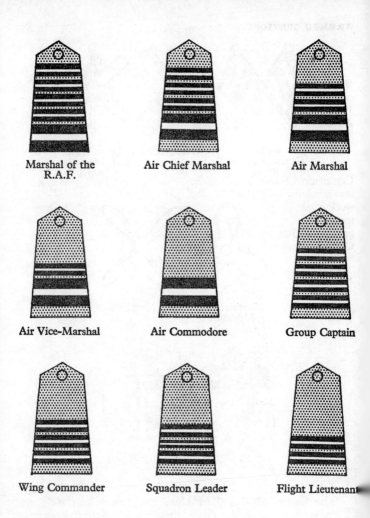

Marshal of the R.A.F.

Air Chief Marshal

Air Marshal

Air Vice-Marshal

Air Commodore

Group Captain

Wing Commander

Squadron Leader

Flight Lieutenant

These are shoulder badges worn with battledress: with No. 1 dress (formal) they are worn on the cuff as in the Royal Navy.

THE ROYAL AIR FORCE

The official head of the Air Force is the Under-Secretary of State for the Royal Air Force, who is responsible to the Secretary of State for Defence. He controls the Service through the Air Force Board, whose senior service member is the Chief of the Air Staff.

HOW THE AIR FORCE IS ORGANISED

The R.A.F. in the United Kingdom is organised into two Commands: Strike and Support. The Commands are divided into sections, each of which deals with a specific aspect of the work of the R.A.F.: operations, intelligence, training, navigation and so on. The Service's fighting units are organised in groups, stations, squadrons and flights. There is one R.A.F. Command overseas, in West Germany.

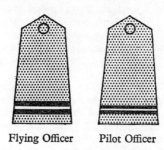

Flying Officer   Pilot Officer

Pilot's Wings

RELATIVE RANKS—SEA, LAND AND AIR

Army	Royal Navy	Royal Air Force
Field Marshal	Admiral of the Fleet	Marshal of the R.A.F.
General	Admiral	Air Chief Marshal
Lieutenant-General	Vice-Admiral	Air Marshal
Major-General	Rear-Admiral	Air Vice-Marshal
Brigadier	Commodore (1st and 2nd class)	Air Commodore
Colonel	Captain	Group Captain
Lieutenant-Colonel	Commander	Wing Commander
Major	Lieutenant-Commander	Squadron Leader
Captain	Lieutenant	Flight Lieutenant
Lieutenant	Sub-Lieutenant	Flying Officer
Second Lieutenant	Acting Sub-Lieutenant	Pilot Officer

The Police

In May 1966, the Home Secretary announced plans to reduce the number of police forces in England and Wales from 117 to 49 (from 105 to 45 in England, and from 12 to 4 in Wales). In England and Wales the police are administered by the Home Office, in Scotland by the Scottish Home Office and Health Department, and in Northern Ireland by the Ministry of Home Affairs.

The main ranks in the police are constable, sergeant, inspector, superintendent and (in London) commander and deputy commander. The head of the Metropolitan Police Force is called the Commissioner; the head of a provincial force is called a Chief Constable.

Policewomen were first recruited during the First World War.

BRANCHES OF THE POLICE

The C.I.D. Most police forces have a Criminal Investigation Department. No officer can be recruited to this section until he has served for at least a few years as an ordinary uniformed constable. Ranks in the C.I.D. are the same as those in the uniformed police: e.g. detective-constable, detective-sergeant and so on.

In London, where one in every ten policemen belongs to this branch, the C.I.D. is controlled by an Assistant Commissioner, with the aid of a Commander and two Deputy Commanders. More than half of the staff of the C.I.D. are attached to police

stations. The headquarters staff consists of Central Office
(which deals with national and international crimes), the
Criminal Record Office and Fingerprint Bureau, the Special
Branch (which in war-time works with the forces in counter-
espionage, and is also responsible for protecting important
public persons), the Flying Squad and the Fraud Squad (whose
job is to detect financial swindles).

The River Police A few forces (e.g. London, Liverpool,
Glasgow) have sections of River Police, whose business is to
prevent and detect stealing from craft on the river and from
waterside premises, to deal with boats found adrift, to help
vessels in difficulty, to come to the aid of drowning persons and
to retrieve dead bodies, to prevent and detect smuggling and to
prevent the pollution of the river.

The Thames Division in London has five river stations—at
Wapping, Blackwall, Erith, Waterloo Pier and Barnes.

The Mounted Police These are used mainly for heading
processions and controlling crowds.

Special Constables These are part-time unpaid men and
women who are employed mainly to help in controlling crowds
on special occasions. They have the same powers as full-time
constables.

Fire Brigades

During the Second World War the 1,059 fire brigades in
England and Wales were amalgamated into a single National
Fire Service, and after the war an Act of Parliament created 125
brigades, each administered by the local authority. At the same
time the 200 Scottish brigades were regrouped into eleven
brigades. The Local Government Act of 1972 made the new
county councils responsible for the fire services. In Scotland, the
Local Government (Scotland) Act, 1973, which came into effect
in 1975, gave responsibility to the nine regions.

In big cities the brigades are manned by full-time firemen;
elsewhere some or all of the crews are part-timers.

The uniform of the British fireman is of dark-blue serge or
cloth, with waterproof leggings and rubber or leather boots. The
brass helmet of earlier times has given place to helmets made of
leather or leather and rubber, which give much better protection
against electric shock.

Decorations and Medals

Victoria Cross (V.C.) (1856). *Ribbon*, crimson. (Until 1918 it was blue for the Royal Navy.) For conspicuous bravery. By order of Queen Victoria, who instituted the decoration, Victoria Crosses were struck from the metal of guns captured at Sevastopol during the Crimean War (see HISTORY: Diary of Events).

George Cross (G.C.) (1940). *Ribbon*, dark blue threaded through a bar adorned with laurel leaves. For gallantry. The G.C. is worn before all other decorations except the V.C., and is intended in the first place for civilians. It is awarded to servicemen, however, for actions for which military honours are not usually granted. It is given only for acts of the very greatest heroism.

The Distinguished Service Order (D.S.O.) (1886). *Ribbon*, red with blue edges. Given in recognition of special services in action to commissioned officers in the three services and (since 1942) the Mercantile Marine. A Bar may be awarded for any additional act of service.

Distinguished Service Cross (D.S.C.) (1914), for Warrant Officers and officers in the Royal Navy below the rank of Captain.

Military Cross (M.C.) (1914), for captains, lieutenants and Class I Warrant Officers in the Army.

Distinguished Flying Cross (D.F.C.) (1918), for officers and warrant officers in the R.A.F. and Fleet Air Arm; awarded for acts of gallantry when flying in active operations against the enemy.

Air Force Cross (A.F.C.) (1918), for acts of courage when flying, though not in active operations against the enemy.

Albert Medal (A.M.) (1866), for gallantry in saving life at sea or on land.

Medal for Distinguished Conduct in the Field (D.C.M.), for warrant officers, non-commissioned officers and men of the Army and R.A.F.

Conspicuous Gallantry Medal (C.G.M.), for warrant

officers and men of the Royal Navy, Mercantile Marine and R.A.F.

George Medal (G.M.) (1940), for acts of gallantry.

Distinguished Service Medal (D.S.M.), for chief Petty Officers, men and boys of all branches of the Royal Navy, Mercantile Marine and Royal Marines.

Military Medal (M.M.), for warrant and non-commissioned officers and men and women of the Army.

Distinguished Flying Medal (D.F.M.) (1918) and the **Air Force Medal** (A.F.M.), the equivalent of the D.F.C. and A.F.C. for warrant and non-commissioned officers and men.

King's Police and Fire Services Medal, awarded for distinguished service.

The Law

What is Law? It is extremely difficult to say exactly what Law is. It is not a logical summing up of experience, like a law in science: it is an accumulation of orders and decisions and compromises, rooted deep in history. You could say that a law is an attempt to change human behaviour by means which ultimately involve the *force* of the State. By law, even a parking offender, if he keeps evading justice, may be brought to heel by *military action*. In fact, all our laws rely on force; but in our complicated society force is very much in the background.

Why do we obey laws? There is always the fear that we might be punished for a criminal offence, or sued for a civil one; but fear of being punished or sued is not even the main reason why we obey the hundreds of laws which affect us at practically every moment of every day. We obey them because we have been brought up to do so; because it is obvious that they are necessary; because this is a democracy and the laws as a whole are roughly how we want them.

It is natural to say 'obey' when we talk about Law, but it is a misleading word. Criminal laws indeed do have to be obeyed, but they are only a fraction of the total. There are many other laws that cannot be obeyed because they are not orders. For example, there is an Act of 1837 called the Wills Act which says that a will must be signed by the testator (the person making the will) in the presence of two witnesses who must be present at the same time. There is nothing in this to 'obey': if the will is not signed in this way, it is not a will: but no one can be punished. There are hundreds of laws of this sort which lay down procedures—that is, they say how things must be done: there are others which give permissions, or make definitions.

As you can see, it is perhaps impossible to say exactly what a law is: luckily this does not prevent us from obeying, using and understanding laws.

Rights, Duties When we look into it we find that much of the Law of England (though not necessarily of other countries) consists of statements about *rights*, *powers*, *duties* and *liabilities*. I have a *duty* not to steal from you—if I do, you automatically have a *power* to have me sent to prison. Again, you have a *right* not to be stolen from, and I am under a *liability* to you if I do.

This reasoning extends from criminal law to the other branches. When a lawyer says that someone *owns* something he means that that person has several rights, powers, duties and liabilities towards the thing. All of these can be dealt with separately: thus the owner of land can sell his *right* to use the land to another person, while keeping for himself the eventual ownership. This is called giving a lease, and under it he may well transfer to the other person the legal *duty* of making the land safe for visitors.

Our law makes very few clear, sweeping statements about life. Instead it consists of thousands of particular rules that often contradict one another. Oddly enough, this is an advantage, for it gives the Judges freedom to pick and choose among all the rules so that justice is done in a way that would be impossible had they to apply a fixed set of laws.

The Courts Part of the business of Government is to provide Courts of Law to keep the peace and to settle disputes. In the old days access to the Courts—that is, getting one's case heard in them—was difficult and expensive; nowadays—at least, in theory—they are free, and will hear the complaint of anyone who is within the United Kingdom.

They work in a formal way; their officers wear traditional clothes, and their methods and language are difficult for anyone who is not a student of the law. Anyone may go and listen to cases being decided—and everyone should, at least once, visit his local County or Magistrates Court, or the Law Courts in the Strand in London.

The Courts do not act of their own accord; cases have to be started either by making a charge in criminal matters or issuing a writ in civil matters. Once set in motion the Courts have considerable powers to compel the parties to a case and witnesses to attend and to give truthful evidence; to punish contempt (which is the legal name given to acts flouting the court's authority; for instance, refusal to give evidence, or to show respect for the judge) and to pronounce decisions and enforce obedience to those decisions.

Partly because the Courts are very traditional bodies, and partly to deal with the great involvement nowadays of Government in private affairs, the Courts are being replaced for some purposes by Administrative Tribunals. These are less formal, more flexible, and equally powerful bodies which differ from Courts in deciding not only *fact* and *law*, but also *policy*. For instance, the question of whether a landlord has allowed his houses to become slums involves more than the *law* defining a slum, and the *fact* of the condition of these houses; it also involves Government *policy* which decides at what point houses are so dilapidated that they have become slums and have to be replaced. Because of their independence of Government—see **Judges** below—the Courts are ill-suited for making this sort of decision. Tribunals decide an enormous variety of questions: from housing, to the siting of atomic power stations, to the release of the mentally ill from hospital.

How the Courts are Organised The supreme Judicial Authority and the ultimate Court of Appeal for Great Britain and Northern Ireland is the *House of Lords* (that is, all the peers who make up the House). In fact, only a dozen specially appointed *Lords of Appeal in Ordinary* hear cases which come before the House. Below them comes the *Court of Appeal*, staffed by the *Master of the Rolls* and eleven *Lords Justices of Appeal*. *The Court of Criminal Appeal* is staffed by the *Lord Chief Justice of England* and the Judges of the *Queen's Bench Division*. These three Courts hear appeals only: cases start in the *High Court of Justice*, which is divided into three Divisions: Queen's Bench, Chancery, Probate Divorce and Admiralty. There are 48 *puisne* Judges in the High Court (a *puisne* Judge is a junior Judge), and they can hear any kind of case. Until 1972, *Assizes* were held by Judges of the Queen's Bench touring the country three times a year. These Courts and the *Quarter Sessions* (part of the system of Lower Courts dealt with below, and consisting of magistrates sitting with a jury and having authority to hear more serious cases) have been replaced by a single Crown Court, served by a new bench of full-time Judges (Circuit Judges) and a limited number of part-time Judges known as Recorders.

Lower Courts The *County Courts* are widely distributed and hear small civil matters—limited in value to £750. They are staffed by 80 County Court Judges who sit periodically in all large towns. Procedure is simpler, quicker and cheaper than in the High Court, and they dispatch vastly more business. *Courts of the Justices of the Peace* hear mainly criminal matters, and are staffed by unpaid, part-time people who have no training in law. They dispatch innumerable petty cases, for example many traffic offences, and they also conduct preliminary examinations of more serious charges; if in such an examination they find there is a case to answer, they refer the matter to the Crown Court. Last of all there are *Coroner's Courts* in which a Coroner, who is a specially appointed barrister, solicitor or doctor, sits with a jury, and holds inquests on 'treasure trove', unexplained death and death in prison.

People in the Courts: The Judge The principal figure in a Court of Law—apart from Magistrates or Coroner's Courts— is the Judge, who has been appointed from among the leading barristers. He holds his office during 'good behaviour', and no English judge has been dismissed in modern times. Judges retire at 75, and are paid a handsome salary to attract the more successful barristers to the Bench and also to protect the Judges against the temptations of bribery.

Barristers Also officers of the Court, though they are employed by their clients, are the barristers—people who have passed examinations in Law, and been 'called to the Bar' by one of the Inns of Court. They are then privileged to appear in any Court on behalf of litigants (that is, persons going to law), who can of course argue their cases for themselves if they wish. Barristers have a double duty: to further their client's case, and to help the Court to enforce the rules of litigation and to come to a just decision. For instance, if a barrister discovered proof that the client he was defending on a criminal charge was guilty, he would be bound to tell the Court. But the barrister's main function is to present his client's case in court as well as he can: what that case is depends on—

Solicitors People who are faced with a court case go first to a Solicitor—a legal practitioner of much the same standing as the Barrister—who helps his clients prepare their cases, and engages barristers for them. In County and Magistrates' Courts, Solicitors can appear directly for their clients, but this is not so in the higher courts. Three quarters of most solicitors' jobs consist in keeping a client out of the courts by advising him, drafting his contracts, wills and leases and many other documents with such skill that disputes do not arise.

Parties There are two sides (parties) in a law case: in civil suits they are the *plaintiff*—who makes the complaint—and the *defendant*. In criminal cases they are the *prosecutor* and *defendant*. In an appeal, the party appealing is called the *appellant* and the other the *respondent*. Any person or corporate body— such as a Limited Company or a City Corporation—can sue or be sued. Children under age have equal rights at law, but they are represented in court by an adult 'next friend'.

Juries In serious criminal trials, and very occasionally nowadays at the request of one of the parties in civil suits, juries sit. A jury consists of twelve householders picked at random, who listen to the evidence and decide the facts of the case in answer to the Judge's questions. Their value lies in preserving common sense among the involved arguments of lawyers.

The Cost of Going to Law The disadvantage of our present system is the great expense of law suits. Although in theory the party at fault has to pay all the expenses of the case, *costs*— as this award is called—very seldom comes to more than a fraction of what has been spent. In civil suits the party with more money has a definite advantage: he can afford, if he loses at first, to appeal to higher and higher courts. Although there is a scheme which gives financial assistance to people involved in Law suits—they apply for *Legal Aid*—it is in general wise to avoid litigation.

The Action (This is the name given to the trying of a case). Every decision given in an English court is the result of a competition between the two sides. Each party brings its evidence and puts its arguments in turn, while the Judge sees fair play. The Judge is allowed in the end to decide the case only on what has been said before him in court—if one side has made a mistake and failed to make out a point which would have given them the decision it is not the Judge's responsibility to do it for them. The course of a trial moves rather like a game of tennis: one side makes a point—it is then up to the other to refute it, or to produce an explanation.

At the end of the evidence and argument the Judge asks the jury—if there is one—for their verdict on the facts; if there isn't a jury he gives his own decision. He then states the law he is going to apply, and makes his award. This takes several forms: in civil suits it is often *damages*—a money compensation for the wrong the defendant did the plaintiff. Less often defendants are ordered by *injunction* to do or to forbear from doing some action, or to deliver or return something of the plaintiff's, or to carry out an agreement. In criminal cases the Judges may—if the defendant is found guilty—discharge him, impose a fine, put him on probation (where he will be free but supervised by a probation officer), sentence him to a term of imprisonment, or, since the 1972 Criminal Justice Act, oblige him to undertake a number of hours of strenuous work for the community. Although criminals can be ordered medical and psychiatric treatment during, or instead of, imprisonment, it is often said that the courts lack sufficient means for dealing with criminals, and that prisons (which are very overcrowded, with a population of over 40,000 in England and Wales) are not the most suitable places for treatment.

Appeals In civil and criminal cases both sides may, with certain safeguards, appeal against the decision. The case is then heard before a Court of Appeal which hears no evidence but reviews the conduct of the trial and the accuracy of the Judge's finding of facts and law. Curiously enough there are many more appeals on points of law than on the facts: this is because finding the right law to apply can be a very difficult and uncertain business. The Appeal Court is free to alter or remove the award or sentence as it thinks fit.

Where the Law Comes From Our law comes from three separate sources: (i) Statutes; (ii) Decided Cases; (iii) Custom.

(i) *Statutes* are the Laws that Parliament makes. Bills—or proposals for new laws—are put before the House, and after they have been passed in three votes, usually after considerable alteration, they receive the *Queen's Assent* and become law. Government Departments make many orders under the authority of Statutes of *Acts of Parliament* which also have the force of law. It is not too difficult to know roughly what a statute means, but the courts are continually having to decide cases that Parliament hadn't thought about, and that might or might not come under a particular Act. Thus: Is a car-park a 'road'? Is a costermonger's barrow a 'place'? These questions look pointless to a non-lawyer, but to the parties involved they may mean imprisonment or great expense.

(ii) Our courts have developed a rule of following earlier decided cases, so that similar facts are treated in similar ways. The difficulty is for the Judge to decide which among the thousands of old cases he will apply. In fact there is considerable freedom of choice, and Judges can choose their cases to do substantial justice' (that is, to give the decision to the party who is really in the right despite legal technicalities which might appear to favour the other side).

Although Parliament has, in theory, a monopoly of law-making, the Judges do in this way make new law. For instance, up to 1932 it was thought that a manufacturer had no legal responsibility to the purchaser of his goods if they were faulty. But then a woman who found a rotten snail in her ginger beer and had become very ill as a result was able to persuade the House of Lords that the manufacturer was responsible for her illness. Although the House said it was following earlier cases, it altered the law in a very necessary way, and as thoroughly as if Parliament had done it.

(iii) Custom is now seldom appealed to. It relates mainly to land, and the alleged custom must be 'ancient, certain, reasonable and continuous'. Or in other words have existed since 1189, the beginning of legal memory.

The Subjects of Law Although the laws form a complete whole, and any Court can apply any part of the law, it is convenient to divide them roughly into groups: *Criminal*—which explains itself, and is much less important than it appears; *Contract*—agreements for selling, hiring, firing; *Tort*—compensation for injuries to person, reputation and property; *Real Property*—the ownership of land; *Personal Property*—the ownership of things; *Trusts*—obligations to hold or do something for another; *Constitutional*—concerned with Government, and the relation between the citizen and the State; *International* —concerned with relationships with foreign states and citizens. There are many smaller divisions.

Scottish Law. Compared with English Law, which applies in England and Wales, Scottish Law differs in a number of particulars and in its application. The supreme civil court of Scotland is still the House of Lords, but below it comes the *Court of Session*, whose Judges have the honorary title of Lord. The Appeal Court is called the *Inner House* and is presided over by the *Lord President* or by the *Lord Justice-Clerk*. Below the Court of Session are the *Sheriff Courts*, one of which is to be found in every county. The supreme criminal court is the *High Court of Justiciary*. There are also the *Burgh Courts* (for criminal cases) where the *Bailies* preside, and the *Justices' Courts* (for criminal and civil cases). In Scotland there are a number of differences in court procedure: for example, the Jury consists of fifteen people and may arrive at its verdict by a majority, and a verdict of 'Not Proven' is allowed. There is no Coroner: the *Procurator-Fiscal* inquires into all suspicious deaths.

Natural History

NATURAL HISTORY

The first thing I do when I get up in the morning is to draw back the curtain and look out through the window at the garden and the new day. If it is a bright summer morning I cannot wait even to get dressed, but go straight downstairs in my dressing-gown. Then I unlock the door and step out into the garden to breathe the fresh morning air 'before many people have used it', as somebody once said. At such times the lawn glitters with beads of dew that glow in different colours, orange, green, turquoise and red, as they reflect separate light waves from the rising sun. A late slug glides towards his shelter, needing to reach it before the sun's heat evaporates the dew and dries the ground. Various flies cluster on sunny patches of the fence to absorb the warming light before they become active, but bumble-bees are already busy at certain flowering shrubs and border flowers, for they are early risers. They set out long before the honey-bees have thought of stirring, and continue to forage later in the evening, sometimes until after sundown. Moreover they fly in light rain or drizzle, which honey-bees never do.

The garden birds, which ceased their singing before sunrise, are now busy collecting food, being hungry after the night. Ladybirds warm their small bodies on sunlit leaves, and a spider circles towards the centre of its orb-web as it spins the last few sticky spirals. Some poppy flowers have split and cast apart their paired sheaths by the delicate pressure of their expanding, crinkly petals—for dawn is their time of opening. I marvel at them, for I can imagine few things so sublimely fresh, or with such a delicately new-born look, as a poppy that has just opened its four satiny, slightly crumpled petals to the rising sun.

So much for a few minutes of sheer enjoyment in my garden at the beginning of the day—but that is what Natural History is about. It is about being aware of the other living things that share this planet with us—the plants that clothe the hills and plains and make them beautiful, and the animals of every shape and size that depend upon the plants for food and shelter. And then, of course, we want to name them, to identify and recognise the many different kinds—but that is not enough. It is no

Poppy

enough to pick a small pink flower by the hedge and say 'This is herb Robert', or to say of a butterfly sunning itself on a bramble in a grassy glade, 'That is a speckled wood', or to point out a jelly-like object on a rock exposed by the ebbing tide and say, 'There is a sea anemone'.

True understanding of Natural History involves enquiry into the whole life of the creatures, their relations with other lives around them, how they feed and reproduce, what are their enemies and by what means they evade them, and how they survive the storms and icy rigours of winter, or the heat and drying winds of summer.

This sort of understanding comes from close contact with living things, and through watching them in the garden, the woods and the open spaces. Books, which contain the accumulated knowledge and observations of devoted men, are of priceless value, of course, and should always be consulted—but nothing can replace the experience of seeing, with your own eyes, the plants and animals in their natural setting. Then there will be other things that you remember, the season and the time of day, the sun that warmed your face, the wind that ruffled your hair, the sudden shower of rain. You will notice how these varying conditions are met, and influence the actions of the creatures that you watch. Thus you will come to know the feel and climate of a creature's life in a direct and personal sense, such as no book alone can ever give you. Then, indeed, you will begin to feel deeply about conserving the wildlife of the earth, and you will want to help in keeping its varied habitats intact and unpolluted for future generations to enjoy.

Now let us return to the subject of gardens, where Nature can be enjoyed simply by stepping out of the back door, or even by gazing through the window. Although gardens are, to a great extent, artificial, man-made habitats, they provide homes and feeding grounds for many wild creatures. In fact, any garden can become a small nature reserve and, as more and more real countryside gets bulldozed away, such private sanctuaries increase enormously in value and importance. Unfortunately, though, there are many kinds of poisons and sprays on the market, and the gardener is urged to use them and to make war on all fronts against aphids, ants, slugs, woodlice, beetles, millipedes, snails and even earthworms, and to scorch and shrivel every kind of weed and wildflower. He is urged to view his garden as a battlefield, where every small creature is a possible threat that must be banished, and where there is little in the way of food for birds.

Such a gardener is apt to wear a worried look and he can never quite relax. Yet, of all places, a garden should be an environment of peace, where one can sit and enjoy the buzz and flutter of wings, the chorus of bird song, the sudden appearance of a shining beetle on the path, as well as the still beauty of the flowers. Surely the peacock butterfly that comes to sip nectar from the herbaceous border is an added bonus, as lovely as any of the flowers on which it sits—but for its caterpillars to feed, there must be nettles.

THE GARDEN AS A WILDLIFE SANCTUARY

Now let us consider how to make your garden a welcome sanctuary for wildlife. It should have a fairly well-clipped lawn where thrushes and blackbirds can find worms, where starlings can probe for leather-jackets, wireworms, little slugs and other grass-root creatures, and where pied wagtails can run and flutter in pursuit of surface insects. A lawn that has a natural variety of short-turf plants is much more interesting than one that has only grass. And if it is not mown too hard or frequently, their short-stemmed flowers will bloom. So leave some daisies to spangle the lawn in spring, and patches of white clover that will attract bees in summer. The closely-clustered flowers of round-leaved speedwell make fresh and lovely sky-blue patches on my own lawn in late spring, and the small, clover-like heads of black medick dot the ground with yellow brightness where it spreads, flowering throughout the summer. Above all, though, I love to see that little gem among the short-turf flowers, the dove's-foot cranesbill, and I can seldom resist squatting on the grass to gaze at its small pink stars.

Dove's-foot Cranesbill

A slenderish kind of tree, planted on the lawn, relieves its flatness, casts an area of shade and gives a feeling of security to smaller birds. They can fly up into its branches if startled while feeding on scattered crumbs. There should also be a fair-sized tree in the garden, for its topmost branches will provide song posts for a song thrush, or perhaps a mistle thrush. Blackbirds tend to sing from lower branches. In fact, the picture that I carry in my mind is of a blackbird singing amid the yellow tassels of a laburnum tree. Nowadays, however, all these birds may choose a television aerial.

A PLACE FOR WILD FLOWERS

I leave an unmown grassy area at the bottom of my garden, where meadow and hedgerow plants can develop freely. Here grasshoppers can live, and their cheerful stridulations enhance my summer days. Here, too, the umbelliferous plants, such as cow parsley and wild carrot, provide feeding platforms for hover-flies, greenbottles, solitary wasps and pollen-feeding beetles. Greater stitchwort, herb Robert, bird's-foot trefoil, knapweed, ragwort, meadow vetch, mallow, poppy, white dead-nettle, spear thistle, ox-tongue and other hedgerow plants may decorate such an area. The flowers of ragwort and knapweed will attract small tortoiseshell and red admiral butterflies, and meadow browns may come to fly floppily over the grasses. The fruiting heads of spear thistle and ox-tongue are likely to give you the joy of seeing goldfinches feeding from them in early autumn.

In this area, too, the underground larvae of swift moths, summer chafers, skipjack beetles and daddy long-legs will thrive, and the close plant cover will shelter such creatures as slow-worms and the larger ground beetles, even, perhaps, a hedgehog. One summer, when I was clipping back some of the taller grasses in my strip of garden meadow, I found a nest of carder-bees. These smallish, brown bumble-bees had made a soft, snug nest of woven moss and grass, rather like a bird's nest, with a covering of moss to protect the cells. Unlike most bumble-bees, which nest in holes, carder-bees make their nests above ground at the base of tall grasses and other plants.

A stand of nettles in a corner of your wild strip of garden will serve as food for the caterpillars of small tortoiseshell, peacock or red admiral butterflies, and may induce a pair of white-throats to nest among the tangled stems if you live in a rural district.

Homes for Soil Creatures

A few small boulders, wide rather than deep, and flattish below, placed in various parts of the garden but not pressed into the soil, will give daytime shelter to centipedes, slugs, woodlice, beetles and ground-dwelling spiders, or roof the nests of garden ants. When you lift such boulders, however, make sure you replace them with extreme care to avoid harming the sheltering creatures. A well built-up rock garden varies the terrain with its different levels. Snails will find homes in crevices between the rocks, while harvestmen, millipedes, springtails and other creatures lurk beneath the mat-like foliage of aubretia, yellow alyssum, mossy saxifrage and other low-growing rock plants.

Another way of altering the terrain of your garden is to make a sand bank. For this, all you have to do is to collect some buckets of sand from a sandy heath, the beach or a builder's yard, mix it with soil to make it firm and bank it up in a sunny corner. In spring and summer, if you keep it fairly clear of weeds, it will attract mining bees and digger wasps to make their burrows.

The first to arrive in spring will probably be the pretty little Andrena bees, easy to recognise by the rich, orange-brown fur on their bodies. These are the female bees, and each will construct a cell at the bottom of her burrow, which she provides

Andrena Bee

with a paste made from pollen and a little honey. Having completed this after several journeys from the flowers, carrying about half her weight of pollen back each time, she lays an egg on the paste and closes the cell. She then makes a few more cells higher up from the tunnel, constructing, provisioning and closing each in turn. Although her offspring emerge from their pupal skins in late summer, they remain resting in their cells until the following spring. This may seem strange, but if they squandered their little store of energy by flying in the autumn sunshine they would be unable to survive the winter months.

One summer I spent a fascinating half hour watching a spider-hunting wasp dragging her paralysed prey to a burrow she had started, under a stone which jutted from the sand bank in my garden. These wasps always seem to be in a desperate hurry. They make short, darting flights, then scurry about on their long legs, poking into crevices as they search for ground-dwelling spiders. This wasp, having already caught her spider, had paralysed it by stinging the nerve centre at the base of its legs.

When I spotted her—only the female wasps hunt spiders—she was running backwards up the slope, dragging the spider along by one leg, gripped in her jaws. Having to move backwards, she could not see very well where she was going, so after dragging the spider a little way, she would drop it and run up the slope to the stone where her burrow was started, to check that she was backing in the right direction. She did not seem able to return in a straight line to the spider, but ran down the

Spider-hunting Wasp

slope to the level where she had left it, then ran to and fro until she found it. On most occasions she dropped the spider on a little ledge of the bank and quickly found it—but twice she dropped the spider on smoothly sloping ground, and it rolled down the bank. Then she would rush feverishly up and down the bank for several minutes, until she finally came across it, and her labours would begin again.

Eventually she made her way up to within a few inches from the stone, dropped the spider for the last time and ran up to complete her burrow. Little jets of sand started to shoot out from under the stone as she dug downwards. I had to wait for about ten minutes before she finally came out to pull the spider up under the stone and into her burrow. There, out of sight, she would lay an egg on the paralysed spider, then fill in the burrow and leave.

When a paralysed spider is left while the wasp explores the terrain or digs her burrow it is liable to be attacked by ants, tiger beetles or other predators. This reminds me of another spider-hunting wasp, of a different species, which I happened to notice while on holiday in Majorca. This wasp had a clever idea. I watched her dragging a spider backwards along the ground. After dragging the spider a little way, she dropped it at the base of a plant stem. Then she ran up the stem, explored its small side-shoots, ran down, gripped the spider, dragged it up the stem and placed it firmly in the fork of a branching side-shoot. Here the spider was fairly safe from attack while the wasp flew off to take her bearings or dig her burrow. Unfortunately I was unable to wait for the wasp's return. The action o this wasp was instinctive rather than thought out—none the less, it was still clever.

Bushes for Birds

Your garden should have some evergreen shrubs or trees, such as laurel, privet, *Euonymus japonica*, yew and holly. These will give protection to small roosting birds through the cold winter months. Holly will also produce some winter food, in the form of berries, for thrushes, blackbirds and starlings—but only if it is a female tree, and only if there is a male tree near by so that its flowers can be pollinated.

Ivy is a very useful evergreen climber if it is allowed to cover part of a garden wall. Spiders of several kinds will spin webs between its leaves, or weave silken traps among its clinging stems. The stick-like caterpillars of the swallow-tailed moth eat its leaves, and in late autumn its rounded clusters of yellow-green flowers provide a last bonanza feast of nectar for wasps, bees, bluebottles, hover-flies, butterflies and many moths, before the cold weather ends their activities. Garden snails will hibernate on the wall between its stems in winter, and wrens may roost behind the shelter of its leaves, while sparrows will sometimes bring dry grass and feathers there, and poke them in their roosts for added shelter. Then, in early summer, the purplish-black berries will be gobbled up by blackbirds, thrushes and even woodpigeons.

Rowan and whitebeam are fine berry-bearing trees to grow in the garden, for they will provide a feast for blackbirds, song thrushes and mistle thrushes in the autumn. Elder bushes will grow anywhere in town or country, and their hanging clusters of shining black berries are quickly cleared by birds. Berberis, pyracantha and cotoneaster are useful ornamental shrubs to have. The oval or cylindrical berries of berberis are rich in vitamins, and the fiery-orange, densely clustered berries of pyracantha make a glorious show in October. These, and the small red berries of cotoneaster, offer a late supply of food for birds when most other berries are over. I have watched blackbirds, thrushes and greenfinches feeding on my cotoneaster bush and one day, to my surprise and joy, a couple of waxwings joined them. The inconspicuous, but nectar-rich, flowers of the cotoneaster cause it to hum with the wings of eager honey-bees in summer.

Waxwing

Flowering Bushes for Insects

You will, of course, want to have some bushes in your garden that are especially attractive to butterflies and other insects. For butterflies, buddleia is the bush *par excellence*. In fact, it is also appropriately known as the butterfly bush. Its long, scented, mauve or purple flower-clusters bloom from July until September, when many other shrubs have ceased to blossom. Small tortoiseshells, large whites, red admirals, peacocks, commas and painted ladies may crowd and jostle each other as they probe the small flowers for nectar, while sunning themselves, spread-winged, on the inflorescences.

Red admirals and painted ladies do not survive the winter in Britain, and those we see in spring and early summer are immigrants from the south—red admirals from southern Europe and painted ladies from North Africa. Both breed in this country. The caterpillars of red admirals feed on nettles, and those of painted ladies feed on thistles, and there is now exciting evidence that some, at least, of the home-bred butterflies migrate south and attempt the return journey in autumn. Whether or not they succeed in doing so has yet to be confirmed, but this is more

Painted Lady

likely to be the case with the painted lady, which is a rapid and powerful flyer, occasionally reaching as far as Iceland on its northward travels.

Another good bush for your garden is the flowering currant. Its multitudes of small pink flowers make a beautiful show in spring, and they are favourites of the big queen bumble-bees. Some years ago I had a bedroom on the ground floor where I was working. There was a large flowering currant bush outside my window, and throughout April I woke each morning to the deep hums and buzzings of the bumble-bees which had been busy among its flowers since dawn. In fact, I always think of the flowering currant as the queen bumble-bee bush. I say 'queen bumble-bee' because bumble-bee colonies are annual affairs, and only the young queens, which have already mated, survive the winter.

Thus, after awakening from hibernation, and restoring her energy with the nectar and pollen of spring flowers, the young queen must find a suitable hole for her nest, and start the new colony all on her own. For the first five or six weeks, she must build the wax cells, lay her eggs, forage for nectar and pollen, feed her growing batch of grubs, lay in a store of honey for wet days, make fresh cells and so on, until the first workers hatch and begin to take over. This is a very different situation from that of the queen honey-bee, who never leaves the hive after her mating flight unless accompanied by a swarm of workers, and who is incapable of building cells, foraging or feeding her young, but must herself be constantly fed and groomed by attendant workers.

Another bush I would recommend is hebe, or veronica, as it is commonly called. It blooms in late summer and the spikes of mauve flowers on my own bushes attract hosts of honey-bees, bumble-bees, hover-flies and silver-Y moths. Most moths fly only after dark, but silver-Y moths are interesting in that they fly in bright sunlight, usually in the afternoon, as well as in the evening and at night. One afternoon, I counted seven of them hovering round the flower-spikes of my veronicas as they probed the small corollas with their tongues. When I came out again at dusk, silver-Y moths were still feeding, impossible to follow as they darted from one veronica bush to the next, but coming suddenly into focus as they hovered, like little swaying ghosts, above the dark foliage. Silver-Y moths do not survive the British winter, but migrants from the Mediterranean regions arrive in late spring, often in great numbers. Their caterpillars feed on various wild and garden plants, and the home-bred moths are believed to make a return flight south in autumn.

Herbaceous Flowers for Insects

Among the summer-flowering herbaceous plants that I grow in my garden, red valerian is one of the best for attracting butterflies, silver-Y moths and others. It is a native of southern Europe, but garden escapes grow wild on railway banks, old walls and cliffs by the sea, at least in the south of England where I live. Red valerian flowers from May throughout the summer, especially if the flower stems are cut right back when the little feathery fruits are forming. Its clustered flowers are great favourites of another immigrant moth from southern Europe and North Africa—the humming-bird hawk-moth. Only recently a friend told me he had seen a humming-bird in his garden, and had called his wife out to have a look. I told him that as all humming-birds are native to America, it must have been the small hawk-moth which flies in bright sunshine and does, indeed, look like a tiny brown and orange bird with a black and white-edged tail tuft. He agreed.

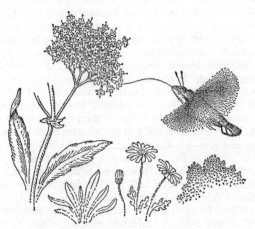

Humming-bird Hawk-moth

I am always thrilled to see a humming-bird hawk-moth come darting into my garden. I love to watch it flick from flower to flower with marvellously controlled flight, and to see it sway and hover, poised for a magic moment on whirring wings, to probe a nectary with its slender tongue. Indeed, there is no creature that seems to burn with such an intense flame of life as this small hawk-moth, that wings its way over continent and sea, to dart among the flowers of English gardens. Its caterpillars feed on lady's bedstraw, and the generation of moths from these may well make the return flight south.

In late September and October, when the blackbirds feast on blackberries and scatter purple droppings in the nearby scrubby wasteland, the ice plant (*Sedem spectabile*), sometimes called the butterfly plant, attracts small tortoiseshells, peacock butterflies and occasional commas to my garden. These three butterflies hibernate as adults in this country, and continue to fly until they must seek shelter for the winter sleep. They feed and sun themselves on the ice plant's pink, flat heads of glistening flowers, or join the big, bee-mimicking drone-flies on the Michaelmas daisies. Both these plants are 'musts' for your garden sanctuary.

Most of the cultivated daisy-type flowers attract butterflies and other insects, that is to say if they are not the double kind, like those chrysanthemums, dahlias and asters that have lost the central disc of yellow florets through artificial selection. The stand of tall white shasta daisies in my garden attracts a multitude of summer insects, such as bees, hover-flies, drone-flies, greenbottles, ichneumon wasps, hunting wasps, soldier beetles, tiny honey-beetles and delicate green capsid bugs, as well as butterflies. Another daisy-type flower, the sunflower, should be grown especially for birds. Its enormous disc, when left to seed, will certainly attract the tits and finches, and if you live in the country near a wood, then nuthatches may join them.

The Garden Hedge

If you are not lucky enough to have a walled garden there should be a wooden fence or a hedge to give it shelter and a feeling of seclusion. Privet makes a good evergreen hedge and if it is occasionally trimmed, but not cut back too hard, it will provide nesting sites for blackbirds, song thrushes and dunnocks. A pair of song thrushes nested in the privet hedge bordering the front garden of my previous house, and I discovered that the rim of their nest was lined with toffee papers that children had dropped on the pavement after visiting the local shop on their way from school. One day, while lightly clipping the same hedge, I found a young caterpillar of the privet hawk-moth. I reared the caterpillar in a large jam-jar and when it was fully grown and ready to pupate, I released it under the hedge. There it could burrow into the soil, construct an earthen cell and cast its skin to become a chrysalis.

Dunnocks and wrens like to search the ground below the privet hedge for spiders and tiny insects; and in June, its heavily scented, creamy-white flower-clusters attract the honey-bees by day and moths at night.

The Garden Fence

My present garden is fenced. Flies like to sun themselves on the south-facing side, and in April and early May a queen wasp comes to scrape wood from the upright fence posts. She scrapes the surface with her jaws, backing downwards as she works, until she has a little ball of shredded wood. This she carries to her underground nest, and mixes with saliva to make wood-pulp for starting the paper nest that will eventually house her first small batch of grubs. Then, in June, the worker wasps arrive, and on throughout the summer they scrape wood-fibre from the fence. They use this to enlarge the paper nest and add cells to the comb, and later to build fresh combs below it and extend the walls around them as the colony expands.

The black-and-white zebra spiders hunt flies and other insects on this south-facing fence, each for ever trailing a hardly-visible

Zebra Spider

line of silk. The little spiders run in short, quick jerks, or twist and swivel to survey the surface round them. When a fly is spotted by a zebra spider she cautiously stalks it until within jumping distance. Then she makes a lightning pounce and, with the fly gripped in her legs and jaws, falls from the fence. However, she falls only an inch or two, because the thread, that she had first fixed to the wall, was spun out as she jumped. If the insect she captures is very small, she grips it with her jaws alone, clutching the fence with her legs to save herself from falling.

Protective Coloration

Garden carpet moths and others choose to rest by day on the north-facing fence, where their sleep will not be disturbed by the heat and brightness of the sun. Garden carpets are common even in town gardens, and may be seen in late spring, and throughout the summer and autumn. The moth rests with its wings spread flat against the surface, in the form of a small triangle. Its greyish white wings are marked with dark patches at the edges. These serve to break up and obscure its outline, and thus prevent it from being easily recognised by a bird, as it rests on a fence or tree. This means of protection, known as 'disruptive coloration', is widely used by moths and other vulnerable creatures.

Garden Carpet Moth

Another means of protection, known as 'mimicry', is used by the angle shades moth. This lovely moth is also extremely common in town and country gardens during early summer and again in the autumn. I usually see an angle shades moth resting on the ground at the base of a wall or fence. Its forewings are delicately coloured in shades of brown, pink and olive green with angle-shaped markings, and their edges are roughly waved and dented. Thus, as the moth rests by day with wings folded over its back, it strongly resembles a dry and partly withered leaf.

Angle Shades Moth

When I am pottering or poking about in the garden I frequently disturb a large yellow underwing. The moth flies rapidly away for a short distance, then drops into a bush or beneath a border plant. It usually rests at the base of plants or low down on the fence where its brown wings, held flat over its back and marked with a few pale lines and darker patches, make it difficult to see. But when the moth flies, its bright yellow hindwings are suddenly displayed, only to vanish as it drops again into the foliage and folds them beneath its forewings. It must be most bewildering to a bird when the yellow-winged moth it was chasing suddenly disappears. The bird may stop to search where the moth plunged, but it continues to look for a yellow moth and misses the concealed brown one. Thus the large yellow underwing is saved from being eaten. This protective device, where vividly marked wings are suddenly displayed in flight, then hidden on alighting, is known as 'flash coloration'.

I have spent several summer holidays abroad in southern Europe. There I like to scramble about among the broom and lavender clumps and pink-flowered cistus bushes on hot, dry, stony hillsides. In such places there are grasshoppers that give very fine displays of flash coloration. The brown, grey or whitish grasshoppers are perfectly camouflaged to match the stony ground where they sit among the sparse dry grasses. As I clamber forwards, they leap up and flutter in front of me, marvellously transformed, and looking like gorgeous butterflies which suddenly vanish as they touch the ground. The broad, gauzy flight-wings of these grasshoppers are brilliant blue or turquoise in some kinds, and vivid red, pink or orange in others, and as the insect alights they suddenly fold like fans beneath its protective forewings. To see them is very well worth toiling up stony tracks, with thorn-scratched arms and legs, in the parching heat of a Mediterannean summer.

Yet another good way to avoid being eaten is to have a nasty taste. However, it is no good being unpalatable if you look much like other creatures that taste nice. You must have distinctive markings that are easily remembered by a predator, and which advertise the fact that you should not be eaten. There are two common garden moths that taste unpleasant, and advertise the fact by means of 'warning coloration'.

One of these is the magpie moth, which I often see resting on bushes in July and August. This attractive moth is very conspicuous. Its body is yellow with black spots, and its broad wings, which are half-spread as it rests, are white with black and yellow spots and marking. When disturbed, it flutters slowly away and settles on the upper surface of a leaf. Not only the moth, but its caterpillar and chrysalis are also distasteful. The caterpillar is marked like the moth, being white with black and yellow spots, and the chrysalis is black with yellow bands. The caterpillars feed on a variety of plants, including the leaves of currant and gooseberry bushes, and I have found them on the euonymus bush in my garden. The chrysalis rests in a very flimsy hammock-like cocoon, which does not hide its yellow-banded form.

The other distasteful moth is the garden tiger. This large and beautiful moth has creamy-white forewings marked with chocolate brown patches, and its hindwings and abdomen are brilliant red with a few black marks. When touched or gently interfered with, the garden tiger does not fly away, but exposes its vivid hindwings and the band of red hairs behind its head. This is its way of saying, 'Leave me alone, I taste nasty.' The furry caterpillar of the garden tiger, commonly known as the 'woolly bear', feeds on dandelions, docks and various other plants.

Aphid Predators

Ladybirds are also distasteful, and their bright red, spotted wing-covers advertise the fact to birds. These little beetles

Garden Tiger Moth

and their larvae feed on the aphids that attack the stems and leaves of roses and other cultivated plants; but when the plants are sprayed with poisons the useful ladybirds are killed. Blue tits, willow warblers and other small birds that like to eat aphids, often suffer too, or even die. Nobody can mistake a ladybird, but its larvae are not always recognised. Ladybird larvae look rather like little flattened caterpillars. They are blackish or bluish-grey, with yellow spots and black legs spread out sideways. When the larva is fully grown it turns into a roundish, black-and-yellow pupa, which is fixed by its tail to a plant stem or leaf. So, when you see these little knob-like objects on rose bushes and other plants, remember what they are. One day, when I was at the south coast, I saw hundreds of seven-spot ladybirds on the breakwaters and the promenade, and crawling over the pebbles of the beach. The probable explanation is that they had flown over from the Continent, and

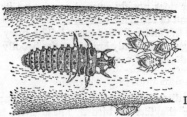

Ladybird Larva

were resting before flying inland to settle in gardens and orchards and continue their search for aphids.

In July and August aphids produce winged forms that fly away to start fresh colonies on other plants. As the winged aphids rise into the air, countless numbers are taken by swallows, house martins and swifts. In fact, swifts have been observed to feed their young on round pellets of compressed aphids, taken on the wing and carried home in their throats.

Myriads of winged aphids, too, get trapped in spider webs, sometimes almost covering each sticky spiral with their tiny forms, only to be left untouched by the sickened spiders. However, plenty will survive to start fresh colonies on garden plants; and other enemies, as well as ladybirds, will eat them as they suck the stems and leaves. The loveliest of these is the green lacewing. This insect has a slender, emerald green body, golden eyes and two long pairs of gauzy, iridescent wings, held roof-wise over its back when not engaged in flight. The green lacewing flies chiefly at night, but on a sunny morning, or in the warm light of evening, I often see one fluttering slowly across the garden with a delightful, twinkling motion of its wings.

Green Lacewing

In late spring and summer you may see tiny, yellowish-green knobs on very slender stalks, that seem to be growing from stems or the underside of leaves. These are the eggs of the green lacewing. They are laid near aphid colonies, for it is in its larval form that the lacewing feeds on aphids. This little creature, not unlike a ladybird larva in shape, is brownish-yellow, and has a pair of sickle-shaped jaws through which it sucks the captured aphids until only their skins are left. When fully grown and ready to pupate, the larva spins a flattish cocoon of white silk on leaves or the trunks of trees.

In late autumn green lacewings seek shelter, often in houses, where they hibernate in corners near the ceiling. It is at this time that a peculiar thing happens. As the weeks pass, the lacewing loses its lovely green colour and becomes drab yellow or reddish-brown. But months later, when hibernation draws to an end, the yellow or red colour disappears, and the lacewing becomes gradually green, then emerald green once more as it flutters out into the mild spring air.

The dainty hover-flies, which are to be seen wherever there is a border of flowers, also lay their eggs near aphid colonies. The yellowish-white or pale green maggot-like larvae which hatch from these are just as avid aphid-eaters as are those of ladybirds or lacewings. The hover-fly larva looks rather like a small, plump caterpillar with suckers instead of legs, but its front part tapers to a very tiny head. When it comes upon an aphid the larva pierces it with its mouth prongs and quickly sucks it dry. The larva then drops the empty skin and pierces another victim. It may consume a dozen or more aphids before taking a short rest to digest its meal. When fully grown the hover-fly larva fixes itself to a leaf or stem and contracts into a little pear-shaped pupa.

If you are an acute observer you may notice a minute insect hovering over a colony of aphids. Keep watching, and you will see it dart down and settle on the colony. This is a braconid wasp, and it is laying an egg in one of the aphids. When the egg hatches, the larva of the braconid wasp will eat its victim from within, until only the empty skin is left. It will then spin a cocoon in the aphid husk and pupate. When ready to emerge, tiny jaws will bite a neat, round hole in the back of the aphid skin, a head will appear, then the little black wasp will struggle out and fly away. However, you need a good pocket lens to watch this happen. I have seen small clusters of aphid skins, still clinging to the stems of plants, each with a round hole in its back where a braconid wasp had left.

Then there is another aphid predator, and a very charming one, that sometimes visits my garden in the autumn. This is the goldcrest, our smallest bird, weighing about six grams or less. I looked out of the front-room window on a dull October morning, and there it was, greenish with a yellow flame along its head, daintily picking aphids from the stems and leaves of my rose bushes. The next day I stood for a quarter of an hour by the sycamore tree in my garden, watching half a dozen goldcrests plucking aphids from the under-surface of the leaves, sometimes hanging on a leaf stalk, or hovering for a few seconds beneath a leaf to do so.

Goldcrest

Well, these are some of the predators of aphids that you may be able to observe in your own garden. One purpose I had in mind in drawing your attention to them, apart from their inherent interest, is to give you some idea of the way a natural balance is maintained by living creatures, preventing any one species from becoming over-numerous. However, where insecticides are used, the predators are killed alongside their prey.

Ants and Aphids

Now let us return once more to the aphid colony. No doubt there is one on a rose bush in your garden, and little black ants are running up and down the stem of the bush between it and their nest. Look closely—you will see ants moving slowly about the colony, tapping or stroking the aphids with their antennae. These ants are inducing the aphids to excrete minute drops of honey-dew, which they greedily lap up. Then with full crops they return to the nest and distribute the liquid, mouth to mouth, among their sister ants. I say 'sister ants' because all worker ants are dwarfed females incapable of mating.

Black garden ants derive much of their food from the honey-dew excreted by aphids. They run up and down the trunk and branches of a sycamore tree in my garden, where their tracks lead to aphid colonies on the leaves. These foraging ants keep closely to invisible tracks, which are really scent trails, laid down and kept fresh by the ants as they travel along. In my previous garden there was a rose bush by the back window. On summer evenings, after sunset, a large toad would come regularly and squat beside the bush. Its tongue would flick out every few seconds and lick up ants from the stem as they ran up and down the track leading to the aphid colonies among the leaves.

Common Toad

Food Chains

A toad and a rose bush—I feel pretty sure that you would never have connected these two things together in your mind. But now you see how a toad may be linked to a rose bush by one item of the food it eats. This sort of who-eats-who linkage is known as a 'food chain'. The rose bush-to-toad food chain may be represented thus: rose bush → aphids → ants → toad. All food chains start with a plant, for only plants can use the sun's energy to trigger the chemical processes that build sugars from the carbon dioxide of air and water from the soil, and only plants can combine the sugars with simple minerals of the same soil water, to make proteins, oils and all the complex matter of their bodies. Thus plants are 'producer organisms', because they produce the food on which all animals depend, whereas animals are 'consumer organisms', for they consume, either directly or indirectly, the various plants. The aphids feed on the rose bush directly, whereas the toad feeds on the rose bush indirectly.

However, rose bushes provide food for mildews, black spot

fungi, caterpillars, sawfly larvae, capsid bugs, gall wasps and thrips, as well as aphids, and are themselves nourished by the dead leaves and stems of plants, dead creatures and the droppings of live ones, when these are all consumed and reduced to compost by earthworms, woodlice, millipedes, springtails, mites, soil bacteria and fungi. Aphids may feed on the sap of other bushes, herbs or trees, as well as roses, and are consumed by special predators as you know, besides providing honey-dew for ants. Garden ants feed on seeds, nectar, tiny insects, dead creatures of all kinds and rotting fruit, as well as honey-dew from aphids, and are themselves eaten by various birds. Toads eat earthworms, slugs, newts, young slow-worms, spiders and many other insects besides ants, and may be eaten by grass snakes, tawny owls and herons.

Food Web

I have mentioned all these creatures to show you that food chains are connected up, linking many kinds of plants and animals in an intricate web of inter-dependence. This is called a 'food web'. The plants and animals that compose a food web are in a delicate state of balance, which can easily be upset by breaking the connecting link provided by any one species. For instance, the spraying of bushes with insecticides over a wide area in summer, when the larvae of ladybirds, hover-flies and lacewings are feeding on aphid colonies, may cause a plague of aphids to develop later in the season. The reason for this longterm adverse effect of the spraying is that aphids give birth, without mating or laying eggs, to active female young throughout the summer. Thus those that survive, or are missed by the sprays, are able to reproduce very rapidly and so build up their numbers far in advance of their predators.

I have already mentioned that, especially in late summer, aphids produce winged forms which fly to fresh host-plants and give rise to new colonies of wingless aphids. These winged aphids may be so abundant that you can hardly prevent them from getting into your eyes when you walk outside, and they smear up the windscreens of cars that travel through the suburbs and along country roads. Now, swifts, being unable to perch or settle on the ground, are entirely dependent on flying insects for their food, and winged aphids form the bulk of their diet. Thus the spraying of trees and bushes with insecticides, when aphid colonies are beginning to produce winged forms, may have a drastic effect on the breeding success of the swifts by forcing them to forage far away from their nesting sites.

Mating Swarm of Ants

Winged males and queens of the black garden ant provide swifts with a rich source of food when the ants are swarming. However, the swarms last only for an hour or two on a few days in late summer when the local weather conditions over a stretch of country are just right. The swarms are mating flights, and at three or four o'clock on a warm, sultry afternoon the worker ants construct larger exit holes in their nest and release the males, and the young queens, which are many times their size. The winged ants climb stems and take off, flying slowly up into the sky, where mating occurs between males and queens from nests all over the district.

One afternoon in August I looked out of the window and saw a group of swifts flying to and fro across my garden. I went

Swifts

straight out and down the garden to where winged ants were streaming upwards from a well-stocked nest. Standing beside the nest, I watched the queens ascend like drifting dots diminishing in the sky, and every dot on which I fixed my gaze was engulfed by a swift before it dwindled from sight. It was a fascinating spectacle. A perfectly-aimed swift would hurtle towards a flying ant, and pass straight on with no apparent loss of speed or checking of its flight. It was as if the swift had never seen the flying ant, but simply hurtled through the space it occupied. I half expected to see the drifting speck still there as the swift shot past, but the space it left was empty. The impression was not of the insect being plucked from the air, but of it being instantaneously absorbed into the body of the speeding swift. A likely explanation is that the swift flies with a gaping bill and the ant gets lodged in a pocket of its throat, to be swallowed later.

Another August, when the same nest swarmed, I watched a group of black-headed gulls flapping and circling over my garden, but no swifts came. It was easy to see the gulls pick the flying ants from the air, and they made a lovely sight as they flapped, veered and circled overhead. However, their performance was clumsy compared with that of the whirling, dashing, cleanly-aimed swifts that homed with such speed on their targets. In fact, as I stood by the nest I saw two gulls make for the same flying ant. Coming from opposite directions, the gulls almost crashed head-on, just veering at the last split-second, the one that missed the ant giving a sudden scream of frightened protest.

The queen ants that have somehow escaped the swifts, swallows, martins, gulls and starlings in the sky come fluttering down to earth, each with a small male clinging to her abdomen. Having landed, the queen ant pushes off the male, who has now finished mating with her. Then she runs a short distance, stops and with her legs starts scraping at the base of her wings, which break away and fall to the ground. Now she runs off to find a suitable hole or crevice, where she digs a small chamber and blocks the entrance with soil. She will spend the rest of her life underground. Her wing muscles disintegrate, and nourishment from these is fed through her mouth to her first small batch of grubs. When these have pupated and emerge as tiny adult workers they make their way out of the chamber, forage for honey-dew and other food, take over the care of eggs and grubs, and feed and groom the queen. Fresh chambers and connecting tunnels are excavated in the soil, and a new ant colony starts to expand.

Making a Garden Pond

The flourishing ant colony beside which I watched the swifts and gulls is under a large stone near my garden pond. A pond adds enormously to the interest of a garden nature reserve. So why not dig one? Ponds used to be an attractive feature of farm-lands and villages, but now most of these have been drained and filled in, and of those still left, many are being poisoned by fertilisers and pesticides that seep in from the surrounding fields, orchards or market gardens. Thus your pond could help, in a small way, to remedy this sad loss. The pond could be rectangular or oval. It does not matter much about the shape, but make it at least half as wide as it is long. For a small pond, four feet by two or two and a half feet would be a suitable size, but it can be as big as you like. Decide on a situation where it gets a fair amount of sunshine, but make sure that it is not too near any tree, or the bottom will soon get clogged with leaves.

A suitable depth for a small pond would be one foot six inches to about two feet, but there is one important point to consider before digging it. This is that you should make one end slope very gradually to the top. It will provide a shallow area where birds can drink and splash in the water. It will also allow little froglets and toadlets to climb out of the water when their tadpole stage is finished. When your pond has been dug and smoothed over, and you have made sure that there are no sharp stones sticking out of the soil, you will be ready to line it with a waterproof material. A sheet of heavy polythene would be suitable for this, but make sure that it is big enough to over-lap and spread for at least six inches round the edges. When you have pressed down the sheet as thoroughly as you can, lay flat stones round the overlapping edges to keep it in place—broken pieces of flagstone will do. Now your pond is ready to be filled and stocked with water-plants and creatures.

Collecting for the Garden Pond

Collecting for your pond will require an expedition into the country. You may find a suitable pond in a low-lying meadow, yellow with buttercups, but wherever your search takes you, make sure that you have a scribbling pad and pencil, so that you can record the various plants and animals you see. You could note down which plants are in flower, the situations where they grow, what insects are seen visiting them and what other creatures are doing—and of course, you should date your observations and record the weather.

I say 'scribbling pad and pencil' because these are rough notes to be made on the spot, and a pencil is quicker to write with than a pen, and useful for making sketches. The notes can be written out properly with a pen in your neat book when you get home; but never rely on memory, or important details of observation may be lost, and others will become distorted and inaccurate. I stress this point very strongly, because it is the most important thing I have ever learned to do in my studies of Natural History.

Now, supposing you discover a fair-sized pond in a meadow. As you approach the pond you will notice that many of the plants in the marshy ground around the pond are different from those in the rest of the meadow. You will see that the plants at the edge of the water are different from those farther back, that those standing in the shallow water are different still and that in deeper water there are plants with floating leaves and others that are completely submerged. This change in the flora from dry ground towards the centre of the pond is called 'zonation'. The plants are zoned according to the amount of water they require. You will notice, too, that there are some animals not seen farther out in the meadow. There may be a moorhen swimming jerkily on the water, a dragonfly cruising to and fro over the pond and some damselflies fluttering around its edges, and you may see some beetles on the leaves of waterside plants that are not found elsewhere.

Waterside Plants

Now let us consider some of the plants you are likely to see in the different zones. There may be scattered clumps of soft rush. It is easy to recognise the stiff, glossy stems, sharply pointed at the top and two or three feet high, each with a small tuft of tiny brown flowers sprouting from one side. You may also see the jointed stems of marsh horsetail standing up from the wet grass, each stem with a whorl of about six slender branches curving upwards from the joints. You will probably find that some of the stems have a brown cone at the tip. The

Marsh Horsetail

cone contains spores, for horsetails are not flowering plants, and like ferns and mosses, they reproduce by spores, not seeds. A spore is an extremely minute reproductive cell which is dispersed by air movement, whereas a seed, which develops from a fertilised ovule, is composed of very many cells, and contains a complete embryo plant with a store of food to give it a start in life. Horsetails are the only representatives left today of a very ancient group of plants. Some of these were large trees that grew in the warm, steamy coal forests, a hundred million years before the first dinosaurs or the first flowering plants appeared on earth.

But back to the present and the marshy zone. If it is spring, the pale, four-petalled, lilac-tinted flowers of lady's smock or cuckoo flower will be in bloom. Its narrow fruit will dry as they ripen and suddenly explode, shooting the little seeds to a distance of four or five feet from the parent plant. In this manner the plants get scattered about the marsh and are saved from crowding each other. Nearer the water's edge some gaudy clumps of kingcups, with flowers like giant buttercups, are sure to catch your eye. Unlike buttercups, however, the flowers of kingcups have no petals, and it is the sepals, green in bud, that turn golden-yellow as they open above the glossy, heart-shaped leaves. If it is early summer you may see ragged robin, another plant requiring marshy ground. Its flowers somewhat resemble those of red campion, which belongs to the same plant family, only the petals appear to be torn or shredded—hence its name.

Kingcups

Closer to the margin of the pond, water forget-me-nots will be coming into bloom. The flowers, on slightly curling branches of the stem, are larger than those of the common forget-me-not, and heavenly blue but pink in bud, each open flower with a yellow eye-spot at its centre. Now, too, at the water's edge, the yellow flags will be showing their first big blooms, on stems that may be six feet tall, arising from thick stands of sword-like leaves.

In high summer, meadow-sweet will hold its frothy bunches of cream flowers three feet or so above the marshy ground. Despite its strong, sweet scent, the flowers of meadow-sweet are without nectar, but you may see little pollen-eating beetles crawling over them. Nearer the ground, the water mint will be showing its globular heads of little lilac flowers. Bend down and pinch one of its leaves, and your finger-tips will smell of peppermint.

Water Plants

Now we have come to the shallow-water zone. Here, at one end of the pond, encroaching inwards from its margin, are the tall ranks of reed-mace where a moorhen may be hiding, or sitting on a nest of broken reed stems. Between the spear-shaped leaves you will see dark green, cigar-shaped flower spikes. These are the densely-packed female flowers, and the portion of stem above them is yellow with the stamens of the male flowers. Soon

Reed-mace

the male flowers wither, and the spike turns chocolate brown as the female flowers start fruiting. Unlike the holly, where male and female flowers arise from separate trees, the male and female flowers of reed-mace are on the same plant. In this case the plant itself is hermaphrodite, but not the flowers. Another plant, not so common, but which I have rejoiced to see on two or three occasions, is the flowering rush. Despite its name, this plant is not a rush, and its tall stem ends in a bouquet of lovely, rose-pink flowers. The flowers have three petals alternating with three sepals of the same bright colour, and the flower stalks all arise from the top of the stem. The flowering rush is, I think, the most beautiful of all the shallow-water plants. Where the water is fairly open, and the reed-mace has not encroached along its margin, you are likely to see water plantains. Their large, plantain-like leaves rise out of the water, and in summer they surround a flower stem about two feet high. This bears loose clusters of small, three-petalled flowers, pale pink or lilac in colour, which open only in the afternoons.

Now look at the plants floating on the surface of the pond. There is probably an area carpeted with bright green patches of duckweed. The little floating discs of duckweed are really flattened stems, and each bears a tiny root which hangs down in the water. In summer new discs are continually being budded and breaking off from the old ones. This is known as 'vegetative

Flowering Rush

reproduction', and it enables the plants to spread quickly over the surface. Another floating plant with roots dangling in the water is frogbit. Its rounded floating leaves look like small waterlily leaves, and in summer you will see its white, three-petalled, male or female flowers raised on short stalks above the water. You are most likely to see frogbit if the pond is based on chalky soil. It spreads along the surface during summer by sending horizontal shoots, called runners, through the water. Each shoot has a bud at the tip, which develops into a new plant and becomes detached as the shoot withers—another case of vegetative reproduction.

Nearer the centre of the pond the gorgeous flowers of the white waterlily form many-petalled floating cups, with wide, polished leaves spread on the water around them. The floating leaves and flowers of the waterlily are carried upwards on long stalks from a thick, horizontal stem, called a rhizome, which is rooted in the mud. The leaves unfurl and the flower buds open only on reaching the water surface.

The submerged plants will not be so easy to see, and you may have to wade in and pull up a few specimens to identify them. But before doing so, test the mud with a stick, for what looks like the solid floor of the pond may be a covering of soft mud or silt, and your foot will sink straight through it.

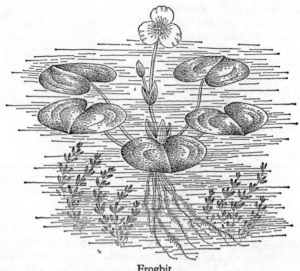

Frogbit

Near the edge of the pond the surface may be studded with small rosettes of leaves like green stars. These are the upper leaves of starwort. The rest of the plant is submerged, with pairs of opposite leaves spaced along its stem. Only at the tip do the leaves grow close to form a floating star. A little farther out, in deeper water, you will see submerged feathery jungles of water milfoil. Pull up a plant, and you will notice that its feather-like

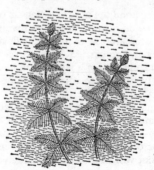

Water Milfoil

leaves are arranged in whorls of four along the stem. In parts of the pond water milfoil may be replaced by even denser growths of Canadian pondweed, which has small leaves in groups of three along its stem. This plant was introduced from North America and has since spread in freshwater all over Britain.

Any of these submerged plants will do for your garden pond, but only put a few specimens in your polythene bags, for they will grow new shoots and spread quickly. Frogbit would be a good floating plant to take home, but not duckweed, for it will spread like a green carpet over the surface.

I have mentioned a few of the typical plants that you may find in and around the pond. There are many other kinds, but what you see depends to some extent on the soil and situation. For instance, in a heathland pond where the soil is peaty and slightly acid, you may find bladderwort in the water, and the beautiful bogbean growing from its shallows, with sphagnum moss, sundew, bog asphodel and cotton grass in the marshy ground around it. Bladderwort and sundew are both carnivorous plants. Bladderwort has little air-filled bladders on its feathery leaves. When minute trigger-hairs on one of the bladders are touched by a water flea or other tiny creature the bladder suddenly fills with water, sucking the creature in, where it is slowly digested. Sundew spreads a rosette of spoon-shaped leaves on the ground. The leaves are covered with long red hairs, each with a drop of sticky fluid at the tip. A fly or other insect, attracted by these glistening globules, gets firmly stuck. The edges of the leaf curl inwards, and the hairs bend over like tentacles to draw the insect to its centre. Here, the soft parts of the insect are gradually digested and absorbed. A possible explanation of this

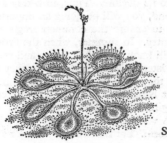

Sundew

unusual habit is that living, as they do, in places where the soil is poor in mineral salts, the plants evolved an ability to trap and digest animal food. Thus they compensate for deficiencies in the soil; but how the change in structure and behaviour came about is not explained at all, and remains a fascinating mystery.

The Common Frog

Now let us take a look at the animal life of the pond. For collecting the various creatures you will need some screw-top jars and a fine-mesh net with a strong frame. If you visit the pond in March or early April you may see rounded masses of frog spawn floating in the shallow water at its edges. Pull off a little spawn to take home for your pond, and leave the rest—on no account take the whole mass of eggs. The common frog, which really *was* common in the early part of this century, has now become relatively scarce. Frogs depend on the still water of ponds for breeding, and along with the ponds that get filled in or built on, the frogs are being squeezed out from large areas

Common Frog

of the country. Also, the toll taken for school and college Biology classes, where the frog is a standard animal for dissection, must have contributed to its decline. Thus, in taking a little spawn for your garden pond, you will be doing an important practical service in helping to ensure the common frog's survival as a species in this country. In summer, when the little frogs leave your pond, they will know it as their home and return there to breed a few years later. Then it will matter that much less if the pond in which they were spawned gets filled in.

A few days after hatching, the tadpole of the common frog develops external gills which show as little tufts on each side behind its head. A week later the external gills wither and internal gills start to form. For the next six weeks or so the tadpole breathes like a fish. Water, sucked in through its mouth, passes over the gills and out through a small opening called a spiracle on its left side. Limb-buds appear by the base of its tail, then, over the next few weeks, a great change occurs. The hind legs gradually take form and the tadpole develops lungs and swims to the surface at times to gulp air. The hind legs lengthen, become functional and assist in swimming, and the front legs break through the skin. Finally, the tail is slowly reabsorbed, and the little frog climbs out on land. This great change from the larval, tadpole form to the adult shape, is known as 'metamorphosis'.

Prehistoric Lobe-fins

Three hundred million years ago an ancient group of fishes known as lobe-fins, because their paired fins were attached to lobe-like, stumpy legs, lived in freshwater pools, swamps and shallow lakes among the coal-forest trees. These lobe-fins developed lungs to help them to breathe when the water became stagnant and poor in oxygen, owing to the rotting portions of tree-ferns, club-moss trees and giant horsetails that gradually littered the mud of their watery world. Thus, whenever pools became clogged or dried up, the fishes were able to make their way overland, with the help of their lobed fins, to fresh bodies

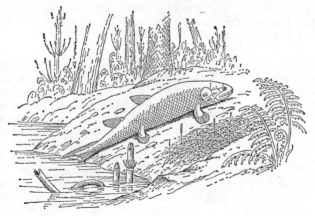

Lobe-fin

of water. Any modifications that made the overland trip easier would be strongly selected, so in the course of millions of years their limbs developed joints, and their bodies became more flexible. Among the ferns and mosses of the forest floor there were hordes of worms, millipedes, early insects and primitive spiders, so the lobe-fins' descendants learned to feed on these, and spent more of their time on land. Their encumbering fringe-fins disappeared, and fingered feet were formed to grip the soil. So, the first amphibians came into being. In the three months of its development in the pond, the common frog re-enacts this age-long evolutionary process.

Mudskippers

Even today there are small fish called mudskippers that spend most of their time on land. Mudskippers live in the mangrove marshes along tropical seashores. They have limb-like front or pectoral fins, by means of which they can lever themselves over the mud quite quickly, assisted by their tails, or climb up on exposed supporting-roots of mangrove trees. Mudskippers have not developed lungs, but they have large gill-chambers which they fill with water before coming on land. However, the water in their gill-chambers has to be renewed at frequent intervals, and they need to keep their skins moist, so they are not able to travel inland from the shore. Mudskippers feed on worms, small crustaceans and insects that they find on the mud flats and the mangrove roots. When disturbed, they go skittering over the mud into the sea.

Mudskipper

Lungfish

There are three kinds of fish, however, that do have lungs as well as gills. These are the three kinds of lungfish living today, one in Australia, one in South America and one in Africa, of which there are four species. Lungfish are closely related in kind to the ancient lobe-fins, and are the only survivors of an equally ancient group. The living lungfish inhabit pools, streams or rivers that tend to become stagnant or dry up during the long dry season. They survive these critical periods because they can breathe air. The South American lungfish tunnels in the mud, leaving just a small breathing hole, when its stream dries up; and two species of African lungfish do likewise and secrete slime, which hardens into a cocoon with a hole at the upper end. In this way they can survive for long periods in mud that has become baked by the sun. This resting state in hot weather is known as 'aestivation'.

African Lungfish

The Australian lungfish, which inhabits rivers in Queensland, and relies more on its gills for breathing, does not aestivate. An interesting point about the African and South American lungfish is that their eggs hatch into larvae with external gills. After a few months their external gill-tufts are absorbed and permanent internal gills develop—a similar change to that we saw in the young frog tadpole. Unlike the lobe-fins, the lungfish, despite their ability to breathe air, were never able to invade the land, and the paired fins of the present-day African and South American kinds are reduced to tentacles.

Development of Toads and Newts

We have travelled a long way in time and space—but now back to the pond. Toads and newts may have spawned in the pond, but their eggs will not be so easy to find. The eggs of the common toad will be in long strings of jelly, tangled round the stems of plants in the deeper water. Newts lay their eggs singly, and stick them on water plants, bending a small leaf round each egg to protect it. The development of toad tadpoles follows a similar pattern to that of frog tadpoles, but newt larvae, which are yellowish in colour, do not grow internal gills. They retain their tufts of external gills until they develop lungs and leave the pond. The front limbs appear first, and their feathery gills are not absorbed until all four legs are well developed.

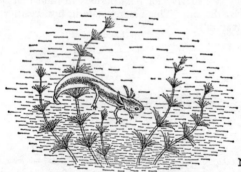

Newt Larva

External and Internal Fertilisation

When frogs and toads reach the pond in early spring, each male mounts a female and clasps her tightly with his forelegs, so that his hands are pressed beneath her breast. The couple remain together, thus, until the female has laid her eggs. The male fertilises the eggs as soon as they emerge from the female's body, after which he releases his hold and they part to make their separate ways back to land. Fertilisation in frogs and toads is external, as it is in fishes and most other water creatures. By this, we mean that the male reproductive cells, called sperms, are shed into the water near the female reproductive cells, or eggs. Each sperm, which can only be seen through a powerful microscope, has a lashing tail, called a 'flagellum', by means of which it swims towards an egg and fuses with it. The fertile egg cell is then able to develop into a new individual creature. Fertilisation in mammals, birds, reptiles and insects is internal. That is to say, the sperms are shed directly into the female's body, where they fertilise the eggs before these are laid. Internal fertilisation is essentially an adaptation of life on land.

Fertilisation in Flowering Plants

Flowering plants overcome this problem of life on land by using insects or wind to carry pollen from the male organs, or stamens, of one flower, to the female organ, or pistil, of another. The pistil consists usually of three parts – the stigma, which is sticky or feathery to trap the pollen; the ovary, which contains the ovules; and the style, not present in all flowers, which is a stem or neck joining the stigma and ovary. After landing on a stigma, each pollen grain of the right kind germinates and sends a pollen-tube containing a male reproductive cell down through the style and into an ovule, where the male cell fuses with an egg cell.

Hermaphrodites

Most flowering plants are hermaphrodite, that is to say each flower has stamens, and a pistil containing the ovules which, after fertilisation, become seeds. As the seeds develop, the ovary grows into a fruit, such as a berry, pod or capsule. However, some flowering plants, such as holly, are either male, having flowers with stamens but no pistil, or female, having flowers with a pistil but no stamens. Some animals, such as earthworms, slugs and garden snails, are hermaphrodite and contain both male and female organs. This means that each earthworm or snail will lay eggs after mating. Slugs and snails lay clusters of round eggs under stones or logs, but earthworms lay theirs in little oval cocoons which can be found in the soil.

Reproduction of Flowerless Plants

Ferns, horsetails and mosses, as mentioned earlier, are not flowering plants and reproduce by spores—but that is not the whole story. The spores of ferns are produced on the underside of the fronds, and those of horsetails on cones at the top of fertile stems. If, after being released in the air, a spore lands on suitable ground it germinates. However, it does not hatch into a baby fern or horsetail, but into a flat, green, tissue-thin, little

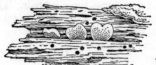

Fern Prothaldi

plant called a 'prothallus', which lies on the surface and attaches itself by tiny root-like structures. I have seen fern prothalli, which are heart-shaped and about a centimetre long, growing on rotting logs in a wood, and at the base of damp shady walls. The fern prothallus forms minute male and female organs on its underside. Each female organ produces an egg and each male organ produces sperms. The sperms swim through wet soil to the female organs and fertilise the eggs. A fertile egg then develops into a minute embryo which is nourished by the prothallus. Soon the baby fern emerges, sending its own roots into the soil, and the prothallus withers.

Alternation of Generations

Here we see a pattern of life that is in one way similar to that of amphibians, such as frogs and newts. Ferns and horsetails, like amphibians, live on land but depend on water for sexual reproduction. The big difference is that these plants reproduce by spores that do not require fertilisation, and it is their offspring, the prothalli, that produce sperms and eggs. This kind of double life-cycle is known as 'alternation of generations'. It occurs, also, in mosses, liverworts and most seaweeds, and in a few animals, such as jellyfish, aphids and certain gall-wasps.

Look at some cushions of moss growing on an old wall in spring. You will see little green or rust-red capsules at the top of slender, pin-sized stalks, rising from some of the moss plants. These stalked capsules are the spore-producing generation of the moss. The moss plant itself is the sexual generation

Moss with Capsules

which develops male and female organs, each in a little cup of leaves at the top of the stem. The sperms swim in rain water or dew to the female organs and fertilise the eggs; and the stalked capsules, which are really separate plants, arise from these. Spores are later shed from the ripe capsules, after which the stalk and capsule wither and fall away. Some of the spores will land on suitable ground and germinate, giving rise to new moss plants.

Now compare this with the life-cycle of a fern, where the spore-producing generation is the fern plant, and the sexual generation is the tiny prothallus, which gives rise to a baby fern and soon withers. But meanwhile the little fern has formed roots in the soil and become independent. Thus the fern can grow to any size, according to its kind, and there are ferns in tropical rain forests that grow into tall trees. In mosses the situation is reversed. Here the sexual generation is the main plant, but it cannot grow big because it depends on rain water for reproduction. Its offspring is the stalked capsule which remains attached to the moss plant, so cannot grow big either. If only the little stalked capsule had learned to get down from its mother's knee and stand on its own feet, so to speak, by forming roots in the soil and growing leaves, then we might have had spore-producing generations of the moss plant as tall as trees.

Liverworts have a similar life-history to that of mosses. A common liverwort is pellia which can be found on the banks of streams and ditches. It has no leaves, and the plant body, called a thallus, is flat and frond-like with a forked tip and lobes at the sides. The male and female organs are on the upper-surface of the thallus and, in early spring, round black spore-capsules are produced on white stalks. Each capsule splits into four segments to release the spores; so what looked like a round-headed pin, opens out like a tiny four-petalled flower.

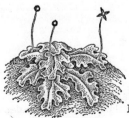

Liverwort with Capsules

The Oak Apple Gall-wasp

An example of alternation of generations in animals is to be seen in the life-history of a little gall-wasp that causes the forma-tion of oak apples on the twigs of oak trees. Oak apples swell rapidly in May, and at that time they are variedly coloured with pale green, yellow and rose pink. As they mature in late June, the galls, for that is what they are, become yellowish-brown suffused with rosy tints and spongy in texture. I collected one of these mature oak apples and placed the twig to which it was fixed in a jar. After covering the top of the jar with a piece of gauze, I placed it on the table in my study and waited. A few mornings later, when I got out of bed and went to my study, I found about three dozen tiny gall-wasps flitting about in the jar, and I saw that the oak apple was pitted with their exit holes. In the evening I took the gall-wasps back to their oak tree and shook them from the jar on to one of its lower branches.

An oak apple develops from one of the buds on a twig, and after hatching from the eggs, the minute grubs set up some sort of irritation which causes the bud to produce the abnormal plant tissue of the gall. Each grub lives in a separate cell, feeding on sap produced by the tree, and when fully grown it pupates in the cell. In late June or July the little gall-wasps, which are either all brothers or all sisters—for the two sexes

Oak Apple with Gall-wasps
emerging

develop in separate oak apples—bite their way out. After a short rest they fly off, eventually meet others of the right sex, and start mating. The fertilised females then make their way into the soil at the base of an oak tree, and lay eggs singly in the tissues of young roots. This results in the formation of root galls, each with a single grub inside. The root galls are about a third of an inch wide when mature, and look like little brown nuts. They take about sixteen months to mature, and the adult gall-wasps emerge in the second winter.

Now comes the surprise. If you visit an oak tree that had oak apples on its twigs, and do so round about Christmas time, you may see a wingless insect that looks rather like a very plump ant, crawling up the trunk or along one of the branches. It is an oak apple gall-wasp, and it is a female, for there are no males in this alternate generation. Moreover, she is larger than the tiny winged forms that emerge from oak apples in summer, and different in appearance. If you are patient enough to watch her movements you will eventually see her start laying her unfertilised, virgin eggs in a bud at the end of one of the twigs. Next summer the bud will become an oak apple, and in it will be little grubs that had a mother but no father.

As in ferns and mosses, the alternate generations are dissimilar—the sexual generation of winged gall-wasps arising from oak apples, and the non-sexual generation of wingless forms arising from root galls. The difference is that in ferns and mosses the non-sexual generation produces spores, whereas in the gall-wasps it produces virgin eggs. These astonishing facts were not known to early naturalists, who called the insects from root galls by one name and those from oak apples by another.

Fertilisation in Newts

So—from my simplified account of reproduction in frogs and toads, the train of my thoughts has taken me to ferny woods, old walls, the banks of ditches and the branches of an oak tree. But now let us return to the pond in early spring. I pointed out that fertilisation in frogs and toads is external, but in the case of newts, despite the fact that they must reproduce in water, fertilisation is internal. Moreover, it is accomplished in an unusual manner, for the sperms from the male are not shed directly into the body of the female.

Smooth newts, being the commonest of the three British species, are the most likely to be found in the pond. You will see them swim to the surface with rapidly beating tails, let go a bubble of air, breathe in a fresh supply and return to the shady underwater jungle. It is easy to distinguish male newts at this season, for they are in full breeding dress. Catch one in a net and place him in a jar of water. You will see that he has a tall wavy crest along his back and tail, a similar crest along the lower edge of his tail and fringes of skin on his hind toes. He is olive brown with a brilliant orange belly, and his lower tail-crest has an orange margin with a stripe of bluish or mother-of-pearl iridescence above it. His body and tail are patterned with black spots and there are black lines along his head. Now, having seen what a splendid creature he is, set him free in the pond, for the bright colours and adornments are there to be flaunted and displayed in courtship.

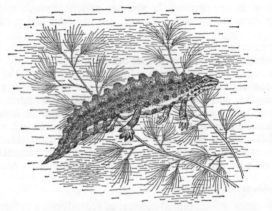

Male Smooth Newt

I have watched male newts courting females in ponds, and it is a charming spectacle. The male moves around the female waving his tail, undulating his crest, nudging her with his snout, and pressing or rubbing it gently along her sides. This may go on for hours, then finally he positions himself in front and, facing her, bends his tail double and vibrates it rapidly so that her body is stroked by the vibrations set up in the water. After repeating this performance a few times, the male newt emits a little capsule of sperms, called a 'spermatophore', on the floor of the pond. He then withdraws and the female newt, who has remained still and passive during the courtship, moves forward until the swollen cavity called the 'cloaca', which opens at the

base of her tail, is directly over the spermatophore. She then
presses her cloaca down on the spermatophore and takes it in.
Once inside her body, the capsule dissolves and the released
sperms fertilise her eggs. When the breeding season is over the
newts climb out on land and move away. The crest and toe-
fringes of the male are reabsorbed, and now he looks much like
the female.

It will be nice to have a few newts for your garden pond, but
it is better not to disturb them in the breeding season. Wait
until the newt larvae have hatched and take home a few of these;
then you will have the pleasure of watching them grow and develop until their metamorphosis is completed in August or
September.

Warm-blooded and Cold-blooded Vertebrates

Newts, frogs, toads and other Amphibians are all backboned
animals that have an internal skeleton. Such animals are called
vertebrates. There are four other classes of vertebrates besides
Amphibians. These are Fishes, Reptiles, Birds and Mammals.
Birds and Mammals are said to be 'warm-blooded' vertebrates,
which means that they have a constant body temperature. Fishes,
Amphibians and Reptiles are said to be 'cold-blooded' vertebrates, which means that their body temperature varies with that
of their surroundings. It does not mean that their blood is
always cold, and a lizard will have warm blood if it is basking
on a rock in full sunshine. Indeed, some reptiles maintain a
fairly constant body temperature, but it is controlled by their
movements and behaviour, and not from inside, like that of
birds and mammals. Take, for instance, the crocodile. When
I went on safari in East Africa I saw crocodiles basking with
their mouths wide open on the banks of the Victoria Nile. They
were not waiting for a meal to walk in, but were regulating
their body temperature.

Crocodiles spend the night swimming about and hunting for
food in the river. At sunrise they climb out of the water and
flop down on a gently sloping beach or a grassy area on top of
the bank. As the sun's heat strengthens, they open their mouths
wide so that evaporating moisture from the membranes lining
the inside of their jaws cools their blood. Around midday, when
the sun climbs overhead, they retire into the shade of trees or
return to the water, either submerging or lying half out of the

water with open mouths. Then for two or three hours in the late afternoon they move back into the sun, and return to the river at sundown. They stay in the water at night to conserve their body heat, because water holds its heat much better than air. By following this sequence of alternating periods in sunshine, in shade and in water, crocodiles are able to maintain a body temperature that varies by only a few degrees.

Back again to our pond in the meadow—the only fish likely to be present is the three-spined stickleback. Take two or three for your garden pond, but do not take too many for they are very voracious. In spring the male three-spined stickleback develops a bright red throat and breast, and his eyes become brilliant blue-green. He scoops out a depression on the floor of the pond and piles bits of weed into this, forming them into a mound with sticky secretions from his body. He then bores a tunnel through the mound and induces females to lay their eggs in it, but drives away all male sticklebacks that enter his territory. He guards and aerates the eggs by fanning water through the nest with his fins, and protects the tiny young for their first few days after hatching.

The other vertebrate inhabiting the pond is the moorhen— a bird with a totally inappropriate name, for moors are one of the few habitats that it invariably avoids. Moorhens usually pair for life, and their nest of dead reeds will be on the mud or water, concealed among the stands of yellow flag or reed-mace. Both parents incubate the eggs, which are whitish with brown speckles, and the black fluffy babies enter the water after hatching, but are fed by their parents for the first three weeks. It is charming to see the parent birds dive in the water, bob up with a morsel of food in their beaks and deliver it gently to their chicks. Moorhens feed chiefly on water plants and insects, and there will only be one pair in the pond unless it is a very extensive one, for they are fiercely territorial.

Invertebrate Animals

The vast majority of animals in the world are invertebrates, and the same applies to the pond. Examples of invertebrate animals are insects, spiders, snails and worms. Vertebrate animals are generally big compared with invertebrates—but if you fill a barrel with apples and then pour peas into the barrel, shaking them down so that they lodge in all the spaces, there will

Moorhen and Chick

be far more peas than apples in the barrel. If, after this, you pour sand into the barrel so that it is filled up with sand, peas and apples, you end up with far more grains of sand than all the peas and apples put together. So it is in any natural environment—there will be far more invertebrate animals than vertebrates, and far more tiny invertebrate animals than there are larger ones.

The peas in the barrel were able to occupy spaces that were not available to the apples, and the sand grains were able to occupy spaces that were not available to the peas. So it is with animals—the smaller they are, the more niches there are in the environment that they can occupy that are not available to larger creatures. The bigger an animal is, the more space it requires to move about in, and the more food it must consume to keep alive. For instance, an African elephant will eat about one and a half hundredweight of vegetation a day, and drink about fifty gallons of water, whereas some chalcid wasps can feed, grow up, pupate and complete their metamorphosis inside the eggs of moths. Thus, a batch of fifty moth eggs, occupying the space of a square centimetre, can supply enough food to nourish fifty chalcid wasps, not for a day but for the whole of their growing lives.

An Invertebrate Phylum

All vertebrate animals are included in one big group or phylum called the 'Chordata', but there are many phyla of invertebrates. I shall describe in brief just one of them which contain familiar animals. This is the phylum 'Arthropoda', which comprises all classes of animals that have segmented bodies, jointed legs and an external skeleton which covers the skin except at the joints and between the body segments. The five main classes of Arthropoda are as follows.

1. *The Crustacea*: With a few exceptions, this class contains all the marine arthropods, and includes crabs, lobsters, shrimps, sandhoppers and water-fleas. It also includes woodlice, which are said to be the only crustaceans able to spend the whole of their lives on land. However, when I was on holiday in Tenerife I found a species of sandhoppers under stones and leaf-litter in the banana plantations well away from the shore.

2. *The Insecta*: This is the only class of invertebrates that have evolved the power of flight. Apart from a few primitive kinds, insects have a larval stage and undergo metamorphosis. They have six legs, and usually two pairs of wings in the adult state.

3. *The Diplopoda*: This is the millipede class. Millipedes feed on fresh and decaying vegetable matter. They are usually long, often cylindrical, and have two pairs of legs on most of their body-segments. The pill-millipedes have short bodies and can curl into tight little balls. They should not be confused with pill-woodlice, which have only seven pairs of legs.

4. *The Chilopoda*: This is the centipede class. Centipedes are carnivorous, and have one pair of legs on most of their body segments, but the front pair take the form of poison-claws and curve round the head. These are used to capture and paralyse their prey. Centipedes are strictly nocturnal creatures, spending the day in hiding and, in some kinds, the mother guards her eggs and the young until they are able to look after themselves. One day in North Africa I turned over a stone, and there was a large centipede, about four inches long, curled round her clutch of nearly white babies. I touched her with a twig, and instead of retreating, she bit at it fiercely, still clutching her group of offspring. In centipedes there is an indirect method of fertilisation similar to that we saw in newts. The male deposits a spermatophore on the soil, which is taken up by the female.

5. *The Arachnida*: This class includes spiders, harvestmen, mites and scorpions. Arachnids have four pairs of legs and are without antennae. All spiders spin silk. Even hunting spiders that do not spin webs, usually trail a line of silk behind them as they move about, and the females enclose their egg-batches in silk cocoons. Wolf spiders carry their egg-cocoons with them, attached to their spinnerets, and many other spiders guard their cocoons. I was able to testify to one instance of this when I was once in Majorca and found a European black-widow spider with her egg-cocoon under a stone on the waste ground behind my hotel. The egg-cocoon, attached by strong threads to some dry stems on the ground, was exposed to the blazing sunshine when I lifted the stone. To save her eggs, the black-widow started feverishly biting free the threads attaching the cocoon. Soon she had to retreat from the hot sun to cool down in the shadow of the lifted stone, but out she came again to sever a few more threads with frenzied haste before being forced back into the shadow by the heat. Out she came a third time, but I could not torment her any further, so I replaced the stone. The black-widow spider is not aggressive, but she can give an excruciatingly painful, and occasionally dangerous, bite when provoked. However, there is no doubt about her merit as a staunch and devoted guardian of her eggs.

Pond Invertebrates

Most of the invertebrate animals that you catch in the pond will belong to the phylum Arthropoda. But before you start collecting any for your garden pond, just stand or squat quietly at the edge of the water and watch the small creatures come and go. Pond skaters will skim over the surface with backward thrusts of their long middle pair of legs. If you move your arm, those nearest will leap away over the surface-film as if they were on a solid base. They do not even wet their feet, for these are covered with extremely minute, water-resistant hairs. There will also be sociable groups of whirligig beetles twisting, turning, swirling, revolving around each other on the surface. Wave your arm, and they will start gyrating at a frantic pace, yet without ever bumping each other. If you wade into the water they will all dive to the bottom, each with a small bubble of air attached to its rear. Return to the side and stand still for a few minutes— you will see them bob up to the surface, one after another, and

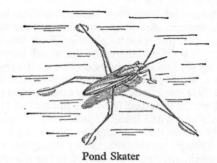

Pond Skater

twist, swivel and wind around each other as before. As the whirligig beetle swims, the under-surface is immersed, but the shiny upper-surface repels water and remains above it. The middle and hind legs of the whirligig are very short, broad and fringed, to form tiny paddles that are vibrated at speed in swimming. These two insects, the first a bug, the second a beetle, have become adapted to occupy a special niche in the pond community, as surface dwellers that feed on insects which fall into the water.

Now gaze down into the water itself. Back-swimmer water-boatmen rest back downwards, suspended from the surface-film, or propel themselves with powerful strokes of their long oar-like hindlegs. Lesser water-boatmen swim in rapid jerks over the muddy floor of the pond, and small water-beetles paddle vigorously above the mud, occasionally diving into it and kicking up little puffs of silt as they go by. Larger water-beetles, streamlined and neatly oval, swim up from the sub-merged jungles of pondweed, tilt themselves head-downwards to break the surface-film with the hind tip of their bodies, pause to renew the air supply beneath their wings, then row them-selves smoothly down again. Bright vermilion water-mites, no more than two millimetres long, swim here and there through the water with a rapid running motion of their legs, and a leech swims past with graceful up-and-down undulations of it flattened body.

You will notice creatures moving on the floor of the pond. Water-snails and small black flatworms glide over the mud, and caddis-fly larvae shuffle along in their cases of cut plant stems

Swimming Leech

leaf sections, small snail-shells or little stones, according to the species. Water-lice crawl over the mud, and freshwater shrimps slither here and there on their sides, or leap up and glide swiftly through the water in a curve that lands them on the mud again. These two crustaceans are scavengers that eat whatever dead or decaying animal or plant material they find. The other pond crustaceans are minute. At the edge of the water milfoil jungle a swarm of water-fleas, or daphnia, floats in mid-water, each tiny unit engaged in a perpetual dance of upward jerks and downward drifts, and little pear-shaped cope-pods jump through the water with sudden back-whisks of their long antennae. These small crustaceans sift microscopic plant-life from the water. The myriads of microscopic plants form the base, or first link, of many food chains in the pond, for the water-fleas which eat them are eaten by water-mites, damselfly nymphs, sticklebacks, newt larvae and small water-beetles.

Now a piece of the mud bottom stirs, and you begin to perceive it for what it really is—the large-eyed head and stout cylindrical body, tapered at the rear, of a two-inch dragonfly nymph. You had not seen it as it rested, alert and watchful, on the mud, for its dingy colours merged with the surroundings. Suddenly the dragonfly nymph's hinged mouth-claw shoots, flash-quick, from beneath its head, and grabs a water-louse. The claw folds back and the nymph's jaws start to munch contentedly.

These are a few of the invertebrate animals that you might see in the pond. If you sweep your net gently to and fro through the thickets of submerged water plants you will find many more that were living among the stems and foliage. Damselfly nymphs, mayfly nymphs, smaller caddis-fly larvae with cases of green leaves that make them hard to distinguish among the plants, and water-scorpions. The latter are not scorpions, but predatory water bugs which capture prey with pincer-like front legs. A large, perfectly dry brown spider might turn up in your net. This is the water-spider which, so far as is known, has the distinction of being the only spider in the world that swims and lives permanently under water. The water-spider spins a curved platform of silk among the submerged plants. This is filled with bubbles of air which the spider carries down from the surface and releases under the web. Finally, a silk dome, filled with air, is formed—a diving-bell-home in which the spider rests. When swimming below the surface of the pond the water-spider appears as a living jewel of glittering quicksilver, for its velvety body is enclosed in a sheath of air.

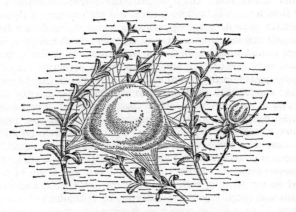

Water-spider with Air-bell

Take home plenty of invertebrate animals for your garden pond, but see that you have far more small invertebrates in your collection than there are larger ones. If you have not already stocked your pond with submergent water plants, fir the stem bases of those you have in small tins of soil, and cover the soil with stones to prevent it from floating out into the water when you lower the plants into your pond. Floating plants like frogbit can be placed straight on the water surface. Do not pour the water creatures from your jars or containers into the pond, but float them out by tilting each jar below the surface and pulling it gently backwards and up.

When the young frogs, toads or newts leave your pond they will find food and shelter in the wild strip of garden. Newts will hide under the large flat-bottomed stones in damp shady parts, and some flower-pots, well concealed and laid on their sides half-buried in the soil, will become permanent day-time shelters for toads throughout the summer months.

Classes and Families

A long, narrow wooden box placed in the shelter of a hedge or large bush in the wild strip, and covered with soil and moss, might tempt a hedgehog to set up home if you fill it loosely with dry grass or hay. Hedgehogs are mammals belonging to the order 'Insectivora', which include the mole and the four kinds of British shrews, one of which is confined to the Scilly Isles. Just as a phylum is split up into separate classes, each containing animals that are more similar to each other than they are to the rest, so each class is split up into separate orders. For instance, dogs, cats, weasels and other flesh-eating mammals that have sharp canine teeth and cutting molars, belong to the order 'Carnivora'. Rats, mice, beavers, squirrels and guinea-pigs belong to the order 'Rodentia', cloven-hoofed mammals such as cattle, sheep, deer, antelopes and giraffes belong to another order, the different kinds of bats to yet another and so on. In the same way, orders are split up into separate families, each containing animals with still closer resemblances. Thus, in the order Carnivora the dog family, 'Canidae', includes wolves, jackals and foxes; the cat family, 'Felidae', includes lions, tigers, leopards and lynxes; and the weasel family 'Mustelidae', includes otters, badgers, polecats and pine martens.

Try to sort out the other orders of mammals, then try to do the same with birds, and then with insects. When you have done your best at this, look them up in books and see how correct you were, and what mistakes you made. Later, try sorting out the orders into separate families. It is a fascinating game to play with a friend, and you will come to understand how different creatures are related to each other and how, in the far distant past, they evolved from common ancestors. Your imagination will be stirred, and you will come to see that by experimenting with different kinds of food, trying out different ways of life and exploring new areas of the environment, the animals were able to avoid competing with each other. Then you will feel an urge to discover all that is known about the processes and pressures, acting over millions of years, that caused the animals to diverge, adapted them to fill new areas of life and initiated the development of structures and behaviour that fitted them for different styles of living.

The Hedgehog

The hedgehog is one of the few wild mammals that most people see sooner or later, even if it is only as a squashed body on the road, for it has adapted well to living in parks and gardens.

Hedgehog

For millions of years, the hedgehog's one means of defence has been to roll up into a prickly ball and, apart from the motor car, its only enemies in Britain are the fox and the badger, both of which have learned how to force it open with their claws. Young hedgehogs are born in early summer and there are usually five to a litter. The babies are blind at birth and have soft white prickles. About five weeks later the mother starts taking them out on foraging expeditions. At dusk, on a mid-summer evening, you might see her leading a string of young ones from the nest.

I very often hear a hedgehog before seeing it, for its search for insects, slugs, snails and other creatures is accompanied by snorts, soft grunts and snuffles. If I approach a hedgehog in the open it immediately stops in its tracks and lowers its snout so that the prickles on its neck and head stand upright. Should I come closer, the hedgehog curls into a ball, but if it is beside thick plant cover it usually makes a hasty retreat. One night in late spring I was woken up by a series of loud puffs, hisses and gurgling noises. I thought a hot-water pipe must have burst, so I got up and rushed downstairs; but not being able to find anything wrong inside the house, I went outside to investigate. My flashlight revealed two courting hedgehogs facing each other on the flower bed. After pausing for a moment they made off into the next garden, and I inwardly cursed myself for being so clumsy and missing the chance of watching their behaviour.

In autumn, hedgehogs accumulate layers of fat around the neck and shoulders to supply the small energy demands of hibernation when their bodies cool and their heart and breathing rates slow down to a life-supporting minimum. Then, towards the end of October, each hedgehog seeks out a dry, well-concealed hollow under a thick hedge, the cavity of an old wasp nest or a garden compost heap, and constructs a nest of leaves and moss which are carried home in its mouth. For the first month or two the hedgehog sleeps intermittently, and on mild evenings it may leave the nest or 'hibernaculum', and wander abroad; but by the new year its sleep has become very deep, and it will not stir until it wakes up in the spring.

Another ground-living mammal which uses spines as a means of protection is the echidna or spiny anteater, of which there are two species in Australia. The echidna looks rather like a hedgehog with a thin snout and large claws. Its snout ends in a tiny toothless mouth, and it feeds on termites and ants which are picked up on its long sticky tongue. The echidna's spines offer good protection against dingoes and other predators and, like a hedgehog, it will roll itself into a ball when disturbed. If the ground is soft, however, the echidna can dig itself vertically down, keeping its spines erect until it disappears beneath the surface. Echidnas are egg-laying mammals belonging to the order 'Monotrema', which also contains the duck-billed platypus. Their single eggs are laid in a pouch; when the young hatches, it is carried in the pouch until its spines start to grow. From then on the mother leaves her baby in a safe hiding place returning at intervals to feed it until it has been weaned.

Echidna

Convergence

The echidna somewhat resembles a hedgehog because it lives a similar kind of life and has evolved the same means of protection. When two different kinds of animals have come to bear certain resemblances because they play similar roles in the living community we call this phenomenon 'convergence'. The echidna shows convergence not only with the hedgehog but with the true anteaters of South America which also have thin snouts, small toothless mouths, long sticky tongues and large claws for opening termite nests.

Adaptive Radiation

The mammals with which we are most familiar are known as 'placental' mammals. That is to say, their young develop in the womb or uterus and are nourished through an organ called the 'placenta', which makes extremely close contact with the mother's blood. However, the majority of Australasian mammals belong to the order 'Marsupialia', or pouched mammals. Many of these show convergence with placental mammals of other continents. The reason for this is that the marsupials entered Australia before it became separated from the Asiatic mainland, and before the more successful placental mammals had reached it. Thus the marsupials were able to branch out, diversify and exploit the various habitats and food resources without serious competition. Some became tree dwellers, some grass eaters, some carnivores, some insect eaters and so on.

This branching out process, where a group of related animals becomes variously changed and specialised for different modes of life, is called 'adaptive radiation'. By adaptive radiation the marsupials came to fill similar niches in the environment to those filled by placental mammals in other parts of the world. A 'niche' is the particular role an animal plays in the living community, and where animals fill similar niches they tend to show convergence. The marsupial mole looks remarkably like any other mole, the marsupial mice look like field mice or wood mice everywhere else, the rat kangaroos look like the jerboas of

Thylacine

North Africa, the Australian native cat is similar to the civets of southern Asia, the wombat, which has rodent-like front teeth, looks like an oversized marmot, the tree-living possums are similar to lemurs, bush-babies and lorises, the flying phalangers or glider possums show remarkable convergence with flying squirrels, the thylacine or marsupial wolf, so tragically exterminated by the early sheep farmers of Tasmania—or probably so, for the last known wild specimen was shot in 1930—really looked like a wolf or hunting dog, and the kangaroos of the grassy plains

have heads resembling those of gazelles and antelopes that
graze the African savannahs. They also have rather similar
stomach structures, containing stomach bacteria and protozoans
to aid the digestion of leaves and grasses.

Nest Boxes

Now back from the ends of the earth to your garden sanctuary.
You have provided a home for a hedgehog, flower-pot shelters
for toads and large flat-bottomed stones for newts and for
insects and other invertebrates—one of the insects you are likely
to shelter will be the handsome violet-bordered ground beetle,
the largest of our common garden beetles. You have also established a self-contained habitat for freshwater creatures. The
next job will be to put up two or three nest boxes for birds to
breed in.

To garden birds, houses with gardens probably appear as
inland cliffs and crags scattered among open woodland and
scrub. Sparrows and starlings nest in crevices of these crags,
and house martins fix their mud cups on the stone surface, in the
shelter of eaves and gutters. Blackbirds, thrushes, finches and
dunnocks will be happy to nest in the trees, bushes and hedges
of this man-made, shrubby woodland, but robins, wrens, tits,
nuthatches, wagtails and flycatchers will be ready to accept nest
boxes, for there is always a housing problem for hole-nesting
birds.

There are two types of nest boxes. One has an open front,
boarded up half-way; and robins, flycatchers and wagtails prefer
this type. The other is an enclosed box with a round entrance
hole, which will suit tits and wrens, and nuthatches if you are
fortunate enough to live near an oak wood. For tits and wrens,
a hole the size of a ten-penny piece will prevent sparrows from
entering and taking over. For nuthatches, the hole must be
larger; but the exact size does not matter, for they will reduce
it to their requirements by applying mud round the edges
and working it in with their bills. Fix the nest boxes to trees,
fences or garden sheds and see that they face in a northerly
direction. If they face south, the nestlings may get over-heated
and die. A little moss, spread on the floor of the boxes will
make them more attractive when prospecting birds visit them in
spring.

Helping Birds in Winter

You will help the birds through the hard winter months by putting out extra food for them. Net bags, such as those used by greengrocers for carrots or oranges, if filled with peanuts and hung from a branch, will be appreciated by tits and greenfinches. Strings of peanuts in their shells, lumps of fat

Blue Tit on Strung Peanuts

or meaty bones, hung from branches, will attract tits, and it is delightful to watch these acrobatic little birds swinging upside-down as they peck away at the food. If you want a bird table, all you need is a wooden platform, twelve inches square, screwed down on a post about five feet high; but I prefer to feed the birds on the lawn where I can scatter the food widely. I collect all bread, cake and biscuit crumbs, chopped leftovers of cheese, meat scraps, skins of roast chicken, bacon rinds and bread soaked in fat from the frying pan.

The sparrows come first, even before I have finished scattering the crumbs, then a couple of collared doves alight and walk towards the crumbs, one or two blackbirds join them and a song thrush appears in the background. Quickly some starlings arrive, and more flutter down from the sky. The sparrows and collared doves peck away at the bread and cheese, the starlings in a close milling flock gobble everything as rapidly as they can, a blackbird spends half his time chasing off a persistent rival, and this is the song thrush's chance until one of the blackbirds sees him and drives him off, but when the larger mistle thrush comes bounding over the lawn the blackbirds themselves must give way. A robin flies in, picks a morsel of cheese, then returns to a bush but comes back for another, and another, and a few chaffinches and dunnocks feed round the fringes of the scattered crumbs. When all the other birds have cleared what they can find and flown away the dunnocks remain for quite a long time, hopping here and there and flicking their wings almost too rapidly to see, as they peck up the minutest bits of crumb that only their bills can gather.

Sometimes a magpie alights at the bottom of the lawn and walks and hops towards the scattered food, alert and wary, with pauses on his way, and head well up, feathers sleeked, and one eye on the window so that I have to stand back and keep quite still. On seeing him the sparrows and small birds scatter into trees and bushes, the blackbird flies up on to the fence and the starlings watch the magpie approach, then stand in a row a couple of yards away, looking very subdued as they wait for him to finish and fly off. On one occasion, however, a collared dove remained feeding, then puffed out its chest and went jumping towards the magpie, driving him off before he reached the crumbs. The magpie flew on to the fence, but came back, and the collared dove repeated its aggressive performance, then flew after him and really saw him off. This was a most surprising piece of behaviour that I should never have expected from a collared dove.

Occasionally some black-headed gulls come circling over the lawn, and then all the small birds scatter. The gulls fly round and round and swoop over the food, but dare not alight or swoop too low. At last one of them swoops down, picks up a piece of bacon rind or chicken skin, slapping the ground with his coral feet as he passes, and swallows the food in flight. The gulls continue to circle over the lawn and then another swoops and grabs some food, a third one follows suit, but none of them dares alight so near the house. Suddenly the gulls fly off, and all the small birds return and flutter down to peck the scattered crumbs.

For the naturalist in the world today, much that he holds most dear seems threatened from all sides. Just as an alpine slope would be bereaved and diminished without its blue gentians, its apollo butterflies, its whistling marmots and its flock of alpine choughs, or as a rock pool would be diminished without its green and scarlet seaweeds, its expanded sea anemones, its starfish and its glass-transparent prawns, so the human species will be bereaved and diminished if it can no longer experience the magic and the pulse of the universe in the clear, sweet trilling of tree-crickets on a warm Mediterranean night, or gasp at the fragile beauty of a wild flower. Natural History is concerned with the quality of life that cannot be registered on the balance sheet of material comforts, for it is about joy and wonder, and the saving and cherishing of this beautiful planet, with its fantastically varied life. In setting up a garden sanctuary, you will be doing something of incalculable value in the world, and come rain, hail or snow, so long as there is a window in your mind and in your house, you will never, never be bored.

Suggestions for Good Books

Rupert Barrington: *The Bird Gardener's Book* (Wolfe)

F. H. Brightman: *The Oxford Book of Flowerless Plants* (O.U.P.)

Michael Chinery: *The Natural History of the Garden* (Collins)

John Clegg: *The Observer's Book of Pond Life* (F. Warne & Co. Ltd.)

T. L. Jennings: *Studying Birds in the Garden* (Wheaton)

Arthur Jewell: *The Observer's Book of Mosses and Liverworts* (F. Warne & Co. Ltd.)

Jean Mellanby: *Nature Detection and Conservation* (Carousel Books)

David Nichols & John Cooke: *The Oxford Book of Invertebrates* (O.U.P.)

Marion Nixon: *The Oxford Book of Vertebrates* (O.U.P.)

Tony Soper: *The Bird Table Book* (David & Charles Ltd.)

Wildlife Begins At Home (David & Charles Ltd.)

Hamlyn All-Colour Paperbacks
  Catherine Jarman: *Evolution of Life*
  Sali Money: *The Animal Kingdom*
  Tony Morrison: *Animal Migration*

John Sparks: *Animals in Danger*
                Bird Behaviour
Ian Tribe: *The Plant Kingdom*

Useful Addresses

XYZ Club, Zoological Society, Regent's Park, London N.W.1
British Naturalists' Association. Branches all over the country.
  Address of local secretary obtainable from Council for Nature,
  Zoological Gardens, Regent's Park, London, N.W.1
Children's Centre, Natural History Museum, Cromwell Road,
  London S.W.7

Miscellany

HOWEVER you divide the contents of an encyclopaedia, there are always essential pieces of information left over that seem to go nowhere in particular. It is these that you will find in this final section of JUNIOR PEARS.

Lantern Clock 1688

Time: Calendars and Clocks

THE DAYS OF THE WEEK

The names of the days—Sunday, Monday, Tuesday (Tiw—the God of War), Wednesday (Woden or Odin), Thursday (Thor), Friday (Frig—wife of Odin) and Saturday come from Old English translations of the Roman names (Sol, Luna, Mars, Mercurius, Jupiter, Venus and Saturnius).

HOW THE MONTHS GOT THEIR NAMES

January From Janus, a Roman God. The Anglo-Saxons called it *wulf-monath*—the month of the wolves.

February From a Roman god, Februus. A.S.: *sprote-cal*—the month when the kale, a kind of cabbage, sprouted.

March Originally the first month in the Roman calendar. From Mars, the god of war. A.S.: *hreth-monath*—the rough month.

April From the Latin *Aprilis*. A.S.: *Easter-monath*—month of Easter.

May From Maia, a goddess. A.S.: *tri-milchi*—the month when the cows were milked three times a day.

June From Juno, mother of the gods. A.S.: *sere-monath*—the dry month.

July Named after Julius Caesar. A.S.: *maed-monath*—meadow-month.

August Named after Augustus Caesar. A.S.: *weod-monath*—the month of vegetation.

September The seventh Roman month. From the Latin word meaning *seven*. A.S.: *haerfest-monath*—harvest month.

October The eighth Roman month. From Latin word meaning *eight*. A.S.: *win-monath*—the month of wine.

November The ninth Roman month. From Latin word meaning *nine*. A.S.: *wind-monath*—month of wind.

December The tenth Roman month. From Latin word meaning *ten*. A.S.: *mid-winter-monath*—mid-winter month.

THE YEAR

The **Equinoctial** or **Tropical Year** is the time the earth takes to go round the sun: 365·422 solar days. The **Calendar Year** consists of 365 days, but a year of which the date can be divided by 4 without a remainder is called a **Leap Year**, with one day added to the month of February. The last year of a century is a Leap Year only if its number can be divided by 400 (e.g. 1900 was not a Leap Year, but 2000 will be one).

The Longest and Shortest Days The longest day is the day on which the Sun is at its greatest distance from the equator; this is called the **Summer Solstice**. It varies between June 21 and 22.

The shortest day is the day of the **Winter Solstice**, and in 1978 falls on December 22.

Dog Days These are the days about the rising of the Dog Star, the hottest period of the year in the Northern Hemisphere. Roughly they occur between July 3 and August 25.

St Luke's Summer is a warm period round about St Luke's Day (October 18).

St Martin's Summer is a warm period round about Martinmas (November 11).

The Christian Calendar Until 1582 the Calendar used in all Christian countries was the Julian Calendar, in which the last year of all centuries was a Leap Year. By the sixteenth century this had caused a difference between the tropical and calendar years (see **The Year**) of 10 days. In 1582 Pope Gregory ordered that October 5 should be called October 15, and that of the years at the end of centuries only every fourth one should be a Leap Year. This new calendar was called the Gregorian Calendar and was gradually adopted throughout the Christian world. In Great Britain and her Dominions it came into use in 1752; by then there was a difference of 11 days between tropical and calendar years, and September 3 of that year was reckoned as September 14.

Easter Day can be, at the earliest, March 22; at the latest, April 25.

Whit Sunday can be, at the earliest, May 10; at the latest, June 13.

The Jewish Calendar dates from October 7, 3761 B.C. In 1978 the Jewish New Year (5739) began on October 2.

The Moslem Calendar dates from the Hejira, or the flight of Mohammed from Mecca to Medina (July 16, A.D. 622 in the Gregorian Calendar). In 1978 the Moslem New Year (1399) falls on December 2.

SUMMER TIME

Summer time—the putting forward of the clock by one hour during the months of summer—was first introduced in the First World War. Its purpose then was to cut down on the use of power for lighting; but in peace-time it was continued so that people might enjoy longer summer evenings.

From February, 1968, summer time was established for a three-year trial period to conform with Central European time. The new title chosen for it was British Standard Time. This experiment was abandoned in October, 1971, when the United Kingdom reverted to Greenwich Mean Time.

Normally, British Summer Time is from the day following the third Saturday in March until the day following the fourth Saturday in October.

TIME ALL OVER THE WORLD

This table shows what the time is in the important cities of the world when it is 12 noon at Greenwich. Places in ordinary type are ahead of Greenwich; those in *italics* are behind Greenwich.

Accra, Ghana .	12 Noon	Baghdad, Iraq .	3.00 p.m.
Adelaide, Australia	9.30 p.m.	*Baltimore, U.S.A.*	7.00 a.m.
Algiers . .	1.00 p.m.	Bangkok, Thailand	7.00 p.m.
Amsterdam,		Belgrade, Yugo-	
Netherlands .	1.00 p.m.	slavia . .	1.00 p.m.
Ankara, Turkey .	2.00 p.m.	Berlin, Germany .	1.00 p.m.
Athens, Greece .	2.00 p.m.	Berne, Switzerland	1.00 p.m.

Bombay, India	.	5.30 p.m.	Montevideo,	
Boston, U.S.A.	.	7.00 a.m.	*Uruguay* .	. 9.00 a.m.
Brisbane, Australia		10.00 p.m.	*Montreal, Canada* .	7.00 a.m.
Brussels, Belgium .		1.00 p.m.	Moscow, U.S.S.R.	3.00 p.m.
Budapest, Hungary		1.00 p.m.	Nairobi, Kenya	. 3.00 p.m.
Buenos Aires,			New Delhi, India .	5.30 p.m.
Argentina	.	9.00 a.m.	*New York*	. 7.00 a.m.
Cairo, Egypt	.	2.00 p.m.	Nicosia, Cyprus	. 2.00 p.m.
Calcutta, India	.	5.30 p.m.	Oslo, Norway	. 1.00 p.m.
Calgary, Canada	.	5.00 a.m.	*Ottawa, Canada* .	7.00 a.m.
Canberra,			*Panama*	. 7.00 a.m.
Australia .	.	10.00 p.m.	Paris .	. 1.00 p.m.
Cape Town, South			Peking, China	. 8.00 p.m.
Africa	.	2.00 p.m.	Perth, Australia	. 8.00 p.m.
Chicago, U.S.A.	.	6.00 a.m.	*Port of Spain,*	
Colombo, Ceylon .		5.30 p.m.	*Trinidad* .	. 8.00 p.m.
Copenhagen,			Prague, Czecho-	
Denmark .	.	1.00 p.m.	slovakia	. 1.00 p.m.
Darwin, Australia .		9.30 p.m.	*Quebec, Canada*	. 7.00 a.m.
Detroit, U.S.A.	.	7.00 a.m.	*Quito, Ecuador*	. 7.00 a.m.
Dublin, Ireland	.	12 Noon	*Reykjavik, Iceland*	11.00 a.m.
Freetown, Sierra			*Rio de Janeiro*	. 9.00 a.m.
Leone	.	12 Noon	Rome	. 1.00 p.m.
Gibraltar	.	1.00 p.m.	*St John's, New-*	
Halifax,			*foundland*	. 8.30 a.m.
Nova Scotia	.	8.00 a.m.	Salisbury, Southern	
Hamilton, Bermuda		8.00 a.m.	Rhodesia .	. 2.00 p.m.
Havana, Cuba	.	7.00 a.m.	San Francisco,	
Helsinki, Finland .		2.00 p.m.	U.S.A. .	. 4.00 a.m.
Hong Kong	.	8.00 p.m.	*Santiago, Chile*	. 8.00 a.m.
Honolulu, Hawaii .		2.00 a.m.	Seoul, Korea	. 8.30 a.m.
Jerusalem	.	2.00 p.m.	Singapore .	. 7.30 p.m.
Johannesburg,			Stalingrad,	
South Africa	.	2.00 p.m.	U.S.S.R. .	. 4.00 p.m.
Karachi, Pakistan .		5.00 p.m.	Stockholm,	
Kingston, Jamaica .		7.00 a.m.	Sweden .	. 1.00 p.m.
Kuala Lumpur,			Sofia, Bulgaria	. 2.00 p.m.
Malaya	.	7.30 p.m.	Suva, Fiji .	. 12 Midnight
Lagos, Nigeria	.	1.00 p.m.	Sydney, Australia .	10.00 p.m.
Leningrad,			Teheran, Iran	. 3.30 p.m.
U.S.S.R. .	.	3.00 p.m.	Tirana, Albania	. 1.00 p.m.
Lima, Peru .	.	7.00 a.m.	Tokyo, Japan	. 9.00 p.m.
Lisbon, Portugal	.	12 Noon	*Toronto, Canada*	. 7.00 a.m.
Los Angeles, U.S.A.		4.00 a.m.	*Vancouver, Canada*	4.00 a.m.
Luxembourg	.	1.00 p.m.	Vienna, Austria	. 1.00 p.m.
Madrid, Spain	.	1.00 p.m.	Warsaw, Poland .	1.00 p.m.
Mandalay, Burma .		6.30 p.m.	Wellington, New	
Melbourne,			Zealand	. 12 Midnight
Australia .	.	10.00 p.m.	*Winnipeg, Canada* .	6.00 a.m.
Mexico City .	.	6.00 a.m.		

BRITISH FLAGS

The Union Jack* was adopted in 1606 following the Union of England and Scotland, and took its present form in 1801, when there was the further union with Ireland (see HISTORY). It consists of three heraldic crosses:

> the cross of St Andrew, which forms the blue and white basis;
>
> upon which lies the red and white cross of St Patrick;
>
> upon the whole rests the red and white cross of St George dividing the flag vertically and horizontally.

The Union Jack

The correct manner of flying the flag is with the larger strips of white next to the flagstaff uppermost.

* Although it has become usual to call this flag the Union Jack on all occasions, it is strictly correct to do so only when the flag is flown at the jackstaff of one of Her Majesty's ships. At all other times it should be called the Union Flag.

The Royal Standard is the sovereign's personal flag, only to be flown above a building when she is actually present. It is divided into quarters, the 1st and 4th containing the three lions *passant* of England, the 2nd quarter containing the lion *rampant* of Scotland and the 3rd quarter containing the harp of Ireland. (*Passant and rampant* are terms in heraldry, and are explained in the section on Heraldry that follows.)

The White Ensign, the flag of the Royal Navy, is a white flag bearing the cross of St George, with a small Union Jack in the top corner next to the flagstaff.

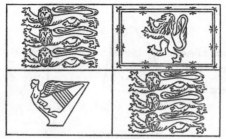

The Royal Standard

The Red Ensign (known as 'the red duster'), flag of the Mercantile Marine. It is a plain red flag with the Union Jack in the top corner next to the flagstaff.

The Blue Ensign (similar to the Red Ensign, but with blue background), flag of the Royal Naval Reserve (R.N.R.).

A NOTE ON HERALDRY

Man has always used symbols to decorate his armour; but heraldry as we know it started in Europe in the twelfth century Knights began to wear helmets which completely covered their wearers' faces, making recognition difficult. So when they met together at tournaments or went on crusades it was necessary that each should have a personal badge. This became known as the knight's **coat-of-arms** because it was worn on his sur-coat over his armour. The most obvious place to put the arms was on the shield. On his helmet a knight sometimes bore another distinguishing badge—the **crest**—which rested on a band of twisted cloth—the **torse**. This held in place a **mantling** to protect the metal from the hot sun. When all these are brought together they form an **achievement of arms** (Fig. 1). Once you have seen them together you are unlikely to make the popular mistake of calling a coat-of-arms a crest.

Because heraldry was formulated so long ago, the language used is a mixture of Norman-French and Latin and English. At first this may seem difficult; but once a few terms are mastered it can be seen to be a very practical language. Describing arms in words is called **blazoning**, and the method is to name the colour or colours of the **field** (the background), then to describe the main **charge** and its colour, and finally to name the subsidiary

FIG. 1

Achievement of Arms

Per pale gules and
argent, a chief
indented ermine

13th century Knight

charges with their colours. Only five **tinctures** are commonly
used—red, called **gules**: blue, called **azure**: green, called **vert**:
purple, called **purpure**: and black, called **sable**. There are two
metals, gold (**or**) and silver (**argent**), and these are usually
represented by yellow and white. In addition there are **furs—
ermine, vair** and numerous variations. A basic rule of heraldry
is that a coloured charge should not be placed on a colour nor a
metal one on a metal.

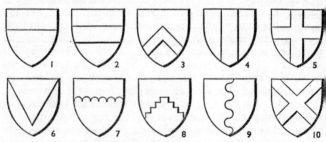

FIG. 2 SOME ORDINARIES AND LINES OF PARTITION

1 Chief: 2 Fess: 3 Chevron: 4 Pale: 5 Cross: 6 Pile: 7 per fess
invected: 8 per chevron indented: 9 per pale wavy: 10 Saltire

All items on a shield are known as **charges** and can be anything and everything from ants to zebras. The main charges
are known as **ordinaries**. Sometimes the field is divided into
more than one colour (as in Fig. 1), and the ordinaries lend their
names to these divisions. The dividing lines can be straight or
wavy-shaped or angular; Fig. 2 shows some of these.

It is possible to tell from a coat of arms to which member of a

Eldest Son
Label

2nd Son
Crescent

3rd Son
Mullet

4th Son
Martlet

5th Son
Annulet

6th Son
Fleur-de Lis

7th Son
Rose

8th Son
Cross Moline

FIG. 3

family it belongs. The head of the family bears plain arms, but his sons must carry a symbol to **difference** his arms from those of his father and his brothers (Fig. 3). Women bear their father's arms on a **lozenge** (a diamond shape), with no difference, and they cannot inherit arms if they have brothers. If a woman marries, her husband **impales** his wife's arms on the **sinister** side of his shield (Fig. 4). (In Latin **dexter** means right and **sinister** left, but in heraldry this refers to the left and right of the man carrying the shield.) If a lady has no brothers, she herself inherits the arms and her husband places them on his own arms on an **escutcheon of pretence.** Their children may **quarter** both parents' arms. Sometimes the quarterings may run into hundreds, but they are not all displayed.

FIG. 4

1 Per pale a chief indented impaling a bend: 2 Per pale a chief indented and on an escutcheon of pretence a bend: 3 Quarterly, 1st and 4th per pale a chief indented 2nd and 3rd a bend. (Note—Colours are omitted in these blazons.)

At first, no doubt, men chose their own symbols; but soon the monarch became the ultimate authority for granting arms. In England this authority is delegated to the Earl Marshal (at present the Duke of Norfolk), who is responsible for arranging great state occasions. To help him he has the College of Arms consisting of the Kings of Arms—Garter, Clarenceux and

Norroy and Ulster—six Heralds and four Pursuivants. In Scotland the principal officer is Lord Lyon, who has three Heralds and three Pursuivants.

Heraldry is a living part of our history. Not only is it found in old manuscripts and in churches and castles, but it can be seen on town halls, banks, company offices and advertisements. Look at your school badge and those of your friends. Some are real arms and have been granted to the school; but most are badges based on the arms of the town or a famous man (Fig. 5). Some, alas, may even have been invented by someone with no knowledge of heraldry.

B.B.C.
A gold band of
communication
surrounding the
Earth

National Coal Board
An heraldic
pictorial
representation of a
coal mine

U.K. Atomic
Energy Authority
Pictorial
representation of an
atomic pile

Barrow Grammar
School badge with
a bee and arrow
from the 'punning'
arms of Barrow
and the roses of
Lancashire

FIG. 5

This is no more than an introduction to the subject and you may want to read more about it. The books listed below are not dry but lively, well-illustrated and in one instance very amusing. Your library may have them. If you want to take your study further, write to the Secretary of the Heraldry Society, 59 Gordon Square, London, W.C.1, who will be pleased to send you information.

Simple Heraldry, by Iain Moncreiffe and Don Pottinger.
Boutell's Heraldry, revised by C. W. Scott-Giles and J. P. Brooke-Little.
Shield and Crest, by Julian Franklyn.
Discovering Heraldry, by R. H. Wilmott.

NOTES ON COINS

Coins as Weights and Measures   A penny weighs 3·564 grams, and has a diameter of 2·0320 cms. The diameter of the 50p coin is 3 cms.

British Coins Our **coppers** are really bronze (97 parts of copper, 2½ parts of zinc and ½ part of tin). The **farthing** (then of silver) was first struck in 1279 and withdrawn at the end of 1960. First **halfpenny** struck, in silver, in 1280: changed to bronze with penny and farthing in 1860: the old halfpenny ceased to exist on August 1, 1969. **Penny** introduced in 8th century: first copper pennies struck in 1797: demonetised on February 15, 1971, when Britain switched to decimal coinage and introduced also the new two pence piece. **Threepence** struck as silver coin in 1551; replaced in 1937 by a twelve-sided brass coin that was demonetised in 1971.

Our **silver** in 1946 became cupro-nickel (75% copper, 25% nickel). The **shilling** (called then a testoon) was first struck as a silver coin by Henry VII: it is now the 5p piece. The **florin** (10p) appeared in 1849, the first step towards putting the English coinage on a decimal basis. (This earlier scheme was abandoned.) The **half-crown** was first struck in the reign of Edward VI: ceased to exist on January 1, 1970.

L.s.d. Librae, solidi, denarii—the Latin for 'pounds, shillings and pence'.

Legal Tender Bank of England notes and gold dated 1838 onwards are legal tender for any sum. Silver (cupro-nickel) coins with values up to and including 10p are legal tender up to £5; 50p coins up to £10, and bronze up to 20p.

American Coins The word **dime** comes from the French dixième, a tenth part, and is the name given to the silver 10 cent coin, which is a tenth part of a dollar. **Nickel** is the popular name for the five-cent American coin, made of copper and nickel. The probable origin of the **dollar sign** ($) is that it is an adaptation of the old Spanish method of recording the peseta or piece of eight as a figure eight between sloping lines (/8/).

DISTANCE OF THE HORIZON

The distance to which you can see depends on the height at which you are standing.

At a height of	You can see
5 ft.	2·9 miles
20 ft.	5·9 miles
50 ft.	9·3 miles
100 ft.	13·2 miles
500 ft.	29·5 miles
1,000 ft.	41·6 miles
2,000 ft.	58·9 miles
3,000 ft.	72·1 miles
4,000 ft.	83·3 miles
5,000 ft.	93·1 miles
20,000 ft.	186·2 miles

THE SEVEN WONDERS OF THE ANCIENT WORLD

1. **The Pyramids of Egypt** The oldest is that of Zoser, at Saggara, built about 3000 B.C. The Great Pyramid of Cheops covers more than 12 acres and was originally 481 ft. high and 756 ft. square at the base.
2. **The Hanging Gardens of Babylon** Adjoining Nebuchadnezzar's palace near Baghdad. Terraced gardens watered from storage tanks on the highest terrace.
3. **The Temple of Diana at Ephesus** A marble temple erected in honour of the goddess about 480 B.C.
4. **The Colossus of Rhodes** A bronze statue of Apollo (see A DICTIONARY OF MYTHOLOGY) with legs astride the harbour entrance of Rhodes. Set up about 280 B.C.
5. **The Tomb of Mausolus** At Halicarnassus, in Asia Minor. Built by the king's widow about 350 B.C. From it comes our word 'mausoleum'.
6. **The Statue of Olympian Zeus** At Olympia in Greece; made of marble inlaid with ivory and gold by the sculptor Phidias, about 430 B.C.
7. **The Pharos of Alexandria** Marble watch tower and lighthouse on the island of Pharos in Alexandria Harbour. Constructed about 250 B.C.

ROMAN NUMERALS

I	.	.	.	.	1	LX .	.	.	60
II	.	.	.	.	2	LXX .	.	.	70
III	.	.	.	.	3	LXXX .	.	.	80
IV	.	.	.	.	4	XC .	.	.	90
V	.	.	.	.	5	IC .	.	.	99
VI	.	.	.	.	6	C .	.	.	100
VII	.	.	.	.	7	CX .	.	.	110
VIII	.	.	.	.	8	CXC .	.	.	190
IX	.	.	.	.	9	CC .	.	.	200
X	.	.	.	.	10	CCC .	.	.	300
XI	.	.	.	.	11	CD .	.	.	400
XII	.	.	.	.	12	D .	.	.	500
XIII	.	.	.	.	13	DC .	.	.	600
XIV	.	.	.	.	14	DCC .	.	.	700
XV	.	.	.	.	15	DCCC .	.	.	800
XVI	.	.	.	.	16	CM .	.	.	900
XVII	.	.	.	.	17	XM .	.	.	990
XVIII	.	.	.	.	18	M .	.	.	1000
XIX	.	.	.	.	19	MLXVI .	.	.	1066
XX	.	.	.	.	20	MD .	.	.	1500
XXX	.	.	.	.	30	MDCCC .	.	.	1800
XL	.	.	.	.	40	MCMLXXVIII	.	.	1978
L	.	.	.	.	50	MM .	.	.	2000
LV	.	.	.	55					

SOME ALPHABETS

Greek

Name	*Letter*		*English equivalent*
Alpha	A	α	*a*
Beta	B	β	*b*
Gamma	Γ	γ	hard *g*
Delta	Δ	δ	*d*
Epsilon	E	ε	short *e* (as in 'egg')
Zeta	Z	ζ	*z, dz*
Eta	H	η	long *e* (as in 'bee')
Theta	Θ	θ	*th*
Iota	I	ι	*i*
Kappa	K	κ	*k* or hard *c*

Name	Letter		English equivalent
Lambda	Λ	λ	*l*
Mu	M	μ	*m*
Nu	N	ν	*n*
Xi	Ξ	ξ	*x*
Omicron	O	ο	short *o* (as in 'box')
Pi	Π	π	*p*
Rho	P	ρ	*r*
Sigma	Σ	σ, s	*s*
Tau	T	τ	*t*
Upsilon	Υ	υ	*u* or *y*
Phi	Φ	φ	*ph, f*
Chi	X	χ	*kh* or hard *ch*
Psi	Ψ	ψ	*ps*
Omega	Ω	ω	long *o* (as in 'dome')

Russian

Letter	English eq	Letter	English eq
А а	*a*	Р р	*r*
Б б	*b*	С с	*s*
В в	*v*	Т т	*t*
Г г	*g*	У у	*u*
Д д	*d*	Ф ф	*f, ph*
Е е	*yeh*	Х х	*kh* as in 'loch'
Ж ж	*zh*	Ц ц	*ts*
З з	*z*	Ч ч	*ch*
И ий	*e*	Ш ш	*sh*
К к	*k*	Щ щ	*shch*
Л л	*l*	Ы ы	*y* as in 'did'
М м	*m*	Э э	*e* as in 'egg'
Н н	*n*	Ю ю	*yu*
О о	*o*	Я я	*ya*
П п	*p*		

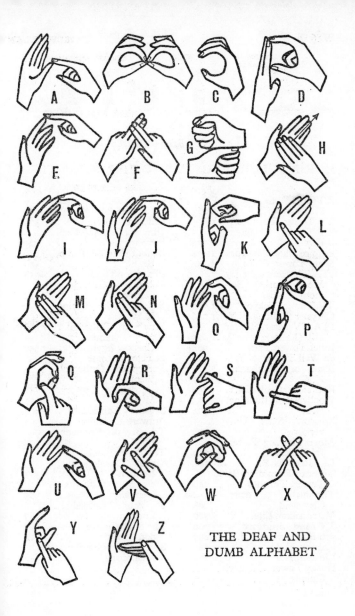

THE DEAF AND
DUMB ALPHABET

Longest and Highest

HIGHEST BUILDINGS AND OTHER STRUCTURES

	Feet		Feet
KTHI-TV mast, N. Dakota	2,063	G.P.O. Radio Tower London	580
TV Tower, Toronto	1,805	Chicago Temple	569
TV Tower, Oklahoma City	1,572	Ulm Cathedral, Germany	529
Empire State, New York	1,472	Bank of State, São Paulo, Brazil	520
Sears Tower, Chicago	1,454	Blackpool Tower	518
ITA TV Masts, Emley Moor (Yorks), Belmont (Lincs)	1,265	Cologne Cathedral, Germany	512
TV Tower, Tokyo	1,082	St John the Divine, N.Y.	500
Chrysler Building, N.Y.	1,046	Strasbourg Cathedral	468
ITA TV Mast, Winter Hill (Lancs)	1,015	The Pyramid of Cheops, Egypt	450
Eiffel Tower, Paris	984½	St Peter's, Rome	448
60 Wall Tower, N.Y.	950	St Stephen's Cathedral, Vienna	441
Bank of Manhattan, N.Y.	927	St Joseph's Oratory, Montreal	414
Rockefeller Centre, N.Y.	850	Salisbury Cathedral	404
Woolworth Building, N.Y.	792	Antwerp Cathedral	397
Moscow State University	787	Torazzo of Cremona, Italy	397
Albert Hertzog Tower, Johannesburg	772	The Tower Block, Millbank Development, London	387
City Bank, N.Y.	741	Freiburg Cathedral, Germany	385
Toronto-Dominion Bank Tower, Toronto	740	St Paul's Cathedral, London	365
Terminal Tower, Cleveland	708	The Shell Centre, London	351
Metropolitan Life, N.Y.	700	St Patrick's Cathedral, Melbourne	340
TV Mast, Stuttgart	700		
500 Fifth Avenue, N.Y.	697		
Chanin, N.Y.	680		
Lincoln, N.Y.	673		
Husky Tower, Calgary, Canada	626		

LONGEST TUNNELS

	Miles		Miles
East Finchley–Morden	17½	Ronco, Italy	5
Golders Green to South		Hauenstein, Switzer-	
Wimbledon	16	land	5
Simplon, Switzerland		Colle di Tenda, Italy	5
to Italy	12½	Connaught, Canada	5
Apennine, Italy	11½	Hoosac, U.S.A.	4½
St Gothard, Switzerland	9¼	Sainte Marie-aux-	
Loetschberg, Switzer-		Mines, France	4½
land	9	Rove, France	4½
Mont Cenis, Italy	8½	Severn, England	4
Cascade, U.S.A.	7¾	Mont d'Or, Switzerland	
Arlberg, Austria	6¼	to France	4
Moffat, U.S.A.	6	Albula, Switzerland	4
Shimizu, Japan	6	Boughton to Cedera,	
Rimutaka, New Zealand	5½	S. Africa	3¾
Ricken, Switzerland	5¼	Totley, England	3½
Grenchenberg, Swit-		Standedge, England	3
zerland	5¼	Woodhead, England	3
Tauern, Austria	5¼	Puigcerda to Aix-les-	
Otira, New Zealand	5	Thermes, France	3

LONGEST BRIDGES

	Length of waterway in ft.		Length of waterway in ft.
Oosterscheide, Nether-		Forth Road, Scotland	6,156
lands	16,476	Rio Dulce, Argentina	5,860
Lower Zambesi, Africa	11,320	Hardinge, Bangladesh	5,380
Storsstrom, Denmark	10,500	Victoria Jubilee, Mon-	
Tay, Scotland	10,290	treal	5,320
Upper Son, India	9,840	Moerdijk, Netherlands	4,700
Godavari, India	8,880	Verazzano—Narrows,	
Forth Railway, Scotland	8,290	New York	4,260
Tay Road Bridge,		Sydney Harbour,	
Scotland	7,365	N.S.W.	4,120
Rio Salado, Argentina	6,700	Jacques Cartier, Mon-	
Golden Gate, San		treal	3,890
Francisco	6,200		

LONGEST SHIP CANALS

	Miles		Miles
Gota, Sweden	115	Elbe–Trave, Germany	41
Suez	103	Manchester	35½
Volga–Moscow	80	Welland, Canada	27½
Albert (Antwerp–Liege)	80	Princess Juliana,	
Kiel	61	Netherlands	20½
Volga–Don, U.S.S.R.	60	Amsterdam	16½
Panama	50		

A Guide to some of the most important Museums in Great Britain

NATIONAL MUSEUMS

The British Museum, Great Russell Street, London, W.C.1.
Victoria and Albert Museum, Cromwell Road, London, S.W.7.
Royal Scottish Museum, Chambers Street, Edinburgh, 1.
National Museum of Wales, Cathays Park, Cardiff.

PREHISTORY AND EARLY CIVILISATION

British Museum, Great Russell Street, London, W.C.1.
Horniman Museum, London Road, Forest Hill, S.E.23.
National Museum of Welsh Antiquities, University College of North Wales, College Road, Bangor.
National Museum of Antiquities of Scotland, Queen Street, Edinburgh, 2.
Pitt Rivers Museum, Parks Road, Oxford.
Ashmolean Museum, Beaumont Street, Oxford.
Fitzwilliam Museum, Cambridge.
Yorkshire Museum, Museum Street, York.
Wells Museum, Cathedral Green, Wells, Somerset.
Museum of the Glastonbury Antiquarian Society, Glastonbury.
Verulamium Museum and Roman City, St Albans, Hertfordshire.
Viroconium Museum, Wroxeter, Shropshire.
Reading Municipal Museum, Blagrave Street, Reading.
Bath Roman Museum, Abbey Churchyard, Bath.
Roman Site and Museum, Corbridge, Northumberland.
Legionary Museum, Caerlon, Gwent, Wales.
Avebury Manor, Avebury, Wiltshire.
Segontium Roman Fort Museum, Beddgelert Road, Caernarvon, Gwynedd.

NATURAL HISTORY AND GEOLOGY

British Museum (Natural History), Cromwell Road, London, S.W.7.
National Museum of Wales, Cathays Park, Cardiff.

Royal Scottish Museum (Natural History Dept.), Chambers Street, Edinburgh, 1.

Zoological Museum, British Museum, Natural History Dept., Akeman Street, Tring, Hertfordshire.

Oxford University Museum, Parks Road, Oxford.

Cambridge University Museum of Zoology, Downing Street, Cambridge.

Geological Museum, Exhibition Road, London, S.W.7.

Horniman Museum, London Road, Forest Hill, S.E.23.

Brooke Museum, Brighton, Sussex.

Robertson Museum and Aquarium, Marine Station, Keppel Pier, Millport, Scotland.

Hancock Museum, Barras Bridge, Newcastle-upon-Tyne, 2.

Marine Biological Station, Aquarium and Fish Hatchery, Port Erin, Isle of Man.

Cannon Hill Museum, Pershore Road, Birmingham.

Royal Botanic Gardens, Kew, London.

Botanic Gardens, Oxford.

University Botanic Gardens, Cambridge.

Zoological Gardens, Regent's Park, London: also in Edinburgh, Manchester and other big cities.

GEOGRAPHY

British Museum (Ethnographical Dept.), Great Russell Street, London, W.C.1.

Imperial Institute, South Kensington, London, S.W.7. (For the countries of the Commonwealth.)

Horniman Museum, London Road, London, S.E.23.

Royal Geographical Society Museum, 1 Kensington Gore, London, W.8.

Pitt Rivers Museum, Parks Road, Oxford.

Cambridge University Museum of Archaeology and Ethnology, Downing Street, Cambridge.

Pitt Rivers Museum, Farnham, Blandford, Dorset.

SCIENCE

Science Museum, Exhibition Road, South Kensington, London, S.W.7.

Museum of the History of Science, Broad Street, Oxford.

Whipple Museum of the History of Science, 14 Corn Exchange Street, Cambridge.

Science and Engineering Museum, Exhibition Park, Great North Road, Newcastle.

Wellcome Historical Medical Museum, 183 Euston Road, London, N.W.1. (Medical science.)

Anatomical Museum, University New Buildings, Teviot Row, Edinburgh, 8. (Medical science.)

Birmingham City Museum, Dept. of Science and Industry, Newhall Street, Birmingham, 3.

AGRICULTURE

Agricultural Museum, Wye College, Wye, Kent.

Rothamsted Experimental Agricultural Institute, Harpenden, Hertfordshire.

Reading University Dept. of Agriculture Museum, Reading, Berks.

Cambridge Agricultural Institute, Cambridge.

The Curtis Museum, High Street, Alton, Hampshire.

West Yorkshire Folk Museum, Shibden Hall, Halifax, Yorkshire.

MOTOR CARS

Science Museum, Exhibition Road, South Kensington, London, S.W.7.

Museum of Carriages, Kent County Museum, Chillington, Manor House, Maidstone, Kent.

Museum of Motor Cars, Beaulieu Abbey, Brockenhurst, Hampshire.

SHIPS

Science Museum, Exhibition Road, London, S.W.7.

National Maritime Museum, Greenwich, London, S.E.10.

Royal United Service Museum, Whitehall, London, S.W.1.

Fisheries and Shipping Museum, Pickering Park, Hull.

RAILWAYS

Railway Museum, Queen Street, York.

AIRCRAFT

Science Museum, London, S.W.7.
Shuttleworth Collection, Old Warden Aerodrome, Old Warden, Bedfordshire.

PUBLIC SERVICES

Imperial War Museum, Lambeth Road, London, S.E.1.
Scottish United Service Museum, Crown Square, Edinburgh Castle, Edinburgh.
Royal Military Academy Sandhurst Museum, Camberley, Surrey.
The Armouries, Tower of London, E.C.3.
Wallace Collection, Hertford House, Manchester Square, London, W.1. (Armour.)
Glasgow Museum, Kelvingrove, Glasgow. (Armour.)
Airborne Forces Museum, Maida Barracks, Aldershot, Hampshire.
Chartered Insurance Institute Museum, 20, Aldermanbury, London, E.C.2. (Firefighting.)
National Army Museum, Royal Hospital Road, S.W.3.
Royal Air Force Museum, Colindale, Hendon.

SOCIAL AND DOMESTIC HISTORY

Victoria and Albert Museum, Cromwell Road, South Kensington, London, S.W.7.
Museum of London, Aldersgate Street, E.C.2.
Cambridge and County Folk Museum, Cambridge.
Welsh Folk Museum, St Fagan's, Glamorgan.
Stranger's Hall Folk Museum, Norwich.
York Castle Museum, Tower Street, York.
Bishop Hooper's Lodging Folk Museum, Gloucester.
Kent County Museum, Chillington Manor House, Maidstone, Kent.
Manx Village Folk Museum, Cregneash, Isle of Man.
Folk Museum, Kingussie, Inverness.

FURNITURE

Geffrye Museum, Kingsland Road, London, E.2.
Old House, High Town, Hereford.

Georgian House, Great George Street, Bristol.
Ham House, Petersham, Surrey.
Temple Newsam, Leeds.
The Pavilion, Brighton.
Iveagh Bequest, Ken Wood, London, N.W.3.

COSTUME

Victoria and Albert Museum, Cromwell Road, London, S.W.7.
Bethnal Green Museum, Cambridge Heath Road, London, E.2.
Gallery of English Costume, Platt Hall, Rusholme, Manchester, 14.
Museum of Costume, The Pavilion, Brighton, Sussex.
Canongate Tolbooth, Edinburgh, 8.

CHILDREN'S MUSEUMS

Bethnal Green Museum, London, E.2. (Dolls, dolls' houses, toys, model theatres, children's books.)
Tollcross Museum, Tollcross Park, Glasgow.
Museum of Childhood, High Street, Edinburgh.

CRICKET

Imperial Cricket Memorial Gallery, Lord's Cricket Ground, London, N.W.8.

THE ARTS

National Gallery, Trafalgar Square, London, W.C.2.
National Portrait Gallery, Trafalgar Square, London, W.C.2,
Tate Gallery, Millbank, London, S.W.1. (Modern art.)
Victoria and Albert Museum, Cromwell Road, London, S.W.7.
Wallace Collection, Hereford House, Manchester Square, London, W.1.
Sir John Soane's Museum, 13 Lincoln's Inn Fields, London, W.C.2. (Architectural drawing.)
Dulwich College Picture Gallery, College Road, London, S.E.21. (Chiefly seventeenth and eighteenth centuries.)
National Gallery of Scotland, The Mound, Edinburgh, 1.

Scottish National Portrait Gallery, Queen Street, Edinburgh, 2.
National Museum of Wales, Cathays Park, Cardiff.
Fitzwilliam Museum, Cambridge.
Ashmolean Museum, Oxford.
Bowes Museum, Barnard Castle, County Durham.
Walker Art Gallery, Liverpool.
Whitworth Art Gallery, Oxford Road, Manchester.
Norwich Castle Museum, Norwich.
City Museum and Art Gallery, Birmingham.
Barber Institute of Fine Arts, The University, Birmingham, 15.
Graves Art Gallery, Sheffield, 1.
Museum of Eastern Art, Broad Street, Oxford.
Royal College of Music, Donaldson Museum, London, S.W.7. (Musical instruments.)

MUSEUMS ILLUSTRATING THE LIVES OF FAMOUS PEOPLE

Jane Austen Jane Austen's House, Chawton, Hants.
J. M. Barrie The Birthplace, Kirriemuir, Angus, Scotland.
The Brontës Brontë Parsonage Museum, Haworth, nr. Keighley, Yorkshire.
John Bunyan Bedford Public Library, Bedford.
Robert Burns Alloway Cottage and Museum, Ayrshire.
Lord Byron Newstead Abbey, Nottinghamshire.
Thomas Carlyle Carlyle's House, 24 Cheyne Row, London, S.W.3.
Sir Winston Churchill Chartwell, Westerham, Kent.
S. T. Coleridge Coleridge's Cottage, Lime Street, Nether Stowey, Somerset.
James Cook Museum of Literary and Philosophical Society, Whitby, Yorkshire.
Charles Darwin Downe House, Downe, Kent.
Charles Dickens Dickens' House, 48 Doughty Street, London, W.C.1.
Dickens' Birthplace, 393 Commercial Road, Portsmouth.
Bleak House, Broadstairs, Kent.
Francis Drake Buckland Abbey, Plymouth.
Thomas Hardy Dorset County Museum, Dorchester.

Samuel Johnson Dr Johnson's House, Breadmarket Street, Lichfield.

Dr Johnson's House, 17 Gough Square, Fleet Street, London, E.C.4.

John Keats Keats Memorial House, Wentworth Place, Keats Grove, London, N.W.3.

David Livingstone Scottish National Memorial to David Livingstone, Blantyre, Scotland.

John Milton Milton's Cottage, Chalfont St Giles, Buckinghamshire.

Horatio Nelson Nelson Museum, New Market Hall, Priory Street, Monmouth.

Isaac Newton The Museum, Grantham.

Cecil Rhodes Rhodes Memorial Museum, Bishop's Stortford.

Capt. Scott Polar Research Institute, Cambridge.

Walter Scott Huntley House Museum, Edinburgh, 8.

William Shakespeare Shakespeare Birthplace, Stratford-on-Avon.

New Place, Stratford-on-Avon.

Anne Hathaway's Cottage, Shottery, Warwickshire.

Mary Arden's House, Wilmcote, Warwickshire.

George Bernard Shaw Shaw's Corner, Ayot St Lawrence, Hertfordshire.

R. L. Stevenson Memorial House, Howard Place, Edinburgh.

James Watt Watt Institution, 15 Kelly Street, Greenock, Scotland.

Duke of Wellington Wellington Museum, Apsley House, Hyde Park Corner, London, W.1.

John Wesley Wesley's House, 47 City Road, London, E.C.1.

William Wilberforce Wilberforce House, Hull.

William Wordsworth Dove Cottage, Grasmere, Westmorland.

Wordsworth Museum, Grasmere, Westmorland.

Wordsworth's Birthplace, Cockermouth, Cumberland.